Conserving Words

Conserving Words

frontier *How American*

garden *Nature Writers*

park *Shaped the*

wilderness *Environmental*

utopia *Movement*

DANIEL J. PHILIPPON

The University of Georgia Press

Athens & London

Paperback edition, 2005

© 2004 by the University of Georgia Press

Athens, Georgia 30602

All rights reserved

Designed by Kathi Dailey Morgan

Set in Electra by

Graphic Composition, Inc., Athens, Georgia

Printed and bound by Maple-Vail

The paper in this book meets the guidelines for

permanence and durability of the Committee on

Production Guidelines for Book Longevity of the

Council on Library Resources.

Printed in the United States of America

09 08 07 06 05 P 5 4 3 2 1

The Library of Congress has cataloged the hardcover

edition of this book as follows:

Library of Congress Cataloging-in-Publication Data

Philippon, Daniel J.

    Conserving words : how American nature writers shaped

the environmental movement / Daniel J. Philippon.

        p. cm.

Includes bibliographical references and index.

ISBN 0-8203-2576-7 (alk. paper)

    1. Natural history literature—United States—History.

    2. Environmentalism—United States—History.   I. Title.

    QH13.45 .P55 2004

    508.73—dc22   2003016938

ISBN 0-8203-2759-X (pbk. : alk. paper)

British Library Cataloging-in-Publication Data available

To Nancy

Contents

Illustrations

Preface

TO EXPLORE HOW American nature writers shaped the environmental movement, I have employed ideas and concepts from a range of academic disciplines, but three disciplines in particular — literature, history, and philosophy — have influenced this project the most. Over the last thirty years, environmental concerns have reshaped each of these fields, spawning an interdisciplinary endeavor known as the "environmental humanities" and initiating a productive new conversation between scholars. I hope this book will contribute to this vital conversation.

Although no book can satisfy the needs of every reader, I hope *Conserving Words* will appeal not only to scholars in each of these fields but also to general readers interested in nature writing and environmental issues. For the academic specialist, I have tried to engage current scholarship and employ original research, but I am sure that some will feel I have not gone into enough detail about their own particular areas of interest. For the general reader, I have tried to write in an accessible, jargon-free style, but I am equally sure that I have not succeeded wholly in this attempt. In each case, I ask the reader's forgiveness.

To bridge the gap between the disciplines, and between my academic and popular audiences, I have chosen a method that integrates biographical and rhetorical criticism. By this I mean that I have tried to tell stories about particular nature writers while also making a larger argument about their roles in the growth of the environmental movement. This focus on individuals is not meant to convey a "great man" or "great woman" interpretation of history. Rather, it is meant to situate these writers in the complex web I call, in the introduction, the "ecology of influence."

The danger of pursuing such an ecological approach too far is that eventually there is no "there" there — all dissolves into vague "connections" and "interactions" and "relationships" without any historical actors. Such an extreme form of ecologism is dissatisfying because it does not ring true to experience. While we are always already in the world, we also retain, cultivate, and value our independent agency. We may live in historically, geographically, and socially specific circumstances, but we still act out of our own free will. As Aviva Freedman and Peter

Medway have pointed out, "To see human relations as ecology or system involves suppressing the consciousness that it is people, experiencing beings like ourselves, and not abstract systemic elements that are the constituents of these networks" (*Genre and the New Rhetoric* 12). As a result, although I discuss the systemic character of the environmental movement in detail, my focus remains on the individual nature writers whose actions had an influence on their—and our—world. This focus also reflects my agreement with Steven J. Holmes, who writes in *The Young John Muir* that "the best way of apprehending the power and dynamics of relationship with nature—or any aspect of human living—is through immersion in the concrete details and narrative shape of a particular life" (16).

In undertaking this integration of biographical and rhetorical criticism, I have attempted to avoid what I have found to be a major weakness of much contemporary criticism, which is that it is *overly* critical—it lacks generosity. All too often, contemporary criticism fails to exhibit much sympathy for its human subjects, not to mention much humor for the situations in which they find themselves. The people depicted in its pages appear as either the unwitting agents of ideology or as selfish, conspiratorial colonizers. And while much contemporary criticism criticizes others for being unaware of their values, or for having the wrong set of values, it often fails to make explicit its own. I have tried to avoid the critic-as-adversary pose. Rather than "interrogating" a subject, for instance, I have simply tried to ask questions about it. Where the lives and work of these individuals deserve praise, I have tried to offer it, and where they exhibit weaknesses—either personal or professional—I have tried to point them out. In so doing, I hope this method exhibits the values of care and compassion that I believe are important corollaries to the search for justice and equity that drives so much current criticism.

Finally, for readers interested in exploring my primary and secondary sources in more detail, I cite most archival material in the endnotes and most published material parenthetically in the text. In the endnotes I also develop some of the points I make in the text and suggest sources for further reading.

Acknowledgments

MANY PEOPLE and institutions deserve my thanks for the help they provided during the research and writing of this book.

For my research on Theodore Roosevelt and the Boone and Crockett Club, I thank William H. Harbaugh of the University of Virginia; Robert W. Lewis of the University of North Dakota; the Manuscripts Division of the Library of Congress; the Sterling Memorial Library at Yale University; Wallace Finley Dailey of the Theodore Roosevelt Collection at Harvard University; and Jack Reneau, Chris Tonkinson, and the staff of the Boone and Crockett Club in Missoula, Montana.

For my research on Mabel Osgood Wright and the National Audubon Society, I offer my gratitude to Christopher Nevins, Alison Olivieri, Robert Braun, Suzanna Nyberg, Lauren Brown, Sherman Kent, and Henrietta and Robert Lachman of the Connecticut Audubon Society; Barbara Austen of the Fairfield Historical Society; Rebecca Abbott of Sacred Heart University; Virginia Lopez Begg of Andover, Massachusetts; Betsy Mendelsohn of the University of Virginia; Peggy Wargo and Tom Geoffino of the Fairfield Public Library; Mary Witkowski in the Historical Collections of the Bridgeport Public Library; Mary LeCroy in the Ornithology Department of the American Museum of Natural History; John Stinson in the Rare Books and Manuscripts Division of the New York Public Library; and George F. Thompson of the Center for American Places.

For my research on John Muir and the Sierra Club, my thanks go to Ronald H. Limbaugh, Sally M. Miller, and Daryl Morrison of the University of the Pacific; Michael P. Cohen of the University of Nevada, Reno; and Steven J. Holmes of Harvard University.

For my research on Aldo Leopold and the Wilderness Society, I am grateful to Paul Sutter of the University of Georgia; Curt Meine of the International Crane Foundation; Michael Nelson of the University of Wisconsin, Stevens Point; Bernard Schermetzler of the University of Wisconsin Archives; Colleen A. Nunn and Robert M. Russell of the Conservation Collection at the Denver Public Library; Rob Nelson of the Aldo Leopold Foundation; and Ann Strohm and the late Tom Watkins of the Wilderness Society. Special thanks to Karen Funk and John Dilts, and to Steve and Joann Dilts, for their hospitality while I was in Denver.

For my research on Edward Abbey and Earth First! thanks to Clarke Abbey; James M. Cahalan of Indiana University of Pennsylvania; Roger Myers, John Murphy, and Mina Parish of the Special Collections Library at the University of Arizona; Dave Foreman of the Wildlands Project; Mike Roselle of the Ruckus Society; Eric Temple of Canyon Productions; Chip Hedgcock of the University of Arizona; Lynn Anderson of the Alternatives Library at Cornell University; Holland Lynch of the New York Public Library; and the Center for the Defense of Free Enterprise.

For my research on the entire manuscript, I received invaluable help from the circulation, reference, interlibrary loan, and special collections staffs of the University of Virginia and University of Minnesota Libraries, as well as the libraries of Macalester College, Hamline University, and the University of St. Thomas. Although their work is often unacknowledged and unappreciated, librarians are among the most important custodians of our culture, and I am forever in their debt.

At the University of Virginia, I offer my deep appreciation to the Graduate School of Arts and Sciences, the Department of English, the Society of Fellows, and Brown College at Monroe Hill for their financial support, and to Robert J. Huskey, Thomas E. Thompson, Carl Trindle, and Erik Midelfort for facilitating that support. Thanks also to Alastair Fowler, Richard Rorty, E. D. Hirsh, Chip Tucker, Hal Kolb, and the late David Levin in the Department of English, and Joe Kett and Cindy Aron in the Department of History, for productive early conversations. Special thanks to Stephen Railton, Jack Levenson, and Tim Beatley for their close attention to the manuscript, and very special thanks to Alan Howard for his continuing support and interest in this project and for his lasting friendship.

At the University of Minnesota, I am indebted to the Office of the Vice President of Research and to the Humanities Institute for fellowship support, and to Billie Wahlstrom, Jerry Miller, Philip Larsen, and Charles Muscoplat for facilitating that support. I am also grateful for the encouragement I have received from my colleagues in the Department of Rhetoric, especially Bill Marchand, Art Walzer, Mary Lay, Laura Gurak, John Logie, Richard Graff, and Lee-Ann Kastman Breuch. Special thanks to Tom Scanlan for his wise counsel. My colleagues in the Departments of American Studies, English, and Fisheries, Wildlife, and Conservation Biology have been equally supportive. Thanks also to the many undergraduate and graduate students who have taken my courses in the environmental humanities over the years, from whom I have learned so much.

For the opportunity to discuss portions of the manuscript, I am grateful to the Association for the Study of Literature and Environment, the American Society for Environmental History, the Society for Conservation Biology, the Society for Utopian Studies, the Connecticut Audubon Society, the Eagle Bluff Environmental Learning Center, the University of New England, the University of the Pacific, and the University of Minnesota's Department of Rhetoric, American Studies Program, History of Science and Technology Colloquium, and Joint Degree Program in Law, Health, and the Life Sciences.

Portions of chapter 2 appeared previously as the introduction to my critical edition of *The Friendship of Nature: A New England Chronicle of Birds and Flowers* by Mabel Osgood Wright and are reprinted here by permission of the Johns Hopkins University Press.

At the University of Georgia Press, I thank Nancy Grayson, Allison Reid, and two anonymous readers whose suggestions helped tighten the manuscript. Thanks to Anne Gibbons for her sharp-eyed copyediting and Kathi Morgan for her elegant design. Special thanks to Jennifer Reichlin — even more interested than me in "conserving words" — for suggesting ways to trim the manuscript. Extra special thanks to Barbara Ras for her many years of encouragement.

Other colleagues, friends, and family members have helped me think through different portions of this project and have provided support in ways large and small. These include Hugh Cloke, Ed Ingebretsen, Daniel Payne, George Hart, Rochelle Johnson, Daniel Patterson, Lawrence Buell, John Elder, John Tallmadge, Scott Slovic, Cheryll Glotfelty, Ian Marshall, Kent Ryden, Randall Roorda, J. Gerard Dollar, Ashton Nichols, Chris Cokinos, SueEllen Campbell, Karla Armbruster, Terrell Dixon, H. Lewis Ulman, Carolyn Merchant, Jennifer Price, Amy Green, Vera Norwood, Alan Taylor, Miles Orvell, Bron Taylor, Holly Doremus, Roger J. H. King, J. Baird Callicott, and Bryan Norton. Thanks also to David W. Teague, Elizabeth Phillips, Anne McIlhaney, Chuck Mathewes, Jenny Geddes, Nancy Hurrelbrinck, Kerry Bolger, Amy Garrou, Dorri Beam, and Ann Woodlief in Virginia; and Karen Warren, Bruce Braun, Bill Cunningham, Capper Nichols, Meredith Cornett, Ethan Perry, Carleen and Nat Pieper, Meredith and Daniel Milowski, and Steve and Beth Claas in Minnesota. Special thanks to Michael P. Branch for his continued friendship and support.

My parents, Ben and Trudy Philippon, have sustained me in more ways than I can count since this project began, and my in-laws, Preston and Mary Dilts, have been equally generous in welcoming me into their lives.

My wife, Nancy Dilts, has been a patient listener, thoughtful guide, and steadfast advocate, and for these qualities and more I dedicate this book to her.

Finally, while I know not what breathed life into the "endless forms most beautiful and most wonderful," as Darwin described them in the magnificent final sentence of *The Origin of Species*, I know that to think on these things is both a privilege and a pleasure, and I give great thanks for the opportunity to have done so.

All errors are, of course, my own.

Conserving Words

The Ecology of Influence

> We are takers of notes, measurers of stone, examiners of fragments
> in the dust. We search for order in chaos wherever we go. We
> worry over what is lost. In our best moments we remember to ask
> ourselves what it is we are doing, whom we are benefiting by
> these acts. One of the great dreams of man must be to find some
> place between the extremes of nature and civilization where
> it is possible to live without regret.
>
> BARRY LOPEZ, "Searching for Ancestors"

I BEGAN THIS BOOK about ten years ago in an attempt to answer a question posed by Scott Slovic in *Seeking Awareness in American Nature Writing* (1992): "How does nature writing influence people's attitudes and behavior?" (181).

Slovic was not the first person to see a connection between nature writing and the beliefs and actions of its readers. Henry Seidel Canby first commented on this relationship in 1917 in the pages of the *Yale Review,* in which he wrote, "How curiously complete and effective is the service of these nature books, when all is considered. There is no better instance, I imagine, of how literature and life act and react upon one another" (767). Since then, and particularly in the last twenty years, many others have made similar observations. In a 1985 essay, "American Literary Environmentalism, 1864–1920," Frederick O. Waage observed that nature writing was a "central force" in the influence early conservation groups had on public environmental awareness (29). In an end-comment to an annotated booklist he compiled for a special issue of the journal *Antaeus* in 1986, Barry Lopez wrote, "I suppose this is a conceit, but I believe this area of writing will not only one day produce a major and lasting body of American literature, but that it might also provide the foundation for a reorganization of American political thought" (Lopez et al. 297). More recently, Lawrence Buell claimed in *The Environmental Imagination* (1995) that "[a]lthough the creative and critical arts may seem remote from the arenas of scientific investigation and public policy, clearly they are exercising, however unconsciously, an influence upon the emerging culture of environmental concern, just as they have played a part in shaping as well as merely expressing every other aspect of human culture" (3). Finally, and most comprehensively, Daniel G. Payne chronicled the relationship between American nature writing and environmental politics in *Voices in the Wilderness* (1996), noting that "[p]erhaps the most remarkable aspect of environmental reform in American politics is the extent to which it has been driven by nature writers" (3).[1]

The more closely I looked at the dynamics of this relationship between nature writers and the environmental movement, the more clearly a pattern emerged. In at least five separate cases, a nature writer was prominently involved in the formation and development of an environmental organization (see page 3). In 1887, two years after Theodore Roosevelt published *Hunting Trips of a Ranchman*, his first book of nature writing, the future president joined with other hunters and sportsmen to found the Boone and Crockett Club, an organization devoted to preserving the western American landscape and the frontier virtues it seemed to them to represent. Mabel Osgood Wright, the author of *The Friendship of Nature* (1894), helped revive the National Audubon Society, originally founded by George Bird Grinnell in 1886, by drawing upon the devotion of her fellow suburban homemakers to their backyard gardens. John Muir, the author of *The Mountains of California* (1894), organized the Sierra Club in 1892 in an effort to defend the newly formed Yosemite National Park from threats to its integrity as a retreat for urban nature lovers. Aldo Leopold, having written many of the wilderness essays that would later be collected in *A Sand County Almanac* (1949), joined with seven other wilderness advocates to form the Wilderness Society in 1935. And, most recently, Edward Abbey provided the practical and spiritual inspiration for the founding in 1980 of Earth First!—the radical environmental group that modeled its utopian activities after scenes from Abbey's rambunctious 1975 novel *The Monkey Wrench Gang*.[2]

Scott Slovic asked how nature writing influenced people's attitudes and behavior, and here seemed at least part of an answer: by contributing to the formation and development of environmental organizations. Wallace Stegner described a similar pattern at work in the history of conservation: "a charismatic and influential individual who discerns a problem and formulates a public concern; a group that forms around him or around his ideas, and exerts political pressure on Congress; legislation that creates some kind of new reserve—national park, national forest, national monument, national wildlife sanctuary or wilderness area; and finally, an increasingly specific body of regulatory law for the protection of what has been set aside" ("It All Began" 39).

Identifying a pattern is not the same as explaining it, however, and this particular pattern merely narrows Slovic's question, leaving its central question—*how*—unanswered. While it is true that nature writing influenced the formation and

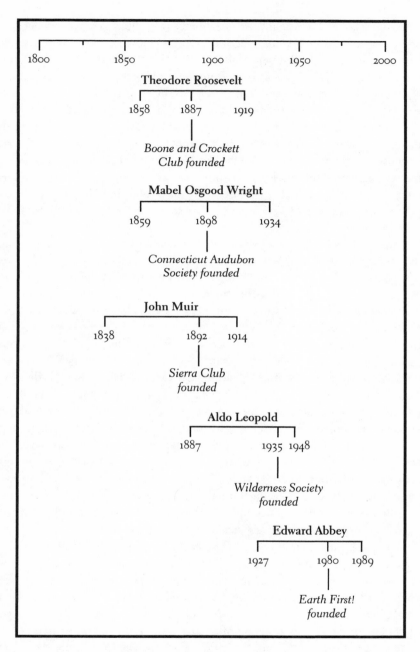

1800   1850   1900   1950   2000

Theodore Roosevelt

1858   1887   1919

*Boone and Crockett
Club founded*

Mabel Osgood Wright

1859   1898   1934

*Connecticut Audubon
Society founded*

John Muir

1838   1892   1914

*Sierra Club
founded*

Aldo Leopold

1887   1935 1948

*Wilderness Society
founded*

Edward Abbey

1927   1980 1989

*Earth First!
founded*

Life spans of nature writers; founding dates of organizations.

development of environmental organizations, to ask "how" is to ask in what manner or way; to what extent, amount, or degree; and for what reason or purpose. In *Speaking for Nature* (1980), one of the earliest surveys of the genre, Paul Brooks observed that the patterns of influence among Progressive Era nature enthusiasts were not quite the one-way street later suggested by Stegner: "The professional careers and personal interests of these men, and of countless others who shared their concerns, were woven together in a complex pattern. Sportsmen collected for the museums; museum curators and university professors provided the scientific base for conservation organizations like the newborn Audubon societies; amateur naturalists supplanted the studies of the professionals; and the writers in both their ranks brought the fruits of their labors before the public. To follow a single thread or an individual career in isolation would be to ignore the cross-fertilization that was constantly going on" (106).[3]

Although Brooks's observation was written before Stegner's, it develops Stegner's in an important way. Influence is a complex system — as Henry Seidel Canby's comment about how "literature and life act and react upon one another" also suggests. At the same time that these nature writers and writings were influencing people's attitudes and behavior, people's attitudes and behavior were exerting a counterinfluence on them, not to mention the influence they were having on the natural world itself and vice versa. In fact, the complexities of these relationships resemble nothing less than an ecosystem, an "ecology of influence" that could be said to encompass all authors, readers, and texts (broadly defined), at all times, in all places. This ecological model allows us to recognize not only that influence circulates in a complex system but also that this system links the natural and social systems that are its component parts.[4] It is not enough, therefore, to ask how nature writing has influenced people's attitudes and behavior, because such writing is but one component in the vast web of relationships that compose this ecology of influence. To more fully understand its effects, we need to consider the wide range of connections that exist between particular authors, readers, and texts at particular times and — most importantly — in particular places.

John Muir famously observed that "[w]hen we try to pick out anything by itself, we find it hitched to everything else in the universe" (*Nature Writings* 245). Not everything is hitched in the same way or to the same degree, however, so we need to explore *how* and *why* things are hitched the way they are. Different disciplines do this in different ways, but increasingly scholars in the humanities and social sciences have turned to the notion of *discourse* to explain this ecology of influence. Discourse is a function of language through which our views of the world are constructed. It is not the *context* for language so much as it is *constituted* by language, enabling this ecology of influence to operate. As Paul Bové has summarized, discourses make possible "disciplines and institutions which, in turn, sustain and distribute those discourses" (57). To study discourses, therefore, is to study "the organized and regulated, as well as the regulating and constituting, functions of language . . . to describe the surface linkages between power, knowledge, institutions, intellectuals, the control of populations, and the modern state as these intersect in the functions of systems of thought" (54–55).

Sociologist Robert J. Brulle has conducted one such study of the discourses of the environmental movement, and in *Agency, Democracy, and Nature* (2000) he argues that the environmental organizations that developed in the United States did so because their members shared a *discursive frame*.[5] Brulle's study is based in part on a large and growing literature known as *frame analysis*, which builds on Erving Goffman's notion of "frames," or the interpretive schemes that enable individuals and groups to organize their experiences and guide their actions.[6] According to Brulle, a discursive frame "enables the construction and maintenance of movement organizations by constituting the social movement's shared version of reality. A discursive frame defines the nature of the problem and how the solution is to be achieved" (*Agency* 78). Brulle draws the discursive frames he discusses from the field of environmental philosophy—specifically, from Max Oelschlaeger's *Idea of Wilderness* (1991). According to Brulle, the major frames operating in the environmental movement are manifest destiny, wildlife management, conservation, preservation, reform environmentalism, deep ecology, environmental justice, ecofeminism, and ecotheology (*Agency* 98–99).[7]

While I admire the scope of Brulle's project and share his interest in frame analysis, *Conserving Words* takes a somewhat different approach. Rather than examining a wide variety of environmental organizations, as Brulle does, I look in detail at a select few, focusing on the relationship between those organizations and the American nature writers involved in their creation. In particular, I argue that *metaphor* is the central figure of speech at work in the discursive frames that enabled these groups to succeed. If we posit social transformation as a kind of "social disturbance" (much like fire is a natural disturbance), we might see metaphor as the agent of that disturbance in the complex system I am calling the ecology of influence.[8] Much like the "strange attractors" of chaos theory, these metaphors offer points of convergence around which individuals and organizations can rally. These metaphors gain currency, moreover, because they carry moral weight. They describe ideal states of the human relationship with the nonhuman world, which in turn have ethical implications. Metaphors are thus vehicles for our worldviews, carriers of our visions of the good. As Donald Worster has written, "metaphors imply worldviews" (*Nature's Economy* 378).

Metaphors enact this cultural work because they enable *narratives* that in turn convey our *values*.[9] In an environmental context, we might say that our environmental values are embodied in the metaphors we use to represent "nature," because these metaphors imply particular stories about how we relate to the "nature" they describe. Furthermore, because these metaphors and their accompanying narratives are socially constructed, they serve as the agents of social change (or social maintenance, as the case may be). As Barbara Novak has written, each view of nature carries with it "a powerful self-image, a moral and social energy that could be translated into action" (*Nature and Culture* 7). Brulle similarly sees narrative as a central component in the creation, maintenance, and transformation of environmental organizations: "The discursive frame provides an interpretation of history that specifies the movement's origins, its heroes, its development, and its agenda. This narrative gives an organization its identity and guides its collective actions. It is a living and contingent framework, created and changed by the participants in the movement" (*Agency* 77).

This narrative interpretation of discourse owes much to Kenneth Burke's theory of dramatism. According to Burke, language can be seen as a kind of symbolic action that takes the form of a drama. By examining the components of this drama, or what Burke called the "pentad" (act, agent, agency, scene, and purpose), the critic can discover the motives underlying the symbolic action.[10] Studying the dramatic character of a social movement's discursive frame can have the same effect. As Brulle has written, "The discursive frame of a social movement takes the form of a moral drama in a quest for salvation in a new social order. The world is seen as a theater in which the drama of human life is played out. This drama unfolds in a sequence in which the old social order falls into corruption. Identification and elimination of the cause of evil follow. A new and redeemed social order emerges, based on a new definition of reality that enters into competition with the dominant discourse" (*Agency* 77). Sylvia Noble Tesh simplifies this summary further, claiming that "all social movement frames are injustice frames. Such frames redefine accepted social conditions as unjust and assign responsibility for that injustice to individuals and institutions other than its victims" (123).[11] (These frames could also be considered "neglect frames" by employing an ethic of care instead of an ethic of justice.)

This interpretive model applies well to the American nature writers and environmental organizations I examine in *Conserving Words* (see page 7). Living in a particular historical context and a particular geographical location, each of these writers understood "nature" through a particular metaphor—frontier, garden, park, wilderness, or utopia—that best fit his or her time, place, and personal history. These metaphors enabled certain narratives that explained how human beings should interact with nature and, in so doing, conveyed certain environmental values. When these writers perceived an injustice or act of neglect hap-

	Theodore Roosevelt	Mabel Wright	John Muir	Aldo Leopold	Edward Abbey
Historical context	closing of the frontier	early eastern suburbs	western tourism	ecological science	post-1960s rebellion
Discursive frame	"nature" as frontier	"nature" as garden	"nature" as park	"nature" as wilderness	"nature" as utopia
Narrative enabled	conquering the frontier	cultivating the garden	visiting the park	studying the wilderness	creating utopia
Values conveyed	recreational/cultural	aesthetic/cultural	aesthetic/religious	recreational/scientific	recreational/political
Objects of injustice/neglect	Yellowstone/wildlife	birds/suburbs	Yosemite/national parks	national forests/wilderness areas	deserts/all of "nature"
Organization founded	Boone and Crockett Club	Audubon Society	Sierra Club	Wilderness Society	Earth First!
Organization type	national, but few members	national and local	national, but began local	national, but began in east	international "disorganization"
Landscape protected	Yellowstone National Park	Birdcraft Sanctuary	Yosemite National Park	national forest wilderness areas	various "wild" landscapes

Conceptual framework of *Conserving Words*.

pening to some portion of the natural world, they used these metaphors, and were used by them, to found organizations devoted to rectifying these problems. Through these organizations, these writers rallied support for their causes, and eventually preserved a portion of "nature" in a way that coincided with their vision of the world. The metaphors these writers used, in other words, functioned as *conserving words*.

Tidy as that framework may be, the reality of nature writing and environmentalism is much more complex, and I devote the bulk of this book to addressing that complexity. For one thing, metaphors of nature are intrinsically general, vague, ambiguous, and tentative. Being metaphors, they are partially, not exhaustively, descriptive, and each has its own strengths and weaknesses. Because the meanings of these metaphors are fluid (not fixed) and contested (not consistent), each of the writers I examine is forced to wrestle with this linguistic uncertainty. In addition, because the meaning of these metaphors is flexible, none is intrinsically linked to any particular ethical framework; each could conceivably be used in the service of a variety of worldviews. Furthermore, metaphors of nature are used not in isolation but simultaneously, and so their contested meanings are dependent on the equally contested meanings of all the other metaphors I discuss. Understanding nature as a "park," for instance, also requires understanding it as a "frontier," "garden," "wilderness," and "utopia." Moreover, these metaphors interact historically, and their meanings change over time. As Donald Worster has observed, "Every generation . . . writes its own description of the natural order, which generally reveals as much about human society and its changing concerns as it does about nature. And these descriptions linger on in bits and pieces, often creating incongruous or incompatible juxtapositions" (*Nature's Economy* 292). Finally, the various ideas of nature expressed through metaphor are only part of the reason these environmental groups formed; many other factors also played a role. Nevertheless, because these ideas of nature were significant contributing factors in the formation of these organizations, I think it both possible and useful to explore how and why they became so.

Given these concerns, it may be best that we recognize the use of metaphor to understand the natural world as part of what the historian Richard White has termed a "protean conversation" between the past, present, and future inhabitants of the land and the land itself. "The conversation is protean," says White, "because both the speakers and what they speak of have changed constantly as the conversation has proceeded. Yet it is still a conversation because what is said remains linked to what was said before" ("Discovering Nature" 877).[12] Any examination of these metaphors, therefore, must of necessity be grounded in history — the history of particular places and particular people at particular moments in time.

The complexity of the stories I examine in this book, and the protean character of the conversation of which they are a part, suggests not only that these writers' words had a conserving effect, but also that we, in turn, should be conserving *them*. "To keep every cog and wheel is the first precaution of intelligent tinkering," Aldo Leopold wrote in "Round River" (*Round River* 146–47), and Leopold's idea has become a well-known rallying cry among advocates for biodiversity.[13] Not until recently, however, have scholars in the environmental humanities begun to recognize the wisdom of Leopold's claim outside of the sciences. In *Hope Is the Thing with Feathers* (2000) Christopher Cokinos has observed that "[h]istories, like species, can go extinct" (12), and in "Saving All the Pieces" (2001), Michael P. Branch has suggested that, just as we are trying to save the pieces of our evolutionary history, we should also be saving the pieces of our literary history. I could not agree more. Although none of the stories and metaphors I examine are in immediate danger of extinction, all of them have their critics, and some of them are more likely to be discarded than others. (Patricia Nelson Limerick, for instance, has called *frontier* the "f-word" and argued that it "is an unsubtle concept in a subtle world" [25].) Some critics even say we would be better off without the idea of "nature" altogether.[14] I disagree, and in the remainder of this introduction I hope to show why we should not only be paying attention to these conserving words but also be conserving them ourselves.

What Is Nature Writing?

> In the history of American writing about landscape, we read in brief the
> history of our thinking about nature and our place in the natural order.
> — Scott Russell Sanders, "Speaking a Word for Nature"

Three questions have confronted critics of nature writing since scholarship on the genre first appeared in the late nineteenth century: what to call the
genre, how to define its contents, and whether its boundaries change over time.[15]
To give but one popular example of the first question, Stephen Trimble describes
nature writing as a tradition of "personal essays about the American landscape" but
admits that "naming that tradition remains difficult": "Nature writers, natural
history writers, landscape essayists, literary naturalists, naturalist writers — no
single tag defines their work. Bookstores find them hard to classify and may shelve
their books under anything from nature, science, conservation, or travel, to an-
thropology, autobiography, political science, fiction, regional writing, and belles-
lettres" (3).

Arriving at a name for the genre, of course, implies an answer to the second
question regarding generic contents. Lawrence Buell, for instance, says he prefers
"'environmental nonfiction' or 'environmental prose' to 'nature writing,' which is
restrictive both in its implied identification of 'nature' as the writer's exclusive field
of environmental vision and in its tendency to exclude borderline cases like eclec-
tic travel and autobiographical and sermonic material" (429 n. 16). Buell then
points to the genre map offered by Thomas J. Lyon in *This Incomperable Lande*
(1989) to identify "most of the discursive strands that seem important" to him. Despite the good intentions of Lyon (as well as those of Peter Fritzell, Don Scheese,
and Patrick Murphy, all of whom also offer maps of the genre), critics of nature
writing would do well to heed Alastair Fowler's warning in *Kinds of Literature*
(1982) that "the whole enterprise of constructing genre maps is theoretically un-
sound. In mimicry of scientific procedure, it invents a spurious objectivity and permanence for entities that in reality are insubstantial and mutable" (249).[16]

If, instead, we follow Fowler in identifying a genre as "a communication system,
for the use of writers in writing, and readers and critics in reading and interpreting" (256), we might turn to the same system of communication described by
Richard White — that is, conversation — for an appropriately expansive definition
of the genre.[17] As Michael P. Branch and I have argued in the introduction to *The
Height of Our Mountains* (1998), "Our appreciation for the natural world and its
representative literature would be better served by a definition of nature writing
that focuses upon the expansive subject — rather than the generic circumscrip-
tion — of this literature" (8). The contemporary nature writer John Daniel shares

our concern about making excessively specific generic distinctions. "I am certainly aware of working in a *tradition* — a conversation we are having, through time, about our feelings toward the North American land," he writes. "It's a vital conversation, vigorous and diverse, imbued with a growing sense of urgency and possibility . . . but I worry that to focus on that conversation as a genre is to specialize it as a thing too merely literary — to miss the point, in perhaps a very subtle way, that what the conversation is about is more important than the conversation itself" (Murray et al. 77).[18]

Although there are virtues in expanding the boundaries of ecocriticism "beyond nature writing," as Karla Armbruster and Kathleen R. Wallace have suggested, there are also virtues in expanding the boundaries of the term "nature writing" to include works of fiction, poetry, and drama, as well as forms of nonfiction other than the essay — such as speeches, diaries, memoirs, and travel narratives. One such virtue is that the constituent parts of the term "nature writing" address the dual issues with which the literary conversation it describes is fundamentally concerned: the definition of "nature" and the problem of language.[19] Nature writing might best be defined, in other words, in terms of its expansive subject: the interaction of nature and culture in a particular place.

An answer to the third question — whether the boundaries of the genre change over time — is, of course, implied in the inherent interactivity of conversation. Ralph Cohen addresses one aspect of this generic interactivity in "Genre Theory, Literary History, and Historical Change" when he says: "Call a genre a family of texts, a communal group of texts, a consortium of texts. Whatever they are called, such texts are dynamic. Their semantic elements are both *intra*-active within the genre and *inter*active with members of other genres" (97). Furthermore, as Fowler has noted, genres are also interactive with so-called extraliterary events (277).

Our difficulty in coming to terms with the generic historicity of "nature writing" illustrates an ongoing tension between essentialism and constructivism in defining the genre: is there an unchanging essence to "nature writing," or do writers and readers construct it over time? John Daniel's comment that "what the conversation is about is more important than the conversation itself" reflects a fundamentally *rhetorical* understanding of genre that embraces the latter, constructivist approach, with which I agree. Such an approach is less concerned with what nature writing *is* than with what it *does*. Furthermore, this approach not only reflects Carolyn Miller's understanding of "genre as social action" but also emphasizes the significance of environmental history in interpreting nature writing. It urges us to move beyond a limited definition of the genre as first-person, nonfiction essays in favor of an analysis of readers and writers who function in history — a history that includes even these writers' seemingly "extraliterary" efforts at environmental reform.[20]

Such considerations of genre animate all the chapters of this book. Theodore Roosevelt, for instance, is often classified as an "outdoor writer" rather than a "nature writer," reflecting the bias Joseph Wood Krutch exhibited when he claimed that "no one can be called a nature writer rather than a sportsman to whom his fellow creatures are . . . consistently merely game" (Krutch 29). Only half in jest, Paul Schullery has similarly pointed out that "[w]hat is called outdoor writing usually involves fishing or hunting. It is distinguished from nature writing (in which the writer hardly ever kills anything) and environmental writing (in which the writer hardly ever has any fun) and is widely regarded as a lower form of written expression — sort of what jockspeak ('O.K., you guys, pair off by threes!') is to regular speech" ("Hope" 1). In contrast to these restrictive definitions, it seems important to include such "outdoor writing" within the purview of "nature writing," if only to demonstrate *all* the ways in which human representations of "nature" are socially constructed. Robert L. Dorman, for instance, has observed that John Muir's "own stories of mountain climbing and glacier exploring, though directed to divergent ethical ends, may not have seemed very different to readers from this emerging genre of outdoor adventure writing" (135). Similarly, although "environmental fiction" is usually excluded from the genre of nature writing, Edward Abbey's *Monkey Wrench Gang* deserves our close attention for precisely the same reason Roosevelt's writing does, although these authors reside at the opposite end of the ideological spectrum. In addition, studying environmental fiction as nature writing helps to remind us that, as David James Duncan has put it, "all writers and readers are full-time imaginers, all prose is imaginative, and fiction and nonfiction are just two anarchic shades of ink swirling round the same mysterious well" (56).[21]

The Definition of "Nature"

The term "nature writing" is useful because it calls attention to the two principal subjects with which the genre is concerned: the definition of "nature" and the problem of language.

Defining "nature," of course, is no easy task, as Raymond Williams recognized when he described it as "perhaps the most complex word in the [English] language" ("Nature" 184). As Williams's comment suggests, the concept of "nature" is not common to all times and all cultures; not only does it have a discernible history, but its history is primarily Western.[22] Nevertheless, it is possible to narrow the many meanings the word has had over time in the West to the "two principal meanings" John Stuart Mill identified in his essay on "Nature" (1874): "In one sense, it means all the powers existing in either the outer or the inner world and everything which takes place by means of those powers. In another sense, it means, not everything which happens, but only what takes place without the agency, or without the voluntary and intentional agency, of man. This distinction is far from exhausting the ambiguities of the word; but it is the key to most of those on which important consequences depend" (375).

In *Uneven Development* (1984), Neil Smith characterizes these two meanings as embodying an essential dualism between "nature" as *external*, in which the word is seen to represent the nonhuman world, and *universal*, in which it is understood to encompass the entire universe, including the human sphere. "These two conceptions of nature are both interrelated and mutually contradictory," claims Smith. For instance, "In our experience of national parks, mountain retreats and weekend vacations in the country, we experience a . . . journey from the externality of nature, as experienced from the city, to the universality of nature in which we endeavour to immerse ourselves. Externality is replaced by universality, at least for the weekend" (14). The interrelated character of these two referents is further illustrated by the opening line of Thoreau's essay "Walking," in which Thoreau announces: "I wish to speak a word for Nature, for absolute freedom and wildness, as contrasted with a freedom and culture merely civil, — to regard man as an inhabitant, or a part and parcel of Nature, rather than a member of society" (93). Inspired by his encounters with the nonhuman world (nature as external), Thoreau celebrates nature as the true home of humans (nature as universal).

To speak of nature as either external or universal is to speak of the reality of its *being* — its material or ontological status. To do so, however, also entails acknowledging our different ways of *knowing* nature — its ideological or epistemological status, and the tension between these two aspects of "nature" is at the heart of current debates about the social construction of nature.[23] To take an oft-cited example, when Bill McKibben mourns the end of "nature" as a consequence of human-induced climate change in *The End of Nature* (1989), he mourns a change in nature's material status — a change that he believes also reflects a change in the definition of "nature." According to McKibben, "We have changed the atmosphere, and thus are changing the weather. By changing the weather, we make every spot on earth man-made and artificial. We have deprived nature of its independence, and that is fatal to its meaning. Nature's independence *is* its meaning; without it there is nothing but us" (58).[24] For McKibben, human modification of the materiality of nature (on an atmospheric level) results in a change in the idea of "nature" (from external to universal, which McKibben regards as no "nature" at all). Thus what for Thoreau was cause for celebration is for McKibben cause for alarm.

Despite their differences, Thoreau and McKibben both share an interest in the empirical, sensory engagement of nature's *being*, whether through personal experience or scientific investigation, and they both recognize the ways in which that "nature" is shaped — both materially and ideologically — by *human* beings. They write of human modifications to material nature, whether on the ground or in the atmosphere, and they reflect on the influence that language and culture can have on our ideas of nature, whether personal or scientific. Thus in different ways and to different degrees, both writers demonstrate their appreciation for the paradoxical character of human existence. Neither all "natural" nor all "cultural," humans are part and parcel of the material world while at the same time being members of particular cultures. This is not to say that human cultures can exist outside of their natural environments, but it is to say that humans never have and never will exist wholly in a "state of nature." To be human is to be as much an inhabitant of culture as an inhabitant of nature. We are both *apart from* external "nature" and *a part of* universal "nature." As Wendell Berry has put it, "Our problem, exactly, is that the human and the natural are indivisible, and yet are different" ("Preserving Wildness" 139).[25]

The Problem of Language

Among the many determinants of culture, language is arguably the most significant, and as a result, it is often considered the principal characteristic that distinguishes the human from the nonhuman.[26] The degree to which this is the case is, as I suggested earlier, the second defining characteristic of nature writing as a genre. This is not to say that all nature writers consciously engage the question of human language use, but it is to say that the problem of language is a dominant theme — whether articulated or not — in most writing about the natural world. The problem cuts two ways: to what degree are humans and nonhumans able to communicate nonlinguistically, and to what degree does language use influence how humans know the world?

Several writers have recently explored both these questions by emphasizing the neglected status of oral communication in human-nonhuman interactions. Christopher Manes, for instance, has argued in "Nature and Silence" (1992) that animistic cultures offer another way of knowing, one in which "human speech is not understood as some unique faculty, but as a subset of the speaking of the world" (342). "To regard nature as alive and articulate," Manes claims, "has consequences in the realm of social practices. It conditions what passes for knowledge about nature and how institutions put that knowledge to use" (340).[27] In *The Spell of the Sensuous* (1996), David Abram extends this argument, suggesting that this epistemological shift from sensory participation *with* the world to abstract thought *about* the world can be traced to the rise of alphabetic literacy.[28] "[O]nly . . . by conceiving language as a purely abstract phenomenon, can we claim it as an exclusively human attribute," Abram argues. "Only by overlooking the sensuous, evocative dimension of human discourse, and attending solely to the denotative and conventional aspect of verbal communication, can we hold ourselves apart from, and outside of, the rest of animate nature" (79). Not only is this sensuous aspect of human language present in the "gesture and bodily expressiveness" of oral discourse, according to Abram, but "[t]he human voice in an oral culture is always to some extent participant with the voices of wolves, wind, and waves — participant, that is, with the encompassing discourse of an animate earth" (116–17). "In indigenous, oral cultures," Abram argues, "nature itself is articulate; it *speaks*" (116).[29]

The problem, of course, is hermeneutic: how to *interpret* what nature is saying. Although knowledge of the world can be gained nonlinguistically, we humans interpret that knowledge linguistically, relying on discourse communities to help us determine its meaning and communicate that meaning to others. Abram admits as much, noting that "there can be no question of simply abandoning literacy, of turning away from all writing" (*Spell* 273).[30] Language is, in short, doubly problematic: it affects our ability not only to *know* nature but also to *represent* it, regardless of whether "nature" is understood externally or universally.

Although the nature writers I discuss strive to re-present the sensory "presentness" of the natural world to their readers (who usually are not present at the place being described), they are never able to do so fully. And although they also seek to represent "nature" in the political arena, to act as representatives for part or all of the nonhuman world, it is never clear that they are, in fact, representing that world as it would wish to be represented (even if the philosophical problems accompanying that concept could be resolved). *Conserving Words* thus attempts to explore the problem of language in two senses: the epistemological question of how these writers know and represent nature, as well as the ontological status of the nature they claim to know and represent. To put it another way, my goal concerns both idealism and materialism; I seek to understand how the idea of "nature" has been constituted in history, as well as how its constitution has affected the material world it purports to name. Not only were these writers representing their own human ideas of nature (as a frontier, garden, park, wilderness, or utopia), the words they employed also had observable effects; they achieved results and mattered in practice. They were *conserving words*.

By emphasizing the necessity of representing a "nature" that cannot represent itself, as well as the ways in which the act of representing "nature" necessarily entails constructing the object of that representation, I do not mean to suggest that nature does not somehow exist. Far from it. Rather, I mean only that our knowledge of nature is always partial and limited, that works of nature writing are not transparent windows onto the world but are always historically and culturally mediated. As Holmes Rolston III has observed, "We need to think about language, about the concept of 'nature.' But this does not mean that we cannot think with such words about the world. There is always some sort of cognitive framework within which nature makes its appearance, but that does not mean that what appears is only the framework" ("Nature for Real" 43). Or as Michael Bruner and Max Oelschlaeger have put it, "To accept the premise that language overdetermines human behavior does not also entail the conclusion that . . . 'it's language all the way down'" (385 n. 31).[31]

In making this claim, I seek to find a middle ground between the reductionist tendencies of what might be termed "hard" versions of both social constructionism and realism. Anna L. Peterson asks the central question in this regard: "can we achieve a balance between the social constructionist critique of the naive idea of an essential, universal nature, on the one hand, and a sense of the independent reality and value of nature, on the other?" (74). Can we, in other words, avoid reducing nature to culture and culture to nature? I believe we can, as scholars in many fields have begun to articulate.[32] Although we can never arrive at an essential "nature," we can nevertheless strive to listen to the "voices" of nature, as expressed through direct experience. Being wholly in the world — living in language, culture, and history — we can never arrive at a complete picture of reality, but by tracing a history of "nature" as an object of discursive practices, of specific attempts to circumscribe a nature unable to be *fully* captured in discourse, we can not only reveal the ecology of influence at work in these representations but also examine them in relation to the soil from which they spring — and which they, in turn, influence. We can, in short, better recognize our own foundations as biological creatures — that is, as creatures of a "nature" we can never wholly access through linguistic means.[33] In the process, of course, we can also acquire a degree of humility.[34]

Achieving a sense of humility about our relationship to nature can in turn have important implications for our material and ideological understandings of "nature." For one thing, it can help us to recognize, as Gary Snyder has written, that "we do not easily know nature, or even know ourselves. Whatever it actually is, it will not fulfil our conceptions or assumptions. It will dodge our expectations and theoretical models. There is no single or set 'nature' either as 'the natural world' or 'the nature of things.' The greatest respect we can pay to nature is not to trap it, but to acknowledge that it eludes us and that our own nature is also fluid, open, conditional" (*No Nature* v).[35] Cultivating a sense of humility can also remind us not to overemphasize the influence environmental ideas have had in history. As J. R. McNeill observes in *Something New under the Sun* (2000), environmental ideas and politics constitute only a fraction of the forces that influence environmental change. "Natural" changes such as tornadoes, volcanoes, and earthquakes alter the dynamics of ecological systems, as do anthropogenic changes occasioned by demographic shifts (such as population growth, migration, and urbanization) and technological developments (such as the advent of the automobile, the jet engine, and the computer). McNeill admits that "what people thought affected the environment because to some extent it shaped their behavior" (326) and that "successful ideas require great communicators to bring about wide conversion" (337), but environmental ideas and politics are only part of the influential forces that have shaped our world. Global ecosystem change and human behavior will always be multicausal phenomena.[36]

What Is Metaphor?

> But maybe that *was* the point, or if not the point . . . then at least the effect: to suggest that nature might be more various than any one of our conceptions of it. That any single view — whether it be wilderness or garden, sublime or picturesque, refuge or prospect — is only that, a version of nature and not the whole of it.
> —Michael Pollan, *A Place of My Own*

According to Lawrence Buell, one important way in which nature writers have exercised an influence on the emerging culture of environmental concern is "through metaphors that have come to seem deceptively transparent through long usage" (3). Indeed, as several critics have observed, the use of metaphor is pervasive at all levels of environmental discourse.[37] Each of the metaphors of "nature" used by the writers I discuss, for instance, refers to nature in terms of a particular place: frontier, garden, park, wilderness, utopia. This hardly exhausts the diversity of such metaphors, which includes terms that describe "nature" as:

friend or family member (self, mother, father, sister, brother, wife, husband, partner)
actor (god or goddess, minister, monarch, lawyer, selective breeder, enemy)
organism (body)
network (web, community, tapestry)
machine (clock, engine, computer, spaceship)
state of being (virgin, harmony, balance)
mode of communication (book)
built object (bank, sink, storehouse, pharmacy, lifeboat, home)
contested landscape (battlefield, commons)

As Buell explained, "We cannot begin to talk or even think about the nature of nature without resorting to . . . [such metaphors], whether or not we believe they are true, and our choice of metaphors can have major consequences" (281).

Why this is the case is suggested by Leo Marx's comment regarding two of the geographical metaphors I explore: the garden and the wilderness. In *The Machine*

in the Garden (1964) Marx observed: "What is most revealing about these contrasting ideas of the American landscape is not, needless to say, their relative accuracy
in picturing the actual topography. They are not representational images. America was neither Eden nor a howling desert. These are poetic metaphors, imaginative constructions which heighten meaning far beyond the limits of fact. And yet,
like all effective metaphors, each had a basis in fact. In a sense, America was *both*
Eden and a howling desert; the actual conditions of life in the New World did lend
plausibility to both images" (43).[38]

The Functions of Metaphor

What, then, is metaphor, and how does it function in environmental discourse?
On the most rudimentary level, a metaphor can be defined as "a figure of speech
in which a word or phrase that ordinarily designates one thing is used to designate
another, thus making an implicit comparison" *(American Heritage)*. Such a definition, however, conceals a rich history of thought about the use and purpose of
metaphor. As Terence Hawkes observed, two fundamental views of metaphor exist: "There is what might be called the *classical* view, which sees metaphor as 'de-
tachable' from language; a device that may be imported into language in order to
achieve specific, pre-judged effects. These aid language to achieve what is seen as
its major goal, the revelation of the 'reality' of a world that lies, unchanging,
beyond it. And there is what might be called the *romantic* view, which sees metaphor as inseparable from a language which is 'vitally metaphorical', and a 'reality'
which is ultimately the end-product of an essentially 'metaphorical' interaction
between words and the 'hurrying of material' they encounter daily. Metaphor, deliberately invoked, intensifies language's characteristic activity, and involves, quite
literally, the creation of a 'new' reality" (90).

Most prominent among the recent "romantic" interpreters of metaphor have
been George Lakoff and Mark Johnson, whose *Metaphors We Live By* (1980) continues to exert a powerful influence on rhetorical studies of language use.[39] Metaphor, they declare, "is pervasive in everyday life, not just in language but in
thought and action. Our ordinary conceptual system, in terms of which we both
think and act, is fundamentally metaphorical in nature" (3). According to Lakoff
and Johnson, metaphors are not only descriptive but also constructive and productive. They help to create meaning and reality and to produce certain effects.
In terms of representations of "nature," metaphors not only explain what nature
is but also structure how we perceive and think about nature and what we do in
nature.

First, metaphors of nature are constructive. As Lakoff and Johnson put it, "The
very systematicity that allows us to comprehend one aspect of a concept in terms

of another will necessarily hide other aspects of the concept. In allowing us to focus on one aspect of a concept, a metaphorical concept can keep us from focusing on other aspects of the concept that are inconsistent with that metaphor" (10). To put it metaphorically, metaphors are like searchlights that illuminate one part of the terrain but leave other parts in the dark (Fill and Mühlhäusler 5). In other words, each of the metaphors for "nature" I discuss has the potential to diminish the influence of different, competing metaphors. Because Theodore Roosevelt saw nature as a frontier, for instance, he had a difficult time viewing its creatures as his friends.

Not all metaphors of nature are inconsistent with one another, however, and each of the writers I examine uses a variety of different but compatible metaphors. Mabel Osgood Wright, for instance, views nature as both a garden and a friend, and John Muir eventually comes to see Yosemite National Park as his home. Thus although the first four metaphors I discuss generally envision "nature" as an external part (frontier, garden, park, wilderness) rather than a universal whole (utopia), such representations need not contradict one another, and in practice they often overlap. Another way to put this is to say that different forms of synecdoche (the substitution of a part for the whole, or the whole for a part) can be mutually compatible.[40] Consider, for instance, how the idea of "God" can be understood as simultaneously external and universal. While some religious traditions consider God to be external to (and thus separate from) human beings, others view God as being internal to (and thus continuous with) human beings; despite this apparent contradiction, many religious believers have little trouble understanding God as existing both "inside" and "outside" human beings.[41]

The second notable function of metaphor is that it is productive. "In most cases," claim Lakoff and Johnson, "what is at issue is not the truth or falsity of a metaphor but the perceptions and inferences that follow from it and the actions that are sanctioned by it. In all aspects of life, . . . we define our reality in terms of metaphors and then proceed to act on the basis of the metaphors" (158).[42] Each metaphor used by the writers I discuss, for instance, contains both an explanation of "nature" and a prescription for human activity. Among other things, a person can conquer a frontier, cultivate a garden, visit a park, study a wilderness, and create a utopia. This being the case, metaphor must necessarily be seen as a political tool, as theologian Sallie McFague has emphasized. "To become aware of the metaphors that govern basic perspectives is, among other things, a political act," McFague observes in *Metaphorical Theology* (1982); "for the possibility of change both at the personal and public levels depends upon consciousness of hidden metaphors" (55–56). It comes as no surprise, therefore, that in his discussion of the Bakhtinian road to ecological insight Michael J. McDowell suggests that one of the most important questions ecocritics can ask is "What does the way a writer uses metaphors reveal about his or her representation of landscape?" (384–85). My argument is that these metaphors reveal how nature writers have attempted not only to come to terms with the meaning of "nature" and the problem of language but also to articulate what will be the focus of environmentalism and what will remain in its peripheral vision.

How and why particular metaphors of nature have come into and gone out of focus is a complicated question. The writers I discuss are not, to be sure, creating such metaphors anew. Rather, they are recasting, reconstituting, transforming, and reacting to already existing conceptions of the natural world. Moreover, the effectiveness of these metaphors depends, as Evelyn Fox Keller has written of scientific metaphors, "not only on available social resources but also on the technical and natural resources that are available" (xiii). Exactly how this process of metaphoric change operates, however, has never been especially clear. As Keller asks: "*Some* relation between the shift in metaphor . . . and the concurrent social transformation seems undeniable, but just how strong is the relationship? . . . [A] great deal more needs to be done to sort out the complex lines of influence and interactions of cultural norms, metaphor, and technical development" (xiv).

Metaphor, Narrative, and Value

One of my central claims in this book is that metaphors have played a critical role in the social transformation called environmentalism because they have enabled narratives that both convey human values about and describe human relationships with the nonhuman world. All descriptions of landscapes, in other words, are also descriptions of human relationships, and each metaphor of nature tells us as much about culture as it does about nature.

Environmental philosophers have traditionally identified two major categories of value: instrumental (or utilitarian) value and intrinsic (or inherent) value. Instrumental value is the value something has when it can be used to attain something else of value, and intrinsic value is the value something has when it is valuable in and of itself and not simply for its uses. All the writers I examine use metaphors of nature that express some form of instrumental values, such as recreational, cultural, aesthetic, religious, scientific, or political.[43] (I identify some of these in the table on page 7.) But some of them also engage, whether implicitly or explicitly, the question of intrinsic value. For example, while the ranch life and hunting books of Theodore Roosevelt are fundamentally utilitarian and anthropocentric, the so-called radical environmentalism of Edward Abbey's nonfiction is nonanthropocentric to the point of being antihumanistic: "I'd rather kill a *man* than a snake," Abbey announces in *Desert Solitaire* (17).

Intrinsic value has been the subject of a great deal of debate among environmental philosophers, who have been concerned with two major questions: which aspects of nature are intrinsically valuable, and where does intrinsic value come from? Of the most prominent intrinsic value theories, *biocentrism* and *ecocentrism* stand out. Generally speaking, a biocentric, or life-centered, ethic attributes value either to individual organisms or to entire species, while an ecocentric, or system-centered, ethic attributes value to individual ecosystems or to the entire ecosphere.[44] Putting aside the various arguments for and against these positions, what is most notable is their metaphorical character. As Lakoff and Johnson wrote of metaphorical sentences, "Each is true for certain purposes, in certain respects, in certain contexts" (165). David Oates develops this pragmatic argument further in *Earth Rising* (1989): "These are metaphors, after all, not statements of fact. Each says what life is *like*, and only indirectly what life *is*. Because of this, there is no reason not to hold various pictures simultaneously — each of them potentially useful, to be chosen as the occasion warrants. Sometimes an individual is an individual. Other times, the organic wholeness of the group or the natural system will present itself as the relevant model. And other times yet, the web-like community of relations" (207–8). Thus, from a metaphoric perspective, the various species of intrinsic value are in fact complementary rather than contradictory.

Where intrinsic value comes from is a knottier, metaethical question, which also involves the meaning of "nature." Does intrinsic value exist objectively in nature, and humans merely recognize it, or is intrinsic value something subjective, which humans actually create, just as they create the idea of "nature"? Are environmental values dependent on environmental facts, or is empirical knowledge of "nature" wholly unreliable? Can an "ought" be derived from an "is"? Important as such questions are, of more immediate interest in this context is the dependence of any understanding of intrinsic value on narration and the relationships it implies. As Roger J. H. King has pointed out, "Abstract moral reasoning presupposes imaginative narrative contexts for their intelligibility, while narrative and metaphorical images provide a rich framework and material for abstract philosophical reflection and critique" ("Narrative" 35). In the context of narration, intrinsic value might also be conceived, as Christopher J. Preston has written, as "less a thing to be discovered in nature by the Kantian, rational subject and more of an affective awakening to the existence of something" ("Intrinsic Value" 255).[45]

The concepts of metaphor and narrative help us to understand the role of value in the development of environmentalism because they remind us that values emerge in practice, in the judgment of right and wrong conduct. Values imply *action* in the world. Geographical metaphors, in particular, have helped to shape the emergence of environmental narratives by suggesting the ways human beings might best know, and act in, nature. The landscapes in which we live, work, and play are thus partially constituted by our metaphors. Frontiers, gardens, parks, and wilderness areas are not merely places; they are also ideas of what those places have been, are, and should be — and how we should act in them. As a result, all these places also embody versions of the metaphor of "nature as utopia." The writers I examine were immersed in these metaphors and narratives in three ways: first, in determining what nature was and how they should act in it; second, in identifying a threat to its value (or in "affectively awakening" to something for which they should care); and third, in advocating for public acceptance of the metaphoric narrative which effectively (or affectively) grounded their values.

These geographical metaphors of nature contextualize human action in place: *this* frontier, *this* garden, *this* park, *this* wilderness, *this* utopia. In doing so, they illustrate Gary Snyder's observation that philosophy is "a place-based exercise. It comes from the body and heart and it is checked against shared experience" (*Practice* 64). By defining the expansive subject of nature writing as the interaction of nature and culture in a particular place, I mean to emphasize the importance of this concept of *place*, which J. Nicholas Entrikin describes as existing between objective fact and subjective experience. The "betweenness" of place, according to Entrikin, is realized in the dynamic suspension between the material and the ideal, between physical landscapes and their human inhabitants. To the degree that the writers I discuss value certain aspects of the natural world intrinsically, they do so based on the place-based stories certain metaphors invoke. As Holmes Rolston III has written, "An ethics should be rational, but rationality inhabits a historical system. The place that is to be counted morally has a history; the ethics that befits such a place will take on historical form; the ethics itself will have a history" (*Environmental Ethics* 342). The metaphors these writers engage, in other words, actually enable two kinds of narratives — human stories and natural stories, personal stories and historical stories — stories that, in practice, act as one. "We cannot create myth from scratch," writes Scott Russell Sanders in *Staying Put* (1993), "but we can recover or fashion stories that will help us to see where we are, how others have lived here, how we ourselves should live" (169).[46]

By emphasizing the interaction of nature and culture in a particular place, nature writing — perhaps more than any other species of writing — helps clarify the ways in which ethics is fundamentally narrative, contextual, historical, and embodied. It demonstrates that the root of our ethics is, in fact, rootedness — emerging in the interaction of self and place, mind and body, reason and emotion, fact and value.[47] Whether rendered as fiction or nonfiction, poetry or drama, nature writing presents individuals living in storied relationship with the natural world, seeking out forms of what Michael Polanyi has called "personal knowledge." As H. Lewis Ulman has written, "nature writing entails a hybrid mode of interpretation — making available to other persons a symbolic model of cognitive, affective, physical, ethical, and pragmatic relationships to the nonhuman world character- istic of an individual or collective human *subject*. This distinctly ethical interpre- tation foregrounds the *ethos* or moral character of the interpreters — in this case, both writers and readers — as it emerges in relation to the nonhuman world mod- eled in the interpretation" (49).[48] This, more than anything, is what makes nature writing so distinctive — it acknowledges and embraces our personhood, the para- doxes of being human, and in so doing, it also foregrounds the uncertainty in- volved in determining not only our values *(ethos)* but also the facts *(logos)* of the world in which we live. This is especially true through its recognition of the hu- mor *(pathos)* involved in misperceiving natural history information and the often confusing task of clarifying one's values in the face of an overwhelming amount of conflicting information.

The uncertainty displayed in nature writing also extends to the metaphors of na- ture and the narratives they enable. As Sara Ebenreck has written, "Rather than pro- ceed as if any one metaphor . . . is the finally correct metaphor, ethicists conscious of the constructive imagination at work in these basic metaphors might be more aware of the limits of any metaphorical construction and more open to the experi- ences and values embodied in alternate metaphoric constructions of the Earth" (14). In fact, environmentalists have long attempted to replace metaphors of nature they hold to be harmful with others they believe to be more appropriate: "machine" with "organism," for instance, or "enemy" with "friend" (Abram, "Mechanical"). As Max Oelschlaeger has acknowledged in *Caring for Creation*, "useful metaphors are likely more important than any other linguistic matter in a time of ecological crisis, since through them Americans might begin to reweave the modern story. Metaphors are essential to recasting our conception of the world and human be- havior in it, and this all the more so when metaphors derive from a foundational mythic structure" (119).[49] This observation is complicated, however, by the con- flicting narratives each metaphor can enable. The metaphor of "nature as woman," for example, can imply quite contradictory images and actions, as Roger J. H. King has pointed out: "At times, nature is the mother, honored for her nurturing support. At times, she is the admired lady on a pedestal, to be gazed upon from a distance. At other times, however, she is the passive and grossly physical other, whose irra- tionality and contingency demand to be controlled, or she is one who should be feared for her chaotic and uncontrollable vengefulness" ("Narrative" 32–33).

Despite this potential indeterminacy, the meaning of the metaphors I examine was in fact significantly constrained by the identity and location of the audience for these writers. Theodore Roosevelt, for instance, contributed to the formation and development of the Boone and Crockett Club not only by fostering a mythology of the frontier but also by employing a form of scientific realism with which his elite, urban audience could identify. The effectiveness of Mabel Osgood Wright's revival of the Audubon Society depended as much on the suburban location of her female readers as it did on her use of the imagery of the garden. John Muir's success at preserving nature in the national parks grew out of his gradual accommodation to the notion of tourism, a practice valued as highly by Muir's national audience as it was by the Sierra Club. If Aldo Leopold had not familiarized the Wilderness Society with the new science of ecology, his effort at broadening the society's definition of "wilderness" would never have succeeded. And Edward Abbey's vision of nature as a utopian space inspired Earth First! in part because Abbey's audience shared his interest in anarchism and the environment of the desert. Metaphors of nature, therefore, were only part of the reason these environmental groups succeeded. (Other factors included the size of the group, its sources of funding, and the political level on which it was operating.)

Similarly, the life and work of these writers was only partly about social protest, and to view their writing through this single lens would be a mistake. The facts of natural history in themselves were as interesting for many writers as any aspect of human society. Recognizing this point, Scott Slovic has distinguished between what he calls the "ingenuous exploration of epistemological issues" and "the explicit voicing of ideology" in nature writing ("Epistemology" 83). Slovic associates "the epistemological mode of nature writing with the rhetorical act of rhapsody (or celebration), for the simple process of expressing deep, ingenuous interest in a subject is, implicitly, a statement of appreciation — a celebration. . . . The more overtly political counterpart of rhapsody is the jeremiad (the warning or critique), the primary goal of which is to persuade its audience to adopt a new perspective by pointing out the problems with readers' current way of thinking" (85). All nature writers, Slovic suggests, "demonstrate a combination of epistemological exploration and persuasive social critique," but the perception of some writers as epistemologists and others as political "environmentalists" can be traced to their divergent use of what Slovic calls "embedded persuasive rhetoric" and "discrete persuasive rhetoric" (86). Nature writers who tend to merge the rhapsodic and the jeremiad work in the embedded rhetorical form, whereas writers who keep these rhetorical modes separate work in the discrete rhetorical form (86). Although "the great advantage of the jeremiad . . . is in the shock effect, which leads to immediate, albeit short-lived awakening," according to Slovic, "the more significant, long-term transformation of values is the work of writers who emphasize fundamental epistemological discoveries and whose political concerns, if any, are blurred with or deeply embedded in the epistemological" (105).[50] The degree to which this is true is the subject to which I now turn.

What Is Environmentalism?

The more clubs, the better. . . .

—John Muir to Theodore P. Lukens, 4 July 1899

In *Habits of the Heart* (1985), the influential study of individualism and commitment in American life, Robert Bellah and his collaborators criticized practitioners of what they called "American nature pantheism" for their tendency to avoid wrestling with the messy details of community practice and to focus instead on the role of the individual in the world. "If the mystical quest is pursued far enough," they noted, "it may take on new forms of self-discipline, committed practice, and community, as in the case of serious practitioners of Zen Buddhism. But more usually the languages of Eastern spirituality and American naturalistic pantheism are employed by people not connected with any particular religious practice or community" (235).

To some extent, this criticism can be applied to American nature writers, many of whom have popularized conservation through book and magazine publication but have not otherwise been politically active. This absence of community activism could be said to have begun with the genre's most visible exponent — Henry David Thoreau — and his fellow New England transcendentalists, who provided Americans with new ways of looking at the natural world but offered no plans or proposals for environmental reform, as Philip Shabecoff has noted (55).[51] "In Thoreau," Wallace Stegner has observed, "there is virtually every idea that later became gospel to the environmental movement, but it is there only as idea, not as action or call to action — unless withdrawal is action. He was not much of a believer in government, and he was the total opposite of a joiner. American as he was, wilderness-lover as he was, he was not a conservationist or environmentalist in our sense" ("Short History" 122). Even Thoreau's most political writing, "Resistance to Civil Government" (1849), offers little in the way of specifically *environmental* resistance.

Such an argument represents a version of the well-known "romance thesis" of American literature, which says that American writers characteristically escape from history and society into "nature."[52] Joyce Carol Oates has offered a version of this thesis in her memorable declaration that the natural world "inspires a painfully limited set of responses in 'nature writers'—REVERENCE, AWE, PIETY, MYSTICAL ONENESS" (236). To attend to "nature," in such a view, is to turn away from history, and so to write about nature is to participate in an ahistorical genre.[53] This thesis has two major faults: it depends upon the notion that aesthetic discourse has no social function, and it neglects the many ways in which nature writers have engaged both history and society.

In place of this thesis, I argue that our vision of the nature writer as romantic individualist is in need of major revision, both in terms of its romanticism and its individualism. Although nature writing in the Thoreauvian tradition stresses the romantic individualist, the relationships between the nature writers and environmental organizations I discuss in this book remind us that nature writing need not necessarily be romantic or individualistic. Rather, the genre has both developed with and helped to define the environmental movement, and it has had as much to say about culture as it has had to say about "nature." As Thomas J. Lyon observed, "Besides incorporating great intellectual currents, nature writing in America has also responded to actual historical conditions, in particular the decline of environmental quality, as the country was settled and relentlessly developed" (*Incomperable* 22).[54]

Organizing the Movement

Exactly what constitutes the "environmental movement" is a topic of considerable debate among scholars.[55] In *Forcing the Spring* (1993), Robert Gottlieb summarized what he called the "charged questions [that] lie at the heart of the problem of how to define environmentalism and its future direction": "What is an environmental group? Who is an environmentalist? How might different kinds of environmental groups influence the state of the environment — and the state of society? . . . Does environmentalism represent new kinds of social movements, democratic and populist insurgencies seeking a fundamental restructuring of the urban and industrial order? Or is it a set of interest groups influencing policy to better manage or protect the environment and help rationalize that same urban and industrial order? Is it a left-wing movement in disguise . . . ? Or is environmentalism apolitical, concerned with science rather than ideology . . . ? Is it a movement primarily about Nature or about industry, about production or about consumption, about wilderness or about pollution, about natural environments or about human environments, or do such distinctions themselves indicate differing interpretations of what environmentalism has been and ought to be?" (315).

Although the differing interpretations Gottlieb describes certainly exist, one point of agreement is clear: whatever else the environmental movement may be, it is largely defined by the environmental organizations that compose it. As Robert J. Brulle has written, "Environmental organizations . . . are virtually synonymous with the idea of the environmental movement in the United States. They are central to the environmental movement, since they serve as developers and carriers of its identity. These organizations are also major actors in environmental politics. Finally, the messages they develop have an important influence on the formation of individual attitudes and behaviors toward the natural environment" ("Environmental Discourse" 58).

Although the "environmental movement" proper is a post–World War II phenomenon, its roots were planted at least as early as the late nineteenth century, and it is this broader history of environmental concern that interests me. Furthermore, given that the nature writers I examine were most concerned with protecting threatened aspects of the nonhuman world — whether particular species or landscapes — it is important to emphasize that this conservationist activity is only part of the contemporary environmental movement, which, as Gottlieb suggests, is as much concerned with protecting human well-being, achieving environmental justice, and fostering sustainable ways of living, not to mention attempting to restore degraded landscapes. Likewise, environmental organizations are not the only means of addressing environmental problems, which can also be remedied by individual actions, government initiatives, and economic reforms. By focusing on these five writers and groups, I do not mean to suggest that they represent the entire scope of environmentalism, nor that other aspects of the environmental movement are unworthy of our attention. I mean only to trace the most prominent examples of one particular pattern in the history of environmental advocacy.

What I call "environmental organizations," then, actually manifest a diverse range of interests that change over time. Although "new groups emerg[e] from old ones to represent each new stage of a deepening political consciousness," the older groups do not just die off; "they remain in existence as points of tension for the new groups" (Killingsworth and Palmer 18). Prior to the founding of the Boone and Crockett Club in 1887, for instance, a number of associations interested in land-use came into being, although none could strictly be called a "conservation" organization.[56] When the Boone and Crockett Club was founded, it became the first sportsman's organization to address conservation issues on a national scale, placing itself in dialogue with these older groups.[57] Likewise, when the Audubon Society (1886) and the Sierra Club (1892) were organized, they introduced yet other voices to the conservation crusade, before eventually being joined by the Wilderness Society (1935), Earth First! (1980), and hundreds of other conservation and environmental groups.

Leading the Conversation

In *Philosophy and the Mirror of Nature* Richard Rorty suggests that conversation may be "the ultimate context within which knowledge is to be understood" (389). "To see keeping a conversation going as a sufficient aim of philosophy, to see wisdom as consisting in the ability to sustain a conversation," Rorty says, "is to see human beings as generators of new descriptions rather than beings one hopes to

be able to describe accurately" (378). Rorty's title for the final section of his book —
"Philosophy and the Conversation of Mankind"—alludes to Michael Oakeshott's
influential essay "The Voice of Poetry in the Conversation of Mankind" (1959), in
which Oakeshott describes "the conversation of mankind" as "the meeting-place
of various modes of imagining" (497). In this conversation, writes Oakeshott, there
is "no voice without an idiom of its own: the voices are not divergencies from some
ideal, non-idiomatic manner of speaking, they diverge only from one another"
(497).

Rorty's suggestion that the aim of philosophy should be "keeping a conversation
going" can also be applied to the work of American nature writers throughout the
last century. If, rather than seeing these writers as representing "nature" in an es-
sentialized sense, we see them instead as "generators of new descriptions," as simultaneously participating in and modifying the metaphoric discourses of their
particular historical moments, we might also understand how what Oakeshott
calls the "voice of poetry" is, for these writers, an attempt to represent the "voice"
of nature in both language and politics. Earlier, I referred to what the historian
Richard White has termed the "protean conversation" that occurs between past,
present, and future inhabitants of the land and the land itself. "The conversation
is protean," White said, "because both the speakers and what they speak of have
changed constantly as the conversation has proceeded. Yet it is still a conversation
because what is said remains linked to what was said before" (877). This expanded
notion of conversation offers a particularly appropriate metaphor by which the
claims of the following chapters may be understood.

To study metaphor as a way of understanding the natural world is to posit the
existence of not one story but multiple stories, told in a dialogue as hesitant, overlapping, and complexly structured as an actual conversation. This conversational
model therefore requires the recognition that "nature" is not singular but plural,
that the "voices" of "nature" in this conversation are many and various. As Michael
Bruner and Max Oelschlaeger have pointed out, the model of a conversation
"does not reduce the biophysical world to language but rather aims, as for example
[Aldo] Leopold's land ethic does, to incorporate the natural world into human discourse" (385 n. 31). This model also echoes John Daniel's definition of nature writing as "a *tradition* — a conversation we are having, through time, about our feelings toward the North American land" (Murray et al. 77). Finally, it compares
favorably to what Mitchell Thomashow has called the "*emerging interpretive tradition* of American environmentalism," within which these nature writers and environmental organizations are working: "*Tradition* means that environmentalism
moves from one generation to the next, both as a series of beliefs and through the
habits of community life. Knowledge is passed on from one person to the next,
either through books and ideas, or through the ecological practices of everyday

life. *Interpretive* signifies that people look to environmentalism as a way to formulate an ecological identity, to learn about appropriate ways of living in nature, to make sense of the world around them, and to construct a moral point of view. *Emerging* describes how environmentalism is still in its formative stages. It is a movement that constantly takes new shape as it generates new ideas" (*Ecological* 28). We might best see nature writers, then, as leading the conversation about "nature" into new realms of ideas and actions, much like a teacher might lead a class discussion, balancing her desire to direct the conversation in ways she believes to be beneficial with her recognition that the best conversations must ultimately evolve organically, from the ground up, and cannot be forced, only nurtured.

How This Book Is Organized

Most historians explain the development of the environmental movement by positing a series of "eras" or "waves" of environmental concern. This book simplifies that history into two parts, which I call "Preserving the Pieces" and "Protecting the Planet."

Part 1, "Preserving the Pieces," examines three Progressive Era nature writers and the organizations they helped to found: Theodore Roosevelt and the Boone and Crockett Club, Mabel Osgood Wright and the National Audubon Society, and John Muir and the Sierra Club. The "pieces" they attempted to preserve are both individual places (now Yellowstone National Park in Wyoming, Birdcraft Sanctuary in Connecticut, and Yosemite National Park in California) and particular creatures and species (the American bison, a variety of songbird species, and the sequoia, among others). These writers relied, in part, upon the metaphors of "nature" current in their time — the frontier, the garden, and the park — to organize these groups and preserve these pieces of the landscape. Although the audiences for these writers overlapped to some degree, particularly with regard to race, they were quite distinct in terms of geography, gender, and class.

Part 2, "Protecting the Planet," explores the gradual globalization of this preservationist impulse brought about by the rise of scientific ecology in the mid–twentieth century and the rebelliousness of the post-1960s era. In this section I examine the relationships of Aldo Leopold and the Wilderness Society, and Edward Abbey and Earth First! Although both these writers remained as committed to protecting particular pieces of the natural world as Roosevelt, Wright, and Muir, they also broadened the scope of environmentalism beyond the particular concerns of the Progressive Era to address the idea of wildness generally and the threats posed to nature by industrialism, urbanization, and militarization. The organizational success of these writers depended, in part, on the metaphors that gave their ideas currency: the representation of "nature" as a wilderness and as utopia.[58]

Finally, in the conclusion, I return to the themes of this introduction and consider how we might choose from among competing metaphors of nature and what the future may hold for nature writers and environmental organizations. In particular, I discuss the growing influence of island biogeography and ask whether the metaphor of nature as island might provide a new discursive frame for twenty-first-century nature writers and environmental organizations — a frame that could potentially demonstrate that preserving the pieces and protecting the planet are, in fact, complementary approaches.

Given my focus on the *interaction* of nature writing, metaphor, and environmentalism, this book does not attempt to provide a comprehensive history of any of these subjects; out of necessity, it omits much more than it includes. Chapter 1 does not discuss Roosevelt's term as president in detail; this topic is covered at length by many other scholars. Chapter 2 does not dwell much on the role of George Bird Grinnell in the founding of the first Audubon Society in 1886. Chapter 3 largely confines itself to Muir's writings about California and does not treat his travels to the Southeast, Alaska, or South America at length. Chapter 4 does not consider Leopold's "land ethic" in detail, despite its centrality to most treatments of Leopold's work. And chapter 5 explores only a few of Abbey's books and does not address most of the other leaders of Earth First!

In addition to the two-part structure of the entire book, the chapters of *Conserving Words* are organized into three sections each. In section 1 I discuss the economic, political, and theological systems out of which the personal philosophies of these writers emerged. In section 2 I discuss the texts these writers produced, especially those that affected the associations with which they were involved, as well as those that were written specifically for these groups. In particular, I explore how nature writing affects the reader not only through *what* it says but also through *how* it says it, paying special attention to the metaphoric emphases evident in each text's rhetorical strategies and narrative structures. I also explore the interaction of text and context, asking how these writers shaped their messages to fit the concerns of their perceived audiences at particular times and places, with both writers and audiences being influenced by sexual, racial, and class-based interests and prejudices. Finally, in section 3, I consider the environmental groups themselves, evaluating their policies and programs and exploring the ways in which they resembled or differed from other environmental organizations. Given my focus on the metaphoric redescriptions of "nature," I principally explore how these groups used the metaphors of nature as a frontier, garden, park, wilderness, or utopia to frame their arguments and accomplish their goals. Examining these rhetorical strategies not only reveals institutional differences but also helps reinforce the idea that so-called literary texts participate in a larger framework of texts, institutions, and discursive practices. The nature writers I examine, therefore, are not merely different authors writing about different issues, but different people using different discourses to speak about "nature"—discourses that influenced, and were in turn influenced by, the environmental organizations these writers helped to found.

PART ONE

Preserving the Pieces

Progressive Conservation

CHAPTER ONE

The Closing of the Frontier

Theodore Roosevelt

and the Boone and

Crockett Club

The geology and the beetles will remain unchanged for ages, but
the big game will vanish, and only the pioneer hunter can tell
about it. Hunting books of the best type are often of more permanent
value than scientific pamphlets.

THEODORE ROOSEVELT TO GEORGE BIRD GRINNELL, 24 August 1897

AVING COMPLETED the manuscript of *Gouverneur Morris* (1888) on
4 September 1887 and having witnessed the birth of his second child
nine days later, Theodore Roosevelt decided the time was right for
another trip west. Convincing his cousin J. West Roosevelt and his friend Frank
Underhill to accompany him, Roosevelt left for the Dakota Badlands early in
November for five weeks of ranching and hunting. Underhill and West Roosevelt
did not last long, returning east on 14 November, so for the next three weeks Roosevelt was left to fend for himself, a circumstance that probably did not bother the
veteran rancher. "As you know," he wrote his sister Anna (or Bamie) the following
year, "I really prefer to be alone while on a hunting trip" (E. Morris, *Rise* 382).[1]

Roosevelt's paper trail uncharacteristically goes blank at this point, and the historian is left to wonder what Roosevelt may have encountered while riding across the
plains he had come to know so well over his previous seven years of western visits. In
The Rise of Theodore Roosevelt Edmund Morris speculates that, as Roosevelt rode
farther and farther afield, "he found the Badlands virtually denuded of big game"
and for the first time "realized the true plight of the native American quadrupeds,
fleeing ever westward, in ever smaller numbers, from men like himself" (378–83).

This inference certainly seems reasonable, given that the only game Roosevelt claims to have encountered during the trip were two black-tailed deer, which with extraordinary luck, he killed with one bullet (*Works* 1:409–10).[2] Lincoln Lang, a rancher who knew the Little Missouri Valley even better than Roosevelt, recalled with despair the ecological effects human intervention had caused in the region by 1887. Nature, Lang lamented, "was beginning to protest forcefully against misusage." Because the beavers had all been trapped out, the dams were letting go, causing ponds full of fish and wildlife to revert to dry streambeds. Desperate to find what water remained, thousands of cattle ate and trampled the grasslands, forming cow paths that increased erosion and made mud holes of what were once clear-running springs. Weed growth increased; migratory bird populations decreased; and game animals appeared less frequently with each passing day (Lang 222–24). Roosevelt himself had been marking the disappearance of big-game animals during his years in the Dakotas, noting in 1885, for instance, that elk and blacktail deer were growing increasingly scarce (*Works* 1:102).

It is not surprising to learn, therefore, that soon after Roosevelt returned to New York on 8 December 1887 he invited ten amateur riflemen to join him for dinner at Bamie's Madison Avenue home, swap hunting stories, and consider a remarkable request.[3] The details of this memorable evening were published two months later on the front page of *Forest and Stream:*

> At a dinner given recently in New York by a well-known gentleman who is interested in big-game shooting in the West, it was proposed to form a club which should bear the title of the Boone and Crockett Club. Only persons who have killed one or more varieties of North American large game with the rifle are to be eligible to membership, and the name, embracing as it does those of two of the best known American rifle shots, sufficiently indicates the character of the organization. It is essentially a club of American riflemen who use the arm for hunting. The suggestion made by their host was warmly welcomed by the gentlemen present, and a few names were suggested of persons who might be glad to become members of such an association. The members of the club, so far as it is developed, are all persons of high social standing, and it would seem that an organization of this description, composed of men of intelligence and education, might wield a great influence for good in matters relating to game protection. It would be premature at present to speak of the possibilities of such a club, but as matters develop in regard to it, the public will be kept advised upon the subject. (Grinnell, "Snap Shots" [1888] 61)

Thus was born the Boone and Crockett Club, which over the years did indeed go on to "wield a great influence for good in matters relating to game protection," and for which, as promised, *Forest and Stream* became the informal journal of record. One of the first voluntary organizations to address conservation issues on a national scale, the Boone and Crockett Club was also the first in a long line of environmental groups to be founded by a nature writer and to use nature writing as a means of increasing public education and fostering political change. As its founder and most prominent member, Theodore Roosevelt wielded considerable influence over the social, literary, and political activities of the club during its first quarter century — a contribution historians of the conservation movement have not always fully acknowledged. Literary scholars have similarly ignored Roosevelt's achievements as a writer, especially as a nature writer, in part because he wrote nonfiction and in part because his writing concerns historical and political events more than personal ones. This is unfortunate, because it was the interaction of Roosevelt's literary efforts with the political goals of the Boone and Crockett Club that helped give the club's efforts so much currency among legislators and the general public.

This chapter examines how Roosevelt's interests in natural history and nature writing developed, how his nature writings about the West helped make possible the formation and development of the Boone and Crockett Club, and how his theory of natural representations influenced the political representations of nature both he and the club put forward during the late nineteenth and early twentieth centuries. Although Roosevelt wrote about nature and natural history throughout his life, I focus mainly on the three books he wrote about the Dakotas in the 1880s and 1890s and the three essay collections he edited with George Bird Grinnell for the Boone and Crockett Club in the late 1890s. I argue that Roosevelt's legacy as a nature writer and a conservationist is twofold: although his integration of frontier romanticism and scientific realism helped further the Boone and Crockett Club's goal of wildlife conservation for utilitarian purposes, the strong aversion he expressed toward any form of sentimentalism discouraged related attempts at grounding an environmental ethic on the basis of compassion for the lives and well-being of nonhuman animals.

The Young Naturalist

"I can no more explain why I like 'natural history' than why I like California canned peaches," Theodore Roosevelt wrote near the end of his life, "nor why I do not care for that enormous brand of natural history which deals with invertebrates any more than why I do not care for brandied peaches. All I can say is that almost as soon as I began to read at all I began to like to read about the natural history of beasts and birds and the more formidable or interesting reptiles and fishes" (*Works* 5:384). In "My Life as a Naturalist" (1918), the essay in which he advances this history of his youth, Roosevelt makes a number of other similarly self-deprecating statements about his considerable achievements as a "faunal naturalist."[4] He balances these comments, though, with statements that also certify and emphasize his authority as a scientist and as a writer. "I never grew to have keen powers of observation," Roosevelt says at one point in the essay. "But whatever I did see I saw truly, and I was fairly apt to understand what it meant. In other words, I saw what was sufficiently obvious, and in such case did not usually misrepresent what I had seen" (*Works* 5:387). Observation, truth, interpretation, and representation: Roosevelt's invocation of these concepts is not merely the wishful thinking of an aging naturalist intent on dignifying his past. They are the keystones around which Roosevelt organized the rhetoric of his life, the refrains that recur throughout his writing on natural history.

"A Natural History of My Own"

As Roosevelt acknowledges in "My Life as a Naturalist," his study of natural history had always been intimately bound up with his habit of reading. David Livingstone's *Missionary Travels and Researches in South Africa*, with its vivid illustrations of giraffes, zebras, and rhinos, was an early favorite, as were the novels of Mayne Reid. Of *Robinson Crusoe*, the young "Teedie" preferred the second part — "with wolves in the Pyrenees" — to the first, and he disliked the *Swiss Family Robinson* "because of that wholly impossible collection of animals met by that worthy family as they ambled inland from the wreck" (*Works* 20:18–19). As he developed as a reader, Roosevelt turned to more technical books about animals, such as those by John James Audubon, Alexander Wilson, Thomas Nuttall, Elliott Coues, and other naturalists, but he also grew to identify with the heroes of Cooper's frontier tales and Longfellow's *Saga of King Olaf*. During the four summers his family spent in Madison, New Jersey, he invented his own adventure stories, which his sister Corinne recalls were "about jungles and bold, mighty and imaginary fights with strange beasts . . . . [T]here was always a small boy in the stories . . . who understood the language of animals and would translate their opinions to us" (E. Morris, *Rise* 45–46).

Roosevelt's decision to become a naturalist as well as a writer came with a discovery he made when he was seven years old, as he recounts in his *Autobiography* (1913): "I remember distinctly the first day that I started on my career as zoologist. I was walking up Broadway, and as I passed the market to which I used sometimes to be sent before breakfast to get strawberries I suddenly saw a dead seal laid out on a slab of wood. That seal filled me with every possible feeling of romance and adventure. I asked where it was killed, and was informed in the harbor. I had already begun to read some of Mayne Reid's books and other boys' books of adventure, and I felt that this seal brought all these adventures in realistic fashion before me. As long as that seal remained there I haunted the neighborhood of the market day after day. I measured it, and . . . I carefully made a record of the utterly useless measurements, and at once I began to write a natural history of my own, on the strength of that seal" (*Works* 20:16). The skull of the seal eventually became the first specimen in the "Roosevelt Museum of Natural History," a collection that, by 1868, had grown to include 250 bird nests, eggs, shells, insects, minerals, and other objects (Cutright, *Making* 8).[5] In subsequent years the museum would continue to expand, although "a rebellion on the part of the chambermaid" forced a relocation of the collections from Teedie's room to a case in the upstairs hallway (*Works* 20:16).[6] As significant as the collection itself is the fact that in the mind of the older Roosevelt — Roosevelt the autobiographer — the Broadway seal combined the romance of the adventure story with the realism of the natural history narrative, a synthesis of aesthetic forms that occurred throughout almost all his writings on nature.

At least as important as the books and creatures that surrounded him, Roosevelt's friends and family members also influenced the type and direction of natural history studies he pursued. His father, Theodore senior, collected scientific specimens and encouraged the proper treatment of animals through his work as a founder of the American Museum of Natural History (1869) and as a generous contributor to societies for the prevention of cruelty to animals (Cutright, *Naturalist* 9). Not only was the "Roosevelt Museum of Natural History" influenced by his father's interests (the charter for the American Museum of Natural History was signed in the Roosevelts' front parlor), but Theodore himself was one of the first contributors to the holdings of the larger museum. In 1871 he donated "1 Bat, 12 Mice, 1 Turtle, 1 skull: Red Squirrel and 4 Birds' Eggs" (Cutright, *Making* 37).

Roosevelt's uncle and next-door neighbor, Robert Barnwell Roosevelt, may also have provided a model for the kind of writer and conservationist Theodore was to become. A hunter and student of wildlife, Uncle Robert wrote such books as *Game Fish of the Northern States of America and British Provinces* (1862) and *Game Birds of the Coasts and Lakes of the Northern States of America* (1866) when Theodore was still a child, and he predicted the eventual demise of game animals if measures were not taken to protect them (Cutright, *Making* 7).[7] Theodore also found kindred spirits in his brother Elliott; two of his first cousins, West and Emlen Roosevelt; and Frederic Osborn, a younger brother of Henry Fairfield Osborn (Cutright, *Naturalist* 9).

Asthma and Nearsightedness

Despite his many advantages as a child, Roosevelt was also faced with two limitations: asthma and nearsightedness. Even these eventually became advantages, though, because the asthma encouraged him to exercise vigorously to improve his health, and the nearsightedness helped him develop an extraordinary sensitivity to sounds. Although the causes of asthma were not known at the time, Roosevelt's parents worked ceaselessly to alleviate his suffering, taking vacations in what they hoped would be more healthful climates, such as Barrytown, Riverdale, and Spuyten Duyvil north of New York City; various European countries; and Egypt and the Holy Land. Nevertheless, the asthma persisted. The first entry in the diary of Roosevelt's 1868 summer vacation in Barrytown reads, "I had an attack of the Asmer," and a recurring entry in the diary of his 1869 voyage to Europe is "I was sick last night" (Cutright, *Making* 4, 17).

During a summer vacation in Dobbs Ferry, New York, in 1872, Roosevelt first learned of his nearsightedness. Having just received his first gun from his father, he found himself unable to see, much less hit, any of the specimens his friends so easily bagged with the same weapon. Finally, when his friends read aloud an advertisement in huge letters on a distant billboard and Roosevelt was unable to see either the letters or the sign, he mentioned the incident to his father, who had him fitted for a pair of glasses. The glasses, Roosevelt said in his *Autobiography*, "opened an entirely new world to me. I had no idea how beautiful the world was until I got those spectacles" (*Works* 20:20).

With his vision corrected and his new gun in hand, Roosevelt was now much better equipped to pursue his goal of becoming "a scientific man of the Audubon, or Wilson, or Baird, or Coues type" (*Works* 20:25). Beginning in the early 1870s he began studying taxidermy with John G. Bell, who had accompanied John James Audubon on a trip to the Upper Missouri in 1841 and whose New York City laboratory was well known to the sportsmen of his day. He also began to frequent museums, visiting the Academy of Natural Sciences on his trips to Philadelphia and the American Museum of Natural History whenever he had the time. He learned to employ the scientific names of species, became familiar with the Linnaean system of classification, and turned his trips at home and abroad into collecting opportunities for his museum, which had grown to one thousand specimens by the spring of 1870 (Cutright, *Making* 30–32).

In addition to the three trips he took with his family to the Adirondacks and the three seasons he spent with them at their summer home in Oyster Bay, Long Island, Roosevelt's most important voyage in the early 1870s was the yearlong tour of Egypt and the Holy Land his family took in 1872 and 1873. For two months they floated up the Nile on a *dahabeah*, or houseboat, with Theodore and his father regularly going ashore in search of specimens. "Teedie and Father go out shooting every day," his sister Corinne recorded, "and so far have been very lucky. Teedie is always talking about it whenever he comes into the room,—in fact when he does come in the room you always hear the words 'bird' and 'skin.' . . . He never rests from his studies in natural history" (Robinson 56–57).

The Abandonment of Science

By the time Roosevelt entered Harvard University in the fall of 1876, he was fully prepared, as he put it, "to make science my life work." During his freshman year Roosevelt explained his plans to his father, who told him that if he "wished to become a scientific man" he could do so, provided he "really intensely desired to do scientific work" and to make it "a serious career" (*Works* 20:26). Though not for lack of desire, Roosevelt eventually changed his plans. As C. Hart Merriam has observed, Roosevelt "lived during the period of the ultra-microscopic specialization in the study of animate nature — the sad period in which the good old term 'natural history' fell into disuse, actually disappearing from text-books and college curricula" ("Naturalist" 183). Roosevelt himself detailed the reasons behind his decision in his *Autobiography*: "Harvard, and I suppose our other colleges, utterly ignored the possibilities of the faunal naturalist, the outdoor naturalist and observer of nature. They treated biology as purely a science of the laboratory and microscope, a science whose adherents were to spend their time in the study of minute forms of marine life, or else in section-cutting and the study of the tissues of higher organisms under the microscope. . . . My taste was specialized in a totally different direction, and I had no more desire or ability to be a microscopist and section-cutter than to be a mathematician. Accordingly I abandoned all thought of becoming a scientist" (*Works* 20:26–27).

Roosevelt's decision was neither as immediate nor as clear-cut as it may appear from this brief, retrospective account. In fact, he seems to have thoroughly enjoyed his scientific studies at Harvard, taking seven courses in science and natural history, all of which he passed with respectable, and sometimes impressive, scores.[8] During breaks in the academic year, he took excursions to the Adirondacks, the Maine woods, and Oyster Bay, publishing detailed lists of his ornithological findings in two small pamphlets, *The Summer Birds of the Adirondacks* (1877) and *The Birds of Oyster Bay, Long Island* (1879). Roosevelt also displayed an affinity for clubs and organizations at Harvard, an affinity that would manifest itself a decade later in his founding of the Boone and Crockett Club. He joined such campus groups as Hasty Pudding, Porcellian, Alpha Delta Phi, Dickey, the art club, the rifle club, the O.K. Club, the glee club, *Harvard Advocate,* and the boxing team; he presented papers to the Natural History Society on the gills of crustaceans and the coloration of birds; and he reported on sparrows to the Nuttall Ornithological Club (Cutright, *Making* 107–9).

Roosevelt's decision to abandon science, which he made sometime during his senior year, was affected by many factors, including his growing interest in political economy; his misgivings about the years of postgraduate study abroad that a scientific career would require; a lack of encouragement from faculty, family, and friends; and his single-minded pursuit of Alice Lee, the woman who would become his first wife (Cutright, *Making* 128). In a 13 February 1880 letter to his friend Henry Minot he said, "I write to you to announce my engagement to Miss Alice Lee; but do not speak of it till Monday. I have been in love with her for nearly two years now; and have made everything subordinate to winning her; so you can perhaps understand a change in my ideas as regards science &c." (Morison 43). One other reason for Roosevelt's break from professional science, however, may be found in the project he had begun during his senior year: writing the first two chapters of *The Naval War of 1812* (1882), his first book.

The Growth of a Writer

When and how Roosevelt developed his skills as a writer remains something of a mystery, but it is notable that almost all his early writing was about nature. His first efforts at composition, attempted at age eight, were the natural history of his Broadway seal and an essay entitled "The Foregoing Ant," based on his reading of naturalist J. G. Wood's *Homes without Hands* (Cutright, *Making* 6). Roosevelt had also been a faithful diarist, letter-writer, and notebook-keeper, all of which helped him refine his prose and increase his knowledge of natural history. In his *Autobiography*, he noted that he also "owed much to the professor of English [at Harvard], Mr. A. S. Hill," though he did not elaborate on Hill's contributions to his literary education (*Works* 20:24).

Whatever formal training Roosevelt may have had, his best prose seems to have resulted not from any academic exercise but from his close attention to objects in his immediate environment. Roosevelt's most compelling piece of college prose was written not for one of his courses but for himself, in the private notebook he kept of his 1877 trip to the Adirondacks. There he heard for the first time the legendary song of the hermit thrush, which John Burroughs has translated as "Oh speral, speral! Oh holy, holy! Oh clear away, clear away; clear up, clear up!" According to Roosevelt,

> Perhaps the sweetest bird music I have ever listened to was uttered by a hermit thrush. It was while hunting deer on a small lake, in the heart of the wilderness; the night was dark, for the moon had not yet risen, but there were clouds, and as we moved over the surface of the water with the perfect silence so strange and almost oppressive to the novice in the sport, I could distinguish dimly the outlines of the gloomy and impenetrable pine forests by which we were surrounded. We had been out for two or three hours but had seen nothing; once we heard a tree fall with a dull, heavy crash, and two or three times the harsh hooting of an owl had been answered by the unholy laughter of a loon from the bosom of the lake, but otherwise nothing had occurred to break the

death-like stillness of the night; not even a breath of air stirred among the tops of the tall pine trees. Wearied by our unsuccess we at last turned homeward when suddenly the quiet was broken by the sound of a hermit thrush; louder and clearer it sang from the depths of the grim and rugged woods, until the sweet, sad music seemed to fill the very air and to conquer for the moment the gloom of the night; then it died away and ceased as suddenly as it had begun. Perhaps the song would have seemed less sweet in the daytime, but uttered as it was, with such surroundings, sounding so strange and so beautiful amid these grand but desolate wilds, I shall never forget it. (Cutright, *Making* 101–2)

Roosevelt's turning point as a writer seems to have occurred in March 1881, almost a year after he had graduated from college, as he was nearing completion of his *Naval War*. In an apparent effort to personalize the adventures he had been rather dryly chronicling for the past two years, Roosevelt prepared an essay chronicling a ducking trip he and his brother Elliott took on the Long Island Sound one cold day in December (probably in 1880). Entitled "Sou'-Sou'-Southerly" after the oldwife or oldsquaw *(Clangula hyemalis)* he encountered on his trip, the essay is Roosevelt's first significant piece of nature writing and his earliest attempt at incorporating natural history into a compelling narrative structure. In it, Roosevelt shows himself to be a careful student of bird life, but he does not overwhelm the reader with detailed scientific information: he avoids using Latin binomials, and he integrates his descriptions of bird behavior into his larger narrative. Like almost all Roosevelt's later writings on nature, the essay is structured around a journey, with its cycle of departure and return; it offers a series of vivid vignettes describing the author's encounters with wildlife; and it displays Roosevelt's obvious joy in living "the strenuous life" in direct contact with nature, whatever the conditions. In short, "Sou'-Sou'-Southerly" shows Roosevelt at age twenty-two to be a gifted and sensitive observer of his environment — a young man well on his way to becoming one of the late nineteenth century's most talented writers on nature.[9]

The Badlands Cowboy

Roosevelt's first trip to the Dakota Badlands occurred in September 1883, when he was twenty-four years old.[10] Three years earlier he and his brother Elliott had gone west to hunt game in Illinois, Iowa, and Minnesota, but for his 1883 trip he was on his own, determined to shoot a buffalo "while there were still buffalo left to shoot" (Hagedorn 9). Motivated in part by Elliott's recent return from India with a sack of big-game trophies, Roosevelt departed New York by train on 3 September and arrived in Little Missouri, 2,400 miles away, on 7 September (E. Morris, *Rise* 198–201). When he left the badlands at the end of September, he had not only his buffalo but also a new occupation — rancher — to add to his growing list of accomplishments. For this honor he had given fourteen thousand dollars to two men he hardly knew and asked them to purchase and maintain four hundred head of cattle for the next seven years (Hagedorn 42–43, 479–80).

To be sure, in 1883 Roosevelt had little intention of becoming a full-time rancher. In the three years following his graduation from Harvard, he had married his college sweetheart, taken up formal residence at 6 West Fifty-seventh Street in New York, studied at Columbia Law School, published *The Naval War of 1812* to nearly unanimous praise, been elected to the New York State Assembly, and undertaken a campaign to become Speaker of the House. He had, as he put it, risen "like a rocket" in public life (E. Morris, *Rise* 184). Nine months after he had left Little Missouri, however, he was back in the Dakotas once again, this time seemingly for good, the result of a double tragedy from which he thought he might never recover. On Valentine's Day 1884, only two days after the birth of his first child, Roosevelt's wife and his mother died unexpectedly, within hours of each other. Overcome with grief, he at first immediately resumed his work in Albany, writing to Carl Schurz, "I think I should go mad if I were not employed." But soon after the legislative session ended, he was en route to the Dakotas, with a plan to go "back into private [life] for a few years" (Morison 66).

During the next three years — 1884 through 1886 — Roosevelt divided his time between New York City and the Dakotas, never fully able to abandon his political ambitions and equally unable to remain in the East for any extended length of time. In the West, Roosevelt found an escape from almost everything he wished to avoid and a setting for almost everything he wished to confront. By going west he could abandon the familiar surroundings that recalled Alice Lee (including responsibility for his daughter, who shared her mother's name), escape the suffocating urban environments that aggravated his asthma, and leave behind the political squabbling that occasionally grew too intense even for his argumentative personality. In exchange, he could immerse himself in solitary hunts through wide-open spaces, try his hand at managing a business (in which he would eventually invest a fifth of his fortune), and devote his free time to writing about his experiences for adventure-starved readers back east (E. Morris, *Rise* 788 n. 13). Roosevelt's enthusiasm about his time in the West is clear from a letter he wrote to Bamie not long after his arrival in Little Missouri in June 1884. "I have just been having a glorious time here, and am well hardened now (I have just come in from spending *thirteen* hours in the saddle). For every day I have been here I have had my hands full. . . . I shall put on a thousand more cattle and shall make it my regular business. . . . The country is growing on me, more and more; it has a curious, fantastic beauty of its own. . . . How sound I do sleep at night now!" (Morison 73–74).

G. Edward White, writing in 1968, framed Roosevelt's career change in terms of Erik Erikson's idea of the "identity crisis," in which "each youth must forge for himself some central perspective or direction, some working unity, out of the effective remnants of his childhood" (52). Though the validity of the "identity crisis" as a generalizable explanation for psychological behavior has been questioned in recent years, White's limited use of the concept still seems an accurate way to characterize Roosevelt's decision to turn west.[11] One of the remnants of Roosevelt's childhood White does not address, however, is Roosevelt's study of natural history, which he had abandoned in part to pursue Alice Lee. Now that she was gone, Roosevelt was free to return to his other passion in life and focus all his energies upon it. From his years at Harvard he knew he did not want to become a "microscopist and section-cutter," so he chose another path toward his goal of becoming a "faunal naturalist" and became a nature writer. As Carleton Putnam put it, "Roosevelt . . . loved the West for the outdoor life it brought him and ranching because it gave that life a raison d'être. In the West he could experiment with a literary career as well as business, the West itself providing a subject for his pen" (507).

The Man in the Buckskin Suit

The first volume to emerge from Roosevelt's western experience was *Hunting Trips of a Ranchman* (1885), which deserves close attention for several reasons. As the only work of nature writing Roosevelt published before the founding of the Boone and Crockett Club in 1887, *Hunting Trips* was an early factor in the creation of his persona as both a hunter and a conservationist. In addition, it set the tone not only for his two other books of nature writing about the West — *Ranch Life and the Hunting Trail* (1888) and *The Wilderness Hunter* (1893) — but also for all his subsequent books on nature. Subtitled *Sketches of Sport on the Northern Cattle Plains*, *Hunting Trips* contains Roosevelt's description of the six or so months of western adventures he accumulated during 1880, 1883, and 1884. Roosevelt wrote a few thousand words of the book at his Maltese Cross ranch in November 1884, but the bulk of the text — ninety-five thousand words — was probably written in the nine weeks between 1 January and 8 March 1885 when he was back in New York (E. Morris, *Rise* 294; Putnam 518). "I have just sent my last roll of manuscript to the printer," Roosevelt wrote to Henry Cabot Lodge on 8 March 1885. "In a fortnight I shall go out West; my book will be out before I return. The pictures will be excellent — as for the reading matter, I am a little doubtful" (Morison 89).

Published in July 1885 by G. P. Putnam's Sons, *Hunting Trips of a Ranchman* first appeared in an expensive, quarto edition limited to five hundred copies.[12] In its review, the *Spectator* noted that *Hunting Trips* was "printed in grand type on thick, creamy, rough-edged paper, two and a half inch margin, lavishly illustrated and bound in gray canvas, gold lettered . . . a setting so costly and yet in such perfect taste" (rev. of *Hunting Trips* 82). The elegance of the book was also acknowledged by the wife of one of Roosevelt's foremen at Elkhorn, who obtained a copy of the book in 1886 and wrote to her sister, "I am reading *Hunting Trips of a Ranchman* by Mr. Roosevelt. It is very interesting and wish you had one at home like it. . . . They are fifteen dollars, so you may know they are a nice book" (Putnam 519). Clearly, this was a book for aristocrats, a book "far too sumptuous for the general public," according to the *Atheneum*, which also described it as "one of the most beautiful hunting books ever printed" (E. Morris, *Rise* 792 n. 7). As Marcus Klein has noted, "when TR spoke of the West, he spoke to the East, and for the sake of the East. . . . He addressed himself to that Eastern Establishment to which he himself belonged more certainly than anybody" (80).[13]

Historian Gail Bederman interprets Roosevelt's awareness of his audience cynically, arguing that *Hunting Trips of a Ranchman* was little more than an elaborate "public relations" scheme developed by the former New York assemblyman to construct "a virile political persona for himself" among his upper-class readers and thereby rescue his floundering political career (171). In *Manliness and Civilization* Bederman specifically identifies the frontispiece of the book, which features Roosevelt posed in a buckskin suit, to make her case that Roosevelt was "publicly measuring the violent power of his own masculinity against the aggressive predation of 'nature'" (176). Bederman is certainly not mistaken about the important connection between violence and manliness in Roosevelt's writing, nor does she misread Roosevelt's intent to reinvent himself in this book, but her quest to uncover the operation of race and gender in *Hunting Trips of a Ranchman* reduces the complex relationship that existed between Roosevelt, the frontier, and natural history into a simple formula of race-based nationalism achieved through male domination. A closer look at the "buckskin suit" episode reveals a more subtle dynamic at work, one that also applies to the book as a whole.

Upon his return to the Dakotas in June 1884, Roosevelt made the acquisition of a buckskin suit one of his most important goals. At Lincoln Lang's suggestion, he visited a Mrs. Maddox ("who made first-class hunting-shirts, leggings, and gauntlets," according to Roosevelt), placed an order, and returned in a few weeks to find himself the proud owner of a buckskin shirt and trousers (*Works* 1:368).[14] The fringed buckskin hunting shirt, Roosevelt later wrote, was emblematic of "[t]he old race of Rocky Mountain hunters and trappers, of reckless, dauntless Indian fighters. . . . It was the most picturesque and distinctively national dress ever worn in America. It was the dress in which Daniel Boone was clad when he first passed through the trackless forests of the Alleghanies and penetrated into the heart of Kentucky. . . . [I]t was the dress worn by grim old Davy Crockett when he fell at the Alamo" (*Works* 1:349).

If the buckskin suit symbolized the romance of frontier life to Roosevelt, it also held a great deal of practical value. "When making a long hunting trip where there will be much rough work, especially in the dry cold of fall and winter," Roosevelt wrote in *Hunting Trips*, "there is nothing better than a fringed buckskin tunic or hunting-shirt. . . . Buckskin is most durable, keeps out wind and cold, and is the best possible color for the hunter — no small point in approaching game" (*Works* 1:28). It also "makes less rustling than any other material when passing among projecting twigs" (*Works* 1:86). It is not, however, a perfect garment, "[f]or wet it is not as good as flannel, and it is hot in warm weather" (*Works* 1:28). As his comments suggest, Roosevelt valued the shirt for its romantic, frontier associations as well as for its realistic usefulness when hunting.

When Roosevelt traveled to a photographer's studio after his return to New York in December 1884, therefore, and posed in his beloved buckskin shirt for a series of publicity photographs (one of which was used to engrave the frontispiece of *Hunting Trips*), he was trying not only to impress his audience with his new masculine character but also, as Bederman suggests, to document the reality of his experience (see page 46).[15] More than just a publicity stunt aimed at tapping into the mythology of the frontier, Roosevelt's posing in his buckskin suit was also a sign of the lengths to which he would go to achieve fidelity to his role as a hunter-naturalist. That Roosevelt's statements about the functional value of the buckskin shirt are no joke can be seen by his response to an 18 July 1907 letter of George Bird Grinnell, in which Grinnell asked if Roosevelt would be willing to donate the shirt for the Boone and Crockett Club's "Collection of American Hunting Arms."[16] Roosevelt still occasionally wore his buckskin shirt on hunting trips, came the reply on 19 July 1907, and thus it "hardly seems worth while to give it permanently."[17] In its place, Roosevelt sent a rifle once owned by Kit Carson.

Frontier Romanticism and Scientific Realism

When Frederick Jackson Turner made his celebrated address on the significance of the frontier in American history at the 1893 Chicago World's Fair, Theodore Roosevelt was not in the audience, but he was one of the first historians to offer enthusiastic praise upon the publication of the address in early 1894 (E. Morris, *Rise* 466). "I think you have struck some first class ideas," Roosevelt wrote to Turner, "and have put into definite shape a good deal of thought which has been floating around rather loosely" (Morison 363). Much of that loose thought was Roosevelt's own, formulated most systematically in *The Winning of the West* (1889–96) — his four-volume survey of the late-eighteenth-century frontier — but also present in his western trilogy, including *Hunting Trips of a Ranchman*. According to Roosevelt, the western frontier was the source of American democracy and character, providing not only the material resources critical to the success of

Theodore Roosevelt in his buckskin suit, 1884. From a series of publicity photographs, one of which was used to engrave the frontispiece of *Hunting Trips of a Ranchman* (1885). (Courtesy Theodore Roosevelt Collection, Harvard University)

the nation but also the sense of limitless opportunity and optimism, the mythic newness originating from so much "free" land and "unspoiled" nature. The frontier seemed also to foster individualism, self-sufficiency, and moral and physical strength, all of which Roosevelt associated with the vigorous manliness he perceived in American civilization. In this way, at the same time as the frontier distinguished American citizens from the effeminate residents of European cities, it also served as the stage upon which Anglo-Saxon domination could proceed, given that the urge to conquer was understood to be a race-based trait among whites.

Roosevelt believed himself to be living through the last wave of frontier activity in which the "ranchman" of his title would "shortly pass away from the plains as completely as the red and white hunters" who passed away before him. "The free, open-air life of the ranchman, the pleasantest and healthiest life in America, is from its very nature ephemeral," Roosevelt claimed in *Hunting Trips*. "It is scarcely a figure of speech to say that the tide of white settlement during the last few years has risen over the West like a flood; and the cattlemen are but the spray from the crest of the wave, thrown far in advance, but soon to be overtaken" (*Works* 1:17). As he would later describe in detail in *The Winning of the West*, Roosevelt saw western settlement as a "natural" phenomenon in *Hunting Trips*, similar to the unstoppable forward motion of water, sweeping away all that lies in its path.

According to Richard Slotkin, who expertly explores the subtleties of Roosevelt's frontier thesis in *Gunfighter Nation*, the mythic subtext of this account of historical succession is "a version of the theme of regeneration-through-regression . . . the passage of a highly civilized man through a revivifying return to the life of an earlier historical 'stage'" (38). Roosevelt gives pride of place in *Hunting Trips* to the frontiersman, "the true old Rocky Mountain hunter and trapper, the plainsman, or mountain man, who, with all his faults, was a man of iron nerve and will" (*Works* 1:25). These "heroes of a bygone age, the men who were clad in buckskin and who carried long rifles" were replaced by the "bronzed and sinewy cowboy," who, though "as picturesque and self-reliant, as dashing and resolute as the saturnine Indian fighters," could never attain to the status of his predecessor, reduced as the cowboy was to hunting only for sport. To Roosevelt, "[t]he old hunters were a class by themselves," and hunting was the consummate frontier activity. "They penetrated, alone or in small parties, to the farthest and wildest haunts of the animals they followed, leading a solitary, lonely life, often never seeing a white face for months and even years together. They were skillful shots, and were cool, daring, and resolute to the verge of recklessness" (*Works* 1:26). Individualistic, masculine, and powerful, the frontier hunter was the ideal American upon which Roosevelt wished to model both himself and the nation.[18]

Although realism and romanticism are often described as opposing traditions in

American literary history, in *Hunting Trips* Roosevelt's frontier romanticism is complemented by his use of scientific realism, a rhetorical strategy Roosevelt had employed ever since that first encounter with the Broadway seal. *Hunting Trips*, for instance, in addition to describing Roosevelt's hunting experiences on the ranch, details his search for grouse in Minnesota in 1880, for buffalo in the badlands in 1883, for antelope on the prairie in 1884, for deer in the Dakotas and on the way to Wyoming in 1884, and for bear and elk in the Big Horn Mountains in 1884. Instead of organizing the book around these hunting trips, though, Roosevelt structured it roughly along taxonomic lines, devoting a chapter to each of the major game animals. After an introductory discussion, "Ranching in the Badlands," the remaining nine chapters map out a hierarchy of species, beginning with waterfowl and continuing through grouse, whitetail deer, blacktail deer, bighorn sheep, buffalo, and elk, and culminating in the grizzly bear. Though hardly ecological, this organization nonetheless shows *Hunting Trips* to be more than just a collection of hunting stories; it is also a scientific description of the animals of the Great Plains. Throughout the book, says Carleton Putnam, "the zoologist vied with the hunter and often eclipsed him" (519).

Roosevelt's natural history in *Hunting Trips* comes from both the library and the field. He mentions only four books by name, explaining that "[n]o ranchman who loves sport can afford to be without Van Dyke's 'Still Hunter,' Dodge's 'Plains of the Great West,' or Caton's 'Deer and Antelope of America'; and Coues's 'Birds of the Northwest' will be valued if he cares at all for natural history" (*Works* 1:11).[19] Each of these books no doubt played a role in Roosevelt's process of composition, but as Stewart Edward White has noted, Roosevelt "preferred to argue from experience rather than authority" (*Works* 2:xxi). Thus most of the facts in *Hunting Trips* derive from personal observation, and some of Roosevelt's most interesting comments concern the challenges posed by the western landscape to scientific observation itself.

Consider, for example, his description of the bighorn sheep: "An old ram is peculiarly wary. The crest of a ridge or the top of a peak is a favorite resting-bed; but even more often they choose some ledge, high up, but just below the crest, or lie on a shelf of rock that juts out from where a ridge ends, and thus enables them to view the country on three sides of them. In color they harmonize curiously with the grayish or yellowish brown of the ground on which they are found, and it is often very difficult to make them out when lying motionless on a ledge of rock. Time and again they will be mistaken for boulders, and, on the other hand, I have more than once stalked up to masses of sandstone that I have mistaken for sheep" (*Works* 1:176).[20]

Like Twain's *Roughing It* (1872), Roosevelt's *Hunting Trips* depicts accurate observation and interpretation as a requirement for survival in the rugged western landscape, a necessity for each animal as well as for the hunter-naturalist. And as Paul Schullery pointed out, "The ability to sort good from bad information was a little-appreciated but surely most important gift for a naturalist, in a day when, with relatively little formal scientific research done on the life histories of most wild animals in North America, a few educated sportsmen and the unschooled mountain men were the main sources of primary material" ("Introduction" 23).

"Savage Realism" and the Rejection of Sentimentality

If Roosevelt's rhetoric of realism in *Hunting Trips* can in part be understood as an attempt to maintain the objectivity expected of scientific writing, it can also be seen as having been influenced by the rise of realism in fiction, which advocated a similar fidelity to observable and testable "facts." In 1885 alone — the year *Hunting Trips* first appeared — the *Century* serialized three monuments of realistic writing: William Dean Howells's *Rise of Silas Lapham,* Mark Twain's *Adventures of Huckleberry Finn,* and Henry James's *Bostonians* (Kolb 6–7). According to Brander Matthews, Roosevelt's writing contained many of the characteristics of these and other realistic novels. "There was no mistaking the full intent of his own words," Matthews wrote. "He knew what he meant to say, and he knew how to say it with simple sincerity and with vigorous vivacity. His straightforwardness prevented his ever employing phrases that faced both ways and that provided rat holes from which he might crawl out. His style was tinglingly alive; it was masculine and vascular; and it was always the style of a gentleman and a scholar" (235). George Bird Grinnell recognized similar characteristics in Roosevelt's work, but he labeled them "scientific." He noted that Roosevelt's natural history studies had taught him "a knowledge of how to observe, and an appreciation of the fact that observations, to be of any scientific value, must be definite and precise. . . . His hunting adventures have not been mere pleasure excursions. They have been of service to science" (Grinnell, "President Roosevelt" 437).[21]

Realism, of course, has long been characterized as a fictional method in which the writer takes a quasi-scientific approach to his or her material. In *Criticism and Fiction* (1891) William Dean Howells famously compared the real grasshopper of the scientist to the wire and cardboard grasshopper of the idealist, claiming that the real grasshopper is "simple, natural, and honest." "I hope the time is coming," Howells wrote, "when not only the artist, but [also] the common, average man . . . will reject the ideal grasshopper wherever he finds it, in science, in literature, in art, because it is not 'simple, natural, and honest,' because it is not like a real grasshopper" (70). Despite Howells's prominent articulation of realist doctrine, realism "barely qualified as a literary movement," as Daniel Borus has pointed out. Realists, he reminds us, "did not uniformly rally around a single set of principles"

(16). There were, in fact, many realisms in late-nineteenth-century America: "the realism of social and moral analysis, and the realism of political indignation, the realism of local colour and the realism of the mean streets and the ghetto, the realism of the fact-laden document, the realism of self-conscious technique" (Bradbury 322).

Roosevelt's own integration of frontier romanticism and scientific realism is perhaps best understood as part of the much larger cultural movement David E. Shi has labeled "savage realism"—"a colorful and controversial new synthesis of realism and romanticism" that developed during this period (211). As T. J. Jackson Lears argued, proponents of both realism and historical romance at this time "contributed to a resurgent 'literature of action,' which encompassed sea-fights, shipwrecks, and Wild West adventure as well as more archaic violence. . . . Whether or not they explicitly voiced the opinion, all agreed that the world of [William Dean] Howells's novels lacked physical and emotional conflict, that it neglected the harsh experience of pain inflicted or endured, that it was devoid of 'real life'" (103). Writing in the *Arena* in December 1893, for instance, Clarence Darrow announced that "[t]he world has grown tired of preachers and sermons; to-day it asks for facts. It has grown tired of fairies and angels, and asks for flesh and blood" (128–29).[22]

Hunting Trips participates in this cultural movement in part through its rejection of sentimentality, which appears both implicitly and explicitly throughout the book.[23] Implicitly, Roosevelt rejects sentimentality through his frequent, vivid descriptions of the violence hunting inflicts on game animals, such as when he describes breaking the back of a doe and then plunging his knife into its throat (*Works* 1:115). Accurate down to the bloodiest of details, Roosevelt does not flinch from graphic descriptions of violence, noting, for example, that "a blacktail will go all day with a bullet through his entrails, and in cold weather I have known one to run several miles with a portion of his entrails sticking out of a wound and frozen solid" (*Works* 1:119). Explicitly, Roosevelt links the "savage realism" with which he renders the killing of animals to the extermination of human "savages," arguing— in an allusion to Helen Hunt Jackson's then-contemporary *Century of Dishonor* (1881)—that "[d]uring the past century a good deal of sentimental nonsense has been talked about our taking the Indians' land" (*Works* 1:16). The slaughter of the buffalo, Roosevelt explains at one point, while "in places needless and brutal," was in fact "the only way of solving the Indian question" (*Works* 1:191). As long as the buffalo existed, Roosevelt argued, "the Indians could simply not be kept on reservations, and always had an ample supply of meat on hand to support them in the event of a war; and its [the buffalo's] disappearance was the only method of forcing them to at least partially abandon their savage mode of life" (*Works* 1:191).

To some writers of the time (mostly women), public sentiment for wildlife protection was best aroused by sentiment itself, by appeals to the sympathies and emotionalism of the reader. To Roosevelt, however, conservation derived not from sentimentalism but from a combination of realism and romanticism that rendered the sport hunter the preeminent animal ethicist and the enemy of all *unnecessary* brutality. "I rarely hunt," Roosevelt explains in *Hunting Trips*, "except for a fine head or when we need meat, and, if it can be avoided, do not shoot at fawns or does" (*Works* 1:126). At one of the most memorable moments in the text, Roosevelt seems to depart from this characteristic realism and nearly embrace sentimentalism in his appreciation of each animal's individuality: "Aside from the thrill and tingle that a hunter experiences at the sight of his game, I by degrees grew to feel as if I had a personal interest in the different traits and habits of the wild creatures. The characters of the animals differed widely, and the differences were typified by their actions; and it was pleasant to watch them in their own homes, myself unseen, when, after stealthy, silent progress through the sombre and soundless depths of the woods, I came upon them going about the ordinary business of their lives. . . . The true still-hunter should be a lover of nature as well as of sport, or he will miss half the pleasure of being in the woods" (*Works* 1:223–24). For any reader so inclined to interpret this passage, however, Roosevelt follows it with a description of his shooting a bull elk twice, once behind the shoulder and once through the lungs and watching the animal as it "staggered gamely on a few rods into the forest before sinking to the ground" (*Works* 1:224). One cannot be more a lover of nature than a lover of sport lest the prey escape with its life intact.[24]

At the same time, Roosevelt's catalog of carnage in *Hunting Trips* is moderated by his disdain for market hunters, those "swinish game-butchers, who hunt for hides and not for sport or actual food, and who murder the gravid doe and the spotted fawn with as little hesitation as they would kill a buck of ten points" (*Works* 1:107). Combining an anticommercial elitism with a concern for the land, Roosevelt claims that "[n]o one who is not himself a sportsman and lover of nature can realize the intense indignation with which a true hunter sees these butchers at their brutal work of slaughtering the game, in season and out, for the sake of a few dollars they are too lazy to earn in any other and more honest way" (*Works* 1:107). Although Roosevelt's model hunter was "the true old Rocky Mountain hunter and trapper, the plainsman, or mountain man" (*Works* 1:25), this frontiersman was not far distant from the indiscriminate market hunter whose practices Roosevelt found so distasteful.[25] Highly inflected by class, Roosevelt's early conservationist leanings thus did not allow him to see past the "privilege" of being able to kill one of the last buffalo in the Dakotas in the fall of 1883 and one of the last elk in the neighborhood of his ranch in the fall of 1884 (E. Morris, *Rise* 788 n. 6; *Works* 1:226–27). Nevertheless, the waste of the West was beginning to dawn on him, and over the next quarter century, Roosevelt would refine his understanding of the obligations of the hunter-naturalist, that "wilderness wanderer, who"—as he noted in 1911, near the end of his hunting days—"to the hardihood and prowess of the old-time hunter adds the capacity of a first-class field-naturalist, and also, what is just as important, the power of literary expression" (*Works* 12:414).

When Roosevelt left the badlands in late September 1886, a chapter of his life closed. Later that December he would marry his second wife, Edith Carow; the terrible winter of 1886 would trim his cattle herds by about 65 percent; and though he would retain his ranches, he would return to them only for his autumn hunting trips, which he would make each year through 1896 (E. Morris, *Rise* 373; G. Edward White 90).[26] "Ultimately," says G. Edward White, "Roosevelt's Badlands excursion, which he had conceived as an interlude and then considered as a way of life, became, of necessity, an interlude again, for its challenge had been mastered" (91). The experience served him well, however, providing material not only for two more books about the West but also for the growth and development of an important friendship and a reconsideration of his duties as a hunter and a sportsman. Roosevelt himself summed up his debt to the years he spent in the Dakotas during a speech he made at Sioux Falls, South Dakota, on 3 September 1910: "I regard my experiences during those years . . . as the most important educational asset of all my life" (Hagedorn 2).

The Boone and Crockett Club

The pursuit of scientific realism first brought Theodore Roosevelt and George Bird Grinnell together in 1885, and that common pursuit remained a focal point of their relationship for the next thirty-four years, until Roosevelt's death in 1919. Together, they were responsible for most of the achievements of the Boone and Crockett Club during these years, including its successful lobbying for the creation of national forest reserves, the protection of Yellowstone National Park, and the passage of Adirondack deer hunting legislation, as well as the publication of the first three Boone and Crockett Club essay collections. Throughout this period, both men also pursued individual projects that benefited the club. Roosevelt wrote two more books of nature writing—*Ranch Life and the Hunting Trail* (1888) and *The Wilderness Hunter* (1893)—and resumed his political career, activities in which he not only influenced public sentiment about conservation but also functioned indirectly as the mouthpiece of club policy. Until 1911 Grinnell served as editor of *Forest and Stream*, in which capacity he provided a regular forum for club announcements and published articles of common concern to club members. In their individual work, as well as in their collaborative efforts, Roosevelt and Grinnell mutually reinforced each other's beliefs in the romance of the frontier life and the realistic representation of nature, from which bases they could argue for the conservation of the nation's dwindling natural resources.

Grinnell had known Roosevelt casually during Roosevelt's term as an assemblyman in the New York legislature, but neither man was on intimate terms with the other until the publication of Grinnell's 1885 review of *Hunting Trips of a Ranchman* in *Forest and Stream*. For the most part, the review was highly favorable. Grinnell identified Roosevelt as "an earnest and energetic politician of the best type . . . a person of exceptionally well-balanced mind, and calm, deliberative judgment." The book itself was rendered in a "very attractive" style, according to Grinnell, and was said to contain much interesting matter. Moreover, because Roosevelt had not "become accustomed to all the various sights and sounds of the plains and the mountains" in the book, "for him all the difference which exists between the East and the West are still sharply defined." Whereas an old-timer might take too much for granted about the West, Roosevelt's accounts of ranch life are "delightful for their freshness" ("Hunting Trips" 451).

Grinnell's main complaint with the book concerned Roosevelt's most valued literary asset: his realism. "Where Mr. Roosevelt details his own adventures he is accurate," wrote Grinnell, "and tells his story in a simple, pleasant fashion, which at once brings us into sympathy with him. We are sorry to see that a number of hunting myths are given as fact, but it was after all scarcely to be expected that with the author's limited experience he could sift the wheat from the chaff and distinguish the true from the false" ("Hunting Trips" 451).[27] Though couched in kind language, this criticism nonetheless troubled Roosevelt greatly, as might be expected. *Hunting Trips* was only his second book — his first attempt at nature writing — so to be accused of printing inaccuracies, myths, and falsehoods was no small matter. As a result, Roosevelt wasted little time in confronting Grinnell, traveling to the *Forest and Stream* offices "not long after the review was printed" to discuss the accusations with him.[28] As Grinnell wrote later, "I knew enough of Theodore Roosevelt — if only from his course in the New York Legislature — to feel that in all that he wrote he wanted to know the truth and to tell it" (*Works* 1:xv).

George Bird Grinnell and *Forest and Stream*

That Roosevelt took a liking to Grinnell despite the confrontational nature of their first meeting is not surprising. "They had much in common," says historian John G. Mitchell: "the patrician blood, Teddy's Harvard and Birdie's [Grinnell's] Yale, the fascination with natural history, the fervor for the hunt, the absentee ownership of western ranches" (91). Like Roosevelt, Grinnell was a central figure in the community of eastern sportsmen. A native New Yorker, Grinnell grew up in one of the houses in "Audubon Park," the former estate of John James Audubon on the Upper West Side of Manhattan, where he received his first lessons about birds from Audubon's widow, Lucy. After receiving his B.A. from Yale in 1870, Grinnell went west to collect fossils for Yale's Peabody Museum with Professor

O. C. Marsh, returning to the West nearly every year thereafter. He served as a naturalist on Custer's exploratory expedition to Yellowstone National Park and the Black Hills of the Dakotas in 1875; he received his Ph.D. in paleontology from Yale in 1880; and like Roosevelt he purchased a western ranch, choosing to locate in the Shirley Basin country of southeastern Wyoming in 1883.

Prior to his meeting with Roosevelt, Grinnell helped set the stage for the coming of the Boone and Crockett Club by his involvement with two significant events in conservation history: the founding of *Forest and Stream* and the formation of the first Audubon Society. Foremost among the many sporting periodicals that arose after the Civil War, *Forest and Stream* was founded on 14 August 1873 by Charles Hallock, who stated the object of his magazine in its inaugural issue: "to studiously promote a healthful interest in outdoor recreation, and to cultivate a refined taste for natural objects" (Hallock 8).[29] Hallock was interested in more than just leisure-time activities, however, as he noted later in the same article: "For the preservation of our rapidly diminishing forests we shall continually do battle. Our great interests are in jeopardy — even our supply of drinking water is threatened, from the depletion of timber-lands by fire and axe" (Hallock 8).[30] Grinnell wrote occasional pieces for *Forest and Stream* from October 1873 until the fall of 1876, when Hallock hired him to replace Ernest Ingersoll as the editor of the natural history column (Reiger, *Passing* 79, 126). Three years later, when Hallock himself resigned, Grinnell became editor of the entire magazine, a position he retained until 1911 (Mott 3:210–11, 4:380–81; Ward 93). By 1879 *Forest and Stream* had a subscription list of about ten thousand with copies being delivered to some twenty-four hundred post offices in the United States and Canada and to a hundred more in thirty foreign countries (Tober 62 n. 20).

The establishment of national sporting magazines such as *Forest and Stream* provided outdoorsmen with a means of communicating with each other, a development that resulted in the rapid growth of group identity as well as the rapid growth of sportsmen's clubs and associations (Reiger, *American Sportsmen* 3).[31] Sporting organizations had existed since the eighteenth century in America, but not until the 1870s with the arrival of the "club movement" did hunting and fishing societies begin to form in earnest.[32] In 1883 Grinnell helped to found the American Ornithologists' Union (AOU) from the Nuttall Club (to which Roosevelt had reported on sparrows as an undergraduate), and as early as 1884 Grinnell had stated in the pages of *Forest and Stream* that "in New York State there ought to be a live association of men bound together by their interest in game and fish, to take active charge of all matters pertaining to the enactment and carrying out of the laws on the subject. There is abundant material for such a body. Why can it not be organized?" (Grinnell, "Game" 301). With the support of such people as Oliver Wendell Holmes, Henry Ward Beecher, and John Greenleaf Whittier,

Grinnell finally organized the group himself, founding the first Audubon Society in 1886.[33] Membership in the society grew rapidly—to nearly thirty-eight thousand in the first year, necessitating the creation of a separate *Audubon Magazine* in 1887 (Pearson, "Fifty Years" 201; Welker 204). In fact, membership grew too rapidly, and Grinnell was forced to disband the group in 1888 when the burdens of editing a magazine and running such a popular organization became too heavy. (See chap. 2 for a discussion of the reformation of the Audubon Society in 1896.)

"An Association of Men Living for the Most Part in New York"

The formation of the Boone and Crockett Club was not without precedent, nor did it depart very far from the elite origins of the AOU and the first Audubon Society. In addition to Roosevelt and Grinnell, the men called to dinner at Bamie's Madison Avenue home on 8 December 1887 included Roosevelt's brother Elliott and cousin J. West, Archibald Rogers, E. P. Rogers, J. Coleman Drayton, Thomas Paton, Col. James E. Jones, John J. Pierrepont, and Rutherford Stuyvesant—upper-class sportsmen all (Trefethen, *Crusade* 16). Roosevelt himself acknowledged the club's elite, urban origins when he stated in 1893 in an important *Harper's Weekly* article about the club that "[t]he Boone and Crockett Club is an association of men living for the most part in New York, but also in other parts of the country" (Roosevelt, "Boone and Crockett" 267). Regular membership in the club was limited to one hundred men who had "killed with the rifle in fair chase, by still-hunting or otherwise, at least one individual of the various kinds of American large game." About fifty associate memberships were also offered to outstanding men who did not meet these qualifications and to important public figures who shared the club's objectives (Trefethen, *Crusade* 356, 18). Over time, the club broadened its membership base to include men from most of the eastern states and many of the western states and territories, including the politicians Henry Cabot Lodge and Redfield Proctor; academics Francis Parkman, Madison Grant, and Henry Fairfield Osborn; artist Frederick Remington; scientist Clarence King; novelist Owen Wister; conservationist Gifford Pinchot; and other well-known figures of the time, such as Henry L. Stimson, J. P. Morgan, Elihu Root, Wade Hampton, T. Gilbert Pearson, and T. S. VanDyke.[34] But the patrician character of the club remained; until the club acquired its own meeting center in 1909, most of the group's gatherings were held at the exclusive University Club in Manhattan and Metropolitan Club in Washington, D.C.

The organization of the club seems to have occurred a few days after the December gathering, at a meeting in which its constitution was adopted and its first president (Roosevelt himself) and secretary (Archibald Rogers) were chosen (Trefethen, *Crusade* 19).[35] The original purposes of the Boone and Crockett Club, according to article 2 of the group's constitution, were to (1) "promote manly sport with the rifle"; (2) "promote travel and exploration in the wild and unknown, or but partially known, portions of the country"; (3) "work for the preservation of the large game of this country, and, so far as possible, to further legislation for that purpose, and to assist in enforcing the existing laws"; (4) "promote inquiry into, and to record observations on the habits and natural history of, the various wild animals"; and (5) "bring about among the members the interchange of opinions and ideas on hunting, travel, and exploration; on the various kinds of hunting-rifles; on the haunts of game animals, etc."[36]

Richard Slotkin has argued that "Roosevelt was not only the founder of the Boone and Crockett Club; . . . he was the author of its myths of origin" (38), and, indeed, Roosevelt's *Harper's Weekly* article suggests that the club relied heavily on his own romantic formulations for establishing its frontier identity. "The club is emphatically an association of men who believe that the hardier and manlier the sport is the more attractive it is, and who do not think that there is any place in the ranks of sportsmen either for the game-butcher, on the one hand, or, on the other, for the man who wishes to do all his shooting in preserves, and to shirk rough hard work," Roosevelt argued in the pages of the journal. He praised "the life of the pioneer settler, the life of the man who struck out into the wilderness as part of the vanguard of civilization, and made his living largely in warfare with the wild game," claiming that such a man represented a characteristic yet evanescent phase in American history. "There is nothing in the history of any other nation which quite corresponds to it," Roosevelt wrote. It was only natural, therefore, that the club be named after "those two typical pioneer hunters Daniel Boone and Davy Crockett, the men who have served in a certain sense as the tutelary deities of American hunting lore" ("Boone and Crockett" 267).

Charting Individual Influence

In a provocative monograph, *American Sportsmen and the Origins of Conservation* (1975; 3d ed., 2001), John Reiger claimed that "American sportsmen, those who hunted and fished for pleasure rather than commerce or necessity, were the real vanguard of conservation" (3). According to Reiger, these hunters and anglers saw themselves as "members of a fraternity with a well-defined code of conduct and thinking" who mounted "the first challenge to the myth of inexhaustibility" with their concern about the disappearance of game fish, birds, and mammals (3–4). The Boone and Crockett Club, and not the Sierra Club, he argues, was "the first private organization to deal effectively with conservation issues of national scope" and its influence proved "far in excess of any ordinary association of similar size" (153). As valuable as the book is, Reiger tends to overstate both the prevalence of the "sportsman's code" and the contributions made by hunters to conservation. In the first instance, while more ethically minded hunters certainly placed limits on the type and extent of their hunting, labeling such self-restraint the "code of the sportsman" suggests such measures enjoyed more unity and authority than they actually did. In fact, one of the greatest achievements of the Boone and Crockett Club has been its success at gradually institutionalizing such ethical standards, both in its own organization and through the legislation for which its members lobbied. As for the contributions of sportsmen to conservation, Reiger "claims far too much for hunters," according to Thomas R. Dunlap. "The early conservationists were hunters, but so were most adult men of that period," Dunlap notes, "and it is hard to see, on the evidence Reiger presents, that hunting led, in quite the direct way he wishes to see, to conservation" (*Saving* 178 n. 11).[37]

Another issue in the book is Reiger's tendency to downplay the influence of Roosevelt on the Boone and Crockett Club while emphasizing that of Grinnell. Although Roosevelt served as president of the club from 1888 to 1894, as vice president from 1911 to 1913, and as a member of the editorial committee from 1888 to 1919, Reiger often characterizes Grinnell as Roosevelt's tutor, not only in matters of club activities but also in terms of governmental policy. For instance, Reiger claims that while Roosevelt's first western books reveal that he "possessed the code of the sportsman, these volumes do not manifest the same commitment to the perpetuation of natural resources so much a part of the later Boone and Crockett book series created and edited by him and Grinnell. Under the latter's tutelage, Roosevelt's love for big-game hunting soon developed into a concern for the future of big game, as he became increasingly aware of the speed with which it was disappearing" (*American Sportsmen* 173). And Reiger suggests that "[f]rom their close association as the leaders of the Boone and Crockett Club, Roosevelt received a thorough exposure to Grinnell's ideas for handling the nation's natural resources. There is little question that he was the original source of many of the concepts Roosevelt later established as national policy" (*American Sportsmen* 181).[38] Although Grinnell was certainly a crucial influence on Roosevelt's emerging conservation ethic, Roosevelt could hold his own about such matters and did so with regularity.

Charting individual influence is a tricky business, of course, because the members of the Boone and Crockett Club "so often acted behind the scenes it was seldom clear whether their accomplishments should have been credited to the men or the organization" (Cart 107).[39] A newspaper article published about the club around the turn of the century suggests that such uncertainty was evident even to Roosevelt's contemporaries, claiming that "[t]he positions held in public life by some of the members, and the wealth and influence of the others, make of the club an organization of power, and this power they use for good."[40] The informality and ambiguity of individual influence in such circumstances presents the student of interest groups with "a severe analytic difficulty"—an example of a problem Robert H. Salisbury calls "elite interaction." "When a corporate executive speaks to a governor, does he represent an organization which can reasonably be included in some list of interest groups? Or is his position itself more ambiguous, part of a general structure of influence relationships but not necessarily an example of interest-group lobbying?" (Salisbury, "Interest Groups" 210). James Tober argues that the Boone and Crockett Club "exercised great influence over a long period of time primarily by using the individual contacts and personal alliances that its well-placed members were able to make" (190), and even Edmund Morris, Roosevelt's biographer, suggests that despite Roosevelt's impressive list of club memberships, "the man was not particularly clubby. By-laws and bad food and big leather chairs held no charm for him" ("Polygon" 26).[41]

In considering Roosevelt's contributions to the Boone and Crockett Club, therefore, it is important to keep in mind the imprecision with which such an analysis must proceed. The effectiveness of the Boone and Crockett Club depended upon several factors, such as its organized constituency, its political power and influence (including access to legislators on local and national levels), and the consequences of the broader social changes of which it was a part. Furthermore, it makes sense to acknowledge the ability of the Boone and Crockett Club to distinguish itself from other constituencies with an interest in wildlife protection, such as market hunters, game dealers, and landowners. Market hunters, for instance, never developed into a powerful interest-group—in part because "the structure of the 'industry' precluded effective mobilization to achieve collective goals" (Tober 55), and in part because most market hunters were immigrants from eastern and southern Europe and thus unfamiliar with American political institutions (Neuzil and Kovarik 7). Some of the success of the Boone and Crockett Club, therefore, can be attributed to the failures of their opposition to organize successfully.

Lobbying for the Land: Parks, Forests, and Hunting

At the end of his "Brief History of the Boone and Crockett Club," first published in 1910, George Bird Grinnell wrote that "the purposes and activities of the Boone and Crockett Club have wholly changed — it might be said, have been reversed," since its establishment in 1887. "Beginning as a club of riflemen, apparently concerned only with their own recreation, it early discovered that more important work was to be done in the field of protection than in that of destruction. No sooner had the Club been organized and begun to consider the subjects which most interested it, than it became apparent that on all hands the selfishness of individuals was rapidly doing away with all the natural things of this country, and that a halt must be called" (490). In the period with which this chapter is concerned — the years before Roosevelt's presidency — the club began to engage in a series of actions that went beyond its first two purposes of promoting "manly sport with the rifle" and "travel and exploration in the wild and unknown, or but partially known, portions of the country." Gradually, according to Grinnell, "the settlement of the country and the sweep of population to the westward" made it more difficult to carry out these first two objects, "while the same causes magnified the importance of the third and fourth" — that is, the preservation of large game through the passage and enforcement of legislation, and the promotion of scientific inquiry into the natural history of wild animals ("Brief History" 437).

During this time, Roosevelt remained active in politics and sport hunting, both of which helped him further the goals of the Boone and Crockett Club. He was appointed to the U.S. Civil Service Commission in 1889 and the New York City Police Commission in 1895, named assistant secretary of the navy in 1897, and commissioned as lieutenant colonel in the First U.S. Volunteer Cavalry Regiment (the Rough Riders) in 1898. In 1899 he was elected governor of New York; in 1901 he was "kicked upstairs" to the vice presidency of the United States; and in September 1901 he unexpectedly ascended to the presidency after President William McKinley was assassinated. During these years, Roosevelt nevertheless managed to take six trips to the mountains west of the Dakotas: to the Big Horn Mountains of Wyoming in 1884, the Coeur d'Alenes of Idaho in 1886, the Selkirks of British Columbia in 1888, the Bitterroots of Wyoming and Idaho in 1889, Yellowstone National Park in 1890, and the Two-Ocean Pass Country in Wyoming in 1891.

Roosevelt's engagement with the Boone and Crockett Club agenda throughout this period can best be seen by tracing his actions on three particular issues: the protection of Yellowstone National Park, the conservation of forest resources, and the advocacy of deer hounding and jacklighting legislation in the Adirondacks.

Roosevelt first came to understand fully the commercial threats facing Yellowstone National Park after his return from a two-week trip to the park in September 1890, during which he introduced his family to the Grand Canyon of Yellowstone, Mammoth Hot Springs, and Tower Falls. As the first national park, established by Congress in 1872, Yellowstone also became the first target of a park "improvement" plan, which included the introduction of mining and timber operations, the construction of a railroad line and several hotels, and the market hunting of game animals — all within the boundaries of the park. Roosevelt was no stranger to disputes over the protection of land — as a New York state assemblyman he had supported a bill to preserve the Adirondacks — and "as soon as he understood about the conditions in Yellowstone Park, he gave time and thought to considering its protection," according to Grinnell (Roosevelt, *Works* 1:xxiii).[42]

Although Roosevelt at first seemed to favor the introduction of railroads into the park, he eventually decided to oppose such development and took action to see the plan defeated. In 1889 he made a personal visit to John W. Noble after Noble was appointed secretary of the interior (Reiger, "Wildlife," 114); in 1890 and 1892 he attended meetings about the park held by the House Public Lands Committee (Grinnell, "Park Bill," "Snap Shots" [1892]); and in 1891 he arranged for Secretary Noble to attend the annual dinner of the Boone and Crockett Club, during which members of the club offered testimonials about the need for preservation of the park (Grinnell, "Boone and Crockett Club Meeting").[43] In his own comments that evening, Roosevelt exhibited the scientific realism for which he was well known, stressing the importance of protecting the entire Yellowstone watershed. As Grinnell explained in *Forest and Stream*, Roosevelt "explained very clearly the way in which the fires in the National Park are started and spread, and called attention to the function performed by the forest floor, which being entirely made up of decaying vegetation retains and gives forth gradually the moisture which it receives from the rains and the melting snows" ("Club Meeting" 3).

Roosevelt's strong feelings about the protection of Yellowstone can also be seen in two letters he sent in the years following this meeting. The first was a letter to Grinnell as editor of *Forest and Stream*, written in 1892 while Roosevelt was a member of the Civil Service Commission. In the letter, which Grinnell published, Roosevelt voiced his powerful support for Grinnell's recent criticism of the plan to run a railroad through the park: "It is of the utmost importance that the park shall be kept in its present form as a great forestry preserve and a National pleasure ground, the like of which is not to be found on any continent but ours; and all public-spirited Americans should join with *Forest and Stream* in the effort to prevent the greed of a little group of speculators, careless of everything save their own selfish interests, from doing the damage they threaten to the whole people of the United States, by wrecking the Yellowstone National Park. So far from having this Park cut down it should be extended, and legislation adopted which would enable the military authorities who now have charge of it to administer it solely in the interests of the whole public, and to punish in the most rigorous way people who trespass upon it. The Yellowstone Park is a park for the people, and the representatives of the people should see that it is molested in no way" (Roosevelt, "Letter to the Editor"). Not only did the railroad plan fail to pass Congress, but the campaign to protect Yellowstone received a boost in March 1893 when a poacher in the park was caught skinning several illegally killed buffalo, an act that elicited widespread outrage and provoked a national discussion about how best to enforce park regulations.

Roosevelt's second letter about park protection was written to Hoke Smith, the next secretary of the interior, on 7 April 1894, after the introduction of a new Park Protection Act by Iowa representative (and Boone and Crockett Club member)

John F. Lacey: "I am very glad of the position the Interior Department has taken in reference to the Yellowstone Park. I am going before Senator Faulkner's Committee to argue against the proposed cutting down of the boundaries of the park and to try to persuade the committee to give you proper police power in the matter. I am president of the Boone and Crockett Club, which is greatly interested in this subject. The next time we give a dinner I shall ask you to be present as our guest, as we much appreciate the stand you have taken in forestry matters and in the preservation of these parks. It will be an outrage if this government does not keep the big Sequoia Park, the Yosemite, and such places under touch" (Morison 371).

After years of lobbying for such protective legislation, Congressman Lacey's "Act to Protect the Birds and Animals in Yellowstone National Park" was finally signed into law by President Grover Cleveland on 7 May 1894. The act made it illegal to kill any animal in Yellowstone, except where necessary to protect human life or property, and it prohibited traffic in living or dead wildlife, the removal of mineral deposits, and the destruction of timber. It also placed the park inside the U.S. judicial district of Wyoming and cleared the way for a park commissioner and a force of U.S. marshals to enforce the law. Never one to sit contentedly after a victory, Roosevelt wrote Grinnell afterward to say he would take "steps to see that good men are appointed for deputy marshals" (Reiger, *American Sportsmen* 164).

The protection of Yellowstone National Park would have been less effective without a related effort by the Boone and Crockett Club to conserve the forest resources that surround it. After his appointment in 1889, interior secretary Noble became convinced — thanks in large part to heavy lobbying by Roosevelt, Grinnell, William Hallett Phillips, and Arnold Hague — that the nation's forests would be rapidly depleted if timber cutting and burning were allowed to continue at their current levels (Reiger, *American Sportsmen* 167–69). As a result, when an "Act to Repeal the Timber Culture Laws" was being pushed through the closing session of the Fifty-first Congress, Noble inserted a final clause to the bill that authorized the president to "set apart and reserve" government-owned timberlands "in any State or Territory having public land bearing forest . . . whether of commercial value or not" (M. Collins 124). Passing through Congress undetected, the rider became law when President Benjamin Harrison signed the Sundry Civil Service Appropriations Act on 3 March 1891, thus creating the federal forest reserve system. With additional pressure from Hague and Phillips, Noble then presented a proposal for the first such forest reserve to President Harrison, who issued the necessary proclamation on 30 March 1891. The Yellowstone National Park Timberland Reserve became the first national forest in the United States, created out of 1.25 million acres of Wyoming land lying to the south and the east of Yellowstone National Park. Soon thereafter, on 8 April, Roosevelt issued a proclamation on behalf of the Boone and Crockett Club, endorsing the action and commending Harrison and Noble for their efforts (Reiger, *American Sportsmen* 170).

The third Boone and Crockett Club issue in which Roosevelt played a part before becoming president was the advocacy of deer hounding and jacklighting legislation in the Adirondacks. Deer hounding is the practice of driving a deer with hounds to deep water and then killing the animal while it is swimming — either by shooting it, clubbing it, or slitting its throat. Jacklighting, also called "fire-hunting" or simply "jacking," entails blinding a deer at night with an artificial light and then shooting it as it stands immobilized in the glare. Both these practices were discouraged by the Boone and Crockett Club, whose constitution explains in article 5 that "[t]he term 'fair chase' shall not be held to include killing bear, wolf, or cougar in traps, nor 'fire-hunting,' nor 'crusting' moose, elk, or deer in deep snow, nor killing game from a boat while it is swimming in the water" (Trefethen, *Crusade* 356). "Fair chase" was important to the sport hunter not only because it introduced an ethical distinction into the hunt but also because it distinguished the sport hunter from the market hunter, whose economic motivations did not admit placing artificial handicaps on the hunt. At the same time, the sport hunter also saw the restrictions of "fair chase" as a means to return to the "authenticity" of the frontier experience, in which the hunter could test his manhood by renouncing the metal traps, artificial lights, and factory-built boats of modern industrial civilization. As George Baxter Ward put it, "'fair chase' . . . gave the animal a sporting chance and required a maximum amount of skill on the part of the hunter" (360). Boone and Crockett Club member William Cary Sanger explained it this way in 1897: "when one is compelled to match his physical endurance, his woodcraft, and his skill as a hunter, against the deer's natural instinct, which enables it to detect, with such wonderful keenness of smell or hearing, the presence of a man, he can feel that he has at least secured his game in a way that can fairly be called sportsmanlike" (278).

Unfortunately, such sportsmanlike conduct was not the norm in the late nineteenth century, and game laws were limited mostly to seasonal prohibitions, sporadically enforced at best. In 1895, for instance, the New York deer season ran from 15 August to 1 November without limit; night hunting was legal; and dogs were permitted to be used from 10 September to 10 October. Salt licks were prohibited, but their use often went undetected (Trefethen, *Crusade* 76).[44] This situation greatly concerned Roosevelt, who wrote to Grinnell from his position on the Civil Service Commission on 13 January 1894: "Don't you think the executive committee plus Madison Grant . . . might try this year to put a complete stop to hounding in the Adirondacks? Appear before the Legislature, I mean. I wish to see the Club do something." His determination on this issue is clear from a second letter he wrote to Grinnell on 30 January, urging him to "meet Madison Grant and have a talk over whether the Club could not take some action . . . about hounding deer in the Adirondacks" (Reiger, *American Sportsmen* 155).

Roosevelt's efforts began to bear fruit at the next annual meeting of the club, held 16 January 1895, during which Roosevelt appointed a committee, chaired by Madison Grant, "to look after legislation in New York State in the interest of game preservation" (Grinnell, "Brief History" 464). Later that year, under pressure from Grant, the legislature approved a law establishing the New York State Fisheries, Game, and Forest Commission, the central administrative body for the management of the state's natural resources and the forerunner of the New York Department of Environmental Conservation.[45] It also passed a compromise bill limiting the use of hounds and jacklights to the first fifteen days of October. Finally, in the 1897 session, again due to lobbying by the Boone and Crockett Club, the New York State legislature passed a bill prohibiting hounding and jacklighting for five years, after which the prohibition was made permanent — and also became a model law for other states (Trefethen, *Crusade* 77–78).

"Far in Advance of the Public Opinion"

If the conservation achievements of the Boone and Crockett Club seem distant from Roosevelt's nature writing and editing, it is worth remembering that throughout the period in which these political battles were being waged, Roosevelt was producing the last two volumes of his Dakota trilogy — *Ranch Life and the Hunting Trail* (1888) and *The Wilderness Hunter* (1893) — and collaborating with Grinnell on the first three conservation and hunting books to be published under the Boone and Crockett Club name: *American Big-Game Hunting* (1893), *Hunting in Many Lands* (1895), and *Trail and Camp-Fire* (1897). Although no textual evidence exists to connect these particular publications with the conservation victories outlined above, the response generated by a subsequent club publication suggests that these early books most certainly helped set the stage for the club's many achievements in the first ten years of its existence.

Published in 1904 *American Big Game and Its Haunts* featured essays on such topics as "Wilderness Reserves" by Roosevelt; "Preservation of the Wild Animals of North America" by Henry Fairfield Osborn; and "The Creating of Game Refuges" by Alden Sampson, as well as listings of all the big-game refuges and forest reserves in North America. Upon the book's publication, the Boone and Crockett Club sent copies to 480 U.S. congressmen and senators and 100 other fish and game officials, along with a letter calling their attention to the three articles by Roosevelt, Osborn, and Sampson and requesting their support for legislation to protect the forests, fish, and game of the nation (Ward 357). Of the many letters of appreciation the club received, most expressed agreement with the aims of the conservation movement and an interest in supporting related legislation, and many of the writers even took the time to share their own observations on hunting, fishing, and camping.[46]

In his "Brief History of the Boone and Crockett Club," first published in 1910, Grinnell argued that "[i]n the years that have elapsed since its organization, the Boone and Crockett Club has accomplished a number of things which entitle it to the lasting gratitude of the American people. Through the efforts of its members have been carried on a number of good things, whose importance the Club saw far in advance of the public opinion of the time, and which in recent years has come to be generally appreciated, though not as yet wholly understood" (438). In essence, much of Roosevelt's work as a writer and editor seems to have been carried out "far in advance of the public opinion of the time," its effect being in part to prepare the public to appreciate the value of resource conservation. Roosevelt's representations of "nature" not only cast this value in terms of frontier romanticism and scientific realism, the combination of which helped advance the cause of conservation, but also disallowed any sympathy for nonhuman animals based on sentimental or emotional reactions.

While *Ranch Life and the Hunting Trail* and *The Wilderness Hunter* both demonstrate the continued importance Roosevelt placed on the accurate observation and description of big game animals, these books also further elaborate the frontier mythology he originally offered in *Hunting Trips of a Ranchman* (a not surprising development, considering that these books were written at the same time that Roosevelt was preparing *The Winning of the West*). *Ranch Life and the Hunting Trail* grew out of a series of articles Roosevelt wrote for *Century* magazine in 1888, the first appearing in February, only two months after the dinner meeting at which the Boone and Crockett Club was established. Other articles followed in March, April, May, June, and October, and in December all six were revised and collected in one volume, which appeared in a deluxe gift edition to enthusiastic reviews. Wholly illustrated by Frederick Remington — the only book by Roosevelt to claim this distinction — *Ranch Life* was published in a quarto edition and bound in tan buckram, its author identified on the title page as "President of the Boone and Crockett Club of New York."[47] Scientifically minded readers, of course, immediately recognized the value of Roosevelt's realism. The *Nation*, for instance, noted that "Mr. Roosevelt's observations on the natural history and the game of the region are thoroughly trustworthy, and consequently possess a considerable scientific importance" (92), and Grinnell himself remarked that Roosevelt's chapter on the mountain sheep was "the best published account of that species" ("President Roosevelt" 437). Less scientifically inclined readers, however, saw the book's evocation of "the West of the great ranch time" as its greatest strength; "anyone who did see that West knows that Roosevelt's account of it is faithful and penetrating," noted Owen Wister (*Works* 1:258).[48]

One passage in particular from *Ranch Life* illustrates especially well the various lenses though which Roosevelt was filtering his western experience in 1888, lenses such as the closing of the frontier, the primitivism of the hunter, and the freedom inherent in the American landscape. At the end of chapter two ("Out on the Range"), Roosevelt declares that "[t]he best days of ranching are over" (*Works* 1:292): "In its present form stock-raising on the plains is doomed, and can hardly outlast the century. The great free ranches, with their barbarous, picturesque, and curiously fascinating surroundings, mark a primitive stage of existence as surely as do the great tracts of primeval forests and, like the latter, must pass away before the onward march of our people; and we who have felt the charm of the life, and have exulted in its abounding vigor and its bold, restless freedom, will not only regret its passing for our own sakes, but must also feel real sorrow that those who come after us are not to see, as we have seen, what is perhaps the pleasantest, healthiest, and most exciting phase of American existence" (*Works* 1:292–3). At the same time as this passage naturalizes the "inevitability" of the westward course of empire, suggesting that both the free ranchland and the primeval forests of the West must succumb to the ax and plow of the agriculturist, it also suggests that preservation of the "vigor" and "freedom" inherent in the frontier experience may eventually require the preservation of the landscapes on which this experience was itself dependent.

Roosevelt further developed this idea in the last volume of his frontier trilogy, *The Wilderness Hunter*, published in 1893, the same year Frederick Jackson Turner declared the frontier closed. Like *Ranch Life*, *The Wilderness Hunter* was recognized for its scientific precision; many reviewers, in fact, considered it Roosevelt's finest achievement. The *Atlantic Monthly*, for instance, noted that the book "stands nearly alone in the literature of sport with large game" and claimed that Roosevelt's chapter on the grizzly bear "is the best essay in existence on its own subject. . . . [N]othing so thorough and satisfactory concerning this animal's way of life and general character has yet appeared" (827, 828). C. Hart Merriam likewise called it "incomparably the best book ever written on the large mammals of America" (246).[49] Also like *Ranch Life*, *The Wilderness Hunter* elicited a similar reaction about Roosevelt's treatment of the frontier. Reviews of the last two volumes of Roosevelt's nature trilogy dwelled less on the idea of the West as a "strange wilderness" and more on its "historic and 'American' qualities" (G. Edward White 186). Roosevelt himself, in the eyes of these reviewers, evolved "from a practical expert on cattle ranching and a teller of strange tales into a chronicler of a phase of American civilization and finally a patriot who saw the legacy of a western experience in some of the ideals of modern America" (190).

A passage from *The Wilderness Hunter* demonstrates the evolution of Roosevelt's thinking about the relationship of conservation to the manly qualities of the hunter and the democratic ideals his freedom to roam the landscape represents.

Near the end of the book, in a chapter on hunting lore, Roosevelt writes, "From its very nature, the life of the hunter is in most places evanescent; and where it has vanished there can be no real substitute in old settled countries. Shooting in a private game-preserve is but a dismal parody; the manliest and healthiest features of the sport are lost with the change of conditions. We need, in the interest of the community at large, a rigid system of game-laws, rigidly enforced, and it is not only admissible, but one may almost say necessary, to establish, under the control of the State, great national forest reserves which shall also be breeding grounds and nurseries for wild game; but I should much regret to see grow up in this country a system of large private game-preserves kept for the enjoyment of the very rich. One of the chief attractions of the life of the wilderness is its rugged and stalwart democracy; there every man stands for what he actually is and can show himself to be" (*Works* 2:353–4).

After *The Wilderness Hunter*, Roosevelt turned his attention from writing to editing, producing three collections of hunting and conservation essays in six years — or a new Boone and Crockett Club book every other year. Working with George Bird Grinnell as his coeditor, Roosevelt helped choose the topics for each volume, solicit the articles from club members, and prepare the texts for publication, often through line-by-line editing. Roosevelt also provided the $1,250 necessary to cover the initial cost of publication, and Forest and Stream Publishing Company, of which Grinnell was controlling owner, agreed to publish the books at cost and advertise them without charge (Trefethen, *Crusade* 25). Following the publication of *Hunting in Many Lands*, the second of these volumes, the *Nation* wrote that the appearance of these books signaled that "the Boone and Crockett Club is really accomplishing something of value, not only to sportsmen, but to the whole country — the protection of game, and incidentally the protection and preservation of its haunts and breeding grounds" (314).

Each volume featured essays by Roosevelt and other prominent contributors. *American Big-Game Hunting*, for instance, included such essays as "The White Goat and His Country" by Owen Wister; "In Buffalo Days" by Grinnell; "The Yellowstone Park as a Game Reservation" by Arnold Hague; and "Coursing the Prongbuck" by Roosevelt. It also featured an editorial on the literature of big game hunting by Roosevelt, a brief description of the Boone and Crockett Club, and a list of forest reservations in the United States.[50] *Hunting in Many Lands* contained essays on game laws by Charles E. Whitehead; the protection of Yellowstone National Park by George S. Anderson; and hunting in the cattle country by Roosevelt; as well as an unattributed article (written by Grinnell) on the Yellowstone National Park Protection Act, accompanied by the full text of the act.[51] *Trail and Camp-Fire* similarly featured such essays as "The Adirondack Deer Law" by William Cary Sanger; "The Origin of the New York Zoological Society" by Madison Grant; and two contributions by Roosevelt: "On the Little Missouri" and "Bear Traits."[52] The preface to *Trail and Camp-Fire* suggests the increasing amount of space Grinnell and Roosevelt decided to allot for the discussion and explanation of conservation issues in these books: "The two earlier volumes of the club's publication, though devoted chiefly to accounts of hunting adventure, contain also considerable matter bearing on the natural history of North American game and forest preservation. In the present volume an effort is made to devote somewhat more space to the natural history side of our large animals, for the publications of the club should contain material of permanent value. Of course, any book, whether on hunting or science, should be interesting, but it should be something else, too. Hunting stories should be more than merely pleasant reading. The purposes of the club are serious, and its published papers should be of a lasting character" (9–10).

Fact and Fiction in Nature Writing

Such a statement suggests that Roosevelt's advocacy of conservation in his later books came to rely less on frontier romanticism than on scientific realism, and the accuracy of this suggestion can be seen quite clearly by reviewing the editorial exchange that occurred between Grinnell and Roosevelt during the creation of *Trail and Camp-Fire*. Reviewing this exchange, moreover, also reveals Roosevelt to be as careful an editor as he was writer, disputing Paul Russell Cutright's claim that the Boone and Crockett Club books betrayed "Roosevelt's lack of editorial experience" (*Making* 180).

Such a review best begins on 24 March 1897, when Grinnell wrote to Roosevelt to inform him that he had "a capital character sketch" called "Cherry" by Lewis S. Thompson. "It is very amusing," Grinnell wrote, "and I think it should go in the book."[53] On 5 May, Roosevelt wrote back to Grinnell, questioning the factual basis of "Cherry": "What kind of character sketch is that by Thompson? I think we should be very cautious of admitting anything in the nature of fiction to our volumes. If it is a description of a real person, put it in, but I should be sorry to see it put in if it is not a real person. . . . The great trouble with American books of this kind has been their admitting articles which are commonly called 'founded on fact.'"[54]

The essay eventually made the cut, but not before Roosevelt further objected to the humor of the piece, as evident in a 30 December letter from Grinnell to Roosevelt: "I think that neither you nor I would object to seeing in an article on sport of any kind, more or less humor. What I object to in the average writer is the unsuccessful attempt to be funny. Now I think that Thompson's article in the B & C book, entitled 'Cherry' is really humorous. It may not be a very high form of humor, but it is certainly a good American form, depending for its effect on absurd exaggerations. As evidence that it is well regarded by others than myself, I may say that our managing editor wants to run it in Forest and Stream."[55]

Earlier that summer, on 2 August, Roosevelt took up the issue of Clay Arthur Pierce's "Newfoundland Caribou Hunt," an article Grinnell had forwarded to him for review. Roosevelt was biting in his criticism, faulting Pierce for puerile prose and ill-fated attempts at humor, but finding value in Pierce's employment of factual precision through photography and measurement: "I have read through the article which I return. How old is young Pierce? He writes as if he were not more than 14. Nevertheless there is much of the article that is really interesting, notably photographing the deer while it was held from the canoe, and some of the accounts of the distances at which the game was shot; but it needs merciless pruning. Wherever the young idiot speaks of papa, father should of course be substituted, and, if possible, the allusion should be left out altogether. It is not advisable to put in nursery prattle. In the next place all of the would-be funny parts must be cut out ruthlessly. If there exists any particularly vulgar horror on the face of the globe it is the 'funny' hunting story. This of course means that we shall have to cut down the piece to about half its present length; but if that is done I think it will be good" (Morison 636). Three weeks later, Roosevelt returned to the Pierce essay in a 24 August letter, telling Grinnell, "If you will send me on Pierce's article I will slash it up into about a third of the space it now occupies, and send it back to you" (Morison 658).

Later in his 24 August letter — while discussing "Books on Big Game," his unattributed collaboration with Grinnell in the volume — Roosevelt offers a justification for his editorial practices in *Trail and Camp-Fire* and the other Boone and Crockett Club books. Claiming that "many of our scientific people don't put enough stress upon hunting, and upon the habits of big game," Roosevelt says he sees the hunting book as providing a valuable factual record — if only it can be saved from writers who value sentiment over science: "The geology and the beetles will remain unchanged for ages, but the big game will vanish, and only the pioneer hunter can tell about it. Hunting books of the best type are often of more permanent value than scientific pamphlets; & I think the B. & C. should differentiate sharply between worthless hunting stories, & those that are of value. Writings by 'Chipmunk,' . . . etc., are not very valuable; but your piece on the buffalo is worth more than any but the very best scientific monographs about the beast" (Morison 658).

Roosevelt was as critical of his own writing as he was of that submitted by the other members of the club. Discussing "On the Little Missouri," his own contribution to *Trail and Camp-Fire*, Roosevelt places his changing views about hunting in the context of his resistance to the sentimentalizing tendencies he sees in the writing of others. He writes to Grinnell on 27 August: "I find that the older I grow the less I care for the actual killing — although, on the other hand, I think we want to beware of getting into the merely sentimental stage. The more I realize what a quantity of bad people [i.e., sentimental writers] we have around, the more I want to see the good people keep a little iron in their blood." Roosevelt then asks Grinnell to review two aspects of "On the Little Missouri": "the case of the bear charging with his mouth open" and the possibility of his having "credited the big wolf with the misdeeds of the coyote." Unsure about the accuracy of these scenes, Roosevelt turns to the metaphor of nature-as-text to describe his frustration at being unable to recall these details with precision: "I have found that it's very easy to misread occasional sentences in the very complicated book of nature and that it's a great help to be able to profit by another student who has closely examined the text."[56]

The following day, he returns the article by Pierce, noting the extensive editing it received. "I enclose Pierce's article. It would really have been easier to rewrite it, for only the most rigorous cutting put it into any kind of shape; but the kid has a genuine eye for scenery, in spite of his florid commercial-drummer way of writing about it." Pierce's article, Roosevelt concludes somewhat sarcastically, "is worth while putting in now that we have cut out about half, and telescoped the remaining paragraphs and eliminated the jokes."[57]

Although Roosevelt's correspondence with Grinnell about *Trail and Camp-Fire* may appear to suggest that he maintained a Gradgrindian insistence on "facts" at the expense of a writer's creativity, nothing could be further from the truth. After Roosevelt had read the proof of "Wolves and Wolf Nature," Grinnell's own contribution to the volume, he was full of praise for the literary aspects of the essay. In a 30 August 1897 letter, Roosevelt contrasted "Wolves and Wolf Nature" to the writings of scientists who lacked Grinnell's eloquence: "I am extremely obliged to you for sending me that proof. I think it is one of the most interesting articles I have ever read. Why in the name of heaven have you never published more of your experiences in book form? They would be worth a hundred times as much as dry-as-dust pedantic descriptions by Shufeldt and a lot of other little half-baked scientists. I know these scientists pretty well, and their limitations are extraordinary, especially when they get to talking of science with a capital S. They do good work; but, after all, it is only the very best of them who are more than brickmakers, who laboriously get together bricks out of which other men must build houses. When they think they are architects they are simply a nuisance."[58]

Roosevelt closed his own essay, "On the Little Missouri," by acknowledging some discrepancies between his own observations of wolves and those of Grinnell in "Wolves and Wolf Nature," again drawing on the metaphor of the book of nature. "The great book of Nature," Roosevelt concluded, "contains many passages which are hard to read, and at times conscientious students may well draw up different interpretations of the obscurer and least known texts. It may not be that either observer is at fault; but what is true of an animal in one locality may not be true of the same animal in another, and even in the same locality two individuals of a species may widely differ in their habits" (219). Notably, Roosevelt's comment echoes the question that first brought Grinnell and Roosevelt together some twelve years earlier.

The achievements of Theodore Roosevelt as president of the United States, particularly in the area of conservation, need no detailed rehearsal here, as they include such well-known acts as the creation of 5 national parks; 16 national monuments, including the Grand Canyon; 13 new national forests; 16 federal bird refuges, starting with Pelican Island, Florida; and the first federal game refuge, at Wichita Forest, Oklahoma (E. Morris, *Theodore Rex* 519). The achievements of the members of the Boone and Crockett Club during and after Roosevelt's presidency have likewise been substantial, including their assisting in the founding of Glacier National Park in 1910, the passage of the Weeks-McLean Migratory Bird Act in 1913, the creation of the National Park Service in 1916, the establishment of the Charles Sheldon National Antelope Range in 1931, the funding and creation of the National Key Deer Refuge in 1957, and their purchase of the Theodore Roosevelt Memorial Ranch in 1986.

Impressive as such accomplishments are, the tension they embody between what Roosevelt calls the iron-blooded "pioneer hunter" and the "merely sentimental" writings "by 'Chipmunk,' . . . etc.," has remained with the organized conservation movement throughout its history. As Matt Cartmill explained in *A View to a Death in the Morning* (1993)—using the term "Romantics" to describe what Roosevelt would call "sentimentalists"—"From the very beginning, the American conservation movement has encompassed two rather different sorts of nature lovers: tender-minded Romantics who want to preserve nature because it is holy, and tough-minded Darwinian types, who want to preserve it because it is healthy. For the Romantics, nature is an open-air chapel in which one can commune with the Infinite and make friends with the forest creatures; for the Darwinians, nature is a kind of vast exercise salon, in which one can get rid of bodily flabbiness and spiritual malaise, work up a glorious appetite, and polish off a couple of those forest creatures for supper. These views are not mutually exclusive, and most nature lovers hold both to varying degrees; but there is a tension between the two attitudes, which sometimes breaks out into fights over such matters as hunting" (149–50).[59]

Just as Roosevelt used a combination of scientific realism and frontier romanticism to create a rhetorical space for the Boone and Crockett Club, Mabel Osgood Wright managed to blend that same scientific realism with the sentimentalism

Roosevelt so despised in order to revitalize Grinnell's Audubon Society after its collapse in 1888. Recognizing the limitations of both these rhetorical strategies, therefore, need not prevent us from saluting their notable achievements, which for both groups exist in abundance.

In his brief history of the Boone and Crockett Club, George Bird Grinnell summarized what may be the supreme achievement of this particular group: simply existing as an activist organization, an achievement he credits largely to Theodore Roosevelt.[60] "It would have been natural and easy for the Club to have confined its activities to meeting at intervals to dine, and discuss abuses and dangers, and to pass stirring resolutions, about them," he admits. "Instead of this, it has had a small body of intelligent men, scattered all over the country, working individually and constantly in behalf of things once laughed at or unknown, but now as familiar to the public mind as household words. The results accomplished by the Boone and Crockett Club bear testimony to the alertness and energy of its members, and to the success of the methods which they have pursued" (Grinnell, "Brief History" 491). Truly, no other testimony need be offered.

CHAPTER TWO

The Garden, You, and I

Mabel Osgood Wright
and the National
Audubon Society

Gardening is the most cheerful and satisfactory pursuit for women
who love outdoors. Field and forest often hold one at bay. We
may admire, worship, love, but neither advise nor argue with them
nor add one cubit to their stature. In a garden one's personality can
come forth, stick a finger into nature's pie, and lend a hand in the
making of it, besides furnishing many of the ingredients.

MABEL OSGOOD WRIGHT, *The Garden of a Commuter's Wife*

O N THE FLOOR, on either side of my fireplace, lie two buffalo skulls,"
wrote George Bird Grinnell in the September 1892 issue of *Scribner's.* "They are white and weathered, the horns cracked and bleached
by the snows and frosts, and the rains and heats of many winters and summers.
Often, late at night, when the house is quiet, I sit before the fire, and muse and
dream of the old days; and as I gaze at these relics of the past, they take life before
my eyes" ("Last of the Buffalo" 267).

It is an irony of fate that these symbols of Grinnell's frontier days, reminders of
his life on the wide-open plains, should now find their home across the street from
what remains of Mabel Osgood Wright's suburban garden — in the Birdcraft Museum and Sanctuary she founded in 1914 while president of the Connecticut
Audubon Society. Not that Grinnell would have been displeased with the donation of these buffalo skulls, along with hundreds of his bird skins and ornithological mounts, to Birdcraft by his nephew Donald Page in 1939. In fact, he most likely
would have encouraged the gesture, given that the museum is a monument to the

resurrection of the Audubon Society he first organized in 1886 and that it lies midway between Audubon Park (his home in New York City) and Yale University (his alma mater). Nevertheless, the presence of these buffalo skulls in their current Fairfield, Connecticut, location also reflects the maturation of the conservation movement from an idea embraced mainly by Grinnell's fellow big game hunters to one that captured the hearts and minds of suburban women across the nation in the late nineteenth and early twentieth centuries.

This chapter explores this shift in emphasis from the western frontier conservation of Theodore Roosevelt and George Bird Grinnell to the "crabgrass frontier" variety of Mabel Osgood Wright.[1] It looks specifically at Wright's involvement in the creation of the Connecticut Audubon Society and her work as a leader of the National Association of Audubon Societies and as associate editor of *Bird-Lore*, the predecessor of *Audubon* magazine. In addition, it discusses the importance of the flower garden as a locus for women's efforts in the conservation movement and examines Wright's use of garden imagery in her nature writing and in the many articles she contributed to *Bird-Lore*. Throughout this chapter, I argue that Wright's work as a writer and conservationist grew out of the ethics and aesthetics of suburban life. By appealing to the patriotic sentiments and untapped energies of suburban women, Wright helped to broaden the audience for environmental reform and deepen the arguments used by its reformers, moving the focus of conservation away from the disappearing frontier of the sportsman and into the backyard gardens of suburban America.

"The Garden of My Girlhood"

One cannot fully appreciate the life of Mabel Osgood Wright without knowing something about her father, Unitarian minister Samuel Osgood (1812–1880), whose love of gardening was rivaled only by his enthusiasm for the intellectual life. A student of Henry Ware and William Ellery Channing, whose work he encountered first at Harvard College and later at the Cambridge Divinity School, Osgood was a tireless writer and speaker, an editor of the Unitarian journals *Western Messenger* and *Christian Inquirer*, a contributor to the *North American Review*, *Putnam's*, *Harper's*, and other periodicals, and the author of six major volumes of essays, sermons, and speeches. A member of William Cullen Bryant's literary circle, Osgood counted among his friends some of the most prominent men of letters in the nineteenth century, including George Bancroft, Oliver Wendell Holmes, Edmund Clarence Stedman, Edwin Arnold, George William Curtis, Edwin Booth, Lawrence Barrett, William Wetmore Story, John Hay, and Joseph Choate.[2]

As pastor of the Church of the Messiah in New York City, Osgood lived most of the year with his family in Greenwich Village, but in 1857, when he bought eight acres of land in Fairfield, Connecticut, he began building Mosswood, an eighteen-room summer home situated close to the train depot and within walking distance of the Long Island Sound. The property was said to have been a tract that one "would hardly accept as a gift, it scarcely being a sheep pasture for quality, overrun with cedars and cumbered with plenty of stones" (Hurd 331). Over the next twenty years, Osgood created extensive gardens on the land, laid out winding sidewalks, dug a lily pool, built smaller summer houses around the main house, placed a half-size Italian statue of Dante on the grounds, and planted a pine tree every time he performed a baptism or marriage ("Fairfield Country Day School"). According to one account, "[t]he apparently worthless natural encumbrances upon the place he converted into ornaments. The stones and rocks made fences, recesses, grottoes, monuments, trellises, and landscape-finishings" (Hurd 331). Many of these rocks were carved with quotations from the Bible and from Osgood's favorite works of literature, as well as with the names of family members, classic poets, and Christian prophets. In a crowning gesture, Osgood built a gazebo-like structure out of cedar and placed it upon a high rock bordering the street. From this wooden pulpit, which came to be known as Union Tower, Osgood preached occasional sermons during the Civil War to crowds gathered in the street below. (Though the tower is now gone, the inscription "God and Our Country 1862" is still visible on Pulpit Rock.) Finally, in the year before his death, Osgood changed the name of the street on which Mosswood was located from Cedar Street to Unquowa Road, using the Indian name for Fairfield, which is said to mean "go further" (Hughes and Allen 171; "Fairfield Estate").

Soon after Mosswood was built, Osgood's youngest daughter, Mabel Gray, was born in New York City on 26 January 1859—a coincidence, Wright insists, that "doubtless accounts for [her] intense love for everything around [the property]" ("MOW Recalls Pleasures").[3] Though she lived most of the year in the family's three-story, brick house on West Eleventh Street in New York, and attended Miss Lucy Green's school for girls at Number One Fifth Avenue, Wright received her true education at Mosswood. As she recalls in "The Story of a Garden," "With my first consciousness, the days were filled with planting and with growth; the pines already hid the walls, and cattle tracks were widened into paths and wound among young maples, elms, and beeches. Then there grew in me a love that made the four garden walls seem like the boundaries of the world" (*The Friendship of Nature* 94–95). She and her father, she once told an interviewer, "had splendid experiences, here in the garden in my girlhood" ("Visit"). Indeed, the garden was so important to Wright that although she and her husband spent the winter months in the Osgood home on West Eleventh Street, in the summers after Wright's father died in 1880 they lived primarily at Mosswood, from which James Wright would commute to work in New York City by train.[4]

Andrew Jackson Downing and the Suburban Domestic Ideal

Samuel Osgood's transformation of his overgrown, stony sheep pasture into a picturesque house and grounds reflects the confluence of two cultural developments in mid-nineteenth-century America, both of which affected Wright's approach to conservation issues: first, the growth of what John R. Stilgoe has identified as "the 'leafy' outer suburbs — or *borderlands* as early nineteenth century intellectuals termed them — of the large eastern cities" (*Borderland* 4), and second, the enthusiasm among the dwellers of these borderlands for the cottage design and landscape architecture of Andrew Jackson Downing (1815–52), the nineteenth century's most influential "apostle of taste."[5]

Prior to the work of historian Kenneth Jackson, the suburbanization of the United States had been discussed mainly in terms of three factors: the technological developments that made possible movement away from the city, the abundance of relatively inexpensive land on the outskirts of urban centers, and the traditional antipathy Americans were said to have harbored against urban life as a result of the nation's agrarian heritage. In *Crabgrass Frontier* (1985) Jackson argued persuasively that the primary factor driving suburbanization was the growth of the city itself, particularly the need for more residential space. In contrast to Jackson's focus on the economic, demographic, and political forces operating in the cities, other historians such as Henry Binford, Clifford Clark, and Robert Fishman have since explained the origins of the suburbs by reference to the architectural, environmental, and cultural characteristics of the suburbs themselves (M. Marsh 2–3).

Of these more recent critics, Robert Fishman has provocatively termed the suburbs "bourgeois utopias," noting that they express values deeply embedded in middle-class culture. According to Fishman, "this 'utopia' was always at most a partial paradise, a refuge not only from threatening elements in the city but also from discordant elements in bourgeois society itself. From its origins, the suburban world of leisure, family life, and union with nature was based on the principle of exclusion. Work was excluded from the family residence; middle-class villas were segregated from working-class housing; the greenery of suburbia stood in contrast to a gray, polluted urban environment. Middle-class women were especially affected by the new suburban dichotomy of work and family life. The new environment supposedly exalted their role in the family, but it also segregated them from the world of power and productivity. This self-segregation soon enveloped all aspects of bourgeois culture. Suburbia, therefore, represents more than the bourgeois utopia, the triumphant assertion of middle-class values. It also reflects the alienation of the middle classes from the urban-industrial world they themselves were creating" (4).

Margaret Marsh deepens Fishman's observations in her discussion of the ideology that drove suburban growth, and particularly the ways in which that ideology changed between the mid–nineteenth century of Samuel Osgood's time to the late nineteenth and early twentieth centuries of Mabel Osgood Wright's adulthood. In *Suburban Lives* (1990) Marsh argues that the suburban ideal first developed independently from the domestic ideal, which held that "the family, over which women presided, was the central institution in American life" (8).[6] According to Marsh, the suburban ideal was largely the creation of middle-class men, and it "stressed separation from urban life, protection of wives and children from city evils (both real and fancied), and property ownership as a safeguard for political independence" (41). The domestic ideal, in contrast, largely the creation of middle-class women, "exalted the spiritual influence of the home, eventually turning the home into a power base from which women would, it was hoped, transform the moral character of the nation, working from the family outward" (41). Similarly, the suburban ideal had at its center a physical space — the residential suburb — while the ideology of domesticity had at its center a cultural institution — the family (xiii). Toward the end of the nineteenth century, however, "as cities grew ever larger and more 'alien,' and as technology made the suburbs more accessible to the city as well as more civilized, the suburban ideal and the ideology of domesticity began to come together," according to Marsh. "Advocates of both increasingly believed that the great city imperiled conventional ideas about the nature of family life as well as traditional American political values" (xiii–xiv). Furthermore, in the years before World War I, a new suburban domestic ideal took hold, which some sociologists have called "suburban familism." "This new suburban vision," Marsh explains, "changed middle-class family life — it reorganized domesticity so that it no longer depended on the strict adherence to separate masculine and feminine roles — and it also redefined the residential suburbs, so that the ruralized suburban vision of the mid–nineteenth century gave way to one emphasizing the importance of place as well as, perhaps moreso than, property ownership" (67–68).

One person who helped facilitate this gradual merger of suburban ideals and domestic ideology was Andrew Jackson Downing, the celebrated landscape gardener and rural architect whom Kenneth Jackson calls "the most influential single individual in translating the rural ideal into a suburban ideal" (63). In the ten years before his death in the *Henry Clay* steamboat disaster of 1852, Downing became one of the most widely read advocates of rural virtue. His *Treatise on the Theory and Practice of Landscape Gardening* (1841) went through eight editions and sixteen printings before 1879, and his *Architecture of Country Houses* (1850) was reprinted nine times before 1886. Borrowing the ideas of Edmund Burke, William Gilpin, Uvedale Price, Humphry Repton, and most significantly, John Claudius

Loudon (whose *Encyclopaedia of Cottage, Farm, and Villa Architecture* first appeared in 1833), Downing proposed a program of rural improvement that blended the aesthetic principles of transcendentalism with the ethical ideals of social conservatism. As William Howard Adams explains, "Downing's message was that the house of correct design surrounded by a virtuous garden would save men from houses of ill-repute, and would shore up the most fragile American institution, the family" (290). Resembling Thomas Jefferson in his linkage of agrarian self-sufficiency and republican virtue, Downing saw the suburbs as the most suitable place for moral improvement, where "men of honor" could find their rationality "strengthened by the natural beauty which architect and gardener had assembled" (Harris 215). "In the United States, nature and domestic life are better than society and the manners of towns," Downing wrote in the *Horticulturist* in 1848. "Hence all sensible men gladly escape, earlier or later, and partially or wholly, from the turmoil of cities" (*Rural Essays* 111).

Echoing the lament of Susan Fenimore Cooper in *Rural Hours* (1850) that young women of her class no longer took an interest in the garden, Downing encouraged women to take a more active role in the cultivation of the landscape, a development he believed would lead naturally to the improvement of their own persons and families. In 1843 Downing edited an American edition of Jane Loudon's *Gardening for Ladies* (1840) in the hope that the book would "increase, among our own fair countrywomen, the taste for these delightful occupations in the open air, which are so conducive to their own health, and to the beauty and interest of our homes" (Loudon iv). And in an 1849 essay "On Feminine Taste in Rural Affairs," which appeared in the *Horticulturist*, Downing bemoaned the fact that "our wives and daughters only love gardens as the French love them — for the results" — arguing that a lady "has been cut off by her mother nature with less than a shilling's patrimony, if she does not love trees, flowers, gardens, and nature, as if they were all part of herself" (*Rural Essays* 46, 52). "What ought to be the most important argument of all," Downing stressed, was that gardening exposed women to exercise, fresh air, and health (*Rural Essays* 53). "[I]f your heart is in the right place for ruralities," he told his female readers, "you will find the occupation so fascinating that you will gradually find yourself able to enjoy keenly what was at first only a very irksome sort of duty" (*Rural Essays* 54).[7]

Suburban Women and Their Flower Gardens

In part because of Downing's influence, women at the end of the nineteenth century no longer needed much encouragement to cultivate their gardens. The suburban ideal merged with domestic ideology, in Margaret Marsh's terms, and women became the primary shapers of borderland life. As John Stilgoe explains, much of this shaping occurred in the garden: "A borderland cottage gracefully embellished with flowers wild, cultivated, and exotic, screened with evergreen hedges perhaps, or half-covered with climbing vines, announced not only the leisure of its mistress, but her developing intellectual and emotional strengths. The garden might originate more in a love of sophisticated botanical study or in notions of floral beauty and messages, or simply in burgeoning love of growing flowers, shrubs, and other nonagricultural plants, but it often reflected a recreation of spirit, a closeness to divinity. Each flower, fragile, delicate, beautiful, thriving in perfect circumstances, wilting in adverse conditions, mirrored the ever more intricate self-image of educated leisured women attempting to rescue their husbands, children, and themselves from the withering blasts of city living" (*Borderland* 37).

Recent scholarship has developed Stilgoe's point, recognizing that a variety of suburbs existed in North America during the late nineteenth and early twentieth centuries and examining how ethnicity and class informed the ways that suburban residents shaped their environments. Mary Corbin Sies, for instance, has observed that "[r]esidents of planned, exclusive suburbs . . . emphasized aesthetics to a much greater degree than is apparent in many working-class suburbs. Manicured 'natural' landscapes, consisting of planned streetscapes, parklike common spaces, and carefully tended flowers or shrubbery at public buildings, were ubiquitous components of affluent suburbs but were seen less frequently in blue-collar enclaves. African American suburbanites articulated their appreciation of the natural surroundings in their neighborhoods, but theirs was a more rural aesthetic. They valued the trees, the creatures, and the open spaces with which their landscape was already furnished, not a meticulously designed parkscape. Although many blue-collar households maintained shrubs and flower gardens, affluent households, on the whole, exerted more aesthetic control over their property, cultivating elaborate pleasure gardens, vistas, and/or exotic plantings" (333). Sies's observation helps clarify the fact that the audience for Mabel Osgood Wright's nature writing and advocacy can be identified not only by their gender but also by their class, race, and ethnicity.

Suburban women who rediscovered the garden in the late nineteenth and early twentieth centuries could be said to have been participants in a long tradition of intimacy involving women and their gardens, particularly women and their flower gardens.[8] Garden historian Eleanor Perényi, for instance, argues that "it was women who invented horticulture in the first place, women who ventured into field and forest in search of wild plants, and women who domesticated them while men were still out chasing wild beasts. Women were the first gardeners; but when men retired from the hunting field and decided in favor of agriculture instead, women steadily lost control" (260). As a result, Perényi claims, men chose to incarcerate women in the flower garden, where they could simultaneously cater to and keep in check their "superstitious fear that women were in league with nature in some way that men were not" (261). Such a claim represents the more essentialist tendencies of feminism, of course, and Jennifer Bennett is right to ask whether men have been "responsible for the incarceration of women in the flower garden, as Perényi suggests, or . . . women themselves [have] freely chosen to work with flowers instead of with other plants or, indeed, rather than not garden at all" (130).

Another point made by Perényi deserves more serious consideration. "Flowers," she notes, "are of all plants the least menacing and the most useless. Their sole purpose is to be beautiful and to give pleasure . . . and as such they are the perfect combination of tribute and demand" (261). Women's identification with the flower garden, therefore, is different from their identification with the vegetable garden because the two gardens have carried different class-bound meanings. Women of the lower classes, more directly concerned with the cultivation of food and the preparation of medicines, have had less time for the beautification of their homes with delicate flowers. These two types of gardens, in other words, have "represented two fundamentally opposed ways of using the soil," as Keith Thomas puts it. "In the one, men [and women] used nature as a means of subsistence; its products were to be eaten. In the other, they sought to create order and aesthetic satisfaction and they showed a respect for the welfare of the species they cultivated" (240). A renewed interest in the flower garden among turn-of-the-century middle- and upper-class suburban women, therefore, symbolizes far more than simply their desire "to rescue their husbands, children, and themselves from the withering blasts of city living," as Stilgoe would have it. More broadly, it suggests that the idea of the flower garden, in particular, is in some sense at odds with the idea of the American nation as garden writ large. If America has been a garden, it most certainly has been a vegetable garden bent on production and not a flower garden grown out of sympathy and respect for the natural world.

"The master symbol of the garden [in America]," Henry Nash Smith famously explained in *Virgin Land* (1950), "embraced a cluster of metaphors expressing fecundity, growth, increase, and blissful labor in the earth, all centering about the heroic figure of the idealized frontier farmer armed with that supreme agrarian weapon, the sacred plow" (123). Smith called this the "Garden of the World" theme in American cultural history, the idea of "a continental empire founded upon agriculture, and associated with various images of the Good Society to be realized in the West" (12). The Good Society, in his formulation, was thus tied to the kind of frontier movement and westward expansion embraced by Theodore Roosevelt. Smith's student Leo Marx further developed his mentor's insight in *The Machine in the Garden* (1964), tracing the history of the garden image in America from *The Tempest* to *The Great Gatsby* and exploring the conflict that arises when technology intrudes into the pastoral ideal. Most important for our purposes, Marx finds in Robert Beverley's *History and Present State of Virginia* (1705) a conflict between the initial image of the New World as a primitive paradise and the incipient image of it as an agricultural ideal. "Beverley," Marx writes, "was groping for the distinction between two garden metaphors: a wild, primitive, or prelapsarian Eden in which he thought to have found the Indians, and a cultivated garden embracing values not unlike those represented by the classic Virgilian pasture" (87).

In taking the flower garden as her point of departure, Mabel Osgood Wright was working to bridge the gap between these two metaphors of nature in America: between the frontier conservation of Theodore Roosevelt and the park preservation of John Muir. While sharing some of the desire for national achievement bound up with the idea of America as an advancing vegetable garden, Wright also argued for the creation of Edenic, parklike spaces where birds and other creatures could find refuge — for what is a park, after all, but a glorified flower garden?

Wright's use of the garden in this manner was less a conscious endeavor on her part than a response to her social, cultural, and political situation. Because so many of her suburban readers maintained their own gardens, the topic guaranteed Wright a sympathetic audience when she switched from discussing the enjoyment of nature to advocating for nature's protection. The topic also allowed her own private garden to take on a public significance, providing her with an image through which she could frame her arguments and a physical location in which she could test her ideas about preservation of local landscapes, much in the same way Mary Kelley has suggested that women's domestic fiction allowed "private women" to speak on a "public stage." By employing the idea of the garden as a domestic space, Wright succeeded not only in celebrating the garden as a realm of nature and virtue but also in justifying the right of women to foster change through both publication and public action.

At the same time, it is important to remember that a garden is defined as much by what it seeks to keep out as by what it seeks to cultivate within. As John Brinckerhoff Jackson points out, "The word *garden*, like the Latin *hortus*, derives from an Indo-Germanic root meaning fence or enclosure" (123).[9] Just as the suburbs described by Robert Fishman were "based on the principle of exclusion," so too were the gardens of Wright and her readers shaped by these women's class, race, and ethnicity. Wright shared the nativist beliefs of many early conservationists, and she cultivated her suburban garden in reaction to immigration as much as urbanization. Although best characterized as upper middle class, Wright also shared the ideology of more upper-class women who "wrote gardening manuals for more middle-class suburbanites, suggesting how they might adapt garden styles of wealthy country places to their smaller plots on the urban fringe" (Norwood 101).[10] Her activism displayed this same sense of noblesse oblige and was enabled by the same leisure that allowed her to write about her garden. Nevertheless, it remains remarkable, if not radical, that Wright achieved so much political success as a conservationist, most of it coming before women received the vote in 1920. Wright's activism may have begun in the garden, but — like Theodore Roosevelt's — it was hardly garden-variety.

Cultivating a Middle Ground

Gardens figure prominently in almost all Wright's books, but a few books in particular deserve special attention: her first book, *The Friendship of Nature* (1894); her two field guides, *Birdcraft* (1895) and *Flowers and Ferns in their Haunts* (1901); her first few children's books; and two of her semiautobiographical novels, *The Garden of a Commuter's Wife* (1901) and *The Garden, You, and I* (1906). Of these, *The Friendship of Nature* provides perhaps the best metaphor for Wright's work as a whole, because its title illustrates her perception that the garden has a unique role in mediating human relationships with the natural world. Whereas the idea of the frontier originates from a domineering anthropocentric perspective, and the idea of the wilderness implies a "nature" where humanity is "only a visitor," the garden is halfway between wilderness and civilization, a place Michael Pollan describes as "a middle ground between nature and culture, a place that is at once of nature and unapologetically set against it" ("Against Nature" 53).[11] Offering neither the absence of nature nor nature "red in tooth and claw," the garden allows human beings to develop an intimacy with nature similar to that found in a good friendship.

Wright's own friendship with nature led her down several garden paths: to establish that friendship, she first cultivated her own garden; to strengthen it, she began a detailed study of backyard birds at the American Museum of Natural History; to introduce others to it, she wrote books, taught classes, and prepared lectures; and to preserve it, she founded the Connecticut Audubon Society and worked tirelessly to place the National Association of Audubon Societies on a solid theoretical and practical footing.

The Friendship of Nature

The Friendship of Nature, Wright's first book, took shape after she and her new husband returned to the United States from a period of travel in Europe.[12] How Wright spent her first few years of marriage in America is largely undocumented, but one newspaper journalist noted that Wright's urge to write "followed experiences of illness and social seclusion. Nature became her comrade, as well as her nurse that aroused new vitality" (Marble). Wright once told an interviewer, "I think that my husband as well as my father expected me to become a writer. But when I would show him some of my efforts he would say: 'See here, Mab, these are green apples. Wait till they ripen a little'" ("MOW Recalls Pleasures"). Despite such feeble encouragement, after six years of married life Wright began to publish nature essays anonymously in the *New York Times* and the *New York Evening Post*, keeping them a secret, at first, even from her husband. In 1925 she recounted the process by which these articles became her first published book: "Edward Clarence Stedman, who was a close friend of us all, strongly urged when he heard of the articles, that they should appear in book form.[13] Other articles were added to those published, and the whole was submitted to George P. Brett, a friend of my husband's, who was then, as he is now, president of MacMillan's.[14] They appeared in April, 1894.[15] Nature books were quite a novelty at that time, and 'Friendships of Nature' [*sic*] as this volume was called, was a great success. My husband was just as much delighted with its success as I was" ("MOW Recalls Pleasures"). Sometime that same year, James Wright also published his wife's translation of *The Bibliomaniac*, a short story by Charles Nodier, in a small-press edition of 150 copies. In her husband's eyes, Wright's apples had finally ripened.

Wright's work was also a success in the eyes of British and American critics, who generally praised *The Friendship of Nature* for its poetic language and accurate representation of the local landscape. "The writer has a sympathetic eye and touch for every face that nature wears in her New England home," said the *Dial*. "[T]hese graceful sketches reflect the changing aspects of the blooming and the waning year, and convince us that the author, though writing prose, is a true poet in the Emersonian sense, namely, in the power to see the miraculous in the common" (rev. of *Friendship of Nature* 159). "Whether we like the author's treatment of flowers or birds the better we do not know," admitted the *New York Times*, "for both subjects are delicately handled. . . . [T]he lady is always in touch" ("Life Out of Doors" 3). Likewise, the reviewer for the *Philadelphia Evening Bulletin* found "much of the feeling of Henry D. Thoreau between the covers of this book" (qtd. in *Birdcraft* 319), and Oliver Wendell Holmes praised Wright for her "charming little book which shall go into my shelves by the side of [Gilbert] White's '[Natural History of] Selbourne'" (Marble).[16]

Some of the most appreciative readers of *Friendship* were the other women writers of Wright's day. "I know of nothing but Alphonse Karr's 'Tour Round My Garden' with which to compare it," Harriet Prescott Spofford told Wright. "I was particularly interested in the 'Story of a Garden,' — but there is not a page without its charm. It is a book that not only must have made you happy in the living and the writing, but which will bring the out-door world into the life of many a housebound reader." Frances Theodora Parsons, whose popular *How to Know the Wild Flowers* (1893) was also written in Fairfield, expressed similar sentiments about *The Friendship of Nature*. "I have read it all through and have found it really delightful," she told Wright. "It seems to me charmingly written and full of thought and affection. The illustrations are peculiarly satisfactory. They seem to get at the very heart of the different spots. I do not believe you can fail to meet with a real success, dear Mrs. Wright, and I congratulate you most heartily."[17]

Friendship consists of eleven related chapters, organized roughly around the passage of the seasons, taking the reader from May Day in spring through summer, fall, and winter. Throughout the book, Wright references a tradition of female engagement with the landscape that links the women of New England both to each other and to their gardens. In a sheltered nook, Wright finds "the little white violets that our grandmothers cherished" (31); she instructs her reader to "fill your basket, your hat, your upturned gown" with roses (49); and she recalls the young women who, rose leaves in their aprons, turned to their mother for the potpourri recipe, only to hear the words of their grandmother's recipe being read (50). Annette Kolodny, Vera Norwood, and other ecofeminist critics have discussed the subtle ways in which American women have turned their intimacy with nature into a source of power, and Wright is very much a participant in this tradition of female empowerment. By the second paragraph of her book she is already asserting her authority over the male poets of New England, noting specifically that "[t]he fringed gentian, set by Bryant in frayed and barren fields, frosty and solitary, usually follows the cardinal flower, in late September" (31).

Wright's most notable stylistic technique, her use of the second person, is both a product and source of this intimacy. "Come into the garden," Wright announces, offering the reader a personal invitation to join her on her walk, as well as a reminder to pay close attention along the way (31). She uses this technique especially well when describing transitions from one environment to another, when one's sensory awareness is heightened and some form of revelation is likely. When moving from orchard to woodland in "When Orchards Bloom," she tells the reader, "Go further yet into the wood; the banks grow steep, the road winds through a glen to the side of a narrow river, which tumbles about restlessly in its rocky bed. All that is pastoral stops. The solemn hush of the forest is irresistible: the characteristics of the flowers and birds have changed; the contrasts of light and shade are keenly dramatic" (41–42). Or later, when walking along the Long Island Sound at night in "Nature's Calm," she instructs the reader, "Step in the current; the black tide looks solid; you marvel the feet can move through it. Wade further in; up the water creeps as you advance. Swim! the cold and resistance seem to lessen as you cleave the liquid moonlight. It is a different world, yourself and Nature, yourself and space, with self a pigmy in it" (90).

In a sense, Wright's use of the second person represents the fundamental trope of her text, the "friendship" that lies at the heart of her philosophical interpretation of nature. Just as the second person point of view implies a relationship of interdependence between writer and reader, speaker and listener, so, too, does Wright's view of nature imply a fundamental connection between humans and the landscape. Though the figure of speech may seem quaint to twenty-first-century readers, the "friendship of nature" could be seen as Wright's own attempt to describe the ecological relationship that has always existed between human beings and their natural environments. People cannot live without nature, Wright might argue, and nature cannot bring forth its bounty without the same kind of patient attention a gardener would give her garden. "If you serve Nature, waiting her moods, taking what she yields unforced, giving her a love devoid of greed, she will be a regal mistress," Wright notes in *Friendship*, "and all she has to bestow will be yours. Exact and say to one little field: 'This year you shall yield this crop or that,' and it becomes a battle-ground, where Nature, well equipped, wages war with man" (65).

Nature, in Wright's view, exists in relationship with human activity. Although people receive only peripheral treatment throughout most of *The Friendship of Nature*, Wright illustrates the relation between humanity and nature near the end of the text by interrupting her description of a picturesque winter landscape to refer to the smokestacks of Bridgeport, the "tall chimneys that breathe flame and cinders"—a moment reminiscent of the "complex pastoral" defined by Leo Marx in *The Machine in the Garden*.[18] "Look at these chimneys also, though they break the harmonious circle, we must wear clothes and we must eat, for we may not all find sweetness in white oak acorns, like Thoreau. In winter, which lays bare the earth, man's needs appear, and intensify his personal limitations. Mutual dependence, and not isolation, was the plan of creation. Man needs the earth, and the earth needs man's stamp of progression" (134). Though the phrase "man's stamp of progression" may trouble modern ears, here Wright seems only to suggest that the pastoral landscape is an incomplete picture, that we cannot isolate "nature" from the products of human activity.

Science and Sentiment

In her nonfiction writing after *The Friendship of Nature*, Wright makes good on this claim, turning increasingly to modern science as a means to identify and describe birds and plants accurately. Until about 1890, as Wright observed in the *Critic*, "it was well-nigh impossible to obtain any inexpensive handbooks upon birds, flowers, trees, stars, or any other of the objects that set the Nature lover's mind at work, that were at once accurate and yet written in a style suited to popular consumption" ("Life Outdoors" 310).[19] Wright's second book, *Birdcraft* (1895), helped fill this gap by providing a catalog of birds arranged in taxonomic order, along with descriptions of each species' appearance, song, and behavior, followed by brief essays of personal observation and anecdote. One of the earliest inexpensive field guides to birds, *Birdcraft* was hailed in 1895 by John Burroughs as "a readable and interesting book." "I wish I could have had the help of such a book when I began my bird studies," Burroughs told her. "I shall take pleasure in recommending it to persons who write me for the name of a handy and reliable book on our birds."[20] Others clearly shared Burroughs's enthusiasm, as *Birdcraft* was reprinted nine times, the last time in 1936, and was eclipsed only by the appearance of Roger Tory Peterson's *Field Guide to the Birds* in 1934.[21]

Birdcraft had a significant impact on many bird-watchers, perhaps none so much as the ornithologist Margaret Morse Nice, who described her childhood encounter with the book in her autobiography, *Research Is a Passion with Me*: "The most cherished Christmas present of my life came in 1895—Mabel Osgood Wright's *Bird-Craft* (1895). For the first time I had coloured bird pictures. . . . The simple descriptions, the charming discussions, the enthusiastic introductory chapters of *Bird-Craft*—all these I pored over and all but learned by heart. Sometimes an author captures the imagination and so stirs anticipation over a particular species that when the bird is finally met there is a glow of satisfaction, a realization that here is a very special character. Thanks to *Bird-Craft*, those were stirring events, when I met my first Magnolia and Blackburnian Warblers and, many years later in Oklahoma, the Yellow-breasted Chat and White-eyed Vireo. . . . *Bird-Craft* had been the first great step in my ornithological education" (5–7).[22]

Unlike many of the male conservationists of her day, and unlike the later generation of female scientists represented by Margaret Morse Nice, Wright was a self-taught naturalist not a university-educated one. Much of Wright's research for *Birdcraft* was based on her observations of bird behavior in Fairfield, but she also drew on her ornithological studies during the winters of 1893 and 1894 studying ornithology at the American Museum of Natural History in New York City, where she received assistance from curator Joel A. Allen and his assistant, Frank Chapman. Wright's letters to Allen show her to be both appreciative of his help and self-deprecating about her own ornithological authority. "Please remember that I consider it a great favor . . . for you to trouble to help me at all," Wright wrote to Allen on 11 May 1894. In October, after Allen had published a positive review of *The Friendship of Nature* in the *Auk*, the scientific journal of the American Ornithologists' Union, Wright told Allen she was "very, very much pleased by the notice itself in such a magazine, but more so that you thought the book deserving of the kindness with which you treated it." The following March she again thanked Allen for his "wonderful" revision of her proof and expressed her fear that "without it . . .

The Auk would have stuck its beak into the book and rent it asunder." In the same letter Wright also asked Allen to tell Chapman that "if he has a chance to say a word for 'Birdcraft' [at a reception for the American Academy of Sciences] and wishes to be satirical he can describe it as being 'sentimental & harmless,'" an indication of her awareness of the challenges facing women who sought recognition from a mostly male scientific establishment.[23]

Both *Birdcraft* and its companion guide to plant life, *Flowers and Ferns in Their Haunts* (1901), reflect Wright's growing awareness not only of science but also of the increasing threats to plant habitat and animal populations in the decades before and after the start of the twentieth century. Birds in particular were being hunted to extinction for sport, for the market, and by hunters employed by milliners, who used the parts, skins, and feathers of the birds to decorate women's hats. Outraged by these abuses, Wright became active in the conservation movement in the late 1890s, and her writings during these years reflected her deepening commitment to the cause. In *Birdcraft*, for instance, she notes that "not only is the wild bird a part of the inheritance of the people, but the people are the trustees of its liberty" (xiii). And in *Flowers and Ferns in Their Haunts* she reminds readers that "wild flowers taken from their surroundings and considered as aggregations of calyx, corolla, stamen and pistil are wholly different from the same flowers seen in their native haunts. . . . The wild flower and fern is only to be truly known where it creeps, clings or sways untroubled in its home" (vii–ix).

Educating the Children

At the same time she was publishing her popular field guides, Wright also began working as a nature educator, writing fact-filled books for children and hosting a group of neighborhood students in her garden for an informal bird class. Though Wright herself had no children, the education of young people was an occupation of which her father certainly would have approved. "[T]he out-door school is the best for the little ones," he wrote in *Mile Stones in Our Life-Journey*, "and the true kindergarten is under the trees with the real objects about them to name and study" (318). Teaching such a bird class was also in line with the "nature study" movement being advocated by Liberty Hyde Bailey, dean of the College of Agriculture at Cornell University, who encouraged educators not only to introduce students to the natural sciences through books but also to take them outside where they could "put the pupil in a sympathetic attitude toward nature for the purpose of increasing the joy of living" (*Nature-Study Idea* 4).[24] For her 1897 bird class Wright read chapters from her *Citizen Bird* (1897) and took the children on field trips to nearby natural areas. She also borrowed various stuffed birds from Frank Chapman at the American Museum of Natural History, perching these birds about her garden and asking the children to locate and identify each species ("Tribute"; "Sixtieth Anniversary").[25]

In her children's books, Wright attempted to achieve a mix of fact and fiction that was faithful to scientific truth but fanciful enough to keep the attention of young readers. Two of her early books — *Tommy-Anne and the Three Hearts* (1896) and *Wabeno, the Magician* (1899), a sequel — constitute "one of the most ambitious works of nature fiction for children published in the nineteenth century — and also one of the best" (Welker 189).[26] Two of her other children's books also feature the work of well-known collaborators. *Citizen Bird*, a bird book for beginners, was written with Elliott Coues and illustrated by Louis Agassiz Fuertes, and *Four-Footed Americans and Their Kin* (1898), a sequel to *Citizen Bird*, was edited by Frank Chapman and illustrated by Ernest Thompson Seton.[27] Although all these works are anthropomorphic, they are not anthropocentric, and Wright took particular care to ensure readers that she did not go beyond the bounds of verifiable facts when depicting the behavior of her nonhuman characters — a particularly sensitive issue at the time, given her vocal criticism of such "nature fakers" as William J. Long.[28] As she noted on the half-title page of *Tommy-Anne and the Three Hearts*, "The lives and habits of plants and animals, however fancifully treated in this book, are in strict accordance with the known facts of their existence."[29]

The Adult Fiction

Wright's transition into adult fiction, which would yield a prolific run of ten works of fiction in twelve years, began with a suggestion from George Brett, following the British publication of Mary Annette Beauchamp Russell's *Elizabeth and Her German Garden* (1898).[30] "Mr. Brett suggested that I write an American garden story [in a] Similar Vein," Wright later recalled. "He and I decided to keep this new venture in the field of adult fiction separate from my children and nature books and so when 'The Garden of a Commuter's Wife' appeared [in 1901], it was under the pseudonym of 'Barbara'" ("MOW Recalls Pleasures").[31] Thus began her series of semiautobiographical "Barbara" books that kept readers guessing for five years as to their authorship.[32] When "Barbara's" identity was finally revealed in 1906 by Jeanette Gilder of the *Critic* and Francis Halsey of the *New York Times*, Wright says she "continued to write all sorts of things, but without that joyous unselfconsciousness and freedom an anonymous author enjoys" ("MOW Recalls Pleasures"). According to the *Bookman*, however, "Wright's anonymity was at best half-anonymity. Almost everybody in touch with literary and publishing circles [was] quite aware of the author's identity from the first" ("Concerning Anonymities" 7).[33]

Although Wright never completely turned her back on her garden, half of her fictional works are more conventional novels, which unfortunately suffer from contrived circumstances, undeveloped characters, and stilted speech. As the *New York Times* commented in a review of her 1909 novel *Poppea of the Post Office*, "Better a week in the garden with Barbara than a cycle of plot with Mrs. Wright" (477). Despite their weaknesses, many of Wright's fictional works offer valuable glimpses of her views on urban and suburban issues, social patterns among the upper classes, and the struggles of women to adapt to changing expectations in public and private life.[34]

Unlike her more conventional novels, most of Wright's "Barbara" books are hybrid texts, mixing discussions of nature and tips on gardening with diary entries, letters, and sketches, all designed primarily for a female audience. *The Garden of a Commuter's Wife*, in particular, explicitly addresses the relationship between women and nature. Wright notes in the book's opening paragraph that "gardening is the most cheerful and satisfactory pursuit for women who love outdoors. Field and forest often hold one at bay. We may admire, worship, love, but neither advise nor argue with them nor add one cubit to their stature. In a garden one's personality can come forth, stick a finger into nature's pie, and lend a hand in the making of it, besides furnishing many of the ingredients" (1–2). Women have a special relationship with nature, according to Wright, because nature itself displays many female qualities. "I think that one of the greatest charms of nature to women," Wright says, "is that she is, like ourselves, a creature of moods, phases, seasons, and not always equally radiant" (124). As she does in *The Friendship of Nature*, Wright claims in *The Garden of a Commuter's Wife* that nature is best approached from the perspective of the patient gardener. "Nature simply despises people who come to her as a last resort and try to squeeze a living from her, or otherwise harry her," Wright says. "She must be wooed understandingly, like any high-spirited woman, not bullied, for she has a capricious temper, and is at once a spendthrift and an economist" (37). Such patience and understanding are not only best cultivated in the country, according to Wright, but they actually *define* country living. "Many of the troubles of country living would disappear," she argues, "if people would only cease dragging in city hours and conventionalities" (204–5).[35]

Although Wright's vision for suburban life at the turn of the century may seem like little more than a perpetuation of Downing's midcentury "rural ideal," it comes in reaction to the rapid growth of Connecticut's "gold coast" and is more than mere nostalgia. Vera Norwood has noted that while residents of the early suburbs of the mid–nineteenth century were as much attempting to carry city amenities out to the country as they were hoping to escape the city and its immigrants, the garden literature of the late nineteenth century "indicates that by the turn of the century, the focus had shifted to protecting some vestige of the country setting within the increasingly congested environments of the suburbs" (303 n. 51).[36] The pastoral and colonial revival photographs Wright included in her books, not to mention the books themselves, certainly testify to Wright's own desire to preserve and protect disappearing landscapes.[37] Her pastoralism, however, unlike that of some of her contemporaries, does not simply look to the past in search of a rural republic but attempts to provide an alternative to what she called, after George Gissing, "the whirlpool"—the ever-agitated life of the city.[38]

As a middle ground between nature and culture, the suburban garden was an ideal landscape for Wright's efforts because it provided a congenial space in which she could link the friendship of nature to the friendship of women. Both women and men, Wright understood, were more likely to protect endangered places and creatures if they could first learn to recognize the fundamental connections between ecological and social communities, a belief well illustrated by the title of Wright's 1906 book *The Garden, You, and I*. In this and other books, Wright sought not merely to celebrate the domestic landscape but also to depict its nonhuman inhabitants as members of a living ecological community, members deserving of the same moral citizenship granted to members of the living social community.[39] Wright's choice of title for her collaboration with Elliott Coues—*Citizen Bird*—suggests that she sought to cultivate this friendship with nature not only through writing but also through civic activism.

The Garden of the World

When the Connecticut Audubon Society celebrated its twenty-fifth anniversary in 1923, the leadership of the organization posed for a revealing photograph outside the cottage of the Birdcraft Sanctuary in Fairfield (see page 90). The foreground of this photograph is dominated by seven dignified-looking men, fully visible to the camera and standing at a comfortable distance from one another. Crowded together on a porch in the background, and partially obscured by a hedge, stand eleven glum-looking women, including the society's president, Mabel Osgood Wright, forced to be photographed in profile by the lack of space. Though histories of the conservation movement often read much like this photograph—men in the foreground and women in the background—the history of the Connecticut Audubon Society is radically at odds with this image (MOW, "Conn. Society" 5).[40]

Early Bird Protection Efforts

Bird protection efforts in the United States began formally with the founding in 1883 of the American Ornithologists' Union, an outgrowth of the Nuttall Ornithological Club of Cambridge (to which Theodore Roosevelt had reported

Leaders of the Connecticut Audubon Society at Birdcraft Sanctuary, Fairfield, Connecticut, 1923. Mabel Osgood Wright is on the porch, third from left. (Courtesy Connecticut Audubon Society)

on sparrows). Primarily a professional organization of ornithologists, the AOU formed a Committee on the Protection of North American Birds in 1884 at the prompting of William Brewster of Harvard's Museum of Comparative Zoology. One of the committee's most significant achievements was the publication of a February 1886 supplement to the journal *Science*, in which several AOU scientists and committee members, including J. A. Allen and William Dutcher, recounted the evidence of the widespread destruction of bird life and issued a plea for bird protection, which included "An Appeal to the Women of the Country in Behalf of the Birds." Featured in the supplement was what may be the committee's greatest contribution to the protectionist cause: the "AOU Model Law," a clear and simple text that conservation advocates could use when proposing state laws to protect birds. Highly successful, the model law was adopted in thirty-two states by 1905 (Palmer, *Chronology*; Pearson, *Fifty Years*).[41]

While Brewster's committee was publishing its supplement and securing the passage of its model law in New York State, George Bird Grinnell was proposing the creation of a new bird protection organization in the pages of *Forest and Stream*. In an editorial in the 11 February 1886 issue, he proposed "the formation of an Association for the protection of wild birds and their eggs, which shall be called the Audubon Society.[42] Its membership is to be free to everyone who is willing to lend a helping hand in forwarding the objects for which it is formed. These objects will be to prevent, so far as possible, (1) the killing of any wild birds not used for food; (2) the destruction of nests or eggs of any wild bird; and (3) the wearing of feathers as ornaments or trimming for dress" ("Audubon Society" 41). Significantly, Grinnell also noted that the work to be done by the Audubon Society would be "auxiliary" to that undertaken by the AOU protection committee and that "reform in America, as elsewhere, must be inaugurated by women, and if the subject is properly called to their notice, their tender hearts will be quick to respond" ("Audubon Society" 41). In part because he offered free membership to anyone who would sign a pledge to fulfill the objectives of the society, Grinnell found himself swamped with requests, especially from schoolchildren. By the end of 1886, membership in the Audubon Society numbered 16,000; by August 1887, nearly 38,000; and by 1888, more than 48,000 (Pearson 201; Welker 204). In fact, the society's popularity was the main cause of its downfall, since Grinnell "had neither the time nor the staff at *Forest and Stream* to keep up with the added correspondence and administrative details," according to Audubon Society historian Frank Graham Jr. (13). Although in 1887 Grinnell had created the *Audubon Magazine*, an independent journal to carry club news and features, both the journal and the organization were forced to fold at the end of 1888, victims of their own success.

Women and the Revival of the Audubon Society

Mabel Wright's awakening to the need for bird protection came in 1886, the same year the AOU committee published its supplement and Grinnell proposed the first Audubon Society. One day that summer, Wright recalled, "I came upon two happy, ragged little boys, sitting on a log in a neighboring bit of open woodland, evidently displaying and gloating over some sort of treasures. I went toward them expecting to find a snapping turtle tied by one foot, or possibly a particularly long snake. Absolutely unabashed, as if no possible objection could be offered, they showed me respectively a quart fruit jar almost full of Robins' eggs, and a tin can a trifle smaller, containing an assortment of robins', wrens', and many other small eggs of the sparrow tribe. 'He ain't pertic'ular' said the robins' egg specialist — 'He'll take any old egg, but I stick to one sort every year, they show up better in the jar.' It was a decided shock to me, wild bird life destroyed and of no more real meaning to their owners than so many bits of bright glass or pebbles" ("Conn. Audubon" 5).

Wright's awakened concern for the birds was typical for the time, and when the Audubon movement was revived in the late 1890s, much of the impetus for the formation of local chapters came from women (Welker 206). Women's involvement in the Audubon movement can be traced to several developments at the turn of the century, including an increased interest in nature generally and birds in particular. Between 1893 and 1898, seventy thousand books on birds were sold, many of which were written by women similar to Mabel Wright, with interests not only in birds but also in gardens and civic organizing (Chapman, "Editorial" [1899] 28). Olive Thorne Miller, for instance, was the author of *Little Brothers of the Air* (1892) and *A Bird-Lover in the West* (1894), but she also published *The Woman's Club: A Practical Guide and Hand-book* (1891).[43] And Florence Merriam Bailey, the author of a number of popular bird books — including *Birds through an Opera Glass* (1889), *A-Birding on a Bronco* (1896), and *Birds of Village and Field* (1898) — was the founder of the Audubon Society of the District of Columbia in 1897. As Felton Gibbons and Deborah Strom point out, "It is not possible to overestimate the effect of this copious literary effort on bird conservation and nature appreciation" (187).

Women's interest in the revival of the Audubon movement can also be traced to their increasing desire to enter the public sphere at the turn of the century, a desire many women were able to fulfill by using their traditional identification with the home and garden to their advantage. As Richard L. McCormick has stated, "Although denied the ballot and considered unfit for the rough and tumble of public life, women increasingly found that protecting 'their' sphere of home and family compelled them to take roles outside the home. . . . Women discovered, too, that so long as they confined — or appeared to confine — their attention to subjects that were traditionally considered within their own sphere, few objections would be raised when they organized for action" (101). For Mabel Wright, as for thousands of other women who became involved with the Audubon movement on the local level, the garden literally offered an "organizing metaphor" for this transition from public to private involvement. As Vera Norwood has observed, women gardeners seemed uniquely suited to recognize that "the little enclosure by the side of the farmstead, in the swept yard, at the rear of the suburban lot, or on the roof of the urban apartment is a model of the whole landscape" (141). *The Friendship of Nature* illustrates this point most clearly; all of Fairfield — indeed, all of New England — becomes Wright's garden. Whenever Wright mentions a border in *Friendship*, for example, it is always a natural border, never a social or political one. Made of grass, flowers, ferns, or trees, these borders always connect environments, never separate them. Wright sees the landscape as one continuous tapestry, in which town and country, public and private are variations on the same theme. For Wright, the activity of planning, designing, and cultivating a garden was but a small step away from tending to the concerns of the larger world.

Robert Gottlieb rightly points out that "[w]ith advocacy about the protection of Nature seen as more directly constituting male concerns, and urban and especially home environments perceived to be part of woman's domain, conservationist and preservationist groups tended to define their work through such gender distinctions, often limiting female roles to the kinds of upper- and middle-class concerns of garden clubs and similar women's organizations" (217–18). This interpretation minimizes the significance of such clubs and organizations, however, which Karen J. Blair has demonstrated to have "provided a significant alternative route toward women's self-development" and to have allowed women to "seize influence beyond the home in the forbidden public sphere" (4). In her study of *The Clubwoman as Feminist*, Blair examines the "literary or culture club, devoted to the systematic study of literature, history, the arts, and current events," and not the numerous women's organizations with specifically political aims, such as the National American Women Suffrage Association, Women's Christian Temperance Union, Women's Trade Union League, National Consumer's League, abolition societies, and female auxiliaries to the Socialist Party. The local chapters of the Audubon movement shared aspects of both kinds of groups, in which women were able to develop "friendships, confidence and knowledge," as well as engage in direct political action (Blair 4).[44]

The Revival Reaches Connecticut

If the first Audubon Society failed in part because of its centralization, its dependence on a single leader, and its lack of financial backing from local groups, the second attempt at establishing an Audubon movement succeeded in part because of the community-based efforts of women (Gibbons and Strom 110–11). The revival began in January 1896 when the Massachusetts Audubon Society was organized in Boston, and it was bolstered when the Pennsylvania Audubon Society was founded later that year in October.[45] In 1897 similar societies were formed in New York, New Hampshire, Illinois, Maine, Wisconsin, New Jersey, Rhode Island, and the District of Columbia, followed by societies in California, Connecticut, Indiana, Minnesota, Ohio, Tennessee, and Texas in 1898 (Graham 14–18).

The Connecticut Audubon Society offers a vivid example of the role played by women in the formation of these local groups, as it was the indirect outcome of a class in parliamentary law held by the Eunice Dennie Burr Chapter of the Daughters of the American Revolution (DAR) in Fairfield. As Wright explained in a 1923 article, "[f]or drill in organization, the technique of forming a society was rehearsed and it was called, for the sake of a name, The Audubon Society" ("Conn. Audubon" 5).[46] The drill became reality when, on 28 January 1898, Wright and twelve other women assembled at the home of Helen Glover in Fairfield to form, officially, the Audubon Society of Connecticut (now the Connecticut Audubon Society).[47] Wright traveled to Fairfield from New York City specifically for this meeting, and she spent the stormy winter night at the home of Mrs. Samuel H. Wheeler, in whose guest book she recorded her enthusiasm about the events of the evening ("Sixtieth Anniversary"). That evening Wright was also elected president of the Connecticut society, a position she retained for twenty-six years, during which time she was the driving force behind most of its activities.

The first annual report of the Connecticut society suggests the variety of causes its membership espoused: "The purpose of the Society is to discourage the purchase or use of the feathers of any birds for ornamentation, except those of the ostrich and domesticated fowl, and game birds used as food. . . . Members shall discourage the destruction of birds and their eggs, and do all in their power to protect them. . . . Members shall use their influence to establish 'Bird-Day' in the schools of the State of Connecticut in connection with Arbor-Day, and do all in their power to encourage the study of Natural History" (Connecticut Audubon Society).[48]

During its first years of existence, membership in the Connecticut society grew rapidly. In its fourth year alone, the organization grew by 1,565 members, many of whom were schoolchildren whose membership fees had been waived. Wright had mounted an aggressive program of youth education, which included sending a Bird-Day program to 1,350 Connecticut schools, preparing slide lectures on such topics as "the birds about home" and "the adventures of a robin," purchasing a parlor stereopticon for projection of these lantern slides, and distributing bird charts and circulating libraries of natural history books to needy schools and libraries. Other activities of the society included petitioning state and local legislatures, distributing bird brochures to farmers, posting notices of game laws, and making contacts with other groups that had similar goals.[49]

Wright was keenly aware of the many demands placed on women who chose to enter the public sphere through such local action. Defending the secretaries of the various state Audubon societies in 1902, Wright seemed to be speaking as much about herself as about them when she announced: "Be it here understood that many of the most active of these secretaries are women with family cares, who conduct a correspondence that amounts to a business wholly without pay" ("Work!" 103–4). Similarly, when her sister Agnes, who had been caring for their mother in the family's Eleventh Street home in New York City, was struck with "nervous prostration" in 1905, Wright told Frank Chapman that she "flatly refused to run that big house and see after mother both, as it would end my work of writing forever."[50] She repeated her preference for professional obligations over domestic duties when she wrote to Audubon leader T. Gilbert Pearson in 1913 after a period of illness: "I'm picking up again but feel that I must concentrate my work in [the] future to what really counts, and let society and inane visiting go, together with many things which the Devil of modern life has invented to kill both time and the people who follow him."[51]

"The Most Influential Woman in the Audubon Movement"

At the same moment she was directing the progress of the Audubon Society of Connecticut, Wright was also becoming involved with the Audubon movement on a national scale, as state societies began to recognize the mutual benefits of association. In 1901, four years after the Massachusetts Audubon Society had been organized, representatives of the state societies and the AOU met in New York City to form a National Committee of Audubon Societies, designed in part to bridge the gap between amateur birders and professional ornithologists. Three years later, Albert Wilcox, a wealthy New Yorker, offered to donate $3,000 annually to a "National Association of Audubon Societies for the Protection of Wild Birds and Animals" if William Dutcher, chair of the National Committee, would devote half his time to the organization. Dutcher agreed, and articles of incorporation were granted to the thirty-five state Audubon societies, plus one in the District of Columbia, by the State of New York in January 1905. When Wilcox died the following year, he left the association a bequest of $320,000—more than $2 million by modern standards (Gibbons and Strom 116–17; Trefethen, *American* 136).[52] As president of one of the state societies, Wright automatically became a member of the National Committee in 1901 and the board of directors of the National Association in 1905.[53] When she finally resigned from the board in 1928 because of health problems, the remaining members informed her that "the unanimous feeling was that this Association, the subject of ornithology, and the cause of

conservation of wild life all owe to you the deepest debt of gratitude for your services in the field of natural history during the past thirty years." T. Gilbert Pearson
also personally offered his "undying gratitude for [her] . . . friendship, loyalty and
support" over the years.[54]

Wright had become "the most influential woman in the Audubon movement"
(Orr 128) in part because for almost three years prior to the formation of the National Committee she had edited the Audubon department of *Bird-Lore*, a bi-
monthly magazine founded by Frank Chapman in February 1899 to function as a
popular alternative to the *Auk*.[55] Chapman was the sole owner, publisher, and editor of *Bird-Lore* for its first thirty-six years, and the magazine was a private venture
throughout his tenure, but *Bird-Lore* maintained many financial and editorial
links to the Audubon movement. For the magazine's first eleven years, Wright as-
sisted Chapman as associate editor, after which she remained an active contributor until her death. From 1899 to 1906 she edited the Audubon department, writing opinion pieces in support of bird conservation and contributing articles about
the habits and haunts of various species; from 1907 to 1910 she edited the school
department, where she continued her campaign to educate young people about
birds by preparing pamphlets, sponsoring contests, and encouraging teachers to
organize Audubon chapters in the schools; and after 1910 she served as a contributing editor, writing occasional articles, but having no direct editorial responsibilities. In his *Autobiography of a Bird-Lover* (1933), written the year before
Wright's death, Chapman called her assistance "invaluable" (188).[56]

In the first few critical years of *Bird-Lore*'s publication, Wright was able to articulate a coherent strategy for environmental reform through her regular column
in the Audubon department. To effect cultural change, she argued, Audubon
members must pursue a dual agenda of education and legislation. "To introduce
people to the bird in the bush is the way to create a public sentiment to keep it
there, and to make it possible to obtain legislative authority for the enactment and
keeping of good bird laws, which are the backbone of protection," Wright informed the readers of *Bird-Lore*'s first issue ("Responsibility" 136–37). She repeated this claim in the magazine's second issue, noting that "the only way to do
permanent good is, on one side, to educate the moral nature so that it will not
desire to do the wrong act, and on the other to work for the establishment and *enforcement* of laws that shall punish those who do the wrong" ("Fees" 64). At the
same time, Wright recognized the limits of her own Connecticut society, writing
to William Dutcher on 3 October 1909 that "[t]o wake the people in general is
what is needed and the campaigns of lectures and libraries is a surer way than lobbying. . . . [O]ur state society can obtain money for charts and libraries or lectures
but when legislative expenses are broached the purses close and a frost settles over
the meeting."[57]

Throughout the issues of *Bird-Lore* Wright time and again emphasized the need for the female membership of the early Audubon movement to exercise restraint in developing appeals based solely on sentiment. "At a time when a great majority look askance at the startling array of societies that they are asked to 'join,' it behooves all Bird Protective bodies to conduct themselves with extreme conservatism, that they may not bear the stigma of being called emotional 'fads,' but really appeal to those whom they seek to interest. . . . Many men (and women also) have many minds, and a form of appeal that will attract one will repel another. It is upon the tactful management of these appeals and the bringing of the subject vitally home to different classes and ages, that the life of the Audubon Societies depends" ("Conducting of Audubon Societies" 64). The need for emotional "conservatism" was a frequent refrain of Wright in these early years. "Be the roads many — illustrated lectures to arouse public sentiment, birdless bonnets, leaflets, thousands of pledge cards signed by ready sympathizers — the goal must be conservative, well thought out legislation, free from any taint of emotional insanity," she wrote in another 1899 column, entitled "The Law and the Bird" (204). Putting the matter more plainly the next year, she reminded her readers that "in all reform movements, especially those where sense and sentiment are interwoven, there is but a step from the sublime to the very, very ridiculous" ("Wanted" 33). Emotionalism, according to Wright, runs the risk of lapsing into exaggeration and thereby alienating potential advocates. As a result, she wrote in 1903, "Audubon workers should realize their responsibility, the importance of accuracy and keep themselves well-informed, — as there is nothing so disastrous as the effect of loose statements and overdrawn claims upon the skeptical" ("Literature" 138).

Politics in Connecticut

Making good on her call for a dual agenda of education and legislation, Wright and the Connecticut society managed over the years to support a wide range of legislative initiatives, including:

presenting a bird bill in the state legislature in 1901;[58]

successfully lobbying for the enactment of a hunter's license law and nonspring shooting law in 1907 (Bowdish 139);

passing a resolution favoring the establishment of national forest reserves in the southern Appalachians and the White Mountains in 1908, and encouraging other state societies to take similar action;[59]

lobbying for the passage of a state bill curbing and regulating the taking of birds and eggs by collectors in 1911 (MOW, *Annual Report*);

working to protect sandpipers and recognize starlings as an alien species in 1912;[60]

pushing for the passage of the Migratory Bird Treaty Act (1918) in 1916 and 1917;

protesting against the offer of a bounty for bald eagles in Alaska with a circular letter
sent to all the state Audubon societies and all the state boards of agriculture in 1919
and 1920;[61]

and lobbying in 1924 for the expansion of Sequoia National Park.[62]

Wright also struggled throughout her presidency of the Connecticut society to balance the interests of songbirds and game birds, a difficult task that mixed the politics of both gender and hunting. In a 28 September 1908 letter to William Dutcher, Wright spelled out the complexities of the issue at length:

> Our Conn Society, with a woman for its president, and an executive board composed largely of women with just enough men to give us balance and counsel, is not prepared to go actively into the politics that surround the sportsmen's interests[,] these having become very acute since the gun license fund has brought money into the protective question. We are keenly alive to any attempt to put any protected birds back on the game list and keep watch over all birds introduced, but we are not prepared to contend with intelligent sportsmen concerning their own best interests. . . . If I remain as president the society must keep close to its original platform of educating the people in the love and protection of its song birds by libraries, lectures and charts, I cannot stand the strain of keeping an intelligent grip upon game law matters except as from time to time the song birds are threatened. If this is to be the main feature of the work of the Conn Society they must elect a male president who can go afield and learn of the various sporting interests *first hand* through his own experience & contact with men and not simply try to judge between the various reports temdered [*sic*], which though from equally trustworthy authorities are often entirely at variance.
>
> If a male president be found, who has sufficient knowledge to take up the work for the game birds, he will doubtless slight the school features to which I have given so much time. So there you are! *My* feeling is to eliminate *active* aggressive work concerning the game birds from the State Society and to simply reserve the right to object to the introduction, by the National Association, of bills that we know from the inside would injure the influence of the Society in the State.[63]

Despite Wright's hesitance to remain active in the protection of game birds in 1908, her draft of the Connecticut society's 1911 annual report describes "sentimentalists who think that the Audubon Societies should begin & end their efforts with the protection of Song Birds." The Connecticut Audubon Society, she claims, "has always stood for the conservative middle course of fair play & fair game bird laws for the sportsmen and we do not forget that it is the result of the game license law that makes it possible to put wardens in the field who also extend their protection to the non-game birds."[64]

Acting Locally: Birdcraft Sanctuary

Involved as she was with such state and national issues, Wright was most successful in her efforts at the local level, where she was able to take a hands-on approach to conservation issues, in much the same manner as she tended her backyard garden. One example of her success in such endeavors was the interest she took in Fairfield's Oak Lawn Cemetery, whose directors she first approached in 1907, convinced that the grounds had become too cluttered and overgrown. According to Thomas J. Farnham, Wright and her sister Agnes hoped to make the cemetery less rustic and more like a park; they wanted to see it become "more open, more spacious, more pastoral, more attuned to the modern tastes" (Farnham 13). By 1914 Wright had begun advocating for cemeteries to be used as bird sanctuaries, an idea also taken up by the national association, from whom Wright felt she did not receive proper credit.[65] Whether or not Wright originated the notion of the cemetery bird sanctuary, she was certainly influenced in her thinking by Andrew Jackson Downing, who had argued for the creation of scenic cemeteries in the early nineteenth century. As Neil Harris notes, for Downing, "[r]ural cemeteries were to be places of beauty and tranquility, secluded spots where bereaved relatives and friends could combine affectionate respect with a love for nature. There families could gather on sunny days, communing with the landscape to show their love for God and their remembrance of the dead" (201). Using cemeteries as bird sanctuaries merely extended the notion of community in nature to include God's creatures.[66]

The premier example of Wright's interweaving of gardening and conservation, however, can be seen in her development of a local songbird sanctuary and museum, the first such facility owned and governed by a state Audubon society. As early as 1901 Wright had been calling for the creation of "song bird reservations," arguing in the pages of *Bird-Lore* that "the day has passed when it is enough to satisfy the demands for bird protection by simply ceasing to kill" ("Song Bird Reservations" 114). By 1910 she had grown even more insistent about the need for such places, noting that "[e]very day the cities and manufacturing towns are growing more solidly packed with human beings; the outlying brush lots and woodland being stripped for fuel, and the many other uses of wood[,] while the land itself is taking on a prohibitory value. Now is the time to secure these oases in what may be called the desert of civilization. In many places it is now or never" ("Bird-Cities" 159–60). In February 1914, after Wright and a group of Fairfield residents attended *Sanctuary*, a masque about the conversion of a plume hunter to a bird protectionist, the interest in creating a local sanctuary reached its peak. The masque, written by Percy MacKaye and staged at the Astor Place Theater in New York City, had originally been performed in 1913 for the dedication of the Helen

Woodruff Smith Bird Sanctuary operated by the Bird Club of Meriden, New Hampshire, and the residents of Fairfield no doubt found themselves spurred into action by the achievements of this rival group.[67]

Annie Burr Jennings, a prominent Fairfield resident and an heiress to part of the Standard Oil fortune, provided the funding for the sanctuary's purchase, but Wright was clearly the driving force behind its creation and the selection of its site. In the minutes of the society, Wright was careful to defer all credit for the donation of the property to Jennings, claiming that "[n]ot only was it entirely spontaneous upon the part of the donor but absolut[e]ly unsolicited."[68] Wright's many published opinions about the matter, however, as well as the recollections of an Audubon Society member, suggest that the idea for the sanctuary was neither spontaneous nor unsolicited but the culmination of Wright's long interest in bird protection and public education. "Mrs. Wright was very anxious to have some such sanctuary," recalled Audubon society member Deborah Glover, "and [she] persuaded Miss Annie B. Jennings to donate it" (D. Glover, "Some of My Memories").

After examining two sites, a hundred-acre plot distant from town and a ten-acre tract close to Main Street, Wright and Jennings decided upon the smaller, more accessible one in 1914, and Jennings purchased and deeded the land to the Audubon Society of Connecticut. Named after Wright's 1895 book *Birdcraft*, the sanctuary was established on a calf pasture that perfectly embodied Wright's ideal landscape for a protected natural area: a "wild untilled land, where leaves have fallen year on year and gone to decay and dead wood been left where it fell" (MOW, "Inviting" 108). Because the site was also located directly across the street from Mosswood, Wright was able to supervise closely the sanctuary's development, including the erection of a catproof fence, the building of stone gate posts, the construction of a bungalow for the caretaker and a museum for exhibitions, the cutting of trails, the dredging of a pond, and the building of birdbaths and birdhouses. Perhaps most important, Wright directed the planting of native trees and shrubs to encourage the ecological well-being of the birds, an idea that has since come to be known as "birdscaping."[69]

As it grew from vision to reality, Birdcraft Sanctuary became a model for local wildlife and habitat preservation efforts throughout the United States. Frank Chapman, writing in *Bird-Lore* in 1915, described the sanctuary as "an object lesson in conservation and museum methods": "[I]n its own field of local bird-life, Birdcraft Sanctuary promises to render a greater and more effective return for the capital invested than can be shown by any museum in this country. One cannot say by any similar institution for we know of none like it. . . . Ten acres cannot harbor many birds nor a little museum in the country be seen by a large number of people . . . but the idea which they embody can reach to the ends of the earth"

(Editorial [1915] 297).[70] Helen Glover, secretary of the Connecticut society, noted in her annual report for 1917–18 that the sanctuary had hosted visitors from Seattle, California, and Cornell University, and in September 1923, when Edith Roosevelt was seeking an appropriate memorial for her late husband, the former first lady traveled to Fairfield, ate lunch with Wright, and "went over the Sanctuary in every detail," noting its beauty and the economy of its management. The result of this and other meetings was the twelve-acre Theodore Roosevelt Memorial Sanctuary in Oyster Bay, Long Island, a direct descendent of Wright's work at Birdcraft (H. Glover, *Report*; "MOW Recalls Pleasures").[71]

Modern conservationists might recoil in horror at the style of "wildlife management" practiced at Birdcraft in these early years, but the removal of so-called problem species from songbird sanctuaries was common practice at the beginning of the twentieth century.[72] In a 1922 letter to Wright from Frederic C. Walcott, president of the Connecticut State Board of Fisheries and Game, Walcott gave Wright "a kind of blanket permission to use your own judgment within the boundaries of your sanctuary and on your own grounds and destroy anything that you think detrimental to the purpose of your sanctuary. . . . I would not hesitate officially or otherwise to encourage the killing of English sparrows, starlings, crows, Cooper and sharp shinned hawks, wandering house cats, weasels, rats, red squirrels, occasionally jays and even chip monks when caught in the act."[73] In the first three years of the sanctuary's existence, its caretaker killed 524 European starlings, 269 English sparrows, 28 purple grackles, and 12 crows, and trapped 14 northern shrikes, 4 sparrow hawks, 4 sharp-shinned hawks, 3 Cooper's hawks, 3 red-shouldered hawks, 2 long-eared owls, 1 barred owl, and 1 screech owl (releasing only the owls and the red-shouldered Hawks). In addition, 107 cats were taken, along with 21 rats, 17 striped snakes, 1 skunk, and 1 weasel (MOW, "Three Years After" 201–10).[74]

Wright's concern about protecting native birds from "problem species" parallels her arguments in *Bird-Lore* about the threat to songbirds from uneducated, insensitive immigrants, particularly those from central and southern Europe. "In appealing to the average child of the public school," Wright claimed in an 1899 column, "it should be remembered of how many races this average child is compounded,—races with instincts concerning what are called lower animals, quite beyond the moral comprehension of the animal-loving Anglo-Saxon" ("Law and the Bird" 203). Likewise, in a later column regarding the posting of game laws, Wright expressed concern about the inability of English-language materials to reach "the newly arrived foreign element unable to read English who, together with cats, are the birds' worst enemies" ("Meditations" 205).[75] Unfortunately, Wright's nativism was shared by many early conservationists and nature enthusiasts, including Andrew Jackson Downing, Henry Fairfield Osborn, and Madison Grant. As Thomas R. Dunlap acknowledged, nature study was "most popular among the descendants of the pioneers — the white, 'Anglo-Saxon,' Protestant people who dominated American society — and their commitment was in part an effort to preserve their culture and its virtues in a new world" (8). Native species, therefore, symbolized both an affirmation of the western European roots of American culture and a resistance to the new influx of immigrants from foreign lands. John Stilgoe posed the question in this way: "If immigrant birds drove out native species, . . . might not immigrant people overwhelm Americans of English, German, and Irish descent, Americans already weakened by stressful urban lives given over to business?" (*Borderland* 296).[76]

Apart from Wright's nativist assumptions and invasive management practices, the basic argument behind the creation of Birdcraft Sanctuary remains compelling. From its founding, the sanctuary sought to integrate a nonanthropocentric philosophy about songbirds with a community-based nature center intended for the education of children and adults alike. Wright outlined the first part of this mission in 1915 when she wrote that "[t]he Song Bird Sanctuary . . . is an oasis in a desert of material things. In it the bird may lead its own life for that life's sake, and the joy of many such lives overflows all arbitrary boundaries in its ethical benefit to the community and state" ("Making" 263). "At Birdcraft," she added later, "we do not seek to humanize birds, or to tame them artificially; we try to look at their lives from their own angle, not ours" ("Little Stories" 195).

The second, educational part of the sanctuary's mission quickly became a difficult task when the songbirds were driven away by the popularity of the sanctuary itself ("Three Years After" 203).[77] As a result, the board of governors had to restrict admission to the sanctuary proper (a practice since discontinued) and bolster the offerings in the museum. One benefit of this decision was the mounting of an exhibition, "Birds of Connecticut," a collection Wright found to be "of greater value to the student than would be a much larger but mixed collection. Such a local group clarifies the mind about the birds of home and is an introduction to study of a wider scope" ("Birdcraft Sanctuary" 403).

This intimate, regional focus is perhaps the most significant aspect of Birdcraft's mission. Unlike large national parks and wildlife preserves, which often appear unconnected to the communities that surround them, Birdcraft has been a familiar feature on the Fairfield landscape since the sanctuary's inception. As one commentator noted in the early twentieth century, "it is passing strange that such a place should have remained to this day in a wild state within easy hearing of the rumbling New Haven road's trains and in sight of the thousands of automobiles that pass that way" ("God's Ten Acres"). Wright herself had proposed keeping the sanctuary close to the railroad station and Main Street for this very reason — so "that those of us who know the land from sea to hills may have before us a bit of what was and the younger generation in its turn feel its inspiration also" ("The End" 105–6).

In 1957, however, when the state government announced that the Connecticut Turnpike was to be constructed through nearly half the sanctuary's land, Birdcraft became a case study in the difficulty of preserving open space within a rapidly growing community. "The first offer made by the State Highway Department was for $20,000," noted the Connecticut Audubon Society's secretary in June 1957. "This offer has been increased to $32,000—the top appraisal. None of these appraisals took into consideration the value of land as a Sanctuary, but considered only the real estate value."[78] Eventually the society received $45,000 in compensation from the state, but the money could not begin to account for the loss of more than 40 percent of Birdcraft's total acreage.[79]

Despite its reduction in size, and the now-constant hum of the thruway to its north, Birdcraft has remained an active facility of the Connecticut Audubon Society, although the society relocated its offices to bigger quarters in 1971.[80] In part because of its ability to survive as a kind of living example of Wright's own determination, Birdcraft was added to the National Register of Historic Places in 1982 and registered as a National Historic Landmark in 1993.

Changing Times

Although Wright fell silent for more than a decade after the founding of Birdcraft in 1914, in her last years she produced three additional works: *My New York* (1926), her autobiography; *Captains of the Watch of Life and Death* (1927), a book about nurses and patients; and *Eudora's Men* (1931), a novel that traces a New England family from the Civil War to World War I. By the 1920s, however, the world seemed finally to have caught up with Wright, both personally and professionally. In the previous decade, she and her husband, James, had sold their beloved Mosswood under financial strain and built Oakhaven, a smaller, eight-room cottage across the street ("MOW Recalls Pleasures").[81] After James died in 1920, even Oakhaven became too difficult for Wright to maintain on her own, and she moved into a nearby cottage, which became known as The Little Brown House on the Hill (Obit. of James O. Wright). The death of her husband affected Wright especially deeply, as her letters to Helen Glover and others bear out. "I simply cannot garden *any more*," Wright wrote to Glover in July 1922. "[I]t is anguish to go out all alone in the cool of the day & work in silence with no one to be glad with me when things do well."[82] For a time in 1933, when Wright found herself facing deepening financial and health problems, she even considered building a bungalow inside Birdcraft Sanctuary itself, where she could live tax free and Audubon Society employees could help her care for her garden. The board of governors of the sanctuary rejected Wright's request, however, despite her having founded the sanctuary itself—a painfully ironic reminder of just how far the Audubon movement had advanced beyond Wright's own vision.[83]

These changes of focus and method were long in coming, of course, and Wright tried her best to keep up with the times. As early as 1911 she was already noting that "[c]ertain methods of interesting school children have undergone a change. Ten years ago the travelling lecture outfits with the colored slides & the easily manipulated oil lanterns were one of our most potent teachers, but with the great improvements in methods, the introduction of moving pictures even in our small town[,] the pictures thrown by the oil lanterns have lost this hold in a great measure" (MOW, *Annual Report*).[84] In a 21 December 1917 letter to Frank Chapman regarding the election of officers to the national association, Wright similarly noted that the "methods and even business principles of recognized efficiency, have so changed within a few years that men of the newer generation only, can meet the requirements of the future."[85] In 1922 Wright was even writing to Chapman that she was "getting weary of hobbling at the head of the Conn. procession." Said Wright, "I sincerely wish a man or a woman of thirty would first take my arm and then slip into my place and let me sit on a fence and be merely a looker on. But the young do not take to this work as we all did in the beginning and I don't see any available material in sight, especially of my own sex, yet if we let the Conn. Society come to an end, Birdcraft, its property, goes to the town for a park — Enter hoodlums, exit birds!"[86]

Three years later, Wright nonetheless chose to resign from the presidency of the state society, and in 1928 she resigned from the national board. "I rather think that my work, such as it is, is done," Wright told Chapman in 1933. "I have no new observations that are worth recording and my view point is too far from the chaotic thought of the present generation."[87]

By the standards of John Muir and the Sierra Club, whose fight against the Hetch Hetchy dam in Yosemite National Park was lost before Birdcraft Sanctuary was even founded, the achievement of Mabel Osgood Wright and the Connecticut Audubon Society may seem like little more than a footnote to the grand narrative of conservation history. It would be a mistake, though, to overlook the significance of Wright's accomplishments, central as they were to the popularization of environmental concern, just as it would be a mistake to overlook the role local conservation efforts have played in the formation of national organizations. Part of a nexus of environmental reformers working in the decades surrounding the turn of the century, Wright was especially successful at crafting rhetorical appeals to women that relied less on the frontier-based conservation of the Dakota cowboy and more on the garden-based conservation of the suburban homemaker. In the end Wright actually began to sound more like John Muir, who argued for wilderness as an antidote to civilization, than she did Theodore Roosevelt, who had been her childhood dance partner (*My New York* 167–69).[88] As she argued in a 1902 article in *Bird-Lore*, "the protection of what is elevating and wholesomely beautiful is one of the most crying human needs of today. What is left for humanity when there is no convenient retreat from where indoors and city and self are fettered together. In today's push and scramble humanity must everywhere have refuge where Heart of Man may realize that however much he may have changed, the fowls of the air and the flowers of the field are as of old, and that Heart of Nature still lives and is working out the plan made him by Heart of God" ("Work!" 104).

CHAPTER THREE

Our National Parks

John Muir and the Sierra Club

Not like my taking the veil — no solemn abjuration of the world.
I only went out for a walk, and finally concluded to stay out
till sundown, for going out, I found was really going in.

JOHN MUIR, *Journal*

I F MABEL OSGOOD WRIGHT'S domestic garden falls somewhere between Theodore Roosevelt's rugged frontier and John Muir's national park, the idea of the "park" nevertheless shares elements of
both these other metaphoric conceptions of "nature." On the one hand, a park
might be seen as a glorified garden, a backyard-style refuge for birds and animals,
although implemented on a much larger scale. On the other hand, a park might
also be understood as possessing the attributes of a frontier, functioning as a kind
of "contained frontier" in the way Yellowstone National Park functioned for the
Boone and Crockett Club. For John Muir, "the father of the national parks," a park
was both these things and more, and the progress of his thinking about the idea of
the "park" in preserving "nature" — particularly through the organization of the
Sierra Club — is the subject of this chapter.

The most prominent example of a nature writer who helped create a conservation organization, Muir has been the subject of no fewer than eleven biographical
studies since William Frederick Badè first published his two-volume *Life and Letters of John Muir* in 1923–24.[1] To provide a comprehensive overview of Muir's work
with the Sierra Club, therefore, is not my intention. Nor do I desire to revisit the
battle over Hetch Hetchy, which raged from 1906 to 1913 and has received wide
treatment elsewhere.[2] Instead, this chapter examines several moments in Muir's
career that were central to his emerging understanding of what a "park" should be
and how to protect it: his early life leading up to his arrival in California, his pub-

lished and unpublished writings prior to the creation of the Sierra Club, and his work with the Sierra Club and the publication of *Our National Parks* in 1901. This chapter closes in 1905—Muir's fateful year—in which the devastating loss of his wife, Louie, was accompanied by the recession of Yosemite Valley to the federal government, a cause for celebration if ever there was one.[3]

Framing the California portion of this chronology are two encounters that suggest the ways in which Muir's thinking about the notion of a national park changed over time: the first, when Ralph Waldo Emerson visited the Yosemite Valley in 1871 and failed to camp with a then-unknown Muir; the second, when Theodore Roosevelt visited the valley in 1903 and spent four days and three nights camping with Muir, who had in the interim become a legendary figure. The contrast between these two events—the first, one of Muir's deepest disappointments; the second, a grand success by all accounts—illustrates my central argument in this chapter: that the development of Muir's conception of what a park should be, and his success at making that idea a reality, rested on the interaction of nineteenth-century notions of domesticity with twentieth-century notions of tourism.

At Muir's invitation, Emerson visited him during a trip to the Yosemite Valley in May 1871, while Muir was living and working at James M. Hutchings's sawmill on the Merced River. There Muir showed Emerson his botanical specimens and pencil drawings and invited the aging philosopher to accompany him on a month-long camping excursion into the Sierra. But Emerson's party would have none of it, according to Muir, and held Emerson to the hotels and trails. "His party, full of indoor philosophy, failed to see the natural beauty and fullness of promise of my wild plan, and laughed at it in good-natured ignorance," Muir recounted in *Our National Parks* (99). In all, Emerson and his party remained "only five tourist days in Yosemite," Muir lamented, after which they left to visit the Mariposa Grove. Muir agreed to accompany them on this last leg of their journey, provided that he and Emerson would camp out in the grove. Initially, Emerson "consented heartily" to this proposition, according to Muir, but when the party arrived at Clark's Station, near the grove, Muir was surprised to see his fellow horseback riders dismount. "And when I asked if we were not going up into the grove to camp they said: 'No; it would never do to lie out in the night air. Mr. Emerson might take cold; and you know, Mr. Muir, that would be a dreadful thing.' In vain I urged, that only in homes and hotels were colds caught, that nobody ever was known to take cold camping in these woods, that there was not a single cough or sneeze in all the Sierra. Then I pictured the big climate-changing, inspiring fire I would make, praised the beauty and fragrance of sequoia flame, told how the great trees would stand about us transfigured in the purple light, while the stars looked down between the great domes; ending by urging them to come on and make an immortal Emerson night of it. But the house habit was not to be overcome, nor the strange dread of pure night air, though it is only cooled day air with a little dew in it. So the carpet dust and unknowable reeks were preferred" (*Our National Parks* 100). The next morning, Muir accompanied Emerson and his party into the grove, where they stayed for "an hour or two, mostly in ordinary tourist fashion," spending what Muir derided as a "poor bit of measured time" with the trees (*Our National Parks* 101). Finally, in the afternoon, Emerson departed, like "a child in the hands of his affectionate but sadly civilized friends," in Muir's estimation, waving a last good-bye from the top of the ridge (*Our National Parks* 101).[4]

Thirty-two years later, Muir was given another opportunity to camp out in the Mariposa Grove, but this time his companion was more enthusiastic about the prospect than Muir himself. Where in 1871 a young, unknown Muir was forced to invite Emerson to visit *him*, it was the president of the United States who in 1903 sought out *Muir* for his camping trip. "An influential man from Washington wants to make a trip into the Sierra with me," Muir wrote Charles S. Sargent, with whom he had been planning a tour of Europe and Asia, "and I might be able to *do some forest good* in freely talking around the campfire" (F. Turner, *Rediscovering* 325). Although not especially enthusiastic about Roosevelt's conduct as president, Sargent agreed to postpone their trip, freeing Muir to take the chief executive camping. A younger Muir might have been overjoyed at the personal note he subsequently received from Roosevelt, in which the president told Muir, "I do not want anyone with me but you, and I want to drop politics absolutely for four days, and just be out in the open with you" (F. Turner, *Rediscovering* 325–26). But this was an older, wiser Muir — author of *The Mountains of California* (1894) and *Our National Parks*, president of the Sierra Club for more than a decade, and veteran of the fight for the forests surrounding the Yosemite Valley — and he knew an invaluable political opportunity when he saw one. Thus Muir led Roosevelt, accompanied by only two rangers and a cook, into the Mariposa Grove, where they camped for the night under the towering sequoias. With Roosevelt, Muir was finally able to make "the big climate-changing, inspiring fire" he offered to light for Emerson, and in exchange his visitor "praised the beauty and fragrance of sequoia flame" as Muir had himself done with Emerson. "Hurrah!" yelled Roosevelt. "That's a candle it took five hundred years to make. Hurrah for Yosemite!" (L. Wolfe, *Son* 291).

When the two men emerged from the forest after two more nights spent camping near Glacier Point and beneath El Capitan, Roosevelt returned to his official duties a changed man, or at least a man whose public statements revealed Muir's considerable influence. "I stuffed him pretty well regarding the timber thieves, and the destructive work of the lumbermen, and other spoilers of the forests," Muir explained to William Trout (L. Wolfe, *Son* 291). The briefing seems to have worked, because when Roosevelt reached Sacramento, he gave what Frederick Turner characterized as "a very Muir-like speech in which he said that trees had not only great and strategic commercial values but aesthetic and moral ones as well." The sequoias deserved protection, Roosevelt claimed, "simply because it would be a shame to our civilization to let them disappear. They are monuments in themselves." Moreover, said Roosevelt, as American citizens his listeners were obligated to keep the distant future in mind when considering the direction in which they were taking the country. "We are not building this country of ours for a day. It is to last through the ages" (F. Turner, *Rediscovering* 328). Illustrating his commitment to this principle, Roosevelt instructed his secretary of the interior to extend the Sierra forest reserve northward to Mount Shasta. When Roosevelt later claimed that Muir was "what few nature-lovers are — a man able to influence contemporary thought and action on the subjects to which he had devoted his life" (*Works* 11:288), the president was speaking from experience, himself having been transformed by the man.[5]

How do these encounters speak to the ways in which Muir's understanding of a "park" was dependent upon the interaction of the domestic and touristic realms? If in 1871 Emerson was the domesticated easterner and Muir the western mountaineer enthralled with the mystery of the forest, in 1903 the tables had turned, with Roosevelt now playing the boyish enthusiast in the woods and Muir the mature advocate for the preservation of California's parks and forests. "I always begrudged Emerson's not having gone into camp with you," Roosevelt wrote Muir a few years after their trip. "You would have made him perfectly comfortable and he ought to have had the experience" (L. Wolfe, *Son* 293).[6] Roosevelt may have been correct, but in 1871 Muir's mind had been set less on comfort than on his "wild plan" for "rough camping"; he had wanted to shake up the "indoor philosophy" of Emerson's party and overcome their dusty "house habit." By 1903, in contrast, Muir had in some ways come around to Emerson's viewpoint, finally recognizing, as Emerson wrote him in 1872, that "solitude . . . is a sublime mistress, but an intolerable wife" (Badè 1:260). Muir still valued the woods more than he did the confines of a house or hotel, but the years he spent as a husband and father in Martinez, California, helped him also understand the ways in which the fate of his beloved Sierra Nevada rested as much on the domesticating influence of civilization as it did on wilderness devotees like himself. And Muir had also learned that much good could come from even the briefest, most touristic visit to the wilderness. A month in the backcountry, in other words, was not always the necessary prerequisite to personal or political transformation.

Many critics and biographers of Muir have observed this general shift in his priorities over time, his move away from an emphasis on the experience of the solitary observer in nature and toward a more lenient understanding of the experience of other humans in the world — both as residents of domestic space and as tourists in the wilderness. Roderick Nash articulates a version of this observation when he describes the change in Muir's rhetoric from his early advocacy of the "rights of nature" to his later use of more anthropocentric arguments. "Why did Muir abandon the environmental ethics approach?" Nash asks. "The reason, it seems clear, is that he got into politics and became pragmatic. Muir believed the only way to save the American wilderness was to persuade the American people and their government of its worth to them. Consequently he tempered his biocentricity and the ethical system it implied, hiding them in his published writing and speeches under a cover of anthropocentrism. It is important to recall that Muir's remarks about the rights of nature appeared first in his private, unpublished journals and not in book form until after his death. Muir knew very well that to go before Congress and the public arguing for national parks as places where snakes, redwood trees, beavers, and rocks could exercise their natural rights to life and liberty would be to invoke ridicule and weaken the cause he wished to advance. So he camouflaged his radical egalitarianism in more acceptable rhetoric centered on the benefits of nature for people" (*Rights* 41).[7]

That Muir tempered his radicalism over time has long been acknowledged as a truism among scholars, but to suggest that Muir was less than forthright with his readers minimizes in important ways the very real changes Muir underwent over the course of three decades. Moreover, such an interpretation rests upon an incomplete understanding of Muir's rhetoric as simply the manipulation of language rather than the negotiation of a complex cultural discourse. A more subtle understanding of Muir's representations of "nature" has begun to be articulated by critics such as Michael L. Smith, Robert L. Dorman, and Steven J. Holmes who emphasize the importance of the domestic in Muir's writing. This chapter contributes to this trend in its argument that Muir's late writings about Yosemite were not an attempt to camouflage his true beliefs but were rather a reflection of the domesticating influence exerted by both his audience and his family. Muir's initial rejection of the domestic life in favor of the wilderness sojourn, and his location of God in the mountains instead of the home, came in reaction to the strict Calvinism imposed on him by his father. Following his marriage to Louie Strentzel in 1880, however, and during the years he spent with her and their daughters in Martinez, Muir gradually came to value the domestic — and its touristic counterpart — as an essential element in the preservation of "nature." With this new perspective, Muir founded the Sierra Club in 1892 "[t]o explore, enjoy, and render accessible the mountain regions of the Pacific Coast; to publish authentic information concerning them; [and] to enlist the support and co-operation of the people and the government in preserving the forests and other features of the Sierra Nevada Mountains," an agenda whose partial fulfillment arrived in 1906 with the recession of the Yosemite Valley to the federal government (Jones, *John Muir* 173).[8]

The Inventions of God

After walking a thousand miles across the American South in 1867, John Muir arrived at Cedar Keys, Florida, on the Gulf of Mexico, but his thoughts were far away.

> *October 23.* To-day I reached the sea. While I was yet many miles back in the palmy woods, I caught the scent of the salt sea breeze which, although I had so many years lived far from sea breezes, suddenly conjured up Dunbar, its rocky coast, winds and waves; and my whole childhood, that seemed to have utterly vanished in the New World, was now restored amid the Florida woods by that one breath from the sea. Forgotten were the palms and magnolias and the thousand flowers that enclosed me. I could see only dulse and tangle, long-winged gulls, the Bass Rock in the Firth of Forth, and the old castle, schools, churches, and long country rambles in search of birds' nests. I do not wonder that the weary camels coming from the scorching African deserts should be able to scent the Nile. (Muir, *Thousand-Mile* 70)

That Muir should have recalled his childhood home in Dunbar, Scotland, after such a voyage is a striking indication of the profound influence of Muir's early experiences in nature upon his eventual renunciation of his father's home in Wisconsin for his own home in the American West.

The Story of My Boyhood and Youth

Born in Dunbar, east of Edinburgh, on the North Sea, on 21 April 1838, John Muir was the third of eight children born to Anne Gilrye Muir and Daniel Muir. The eldest son of the family, Muir would often attempt to protect his brothers and sisters from danger during his childhood years, but he also had a knack for leading them astray — not in the moral sense, but in the geographical. In *The Story of My Boyhood and Youth* (1913), Muir recalls how he and his brother David would steal away "like devout martyrs of wildness . . . to the seashore or the green, sunny fields with almost religious regularity," despite the entreaties of their father to remain in the safety of the backyard and garden.[9] The sea, especially, seems to have captured Muir's attention; he recalls wandering along the seashore "to gaze and wonder at the shells and seaweeds, eels and crabs in the pools among the rocks when the tide was low; and best of all to watch the waves in awful storms thundering on the black headlands and craggy ruins of the old Dunbar Castle when the sea and the sky, the waves and the clouds, were mingled together as one" (NW 7). From his playground at school, Muir and his fellow students could see the sea, and they "loved to watch the passing ships and, judging by their rigging, make guesses as to the ports they had sailed from, those to which they were bound, what they were loaded with," and other such unknown quantities (NW 23). Sometimes, if they were fast enough, they could even find the answers to these questions by recovering the cargo of a ship that had foundered upon the rocky Scottish shore.

Nevertheless, as Frederick Turner suggests, "the real locus of his Dunbar memories is not the sea, wild and wonderful as it was in its moods, but the hill country he could see from his back window: the long, broad folds of the Lammermuirs, the deep green, the copses like shadows, the brown, regular lines traced by the stone walls." According to Turner, Muir's "long runs and rambles into the heart of that landscape were mental and spiritual escapes as much as they were physical ones. Here the boy developed the intuitive ability to take instruction, comfort, and deep pleasure from the natural world" (*Rediscovering* 26). From the beginning of his life, in other words, Muir's sympathy for "nature" derived in part from his need to escape — mentally, spiritually, and physically — from the world around him.

The two principal tensions from which the young Muir felt the need to escape were his grammar school and his father. In *The Story of My Boyhood and Youth* Muir remarks at length upon his struggles with both these influences, each of which strongly emphasized rote memorization and the power of strict discipline. Required to memorize French, English, and Latin grammar in school, Muir says he was thrashed for "everything short of perfection" (NW 20). Similarly, his father daily made him learn so many Bible verses that by the time he was eleven years old, Muir notes, he had "about three fourths of the Old Testament and all of the New by heart and by sore flesh" (NW 20). What Muir says of the educational philosophy of his school teachers could apply equally to his father: "If we failed in any part, however slight, we were whipped; for the grand, simple, all-sufficing Scotch discovery had been made that there was a close connection between the skin and the memory, and that irritating the skin excited the memory to any required discovery" (NW 21). To his credit, Muir used such suffering to his advantage, noting that "no punishment, however sure and severe, was of any avail against the attraction of the fields and woods. . . . Wildness was ever sounding in our ears, and Nature saw to it that besides school lessons and church lessons some of her own lessons should be learned, perhaps with a view to the time when we should be called to wander in wildness to our heart's content" (NW 28).

That opportunity came one step closer to reality when Muir's father decided to immigrate to North America in 1849, when Muir was eleven. That spring, John, his older sister Sarah, and his younger brother David accompanied their father across the Atlantic, after which Anne Muir and the other children planned to re-unite with the rest of the family on their newly established homestead in the fall. Although he originally expected to settle in Canada, Daniel Muir learned of new settlements in Wisconsin during the voyage to America, and so upon reaching New York City he decided to travel to Buffalo via the Erie Canal and then to Milwaukee via Lake Erie. Soon, he was the owner of eighty acres of unimproved land near Portage, Wisconsin, land that eventually became known as the Fountain Lake farm. At first, this landscape seemed to embody the renewal symbolized by springtime for John Muir: "This sudden plash into pure wildness — baptism in Nature's warm heart — how utterly happy it made us! Nature streaming into us, wooingly teaching her wonderful glowing lessons, so unlike the dismal grammar ashes and cinders so long thrashed into us. Here without knowing it we were still at school; every wild lesson a love lesson, not whipped but charmed into us. Oh, that glorious Wisconsin wilderness!" (NW 34).

Unlike Roosevelt in the Dakotas, however, it was not long before Muir felt the pains as well as the pleasures of frontier life. "Those first days and weeks of unmixed enjoyment and freedom," writes Muir, "reveling in the wonderful wildness about us, were soon to be mingled with the hard work of making a farm" (NW 40–41). Furthermore, the thrashings that used to accompany his failed attempts at memorization now accompanied even the smallest act of disobedience or forgetfulness. Most of these whippings were "outrageously severe," according to Muir, and it is remarkable that his published writings are so restrained in their criticism of his father (NW 44). Yet a letter Muir wrote years afterward to a boyhood friend suggests some of the inner anguish Muir must have felt at the unjust treatment he received from his father: "When the rod is falling on the flesh of a child, and, what may oftentimes be worse, heart-breaking scolding falling on its tender little heart, it makes the whole family seem far from the Kingdom of Heaven. In all the world I know of nothing more pathetic and deplorable than a broken-hearted child, sobbing itself to sleep after being unjustly punished by a truly pious and conscientiously misguided parent" (F. Turner, *Rediscovering* 41).

As in Dunbar, Muir found escape from such treatment in the fields and forests around Fountain Lake. Much of *The Story of My Boyhood and Youth*, in fact, is composed of Muir's recollections of the plants, animals, and places he encountered in rural, nineteenth-century Wisconsin. Muir's subheadings for three of his Wisconsin chapters include the following items, which suggest the breadth of his interests: oxen, ponies, snakes, mosquitoes, fish, lilies, lakes, prairie chickens, waterfowl, loons, passenger pigeons, deer, woodpeckers, muskrats, foxes, badgers, raccoons, squirrels, gophers, and shrikes. On Sunday afternoons, which were Muir's only time off from the constant drudgery of wresting a home from the northern plains, he and his brothers David and Daniel would head for the hills — not the Lammermuirs this time, but perhaps nearby Observatory Hill or Wolf Hill. They would go berry-picking and duck-hunting, or swimming and fishing in Fountain Lake, for which they built a boat from planks their father gave them in a rare act of generosity (F. Turner, *Rediscovering* 46; NW 58–60, 85–86). Ultimately, however, the land hunger of Daniel Muir Sr. was not satisfied by his family's achievement at Fountain Lake, and so in 1857 he bought a second farm, five miles to the southeast, which he christened Hickory Hill.

Of all his father's actions, the purchase of Hickory Hill seems to have discouraged Muir the most. He later wrote: "After eight years of this dreary work of clearing the Fountain Lake farm, fencing it and getting it in perfect order, building a frame house and the necessary outbuildings for the cattle and horses, — after all this had been victoriously accomplished, and we had made out to escape with life, — father bought a half-section of wild land about four or five miles to the eastward and began all over again to clear and fence and break up other fields for a new farm, doubling all the stunting, heartbreaking chopping, grubbing, stump-digging, rail-splitting, fence-building, barn-building, house-building, and so forth" (NW 109). Even more than having to repeat the backbreaking labor of clearing another farm, his father's purchase of the Hickory Hill farm was nearly fatal for Muir, who almost died from "choke damp" when digging a ninety-foot well at his father's command. In fact, the accident was symbolic of the dichotomy that had developed over the years between Muir and his father, with Muir's appreciation for the gift of nature — "living water," as Muir called Fountain Lake (NW 111) — contrasting sharply with his father's desire to impose his will upon the landscape and its inhabitants. "Constant dropping wears away stone," Muir observed. "So does constant chipping, while at the same time wearing away the chipper" (NW 113).

Education for Independence

Of all the possible moments, then, from which one might date the beginning of Muir's departure from his father's control, this near-death experience in the well may be the most compelling, for it was at about this time that Muir began to take charge of his own education. Until age sixteen, when Muir had asked for and received a mathematics book from his father, he had been without books or schooling in America. With the help of friendly Scottish neighbors, however, he found himself increasingly able to turn to literature for companionship, discovering in Shakespeare and Milton a love of biblical language, and in the romantic poets a love of the natural world. Like Roosevelt, Muir began by reading histories, natural histories, and travel narratives, displaying a special interest in stories of scientific exploration and foreign adventure, such as George Wood's *Natural History*, Mungo Park's *Travels in the Interior Districts of Africa*, and Alexander von Humboldt's *Personal Narrative of Travels in the Equinoctial Regions*. Over his father's objections, Muir even read Thomas Dick's *Christian Philosopher*, in which Dick attempted to reconcile Christian theology with nineteenth-century science (F. Turner, *Rediscovering* 59–67). During this time Muir also struck a deal with his father, who allowed Muir to have as many hours to himself as he could manage to squeeze out of the early morning, before the rest of the family awoke. Given to mechanical invention, Muir used the extra time to build himself a self-setting sawmill, an automatic horse feeder, several clocks, a barometer, a thermometer, and a variety of other devices (NW 117–22).

What began as mere tinkering in the basement eventually became Muir's ticket out of his father's sphere of influence, when Muir was encouraged to display some of his devices at the Wisconsin State Fair in Madison. The exhibition was a great success, and as a result Muir was invited to work in a machine shop in Prairie du Chien, where he remained through the winter of 1860. By the spring of 1861, he had earned enough money to enroll at the University of Wisconsin, Madison — his first experience with formal education since leaving Dunbar. There he encountered Ezra S. Carr, professor of chemistry and natural history, who stressed the importance of fieldwork, as well as his wife, Jeanne C. Carr, with whom Muir later developed a long-standing correspondence. He also studied with classics professor James Davie Butler, who urged his students to keep a commonplace book of thoughts and observations, a suggestion Muir himself would soon embrace (F. Turner, *Rediscovering* 106–7).

In all, Muir spent two and a half years in Madison, during which time he studied chemistry, geology, and botany, and was exposed to the writings of Emerson and Thoreau, crucial signposts on Muir's road to independence.[10] Emersonian philosophy in particular seems to have had a great influence on Muir, especially Emerson's philosophical optimism, which brightened Muir's outlook considerably. In his copy of Emerson's "Self-Reliance," for instance, Muir marked the passage: "Welcome evermore to gods and men is the self-helping man. For him all doors are flung wide; him all tongues greet, all honors crown, all eyes follow with desire. Our love goes out to him because he did not need it. We solicitously and apologetically caress and celebrate him because he held on his way and scorned our disapprobation. The gods love him because men hated him" (F. Turner, *Rediscovering* 217). Both the Carrs and Butler were native New Englanders, and their devotion to Emerson no doubt rubbed off on Muir, who shared Emerson's inherited Calvinism, as well as Thoreau's habit of close observation of the natural world (Albanese 95). As his life progressed, Muir's cultivation of Emersonian confidence and his developing scientific appreciation for what he called "the great book of Nature" would merge to yield a new understanding of "nature" in which God, humanity, and the natural world were part and parcel of one another, a transcendental unity whose patterns could nonetheless be discerned, comprehended, and described.[11]

In 1863, however, when Muir traveled down the Wisconsin River valley and into Iowa, exploring the Mississippi River bluff country, such an understanding was still incomplete. Likewise for the years 1864 to 1866, much of which Muir spent walking across eastern Canada (in an attempt to avoid being drafted for service in the Civil War) and working in a broom and rake factory in Meaford, Ontario.[12] Nevertheless, one incident in Canada gives an indication of the direction of Muir's thinking about his relationship with the natural world at this time. One late afternoon in June 1864, while walking through a dense swamp, Muir came upon the rare orchid *Calypso borealis* growing on the bank of a stream, and he found comfort in the similarities between this hidden, solitary flower and his own mental and physical isolation. "I never before saw a plant so full of life," Muir wrote to Jeanne Carr; "so perfectly spiritual, it seemed pure enough for the throne of its Creator. I felt as if I were in the presence of superior beings who loved me and beckoned me to come. I sat down beside them and wept for joy" (Fox, *John Muir* 43; Gisel 41). As Stephen Fox observes, although the flowers did nothing "useful," they reassured Muir "simply by existing for themselves" (*John Muir* 43–44). That Muir later ranked this moment as one of the two greatest encounters of his life — the other being his meeting with Emerson in 1871 — suggests the importance of this particular stage of Muir's philosophical development (L. Wolfe, *Son* 146–47).[13]

When Muir returned from Canada in the spring of 1866, he accepted a position in an Indianapolis carriage wheel factory, which seemed to satisfy him with its opportunities for invention, improvement, and efficiency. In the fall, at his employers' request, he made a time-and-motion study of the shop, with the goal of increasing production through better coordination and regularization of the manufacturing process. On 6 March 1867, however, while he was attempting to tighten new belting that had been installed on one of the machines, the sharpened end of a file Muir was using punctured his right eye, and Muir's world changed forever. The file released the aqueous humor of Muir's right eye into his cupped hand, causing his left eye to go blind in sympathetic reaction. An assistant at the factory overheard Muir remark at the time, "My right eye is gone, closed forever on all God's beauty" (F. Turner, *Rediscovering* 125).

The accident sent Muir into physical and mental shock. Confined to a dark room for weeks, certain that his right eye was lost, Muir feared he might never again see the world in the same way. He wrote to Jeanne Carr on 3 April 1867: "You have, of course, heard of my calamity. The sunshine and the winds are working in all the gardens of God, but I — I am lost. I am shut in darkness. My hard, toil-tempered muscles have disappeared, and I am feeble and tremulous as an ever-sick woman" (*Letters* 15; Gisel 44).[14] Good news eventually came his way: sight would soon return in the left eye, and the right eye would also recover much of its function, though it would never again yield perfect vision. By April Muir was up and around, once again able to revel in "all God's beauty" and no longer blind to the limitations of factory work. He quit his job, packed his belongings, and returned to Portage, Wisconsin, where he spent the summer recovering, botanizing, and preparing for what was to be the greatest journey of his life. "God has to nearly kill us sometimes, to teach us lessons," Muir later noted (L. Wolfe, *Son* 105).[15]

A Thousand-Mile Walk to the Gulf

Muir's recovery of his vision marks the beginning of what Ronald H. Limbaugh has called "the rebellious middle period from 1868 to 1880—the young bachelor years of the 1,000 Mile Walk and the Sierra explorations" ("Nature" 19). Shaken by his temporary blindness, and dissatisfied with the direction his life was taking, Muir decided in August 1867 to embark on a one-thousand-mile walk to the Gulf of Mexico, beginning in southern Indiana and concluding on the Gulf Coast of Florida, after which, Muir speculated, the future would take care of itself. "As soon as I got out into Heaven's light," Muir recalled in his later years, "I started on another long excursion, making haste with all my heart to store my mind with the Lord's beauty and thus be ready for any fate, light or dark. And it was from this time that my long continuous wanderings may be said to have fairly commenced. I bade adieu to mechanical inventions, determined to devote the rest of my life to the study of the inventions of God" (Badè 1:155). Muir's decision—a leap of faith—parallels the activity of "surrender" that has marked the autobiographies of many religious figures throughout history.

William James describes the process of salvation by surrender in the fourth and fifth lectures of *The Varieties of Religious Experience* (1902), in which he states: "Official moralists advise us never to relax our strenuousness. 'be vigilant, day and night,' they adjure us; 'hold your passive tendencies in check; shrink from no effort; keep your will like a bow always bent.' But the persons I speak of find that all this conscious effort leads to nothing but failure and vexation in their hands, and only makes them twofold more the children of hell they were before. The tense and voluntary attitude becomes in them an impossible fever and torment. *Their machinery refuses to run at all when the bearings are made so hot and the belts so tight.* Under these circumstances the way to success, as vouched for by innumerable authentic personal narrations, is by an anti-moralistic method, by the 'surrender' of which I spoke in my second lecture. Passivity, not activity; relaxation, not intentness, should now be the rule. Give up the feeling of responsibility, let go your hold, resign the care of your destiny to higher powers, be genuinely indifferent as to what becomes of it all, and you will find not only that you gain a perfect inward relief, but often also, in addition, the particular goods you thought you were renouncing" (101; emphasis added). The parallels between this passage and the trajectory of Muir's life until now are striking: a moralistic father, repeated exhortations to vigilance, the tightening of a machine belt and the machine's refusal to run properly, the subsequent rejection of moralism, and the surrender of responsibility to a higher power.

Other commentators have seen in Muir's journey a purposelessness and lack of direction, but such an interpretation diminishes the real religious power of Muir's surrender. Herbert F. Smith, for instance, claims that "[u]ncertainty is the most striking aspect of *A Thousand-Mile Walk to the Gulf*. It is a narrative of a man who had not yet made up his mind" (35). Much of Muir's *Thousand-Mile Walk* certainly offers evidence for the accuracy of this reading, such as Muir's initial announcement that "[m]y plan was simply to push on in a general southward direction by the wildest, leafiest, and least trodden way I could find, promising the greatest extent of virgin forest" (1).[16] But a letter Muir wrote to Jeanne Carr from Indianapolis on 30 August 1867, just before embarking on his walk, suggests not uncertainty but a surrender to what Muir calls "the spirit": "I wish I knew where I was going. Doomed to be 'carried of the spirit into the wilderness,' I suppose. I wish I could be more moderate in my desires, but I cannot, and so there is no rest" (*Letters* 32; Gisel 57).

Muir's surrender to the spirit freed him to explore alternatives to the Calvinist faith of his father, which Muir identified with the unpleasant harshness of his father's physical discipline.[17] Originally a conventional Presbyterian, Daniel Muir had become a member of the Disciples of God, a sect of Campbellites, prior to his immigration to North America. According to Donald Worster, "[t]he peculiar, distinguishing quality of the Campbellites was their amalgamation of two quite contrary tendencies: Enlightenment rationalism, which denounced all tyranny over the individual mind, and evangelical piety, or what we would now call fundamentalism" (*Wealth* 192). "We became skeptics in everything sectarian — in everything in religion — but the Bible," explained Alexander Campbell, one of the sect's founders (Worster, *Wealth* 192). For Daniel Muir, the consequence of such a view, when combined with the necessities of frontier life, was that "nature" assumed a strictly utilitarian function (Stoll 74). As outlined in the book of Genesis, humans were to "replenish the earth, and subdue it; and have dominion over the fish of the sea, and over the fowl of the air, and over every living thing that moveth upon the earth" (1:28). Much of Muir's life, as Worster notes, thus became a process of "working out some of the tendencies in his father's logic and emotion" (*Wealth* 194).

While no one questions whether Muir eventually did work out these tendencies, exactly *how* he did so has kept readers and critics guessing for more than a decade. Popularly, Muir is often seen as a pantheist: "pantheism at its purest," as one *U.S. News* reporter termed it (Parshall 57). Even within the scholarly community, Muir's religion has led to a wide variety of interpretations, with Stephen

Fox arguing that Muir "made a permanent break from Christianity" (*John Muir* 50), Michael P. Cohen suggesting that Muir may be the "Taoist of the West" (*Pathless* 120), and Bill Devall claiming that Muir "used Christian symbols and rhetoric brilliantly to cloth[e] his pantheistic conception of nature" (75). Such conclusions miss the mark widely, removing Muir from his historical context and anachronistically imposing a modern interest in Eastern religions onto a wholly nineteenth-century Westerner. As Worster observes, Muir himself is partially responsible for the scholarly neglect of his Christian background, since even he "never quite acknowledged its hold on him" (*Wealth* 193). Yet the young Muir was more than just a passive receptacle for his father's religion. According to Dennis Williams, one of several Muir scholars who have recently refocused attention on the continuity of Muir's Christian faith: "As a young man he evangelized his friends. His peers elected him president of the Young Men's Christian Association at the University of Wisconsin. He preached piety to the Union volunteers camped in the fairgrounds at Madison" ("Christian" 84).[18]

Muir's surrender to the spirit in 1867, therefore, was less a rejection of Christianity than a rejection of strict denominationalism, particularly the harsher aspects of his father's Campbellite faith (Limbaugh, "Nature" 19–20). It was, in some ways, the extension of a belief Muir first expressed in a letter to Jeanne Carr in January 1866, in which Muir confessed to taking "more intense delight from reading the power and *goodness* of God from 'the things which are made' than from the Bible" (*Letters* 1; Gisel 34–35).[19] These, indeed, were the "inventions of God" to which Muir had now dedicated his life. Nevertheless, this focus did not prevent Muir from recognizing that the Good Book and the book of nature "harmonize beautifully, and contain enough of divine truth for the study of all eternity" (*Letters* 1; Gisel 35). Like a child attempting to find his place in the cosmos, Muir inscribed his name and location inside the cover of his journal — "John Muir, Earth-planet, Universe" (F. Turner, *Rediscovering* 130)—and set off on his journey, taking notes on the plant, animal, and human life he encountered along the way. That Muir chose to carry with him on his trip a copy of the New Testament and not the Old suggests his greater inclination to find evidence of divine love than divine wrath in the natural world (F. Turner, *Rediscovering* 146).[20]

Muir was not disappointed. Climbing the Great Smoky Mountains on September 18, he found the scenery far grander than he had ever beheld before, nearly leaving him at a loss for words: "Such an ocean of wooded, waving, swelling mountain beauty and grandeur is not to be described. Countless forest-clad hills, side by side in rows and groups, seemed to be enjoying the rich sunshine and remaining motionless only because they were so eagerly absorbing it. All were united by curves and slopes of inimitable softness and beauty. Oh, these forest gardens of our Father! What perfection, what divinity, in their architecture! What simplicity and mysterious complexity of detail! Who shall read the teaching of these sylvan pages, the glad brotherhood of rills that sing in the valleys, and all the happy creatures that dwell in them under the tender keeping of a Father's care?" (*Thousand-Mile Walk* 23). It could not have been far from Muir's mind that the surrender of which his walk was visible evidence could in fact be leading him toward his vocation, his calling, toward "the particular goods he thought he was renouncing," in the words of William James. If Muir were himself to read the teaching of these sylvan pages, might he not in response also feel compelled to teach that reading?

Muir's interpretation of the book of nature (a metaphor of which he was particularly fond) grew less and less orthodox the farther south he walked. Upon seeing his first palmetto on 15 October, Muir noted, "They tell us that plants are perishable, soulless creatures, that only man is immortal, etc.; but this, I think, is something we know very nearly nothing about. Anyhow, this palm was indescribably impressive and told me grander things than I ever got from a human priest" (*Thousand-Mile Walk* 53). Like Henry David Thoreau before him, whose speculations on the immortality of a pine tree in an article he wrote for *Atlantic Monthly* were deleted by editor James Russell Lowell, Muir was moving further away from narrow anthropocentrism and closer to an all-encompassing environmental ethic, in which every part of God's creation was connected and worthy of moral value. The following day, for example, Muir noted: "Many good people believe that alligators were created by the Devil, thus accounting for their all-consuming appetite and ugliness. But doubtless these creatures are happy and fill the place assigned them by the great Creator of us all. Fierce and cruel they appear to us, but beautiful in the eyes of God. They, also, are his children, for He hears their cries, cares for them tenderly, and provides their daily bread. . . . How narrow we selfish, conceited creatures are in our sympathies! how blind to the rights of all the rest of creation! With what dismal irreverence we speak of our fellow mortals! Though alligators, snakes, etc., naturally repel us, they are not mysterious evils. They dwell happily in these flowery wilds, are part of God's family, unfallen, undepraved, and cared for with the same species of tenderness and love as is bestowed on angels in heaven or saints on earth" (*Thousand-Mile Walk* 56). Though close to heresy at the time, Muir's belief in the moral goodness of snakes and alligators was merely an extension of a humanistic Christian ethic to the rest of creation.[21]

As he neared the end of his walk, Muir took this extension to its logical conclusion, criticizing human beings for effectively displacing God as the ultimate referent in the universe. "I have precious sympathy for the selfish propriety of civilized man," Muir wrote in a now-famous passage, "and if a war of races should occur between the wild beasts and Lord Man, I would be tempted to sympathize with the bears" (*Thousand-Mile Walk* 69). Equating civilization with selfishness, Muir took to task the self-centeredness of "Lord Man," who celebrates himself at the expense of other creatures. "The world, we are told, was made especially for man — a presumption not supported by all the facts," Muir concluded upon reaching Cedar Keys. "A numerous class of men are painfully astonished whenever they find anything, living or dead, in all God's universe, which they cannot eat or render in some way what they call useful to themselves. . . . Now, it never seems to occur to these far-seeing teachers that Nature's object in making animals and plants might possibly be first of all the happiness of each one of them, not the creation of all for the happiness of one. Why should man value himself as more than a small part of the one great unit of creation? And what creature of all that the Lord has taken the pains to make is not essential to the completeness of that unit — the cosmos? The universe would be incomplete without man; but it would also be incomplete without the smallest transmicroscopic creature that dwells beyond our conceitful eyes and knowledge" (*Thousand-Mile Walk* 77–79). In what could be seen as a reinterpretation of the Genesis story, Muir stresses not the dominion of humans over the earth, but rather the limitations placed upon them by God, who does not give humans animals to eat, but only "every herb bearing seed, which is upon the face of all the earth, and every tree, in the which is the fruit of a tree yielding seed" (1:29). Likewise, Muir is not selective about those creatures he values; instead, he follows the Lord, who "saw every thing that he had made, and, behold, it was very good" (1:31).

By the end of his thousand-mile walk, when Muir found himself bound for California, this son of a Campbellite follower had wrestled with and found wanting the orthodox emphasis on human civilization as the apex of God's unfolding creation. At the same time, however, he had grown more certain than ever of the sacredness of that creation, of the value and worth of all God's creatures, whether "beautiful" or "ugly," human or nonhuman, large or small. It should come as no surprise, then, that to Thoreau's dictum, "[i]n Wildness is the preservation of the World" ("Walking" 112), Muir eventually added God: "In God's wildness lies the hope of the world" (L. Wolfe, *John* 317). No Taoist or pantheist or religious renegade he, John Muir remained fiercely Christian — progressive though he was — until the very end. As John Burroughs wrote in a review of *The Yosemite* (1912), Muir's late collection of essays about the park he was soon to celebrate, "All his streams and waterfalls and avalanches and storm-buffeted trees sing songs, or hymns, or psalms, or rejoice in some other proper Presbyterian manner. One would hardly be surprised to hear his avalanches break out with the Doxology" (1165).

Domesticating the Sacred

"I am sure you will be directed by Providence to the place where you will best serve the end of existence," Muir wrote Jeanne Carr on 1 November 1868, after having spent his first summer in the Sierra (*Letters* 48; Gisel 80). Muir could just as easily have been talking about himself, as his surrender of the previous year seems to have paid off richly indeed, leading him to the Yosemite Valley he had first read about in 1866, and which would soon become the chief reason for his own existence (*Letters* 20; Gisel 50). If Providence was leading Muir to Yosemite, it could also be said to have been leading Yosemite to national park status, because, as Bron Taylor has noted, although "Muir is best known as the founder of the Sierra Club, . . . his foremost legacy is the National Park System, where his preservationist ideals found institutional expression" ("Resacralizing" 141 n. 13). Like Muir himself, the idea of the "park" had a long history before being applied to the Yosemite Valley, and a brief examination of this history will help place Muir's achievement in its proper context.

The Idea of the "Park"

"Parks have varied widely," according to environmental historian Thomas R. Cox, and "the very term 'park' has been used in a host of ways." As intellectual and social currents have shifted, so too have the conceptions of parks, making it possible for the idea of the "park" to serve as "a barometer of changing attitudes and perceptions" (Cox 14).[22]

According to the *Oxford English Dictionary*, the oldest usage of the term "park," which dates to the thirteenth century, is for "[a]n enclosed tract of land held by royal grant or prescription for keeping beasts of the chase." This was subsequently extended to encompass "a large ornamental piece of ground, usually comprising woodland and pasture, attached to or surrounding a country house or mansion, and used for recreation, and often for keeping deer, cattle, or sheep." By the seventeenth century, the term "park" was being used to designate land held for public as well as private use, such as "[a]n enclosed piece of ground, of considerable extent, usually within or adjoining a city or town, ornamentally laid out and devoted to public recreation" or "where animals are exhibited to the public." Not until the nineteenth century, and the discovery of the vast western landscapes of the United States, did the term "park" come to acquire its most familiar contemporary meaning as "[a]n extensive area of land of defined limits set apart as national property to be kept in its natural state for the public benefit and enjoyment or for the preservation of wild life."

What kind of "shifting intellectual and social currents" do these changing definitions suggest? Roderick Nash makes the important observation that "[u]ntil the American invention of national parks, the word 'park' (or its equivalent in other languages) was understood as being synonymous with 'garden.' Nature was supposed to be pleasant. . . . Gardening or park-making consisted of shaping the environment to man's will. The idea of a wild park was self-contradictory. The ideal environment, and the one a park was intended to display, was the pastoral, the arcadian. Wilderness was the frightening, unordered condition from which man was relieved to have emerged. Parks were symbols of this emergence, of control over nature" ("American Invention" 726–27). Landscape historian Paul Shepard concurs, observing that "[t]he 'natural' garden or 'park' was the estate grounds, landscaped to blend into the rural countryside. The park was a particular association — planned randomness — of scattered trees, lawn, and winding streams connecting lakes. It looked somewhat like paintings of Arcadia or of paradise. It was both an abstraction from nature and a figment of human experience, roughly equivalent to the pastoral landscape of mixed forest and meadow from which modern European man emerged" (255). Thus the roots of the "park" idea can be found in the idea of the "garden" embraced by Mabel Osgood Wright; just as her Birdcraft Sanctuary could be said to resemble a park, so does the Yosemite Valley share characteristics of the garden.

Yet parks did not spring fully formed out of California like some towering redwood newly encountered. As historian Hans Huth has described, "[t]o a limited degree there had been 'public' parks in this country since the beginning of colonization. When [William] Penn laid out the original plan of Philadelphia he assigned for public use a number of squares, the largest of which had measured ten acres. These were to be graced with trees and not to be built over, except perhaps with a few public buildings. Likewise there were 'commons' such as those in England in most of the New England settlements. Primarily intended to serve as pastures, they were also used as parade grounds or for recreational purposes" ("Yosemite" 61–62). In the early nineteenth century, garden parks such as those found on Andrew Jackson Downing's Hudson River estates, in Frederick Law Olmsted's Central Park, and in the rural cemeteries near Boston and Philadelphia also reflected the English style of the cultivated, pastoral landscape. By midcentury, however, Americans had encountered what Shepard describes as "the visual surprise of the western wilderness: truly wild places that resembled civilization's most ornamental achievement — the estate park — which was, in turn, linked with an image of paradise" (256).

Not surprisingly, the earliest call for a national park came from the West, from the artist George Catlin who, looking out over present-day South Dakota in 1832, exclaimed: "what a beautiful and thrilling specimen for America to preserve and hold up to the view of her refined citizens and the world, in future ages! A *nation's*

Park, containing man and beast, in all the wild[ness] and freshness of their nature's beauty!" (Catlin 1:2–3).[23] Although national park historian Richard West Sellars argues that Catlin's proposal had "no influence" upon the subsequent development of the national park system in America (293 n. 2), Catlin's sentiments nevertheless reflect the leading edge of Americans' changing assumptions about the meaning and purpose of wildlands. To most Americans, wilderness was meant to be subdued, not preserved — a belief effectively illustrated by the activities of Muir's father. Yet as the nation moved westward and land grew increasingly scarce, more and more people began voicing a different opinion, that perhaps some western lands should be preserved, for such reasons as recreation, aesthetics, and inspiration. Such was the case with what was to become Yosemite National Park.[24]

Yosemite before Muir

At the time of the California gold rush, John Muir was eleven, just beginning his voyage from Scotland to Wisconsin. The forty-niners, on the other hand, were migrating westward in search of gold, which they found in the foothills of the Sierra Nevada, or "snowy mountains" — a range of mountains in eastern California running about four hundred miles north and south between the Sacramento and San Joaquin Valleys and the Nevada border.[25] There the miners also encountered American Indians, and it was the dispossession of these Indians that led to the first European American exploration of the Yosemite Valley in 1851. Late in the afternoon of 27 March, the members of the Mariposa Battalion, a unit of mounted volunteers, were pursuing a band of Ahwahneechee Indians some two hundred miles west of San Francisco when they came to a clearing in the trees near what is now Inspiration Point. From that perspective, they could see down into a narrow, flat valley surrounded by dramatic granite cliffs and majestic waterfalls, a view not easily forgotten (Runte, *Yosemite* 10). "The grandeur of the scene was but softened by the haze that hung over the valley, — light as gossamer — and by the clouds which partially dimmed the higher cliffs and mountains," recalled expedition member Lafayette Bunnell in 1880. "This obscurity of vision but increased the awe with which I beheld it, and as I looked, a peculiar exalted sensation seemed to fill my whole being, and I found my eyes in tears with emotion" (54).[26]

Bunnell's memory of the scene, influenced as it no doubt was by the other accounts of the valley that had appeared by the time of its publication, nevertheless reflects the primary means by which Yosemite was first appreciated: the aesthetic. Prior to Muir's arrival, the valley's most enthusiastic promoter was James Mason Hutchings, an Englishman who had traveled to California during the gold rush. Hutchings first visited the Yosemite Valley in 1855, and the following year he founded *Hutchings' Illustrated California Magazine*, in which he intended to foster public appreciation for the Yosemite and other California landscapes. In 1859 Hutchings settled permanently in the Yosemite Valley, where he established a hotel, served as a tour guide, and published several books about the valley, including *Scenes of Wonder and Curiosity in California* (1860), which included a thorough introduction to the valley for the interested tourist. Eastern journalists such as Thomas Starr King, Albert D. Richardson, and Samuel Bowles also toured the region and sang its praises. In 1859, for instance, Horace Greeley, editor of the *New York Tribune*, famously visited Yosemite Valley and declared it "the most unique and majestic of nature's marvels" (Greeley 306). But it was the painters, engravers, and photographers who had the most wide-reaching effect on the public's knowledge of the valley. Hutchings published the first views of the valley in 1855; the photographer Carleton E. Watkins visited the Yosemite in 1861; and Albert Bierstadt spent seven weeks in August and September 1863 making sketches for what were to become two of his best-known paintings: *Valley of the Yosemite* (1864) and *Domes of the Yosemite* (1867).[27]

As the publicity surrounding Yosemite continued to grow, a parallel movement arose advocating for its preservation. In the winter and spring of 1864, just as John Muir was beginning to explore eastern Canada, the junior senator from California, John Conness, was introducing legislation to close forever from commercial development a large tract of the Sierra, including the Yosemite Valley and the Mariposa Grove. Wary of allowing the valley and its magnificent Sierra redwoods to fall into private hands, as had Niagara Falls, Conness and a small group of concerned Californians lobbied Congress to set aside approximately forty square miles of the Yosemite Valley and its surrounding peaks, and four square miles of Sierra redwoods, including the Mariposa Grove. The land was to be turned over to California for administration as a state park, not kept by the federal government. The measure passed, and on 30 June 1864, President Lincoln signed the Yosemite Park Act granting the prescribed area to the State of California as a state park "for public use, resort and recreation" to be held "inalienable for all time."[28]

Several factors influenced the success of Conness's legislation. First, Conness stressed what has since come to be known as the "worthless lands" thesis: that the valley contained no commercially valuable resources other than its beauty.[29] Second, he played on anti-British sentiment generated by England's sympathy for the Confederacy by reminding senators that because the British had earlier denied the existence of the giant sequoias, a grove of them must be preserved from destruction to sustain the nation's pride. Third, he emphasized the expense-free nature of the grant, noting that no appropriation would be necessary to maintain and support the park — an important argument, given the extraordinary expense involved in fighting the ongoing Civil War (Runte, *Yosemite* 19–20).

Although Arkansas Hot Springs had been set aside as a "national reservation" in

1832, it was really the approval of Yosemite, thanks to Conness's savvy rhetoric, that inaugurated what was to become the National Park System in America. Arkansas Hot Springs had been preserved because of its medicinal value and not its scenic qualities, and although Yosemite existed as a state park for its first quarter century, it could certainly be argued—as national parks historian Alfred Runte convincingly has—that "[i]n fact, . . . if not in name, Yosemite was the first national park" (*National Parks* 30). "Yellowstone," Runte notes, "merely reaffirmed the ideals and anxieties of 1864" (*National Parks* 34). As Kenneth R. Olwig has observed, "National parks would seem to be as much about the nature of national identity as about physical nature" (380).

One of the most farsighted early advocates of the new Yosemite park was Frederick Law Olmsted, whom California governor Frederick F. Low appointed to the park's board of commissioners in 1864 (Runte, *Yosemite* 21). In an important report he prepared for the park commission, Olmsted noted the existence of "the most tranquil meadows, the most playful streams, and every variety of soft and peaceful pastoral beauty" in Yosemite (16), but he also warned that such scenes "might become private property and . . . their value to posterity be injured" (14). To prevent this, Olmsted recommended that free access to the valley be preserved, that a public road be constructed to provide better transportation to the valley, that a circuit trail for carriages be built around the valley, and that five rental cabins also be built within the valley (23–25). In perhaps his most farsighted observation, Olmsted also predicted that the then-hundreds of visitors to Yosemite "will become thousands and in a century the whole number of visitors will be counted by the millions" (22).[30]

As Olmsted warned in his report, in the seven years between the passage of the Yosemite Park Act of 1864 and John Muir's first published writings about the valley in 1871, Yosemite underwent a profound transformation due to the efforts of park promoters to publicize its existence and the arrival of tourists to explore its natural wonders. Eadweard Muybridge produced a series of photographs of Yosemite between 1867 and 1872; Josiah Dwight Whitney of the Geological Survey of California published the *Yosemite Guide-Book* in 1869; and survey member Clarence King described his experiences in and around the valley in *Mountaineering in the Sierra Nevada* in 1872. Throughout this period, tourism to Yosemite increased steadily, with sightseers from San Francisco traveling across the San Joaquin Valley by train and stagecoach, into the foothills of the Sierra by wagon, and into the Yosemite Valley by horseback.[31] As historian Richard West Sellars explains, "much of the valley floor was developed to satisfy the whims of the tourist industry. Under lax state management, the Yosemite Valley emerged as a crazy quilt of roads, hotels, and cabins, and pastures and pens for cattle, hogs, mules, and horses. Tilled lands supplied food for residents and visitors, and feed

for livestock; irrigation dams and ditches supported agriculture; and timber operations supplied wood for construction, fencing, and heating" (18). Most outrageous were the promotional activities of hotel owner James McCauley, who in the
early 1870s constructed a trail to Glacier Point — thirty-two hundred feet above the
valley floor — off of which he daily began to throw a chicken, and later the smol-
dering embers of a fire, for the amusement of the spectators below (Runte, *National Parks* 163–65).

What seemed to have escaped all the early explorers, preservers, and promoters
of Yosemite, however, was the degree to which their perceptions of the valley as a
garden park had been influenced by the presence of its original gardeners, now ex-
pelled from what had been their home. As Rebecca Solnit observes, "when Bunnell, Olmsted, and their peers rode into the valley and wondered at it for its re-
semblance to an English landscape garden, it resembled such a garden because it
was one, an explanation that never occurred to them and their successors. Had it
truly been uninhabited wilderness, they might have instead entered a forest so
dense that the waterfalls and rock faces they glimpsed from above would not have
been easily visible from the valley itself. . . . The touchstone for wilderness turns
out to be an artifact of generations of human care. So the model for all the park
preserves of wilderness or pure nature around the world turns out to be no more
independent than any other garden, and the deterioration of its ecology is as much
the story of a garden gone unweeded as a wilderness civilized" (307–8).[32] Such was
the context into which John Muir walked when he first arrived in California on 27
March 1868.

Summering in the Sierra

Nearly thirty years old and still without a "respectable" occupation, John Muir
arrived in San Francisco on 27 March 1868 and immediately inquired about the
nearest way out of town. "But where do you want to go?" replied the man to whom
Muir had posed this pointed question. "To any place that is wild," Muir says he
replied (*Yosemite* 1).[33] Muir's wanderings eventually brought him to Yosemite,
which for the next five years — roughly until 1873 — became "his life's center, its focus, its spiritual home" (Engberg and Wesling 5). One of Muir's earliest responses
to the valley indicates the refrain that would appear throughout his writings from
and about this period. "It is by far the grandest of all the special temples of Nature
I was ever permitted to enter," Muir wrote to Jeanne Carr on 26 July 1868. "It must
be the *sanctum sanctorum* of the Sierras [*sic*]" (*Letters* 43; Gisel 74).

Exactly when and how Yosemite became Muir's "spiritual home" has been the
subject of considerable discussion among scholars. Thomas J. Lyon, for instance,
has argued that the first full summer Muir spent working as a shepherd in the

Sierra was one of the two or three critical periods of his life. "The summer of 1869 was a revelation to him, a lifelong touchstone," Lyon says; "it was the great immersion" ("John Muir's Enlightenment" 52). *My First Summer in the Sierra* (1911), the book that emerged from the journals of Muir's experience, seems to support such a view, particularly in its use of the language of conversion, as John Tallmadge and others have observed.[34] "We are now in the mountains and they are in us, kindling enthusiasm, making every nerve quiver, filling every pore and cell of us," Muir writes in *My First Summer.* "Our flesh-and-bone tabernacle seems transparent as glass to the beauty about us, as if truly an inseparable part of it, thrilling with the air and trees, streams and rocks, in the waves of the sun, —a part of all nature, neither old nor young, sick nor well, but immortal. Just now I can hardly conceive of any bodily condition dependent on food or breath any more than the ground or the sky. How glorious a conversion, so complete and wholesome it is, scarce memory enough of old bondage days left as a standpoint to view it from! In this newness of life we seem to have been so always" (NW 161).

Recently, Steven J. Holmes has argued, based on a detailed analysis of *My First Summer* and the notebooks upon which it is based, that neither of these texts offers a reliable account of what Muir experienced that first season. In particular, Holmes claims, "many of the most characteristic elements that have long been associated with Muir's 1869 entry into Yosemite — including his language and experience of becoming 'a part of all nature,' through a dramatic, ecstatic 'conversion' and total reorientation of his life — must be understood not as his immediate, intuitive responses to Yosemite but rather as the self-conscious results of his later literary and philosophical development" (7). This is a helpful corrective to the tendency to read too much into a single passage or moment in Muir's life, but as Holmes himself points out, "it seems quite likely that . . . [Muir] had a powerful experience of *some* sort at this point, perhaps on a milder scale than the present language suggests but nevertheless of importance in the development of his perceptions of and feelings toward the mountain environment" (205). According to Holmes, Muir "came to his eventual relationship with Yosemite not through a sudden, dramatic 'conversion' but rather through a gradual process that would develop only over years of living in that place and that was grounded in specific patterns and images that were deeply rooted in the experiences and relationships of his entire life" (207).

Whether it happened over the course of a summer or over the course of several years, the spiritual change that took place in Muir remains significant. The Yosemite, he came to realize, was a sacred landscape, a place where he could become cleansed of his father's religious influence as if in a new baptism. "If there is such a thing as an awakening," Michael P. Cohen writes, "Muir's eyes were opened by the mountains in the early seventies. His journals and letters from

Yosemite are filled with references to baptism in light and water. Rock, water, and sunlight were instinct with God. . . . He was living in a sacred world, and as he partook of its reality and being he became a part of a world which was not a chaos, but a cosmos" (*Pathless* 65). (Holmes, too, notes that "baptism would have carried much more theological weight and personal resonance than conversion" for Muir, at this time of his life [214].)

But once again it would be a mistake to emphasize the pantheistic tendencies of Muir's thought over his continuing reliance upon a more traditional religious understanding of natural beauty. On the one hand, Muir's Christianity clearly tended toward the mystical, as a comment Muir made (probably in 1870) in a letter to his brother David suggests: "I have not been at church a single time since leaving home. Yet this glorious valley might well be called a church for every lover of the great Creator who comes within the broad overwhelming influences of the place fail not to worship as they never did before" (D. Williams, "John Muir, Christian Mysticism" 89). On the other hand, an entry from Muir's journals of September and October 1872 reveals such mysticism to be not nearly as unorthodox as some critics have suggested. "I never found the devil in the Sierras nor any evil," Muir wrote, "but God in clearness and the religion of Jesus Christ" (D. Williams, "John Muir, Christian Mysticism" 95).

Yosemite was the ideal landscape for Muir's 1870s transformation in part because it so closely fit the Edenic, gardenlike model of the sacred space to which he was accustomed: "the natural paradise or garden park," as Paul Shepard has described the valley (257). In *The Story of My Boyhood and Youth*, Muir described his father's attempt to make the backyard garden of his house in Dunbar "as much like Eden as possible" (NW 12), and in *My First Summer* he characterized his first view of Yosemite Valley from the top of Yosemite Falls in much the same way: "The level bottom seemed to be dressed like a garden, sunny meadows here and there, and groves of pine and oak; the river of Mercy sweeping in majesty through the midst of them and flashing back the sunbeams" (NW 220). Muir's focus on the pastoral aspects of the valley — and his failure to mention at all the trails, fences, barns, and houses that littered the landscape below (Runte, *Yosemite* 5) — suggests the power this cultural model held for him at the time he wrote *My First Summer*, if not also when he claimed to have first seen the valley (15 July 1869).

Despite his selective editing of this view in *My First Summer*, Muir certainly was aware of the presence of tourists in and around the valley. One of Muir's early letters (16 May 1869) to Jeanne Carr from Yosemite even provided her with touristic instructions and detailed the necessary preparations for a visit to Yosemite, including preferred roads, provisions, and outfitters; estimated costs; and suggested camping places (*Letters* 54–59; Gisel 84–86). Nevertheless, Muir's chief concern about tourists was their potential to profane the sacred Sierra landscape. "Most persons visiting the sequoia grove," he told Carr on 20 May 1869, "spend only a few hours in it and depart without seeing a single tree, for the chiefest glories of these mountain kings are wholly invisible to hasty or careless observers" (*Letters* 60; Gisel 87). Just as he chides the tourists who fail to tarry long enough with the big trees to appreciate them fully, in *My First Summer* he also criticizes those visitors who so eagerly anticipate the view of the Yosemite Valley that they fail to see the beauty of the rest of the Sierra range. In a 12 July 1869 entry, Muir remarks that "[s]omehow most of these travelers seem to care little for the glorious objects about them, though enough to spend time and money and endure long rides to see the famous valley. And when they are fairly within the mighty walls of the temple and hear the psalms of the falls, they will forget themselves and become devout. Blessed, indeed, should be every pilgrim in these holy mountains!" (*NW* 212).

Most notable among Muir's early condemnation of tourists is a letter to Jeanne Carr he wrote on 29 May 1870, in which Muir explains that "[a]ll sorts of human stuff is being poured into our Valley this year, and the blank, fleshy apathy with which most of it comes in contact with the rock and water spirits of the place is most amazing" (*Letters* 80; Gisel 110). The horseback-riding tourists, Muir laments, "climb sprawlingly to their saddles like overgrown frogs pulling themselves up a stream-bank through the bent sedges, ride up the Valley with about as much emotion as the horses they ride upon, and comfortable when they have 'done it all,' and long for the safety and flatness of their *proper homes*" (*Letters* 81; Gisel 110; emphasis added). To Muir in 1870 such tourists were out of place in the mountains of California; their homes were in Boston or New York, not in the wild spaces of the Sierra.[35] Yet Muir assures Carr that "the tide of visitors will float slowly about the *bottom* of the Valley as a harmless scum, collecting in hotel and saloon eddies, leaving the rocks and falls eloquent as ever and instinct with imperishable beauty and greatness" (*Letters* 81; Gisel 110). Equally telling, in another letter to Carr on 29 July 1870, Muir declares that "[t]he Valley is full of people but they do not annoy me. I revolve in pathless places and in higher rocks than *the world* and his ribbony wife can reach" (*Letters* 85; Gisel 114). Not only does Muir distinguish between his own home in the mountains and the rest of civilization in the valleys, but he also feminizes the civilized world by reference to "his ribbony wife."

This vertical morality can been seen throughout Muir's writing from the early 1870s. In a 2 April 1872 letter to Emily Pelton, Muir writes: "You mention the refining influences of society. Compared with the intense purity and cordiality and beauty of Nature, the most delicate refinements and cultures of civilization are gross barbarisms. As for the rough vertical animals called men, who occur in and on these mountains like sticks of condensed filth, I am not in *contact* with them; I do not live with them. I live alone, or, rather, with the rocks and flowers and snows and blessed storms; I live in blessed mountain *light*, and love nothing less pure" (Badè 1:325). Perhaps most famously, when Muir returned to the Sierra in September 1874 after a ten-month stay in Oakland, he announced to his journal: "All are more or less sick; there is not a perfectly sane man in San Francisco" (L. Wolfe, *John* 191). Then, recalling his brush with death from choke damp in his father's well, Muir wrote, "in just this condition are those who toil or dawdle or dissipate in crowded towns, in the sinks of commerce or pleasure" (L. Wolfe, *John* 192). These passages also parallel *My First Summer*, in which Muir chides "the poor Professor [Butler] and General [Alvord], bound by clocks, almanacs, orders, duties, etc., and compelled to dwell with lowland care and dust and din, where Nature is covered and her voice smothered, while the poor, insignificant wanderer [Muir himself] enjoys the freedom and glory of God's wilderness" (NW 261).

"Going to the Mountains Is Going Home"

In the early 1870s Muir's identification of mountain landscapes with God's light and lowland civilization with the darkness of evil was a vivid and clear-cut reversal of the Calvinist dichotomy of his father, who instead attempted to bring the light of civilization to the darkness of the wilderness (Brooks 29; Lyon, *John Muir* 16). "Heaven knows that John Baptist was not more eager to get all his fellow sinners into the Jordan than I to baptize all of mine in the beauty of God's mountains," Muir wrote in his journal in October 1871 (L. Wolfe, *John* 86). As time passed, however, the starkness of Muir's dichotomy softened considerably. As Stephen Fox observes, the truth of Muir's sentiments is to be found somewhere in between these two extremes. "At one pole he always overstated the nature of the opposite extreme. He neither loved the wilderness nor hated civilization as much as he claimed" (*John Muir* 54). Steven J. Holmes agrees, observing that Muir never really *lived* the dichotomy between wilderness and civilization that he constructed; "leaving all his human contacts for 'pure nature,' for good, was never a real possibility for him. Instead, his emotional bonds to home cut across 'wilderness' and 'civilization,' or rather the natural, human, and divine realms, resulting in complex and shifting configurations of the desired and the defiled" (246).[36]

Michael P. Cohen attributes this softening to Muir's discovery of his calling as a writer. In December 1871 Muir published his first article, "Yosemite Glaciers," in the *New York Tribune*, followed the next month by another contribution to the *Tribune*, "Yosemite in Winter." Three months later, in April 1872, his first magazine article, "Yosemite Valley in Flood," appeared in the *Overland Monthly*. The title of this last article was telling, because over the next ten years Muir himself would release a flood of articles on the Yosemite and surrounding regions, publishing them in some of the nation's leading periodicals and newspapers, such as

Overland Monthly, Harper's Monthly, Scribner's, and the *San Francisco Bulletin.* How was it possible, Cohen asks, for Muir to write for such popular magazines without uprooting himself? "What we now know — that working[in and through a medium, with its own conventions, has a way of shaping the mind of the creator — Muir also suspected. Popular literature and industrial tourism have this in common: they vulgarize the writer and the tour guide as well as the reader and the tourist. Muir was on the brink of a very dangerous abyss. . . . By falling into the occupation of a popular writer he could endanger the very message he had a sacred mission to convey. He would have to stand astride the abyss between wilderness and civilization and mediate between the vision he had gained in the mountains and the expectations of his readers" (*Pathless* 132).

Part of the way Muir accomplished this mediation was by domesticating the sacred.[37] Rather than invoking the discourse of Mabel Osgood Wright and other nineteenth-century women writers, who identified the home as a sacred space, Muir turned to the spaces he already knew to be sacred and made them seem more like home. In so doing, Muir helped to convince Americans that "useless lands" were valuable not because they held little utilitarian value but because their value as "sacred spaces" was inseparable from their value as "domestic spaces." As Steven J. Holmes points out, this process was part of Muir's own coming-to-terms with Yosemite as a home. "It was only after repeated experiences of leaving and then returning to Yosemite throughout the 1870s that he came to commonly refer to that specific place as his 'true mountain home'; this process was especially powerful after he had begun to make a literary career on the basis of his descriptions of Yosemite and had begun to be strongly associated with that place in the public mind. . . . Yosemite took on the force of a symbolic center only after he had left and then returned to it — with no plans of actually staying there to live. Thus, Yosemite gained meaning precisely through marked *contrast* with his actual homes of the period; freed of many of the requirements for a literal home, Yosemite could serve as a locus of religious and symbolic meanings in the context of a developing literary career and personal identity" (Holmes 242).

Muir made his argument about Yosemite's sacred domesticity by adopting one of the literary techniques of Thoreau, which Emerson first identified as the "old fault of unlimited contradiction" in an important journal entry from 25 August 1843. "The trick of his rhetoric is soon learned," Emerson wrote of Thoreau. "It consists in substituting for the obvious word & thought its diametrical antagonist. He praises wild mountains & winter forests for their domestic air; snow & ice for their warmth; villagers & wood choppers for their urbanity[;] and the wilderness for resembling Rome & Paris" (Emerson, *Journals* 9). Muir's adoption of this technique suggests that Thoreau's use of "unlimited contradiction" was no trick, though. As Cecelia Tichi observes about *Walden*, "the premise of a domesticated environment . . . frees Thoreau to explore and celebrate wildness as a tonic for thought. . . . His wildness is held in a domestic embrace" (166–67).[38]

Despite the different objects of their attention, Muir shares with Mabel Wright an emphasis on the *friendship* of nature. "Throughout his work," observes Lawrence Buell, "Muir insisted to the point of obsessiveness on nature's companionableness, no matter how superficially forbidding. . . . Such transformations of images of harshness into images of shelter and comfort are typical of Muir; they show how important to him it was, for whatever reason, to think of nature as his friend" (193–94). One of the reasons this was important, of course, was rhetorical. Nature was not just Muir's friend; it was to be the reader's friend, and no reader wants to neglect his or her friends in their time of need. Sherman Paul explains that one of the ways Muir makes himself at home is "by speaking of 'Nature's carpeted mountain halls,' by frequently considering landscape and natural phenomena in terms of rugs, lacework, and embroidery. He reminds us that nature, even though God makes it, is 'feminine,' with all that this has immemorially meant for our dwelling there" (255). Like Wright, Muir even disregarded the "pathetic fallacy" and personified the plants, animals, and even landscape elements he encountered, making them all seem "familiar," like members of the human family (Tallmadge, "John Muir" 72–74).[39]

The first instance of Muir's best-known example of "unlimited contradiction" appeared on 3 August 1875, as part of Muir's series "Summering in the Sierra" for the *San Francisco Bulletin*. Muir began the article, titled "In Sierra Forests," by announcing that "[g]oing to the mountains is going home" (Engberg 79). On 24 August 1876 Muir expanded on this statement, noting that "[t]he regular tourist, ever on the flow, is one of the most characteristic productions of the present century; and however frivolous and inappreciative the poorer specimens may appear, viewed comprehensively they are a most hopeful and significant sign of the times, indicating at least the beginning of our return to nature, — for going to the mountains is going home" (Browning 34–35). Remarkably, Muir expanded on the meaning of his statement by making one of his earliest declarations of hope in the possibility of tourism, a sure sign that his attempt at mediation between the wilderness and civilization would come through the domestication of the sacred.

The interaction of the domestic and the sacred was a prominent theme for Muir from his earliest days in Yosemite, and it remained so until the end of his life in 1913. Robert Underwood Johnson, for instance, recounts that when Muir wrote for the first time to a young admirer, he "expressed the hope that she would 'find that going to the mountains is going home and that Christ's Sermon on the Mount is on every mount'" (*Remembered* 286). One of Muir's better-known statements, however, may best demonstrate the continuity of Muir's thinking about this topic. In a late journal entry from around 1913, Muir summed up the course of his life by stating: "Not like my taking the veil — no solemn abjuration of the world. I only went out for a walk, and finally concluded to stay out till sundown, for going out, I found was really going in" (L. Wolfe, *John* 439). Michael P. Cohen claims that "[s]uch was simply not the case. He was abjuring the world when he went out, and those who cared about him were constantly trying to bring him back in" (*Pathless* 148–49). Yet Muir specifically notes that he is *not* renouncing the world here, and the language of the second sentence seems to support his assertion; close attention to its implied referents suggests that Muir may have meant that going out [of his own house] was really going in [to God's house], a place of worship, and one that Muir increasingly attempted to entice others to enter.[40]

On the literal level, Muir was himself becoming more domesticated by the end of the 1870s, and his life as a husband and a father in the following decade changed him visibly, making him better able to communicate with middle- and upper-class readers and more willing to accede to the actual domestication of Yosemite through tourism. John P. O'Grady observes that Muir "never divested himself — even during his pilgrim years — of the domestic urge" (60), a fact borne out by a letter to his sister Sarah written on 12 January 1877: "Little did I think when I used to be, and am now, fonder of home and still domestic life than any one of the boys, that I only should be a bachelor and doomed to roam always far outside the family circle" (Badè 2:62). Indeed, Muir often expressed his loneliness in letters and his journal throughout the late 1860s and early 1870s. "I am lonely among my enjoyments," Muir wrote Jeanne Carr on 17 May 1870; "the Valley is full of visitors, but I have no one to talk to" (*Letters* 77; Gisel 106). And to his journal in October 1872 Muir confided: "There perhaps are souls that never weary, that always go unhalting and glad, tuneful and songful as mountain water. Not so, weary, hungry me. In all God's mountain mansions, I find no human sympathy, and I hunger" (L. Wolfe, *John* 89).[41]

With more than a little prodding from Jeanne Carr, Muir eventually settled down at age forty-one and married Louie Wanda Strentzel on 14 April 1880, receiving the Strentzels' seventeen-room ranch in Martinez as a wedding gift and later taking over the responsibilities for their twenty-six-hundred-acre fruit farm (F. Turner, *Rediscovering* 262–63).[42] In late interviews and conversations, Muir tried to emphasize that his true "home" remained in the wilderness despite his marriage. In 1906, for instance, Muir told the *World's Work* that "[h]ome is the most dangerous place I ever go to. . . . As long as I camp out in the mountains, without tent or blankets, I get along very well; but the minute I get into a house and have a warm bed and begin to live on fine food, I get into a draft and the first thing I know I am coughing and sneezing and threatened with pneumonia, and altogether miserable. Outdoors is the natural place for a man" (Strother, "Conversation" 8249).[43] And Ray Stannard Baker recounts Muir speaking of his home in Martinez as "a good place to be housed in during stormy weather, to write in, and to raise children in." But, Muir told Baker, "it is not my home. Up there is my home," he said, pointing toward the Sierra (377).[44]

Nevertheless, several critics suggest that Muir's domestic life was in fact quite beneficial to his long-term goal of wilderness preservation. "Muir scholars tend to exaggerate the frustrations Muir experienced in the 1880s," notes Ronald H. Limbaugh. "Exchanging the wild Yosemite days for a prosperous life in Alhambra Valley was a willful act that brought with it security and fortune, things he had never known before" ("Stickeen" 26). Robert L. Dorman similarly observes that "Muir hagiographers are sometimes puzzled by this interregnum of domesticity and conventionality" in Muir's life, suggesting instead that the 1880s merely represent the surfacing of several conventional Victorian elements Muir had always embodied. "Many habits of the Victorian mind, Muir's Victorian mind — his secularized Christian worldview, his belief in evolutionary progress, his faith in objective science, his genteel aesthetic and literary tastes — were to guide him in the wilderness and allow him to interpret it for a mainstream audience who read him avidly because they shared these comfortable assumptions," Dorman claims (111–12). Another critic, Harold Simonson, argues that Muir's later years tempered his early romanticism. The "purity" of the mountains, Muir realized, could no more provide salvation than could the "sickness" of the lowlands. In fact, Muir discovered that the lowlands offered him the opportunity for experiencing the fullness of human experience: social and political service, a happy family life, a successful career, and many rich friendships (238). As Simonson puts it, "[t]o turn away from human society in hopes of achieving spiritual purity denied the claims of time and place and denied as well the need for human love. . . . In wildness the soul comes to know a certain weariness that the lowlands, for all their ills, can alleviate" (239). Linnie Marsh Wolfe, Muir's early biographer, sums up the contributions of these "lost years" of Muir's life by noting that "when one considers the great work of the ensuing quarter century, during which, largely owing to his leadership, the national park and forest reserve systems were established in America, it is apparent that the six or seven years of withdrawal contributed their necessary share to the pattern and purpose of his life. For it was then he learned to live and work with men and women, and to understand and utilize social institutions. When he emerged in 1889, to take up his public work, he was no longer 'an unknown nobody in the woods,' but a shrewd, practical man of the world, and a lover of his fellow man" (*John* xiv).

The Sierra Club

Although Muir did lower his profile considerably during the 1880s, he did not disappear completely, nor did his conservation work during the subsequent decades emerge without precedent. As early as 19 September 1873, for instance, Muir was making connections in his journal between conservation and public policy, declaring that "[n]ine-tenths of the whole surface of the Sierra has been swept by the scourge [of sheep]. It demands legislative interference" (L. Wolfe, *John* 174). In August 1875 the wholesale destruction of plants and trees in the Sierra led Muir to speculate further in his journal about the future of the mountains he loved: "I often wonder what man will do with the mountains — that is, with their utilizable, destructible garments. Will he cut down all the trees to make ships and houses? If so, what will be the final and far upshot? Will human destructions like those of Nature — fire and flood and avalanche — work out a higher good, a finer beauty? Will a better civilization come in accord with obvious nature, and all this wild beauty be set to poetry and song? Another universal outpouring of lava, or the coming of a glacial period, could scarce wipe out the flowers and shrubs more effectively than do the sheep. And what then is coming? What is the human part of the mountains' destiny?" (L. Wolfe, *John* 215).

Muir decided it was time to ask such questions publicly six months later, when he published his first protest of forest destruction — an article entitled "God's First Temples" — in the *Sacramento Daily Union* on 5 February 1876. He took the main part of his title from William Cullen Bryant's "Forest Hymn," and in his subtitle asked his readers, "How Shall We Preserve Our Forests?" Using the sequoia as a case study, Muir offered a two-part answer: first, the government must survey the forests and the forces acting upon them; second, it must pass and enforce protective legislation based on the results of this survey. As informed as anyone about California's forests, Muir helped draft legislation for this purpose in 1881: a bill to enlarge the state park that contained Yosemite and the Mariposa Grove, and another to preserve the Kings River region of the southern Sierra. Although neither bill got past the Senate Public Lands Committee, Muir remained undaunted, later urging in *Picturesque California* (1888) that the Mount Shasta region of the state be made a national park "for the welfare and benefit of all mankind, preserving its fountains and forests and all its glad life in primeval beauty" (L. Wolfe, *Son* 227–28, 239). In the years that followed, Muir became much more actively involved with the preservation of wilderness through its designation as a "park," and the domesticating influence of civilization served him well. Though never fully at ease with the twentieth-century notion of tourism, Muir eventually came to appreciate — as did the Sierra Club he founded — that wilderness protection could not occur without "park" status, and that "park" status could not occur without tourism.

Yosemite National Park

For Muir, of course, the consummate "park" was Yosemite National Park, established in 1890 thanks in part to the combined efforts of Muir and Robert Underwood Johnson, associate editor of the prestigious *Century* magazine, the successor to *Scribner's*, in which Muir had published a popular series of articles in the late 1870s and early 1880s. After Muir ceased journal publication in the 1880s, Johnson had continued to correspond with him, hoping to encourage Muir once again to pick up his pen. "Have you abandoned literature altogether?" Johnson asked him on one occasion. "Has the ink in your fountain entirely dried up? . . . Have you put your hand to the plow, and then turned back?" (L. Wolfe, *Son* 232). Not receiving the response he wanted, Johnson arranged to meet Muir during a visit he made to California in the spring of 1889. This time, Johnson had better luck. "My great discovery here is John Muir," he wrote home (Fox, *John Muir* 87).

Encouraged by their initial conversations, Johnson agreed to accompany Muir on a trip to Yosemite and the High Sierra in early June 1889. What he saw in the mountains both impressed him and motivated him to act. "[O]ne does not know trees till he has visited California," Johnson wrote in his memoir, *Remembered Yesterdays* (1923). "The imagination is staggered in the endeavor to realize the antiquity of these primeval structures, that have grown with the centuried growth of the human race while dynasties have risen and fallen" (280).[45] After visiting the big trees, the men traveled into the valley itself and up into the higher mountains. Unlike Muir, Johnson was no seasoned outdoorsman, and he soon found himself the butt of Muir's jokes when he floundered in a manzanita thicket. Once the two returned to camp, however, Muir revealed his domestic side, showering Johnson with "little attentions" and tucking him into bed "with the tenderness that he gave to children and animals," as Johnson recalled (283–84).

During their time in the mountains, Johnson noted the absence of meadows, about which Muir had written so eloquently, and Muir attributed their loss to the presence of sheep — "hooved locusts," Muir called them — who not only ate all the plants but also dug up most of their roots "so that nothing but barrenness was left," as Johnson described the scene. Furthermore, Muir explained that because the state park did not include the headwaters of the streams that fed the three great falls — the Yosemite, the Nevada, and the Bridal Veil — the sheep were free to graze these lands, resulting in torrential floods each spring when the snowpack melted, and also in the reduction of the waterfalls to comparative trickles each summer. "Obviously the thing to do is to make a Yosemite National Park around the Valley on the plan of Yellowstone," Johnson recalls telling Muir beside the campfire at Soda Springs (*Remembered* 287).[46]

Muir had no doubt considered and dismissed such a possibility before, and he at first expressed his skepticism of the plan. But Johnson's enthusiasm, as well as his influence as editor of one of the most respected journals of the day, eventually won Muir over. Muir agreed to prepare a map of the region and write two articles for the *Century*: one on the treasures of the Yosemite ("to attract general attention," as Johnson explained), the other on the features of the proposed Yosemite National Park (*Remembered* 288). Knowing the high social and editorial standards of the *Century*, and aware of its two hundred thousand subscribers, Muir may well have thought that perhaps the time had finally come for Yosemite to get the protection it deserved (Mott 3:475).

"The love of Nature among Californians is desperately moderate; consuming enthusiasm almost wholly unknown," Muir wrote Johnson on 4 March 1890 as he was preparing his articles for publication ("Creation of Yosemite" 52). As Muir's comment suggests, westerners in the late nineteenth century were less interested in the preservation of the land than in how they might best put that land to economic use. Muir knew that for his plan to succeed he would need to craft aesthetic arguments for the park and direct them toward an eastern audience; park preservation would need to go hand in hand with its development as a tourist attraction. Of course, as Michael P. Cohen points out, "Muir's idea of a Yosemite national park was essentially ecological, since it began with the preservation of the complete watersheds of the Merced and Tuolumne rivers" (*Sierra* 6). Muir may even have been influenced by George Perkins Marsh, whose *Man and Nature* (1864) "urged care of the nation's mountainside forests in the interest of regulating the hydrologic cycle and preventing the lowlands from becoming deserts" (Nash, *Rights* 40). Yet even this ecological aspect of Muir's proposal fell under the influence of Muir's aesthetics. "As I have urged over and over again, the Yosemite Reservation ought to include all the Yosemite fountains," Muir explained to Johnson in an 8 May 1890 letter. "They all lie in a compact mass of mountains that are glorious scenery, easily accessible from the grand Yosemite centre, and are not valuable for any other use than the use of beauty" ("Creation of Yosemite" 58).

In embracing his aesthetic argument wholeheartedly, Muir understood the needs and desires of his audience. As Christine Oravec has noted, Muir succeeded in his *Century* articles in "transforming his readers' imaginative experience of scenic grandeur into an obligation to support preservationist legislation" (246). "The Treasures of the Yosemite," Muir's first article for the *Century*, appeared in August 1890 as part of the magazine's "Midsummer Holiday Issue" and is to many critics one of the finest essays Muir ever wrote (Kimes and Kimes 73). Based in part on the notes and journals from Muir's first summer in the Sierra, "Treasures" focused on Yosemite's watershed and included vivid pictures of the valley's devastation from farming and timber-cutting. Although the bulk of the essay detailed the ways in which "into this one mountain mansion Nature had gathered her choicest treasures" (485), Muir also noted that "[s]teps are now being taken towards the creation of a national park about the Yosemite" and that, because "the branching cañons and valleys of the basins of the streams that pour into Yosemite are as closely related to it as are the fingers to the palm of the hand," the entire region above Yosemite should be included in the park (487–88). "Features of the Proposed Yosemite National Park," which followed in September, was more practical. While its illustrations and most of its text depicted the beauty of the region, the essay closed with an appeal to the tourist, warning that "[u]nless reserved or protected, the whole region will soon or late be devastated by lumbermen and sheepmen, and so of course made unfit for use as a pleasure ground" (667).

Among his eastern readership, Muir had two specific audiences in mind: general readers and congressional legislators. He reached the first group with little trouble. "Everyone has been so delighted to find Mr. Muir again in print," a woman from Washington wrote Louie on 31 December 1890. "I hope that you will keep him to it" (Fox, *John Muir* 106). As for the second group, the articles seem to have appeared just in time.

On 18 March 1890, after some preliminary editorializing in the *Century* by Johnson, Representative William Vandever of Los Angeles introduced a bill for the establishment of a national park out of the government-held territory still surrounding the state grant. Unfortunately, Vandever's plan for the park encompassed only 230 square miles of new land — as opposed to Muir's proposed 1,500 — and it excluded Lake Tenaya and the Tuolumne River watershed. Familiar with the ways of Washington from his two successful years of lobbying for an international copyright law in the late 1880s, Johnson knew what it would take to get an alternative bill through Congress. To start, he rallied support for the idea among influential friends, such as John W. Noble, secretary of the interior, and Frederick Law Olmsted, who voiced his approval for Muir's plan in an open letter that appeared in several newspapers. Johnson then presented an alternate proposal to the House Public Lands Committee on 2 June 1890, quoting from Muir's forthcoming articles and displaying photographs of the region. Muir's articles, when they appeared in August and September, seem to have had the desired effect, because a substitute bill authorizing a preserve of 1,512 square miles was introduced that September and passed through both houses of Congress on the last day of the first session. The preserve it outlined — five times larger than that contained in the original bill — followed almost exactly the lines first proposed by Muir. With the signature of President Benjamin Harrison, the bill became law on 1 October 1890 (Jones, *John Muir* 43–47).

The credit for this legislative victory, however, may need to be shared with Daniel K. Zumwalt, a friend of Representative Vandever and a land agent for the Southern Pacific Railroad in the San Joaquin Valley. Though the full truth may never be known, Zumwalt was in Washington at the time and recognized the value of the park for the railroad — not only as a potential tourist destination but also as a means of protecting the watershed of California's Central Valley, upon whose farmers the Southern Pacific relied for business. According to historian Richard J. Orsi, Zumwalt seems to have been the invisible hand behind the expanded bill, introducing the amended legislation through Vandever, lobbying door-to-door for its approval, and orchestrating its passage in the last-minute legislative scramble (147–48). "Even the soulless Southern Pacific R. R. Co., never counted on for anything good, helped nobly in pushing the bill for this park through Congress," Muir later noted at an 1895 Sierra Club meeting ("National Parks" 275).

"The Church . . . That Muir Built"

That he could not protect the Yosemite single-handedly may have been the most important lesson Muir learned in the fight to establish Yosemite National Park. Johnson recognized this point early on, suggesting in a 21 November 1889 letter to Muir that he start "an association for preserving California's monuments and natural wonders — or at least Yosemite" (Fox, *John Muir* 106; L. Wolfe, *Son* 254). As with Johnson's plan for the park, Muir was skeptical at first, replying on 6 December: "I would gladly do anything in my power to preserve Nature's sayings and doings here or elsewhere but have no genius for managing societies" (Fox, *John Muir* 106). Despite Muir's initial apprehension, Johnson kept the idea alive, writing in 1891 to George Bird Grinnell, Arnold Hague, and others, asking whether they would be interested in the formation of a Yellowstone and Yosemite Defense Association. Not surprisingly, Grinnell replied on 6 May that the Boone and Crockett Club might be able to function as exactly the kind of association Johnson had in mind. Hague, though, disagreed, replying to Johnson on 5 June that the Boone and Crockett Club would function best if its focus was limited to the Rockies. "Those especially interested in the Yosemite Park could form an association having for its object the maintenance of the California parks," wrote Hague. "When necessary, this latter association could unite with the Boone and Crockett Club in any work in which they were both interested. Many members might belong to both clubs" (Jones, *John Muir* 8).

While Johnson was testing the waters for a defense association, several Californians were contemplating the formation of another kind of association: a mountaineering club, whose members would gather to explore the upper reaches of the Sierra Nevada. Similar organizations had been formed elsewhere in the previous three decades, including the Little Alpine Club in Williamstown, Massachusetts, in 1863; the White Mountain Club in Portland, Maine, in 1873; the Rocky Mountain Club in Colorado Springs in 1875; the Appalachian Mountain Club in Boston in 1876; and the Oregon Alpine Club in 1887 (Jones, *John Muir* 4). Muir had been in contact with William D. Armes, an English professor at the University of California at Berkeley, as early as 1890 about the formation of such a club, and the name "Sierra Club" had been proposed for the association. Philology professor J. Henry Senger, also of Berkeley, had similarly contacted Muir, who replied, "I am greatly interested in the formation of an Alpine Club. I think . . . the time has come when such an club should be organized. You may count on me as a member and as willing to do all in my power to further the interests of such a Club" (Jones, *John Muir* 9).

Out of these parallel discussions about both a Yosemite defense association and a mountaineering club, the Sierra Club emerged on 28 May 1892, when an organizational meeting was held in the San Francisco office of Attorney Warren Olney. The next month, on 4 June, the club was legally incorporated in Olney's office. Twenty-seven men, all from northern California, were in attendance, and Muir was unanimously elected president (Jones, *John Muir* 9). The articles of association, written by Olney, outlined the club's mission, which reflected the variety of scientific, educational, developmental, and recreational goals its membership embraced: "To explore, enjoy and render accessible the mountain regions of the Pacific Coast; to publish authentic information concerning them; [and] to enlist the support and co-operation of the people and the government in preserving the forests and other natural features of the Sierra Nevada Mountains" (Jones, *John Muir* 173).[47] Samuel Merrill, who had been staying at the Muir ranch in the summer of 1892, recalled in 1928 the day "when Mr. Muir returned from San Francisco and announced to us all at the supper-table that the Sierra Club had been organized and that he had been chosen its first president. I had never seen Mr. Muir so animated and happy before. . . . [I]t was not Muir's success as an author, or the honors that were conferred upon him in this country and abroad, that gave him the keenest pleasure, but the happiest day in his life, I venture to say, was the day in San Francisco in the summer of 1892, when he found himself the center of a devoted and loyal group of citizens who organized themselves into the Sierra Club and made him president" (29–30). Fifty-four years old when the Sierra Club was founded, Muir remained its president for twenty-two years until his death in 1914, leading Donald Worster to describe the Sierra Club as "the church . . . that Muir built" (*Wealth* 191).

In *Wilderness as Sacred Space* (1976) Linda H. Graber points out that "Muir's glorification of Yosemite fell on fertile soil in the San Francisco of the 1880's and 1890's" (23), and the success Muir achieved in attracting new members to the Sierra Club certainly supports this claim. By October 1892 the club boasted 182 charter members, but membership quickly rose to 283 in 1893; 350 in 1897; 480 in

1900; 663 in 1903; and 1,000 in 1908 (M. Cohen, *History* 9; Jones, *John Muir* 10, 20; T. Turner, *Sierra* 276). Two factors unique to fin-de-siècle California helped make such gains in membership possible. First, San Francisco contained a large number of native New England families, such as Ezra and Jeanne Carr, who never lost their eastern reverence for wilderness. As John Brinckerhoff Jackson observes in *American Space* (1972), "[w]ithin a hundred mile radius of San Francisco a transplanted East had evolved. . . . Whatever educated circles in the East thought and did, educated circles in the Bay Region were prompt to think and do" (182). Second, the same large-scale agricultural production that helped bring about the establishment of Yosemite National Park (and that helped John Muir achieve financial independence) also helped create a dualistic perception of landscape in California, in which Muir himself shared. With the rural spaces of the Central Valley given over solely to wheat production, as Jackson explains, "[d]isdain for the dull workaday utilitarian countryside . . . became characteristic of a peculiarly California environmental philosophy: a philosophy which to this day persists in seeing two, and only two, significant aspects of the world: the city and the wilderness" (194).[48] It should come as no surprise, therefore, that a list of the charter members of the Sierra Club is dominated by city dwellers — "almost a *Who's Who* of the San Francisco region in 1892," as Harold Gilliam points out (xx). It includes such figures as Charles F. Crocker, builder of the Southern Pacific railroad; William T. Coleman, leader of the Vigilance Committee of 1856; George Davidson, pioneer scientist; William Hammond Hall, founder of Golden Gate Park, and California's first state engineer; William Keith, landscape artist; David Starr Jordan, president of Stanford; and Adolph Sutro, the city's mayor.

It wasn't long before the resolve of this new organization was put to the test by the first of many attacks on the boundaries of Yosemite National Park. Although the language of the 1890 park bill declared Yosemite to be "reserved forest lands," Secretary of the Interior John W. Noble decided to manage Yosemite as a park, prohibiting grazing and tree-cutting and putting the U.S. cavalry in charge of enforcing park regulations, as was also being done in Yellowstone. In an 1895 *Century* forum, "Forest Preservation by Military Control," Muir extolled "[t]he effectiveness of the War Department in enforcing the laws of Congress. . . . The sheep having been rigidly excluded, a luxuriant cover has sprung up on the desolate forest floor, fires have been choked before they could do any damage, and hopeful bloom and beauty have taken the place of ashes and dust. . . . [O]ne soldier in the woods, armed with authority and a gun, would be more effective in forest preservation than millions of forbidding notices" (Letter 631).[49]

Not everyone, however, was happy with this state of affairs, and U.S. representative Anthony Caminetti found himself under increasing pressure to return the park to its previous state. His district included the counties surrounding Yosemite, and his constituents included the cattle, sheep, and timber interests whose local forests and grazing lands were withdrawn from the public domain when the park was created. At the same time as the Sierra Club was being formed, its organizers learned that Caminetti had introduced a bill in Congress to reduce the area of the park by nearly half, and the new club swung into action (Jones, *John Muir* 11–12).

At the club's second general meeting, held on 14 October 1892, Henry Senger explained the provisions of the bill to the more than five hundred people in attendance — most of whom had come to hear John Wesley Powell, director of the U.S. Geological Survey, recount his 1869 and 1871 expeditions through the Grand Canyon. Three weeks after Powell's lecture, the officers called a special meeting to organize opposition to the Caminetti bill. They drafted a resolution in protest and began a letter-writing campaign to the House Committee on Agriculture, to which the bill had been referred. Muir, meanwhile, sent telegrams to legislators and gave newspaper interviews that were reprinted in the eastern press (Jones, *John Muir* 12–15; F. Turner, *Rediscovering* 292; L. Wolfe, *Son* 255). Although the bill eventually died in committee — to the great relief of club leaders — the fight against it nevertheless brought to the foreground the question of exactly what a "national park" should be. As Michael L. Smith observes, in the absence of a working definition of a "park," club leaders were forced to formulate one of their own. Over the next few years, Smith argues, they came to realize that in a park, "human alteration of the landscape should be minimized. . . . A park, unlike any other variety of American landscape, should be exempt from commerce" (153).

The Mountains of California

As Donald Worster's comment about the Sierra Club being "the church . . . that Muir built" suggests, Muir has come to occupy an increasingly prominent place in the history of environmentalism. It is not always clear, however, whether Muir deserves more credit for his work as a writer or for his contributions as an activist. Herbert F. Smith, writing in 1965, claimed that "Muir exists primarily as a person, and it is as a folk hero, as a historic figure, as a remarkable manifestation of one element of what we like to consider as the American character that he has been studied" (7). Linda H. Graber, writing a decade later in 1976, argued in contrast that Muir "is better remembered today as a nature writer than as a scientist or as a political activist" (68). Both these comments point to the difficulty of evaluating the elements of Muir's legacy in isolation from one another, so tightly were they woven together in life. As Muir himself wrote in *My First Summer*, "[w]hen we try to pick out anything by itself, we find it hitched to everything else in the universe" (*NW* 245).

The question of Muir's legacy becomes particularly relevant following the 1894 publication of *The Mountains of California*, Muir's first book-length work, issued when he was fifty-six. The appearance of this volume is notable in part because the reviews that accompanied it almost all stressed the self-effacing aspects of Muir's prose. The reviewer for the *Nation*, for instance, claimed in 1894 that "Mr. Muir never poses like Thoreau, whom he otherwise resembles in his worship of nature and intimacy with wild animals; he keeps his personality in the background, nor does he, like Thoreau, constantly drag in human analogies, and moralizings on man and his ways. The beauties and sublimities of the California mountains have for him such an absorbing fascination that man is crowded out, and even the writer disappears from sight. We have here nature pure and unadulterated" ("Mountain Enthusiast" 366). Alice Morse Earle writing the next year in the *Dial*, similarly observed that "[t]he book is wholly self-forgetful, — in that respect a keen contrast to the self-conscious nature-studies of Thoreau. It is almost man-forgetful" (77). Although Earle was obviously influenced by the reviewer for the *Nation*, her decision to emphasize this aspect of Muir's writing in her own review indicates the willingness with which she, too, could assent to such an evaluation. The reviewer for the *Critic* also chose to stress the evasiveness of Muir's presence in *Mountains*: "He has lived so long amid the mysteries and splendors of the lakes, cañons and peaks that he seems to have become part of the landscape itself, while yet maintaining his unique personality" ("Book of Nature" 4).[50]

What role did Muir's "unique personality" have in *The Mountains of California* and in the conservation work of the Sierra Club during the next decade? To begin with, it is important to note that *The Mountains of California* was less a creation of the 1890s than it was a portrait of Muir in the late 1870s and early 1880s, when the articles upon which the volume is based were first published in *Scribner's*. Nevertheless, Muir worked hard during the early 1890s to tighten and polish these essays and assemble them into a book of which he could be proud. In a letter to Johnson, who was coordinating the book's publication for the *Century*, Muir wrote: "I have worked hard . . . adding lots of new stuff, and killing adjectives and adverbs of redundant growth — the *verys*, *intenses*, *gloriouses*, *ands*, and *buts*, by the score" (Badè 2:287). Muir's effort was repaid richly, as the book sold out of its first printing in a few months and went on to sell about ten thousand copies total (Fox, *John Muir* 117).

That Thomas J. Lyon has described *The Mountains of California* as Muir's "most carefully written yet ecologically revolutionary book" (*John Muir* 43) and Michael P. Cohen has said that *Mountains* "became the Sierra Club's chief text, a political book" (*Pathless* 284) suggests that Muir's dual persona as a writer and an activist were connected most visibly by his *ecological vision*, to which the comments of Muir's reviewers were able to allude but never identify. On the one hand, this ecological vision could be seen as strictly scientific, as is evident in his articles on the "treasures" and "features" of the Yosemite, with their emphasis on watersheds. On the other hand, Muir's ability to see connectedness and relationships also had humanistic implications — namely, the diminution of the human figure from the heroic to the commonplace or, to put it in the words of Aldo Leopold, "from conqueror of the land-community to plain member and citizen of it" (*Sand County* 204). For Muir, of course, such a seeming "reduction" in human status was nothing of the sort; if all creation was sacred, then humankind shared in that sacred status, no worse off than any other plant or animal, though no more privileged either. Muir may best have expressed this state of affairs in the final sentence of an earlier essay, "Twenty Hill Hollow," which first appeared in the *Overland Monthly* in July 1872 and which William Badè included as the last chapter of Muir's *Thousand-Mile Walk to the Gulf:* "You cannot feel yourself out of doors; plain, sky, and mountains ray beauty which you feel. You bathe in these spirit-beams, turning round and round, as if warming at a camp-fire. Presently you lose consciousness of your own separate existence: you blend with the landscape, and become part and parcel of nature" (*Thousand-Mile Walk* 120).[51]

More than any other of Muir's works, however, *The Mountains of California* illustrates the problematic nature of representing such connectedness in prose. In attempting to avoid what Donald Wesling has called the danger of "hectoring the reader into a moral response" (42), Muir instead chose to act as a learned tour guide, developing a persona that he hoped "would establish a human perspective upon the complexity of nature and ground his descriptions in scientific fact" (Oravec 250). Like Roosevelt before him, and even more strongly like Abbey after him, Muir was thus forced to become the protagonist of his own adventures, a role not always compatible with the ecological vision he wished to convey. In his study of narrative in American nature writing, Randall Roorda has effectively described the tension such a role embodied, noting that "in recognizing the writer *as* a protagonist, we are posed in dramatic contradistinction to the writer; we both 'move through [the landscape] with' and come up against that writer. . . . Thus we enthuse with a writer like Muir, through his eyes; but part of us gapes at him, too, as at a spectacle; and there is drama in this encounter" (*Dramas* 18).[52] As a collection of Muir's *Scribner's* articles, *The Mountains of California* functions as a kind of anthology of such moments, the best known of which are Muir's ascent of Mount Ritter in "A Near View of the High Sierra" (chap. 4) and his climbing of a Douglas spruce in "A Wind-Storm in the Forests" (chap. 10). In *Mountains* Muir was able to transcribe the oral narratives for which he had become legendary among his circle of listeners and offer them to a wider audience of readers, crafting in the process a literary persona — "John o' the Mountains" — through which readers could vicariously experience the mountains without ever leaving their armchairs.[53] The result, for many readers, was equivalent to the reaction of Muir's friends whenever the mountaineer came down from his Sierra rambles. "We almost thought he was Jesus Christ," the artist William Keith told William Colby. "We fairly worshipped him!" (L. Wolfe, *John* 154).

Muir's role as a tour guide in *The Mountains of California* took on a quite literal status in 1901 with the beginning of the Sierra Club's outing program, still in existence today (see page 147). An early indication of just how far Muir had traveled since his solo mountaineering days came during the first official annual meeting of the club, held on 23 November 1895, at which Muir was asked to deliver a speech on the national parks and forest reservations. Said Muir: "It is encouraging to learn that so many of the young men and women growing up in California are going to the mountains every summer and becoming good mountaineers, and, of course, good defenders of the Sierra forests and of all the reviving beauty that belongs to them. For every one that I found mountaineering back of Yosemite in the High Sierra, ten years ago, I this year met more than a hundred. Many of these young mountaineers were girls, in parties of ten or fifteen, making bright pictures as they tramped merrily along through the forest aisles, with the sparkle and exhilaration of the mountains in their eyes — a fine, hopeful sign of the times" ("National Parks" 280). Clearly, this was a father of daughters speaking! And it was during this speech that Muir delivered what has become the unofficial motto of the outings program: "Few are altogether deaf to the preaching of pine-trees. Their sermons on the mountains go to our hearts; and if people in general could be got into the woods, even for once, to hear the trees speak for themselves, all difficulties in the way of forest protection would vanish" ("National Parks" 282–83).

Just prior to the first annual meeting, Muir lamented in his journal (24 June 1895) that "[t]he club seems to be losing ground," and on 28 December 1898 he wrote T. P. Lukens that "[o]ur Sierra Club seems half dead" (Fox, *John Muir* 119). Two other mountaineering clubs — the Appalachian Mountain Club and the Mazamas of Oregon (formed in 1894) — had run outings before 1901, but not until William Colby joined the Sierra Club did it began its own outings program.[54] "It was from John Muir . . . that I received the warmest encouragement," Colby wrote in a memoir of his years with the club. "He was highly enthusiastic, and told me that he had long been trying to get the Club to undertake just such outings" ("Twenty-Nine Years" 2). The first of these annual outings took place in Yosemite National Park's Tuolumne Meadows in the summer of 1901. Ninety-six men and women attended, including — notably — both Muir's daughters. During the day, individuals and groups hiked to various parts of the High Sierra, and at night they returned to the base camps, where supply wagons, mule trains, and full-time chefs provided the necessary food and equipment. Muir and faculty members from Berkeley and Stanford gave campfire lectures on natural history, including talks by William R. Dudley on forestry, C. Hart Merriam on birds and animals, and

John Muir and Sierra Club group on the trail to Hetch Hetchy, 1909.
Note the large number of female hikers. (Courtesy John Muir Papers,
Holt-Atherton Special Collections, University of the Pacific Libraries,
© 1984 Muir-Hanna Trust)

Theodore Hittle on the history of Yosemite (Demars 75). Furthermore, Colby recommended that the participants read Muir's *Mountains of California* beforehand,
along with Joseph LeConte's *Ramblings through the High Sierra* (Colby, "Proposed" 253). "The Club outing is a great success," Muir wrote Louie on 20 July
1901. "God's ozone sparkles in every eye. I never before saw so big and merry a
camp circle, a huge fire blazing in the center. I had, of course, to make a little
speech" (Fox, *John Muir* 120).

In his proposal for this first outing, Colby had declared that "[a]n excursion of
this sort, if properly conducted will do an infinite amount of good toward awakening the proper kind of interest in the forests and other natural features of our
mountains, and will also tend to create a spirit of good-fellowship among our
members" ("Proposed" 250). Such seems to have been the case, as fifty new club
members resulted from the first outing, and roughly two hundred had joined by
the following summer (Strong 1:13). The persona for which Muir had become well
known by this time had more than a little to do with this surge in membership. As
Colby told Muir when he began planning the following year's outing, "[t]hey all
ask, the first thing, if you are going to be with us'" (Fox, *John Muir* 120).

Our National Parks

"[H]ow many of us know that there are now in the United States five great national parks and thirty-eight reservations, most of them easily accessible?" asked
the *Nation* in its review of *Our National Parks*, published shortly after the conclusion of the first Sierra Club outing (294). Following the establishment of
Yellowstone and Yosemite, three other national parks — Sequoia (1890), General
Grant (1890), and Mount Rainier (1899) — had been formed, along with the thirty-
eight forest reserves — the predecessors to today's national forests — mentioned by
the *Nation*'s reviewer. *Our National Parks* (1901), which went through a dozen
printings in six years, is Muir's attempt to wrestle with the emerging distinction between these two cultural definitions of "nature" (Fox, *John Muir* 117).

Concerns about the nation's dwindling resources following the census report of
1890 led Congress in March 1891 to create the federal forest reserve system, giving
the president the power to withdraw areas from the public domain to create forest
reservations.[55] The act creating the forest reserves, however, said nothing about
"what specifically the new reserves would be for, how they were to be protected,
or how many in the future might be created," as Frederick Turner has noted (*Rediscovering* 307). To begin to answer these questions, in 1896 Congress funded a
Forestry Commission, under the direction of the National Academy of Sciences,
on which Muir was asked to serve in an ex officio capacity. Although the commission as a whole agreed about the necessity for federal protection of the forests, its

individual members — Charles S. Sargent (chairman), Gifford Pinchot (secretary), Henry L. Abbot, Alexander Agassiz, William H. Brewer, Arnold Hague, and Wolcott Gibbs — disagreed sharply about the character and method of that protection. As a result, their final report was a compromise document reflecting the interests of both factions: those favoring utilitarian conservation of the forests (Pinchot) and those favoring a stricter kind of preservation (Muir and Sargent), in which logging, grazing, and mining would be prohibited as in the national parks.

Of the ten essays that compose *Our National Parks,* two in particular illustrate Muir's attempt to publicize his preservationist vision for the national forests. Like *The Mountains of California, Our National Parks* collects essays Muir had originally published in a national periodical — not *Scribner's* this time, due to Muir's dissatisfaction with Johnson's editing of his work, but the *Atlantic,* in whose pages they appeared from 1897 to 1901. "The Wild Parks and Forests Reservations of the West," the opening essay in the book, first appeared in the *Atlantic* in January 1898, and "The American Forests," the closing essay, a few months earlier in August 1897. Sandwiched between these two essays are eight chapters on four of the national parks — six on Yosemite, one on Yellowstone, and one on Sequoia and General Grant — but it is only in the context of the two surrounding forestry essays that Muir's discussion of the parks can fully be understood.[56]

Two divergent threads of Muir's philosophy — conservation and tourism — come together in the framing essays of *Our National Parks.* On the one hand the book is Muir's most explicitly conservationist work, a point stressed by the *Dial* in its review. "No one has done more to draw the attention of the public to the desirability and necessity of forest preservation than Mr. John Muir," and *Our National Parks* "embodies some of his most trenchant appeals for public interest and legislative action" (rev. of *Our National Parks* [1902], 163).[57] On the other hand, the book also contains some of Muir's strongest statements about the value of tourism, a fact recognized by an anonymous reader in New York, who wrote to Muir on 10 August 1903: "This is the first of your published works I have met, and being of stern necessity tied up to an office business, with the hills and streams out of sight and the love of them strong in me, imagining the delight of seeing the Sierras, of breathing the fine clean air, of making acquaintance with those blessed trees of yours . . . ah, it is a treat, a vacation more enjoyed than many" (Fox, *John Muir* 117). If government action would not preserve the forests, Muir reasoned, then perhaps tourism would; perhaps getting people into the forests would demonstrate to them that nature was indeed a utilitarian resource — though one for spiritual, not consumptive purposes.[58]

When "The Wild Parks and Forests Reservations of the West" originally appeared in the *Atlantic,* the magazine's editor reported that the article increased the magazine's circulation "enormously" (L. Wolfe, *Son* 277). It is easy to see why this was the case. "Wild Parks" not only offered readers a whirlwind tour of western America but also validated whatever desires they may have had to see these spaces for themselves. "The tendency nowadays to wander in wildernesses is delightful to see," Muir announced at the beginning of his essay. Then, turning again to his own version of Thoreau's "unlimited contradiction," he noted that "[t]housands of tired, nerve-shaken, over-civilized people are beginning to find out that going to the mountains is going home; that wildness is a necessity; and that mountain parks and reservations are useful not only as fountains of timber and irrigating rivers but as fountains of life" (1). Whereas such a statement was perfectly in keeping with the Muir of the 1870s, his subsequent extension of this thought would hardly have been thinkable thirty years earlier. Certainly the younger Muir would have bristled at the notion that "[e]ven the scenery habit in its most artificial forms, mixed with spectacles, silliness, and kodaks; its devotees arrayed more gorgeously than scarlet tanagers, frightening the wild game with red umbrellas — even this is encouraging, and may well be regarded as a hopeful sign of the times" (2). Yet the 1901 Muir even goes so far as to stress the "good roads" by which a visitor can reach the wilderness (2). Still, the older Muir does not hesitate to follow this statement with a description of the destruction caused to the nation's flora by several groups: farmers in the Central Valley of California, loggers and shepherds in the Sierra, and cattlemen in the southwestern deserts. Muir next takes his readers on a tour of the forest reserves, anticipating all the while their possible objections to his enthusiasm. "No American wilderness that I know of is so dangerous as a city home 'with all the modern improvements,'" he assures his audience. "One should go to the woods for safety, if for nothing else" (21). Finally, defining "parks" as "places for rest, inspiration, and prayers" (23), he argues for the transformation of many of the forest reserves he has surveyed into such parks, often using the "parklike" openings of such a reserve as the Grand Canyon to argue for its designation as an authorized "national park" (26).

"The American Forests" closes *Our National Parks* by providing a different perspective on the forests than that offered by "Wild Parks." Rather than taking readers around to the various forest reservations in the West, Muir celebrates the American forests generally, employing the metaphor of the "park-as-garden" to collapse the distinction he had been drawing between the forest reserves and the national parks. "The forests of America, however slighted by man, must have been a great delight to God; for they were the best he ever planted," Muir begins. "The whole continent was a garden, and from the beginning it seemed to be favored above all the other wild parks and gardens of the globe" (248). The survey of forests that follows is not geographical but historical, starting with the presettlement landscape ("American forests! the glory of the world!" [250]), turning to the arrival of the early settlers (who, "claiming Heaven as their guide, regarded God's trees as only a larger kind of pernicious weed" [251]), and concluding with a plea to stop the current destruction ("Clearing has surely now gone far enough; soon timber will be scarce, and not a grove will be left to rest in or pray in" [252]). With this historical background, Muir then turns to more practical matters, comparing American forestry practices to those in Prussia, France, Switzerland, Russia, Japan, and India, and cataloging the current U.S. timber laws and the destructive uses of the forest they have allowed. Finally, in what may be Muir's most powerful statement in support of government conservation, Muir closes his essay with the observation that "[a]ny fool can destroy trees. They cannot run away. . . . Through all the wonderful, eventful centuries since Christ's time — and long before that — God has cared for these trees, saved them from drought, disease, avalanches, and a thousand straining, leveling tempests and floods; but he cannot save them from fools — only Uncle Sam can do that" (272).

Recession

As the inclusion of six chapters on Yosemite in a book supposedly about "our national parks" suggests, Muir remained committed to publicizing the glories of the Yosemite above all other scenic wonders. Indeed, part of Muir's purpose in writing *Our National Parks* was to aid the cause of the recession of Yosemite Valley and the Mariposa Grove to the federal government. In "The American Forests," for instance, Muir notes that the Mariposa Grove is still managed by the state of California and can only be returned to the government "by gift or purchase," a transfer he quite clearly wishes to see occur (262–63). In fact, Muir had been wanting to see the recession of the state park ever since the creation of Yosemite National Park in 1890. Despite the provision of national park status to the lands surrounding the Yosemite Valley, the valley itself had remained in state hands, and had been poorly managed, throughout the 1890s. Summarizing the neglect of the valley under state control, Robert Underwood Johnson recalled how parts of the valley had been turned into hayfields for horses, trees had been indiscriminately cut to allow for a better view of Yosemite Falls from one of the hotels, and garbage dumps had been permitted to litter the valley floor. In addition, a proposal had even been made to shine colored lights upon the falls at night and to cut the underbrush on the valley floor so as to see clearly the approach of the stagecoach (R. Johnson, *Remembered* 289). Writing to Johnson on 4 March 1890, Muir employed a vivid domestic metaphor to explain the resistance of the state commissioners to return the valley to the federal government: "A man may not appreciate his wife, but let her daddie try to take her back!" ("Creation of Yosemite" 52).

Throughout the 1890s the Sierra Club remained divided over the issue of recession, with some of its members hesitant to criticize friends who sat on the

Yosemite commission, and others concerned that California would lose prestige over the transfer of lands. In addition, the same vested interests that had fought against the establishment of the national park—the loggers, sheep herders, and miners—also fought against recession. In 1903, however, Muir gained a strong ally in Theodore Roosevelt, who assured Muir after their camping trip that he would sign a recession bill if one arrived on his desk. Likewise, California governor George Pardee also favored recession; he not only promised to sign a recession bill, but he even had his staff help the Sierra Club plan their strategy to get such a bill through the state legislature (F. Turner, *Rediscovering* 330). Recession, in other words, was to be a two-step process: first California's legislators would need to approve the transfer of land, and then Congress would need to accept that transfer from the state.

In 1905 the movement finally gained momentum, as Californians inside and outside the Sierra Club began to realize not only that the valley was being poorly managed but also that Yosemite was becoming an economic liability (Jones, *John Muir* 63). Helped by William H. Mills, the chief land agent for the Southern Pacific Railroad, William Colby drafted a recession bill that was introduced in the state legislature in January 1905 (Colby, "Yosemite" 13; Jones, *John Muir* 67). Further aided in their lobbying efforts by William F. Herrin, the Southern Pacific's lead attorney in California, the Sierra Club began a letter and telegram campaign in support of the new bill (Colby, "Yosemite" 16). Notably, when Muir and Colby prepared the statement voicing the support of the Sierra Club for recession, they emphasized the benefits to tourism that recession would bring: "The result would be the improvement of the valley and National Park by the construction of the best of roads, bridges, and trails. Ample hotel accommodations of the best quality would be provided. A telephone system for the entire park to guard against forest fires would be inaugurated. The patrol system of the National Park would be rendered far more effective and the valley itself placed under the same system, so that perfect order would prevail, no matter how great the number of visitors. The toll road system would be abolished, and in all probability a splendid boulevard constructed up the Merced Canyon, which would reduce the time and expense of travel one half and greatly increase the comfort" (Muir et al., "Statement" 246). Printed as a leaflet, the statement was distributed to members of the California legislature just before the start of the January 1905 session (Jones, *John Muir* 65).

As with the 1890 designation of the land surrounding the valley as a national park, the Southern Pacific Railroad was a powerful force behind the movement for recession, as its involvement with the bill's introduction indicates. Muir had met the latest head of the railroad, industrialist Edward H. Harriman, on an 1889 expedition Harriman had sponsored to Alaska, and Muir did not hesitate to call upon the resources of his friend when he thought it could *"do some forest good,"* as he had written to Charles Sargent about his meeting with Roosevelt. So, in what Richard J. Orsi calls Muir's "partial rapprochement with modern industrial life" (141), Muir appealed to Harriman for assistance with the measure as early as 5 January 1905. Harriman, of course, knew that the Southern Pacific would benefit from recession, given that improvements to facilities in the valley would bring an increase in travel on its passenger service.[59] Thus while Muir and Colby made nine lobbying trips to Sacramento, they were also aided by Harriman, whose contacts in the state legislature helped bring about a successful California vote on 2 February 1905. "I am now an experienced lobbyist; my political education is complete," Muir wrote to Johnson on 24 February. "Have attended Legislature, made speeches, explained, exhorted, persuaded every mother's son of the legislators, newspaper reporters, and everybody else who would listen to me. And now that the fight is finished and my education as a politician and lobbyist is finished, I am almost finished myself. Now, ho! for righteous management" (Colby, "Yosemite" 18; Badè 2:356).

The final stage of recession victory came on 3 March 1906, when President Roosevelt signed the Senate joint resolution calling for the federal acceptance of the valley and an annual appropriation of twenty thousand dollars for its administration. On 11 June 1906 the Yosemite Valley formally became a part of the surrounding national park (F. Turner, *Rediscovering* 331). "Yes, my dear Johnson, sound the loud timbrel and let every Yosemite tree and stream rejoice!" Muir wrote to his friend on 16 July 1906. "You may be sure I knew when the big bill passed. Getting Congress to accept the Valley brought on, strange to say, a desperate fight both in the House and Senate. Sometime I'll tell you all the story. You don't know how accomplished a lobbyist I've become under your guidance. The fight you planned by that Tuolumne camp-fire seventeen years ago is at last fairly, gloriously won, every enemy down derry down" (Badè 2:357).

It was, to be sure, a bittersweet victory, though one understood fully only with the leisure of hindsight. For the Sierra Club, the success of the vote in California was offset by the achievement of the timber and mineral industries in redrawing the boundaries of the park. On 7 February 1905, only five days after the California assembly voted for recession, Congress removed 542 square miles from the park — land that contained timber and mineral claims — thus eliminating several townships on the corners of the park. Although Congress also extended the northern boundary to include 113 miles of mountainous terrain, with the goal of protecting the Tuolumne River watershed, the net loss of 429 square miles was especially troubling to the club, given that the territory being removed was to be placed in a forest reserve and effectively opened to development (Runte, *Yosemite* 74–76). To make matters worse, the final 1906 recession bill passed by Congress also included an amendment that reduced the park by yet another 16 square miles (Runte, *Yosemite* 86).

For Muir himself, the recession victory was tempered by the loss of his wife to lung cancer on 6 August 1905. Although Muir left no written memories of Louie, "her death marked a major transition in his life," according to Michael P. Cohen. "For several years he immersed himself in a study of the petrified forests of Arizona as a kind of consolation, and wrote about nothing" (Cohen, *Pathless* 341). It was, to be sure, the beginning of the end for Muir, and although the subsequent loss of the Hetch Hetchy Valley to San Francisco for a reservoir in 1913 appears to have hastened his final days, the death of his wife marked a clear turning point for him, after which he spent much of his time living in the past, working on the autobiographical manuscripts for *My First Summer in the Sierra* (1911), *The Story of My Boyhood and Youth* (1913), and the posthumously published *Travels in Alaska* (1915).

For the conservation movement as a whole, the recession of Yosemite Valley reflected the compromises that would increasingly become necessary for the preservation of the national parks — and no compromise better embodied this dilemma than the domestication of nature through tourism. As John A. Jakle writes, "The quest to protect nature inviolate provided much of the intellectual and emotional drive behind park development, but the tourist, as consumer, and as responsive citizen, provided the economic and political rationale needed to translate philosophy into accomplishment" (69). Muir certainly recognized this fact, and the older he grew, the more generous he became with tourists, eventually even accommodating himself to the idea of cars in Yosemite. In a 12 December 1912 letter to Howard Palmer, for instance, Muir noted that there was no use in trying to keep those "useful, progressive, blunt nosed mechanical beetles" out of Yosemite. "Good walkers can go anywhere in these hospitable mountains without artificial ways," Muir told Palmer, "but most visitors have to be rolled in on wheels with blankets and kitchen arrangements" (Badè 2:378–79). With the arrival of the automobile, and its portable domesticity, going to the mountains had truly become going home.

As his comments to Palmer indicate, Muir had strong reservations about the transformation of Yosemite into what David Louter has termed a "windshield wilderness," but he also recognized the positive effect automobile tourism could have on park preservation efforts. William Colby shared Muir's optimism with the second National Park Conference, held at Yosemite in October 1912, when he stated the Sierra Club's position on automobile tourists in national parks: "We hope they will be able to come in when the time comes, because we think the automobile adds great zest to travel and we are particularly interested in the increase of travel to these parks." For Yosemite, Colby added, the proper time was "very close at hand" (Lillard 31).[60] Muir and the Sierra Club, says David Louter, "embraced the automobile as a way to expand the political support of parks and meet utilitarian arguments with their own that auto tourism to national parks would promote economic growth. . . . Evidently, Muir saw automobiles the way Emerson saw trains. Cars seemed to present a lesser menace than grazing sheep in Yosemite or flooding one of its valleys" (257). Ironically, the political support Muir hoped those auto tourists would bring could not be marshaled in time to prevent the flooding of Hetch Hetchy Valley. In 1913, the same year Interior Secretary Franklin K. Lane lifted the ban on automobiles in Yosemite National Park, he also approved San Francisco's proposal to dam the valley for a reservoir (Louter 256).

A Mixed Legacy

In the John Muir Memorial Number of the *Sierra Club Bulletin*, published in 1916, Robert Underwood Johnson articulated his sense of Muir's legacy to the citizens of the United States: "Muir's public services were not merely scientific and literary. His countrymen owe him gratitude as the pioneer of our system of national parks. Before 1889 we had but one of any importance — the Yellowstone. Out of the fight which he led for the better care of the Yosemite by the State of California grew the demand for the extension of the system. To this many persons and organizations contributed, but Muir's writings and enthusiasm were the chief forces that inspired the movement. All the other torches were lighted from his" ("John Muir" 12).

Nearly seventy-five years later, in April 1988, the *Los Angeles Times* published a lengthy analysis of what it titled "The Muir Mystique" in acknowledgment of the 150th anniversary of Muir's birth. The article's subtitle suggested how thoroughly Johnson's estimate of Muir's legacy had been accepted: "After 150 Years, the Naturalist Has Become Patron Saint to All Environmental Factions, but His Legacy Is Still in Dispute" (Sipchen 1). The dispute was not about the significance of Muir's legacy; that, according to writer Bob Sipchen, was "beyond dispute." Rather, the dispute was about which end of the environmental spectrum Muir would now be on. Was he a mainstream environmentalist or a radical? Would he still be a member of the Sierra Club or would he have joined Earth First!? These are certainly good questions, especially considering that Dave Foreman, one of the founders of Earth First! himself served on the Sierra Club Board of Directors in the 1990s.

What the article fails to acknowledge, however, were the problems inherent in Muir's notion of the national parks and the unintended consequences of his reconciliation with tourism. Like the idea of "wilderness" (explored at length in chap. 4), the idea of the "park" implies as much about "culture" as it does about "nature" — not only in its exclusion of the original inhabitants but also in its exclusion of *any* inhabitants whatsoever. "To say that Yosemite is Eden is to say that everywhere else is not," writes Rebecca Solnit. "'This place shall we set aside and protect' implies 'all other places shall we open up and use'" (246). To be fair, the protection of certain landscapes from industrial development is hardly such a black-and-white endeavor, and like development itself, it occurs in degrees. Many landscapes — including the national parks — involve a mixture of both, and developing some landscapes less intensively need not imply developing others that much more so.

If anything, the problem is not that the national parks have enabled the destruction of the rest of the landscape but that the national parks have never quite been as protected as we believed them to be. As David Robertson and many others note, Yosemite's "very popularity may be its undoing. The conveniences we require, whether trail and tent or highway and motel, are taming the valley. In fact, domestication has proceeded so far by the early 1980s that the status of Yosemite as wilderness is seriously questioned" (xvi). In the early 1990s Solnit herself visited Yosemite repeatedly, and her account of those experiences may best summarize the unintended consequences of Muir's advocacy for the park. "In a lot of ways, it wasn't a great place to go see Nature, whatever that is, but it was the best place to go see people going to see Nature, the Park Service presenting them with the official version of Nature, and the accretion of Nature's artifacts and souvenirs — human nature. It was a strange place, full of crowds and people — families, tour groups, gatherings — in the brightly colored clothes that signify leisure and pleasure, more intent on having recreation than on pursuing the sublime, or perhaps pursuing the sublime as a quick recreational interval. The more time I spent in the place the more it seemed like a suburb without walls rather than a wilderness with amenities, as though one weekend night all the fences and buildings had disappeared, but the residents went on as usual with their cards, their cooking, washing up, dozing, tossing balls, and scolding children" (228–29).

Like Mabel Wright's suburban garden, caught somewhere between a tamed frontier and a miniature park, John Muir's national park attempts both to preserve the frontier experience and protect the aesthetics of Eden. That all three of these metaphors for nature have also helped to enable industrial progress should hardly come as a shock, since they gained currency at the very moment the United States was itself being transformed by industry. As Robert G. Athearn observes, "Muir's blind spots . . . tell a lot about the early preservation movement. He often seemed to have nothing particular against the coming of big business to the West, and the admiration for progress and technological wizardry never quite died in him. . . . In 1900, it was hard to foresee what development and tourism would bring" (196–99). By 1935, when the Wilderness Society was formed, and by 1980, when Earth First! was founded, the consequences of development and tourism had become quite clear, and the work of Aldo Leopold and Edward Abbey changed accordingly.

PART TWO

Protecting the Planet

Modern Environmentalism

CHAPTER FOUR

The Call of the Wild

Aldo Leopold
and the
Wilderness Society

The test of the wilderness ethic is not how truthful it is,
but how useful it is in doing what we want to do —
in protecting and improving the environment.
MICHAEL POLLAN, *Second Nature*

OST READERS KNOW LITTLE of Aldo Leopold's work beyond his authorship of a single book of nature writing, *A Sand County Almanac*,
first published in 1949. Similarly, most readers of *A Sand County Almanac* know little of Leopold's wilderness philosophy beyond what is contained
in a single essay, "Wilderness," which serves as the penultimate chapter of that
book. Part of "The Upshot"—a series of four philosophical essays that concludes
with Leopold's most famous essay, "The Land Ethic"—"Wilderness" articulates
three principal reasons for the preservation of wilderness: wilderness for recreation, for science, and for wildlife. What the essay does not articulate, however, is
that these three reasons are not simply some abstract justifications Leopold developed one day while mulling the matter over in his office. Rather, they are the product of a lifetime of engagement with the idea of wilderness, and they represent the
evolution of more than thirty years of Leopold's thought, writing, and activism on
the issue.[1]

If there is agreement on anything about Leopold's thinking, it is that his thinking was always evolving. As Dave Foreman, cofounder of Earth First! put it in his
characteristically straightforward style, "Aldo Leopold was a big man. He thought
deeply, and he thought about a lot of things. His ideas changed during his life as
his experience and wisdom grew (we should all be so fortunate)" ("Wilderness"

397).[2] Beyond the plain fact of its evolution, though, Leopold's wilderness philosophy deserves our attention for at least two other reasons. In the first place, as Curt Meine and Richard L. Knight have observed, Leopold's essence is located "not just in the conclusions he reached but in the process by which he reached them" (xvii). *How* Leopold's wilderness ideas evolved, in other words, is as important as the ideas themselves. Furthermore, while the trajectory of Leopold's wilderness thought was certainly unique to him, it nevertheless evolved alongside a significant set of changes in cultural and scientific understandings of nature in the mid–twentieth century. Critics again agree upon this point, with Max Oelschlaeger claiming that Leopold "mirrors his time almost as perfectly as any person can" (*Idea* 210) and Susan Flader observing more specifically that Leopold's "intellectual development mirrors the history of ecological and evolutionary thought" (*Thinking* 5). Summarizing the content of this changing history, Donald Worster identifies Leopold as belonging "essentially to the middle generation of that transition period from a utilitarian to an ecological approach to conservation" (*Nature's Economy* 284).

Of Leopold's sixty-one years, 1935 seems to have been the crucial year, a clear turning point in his evolving understanding of nature. Curt Meine calls it "a landmark year" (*Aldo Leopold* 360), and Susan Flader claims it "marked a reorientation in his thinking from a historical and recreational to a predominantly ecological and ethical justification for wilderness" (*Thinking* 29). In some ways this certainly appears to be the case, as 1935 was the year Leopold helped found the Wilderness Society, the year he purchased his Sauk County "Shack," the year he made his only overseas trip (to Germany), and the year he first publicly used the term "land ethic." Yet it would be a mistake to make too much of this year, just as it would be a mistake to make too much of Leopold's legendary conversion experience in the essay "Thinking Like a Mountain," in which he describes watching the "fierce green fire" die in the eyes of a wolf he had shot. Leopold scholars have been careful not to make such a claim, with Flader admitting that "no single event can cause a transformation in the intellectual development of so integral a thinker as Leopold" (*Thinking* 30), and Worster observing that "Leopold's conversion . . . was not exactly a sudden awakening on the road to Damascus" (*Nature's Economy* 284). But it remains tempting to do so, especially given that when Mabel Osgood Wright died in 1934, Progressive conservation could then be said to have died along with her. The truth of the matter, however, is more complicated.

As my several references to existing scholarship on Leopold suggest, I am hardly alone in wanting to explore the evolution of Leopold's wilderness thought in all its richness. Beginning with Roderick Nash's chapter on Leopold in *Wilderness and the American Mind,* and continuing with articles and chapters by Craig Allin ("Leopold Legacy"), Susan Flader ("Aldo Leopold"), Max Oelschlaeger (*Idea* 205–42), Curt Meine ("Utility"), and Paul Sutter (*Driven* 54–99), several scholars have attempted to place Leopold's wilderness philosophy in its historical and philosophical context. For the most part, however, these attempts have not fully appreciated the *rhetorical* context of Leopold's wilderness ideas, particularly the extent to which his thought, writing, and activism on the issue were inextricably linked. Leopold could hardly act without thinking, and hardly think without writing, and his writing was almost always composed with a particular audience in mind.

Looking at *A Sand County Almanac* in isolation, one might imagine that Leopold, like Muir, was a "late-bloomer," turning to writing only later in life. But such a view would be mistaken. As J. Baird Callicott and Susan Flader point out in the preface to *The River of the Mother of God*, their collection of Leopold's early essays, "the strength of . . . [Leopold's] reputation and the credibility of *Sand County Almanac* rest upon a lifetime of extraordinary professional achievement and a large body of other writing."[3] Callicott and Flader recognize the significance of Leopold's rhetorical context, noting that "Leopold was keenly aware of his different audiences and varied his rhetoric accordingly" (*RMG* xi), but they do not address the strengths and weaknesses of his writing in detail. David E. Brown and Neil B. Carmony, editors of *Aldo Leopold's Wilderness*, another collection of Leopold's early writings, similarly claim that "[m]uch of Leopold's success as a policymaker and organizer was due to his effective writing," but they generally limit their observations to the content and historical context of his essays (9). In contrast, I believe that no other nature writer so thoroughly explored the implications of a metaphor for "nature" than Leopold did with "wilderness," and that Leopold's exploration of the meanings of that idea cannot be understood outside the rhetorical context of his written work.

Such a claim, of course, foregrounds Leopold's identity as a writer, but as with all the writers I discuss, Leopold himself may not have "agreed with such a view," to borrow a phrase from "Thinking Like a Mountain" (129). Peter Fritzell, for instance, notes that Leopold "did not consider himself a nature writer, and he did not live to know his reputation as such. . . . Neither, while he was alive, did Leopold's contemporaries consider him a nature writer" ("Aldo Leopold" 525). In this sense Leopold most resembles Theodore Roosevelt, whose political achievements overshadowed his literary ones, just as Leopold's work as a forester and wildlife biologist overshadowed the essays he composed while pursuing these vocations.[4]

The genre of nature writing was certainly alive and well during Leopold's lifetime, but the attention he paid in his wilderness essays to public policy issues, and the venues in which he published them, prevented both Leopold and his readers (and potential readers) from categorizing his work as "literary," at least in the popular sense of the term. The effect was similar to that created by Leopold's more "scientific" writings, such as his textbook *Game Management*, which continues to be read, but primarily for its content and not for its style. Randall Roorda articulates the issue well in *Dramas of Solitude*: "How do we say in the case of the biologist, for instance. . . , that such an individual defines him/herself *first* as a writer? Cannot such a person write appealing, jargon-free, 'elegant prose' while cultivating the role of biologist as primary occupation and not something 'else' in addition to an identity as writer? What could it mean to regard oneself 'as a writer first' while still discharging the professional functions of a biologist? How do we tell the difference?" (149). The "drama" of Leopold and other scientist-writers, according to Roorda, "resides in the sense of their having come to writing out of needs and recognitions originating in their fronting of nature, and not the reverse" (150). While this may be true if we look exclusively at *A Sand County Almanac*, its accuracy is less certain the further back we go in Leopold's life history. From the beginning, Leopold's attention to, understanding of, and activism on behalf of "nature" have been inextricably linked to his writing.

In this chapter, therefore, I argue not that the founding of the Wilderness Society helped to move Leopold's thought in an ecological direction, but rather that Leopold's principal contribution to the Wilderness Society was to move *its* thought in the ecological direction Leopold's own thought had already been moving for quite some time. Another way to put this is to say that when Bob Marshall and others asked Leopold to join them in organizing the Wilderness Society, what they wanted was Leopold the forester and wildlife manager, but what they got was Leopold the ecologist. As cofounder Harvey Broome observed in 1945, "In those days we were more engrossed with the setting aside and protection of wilderness areas than with their possible uses. But in the scientific articles of Leopold, . . . we observe a steadily growing emphasis upon the importance of wilderness to science" ("Last Decade" 16). Moreover, I suggest that Leopold's repeated call for an ecological justification for wilderness did not merely provide the Wilderness Society with a new argument for preserving wilderness areas but more importantly led to a new understanding of "wilderness" that would forever change the way the Wilderness Society — and society in general — represented, and thus defined, "nature." T. H. Watkins, the former editor of *Wilderness* magazine, wrote of Leopold in 1985, "Until his death, he was The Society's intellectual heart, and the power of his idea continues to inform the work we do here" ("Shadow" 3). Today Leopold's legacy lives on not only in the Wilderness Society but in its offshoot, Earth First! and in the thousands of local groups for whom ecology and environmentalism are one and the same.

Frontier to Wilderness

In 1924, when a thirty-seven-year-old Aldo Leopold moved to Madison, Wisconsin, after spending fifteen years in the American Southwest, he took up residence, as chance would have it, only two houses away from Frederick Jackson Turner.

Turner had been born in Portage, the town of John Muir's youth, in 1861, and he had returned to the University of Wisconsin, his alma mater, after teaching at Harvard for fourteen years. If the two men swapped stories during Turner's latest stay in Madison, they may well have reminisced about both growing up in the Midwest: Turner sharing stories of Portage at the end of what he called its "frontier phase" and Leopold telling tales of his youthful expeditions to frontierlike lands he hoped one day might be designated wilderness (Cronon, "Landscape" 93; Meine, *Aldo Leopold* 233).[5]

Burlington, Lawrenceville, New Haven

Twenty-six years younger than Turner, Leopold was born in Burlington, Iowa, on 11 January 1887, the same year that Theodore Roosevelt founded the Boone and Crockett Club. The first of four children born to Carl and Clara Starker Leopold, Rand Aldo Leopold (the "Rand" was quickly dropped) was raised in affluence on the family's Prospect Hill estate, a three-acre tract of land overlooking the Mississippi River. Aldo spent much of his youth outdoors — walking in the woods with his father, who was an amateur naturalist; traveling to a southeast Iowa prairie or a western Illinois lake for a family picnic; and helping his grandfather, Charles Starker, manage the gardens around the Starkers' large Italianate home. His grandparents on both sides were German immigrants, and German was Aldo's primary language, although he learned English before entering school. He read German literature, philosophy, and poetry, but he was most captivated by the outdoor writings of the day, including the adventures of Hiawatha and Daniel Boone, the features of *Outing* magazine, and the literary accounts of Ernest Thompson Seton, Stewart Edward White, and Jack London (Meine, *Aldo Leopold* 12–16).[6]

The parallels between Leopold and the young Theodore Roosevelt are striking, none more so than their interest in birds. "I like to study birds," an eleven-year-old Leopold wrote in his school composition book. "I like the wren best of all birds. . . . I like wrens because they do more good than almost any other bird, they sing sweetly, they are very pretty, and very tame. I could have caught them many a time if I wanted to" (Meine, *Aldo Leopold* 17). Leopold observed thirty-nine species of birds that year, a fortunate consequence of growing up on the Mississippi flyway, and he listed them all in his composition book. At thirteen he received a copy of Frank Chapman's *Handbook of Birds of Eastern North America* from his parents, and that became his bible (Meine, *Aldo Leopold* 17; Lorbiecki 14). In 1902 he began the first of a lifetime's worth of ornithological journals, and for the next two years he kept careful track of all the feathered activity on Prospect Hill, as well as that which occurred in nearby caves and ravines, and along the Mississippi bottomland. As Curt Meine indicates, "Leopold's early study of birds had a pronounced effect on his perception of the natural world and, incidentally, on his writing. Spying the birds trained his eye to concentrate on even the most fleeting phenomena, while identifying them forced him to hone his descriptive talents" (*Aldo Leopold* 26–27).

Like Roosevelt, Leopold was also a hunter of birds, a practice he learned from his father at an early age. At first, Aldo carried a carved stick to accustom himself to the weight and feel of a shotgun; later, he graduated to the real thing, first unloaded, and then loaded. Carl took all three of his sons hunting, usually one at a time, to several locations around Burlington, but most often they found themselves traveling east across the Mississippi to the Crystal Lake Hunt Club or the Lone Tree Hunt Club on the Illinois side of the river. Also like Roosevelt, Leopold learned much of his conservation philosophy from his father, who watched the decline of Iowa's migratory wildfowl throughout the 1880s and 1890s. A member of the Boone and Crockett Club, Carl placed voluntary restrictions on the kinds and numbers of birds he would shoot, the techniques he would use to do so, and the times and seasons during which he would hunt. He shot only what his family could eat, and he declined to hunt endangered species. To ensure he could kill any animal he had wounded, he always used a double-barreled shotgun, and he refused to carry one of the new automatic or pump guns, which he believed to be too powerful for a sportsman's needs. To avoid losing a bird, he hunted only during daylight hours, and eventually he stopped spring shooting altogether, so that yet-unborn birds would have a fighting chance (Meine, *Aldo Leopold* 17–19; Lorbiecki 10–12).[7]

His father's code of sportsmanship left its mark on young Aldo, and over time this developed and broadened into a wilderness ethic. It certainly couldn't have hurt that some of Leopold's early experiences with hunting occurred in wild and semiwild locations. In the summer the Leopolds vacationed at Les Cheneaux Club on Marquette Island at the north end of Lake Huron, which became a base camp for ruffed grouse and goldeneye duck hunting in the fall. Although the recently cutover Michigan mainland was not a wilderness, some isolated stands of old-growth hardwoods still remained, and miles of abandoned logging trails wove through a rich tapestry of second-growth woods. "In our young minds," Leopold's brother Frederick recalled, "we imagined that we were at the jumping-off place where to the north an endless wilderness extended to Hudson Bay and the arctic" (Meine, *Aldo Leopold* 22–24). In the summer of 1903 Aldo got a taste of the wilderness he had imagined when he and his father traveled to Montana with some family friends for a big game hunt. They encountered bears, antelope, and elk in Yellowstone National Park and hunted in the nearby Hoodoo Mountains. Despite heavy snow, a sick guide, and poor luck in the hunt, Aldo was not deterred. He added forty new species to his life list of birds and wrote in his journal that he could think of "no better possible vacation" (Meine, *Aldo Leopold* 28–29; Lorbiecki 10–12).

Leopold was a junior in high school when he returned home from the hunt, but he was not long for Burlington. In January 1904, at the urging of his mother, he left for the Lawrenceville School in New Jersey, where he prepared for admission into Yale University's new school of forestry, created by Gifford Pinchot. Theodore Roosevelt was in the White House; Pinchot was director of the Division of Forestry in the Department of Agriculture; and both Aldo and his parents recognized that this new field of forestry held great promise (Lorbiecki 24–25).

Most notable while Leopold was away were his letters home — some ten thousand pages during his first few years at school and later at work, sometimes arriving at a rate of four or five letters a week. "Aldo's correspondence was his reprieve from schoolwork, his literary training ground, his naturalist's notebook, and his private connection to the family and to Prospect Hill," notes Curt Meine (*Aldo Leopold* 34). The letters are also our principal source of information about Leopold's early years, during which much of his personal growth occurred out of the sight of others. Of particular interest are Leopold's daily "tramps," the excursions he took whenever possible into the fields and forests around Lawrenceville. On 9 January 1904, two days after his arrival, Leopold described his first such attempt at nature study: "I went north, across the country, about seven miles, and then circled back toward the west. Here every farm has a timber lot, sometimes fifteen or twenty acres, so it is a fine country for birds. It is about like Iowa high prairie, but the timber is more like the Michigan hardwood, the commonest trees being oak, beech, ash, hickory, chestnut, red cedar, and some elm. In some places, notably old orchards, young red cedars cover the ground. Nearly all the undergrowth in the woods is sapling and briars. There is little indiscriminate chopping of timber here" (Meine, *Aldo Leopold* 36). As the tramps grew longer, so did the letters, which came to resemble Thoreau's journal in both content and function. He described landscapes, birds, plants, the weather, and the relationships between them. As his reading widened to include Darwin's *Naturalist's Voyage around the World* ("very instructive and interesting") and Asa Gray's *Manual of Botany*, so did the scope of his letters. In a remarkable 21 May 1905 letter, written just a few days before he was to graduate, Leopold confessed to confronting what Walt Whitman called the "inimitable" nature of nature.[8] "I almost fear to begin on the news of the woods and fields for the past week," he wrote. "In fact, I sadly fear my attempts are too frequently narrow and dry. We can put on paper that such-and-such flowers are added to the list, that these birds have arrived and those are nesting, but who can write the great things, the deep changes, the wonderful nameless things, which are the real object of study of any kind" (Meine, *Aldo Leopold* 35–44).

After Lawrenceville, Leopold spent three years as an undergraduate at Yale's

Sheffield Scientific School and a year at the Yale Forest School, from which he graduated with a master's degree in forestry in 1909. While in New Haven, Leopold read Roosevelt's *Outdoor Pastimes of an American Hunter,* and like Roosevelt he reveled in natural history but hated microscopic science. "You sit four hours a week squinting through a microscope at a little drop of mud all full of wiggly bugs and things, and then draw pictures of them and label [them] with ungodly Latin names," he wrote of his plant morphology course. "One cannot help wondering what the *Cyanophycens oscillatorius* has to do with raising timber" (Meine, *Aldo Leopold* 72).[9] What most stood out in Leopold's memory, though, when he looked back on his college years after four decades of conservation work, was neither the books he read nor the courses he took but the damage that had been done to the land he loved. In the 1947 foreword to "Great Possessions," the manuscript that became *A Sand County Almanac,* Leopold writes: "My first doubt about man in the role of conqueror arose while I was still in college. I came home one Christmas to find that land promoters, with the help of the Corps of Engineers, had dyked and drained my boyhood hunting grounds on the Mississippi River bottoms. The job was so complete that I could not even trace the outlines of my beloved lakes and sloughs under their new blanket of cornstalks. I liked corn, but not that much. Perhaps no one but a hunter can understand how intense an affection a boy can feel for a piece of marsh. My home town thought the community enriched by this change, I thought it impoverished. It did not occur to me to express my sense of loss in writing" (Leopold, Foreword 282).[10] What Leopold saw that Christmas would become his life's work, which no doubt accounts for how vividly he retained the episode in his memory. Across the continent, lands were being drained and forests being cut in the name of "progress," and writing would become the means by which Leopold would not only express his sense of loss at such changes but also try to stop them.

Conservation in the Southwest

When Leopold's grandfather Charles Starker first settled in Burlington in 1850, only four years had passed since Iowa had become a state. When Leopold traveled to the Southwest in 1909 to join the U.S. Forest Service, another three years would have to pass before Arizona and New Mexico would be admitted to the Union. Sixty years separated the two men's actions, but Leopold still beat his grandfather in the competition for earliest residence in a state.

That statistic should give some idea of the challenge Leopold faced when he boarded the train in Iowa for Albuquerque in the summer of 1909. The U.S. Forest Service itself was only four years old, and hardly a year had passed since Gifford Pinchot had organized his new domain into six separate districts. Leopold had asked for and received an appointment in district 3, which included twenty-one forests in the southern and southwestern United States. Thus not only was Leopold new to forestry in the Southwest, but so, too, was the Forest Service.

From 1909 to 1910 Leopold served as a forest assistant in the Apache National Forest in northeastern Arizona Territory, leading reconnaissance parties to survey and map the forest's recently acquired land. As green as he was, Leopold nevertheless managed to impress his superiors, especially Arthur Ringland, the district supervisor, who in 1911 made him deputy supervisor of the Carson National Forest north of Santa Fe. The next year brought a flurry of activity: Leopold became editor of the *Pine Cone*, the Carson's newsletter; he married Estella Bergere, the daughter of a prominent Santa Fe family; he was promoted to supervisor of the Carson; and he and his new bride settled into a new house overlooking the Upper Rio Grande. By the spring of 1913, it was fair to say, Leopold's future looked bright, if not entirely certain (Meine, *Aldo Leopold* 87–122).

As often happens at such moments, however, the future that Leopold expected was not to be. On a horseback trip to resolve some grazing disputes in the Carson, Leopold grew ill, his knees swelling up so much that he had to slit his riding boots to ease the pain. At first misdiagnosed as a case of rheumatism, and then correctly diagnosed as an attack of acute nephritis (also known as Bright's disease), the illness forced Leopold to take a six-week unpaid leave, which eventually stretched into an absence of sixteen and a half months (Meine, *Aldo Leopold* 123). Similar in significance to Roosevelt's childhood battle with asthma, the disease had unexpected advantages; it gave Leopold a new perspective on his work, and it enabled him to read widely about nature. Home in Burlington to rest, he edited the *Pine Cone* from afar, noting that "[a]fter many days of much riding down among thickets of detail and box canyons, it sometimes profits a man to top out [on] the high ridge leave without pay, and to take a look around" (Meine, *Aldo Leopold* 126). During his recovery he made his way through his parents' back issues of the *Atlantic Monthly* and *National Geographic*; an account of a Grand Canyon hunt by Roosevelt in *Outlook*; and several books, including Thoreau's *Journals* and William Temple Hornaday's *Our Vanishing Wildlife* (Meine, *Aldo Leopold* 128). And to his commonplace book he added a notable quotation from Thoreau's "Walking": "In wildness is the preservation of the world" (Lorbiecki 61).

When Leopold returned to work in September 1914, he was a changed man, and fortunately, the Forest Service was changing with him, albeit slowly. Not only had Leopold become a father but he had also grown more reflective about his role as a forester, seeing in the national forests an opportunity to further the cause of game protection. As acting assistant district forester in the grazing office in Albuquerque, Leopold was able to spend some of his time on game-related issues, but not until the following year — when Arthur Ringland reassigned him to work on fish and game, recreation, and publicity concerns in district 3—did Leopold's broadening vision for the national forests find a suitable home. Ringland gave Leopold wide latitude to carry out his duties, enabling him to spend part of 1915 and 1916 organizing local branches of the American Game Protection Association, a sportsman's association originally created by the Winchester Repeating Firearms Company, whose business interests depended upon the protection of game. Leopold devoted most of his time to the Albuquerque branch of the group, publishing its newsletter (which he also titled the *Pine Cone*) and lobbying for the appointment of a state game warden sympathetic to its progressive platform (Meine, *Aldo Leopold* 128–58). No doubt Leopold was pleased when he received the following letter praising his efforts:

> My dear Mr. Leopold,
>
> Through you, I wish to congratulate the Albuquerque Game Protective Association on what it is doing. I have just read the Pine Cone. I think your platform simply capital, and I earnestly hope that you will get the right type of game warden. It seems to me that your association in New Mexico is setting an example to the whole country.
>
> Sincerely yours,
> Theodore Roosevelt (Meine, *Aldo Leopold* 158)

Neither the protection of fish and game nor the development of recreational activities were the primary mission of the U.S. Forest Service, but in devoting some of its resources to these activities, the Forest Service was responding to pressures both internal and external. According to the first field manual of the Forest Service, the national forests existed "for the purpose of preserving a perpetual supply of timber for home industries, preventing destruction of the forest cover which regulates the flow of streams, and protecting local industries from unfair competition in the use of forest and range" (Meine, *Aldo Leopold* 77). In advocating for game protection as another important purpose of the Forest Service, Leopold was pressing against the limits of its legislative mandate from the inside.[11] At the same time, external pressure to add recreational objectives to the Forest Service's mission was coming from the formation of the National Park Service in 1916 and from an increase in recreational activity in general.[12]

After the loss of Hetch Hetchy in 1913 and the death of John Muir in 1914, many preservationists—including the Sierra Club and its members—called for the creation of a federal agency to manage and protect the national parks. What distinguished their success from the failure of Hetch Hetchy's advocates to protect the valley from flooding was the increased emphasis they placed on the economic potential of scenic preservation. Preserving the aesthetic integrity of the national parks mattered, these advocates claimed, because outdoor recreation would promote the economic well-being of the nation, and the best way to take advantage of this "scenery business" would be to create a centralized government agency to manage the national parks efficiently. As landscape architect Mark Daniels put it at a 1915 national park conference, "economics and esthetics really go hand in hand" (Sellars 28–29). The result of this tactic was that when the National Park Service Act was passed in 1916, it clearly distinguished the mission of the national parks from that of the national forests. The "fundamental purpose" of the parks, it said, is "to conserve the scenery and the natural and historic objects and the wild life therein and to provide for the enjoyment of the same in such manner and by such means as will leave them unimpaired for the enjoyment of future generations" (Runte, *National Parks* 104).[13] Thus, as Dennis Roth observes, the National Park Act "was as much a mandate for development as it was for preservation. It called upon the newly created Park Service to protect the natural integrity of the parks but at the same time make them accessible for use by the public" (112).

Despite the apparent difference in their mission statements, the Forest Service nonetheless considered the Park Service its rival for control of prime scenic lands, so any actions it could take to integrate recreational use into its stated mission would give it leverage against the appropriation of its domain for new national parks (H. Rothman). Two types of recreation in particular helped distinguish the national forests from the national parks: patrons of the national forests could hunt and could lease sites for summer homes and commercial recreational facilities, activities that were prohibited in the national parks (Flader, *Thinking* 14). Moreover, national forests had the potential to provide a kind of environment that was growing increasingly difficult to find in the national parks: a primitive wilderness, free from roads and tourist accommodations (Meine, "Utility" 151).

In his new position devoted to fish and game, recreation, and publicity concerns in the Southwest, Leopold spent much of the fall of 1916 preparing a report on recreational policy for the Grand Canyon, which at the time was administered by the Forest Service. Leopold had visited the south rim of the canyon in June 1915, where he found a touristic landscape similar to Yosemite Valley in the 1870s. On a visit to the Grand Canyon in 1903 Theodore Roosevelt had warned that "man can only mar it," and Roosevelt's words were proving sadly prophetic. Curt Meine catalogs some of the abuses: "Gaudy electric advertisements lit up the rimtop nights. Hawkers for competing travel companies squalled through megaphones at the break of dawn, persevering until the tourists surrendered their patronage. Shifty concessionaires continually feuded, with visitors caught in the cross fire" (*Aldo Leopold* 144–45). In his report on the canyon, cowritten with Don Johnston, Leopold expressed concern about the effects of recreational development on the "great spectacle of nature" to be found there and called for specific changes to correct some of the more egregious abuses (Meine, *Aldo Leopold* 157).[14] It was an early indication of what would become, in a few years, a much more far-reaching critique of outdoor recreation.

In the meantime, Leopold was beginning to find a broader audience for his writing, as he adapted the *Pine Cone* from a Forest Service newsletter to the bulletin of the New Mexico Game Protective Association. In 1916 he broadened this audience even further, publishing his first article for a general readership: "Game Conservation: A Warning, also an Opportunity" in *Arizona* magazine. On the basis of titles alone, Leopold's next major article would appear to have been about wilderness: "The Popular Wilderness Fallacy: An Idea That Is Fast Exploding," published in 1918 in *Outer's Book — Recreation*, a magazine for sportsmen. However, "The Popular Wilderness Fallacy" is not about wilderness so much as it is a continuation of Leopold's concern about wildlife.

In it, Leopold sought to overturn what he believed to be a popular assumption at the time: "that the abundance of game must bear an inverse ratio to degree of settlement" (*RMG* 49). While in theory an argument against the destruction of wildlife, the essay is in fact an apologia for economic progress from what might be called the "preecological" Leopold. Although economic progress "has inevitably brought into operation many factors inimical to wild life, a careful analysis of each will almost invariably reveal an accompanying counter-influence decidedly beneficial to wild life perpetuation," Leopold argues (*RMG* 50). Thus hunting, agriculture, drainage, overgrazing, fire, disease, urbanization and industrialization — all can be said to benefit wildlife populations at least as much as they harm them. American sportsmen need not rethink their commitment to civilization to protect wildlife, Leopold concludes; they simply must refrain from "indiscriminate slaughter" (*RMG* 52).

Although only tangentially about wilderness, this essay deserves note not only as a landmark by which to measure the evolution of Leopold's wilderness thought but also as a reference point in the evolving scholarly discussion of Leopold's relationship to wilderness. In his 1991 essay "The Wilderness Idea Revisited," J. Baird Callicott notes that he and Susan Flader initially disagreed about whether to include this essay in *The River of the Mother of God*, their collection of Leopold's early writings. Flader argued for its inclusion, given that it revealed an early indication of Leopold's interest "in managing humanly inhabited and used land," but Callicott argued for its suppression, so as not to publicize the fact that Leopold "was also at first a Philistine on the wilderness issue" ("Wilderness" 338). Flader eventually prevailed in her wish to include the essay in the collection, and Callicott has since changed his mind — he no longer thinks the essay is "as aberrant as at first it seemed" ("Wilderness" 338). Instead, Callicott now believes "that Leopold envisioned throughout his career an ideal of human unity and harmony with nature, rather than a trade-off between human and economic activities and environmental quality." This is unquestionably true, but as Callicott further suggests, Leopold also "eventually came to see and expressly to formulate the important and absolutely vital role that wild refugia had to play in biological conservation" ("Wilderness" 339). Even the young Leopold would, I think, agree with Dave Foreman, who, in a reply to Callicott's article, says, "There does not have to be a Cartesian dualism here at all; we do not have to pick one or the other [wilderness or sustainable agriculture] ("Wilderness Areas" 397).

Foreman also says he is glad Flader and Callicott included "The Popular Wilderness Fallacy" in *The River of the Mother of God* because it "underscores Leopold's wonderful ability to grow intellectually" ("Wilderness Areas" 407 n. 1). One need not look far to see that growth occur. After a brief period working for the Albuquerque Chamber of Commerce during World War I, Leopold rejoined district 3 in August 1919 as assistant district forester in charge of operations, a position that would lead to his becoming a pioneer in the cause of wilderness preservation.

A Wilderness Pioneer

Of all the metaphors for nature examined in this study, "wilderness" is surely the most contested, in part because its meanings are so varied. To speak of "wilderness" as if the word signified a single, stable, commonly agreed-upon entity would be a mistake. The many debates about "wilderness" are the result of the many different interpretations of the word, and even Leopold himself changed the way he defined it over time. It is thus important to note that "wilderness" is not a real thing that exists out in the world, which some definitions get us "closer to," but that it is a thing we make — both as place and as idea — through our definition of it. Understanding "wilderness" this way — as a rhetorical construct — does not necessarily diminish its importance, but it does help us recognize that both wilderness areas and the idea of wilderness are only as important as our definitions are persuasive, and that the persuasiveness of our definitions depends in large part upon their historical context, including the scientific, political, recreational, intellectual, and institutional factors at work in a particular historical moment. Understanding the relative success of Leopold and the Wilderness Society, therefore, involves understanding the ways in which they interacted not only with each other but also with their changing times.

Naming "Wilderness"

The word *wilderness* derives from the Old English *wilddeor*, "wild beast," and therein lie two of the principal relationships that have characterized the meaning of the word throughout its history: the relationship between "wilderness" and the "wild," and between "wilderness" and the "wildlife" that inhabits it. R. Edward Grumbine argues that "Leopold saw wilderness as a cultural construct flowing from and dependent on wildness," but this was true more for the later Leopold than for the earlier ("Wild" 7). The well-known opening of the foreword to *A Sand County Almanac* certainly supports Grumbine's interpretation — "There are some who can live without wild things, and some who cannot. These essays are the delights and dilemmas of one who cannot" (vii) — but perhaps more importantly it suggests the close connection that came to exist for Leopold between the specific "wild things" of which he speaks: wildlife and wilderness, which together make up half the subjects of "The Upshot."

Leopold's celebration of these correlates — wilderness, the wild, and wildlife — reflects a cultural shift hardly a century old that transformed their definitions from ones based in fear to ones based in respect. As Roderick Nash indicates, "Ancient biases against the wild are deeply rooted in human psychology and in the human compulsion to understand, order, and transform the environment in the interest of survival and, later, of success. Wilderness was the unknown, the disordered, the uncontrolled. A large portion of the energies of early civilizations was directed at defeating the wilderness in nature and controlling it in human nature. Americans knew these imperatives firsthand: the European colonists reexperienced in America their old, insecure relationships to wilderness. There was too much wilderness for appreciation. The first white visitors regarded wilderness as a moral and physical wasteland fit only for conquest and fructification in the name of progress, civilization, and Christianity. Wilderness *recreation* was the last thing on Coronado's or John Winthrop's mind" (xi–xii). Only with the rise of romantic aesthetics and cultural nationalism in early-nineteenth-century America, and with the reduction of actual wilderness areas (and the corresponding growth of cities) that accompanied the closing of the frontier in 1890, did the notion of wilderness appreciation begin to take root (Nash, *Wilderness* 44–83, 141–60). It was, as Nash points out, "one of the most remarkable intellectual revolutions in the history of human thought about land" (*Wilderness* xii).

The only revolution that rivals it is the creation of the idea of "wilderness" itself, which has become the principal basis for modern criticisms of the concept. As Nash also points out, and as many other historians and anthropologists have acknowledged, prior to the advent of herding and agriculture some fifteen thousand years ago, "wilderness" did not exist because "nature" did not exist. "Until there were domesticated animals it was impossible to distinguish them from wild ones. Until there were fenced fields and walled cities 'wilderness' had no meaning. Everything was simply habitat, which man shared with other creatures" (*Wilderness* xiii). This "received wilderness idea," as J. Baird Callicott and Michael P. Nelson term it, has come under fire mainly because of the fundamental dichotomy between man and nature it appears to embody. In the view of many of these critics, whose writings Callicott and Nelson have helpfully anthologized, "wilderness" is a problematic idea not only because it is based on a dualism between human culture and nonhuman nature but also because it created landscapes of exclusivity in nineteenth- and twentieth-century America: places for rich, white men to visit that were sexist (not for women to visit), elitist (not for the poor to visit), and racist (not for native people to live and work in).[15]

There is much merit to these criticisms, and Leopold — as "an architect of the received wilderness idea," as Callicott and Nelson term him (15) — is certainly not beyond reproach. At the same time, however, the notion of "wilderness" that he and the Wilderness Society began to formulate by the end of his life continues to have a great deal of redeeming value. More than anything else their wilderness proposals arose as a reaction against the very modern civilization that enabled subsequent criticisms of the wilderness idea to arise. Furthermore, Leopold's eventual justification of the wilderness idea for recreation, for science, and for wildlife suggests that there may be several good reasons to preserve the *places* we call wilderness areas despite whatever negative connotations may accompany certain aspects of the *idea* of wilderness.

Writing "Wilderness"

"Wilderness" (as the idea of an uninhabited, uncultivated region) certainly existed before 1924, in both the national parks and the national forests, but "wilderness" (as a federally designated land classification) did not, and for initiating the latter Aldo Leopold has been called the "Father of the National Forest Wilderness System" (J. Gilligan 1:82).

According to Dennis Roth, Leopold had discussed the idea of setting aside particular tracts of land as wilderness areas with Elliott Barker, a ranger on the Carson National Forest, as early as 1913 (113). And in December 1919 Leopold had an important, daylong conversation with Arthur Carhart, the first landscape architect to be employed by the Forest Service, regarding the preservation of Trappers Lake, Colorado, in an unimproved state.[16] But not until 1921 did Leopold publish his first substantial discussion of the wilderness idea in the Society of American Foresters' *Journal of Forestry*.

"The Wilderness and Its Place in Forest Recreational Policy," published in the journal's November issue, was by no means Leopold's first attempt to communicate with his fellow foresters in the pages of their professional journal.[17] Since 1918 Leopold had published six articles in the *Journal of Forestry* — most recently an article on erosion for the March 1921 issue — so his audience was certainly familiar with both his name and his style of writing. Similarly, Leopold was aware of the expectations and limitations of his audience, and he clearly adapted his argument to fit their needs and desires. The pivot around which the entire article turns is Leopold's acknowledgment, in the fourth paragraph, that many of his forestry colleagues will likely greet his proposal with skepticism — the anticipation of which drives Leopold's rhetorical strategy. "It is quite possible," he admits, "that the serious discussion of this question [of wilderness preservation] will seem a far cry in some unsettled regions, and rank heresy to some minds." Nevertheless, his proposal deserves consideration, because "[l]ikewise did timber conservation seem a far cry in some regions, and rank heresy to some minds of a generation ago" (*RMG* 79). The historical parallel holds the key to Leopold's argument: because wilderness recreation and timber production are both forms of land use, the doctrine of "highest use" should apply to each.

Much of Leopold's article consists of defining the three terms of his argument: "wilderness," "development," and "use." He opens the article by recognizing that wilderness has traditionally been perceived as undesirable by foresters as well as their opponents. When the national forests were created, Leopold observes, Gifford Pinchot had to assure his opponents that the forests "would neither remain a wilderness by 'bottling up' their resources nor become one through devastation" (*RMG* 78). In the first case, "wilderness" is defined as a dense forest created by nonuse; in the second, as a barren desert created by overuse. In both cases, however, wilderness has a negative connotation. To prevent the formation of this kind of landscape, Pinchot promised "development" of the forests by putting them to their "highest use," which was to be determined by John Stuart Mill's utilitarian calculus of providing "the greatest good to the greatest number" (*RMG* 78). In response to user demand, this "industrial development" had grown by 1921 to include not only the lumber industry but also the tourist industry; to include roads and buildings not only for timber-cutting but also for vacationing.[18] Leopold's heresy is to ask "whether the policy of development . . . should continue to govern in absolutely every instance, or whether the principle of highest use does not itself demand that representative portions of some forests be preserved as wilderness" (*RMG* 78).

The remainder of the article consists of Leopold's redefinition of "wilderness" in more favorable terms and an explication of the purpose, size, location, and character of his proposed wilderness areas. "By 'wilderness,'" Leopold writes, "I mean a continuous stretch of country preserved in its natural state, open to lawful hunting and fishing, big enough to absorb a two weeks' pack trip, and kept devoid of roads, artificial trails, cottages, or other works of man" (*RMG* 79). Two factors are at work here: an *idea* of wilderness as uninhabited, undeveloped land in its "natural state," and actual *places* called wilderness areas, which are defined by a variety of additional factors:

Purpose: "The argument for such wilderness areas is premised wholly on highest recreational use," Leopold writes (*RMG* 79). In particular, wilderness areas should be created in response to the demands of users who desire both positive and negative freedoms. These include the *freedom to* experience "the horses, packing, riding, daily movement and variety found only in a trip through a big stretch of wild country" (*RMG* 80), as well as the *freedom from* the modern conveniences desired by the majority of tourists. According to Leopold, "it is our duty to vary our recreational development policy, in some places, to meet the needs of the minority also" (*RMG* 79). By continuing to allow hunting in these wilderness areas, the national forests also provide a recreational experience not available to visitors to the national parks, further evidence that "highest use is a very varied use, requiring a very varied administration, in the recreational as well as the industrial field" (*RMG* 80).

Size: The size of these wilderness areas is determined by their purpose. Leopold defines them as being "big enough to absorb a two weeks' pack trip," and he argues that "any number of small patches of uninhabited wood or mountains are no answer to the real sportsman's need for wilderness" (*RMG* 81).

Location: Leopold envisions wilderness areas throughout the national forests, but he suggests that the impact of these will be minimal: "such wilderness areas should occupy only a small fraction of the total National Forest area — probably not to exceed one in each State" (*RMG* 79).

Character: Beyond the basic idea of wilderness as uninhabited, undeveloped land, wilderness areas "should be representative of some type of country of distinctive recreational value, or afford some distinctive type of outdoor life, opportunity for which might disappear on other forest lands open to industrial development" (*RMG* 79).

Making a convincing case for wilderness to his audience required Leopold to define not only what these areas should be but also what they should *not* be. The most important qualification Leopold notes is that wilderness areas should not interrupt the business of the forests: "only areas naturally difficult of ordinary industrial development should be chosen" (*RMG* 79). Using the headwaters of the Gila River in the Gila National Forest as an example, he notes that "no net economic loss would result" from a policy of withholding further industrial development from this region, with the exception of keeping timber inaccessible to all but local consumers (*RMG* 81). Furthermore, some resource uses, such as cattle grazing, could continue uninterrupted, since "cattle ranches would be an asset from the recreational standpoint because of the interest which attaches to cattle grazing operations under frontier conditions" (*RMG* 81).[19]

Leopold's first wilderness proposal differs greatly not only from contemporary ideas of wilderness but also from Leopold's later conceptions of what a wilderness area should be. As Susan Flader observes, "Leopold's initial vision of wilderness was not exactly 'pure.' He would have allowed more development than under the 1964 Wilderness Act" ("Let the Fire Devil" 90). Furthermore, Leopold's wilderness was exactly the kind of exclusive landscape that recent critics have taken wilderness advocates to task for embracing: a place for rich, white men to visit. Throughout his life, Leopold would return again and again to these defining components in his writings on wilderness, modifying some, yet standing firm on others. For instance, Leopold soon qualified his argument about "the needs of the minority" in response to charges that such a claim was elitist and undemocratic. More significantly, he later departed from a strictly utilitarian defense of wilderness areas and broadened his justification of them to include more than just recreational value.

Despite these differences, Leopold's wilderness proposal remains a significant achievement, not only because Leopold was the first to argue for the preservation of wilderness on such a large scale but also because his proposal led to the creation of the first federally designated wilderness area. In an inspection report of the Gila National Forest completed in July 1922, Leopold formally proposed the creation of the wilderness area he had used as an example in his article: a 755,000-acre tract encompassing the headwaters of the Gila River in the Mongollon Mountains of the Gila National Forest. In a more complete report on his wilderness proposal submitted later that October, Leopold suggested that the land be designated "The Gila Wilderness Area or Gila National Hunting Ground" (Meine, *Aldo Leopold* 200, 557 n. 72). On 3 June 1924 district 3's chief forester, Frank C. W. Pooler, approved Leopold's recreational working plan for the region, thus initiating the establishment of the first wilderness area in the U.S. Forest Service.

While it might be nice to think that Leopold's proposal was approved due to his skills as a writer, Leopold's rhetorical ability was only partly responsible for the implementation of his wilderness plan. His Forest Service superiors agreed to the proposal not simply on its merits, or because of Leopold's personal influence, or even because it was presented in a well-crafted argument, although all these factors played a role. They also approved it partly because it was to their advantage to do so, given the circumstances in which they found themselves. Designating land as "wilderness" allowed the Forest Service to argue that these areas should remain under its control rather than be transferred to the Park Service, since the Forest Service would not just be providing recreational access to these areas but would in fact be preserving them better than the Park Service ever could, given the touristic orientation of the national parks. Furthermore, the Forest Service could do so without making any significant changes in its management of these areas. Wilderness cost little to maintain; its establishment did not alter any existing sources of revenue; and it had the support of local ranchers (Allin, "Leopold Legacy" 30–31; Brown and Carmony 153–54).

Similarly, while it might be nice to think that the creation of wilderness areas was the result of the dawning of Leopold's ecological awareness, this is far from the case. As Susan Flader indicates, "Although Leopold was unquestionably familiar with the concepts of plant ecology emanating from the universities of Chicago and Nebraska, particularly as they described the distribution and succession of vegetation types, his thinking does not seem to have been dominated by them" (*Thinking* 17). Leopold first used the word "ecological" in a 1920 *Journal of Forestry* article entitled "The Forestry of the Prophets" (*RMG* 76), and in an early 1920s memo he even indicated an interest in an ecological justification for wilderness, as Paul Sutter has pointed out (72–73). But Leopold's early interest in protecting a portion of nature as "wilderness" primarily came not because of his exposure to ecological thinking but because of his interest in preserving a particular kind of recreational experience, one most evocative of Theodore Roosevelt's notion of the frontier.

That this is the case can be seen nowhere more profoundly than in "The River of the Mother of God," a 1924 essay Leopold sent to the *Yale Review* that was rejected and remained unpublished during his lifetime. Leopold's first attempt at self-consciously "literary" expression as an adult, "The River of the Mother of God" argues for the preservation of wilderness areas from motorized tourism on the basis of what he believes to be the basic impulse behind outdoor recreation: the need for adventure.

The title refers to El Río Madre de Dios, the South American river that rises in Peru's southern Andes and flows eastward into Brazil, where it joins the Río Madeira, which then empties into the Amazon.[20] Since Leopold had first heard of it, the river had always possessed a duality of meaning. On the one hand, its cartographic image, which early maps portrayed as "a river without beginning and without end"—a "short heavy line flung down upon the blank vastness of tropical wilderness"—had always seemed "the perfect symbol of the Unknown Places of the earth" (*RMG* 123). On the other hand, its name, "resonant of the clank of silver armor and the cruel progress of the Cross, yet carrying a hush of reverence and a murmur of the prows of galleons on the seven seas," seemed to symbolize "the Conquest that has reduced those Unknown Places, one by one, until now there are none left" (*RMG* 123–24). Writing in 1924, Leopold believed he saw the frontier closing on a global scale and western culture extending its reach everywhere. The rise of mechanized transportation, he laments, "marks a new epoch in the history of mankind, an epoch in which Unknown Places disappear as a dominant fact in human life." History, he writes, "is but a succession of adventures into the Unknown. . . . And now, speaking geographically, the end of the Unknown is at hand" (*RMG* 124)

The reader looking to fault Leopold for failing to see the colonialist implications of wilderness need look no further than this essay. The "blank vastness of tropical wilderness" is of course blank only to western eyes, and the "Unknown Places of the earth" are unknown only to those who do not live in them. But Leopold was after something else, as his reference to "the Conquest" suggests. He was certainly aware of the human costs of imperialism, which he references as "the cruel progress of the Cross," but it was the "hush of reverence" and the "murmur of the prows of galleons on the seven seas" that interested him more. It was, in short, the loss of adventure that had him concerned. "It is this same reaction against the loss of adventure into the unknown," Leopold notes, "which causes the hundreds of thousands to sally forth each year upon little expeditions, afoot, by pack train, or by canoe, into the odd bits of wilderness which commerce and 'development' have regretfully and temporarily left us here and there" (*RMG* 124–25). Leopold saw the need for adventure through the lenses of his own ethnic and gender identity, to be sure. He claims that it allows for the "expression of racial instincts" that characterize hunting, and it motivates men to "venture forth, as becometh men, into remote lands" (*RMG* 125). Yet adventure need not have these characteristics, as Leopold would soon come to see, and what he here glosses as "adventure" would later become "perception," a change that would make all the difference.

To read "The River of the Mother of God" as a naive celebration of the frontier impulse would be to misread what is arguably Leopold's most insightful meditation on the meaning of wilderness. Whether described as the pursuit of "adventure" or "perception," the desire to know is perhaps the most defining of all human passions.[21] Likewise, wilderness is defined by its unfamiliarity to us, and as our knowledge of it grows, its essential character is irreversibly altered. How much, Leopold seemed to be asking, does our ability to wonder about the mystery of the world depend in part on our having mysterious places to wonder about? "Is it to be expected that . . . [the unknown] shall be lost from human experience without something likewise being lost from human character?" (*RMG* 124). Although Leopold would later broaden his notion of wilderness to encompass many more landscapes of mystery, he never surrendered the fundamental claim he made in this essay: that the question of wilderness is ultimately "a question in self-control of environment" (*RMG* 126). Should we fail to preserve some remnants of these landscapes, he warned, "[w]e fall back into the biological category of the potato bug which exterminated the potato, and thereby exterminated itself" (*RMG* 127).[22]

"Wilderness Is a Relative Condition"

In 1924 Leopold left the southwestern landscape he had come to call home and returned to his native Midwest to accept a position as associate director of the U.S. Forest Service's Forest Products Laboratory in Madison, Wisconsin. Nearly fifteen years had passed since he first arrived in Albuquerque, and during that time the Southwest had come to possess the same duality of meaning he once saw in the River of the Mother of God. Back in 1909 Arizona and New Mexico were still Unknown Places in the eyes of the Forest Service, but by the time Leopold had left, they too had become victims of the Conquest — surveyed, mapped, and cataloged, in part by his own hand. The idea of preserving some of these places from further development by designating them "wilderness" thus held special significance for him, functioning as a kind of reparation for his own participation in transforming these places from Unknown to Known.

It should come as no surprise, therefore, to learn that when Leopold left the Southwest he could hardly leave wilderness behind. In the year following his departure, Leopold published five articles on the subject, each to a different audience and each in a different publication.[23] Despite their rhetorical variety, all five pieces had a common purpose: to develop Leopold's justification for the wilderness idea and to address the objections of his critics. These articles are interesting not only because of *what* Leopold had to say about wilderness but also because of *how* he chose to say it, using the most appropriate language, structure, and tone for his various audiences. In a sense, all five articles demonstrate that "wilderness is a relative condition"—as Leopold put it in "Wilderness as a Form of Land Use"—since their differing arguments illustrate the ways in which wilderness is as much a rhetorical construction as a physical place.

At the same time, it is helpful to keep in mind that wilderness does indeed *take place*, and it is the future of those places that had Leopold concerned. As Curt Meine indicates, Frank Pooler's designation of the Gila Wilderness Area was hardly set in stone. "The Gila itself, for all its ruggedness and grandeur, was only marginally more secure than it was before. Its protection was by administrative fiat only, and assigned it merely to another category of land use. Washington had no say in its establishment, and the designation could be altered at any time. Opposition to the whole idea remained, both within and beyond the Forest Service" (*Aldo Leopold* 227). Particularly disappointing to Leopold was the omission of any discussion of wilderness during the first National Conference on Outdoor Recreation, a three-day meeting held in Washington in May 1924. As a result of that exclusion, and out of concern for the future of the wilderness idea, Leopold worked to build support for the designation among his colleagues and the general public, using the Gila as an example of how the concept of wilderness might be extended to cover other Forest Service lands around the country.

"Conserving the Covered Wagon," the first of Leopold's five essays, appeared in the March 1925 issue of *Sunset*, the magazine of the Southern Pacific Railroad.[24] The previous year *Sunset* had published Leopold's "Pioneers and Gullies" (an article on soil erosion in the Southwest), and "Conserving the Covered Wagon" was a kind of companion piece, continuing the pioneering theme. In it, Leopold argued for the preservation of wilderness from the perspective of the urban tourist seeking an "authentic" frontier experience. "Our fathers set great store by this Winning of the West, but what do we know about it?" Leopold asked. "If we think we are going to learn by cruising round the mountains in a Ford, we are largely deceiving ourselves" (*RMG* 128). Instead, Leopold suggested that Americans should "preserve a sample of the Covered Wagon Life," because "the measure of civilization is in its contrasts." Once in a while, if the city man "has the opportunity to flee the city, throw a diamond hitch upon a packmule, and disappear into the wilderness of the Covered Wagon Days, he is just that much more civilized than he would be without the opportunity. It makes him one more kind of a man — a pioneer" (*RMG* 129).

Leopold's principal opponent in all five essays was the Good Roads Movement — a catchall term to describe those individuals and organizations that lobbied for a system of national roads in the first decades of the twentieth century. The movement began in the 1880s and 1890s as a series of local efforts to improve road conditions for bicyclists, but with the arrival of the automobile at the turn of the century, advocates began calling for a nationwide system of good roads to foster interstate commerce and promote recreational travel. Like the Good Roads Movement, road-building in the United States also began as a local phenomenon, with individual towns and states responsible for building and maintaining their own roads. Although an Office of Road Inquiry was established in the Department of Agriculture in 1893, the national funding of roads did not begin until 1912 with the Post Office Appropriation Act. Soon thereafter, federal aid for highways became national policy with the passage of the Federal Aid Road Act of 1916 and the Federal Aid Highway Act of 1921. Roads began spreading everywhere, including in the national forests.

Leopold had been highly critical of the Good Roads Movement in "The River of the Mother of God," which may have been one of the reasons the article was rejected by the *Yale Review*. In the last few paragraphs of that essay, his tone changed dramatically as he blasted "that Frankenstein which our boosters have builded" for "choking out the wilderness" (*RMG* 126).

> This movement, entirely sound and beneficial in its inception, has been boosted until it resembles a gold-rush, with about the same regard for ethics and good craftsmanship. The spilled treasures of Nature and of the Government seem to incite about the same kind of stampede in the human mind.
>
> In this case, the yellow lure is the Motor Tourist. Like Mammon, he must be spelled with a capital, and as with Mammon we grovel at his feet, and he rules us with the insolence of a new god. We offer up our groves and our greenswards for him to camp upon, and he litters them with cans and with rubbish. We hand him our wild life and

our wild flowers, and humbly continue the gesture after there are none left to hand. But of all offerings foolish roads are to him the most pleasing of sacrifice. . . .

And of all foolish roads, the most pleasing is the one that "opens up" some last little vestige of virgin wilderness. With the unholy zeal of fanatics we hunt them out and pile them upon his altar, while from the throats of a thousand luncheon clubs and Chambers of Commerce and Greater Gopher Prairie Associations rises the solemn chant "There Is No God but Gasoline and Motor Is His Prophet!" (*RMG* 126–27)[25]

Leopold had to be much more careful with his words in *Sunset,* which was created in 1898 by the passenger department of the Southern Pacific Company to promote western tourism and development.[26] Although the magazine began to feature more controversial subjects after the company sold the magazine to its staff in 1914, *Sunset* never strayed far from its roots as a booster of the West (Gotliffe 305–6). The same March issue that featured Leopold's essay, for instance, also included two articles written in support of good roads. In an article celebrating the transcontinental motor trails of the far West, complete with road map, Walter V. Woehlke proclaimed, "It's a wonderful thing, this endless procession of heavily loaded cars going east and going west, going south and going north" (25). Another article, by C. P. Knight, related the "experiences of a motorist with human nature on desert trails" (49).

In "Conserving the Covered Wagon," Leopold treads much more lightly than in "The River of the Mother of God," offering concession after concession to his tourism-oriented readers. "Motor cars and highways are of course the very instruments which have restored to millions of city dwellers their contact with the land and with nature. For this reason and to this extent they are a benefaction to mankind," Leopold writes. "But even a benefaction can be carried too far" (*RMG* 129). "To my mind the Good Roads Movement has become a Good Roads Mania; it has grown into a pleurisy. We are building good roads to give the rancher access to the city, which is good, and to give the city dweller access to recreation in the forests and mountains, which is good, but we now, out of sheer momentum, are thrusting more and ever more roads into every little remaining patch of wilderness, which in many cases is sheer stupidity. For by doing so we are cutting off, irrevocably and forever, our national contact with the Covered Wagon days" (*RMG* 130). Granting the many "goods" the Good Roads Movement has achieved, Leopold suggests—as he did in "The River of the Mother of God"—that its pioneering spirit must ultimately be restrained, lest it undermine itself.

Another reason Leopold had to temper his criticism of the Good Roads Movement was that he needed it to counter those opponents who claimed his wilderness plan was elitist. As Christopher J. Huggard observes about Leopold's "substantial minority" argument, "Leopold was treading on shaky political ground.

The argument to set aside wilderness for 'minority wants' provided ammunition for preservation opponents who for the remainder of the century would claim this was an elitist argument for wilderness and contrary to the Forest Service's democratic mandate" (137). Not damning the Good Roads Movement in toto allowed Leopold to claim that nearby wilderness would give the average American somewhere to go in his motor car, so long as the road stopped at the boundary of the wilderness. Leopold asks: "have . . . well-to-do travelers in foreign wilds a monopoly on the Covered Wagon blood? They have not. In every village and in every city suburb and in every skyscraper are dozens of the self-same blood. But they lack the opportunity. It is the opportunity, not the desire, on which the well-to-do are coming to have a monopoly. And the reason is the gradually increasing destruction of the nearby wilderness by good roads. The American of moderate means can not go to Alaska, or Africa, or British Columbia. He must seek his big adventure in the nearby wilderness, or go without it" (*RMG* 130).

The accusation that wilderness advocates were antiroad could be heard both inside and outside the Forest Service, and Leopold's second missive in his wilderness campaign was addressed to his fellow foresters. In "The Pig in the Parlor," a short piece that ran in the mimeographed *USFS Service Bulletin* in June 1925, Leopold was responding to a notice in the 11 May *Service Bulletin* that dismissed the wilderness idea as "antiroad," an assumption that Leopold claims is incorrect.[27] "I do not know of a single 'enthusiast' for wilderness areas who denies the need for more forest roads. It is not a question of how many roads, but a question of distribution of roads," he argues. "Roads and wilderness are merely a case of the pig in the parlor." Like the rest of the piece, Leopold's conclusion struck a familiar tone, with an added dose of wit. "We now recognize that the pig is all right — for bacon, which we all eat. But there no doubt was a time, soon after the discovery that many pigs meant much bacon, when our ancestors assumed that because the pig was so useful an institution he should be welcomed at all times and places. And I suppose that the first 'enthusiast' who raised the question of limiting his distribution was construed to be uneconomic, visionary, and anti-pig" (*RMG* 133).

Leopold's third wilderness article, "The Last Stand of American Wilderness," reached a much wider audience, given its publication in the October issue of *American Forests and Forest Life*, the illustrated journal of the American Forestry Association, which was popular not just among foresters but also among a broad range of conservation-minded readers.[28] It was also abstracted as "The Vanishing Wilderness" in the August 1926 issue of the *Literary Digest*, ensuring an even wider readership.[29] While it rehearsed many of the arguments Leopold had made elsewhere about the importance of wilderness recreation, "The Last Stand of American Wilderness" much more explicitly solicited public support for the wilderness idea. Sounding strikingly similar to a modern-day wilderness advocate, Leopold reminded his readers of the practicalities of forest management and called on them to voice "definite expression of public opinion" in support of wilderness designation. "The point is that governmental policies can not be actually applied without many decisions by administrative officers involving the adjustment of conflicting interests. In such conflicts individual or economic interests may always be counted upon to be articulate. Group or public interests must likewise be made articulate, else they place the government executive in the thankless and often untenable position of being at once judge of the conflict and counsel for an absentee. The public interest must 'speak up or lose out'" (603). Writing to a diverse audience of recreationists and resource managers, Leopold did not dwell on the "minority rights" argument for wilderness, citing instead the fellow of "lesser pocketbook" who "probably has more real need of recreation" than the well-to-do sportsman. In fact, Leopold did not ask any specific constituency to come to the aid of the wilderness, which may have been part of his article's wide appeal. The most politically successful of Leopold's five articles, "The Last Stand of American Wilderness" not only broadened the base of support for Leopold's cause but also had a clear effect on policy. It was quoted extensively and approvingly by *Recreation Resources of Federal Lands*, the 1928 Report of a Joint Committee of the American Forestry Association and the National Parks Association commissioned by the 1924 National Conference on Outdoor Recreation to study the use and potential use of federal lands for recreation.[30]

Not everyone agreed with Leopold about the value of wilderness, and "The Last Stand of American Wilderness" occasioned a prominent reply from Howard R. Flint, a fellow forester. In "Wasted Wilderness," published in *American Forests and Forest Life* the following July, Flint leveled several common complaints about the wilderness idea. His principal criticism is implied by his title: that wilderness is a "thoughtless waste" of marketable timber (410). According to Flint, "the nature lover, the sentimentalist, and the average citizen" are no match for the forester when it comes to knowing how best to manage the forest, which is to "wisely harvest" it for economic purposes (409). Challenging Leopold's definition of wilderness, Flint suggests that "it may be possible to keep most of our cake and eat it too"—that a wilderness area could peacefully coexist with roads, timber-cutting, and grazing. If nothing else, Flint argues, it would be wise "not to commit ourselves to a 'cast-iron' policy" of permanently closing wilderness areas from development. Flint's most pointed criticism comes in his final paragraph: "Perhaps if one closely analyzes the arguments of the true 'wilderness' advocate it will become apparent that it is not roads but people that he objects to. Perhaps he wants the 'wilderness' to himself and the elect few, and objects to roads because they inevitably bring other people" (410).

Leopold's response, which followed Flint's reply, addresses each of his criticisms in turn. To the economic argument that wilderness was a waste of timber, Leopold reminds his readers that most of the national forests were already being conserved for just such uses. "While it would be theoretically possible to overdo the wilderness idea," Leopold writes, "the actual present question is not whether the establishment of wilderness areas will be overdone, but whether it will be done at all." As for wilderness areas being redefined to accommodate a blend of economic and recreational uses, Leopold argued that the wilderness idea was an attempt to preserve "the distinctly American idea of *facing nature alone*, without any hotels, guides, motors, roads, or other flunkeys or reinforcements." Such a claim also allowed Leopold to answer Flint's final criticism that wilderness advocates perhaps objected not to roads but to people. "Why 'perhaps?'" replied Leopold. "I would say *surely* it is people." Turning Flint's criticism on its head, he argued that the wilderness idea was not elitist but rather *anti*elitist. Wilderness advocates do not object to having people other than themselves use the wilderness, Leopold claimed. They do, however, object to people who "buy their way into the wilderness by building roads, or riding in motors, or hiring guides" rather than "*working their way*" into it. "All that we wilderness cranks are asking for," he concluded, "is a few roadless areas where we can go once and a while, and where we will at least have a chance of escaping the man who buys his way" ("Comment" 411; emphasis in original).

If "The Last Stand of American Wilderness" was the most successful of Leopold's writings on wilderness in 1925, the most comprehensive was "Wilderness as a Form of Land Use," which appeared in the scholarly *Journal of Land and Public Utility Economics* in October.[31] Not surprisingly, Leopold framed the wilderness idea in economic terms in this article, arguing that wilderness entailed "very low costs" and represented a "good balance" between competing interests: between economic and social uses of the land, and between motorized and nonmotorized forms of recreation (RMG 136, 140). In so doing, Leopold also offered his most thorough defense of the cultural value of wilderness, arguing — along with Frederick Jackson Turner and Theodore Roosevelt — that the pioneer wilderness environment "determined the character of our development; . . . it is the very stuff America is made of. Shall we now exterminate this thing that made us American?" (RMG 137). "I can only picture the day that is almost upon us," he observes, "when canoe travel will consist in paddling in the noisy wake of a motor launch and portaging through the back yard of a summer cottage. When that day comes, canoe travel will be dead, and dead, too, will be a part of our Americanism" (RMG 141).

"Wilderness as a Form of Land Use" also represented an important step forward in Leopold's own understanding of wilderness, because it contained his most sophisticated definition of the concept since his 1921 article in the *Journal of Forestry*. "Wilderness is a relative condition," Leopold admits. "As a form of land use it cannot be a rigid entity of unchanging content, exclusive of all other forms. On the contrary, it must be a flexible thing, accommodating itself to other forms and blending with them in that highly localized give-and-take scheme of land-planning which employs the criteria of 'highest use'" (*RMG* 135–36). Perhaps most significant was the new flexibility Leopold revealed in assessing the size and location of wilderness areas. "[W]ilderness exists in all degrees," he declares, "from the little accidental wild spot at the head of a ravine in a Corn Belt woodlot to vast expanses of virgin country" (*RMG* 135). As a result, "the application of the wilderness idea [should] vary in degree from the wild, roadless spot of a few acres left in the rougher parts of public forest devoted to timber-growing, to wild, road-less regions approaching in size a whole national forest" (*RMG* 136). Though unannounced as such, this was a major broadening of the wilderness idea that would soon make its way into Forest Service policy.

The final article Leopold published on wilderness in 1925 was "A Plea for Wilderness Hunting Grounds," which appeared in the November issue of *Outdoor Life*.[32] Addressed to his fellow hunters — the core supporters of his wilderness idea — the article used the language of the sport itself to plead "for establishing in each of the Rocky Mountain states at least one area in which there shall be a permanent closed season on roads" (Brown and Carmony 155). Once again Leopold made the case for wilderness, but for these readers he added a new justification, beginning with a qualification: "It should require no explanation that this proposal of wilderness areas is not primarily a game conservation measure. Certainly 99 percent, figuratively speaking, of our country should and must have roads. We must learn to raise game and build roads on the same ground, or go gameless. It so happens, however, that the establishment of wilderness areas would provide an opportunity to produce and hunt certain kinds of game, such as elk, sheep, and bears, which do not always 'mix well' with settlement, but the majority of game species can and must be produced on all the grounds suitable for them" (Brown and Carmony 160). Leopold knew better than to suggest that wilderness areas could be defended solely on the basis of game management, but his comment raises several questions about the role of hunting in his idea of wilderness. In many ways, Leopold can be seen as a bridge between the interest of Theodore Roosevelt and Mabel Osgood Wright in wildlife conservation and the interest of John Muir in land preservation. As Michael Nelson points out, however, the "wilderness as hunting ground" argument pertains only to some wilderness areas and not to others. "Places inhabited by animals that humans desire to hunt or have a historical predator/prey relationship with are worth preserving as wilderness, but those that are largely devoid of big game are not" (158). As a result of this dilemma, Leopold gradually distanced himself from this argument for wilderness preservation over the years, particularly as he developed other arguments stressing wilderness as a land laboratory and a wildlife reserve. Indeed, Leopold's admission that "[w]e must learn to raise game and build roads on the same ground, or go gameless" prefigured this change in his priorities, which would begin to take effect in the next several years.

"The Most Salient Manifestation of Naturalism"

In the ten years between Leopold's 1925 articles on wilderness and the 1935 founding of the Wilderness Society, wilderness advocacy receded into the background of his consciousness, but the movement he initiated continued to grow.

In January 1926 Leopold was invited to address the Second National Conference on Outdoor Recreation, where he described wilderness as "the fundamental recreational resource" and declared that "the conservation of wilderness is the most urgent and difficult of all the tasks that confront us." But Leopold also admitted that "evolving a wilderness policy and putting it into practice is a more difficult matter than justifying such a policy in theory" (National Conference 63). In particular, he urged his listeners not to make the error of assuming "that an area is either wild or not wild, that there is no place for intermediate degrees of wildness. All land planning must deal in intermediate degrees and especially in the skillful dovetailing of many uses in a single area. . . . The wilderness idea is merely a proposition in good land use planning" (National Conference 64).

In the next few years Leopold's Forest Service colleagues began to wrestle with those very issues. In 1926 William B. Greeley, chief forester since 1920, endorsed the Gila Wilderness Area and called for the creation of more such areas in all the western districts of the Forest Service. By 1928 more than 5 million acres of Forest Service land had been designated wilderness (Allin, *Politics* 72–73). The following year, new chief forester R. Y. Stuart issued the Forest Service's first official wilderness policy, known as the "L-20" regulation, which established "a series of areas to be known as primitive areas, . . . within which will be maintained primitive conditions . . . with a view to conserving the values of such areas for purposes of public education and recreation" (Allin, *Politics* 74). The regulation redesignated most wilderness areas as "primitive areas," but it did not expressly prohibit grazing, logging, or road-building in these areas, nor did it require the new designations to become permanent.

Leopold's advocacy certainly played a role in the adoption of the L-20 regulation, but the Forest Service's rivalry with the National Park Service remained a significant factor. On the one hand, as several historians suggest, fear of National Park Service expansion at the expense of Forest Service lands likely motivated foresters to support the designation of wilderness areas in the national forests (Allin, *Politics* 75–76; Roth 115).[33] On the other hand, as others argue, the Forest Service's reluc-

tance to make the wilderness designation permanent may also have been motivated by the opposite fear: that the permanent designation of wilderness areas
would make them the equivalents of national parks and thus facilitate the Park
Service's acquisition of these areas (Dana and Fairfax 156; Sutter 85).

The L-20 regulations also symbolized the rhetorical dimensions of the Park Service–Forest Service rivalry. Two years before the L-20 regulation was announced,
the National Park Service had begun to set aside land in some national parks as
"primitive areas" for scientific study (J. Gilligan 1:119). After the Forest Service
changed the name of its "wilderness" areas to "primitive" areas, the Park Service
then changed the name of its own "primitive" areas to "wilderness" areas (Allin,
Politics 72–74). This terminological flip-flop signified more than just an intera-
gency rivalry, as a 30 April 1940 letter from Robert Sterling Yard to Leopold reveals.
Yard, who was executive secretary of the National Parks Association at the time
(before he became president of the Wilderness Society), discovered that the roots
of the conflict lay in the very definition of "wilderness": "I recall going to Chief
Stuart in some vexation when this announcement [of the L-20 regulations] was
made and protesting that this apparently set up a Forest Service rival to the Park
Service primitive areas concerning which much was being said and written at the
time. But he and [head of National Forest Recreation Planning Leon F.] Kniepp
were immovable. They said that somebody had objected that 'wilderness' was a
horrid kind of name suggesting dangerous brutes and might scare people off. I
could scarcely believe them in earnest, and laughed when [National Park Service
director Horace] Albright announced that the Forest Service was welcome to
'Primitive' if it wanted it; thereafter National Park lands were to be called 'Wilderness.'"[34] In a telling reply, Leopold wrote to Yard on 8 May: "This squabble over
official labels has never interested me, but your story does; it throws light on some
unsuspected 'tender spots' in forester-psychology."[35]

Leon F. Kniepp, who drafted the L-20 regulation, offered a more formal explanation for the change from "wilderness" to "primitive" in the first *American
Planning and Civic Annual*. Kniepp argued that the colloquial term "wilderness"
was "a misnomer for areas prospected, grazed, logged, or otherwise occupied or
utilized for a half-century, threaded with trails and telephone lines, bounded by
highways, scrutinized daily during the fire season by lookouts and now traversed
frequently by airplanes." Likewise, the terms "virgin," "primeval," and "pristine"
could not apply to the areas under consideration for L-20 regulation, and the term
"natural," according to Kniepp, "creates a false distinction." The term "primitive,"
however, implies conditions "characteristic of earlier stages of the Nation's
growth," which was the objective "actually sought by the nature-lover and aimed
at by the Forest Service" (35). Thus, concluded Kniepp, "primitive" is "the term
most completely descriptive and expressive of their character" (36).

Ironically, just as the Forest Service was doing the difficult work of "evolving a wilderness policy and putting it into practice," as Leopold had suggested, Leopold himself left the Forest Service, resigning from the Forest Products Laboratory after four years of less-than-satisfying work. From 1928 to 1933 he served as a private forestry and wildlife consultant, making game surveys of the north-central states for the Sporting Arms and Ammunition Manufacturers Institute, until the Depression eroded his financial support. Finally, in 1933, with the support of many friends and colleagues, Leopold was appointed professor of game management at the University of Wisconsin, the first such position in the nation. It was a nontraditional appointment, since Leopold did not hold a Ph.D., but few could question his legitimacy, as he had just published *Game Management*, the only textbook in this emerging field (Meine, *Aldo Leopold* 256–310).

In that book, Leopold defined game management as "the art of making land produce sustained annual crops of wild game for recreational use," and he justified this agronomic approach with the same democratic rhetoric he had used in his wilderness advocacy (3). "It seems reasonable," he writes in *Game Management*, "to accept some moderate degree of control, rather than to lose species, or to suffer the restriction of sport to those financially able to follow the wholly wild game of the shrinking frontier into other lands" (4). He admits that "effective conservation requires, in addition to public sentiment and laws, a deliberate and purposeful manipulation of the environment — the same kind of manipulation as is employed in forestry" (21). But his version of manipulation — what he calls "agricultural art" (3) — involved working with the processes of nature rather than against them. Leopold endorsed a philosophy of "naturalism," which he described as "an effort to avoid artificiality in the manipulation of natural processes for conservation purposes" (396). Citing several examples of "artificial" forestry management practices that failed — such as clear-cutting instead of logging selectively — Leopold suggested that "the movement to establish permanent wilderness areas in the National Forests and Parks . . . is perhaps the most salient manifestation of naturalism so far apparent in conservation affairs" (396–97).

Leopold further developed this idea in "The Conservation Ethic," an address he delivered to the Southwestern Division of the American Association for the Advancement of Science in May 1933. The talk, published later that year in the *Journal of Forestry*, was one of Leopold's most important essays, which eventually became part of "The Land Ethic."[36] In it, Leopold attempted to articulate the relationship of human beings and the natural world by defining civilization "as a state of *mutual and interdependent coöperation* between human animals, other animals, plants, and soils" (*RMG* 183; emphasis in original). In a key passage, Leopold argued that flora and fauna can be preserved by "modifying the environment with those same tools already used in agriculture and forestry. . . . [T]his idea of controlled wild culture or 'management' can be applied not only to quail and trout, but to any living thing from bloodroots to Bell's vireos. . . . A rare bird or flower need remain no rarer than the people willing to venture their skill in building it a habitat" (RMG 190–91). At first glance, this notion of "management" might seem at odds with Leopold's claim throughout his articles of 1925 that wilderness was irreplaceable — that the possibility of ecological restoration in the future should not be used to justify the modification of wilderness in the present. But this was not what Leopold was arguing. Rather, he was elaborating on the point he made in "A Plea for Wilderness Hunting Grounds" that "we must learn to raise game and build roads on the same ground, or go gameless." It was an argument that people should be attending to the rest of the land *as well as* to wilderness, that they should be attempting to make the rest of the land as healthy as Leopold perceived the wilderness to be.

Although his focus had shifted from forestry to wildlife throughout the late 1920s and early 1930s, the idea of wilderness remained at the core of Leopold's message. At the same time, the place where the wilderness idea began — the Gila — had come under attack. In the late 1920s the Gila's deer population had exploded, due in part to a predator-control policy Leopold had helped to formulate, and the resulting overbrowsing of vegetation began to threaten the forest itself. Much to Leopold's dismay, one proposed measure to reduce the deer herd was to reconstruct the North Star Road, an old wagon trail, to make the Gila more accessible to hunters. Despite Leopold's objections, District Forester Frank Pooler approved this proposal in June 1929 and the road reopened in 1931 (Meine, *Aldo Leopold* 271).[37] Looking back on the episode in the 1947 foreword to "Great Possessions," Leopold had a striking slippage of memory: "The Forest Service," he writes, "in the name of range conservation, ordered the construction of a new road splitting my wilderness area in two, so that hunters might have access to the top-heavy deer herd. I was helpless, and so was the Wilderness Society. I was hoist of my own petard" (Leopold, Foreword 284).[38] Although the Wilderness Society was not formed until six years after the road was approved, so large did the Wilderness Society loom in Leopold's mind at the end of his life that he failed to notice the anachronism.

The Wilderness Society

Historians have tended to minimize Leopold's role in the Wilderness Society, acknowledging his intellectual contributions but crediting Bob Marshall and others with the society's day-to-day operations. Stephen Fox, for instance, says that Leopold "had probably the finest mind in conservation" but claims that he was too busy with the many other organizations he helped to start to do much for the

Wilderness Society.[39] "[H]e seldom came to Washington," Fox notes, "and never even met Bob Yard in person" ("We Want No Straddlers" 8, 10).[40] While this may be true, it certainly does not tell the whole story. As I suggest at the beginning of this chapter, Leopold made two critical contributions to the Wilderness Society that deeply affected its choice of scope and direction. First, he encouraged his fellow councilors to broaden the society's justifications for wilderness preservation to include ecological criteria, particularly through collaboration with the Ecological Society of America, and second, he encouraged them to broaden the society's notion of "wilderness" to extend beyond traditional aesthetic notions and incorporate other kinds of land use.

"Welcome News"

Leopold's involvement with the Wilderness Society began, as did many of his organizational commitments, by invitation, but it was an invitation whose genesis he had unknowingly helped shape. As his fellow organizer Harvey Broome put it in a 1940 account of the origins of the Wilderness Society, "Unquestionably, Aldo Leopold was the Jeremiah of wilderness thinking. . . . But if Leopold was the prophet of the wilderness movement, [Bob] Marshall was the first to suggest organization" ("Origins" 13). Marshall had first called for an "organization of spirited people who will fight for the freedom of the wilderness" in "The Problem of the Wilderness," a landmark article in the February 1930 *Scientific Monthly* in which Marshall quoted approvingly from Leopold's "Last Stand of American Wilderness" (142).[41] Marshall sent copies of his article far and wide — in an early correspondence with Leopold, Marshall called him "the Commanding General of the Wilderness Battle" — but not until 1934 did anything come of his proposal.[42]

One of the recipients of Marshall's 1930 article was Benton MacKaye, a forester with the Tennessee Valley Authority and the originator of the idea for the Appalachian Trail in 1921.[43] In 1934 MacKaye himself published an article in the journal *Appalachia*, expressing his dismay at several proposed "scenic roads" that threatened to undermine the trail he and others had been working to develop ("Flankline"). But MacKaye had not forgotten Marshall's idea of an organization of wilderness advocates, and when news came that Marshall would be visiting MacKaye's hometown of Knoxville in August, MacKaye contacted Harvey Broome, a local attorney and member of the Smoky Mountains Hiking Club, to arrange a meeting. Perhaps Marshall could be convinced to help organize a federation of hiking clubs to combat road-building in the vicinity of the trail — an idea first developed by Harold C. Anderson, secretary of the Potomac Appalachian Trail Club. Marshall, in fact, was in Knoxville for precisely the opposite reason. As director of forestry for the Department of the Interior's Office of Indian Affairs, he was there to study Park Service plans to route MacKaye's bête noire — the Blue Ridge Parkway — through the southern Appalachians. Nevertheless, Marshall was not only receptive to MacKaye's proposal, he also broadened it to resemble his original suggestion of a national organization of wilderness defenders. MacKaye quickly began drafting a statement of principles (Broome, "Origins" 13–14).

When Marshall returned to Knoxville in October for the meeting of the American Forestry Association, plans for the Wilderness Society began to take formal shape. But with Marshall and MacKaye both busy with conference proceedings, the organizers were pressed for time, so they ended up discussing MacKaye's statement of principles while driving to a CCC camp north of Knoxville for a conference field trip. In the car that day were Marshall, MacKaye, Broome, Bernard Frank (another forester with the Tennessee Valley Authority), and Frank's wife, Miriam. At one point, when the discussion must have become quite animated, the group pulled off the road and climbed a nearby bank to review MacKaye's draft in detail while the other conventioneers drove past. "One by one," recalled Broome, "we took up matters of definition, philosophy, scope of work, name of organization, how we should launch the project, the names of persons who should sign the statement and those to whom it should be sent." Eventually, the four men decided that they themselves should be the ones to sign it, and they sent the statement to six other prospective organizers, four of whom agreed to join the organization: Harold C. Anderson, whose idea had helped rekindle Marshall's enthusiasm for the plan; Ernest Oberholtzer, leader of the fight for the Quetico-Superior; Robert Sterling Yard, former editor of *Century* magazine and former head of the National Parks Association; and Aldo Leopold (Broome, "Origins" 14).

In his letter to Leopold, dated 25 October 1934, Marshall asked him to consider joining "a small group of people who have thought keenly and felt deeply about the value of preserving the primitive." The accompanying invitation detailed the society's goals: "We desire to integrate the growing sentiment which we believe exists in this country for holding its wild areas *sound-proof* as well as *sight-proof* from our increasingly mechanized life." The organizing committee, Marshall noted, would be judicious in extending additional invitations. "We want no straddlers, for in the past they have surrendered too much good wilderness and primevil [*sic*] areas which should never have been lost." The result, he indicated, would be a national organization of principled members able to respond to local battles at a moment's notice. "It will be no longer a case of a few individuals fighting but of a well organized and thoroughly earnest mass of wilderness lovers."[44]

Leopold's reply clearly indicated the direction his own thought had been taking in the ten years since his fight for the Gila. Marshall's letter was "welcome news," Leopold wrote, and he agreed to join the organizing committee. But he asked whether the society should include "only those interested in wilderness from the esthetic and social point of view, or whether it should also include those desiring wilderness for ecological studies. My hunch is that the ecological group should be included, but with a minor emphasis" and suggested that Marshall contact John C. Merriam for the names of additional prospective members.[45] Although Leopold's suggestion that ecological concerns should receive only a "minor emphasis" in the society illustrates that Leopold was still in the early stages of his own ecological education, the fact that he raised such concerns at all is worthy of note, not only because it showed how far Leopold had already come in his thinking, but also because it foreshadowed his later efforts to integrate the "ecological group" more systematically into the work of the Wilderness Society.

When the organizing committee held its first meeting at the Cosmos Club in Washington, D.C., on 20 and 21 January 1935, Leopold was unable to attend due to the concurrent meeting of the Twenty-first American Game Conference in New York. He wrote to Marshall prior to the gathering, however, saying: "Call on me when it [is] my turn to act."[46] Soon thereafter, Leopold was asked to comment on a nine-page typewritten statement about the society prepared by MacKaye, Broome, Yard, Anderson, and Marshall, all of whom were in attendance in Washington. Leopold suggested three changes that demonstrate his commitment to ecological value and his attention to the likely audience for such a document. First, he asked that the document's description of "extensive wilderness areas" include not only "timber, range lands, bare rocks, or snowfields" but also "marsh or desert." According to Leopold, "We are fighting not only mechanization of country, but the idea that wild landscape must be 'pretty' to have value." Second, aware of potential readers in the Forest Service, he suggested that a ban on "roads for autos" in wilderness areas be broadened to include "roads for motors," since "[s]ome forester will say a fire truck is not an auto." Finally, he asked that a line regarding the prohibition of erosion control "in the case of normal geological erosion" be struck, because "[t]here is no control of 'normal' erosion going on or in prospect, as far as I know."[47]

"He Would Make a Swell President"

In Washington, the other committee members appointed Marshall to serve as president of the society, but his work for the Department of the Interior posed a conflict of interest, according to Secretary of the Interior Harold Ickes. Why not do the work of a president, Ickes asked Marshall, "and let somebody else get the title." Marshall agreed that the proposal seemed like "a very sound idea" (J. Glover 182). Who better than Leopold, Marshall told Broome in a 28 February letter, since Leopold had "proposed the setting aside of extensive wilderness areas for the first time, to my knowledge. He has been head over heels in the fight ever since and he is entirely outside the government" (J. Glover 182). Marshall wrote to Leopold on 14 March: "It was my strong belief at the time that you would make a better President than I. The others . . . all agree that you would make a splendid President, therefore, may I in [*sic*] behalf of your coörganizers of the Wilderness Society, request, urge and implore you to accept the presidency of this Society."[48]

Initially, Leopold expressed only mild hesitation at the request, replying to Marshall on 25 March: "I have a great deal more than I can carry and would have to drop things to take on anything of this kind. . . . I would much prefer not to take it on. . . . What about Sterling Yard? Most policy affecting our interest is made in Washington. It is a long way from here to Washington and I hope at least to avoid very many trips there." Two days later, he wrote Marshall again, his hesitancy stronger: "It seems to me that the presidency ought to be in Washington. If my advice is valuable on matters of general policy, it can be made available to the Society just as well without any office or title." Marshall's request must have continued to weigh heavily on Leopold's mind, given his other responsibilities, because a week later he wrote to Marshall again, this time much firmer in his resolve: "Unless you have already taken action, I want to express the opinion that my taking the presidency of the Wilderness Society would be simply an absurdity. It necessarily involves a lot of lobbying on current departmental actions and bills of which I know nothing whatsoever and I lack both the time and the desire to find out."[49]

Leopold appears to have convinced his fellow organizers of his unsuitableness for the presidency, but a 9 April 1935 letter from Marshall to Benton MacKaye suggests that Leopold's many obligations may not have been the only reason the rest of the organizing committee did not press the point. "I have also been made aware from several sources that there is a considerable feeling against Leopold [as president] because of his activities with the Ammunition Institute, or whatever it was called," Marshall wrote, referring to Leopold's game surveys for the Sporting Arms and Ammunitions Manufacturers' Institute. "A lot of the game conservationists feel that he was working for the propagation of game merely that it might be slaughtered. I do not subscribe to this view and think he would make a swell president if he had the time but nevertheless it is something that should be considered."[50] In the face of Leopold's refusal of the nomination, the committee decided not to appoint anyone as president, but instead voted to appoint Bob Yard as permanent secretary, a position he maintained until the society incorporated in 1937, when he added the title of "president" to his résumé (Broome, "Origins" 15; J. Glover 183).[51]

One of the reasons Marshall felt Leopold would make a "swell president," despite others' concerns, was his knowledge that, as he wrote to Alvin G. Whitney on 1 May 1935, Leopold "had done some of the most effective work yet done to save various areas from mechanical invasion" (Fox, *John Muir* 210). Stephen Fox summarizes Marshall's interest in Leopold in his observation that "[m]ore than any other provocation, the founders of the Wilderness Society were worried about one overriding threat to the wilderness: the internal combustion engine in all its forms, as airplanes, motorboats, and — especially — automobiles. All were intrusions, all were ugly" ("We Want No Straddlers" 8). Yet Marshall and the other organizers either did not know or did not fully appreciate just how far Leopold had come since his early days in the Forest Service. As Curt Meine says of Leopold, "When he returned to an active role in the wilderness preservation movement in the mid-1930s, he did so with all the additional insight that his intellectual evolution could bring to the cause. The significance of wild lands was no longer just aesthetic, recreational, cultural, historical, or social, but scientific and ecological" ("Utility" 156).

A Momentous Year

Among the activities that contributed to Leopold's evolving idea of wilderness were his purchase of a worn-out, abandoned farm on the Wisconsin River in April 1935, his delivery of a lecture on land pathology later that same month, and his study of forestry practices in Germany for three months later that fall.

Leopold's purchase and transformation of his Wisconsin River property has been described at length elsewhere, not least of all in his own *Sand County Almanac*, but what marks its significance in this context is the potential Leopold must have seen in it in 1935 for reestablishing a bit of midwestern wilderness, the loss of which he had been mourning for almost thirty years. T. H. Watkins has described the Shack property as Leopold's "tiny imitation wilderness" ("Signature" 54), and William Cronon has suggested that the intensive tree-planting the Leopold family practiced there was in effect a form of ecological restoration "in a reversal of Turnerian progress, returning the land to health by recreating its former wildness. In a move that would have been quite alien to Turner or Muir, the Leopolds became gardeners of the wild" ("Landscape and Home" 103).

Leopold was too busy to begin this process of "rewilding" in 1935, in part because he was preoccupied with articulating the underlying philosophy for such action. On 15 April he delivered a talk to the University of Wisconsin's chapter of Sigma Xi, a scientific honor society, on the subject of land pathology. Leopold began his lecture by defining conservation as "a protest against destructive land use" that "seeks to preserve both the utility and beauty of the landscape" and that "now invokes the aid of science as a means to this end" (*RMG* 212). What, he asked, might scientists do to further this worthy goal? "In my opinion, there are two possible forces which might operate *de novo*, and which universities might possibly create by research. One is the formulation of mechanisms for protecting the public interest in private land. The other is the revival of land esthetics in rural culture. The further refinement of remedial practices is equally important, but need not here be emphasized because it already has some momentum. Out of these three forces may eventually emerge a land ethic more potent than the sum of the three, but the breeding of ethics is as yet beyond our powers. All science can do is safeguard the environment in which ethical mutations might take place" (*RMG* 215). It was the first time, apparently, Leopold used the term "land ethic," but he was as yet uncertain how such an ethic might be cultivated. The most scientists can do, he indicated, was to preserve "the land which is its medium" (*RMG* 212). Leopold's subject being private land, he concluded his talk by calling "for positive and substantial public encouragement, economic and moral, for the landowner who conserves the public values — economic and esthetic — of which he is the custodian" (*RMG* 216). But Leopold could not resist taking aim at the failure of one kind of public ownership: the parks. "A few parcels of outstanding scenery," he notes, "are immured as parks, but under the onslaughts of mass transportation their possible function as 'outdoor universities' is being impaired by the very human need which impelled their creation. Parks are over-crowded hospitals trying to cope with an epidemic of esthetic rickets; the remedy lies not in hospitals, but in daily dietaries" (*RMG* 216). Another remedy he might have mentioned lay in wilderness areas.

The opportunity to discuss this additional remedy came on 23 June, when Leopold received a request from Bob Yard to prepare a brief article for the Wilderness Society's new magazine, *Living Wilderness*, articulating "the fundamental need or purposes of the Society."[52] The article Leopold prepared — entitled "Why the Wilderness Society?" — appeared in the magazine's first issue in September 1935, the first of five such articles Leopold would contribute to *Living Wilderness*.[53] Leopold began the article on familiar ground, proclaiming the cultural value of wilderness and declaring it threatened by road development. "This country," he writes, "has been swinging the hammer of development so long and so hard that it has forgotten the anvil of wilderness that gave value and significance to its labors. The momentum of our blows is so unprecedented that the remaining remnant of wilderness will be pounded into road-dust long before we find out its values" (6). New Deal spending for work relief posed a particularly pressing threat to wilderness areas, Leopold claimed, and "[u]nder these circumstances it is fitting that those who perceive one or more of these values should band together for purposes of mutual education and common defense" (6).

Leopold carefully laid the groundwork for a new justification for wilderness, one whose full significance even the society's founders seem not to have recognized fully. Writes Leopold: "The recreational value of wilderness has been set forth so ably by Marshall, Koch, and others that it hardly needs elaboration at this time. I suspect, however, that the scientific values are still scantily appreciated, even by members of the Society. These scientific values have been set forth in print, but only in the studiously 'cold potato' language of the ecological scientist. Actually, the scientific need is both urgent and dramatic. The long and short of the matter is that all land-use technologies — agriculture, forestry, watersheds, erosion, game, and range management — are encountering unexpected and baffling obstacles which show clearly that despite the superficial advances in technique, *we do not yet understand and cannot yet control* the long-time interrelations of animals, plants, and mother earth" (emphasis in original). Citing the work of University of Nebraska botanist and plant ecologist John E. Weaver on the importance of native prairie plants to soil stability, Leopold suggested that only "those who see the values of the wilderness" could care "a hang about preserving prairie flora."[54] Recalling Leopold's earlier, private response to Bob Marshall — in which he argued that the Wilderness Society should be "fighting not only mechanization of country, but the idea that wild landscape must be 'pretty' to have value" — Leopold was now clearly taking his campaign public, urging the new society to broaden its philosophical and political scope. Leopold ends his article by describing the society as he wanted it to be rather than as it was. "The Wilderness Society," he writes, "is, philosophically, a disclaimer of the biotic arrogance of *homo americanus*. It is one of the focal points of a new attitude — an intelligent humility toward man's place in nature" (6). It would take more than wishful thinking, however, to turn Leopold's prescription for the society into an accurate description. In fact, it took a radical change of place even for Leopold himself to grasp the full consequences of this new attitude he had named.

The day after Leopold received Bob Yard's invitation to contribute to *Living Wilderness*, another invitation arrived, this one from the Oberlaender Trust, inviting Leopold to spend three months studying forestry methods in central Europe. (The trust was part of the Carl Schurtz Memorial Foundation, devoted to furthering German-American cultural relations, particularly in forestry.) Leopold accepted, and spent August, September, and October 1935 traveling through Germany and Czechoslovakia, studying the relationship between wildlife management and forestry (Meine, *Aldo Leopold* 351–60). Although the trip resulted in two of Leopold's better-known articles on nature protection and "permanent forests" in Germany, a handwritten paper titled, simply, "Wilderness" seems best to capture the essence of Leopold's experience.[55] In it, Leopold draws a distinction between the particular geographic spaces Americans called "wilderness areas" and a certain quality he called "wildness." "I did not hope to find in Germany anything resembling the great 'wilderness areas' which we dream and talk about, and sometimes briefly set aside, in our National Forests and Parks.[56] Such monuments to wilderness are an esthetic luxury which Germany with its timber deficit and the evident land-hunger of its teeming millions cannot afford. I speak rather of a certain quality which should be but is not found in the ordinary landscape of producing forests and inhabited farms, a quality which in some measure persists in some of the equivalent landscapes of America, and which we I think tacitly assume will be enhanced by rather than lost in the hoped-for practice of conservation" (*RMG* 226–27). Later in the paper Leopold identifies this "certain quality," this "wildness," as "a certain exuberance which arises from a rich variety of plants fighting with each other for a place in the sun"—a quality his daughter Nina now identifies as "biodiversity" (*RMG* 229; Bradley 4).[57] More important than its name, however, is Leopold's recognition that this quality can be present in any landscape. To say so is not to diminish the importance of preserving wilderness areas but rather to increase the importance of conserving ordinary land, more commonly known as "real estate." As Leopold himself put it in "Wilderness," "The impulse to save wild remnants is always, I think, the forerunner of the more important and complex task of mixing a degree of wildness with utility" (*RMG* 227).

"Beauty, in the Broadest Ecological Sense"

Leopold's characterization of American wilderness areas as "an esthetic luxury" for Germans could easily be misread to suggest that Leopold saw the mission of the Wilderness Society as simply one of preserving beauty. In fact, Leopold encountered such a misreading not more than a month after he returned home from Germany, when an editorial critical of the Wilderness Society in the *Journal of Forestry* caught his eye. Entitled "The Cult of the Wilderness," the editorial was the work of Herbert A. Smith, editor in chief of the journal and one of Leopold's friends. Smith accused the society of basing its platform on a questionable assumption: "that the primitive wilderness possesses an exquisiteness and richness of beauty which, once lost, can never be recovered." The implications of Smith's assertion were twofold. First, it suggested that the society's platform was based not on science but on aesthetics—a fact, Smith argued, that "removes the subject from the field in which foresters can claim to be qualified as experts for passing judgment." Second, it opened the society up to the charge of "false sentimentality" and "loose thinking" in aesthetics, according to Smith, since even experts such as landscape architects know that humans must sometimes make "judicious use of the ax" to achieve beauty in the landscape. Smith's conclusion, not surprisingly, was that scientific forestry had been doing it right all along. "A sound basis for public policy in determining where and to what extent wilderness should be preserved," he writes, "is to be sought not in transcendental or pantheistic nature idolatry but in our good old doctrine of obtaining, through wise use, the largest measure of contribution to the welfare of everybody in the long run" (957).

In a 20 December 1935 letter to the editor, excerpts of which appeared in the April 1936 issue of the journal, Leopold was careful not to offend Smith, expressing his gratitude that the *Journal of Forestry* "should at last lift its eyes, editorially, above the daily technical chatter of acres, authorizations, and acts of Congress" and labeling the piece "a brand new contribution" whose literary expression was "very pleasing indeed."[58] Furthermore, in his criticisms of the editorial, Leopold chose not to address Smith's assertion that the Wilderness Society embraced a "romantic sentimentalism" that viewed "the undisturbed handiwork of nature as supremely beautiful" (957)—perhaps because he suspected this was indeed true for some members. Instead, he sought to undermine both of the implications of Smith's argument by complicating his notion of beauty.

Leopold began with the first implication, that foresters lacked the expertise to judge beauty. "I suspect there are two categories of judgment which *cannot* be delegated to experts," Leopold writes, "which every man *must* judge for himself, and on which the intuitive conclusion of the non-expert is perhaps as likely to be correct as that of the professional. One of these is what is right. The other is what is beautiful." Furthermore, Leopold argued that beauty must be evaluated not simply according to traditional aesthetic measures but by ecological criteria as well. "The question of the 'highest use' of remaining wilderness is basically one of evaluating beauty, in the broadest ecological sense of that word." By linking beauty and ecology, Leopold not only undermined Smith's conclusion that "highest use" was to be determined through utilitarian calculations but also echoed and developed his own 1921 claim in the *Journal of Forestry* that "highest use" was recreational use. Now, Leopold was saying, highest use should be considered aesthetic use, but the measure of beauty should include ecological health. Finally, Leopold took issue with the second implication of Smith's argument, writing, "I am not much impressed with your logic in pitting wilderness beauty against landscaped beauty. Why argue whether the domestic fowl is more or less beautiful than the ivory-billed woodpecker? The question is irrelevant. The thing that matters is that the ivory-bill is beautiful, and, like the wilderness, irreplaceable and almost gone. Call this assertion a cult if you will,—that does not change its irrefutable logic" (Leopold, Letter). Beauty, ecological health, wildness, biodiversity—whatever the name, Leopold was more and more coming to the conclusion that the land in all its variety, from wilderness to agricultural landscapes, deserved more attention than it was receiving.

That Leopold knew not all the members of the Wilderness Society agreed with him that ecological health should be considered a measure of beauty is clear from his 6 January 1936 reply to Robert Sterling Yard, who had written to Leopold expressing concern about Smith's labeling the Wilderness Society a "cult." Writes Leopold: "I can imagine nothing better calculated to stimulate real thinking in our own ranks, and I certainly admit that such stimulation is needed in our own ranks as well as among our opponents."[59]

The Quality of Cranes

As with other newly organized groups, a key issue for the fledgling Wilderness Society was how to recruit new members. Initially, prospective members were identified by nomination, but this method proved only moderately successful and also tended to produce inbreeding. By April membership had reached a meager 85, and the majority of these members lived on the East Coast — with a full 30 percent of them living in Washington, D.C.[60] Although 45 more members joined in May, Yard became concerned about the society's slow growth but was uncertain how to proceed. "Is a more rapid method safe?" he wondered aloud in the society's May newsletter. "Members who will not work enthusiastically whenever opportunity offers are deceiving and a burden. . . . If any of us has a speedier substitute for our present plug-along method of member-getting, will you please tip us off?"[61] Gradually, as news of the organization spread, membership increased beyond this core group of devoted enthusiasts. By October it had reached 230; in 1937, it was at 576; and by 1941, it had grown to 796. Even compared to regional organizations such as the Connecticut Audubon Society, this clearly remained an elite group, much like the Boone and Crockett Club in both size and influence. As T. H. Watkins indicates, the society was "effective far beyond its paltry numbers, which in Leopold's lifetime never surpassed two thousand members" ("Signature" 60). "Its members," observes Curt Meine, "though few in number and diverse in personality, were headstrong, well-placed, and knowledgeable in the ways of land-use politics" (*Aldo Leopold* 344).

Exactly what this new society was supposed to do was another important issue in the first years of its existence, and Leopold seems to have been as challenged by this question as anyone. In a 20 January 1936 letter to Gaston Burridge he speculated, "I think the function of the Wilderness Society in relation to an area like the Gila is one of intelligent criticism. . . . Our job is to know enough about the various wilderness areas to be able to give them either support or criticism when some new question arises or some new policy is launched."[62] As the society grew, however, it became clear that "intelligent criticism" could be only one of its functions. Reporting on the first organizing meeting of the full membership in April 1937, the May 1937 newsletter observed, "All the members felt that, splendid as the activities of the Society have so far been, they have been largely of a negative type, fighting proposed invasions. It was agreed that there should also be positive campaigns launched to stimulate national interest in the preservation of wilderness in general without reference to specific invasions."[63] This was an important step forward for

the society, and while Leopold chose to plant trees at the Shack instead of traveling to Washington for the meeting, he nevertheless helped to revise the society's
bylaws that year, and would continue to contribute from afar.

Positive campaigns being more difficult than fighting proposed invasions, it
took several years for Leopold to find his cause célèbre in the Ecological Society
of America. In the meantime he continued exploring the linkage between aesthetics and ecology, wilderness and wildness. In October 1937 *American Forests*
published "Marshland Elegy," Leopold's paean to the sandhill cranes of Wisconsin, an essay that eventually became part of *A Sand County Almanac*.[64] In eloquent, evocative prose, Leopold enclosed the cranes in a vast circle of time, using
them as symbols of the broad sweep of evolutionary history that must ultimately
contain both ethics and aesthetics. Notably, Leopold struggled here, as he did in
his unpublished paper "Wilderness," to describe the certain "quality" in nature he
eventually came to call "wildness": "Our ability to perceive quality in nature begins, as in art, with the pretty. It expands through successive stages of the beautiful
to values at yet uncaptured by language. The quality of cranes lies, I think, in this
higher gamut, as yet beyond the reach of words. This much, though, can be said:
our appreciation of the crane grows with the slow unraveling of earthly history. His
tribe, we now know, stems out of the remote Eocene. The other members of the
fauna in which he originated are long since entombed within the hills. When we
hear his call we hear no mere bird. We hear the trumpet in the orchestra of evolution. He is the symbol of our untamable past, of that incredible sweep of mil-
lennia which underlies and conditions the daily affairs of birds and men" (*SCA*
96). Here, unlike in "Wilderness," Leopold speaks in more detail about the need
to preserve not only wildness but also specific wilderness areas from human in-
trusion. Moreover, he begins to link the ecological justification for wilderness to
the more traditional objections of his Wilderness Society colleagues to road-
building in recreational areas. "To build a road is so much simpler than to think
of what the country really needs. A roadless marsh is seemingly as worthless to the
alphabetical conservationist [Leopold's term for New Deal CCC and WPA con-
servationists] as an undrained one was to the empire builders. Solitude, the one
natural resource still undowered of alphabets, is so far recognized as valuable only
by ornithologists and cranes. Thus always does history, whether of marsh or market place, end in paradox. The ultimate value in these marshes is wildness, and the
crane is wildness incarnate. But all the conservation of wildness is self-defeating,
for to cherish we must see and fondle, and when enough have seen and fondled,
there is no wildness left to cherish" (*SCA* 101).[65]

Leopold's understanding of wilderness received an unexpected jolt from two
vacation trips he took in September 1936 and December 1937 to the Sierra Madre
of northern Chihuahua, Mexico. There he found a landscape similar in topogra-

phy and vegetation to the Gila but strikingly different from the heavily managed German forests he had recently observed. Wildlife was abundant, soils and vegetation were stable, and watersheds were intact. In "Conservationist in Mexico," published in *American Forests* in March 1937, Leopold described his first trip there with rapturous delight. "To my mind these live oak-dotted hills fat with side oats grama, these pine-clad mesas spangled with flowers, these lazy trout streams burbling along under great sycamores and cottonwoods, come near to being the cream of creation" (*RMG* 240). The land, he wrote, is "a picture of ecological health" (*RMG* 239). In the 1947 foreword to "Great Possessions," Leopold recognized the significance of these trips to his life and thought: "It was here that I first clearly realized that land is an organism, that all my life I had seen only sick land, whereas here was a biota still in perfect aboriginal health. The term 'unspoiled wilderness' took on a new meaning" (Leopold, Foreword 285–86). Whereas in 1935 he had concerned himself with "land pathology," increasingly he would turn his attention to "land health" (Meine, *Aldo Leopold* 368).

What may be most striking about Leopold's trips to Mexico, however, is the degree to which they forced him to wrestle with the relationship of wilderness to human inhabitation. In Chihuahua, Leopold found what he admits may at first have appeared "absurd" to the reader of "Conservationist in Mexico": that where the "predatory Apache" were "allowed to run at large," the Sierra Madre "still retains the virgin stability of its soils and all the natural beauty that goes with that enviable condition." It is ironic, Leopold admits, "that Chihuahua, with a history and terrain so strikingly similar to southern New Mexico and Arizona should present so lovely a picture of ecological health, whereas our own states, plastered as they are with National Forests, National Parks and all the other trappings of conservation, are so badly damaged that only tourists and others ecologically color-blind, can look upon them without a feeling of sadness and regret" (*RMG* 239).

Leopold's most sustained discussion of a native population's effect on its environment, "Conservationist in Mexico" never fully engages the question of whether healthy land and human inhabitation can coexist, nor does it directly address the philosophical justification for excluding native populations from wilderness areas. Nevertheless, in his juxtaposition of prehistoric Indian agricultural practices with the erosion, overgrazing, and overhunting that accompanies modern settlement, Leopold clearly understood the importance of these issues and worried over what he called "the inexorable process of losing quality to gain quantity" (*RMG* 243). In a haunting set of questions, he asked: can the Sierra Madre "arrest and control the wasteful and predatory nature of what we call 'development?' The self-defeating nature of mass-use of outdoor resources? Or are these evils inherent in industrial civilization?" (244). Unable to answer such questions, he sought refuge in a set of questions he thought he could answer. The Sierra

Madre, he claimed, "offers us the chance to describe, and define, in actual eco-logical measurements, the lineaments and physiology of an unspoiled mountain landscape. What is the mechanism of a natural forest? A natural watershed? A natural deer herd? A natural turkey range?" (244). It would be easy — too easy — to accuse Leopold of racism in his exclusion of indigenous populations from this definition of a "natural" wilderness area. Better to recognize the origin of this defi-nition in its fullest biographical and historical context: as coming from a man searching for solutions to humanity's toughest philosophical question and hoping to find at least a portion of the answer in the preservation of land from what he called "the Juggernaut" (240).[66]

"The Biota as a Whole Is Useful"

As Leopold returned to writing about the subject of outdoor recreation that he first addressed in his essays from the 1920s, he now began approaching the subject not only from the perspective of ecological science but also in a more literary style that would appeal to a broader audience. While both "Marshland Elegy" and "Conservationist in Mexico" appeared in *American Forests* — the continuation of *American Forests and Forest Life*, which published "Last Stand of American Wilderness" in 1921 — his next major essay appeared in *Bird-Lore*, Frank Chap-man's journal, which had been bought by the National Association of Audubon Societies in 1935. "Conservation Esthetic," published in the spring of 1938, also eventually became part of *A Sand County Almanac* — the first complete essay in what would become "The Upshot," the book's final, most philosophical section.[67]

"Conservation Esthetic" is in many ways a development of Leopold's lament in "Marshland Elegy" that "all the conservation of wildness is self-defeating." Indeed the meaning of the entire essay can be discerned in its final two, memorable sen-tences: "It is the expansion of transport without a corresponding growth of per-ception that threatens us with qualitative bankruptcy of the recreational process. Recreational development is a job not of building roads into lovely country, but of building receptivity into the still unlovely human mind" (SCA 176–77). Leopold began the essay by turning to history, noting that recreation "became a problem with a name in the days of the elder Roosevelt, when the railroads which had ban-ished the countryside from the city began to carry city-dwellers, *en masse*, to the countryside" (SCA 165). The automobile, he continued, "has spread this once mild and local predicament to the outermost limit of good roads — it has made scarce in the hinterlands something once abundant on the back forty. But that something must nevertheless be found" (165). Indeed, it is the search for that "something" — that quality Leopold had previously identified as "wildness" — that led Leopold to describe recreation as "a self-destructive process of seeking but never quite finding, a major frustration of mechanized society" (166). Yet not all outdoor recreation is the same, according to Leopold. "Equally conscientious citizens hold opposite views on what it is and what should be done to conserve its resource-base. Thus the Wilderness Society seeks to exclude roads from the hinterlands, and the Chamber of Commerce to extend them, both in the name of recreation" (SCA 168).

Hoping to resolve such conflicts, Leopold classifies outdoor recreation into five distinct components: (1) the hunt for a trophy, whether physical or photographic, (2) the search for the feeling of isolation in nature, (3) the search for fresh air and a change of scene, (4) the study of nature, and (5) the development of a sense of husbandry in the wild. To Leopold, these components exist on a moral spectrum, from least desirable to most desirable: "It would appear, in short, that the rudimentary grades of outdoor recreation consume their resource-base; the higher grades, at least to a degree, create their own satisfactions with little or no attrition of land or life" (SCA 176). What distinguishes the most-desirable from the least-desirable components of outdoor recreation is the quality of perception that a knowledge of ecology brings to the individual. "Recreation," writes Leopold, "is not the outdoors but our reaction to it. Daniel Boone's reaction depended not only on the quality of what he saw, but on the quality of the mental eye with which he saw it. Ecological science has wrought a change in the mental eye. It has disclosed origins and functions for what to Boone were only facts. It has disclosed mechanisms for what to Boone were only attributes. We have no yardstick to measure this change, but we may safely say that, as compared with the competent ecologist of the present day, Boone saw only the surface of things" (SCA 173–74). While significant in itself, this point gains particular importance as a result of the consequences that follow from it. Later in "Conservation Esthetic," Leopold writes: "Like all real treasures of the mind, perception can be split into infinitely small fractions without losing its quality. The weeds in a city lot convey the same lesson as the redwoods; the farmer may see in his cow-pasture what may not be vouchsafed to the scientist adventuring in the South Seas. Perception, in short, cannot be purchased with either learned degrees or dollars; it grows at home as well as abroad, and he who has a little may use it to as good advantage as he who has much."[68] This statement represents a crucial shift for Leopold, because it suggests that not all recreational wilderness areas need be "big enough to absorb a two week's pack trip." The net impact of Leopold's point is not that large wilderness areas are unnecessary—the desire for the feeling of isolation in nature, not to mention scientific reasons, suggest otherwise—but rather that the "wildness" of life itself can be found anywhere, if you know how to look. He had made a similar point in his unpublished "Wilderness" essay of 1935, but not nearly so eloquently, nor so publicly.

The following summer, Leopold further articulated the scientific reasons for the preservation of wilderness in one of the most important speeches of his career, a plenary address to a joint meeting of the Society of American Foresters and the Ecological Society of America on 21 June 1939. Published in September as "A Biotic View of Land" in the *Journal of Forestry*, the address offered what R. Edward Grumbine describes as "one of the first inclusive definitions of biodiversity," citing Leopold's conclusion that "the biota as a whole is useful, and biota includes not only plants and animals, but soils and waters as well" (Grumbine, "Biodiversity" 74; *RMG* 267). Major portions of the address also eventually became part of "The Land Ethic" in *A Sand County Almanac*.[69] Most interesting in this context, however, is Leopold's observation that "[t]he wilderness movement, the Ecological Society's campaign for natural areas, the German *Naturschutz*, and the international committees for wildlife protection all seek to preserve samples of original biota as standards against which to measure the effects of violence" (*RMG* 272). Leopold had argued for the scientific value of wilderness in "Why the Wilderness Society?" but he had never before made the case for wilderness in such specific ecological terms. Now the full richness of his message was becoming clear: large tracts of undeveloped land should be preserved for recreational purposes, certainly, but also — and perhaps more importantly — as samples of vanishing biotic systems.

Recreation Meets Ecology

By the end of the summer of 1939, Leopold had survived a budget battle between the University of Wisconsin and the legislature and — thanks to the support of friends and colleagues — been named chairman of his own, one-man Department of Wildlife Management (Meine, *Aldo Leopold* 396). In the meantime, two important developments had taken place that would affect the future direction of the Wilderness Society — and Leopold's influence on it.

The first was the hiring of Bob Marshall as head of the Forest Service's Division of Recreation and Lands in May 1937, which led to the approval in 1938 of a new Forest Service wilderness policy Marshall helped to develop. The policy attempted to address the weaknesses of the "L-20" regulation, which governed the seventy-six primitive areas that had been created on more than 13 million acres of Forest Service land. It directed the Forest Service to preserve "substantial areas of wilderness under as many different conditions of topography and forest type as is reasonably possible" and ordered regional foresters to resurvey these primitive areas and reclassify them into two new categories: "wilderness areas," which encompassed more than 100,000 acres, and "wild areas," which contained from 5,000 to 100,000 acres. Whereas the L-20 regulation had allowed grazing, logging, and road-building in many of the primitive areas, the new policy closed both the wilderness and wild areas to motorized transportation and excluded "motor homes, resorts, organization camps and commercial logging" from them (J. Gilligan 1:193–97; J. Glover 232). In September 1939, Secretary of Agriculture Henry A. Wallace formally approved what became known as the "U" regulations, endorsing this new Forest Service policy and requiring a ninety-day period of public notice (and public hearings, if demanded) before any changes to wilderness and wild areas could be made (J. Glover 264–65).[70]

Although the U regulations were the result of many forces, including the ongoing rivalry between the Forest Service and the Park Service for control of the public lands, Bob Marshall nevertheless deserves much of the credit for their existence (Allin, *Politics* 85; J. Glover 265). When Marshall died unexpectedly in November 1939, just two months after the new regulations were approved, Leopold proclaimed his passing "a loss to the Wilderness Society, not to mention the Forest Service and conservation in general."[71]

The second development that would affect the Wilderness Society in the last decade of Leopold's life was the growth of the Ecological Society of America (ESA) and its Committee on the Preservation of Natural Conditions. The ESA was founded in 1915 as a national scientific organization to "promote the interests of ecology," and from its beginning many of its members believed these interests included advocacy. In 1917 the ecologist Victor Shelford worked to establish a committee to advocate for "the preservation of natural conditions," and for more than twenty years his committee sought to influence legislation, federal and state agencies, and the general public to preserve nature for biological research. In a 1921 progress report Shelford and his colleagues noted several reasons for preserving natural areas, including aesthetic and recreational justifications, but they stressed that natural areas were "living museums" upon which the future of ecological research depended (Croker 120–23; Ecological Society; Shelford).

Since delivering his address on biotic land use to the ESA's joint meeting with the Society of American Foresters in June 1939, Leopold appears to have become increasingly frustrated by the disconnect between the preservationists in the ESA, who worked to protect wilderness for scientific reasons, and his fellow councilors in the Wilderness Society, who remained focused on the recreational uses of wilderness. On 4 June 1940 Leopold wrote to Robert Sterling Yard suggesting that the Wilderness Society "attempt in some way to join forces with the ecologists who are conducting an independent but parallel campaign for wilderness areas."[72] Four days later he wrote to the naturalist Robert Cushman Murphy and invited him to attend the upcoming annual meeting of the Wilderness Society in Washington, telling him that the society needs "counsel of the kind you can give": "One of the points I have in mind is this: the Society as now constituted is interested mainly in wilderness *recreation*. Another group, the Ecological Society, is interested mainly in wilderness *study*. There is little or no cooperation between the two groups, though both need the same changes in public policy. What needs to be done, I think, is to persuade both groups that wilderness recreation is destined to become more and more 'studious,' and wilderness studies more appreciative of esthetics, i.e., recreation."[73] Neither Leopold nor Murphy were able to attend the meeting, but Leopold sent a resolution to be considered, stating "that the Wilderness Society hereby invites the Ecological Society to attend its meetings and use its journal, and suggests to the Ecological Society a possible joint committee on cooperation."[74] Yard wrote back to Leopold following the meeting, saying, "Your suggestion went big for a combination with the Ecological Society, was universally approved, and your resolution passed."[75]

The following March, after a meeting of the Wilderness Society's executive committee, Yard detailed in the minutes how Leopold's suggestion had been pursued: "Last July [*sic*], Aldo Leopold had undertaken to bring about activity in common with a group of ecologists, and, at the beginning of this year, Irving Clark had established an understanding with the National Research Council's Committee for Preservation of Natural Conditions. Mr. Yard also had furthered negotiations for activity in common with the Committee for Preservation of Natural Conditions of the Ecological Society of America. The majority of the members of both these committees are discovered to be members of The Wilderness Society. Also we have renewed relationship with Dr. Victor E. Shelford, who just organized preservation in the Ecological Society, a member of The Wilderness Society; and Dr. Robert F. Griggs of George Washington University and the Research Council. Dr. Griggs has joined The Wilderness Society. It is my plan to have the combined ecological activities under Aldo Leopold's chairmanship."[76]

Although it is unclear how active Leopold was in pursing these activities, the Wilderness Society not only became an institutional member of the ESA, but it soon agreed, with Leopold's prodding, to give greater weight to scientific arguments for wilderness preservation.

Ironically, at the same time the Wilderness Society was embracing the arguments of the ESA's Committee on the Preservation of Natural Conditions, the Executive Committee of the ESA was recommending that the preservation committee be discontinued. In a 21 September 1944 letter to the Executive Committee of the Wilderness Society, ESA President Robert Griggs explained the reason for the recommendation, observing that "there has been a long standing difference of opinion in the Ecological Society concerning propagandizing for the preservation of natural conditions" and that "there is a feeling among some of the past presidents that a scientific society such as the Ecological Society of America would be in a stronger position if it delegated propaganda activities to other agencies organized for that purpose."[77] In 1945 the ESA membership agreed with the Executive

Committee, voting to deny the Committee on the Preservation of Natural Conditions "authority to take direct action designed to influence legislation," effectively ending the ESA's involvement in wilderness activism (Croker 143). Not all ecologists agreed with Griggs that "a differentiation between scientific and propaganda objectives would be desirable," however, and in response to the ESA's decision, a splinter group of ecologists formed the Ecologists' Union in 1945 to continue their lobbying efforts for wilderness preservation. In 1950 the group changed its name to the Nature Conservancy (Croker 144–46).[78]

"A Base-Datum of Normality"

Leopold became increasingly active in the Wilderness Society throughout the 1940s, most notably in the publication of several essays in *Living Wilderness* urging the society to broaden its notion of "wilderness."

In the spring of 1940 Leopold wrote "Origin and Ideals of Wilderness Areas" for the July issue of *Living Wilderness*, in which he related the history of the wilderness movement in the Southwest prior to 1926.[79] In perhaps the most important part of the essay, Leopold outlined "four jobs for the future now in sight" in the Southwest: (1) "to make the system of wild areas mean something in terms of particular rare plants and animals"; (2) "to guard against the disruption of the areas still wild"; (3) "to secure the recognition, as wilderness areas, of the low-altitude desert tracts heretofore regarded as without value for 'recreation' because they offer no pines, lakes, or other conventional scenery"; and (4) "to induce Mexico to save some samples of what we no longer have on our side of the border" (7).

In "Wilderness as a Land Laboratory," published the following July in *Living Wilderness*, Leopold clarified the scientific rationale for wilderness protection. Noting that "[t]he recreational value of wilderness has been often and ably presented, but its scientific value is as yet but dimly understood," Leopold asserted that wilderness was necessary as "a base-datum of normality, a picture of how healthy land maintains itself as an organism" (*RMG* 288). Describing wilderness as the "most perfect norm" for land health, Leopold relied on then-current notions of stability as an indicator of healthy land to advocate for the importance of wilderness areas to science. "Paleontology offers abundant evidence that wilderness maintained itself for immensely long periods; that its component species were rarely lost, neither did they get out of hand; that weather and water built soil as fast or faster than it was carried away" (*RMG* 288–89). Acknowledging that no healthy wilderness remained in the United States, Leopold recalled his experience in the Sierra Madre, noting that it "retains its full flora and fauna (save only the wild Indian) and . . . has only one intruded species (the wild horse). . . . Its preservation and study, as a norm for the sick lands on both sides of the border, would be a good neighborly act well worthy of international consideration" (Flader, "Let the Fire Devil" 93; *RMG* 289).

Further articulating the ideas he developed in "A Biotic View of Land," Leopold made two specific claims regarding the need for wilderness areas. First, he noted that a few isolated wilderness areas are not enough: "One cannot study the physiology of Montana in the Amazon; each biotic province needs its own wilderness for comparative studies of used and unused land" (*RMG* 289). Second, taking a page from the Forest Service's new U regulations, he acknowledged that not all wilderness areas need be as large as one hundred thousand acres: "All wilderness areas, no matter how small or imperfect, have a large value to land-science. The important thing is to realize that recreation is not their only or even their principal utility. In fact, the boundary between recreation and science, like the boundaries between park and forest, animal and plant, tame and wild, exists only in the imperfections of the human mind" (*RMG* 289).

"Wilderness as a Land Laboratory" was significant in that it allowed Leopold to synthesize his thinking on wilderness since his return to the issue in the mid-1930s. He returned again and again to the essay in the coming years, no doubt because it provided a compact statement of his strongest argument for wilderness preservation from a scientific standpoint. Most notably, he incorporated portions of the statement into his essay "Wilderness" in *Sand County Almanac*. More immediately, he used it as a reference point in discussions with his fellow Wilderness Society councilors about developing a standard definition of "wilderness areas." On 26 January 1942 Leopold wrote to Robert Sterling Yard: "Yes, I agree that the Society should have some well thought out definitions of wilderness areas, and I think the Forest Service definitions . . . are sound, and will serve as a foundation. I think another term should be used for areas smaller than 100,000 acres but of the same general intent. I suggest that the definition of purpose include scientific research in ecology as well as history, education, and recreation."[80] Reiterating his point on 13 February, Leopold again wrote to Yard: "The correspondence on Wilderness Area definitions is very illuminating, and proves again how hard it is to standardize. . . . When a new definition is drafted, I hope the scientific value will be included. My paper 'Wilderness as a Land Laboratory' might supply the framework for whatever definition is needed."[81]

Two other articles by Leopold appeared in *Living Wilderness* in 1942, both of which reiterated the messages of "Wilderness as a Land Laboratory," but to very different audiences. The first, "Wilderness Values," appeared in March and was reprinted from the 1941 *Yearbook* of the National Park Service.[82] Originally written for Park Service administrators, "Wilderness Values" cast the scientific argument for wilderness not only as a problem of perception (as in "Conservation Esthetic") but also as the natural inheritance of the twentieth-century frontiersman: "What matters is our ability to see the land as an organism. Most civilized men do not re-

alize that science, in enabling us to see land as an organism, has given us something far more valuable than motors, radios, and television. It is the intellectual exploration of land, including aboriginal land or wilderness, that constitutes the
frontier of the present century. Unless we can see the full gamut of landscapes
from wild to tame, we lose a part of our explorer's birthright" (24). In so doing, Leopold sought to assure recreation managers that scientific justifications are not the
province only of scientists. Reiterating a point he made privately to Robert Sterling
Yard in 1940, Leopold wrote that "[the] false cleavage between studies and sports
explains why the Natural Area Committee of the Ecological Society does not cooperate with the Wilderness Society, though both are asking for the perpetuation
of wilderness. 'Serious' ecological studies of a professional nature are, of course,
important, and they of course have a place in wilderness areas. The fallacy lies in
the assumption that all ecology must be professional, and that wilderness sports
and wilderness perception are two things rather than one. Good professional
research in wilderness ecology is destined to become more and more a matter of
perception; good wilderness sports are destined to converge on the same point"
(24). Finally, Leopold made perhaps his most forceful appeal for a broadening of
the wilderness idea beyond large tracts of undisturbed country. "One of the symp-
toms of immaturity in our concept of recreational values is the assumption, frequent among administrators, that a small park or forest has no place for wilderness.
No tract of land is too small for the wilderness idea. It can, and perhaps should, fla-
vor the recreational scheme for any woodlot or backyard. Of course, such small
wild places lack the scarcity value of large ones, and should not constitute an ex-
cuse for sacrifice of large ones. Small areas are not wild in any strict ecological
sense, but they may nevertheless add much to the quality of recreation" (25).

Leopold's final article for *Living Wilderness*, "The Last Stand," appeared in December 1942 and was reprinted from the May–June issue of *Outdoor America*.[83] A
plea for the preservation of the last stand of old-growth hardwoods in the Great
Lakes area, located in the Porcupine Mountains of the Upper Peninsula of Michigan, "The Last Stand" provides a concrete example of what Leopold termed the
"scarcity value" of large wilderness areas. The area deserved to be preserved, Leopold wrote, "as an act of national contrition, as the visible reminder of an unsolved
problem, and as an educational exhibit" (26). Among other things, the last stand
offered what Leopold called "the best schoolroom for foresters to learn what remains to be learned about hardwood forestry: the mature hardwood forest. We
know little, and we understand only part of what we know" (25). In its original publication in *Outdoor America*, the essay appeared with a sidebar containing details
of pending legislation and asking readers to write their congressmen. With the
assistance of the Wilderness Society, Leopold lobbied hard for the Porcupine
region, writing to the Michigan Department of Conservation, gathering legislative support, and giving public talks on the issue (Meine, *Aldo Leopold* 413, 434–

35). In 1943 the effort paid off, when the Michigan legislature purchased the area for a state park at a cost of $1 million (Flader and Callicott 290). Leopold had been pessimistic about the success of the preservation effort in wartime, predicting in "The Last Stand" that "[t]he war will surely outlast this remnant of forest" (25). Fortunately, he was mistaken.

The tenth anniversary of the Wilderness Society in 1945 occasioned concern for the future more than for the past, given the death of Robert Sterling Yard on 17 May, just nine days after VE-Day. At a 14 July 1945 meeting of the governing council in Washington, D.C., Benton MacKaye asked the councilors, "What is our function in the post-war period we are entering? Is it big or little? If 'little' we should liquidate. But I am assuming it is 'big' — if for no other reason than the condition of our average returning fighter from this war — his need for a place wherein serenity shall quell confusion."[84] Aware of the need for leadership, and perhaps seeing an opportunity to advance his own agenda, Leopold finally accepted an official role in the society at this meeting, becoming vice president — an office he would retain until his death — while Benton MacKaye became president, Howard Zahniser became executive secretary, and Olaus Murie became director (Fox, "We Want No Straddlers" 10; Meine, *Aldo Leopold* 471). The following June, he met with the councilors again at their annual meeting, held this time at the foot of Old Rag Mountain in Virginia (see page 211).

In a retrospective of the society's first thirty years, Harvey Broome described Leopold as "a warm, considerate, and resourceful colleague" who also held "uncompromising views" — a description that seems to fit the evidence quite well (Broome, "Thirty Years" 17). Leopold appeared not to fear being "out of step with the company" when necessary, and as vice president he continued to press his fellow councilors to think beyond the recreational use of wilderness.[85] In a 1 May 1946 letter to MacKaye, Leopold made his postwar priorities vividly clear: "I am thoroughly convinced of one basic point: that wilderness is merely one manifestation of a change of philosophy of land use and that the Wilderness Society, while focusing on wilderness as such, cannot ignore the other implications and should declare itself on them, at least in general terms."[86] When the society did attempt to do so, however, Leopold remained a careful critic, such as when Howard Zahniser polled the governing council in November 1946 on whether the Wilderness Society should support the move for federal regulation of timber cutting on private land. Leopold was the only councilor to vote against the proposal, telling Zahniser: "The issue is so far reaching that I do not think the argument of timber exhaustion is more than a small fraction of the question. I am not yet convinced that federal regulation is workable. I think the agitation for it has been useful in stimulating the states to 'shake a leg.'"[87]

In 1947 Leopold finally seems to have made his mark on the Wilderness Society, convincing his fellow councilors to begin a new campaign for a coordinated

Aldo Leopold and fellow Wilderness Society councilors at the 1946 annual meeting, held 21–23 June at the foot of Old Rag Mountain, Virginia. *Left to right:* Harvey Broome, Benton MacKaye, Leopold, Olaus J. Murie, Irving M. Clark, George Marshall, Laurette Collier (staff), Howard Zahniser, Ernest C. Oberholtzer, Harold C. Anderson, Charles G. Woodbury, Robert F. Griggs, Ernest S. Griffith, and Bernard Frank. (Courtesy The Wilderness Society)

system of wilderness areas throughout North America. In a July 1947 press release following the governing council's meeting in northern Minnesota, the council presented the campaign as primarily recreational in intent, but its practical effect was clearly ecological. The press release began by stating that such areas "have unique scientific values and are of historical and educational importance but their outstanding value is in 'preserving for all Americans the choice they now have of finding recreation in the wilderness if they so wish.'" It followed this statement, however, by quoting Leopold extensively. "Already it is too late to save a sample area of every type of primitive America. Gone entirely are all large stretches of the primitive prairie," he was said to have declared. Although "for about half of the types of primitive America all substantial remnants have already disappeared," and although "it will be most difficult to find areas of some other types," there is still opportunity "to preserve a wilderness system that will be of inestimable value to future generations, as well as to the present." Benton MacKaye thus "called for aggressive action that would secure in a continental system representative units of every type of wilderness now remaining." Wilderness areas were sought in eleven principal land and water types — lake state pines, short-grass prairie, Rocky Mountain conifer, northwest conifer, southwest bushfield, southwest desert, coastal prairie, coastal swamp, south Appalachian, northwest conifer, and tundra — and small natural areas were sought in seven other types — lake state hardwood, oak hickory, high-grass prairie, coastal pine, piedmont, Atlantic coastline, and Pacific coastline. In addition, the society announced its desire to cooperate with other organizations — conservation organizations, educational and scientific institutions, civic groups, governments — "in preserving before too late representative remnants of the once extensive and greatly varied American wilderness."[88]

It was as if everything Leopold had been saying about wilderness for the last twelve years had finally come to fruition. There was the recognition of the scientific value of wilderness. There was the system of interconnected wilderness areas representing distinct ecosystems. There was the call for cooperation with other organizations, such as the Ecologists' Union. There was the evidence that "wilderness" meant more than aesthetically pleasing landscapes. And, perhaps most strikingly, there was the claim that "wilderness" meant more than areas big enough to sustain a week's pack trip. In a 9 November 1947 memo to all the members of the Wilderness Society describing the launch of the campaign, MacKaye noted that "[t]he spots of wilderness that would result should be in every type of country from Alaskan tundra and Canadian conifer to Florida everglade. They should be large and small. The large spots require the special attention of The Wilderness Society Council and staff. The small spots should concern our individual members in their respective neighborhoods." Asking members to find and protect "small areas of ridge, marsh, intervale, and other wildland patches" in their home localities, MacKaye explained, "Here is a project for the membership rather than the staff — a little job for each in his own back yard."[89] As J. Baird Callicott and Susan Flader indicate, "The idea that each state should have one wilderness preserve for the affordable experience of its residents was transformed into the idea that each biome should have a wilderness preserve as a benchmark of health and stability against which ecologists might measure the disorganizing impact of land-use technologies in similar biotic communities elsewhere" (RMG 27).[90]

A Sand County Almanac

The June meeting of the Wilderness Society councilors must have gone well for Leopold on a personal as well as programmatic level, because in August he sent a letter to Howard Zahniser requesting assistance from both Zahniser and Olaus

Murie: "I am compiling my essays for publication and as you remember there are several on wilderness. Many of the allusions to current issues are out of date and there is also some duplication, hence I have tried to combine them into one essay which attempts to sketch all of the important ideas about a wilderness program. . . . I need your critical scrutiny and also Olaus'. What is omitted? What should be added? Are the illustrative cases well selected? What parts lack force?"[91] The compilation, of course, became *A Sand County Almanac*, and the essay in question became "Wilderness," the penultimate essay in "The Upshot."

"Wilderness" had not always occupied the next-to-last position in the book. In Leopold's original manuscript of *A Sand County Almanac*, entitled "Great Possessions," "Wilderness" appeared as the final essay, and it was only in the editorial discussions following Leopold's death in 1948 that the decision was made to move "The Land Ethic" from its original position as the first essay in "The Upshot" to its current position following "Wilderness."[92] Part of the impetus for this change may have come from Alfred G. Etter, a graduate student in botany at Washington University, who was asked to review the manuscript of "Great Possessions" prior to publication. Etter's comments on "Wilderness" in his reader's report are particularly noteworthy, as they reveal his limited understanding of the role of wilderness advocacy in the conservation movement and suggest that Leopold may in fact have had some very good reasons for positioning "Wilderness" where he did, especially considering his recent successes with the Wilderness Society: "With reference to this essay, I feel strongly that it is not the proper piece for the ending. It is on a limited phase of conservation, it refers to a particular society as though the book were written with the intention of advertising it, and the convictions and hopes of the professor are not nearly so well infused into this work as in the "Land Ethic." The Foreword refers seemingly almost specifically to the concepts in this latter essay. I cannot understand why the Professor would not have chosen this essay to proclaim his most important message to 'our bigger-and-better society.' *Wilderness* might very well become the first in the group 'The Upshot,' and the Land Ethic the last."[93] Whether or not "The Land Ethic" is in fact better suited in its current position is not the issue, so much as why Leopold may have placed "Wilderness" where he did and how differently we would perceive his relationship to the wilderness idea had the essay remained in its original location.

On 2 November 1943, at about the time he was beginning to assemble what became *A Sand County Almanac*, Leopold made some "notes for a paper on writing," in which he described the difference between commentary and exposition: "One of the most frequent (and sometimes the most damaging) errors in writing is to forget just what the reader knows, as compared with what you know, and to launch into commentary before exposition has been completed. If both you and your reader know the facts at issue, then you may discuss, appraise, and interpret them without describing them. Such writing is *commentary*. . . . If only you know the facts at issue, then you must first describe the facts before you can discuss, appraise, or interpret them. Such setting forth of facts is *exposition*. It is a necessary prelude to commentary."[94] As Dennis Ribbens has observed, *A Sand County Almanac* is a working out of these notes: "It begins with the facts and descriptions of land and of man at the shack. Only then does it move on to discussion, appraisal, and interpretation" (105). How different might that interpretation have been had it ended with "Wilderness"?

For one thing, Leopold's reputation as an ecological philosopher might have been deepened by a greater recognition of his political activism. William Cronon has said of *A Sand County Almanac* that "[o]ne gets the sense that the author would be much happier getting out into the woods with his dog than finding himself mounting the barricades on behalf of a political cause" ("Voice" 9). And Sylvia Noble Tesh has observed that, with the exception of "The Land Ethic," the essays in *A Sand County Almanac* consist of "the stuff of poetry and of religion, not the stuff of social movements. They inspired reverence in readers, not collective action" (45). Both these points about the contemplative tone of *A Sand County Almanac* are well taken, but I wonder whether ending the book by referring "to a particular society as though the book were written with the intention of advertising it" might have altered that tone in a modest, yet significant way. Political activism takes many forms, and while few literal barricades were erected on behalf of wilderness preservation until Earth First! appeared in the early 1980s, Leopold was as dogged in pursuit of political change as he was in pursuit of canvasbacks, and his essay on wilderness reflects that fact better than any.

Imagine having read through the "Sand County Almanac" of part 1, the wide-ranging sketches of part 2, and the rest of "The Upshot" in part 3, all before reaching the book's final essay on "Wilderness." What would one find?

One would find a brief essay consisting of six parts: an unlabeled introduction, a categorization of "the remnants" of remaining wilderness, a section for each of Leopold's justifications for wilderness (recreation, science, and wildlife), and a final section on the defenders of wilderness.

Leopold begins his essay by making two foundational claims about the relationship of wilderness to human culture. "Wilderness is the raw material out of which man has hammered the artifact called civilization. Wilderness was never a homogeneous raw material. It was very diverse, and the resulting artifacts are very diverse. These differences in the end-product are known as cultures. The rich diversity of the world's cultures reflects a corresponding diversity in the wilds that gave them birth" (SCA 188). While one should rightly be suspicious of an over-reliance on environmental determinism, that is not what Leopold is doing here. Rather, he is reminding readers of the biological basis for human cultural evolution, his point being that the proper end product of that evolution is "the development of the perceptive faculty" detailed earlier in "The Upshot" in "Conservation Esthetic" (SCA 174). As Leopold indicates at the close of the introductory section of "Wilderness," "to the laborer in repose, able for a moment to cast a philosophical eye on the world, . . . [wilderness] is something to be loved and cherished, because it gives meaning and definition to his life. This is a plea for the preservation of some tag-ends of wilderness, as museum-pieces, for the edification of those who may one day wish to see, feel, or study the origins of their cultural inheritance" (SCA 188).[95]

Leopold catalogs these tag ends in "The Remnants," noting that "in any practical program the unit areas to be preserved must vary greatly in size and in degree of wildness" (SCA 189). Wilderness may thus be found anywhere, according to Leopold, and should not be defined by "that under-aged brand of esthetics which limits the definition of 'scenery' to lakes and pine trees" (SCA 191). Wilderness exists in prairies, forests, coastlines, deserts, and Arctic landscapes, and one must always remember that federally protected wilderness areas "are not so secure as the paper record might lead one to believe" (SCA 190).

Leopold's justifications for wilderness on the basis of recreation and science in the next two sections recast familiar arguments from "Wilderness as a Form of Land Use" and "Wilderness as a Land Laboratory" and need not be repeated here. The section of the essay on "Wilderness for Wildlife," however, offers a new argument — based on Leopold's 1936 essay "Threatened Species"[96] — that links wilderness preservation to endangered species protection. Claiming that the national parks are too small to support large carnivores such as the grizzly bear, Leopold makes the point — now well documented by conservation biologists — that many animal species "do not seem to thrive as detached islands of population" (SCA 198). The solution, says Leopold, is "for the wilder parts of the National Forests, which usually surround the Parks, to function as parks in respect of threatened species" (SCA 198) — a proposal now formalized by those same conservation biologists in the concept of "buffer zones" to surround core species habitat.

Linking wilderness preservation to endangered species protection has important ethical implications, of which Leopold was also aware. Echoing an argument he first made in 1937 in "Marshland Elegy," which became the lead essay in part 2 of *A Sand County Almanac,* Leopold claims that a nonanthropocentric environmental ethic ultimately rests on an evolutionary perspective of history: "Permanent grizzly ranges and permanent wilderness areas are of course two names for one problem. Enthusiasm about either requires a long view of conservation, and a historical perspective. Only those able to see the pageant of evolution can be expected to value its theater, the wilderness, or its outstanding achievement, the grizzly" (SCA 199). In *The Arrogance of Humanism,* David Ehrenfeld calls this argument the "Noah principle": "This non-humanistic value of communities and species is simplest of all to state: *they should be conserved because they exist and this existence is itself but the present expression of a continuing historical process of immense antiquity and majesty*. Long-standing existence in Nature is deemed to carry with it the unimpeachable right to continued existence" (208; emphasis in original). In *Confessions of an Eco-Warrior*, Dave Foreman puts it more colloquially: "We are not talking about a football game or a high-school debate here; we are discussing the continuation of three and half billion years of evolution" (123). "Wilderness for Wildlife" thus serves an important function in Leopold's overall argument in "Wilderness," adding a third justification to his defense of wilderness and grounding it in a nonanthropocentric, evolutionary ethic.

The final section of the essay, entitled "Defenders of Wilderness," articulates the political implications of Leopold's three wilderness justifications and, as Alfred G. Etter correctly noted, "refers to a particular society as though the book were written with the intention of advertising it." Wilderness, Leopold observed, "is a resource which can shrink but not grow. . . . It follows, then, that any wilderness program is a rear-guard action, through which retreats are reduced to a minimum. The Wilderness Society was organized in 1935 'for the one purpose of saving wilderness remnants in America.' It does not suffice, however, to have such a society. Unless there be wilderness-minded men scattered through all the conservation bureaus, the society may never learn of new invasions until the time for action has passed. Furthermore, a militant minority of wilderness-minded citizens must be on watch throughout the nation, and available for action in a pinch" (SCA 200).[97] In the final paragraph of the essay, which was to be the final paragraph of the book, Leopold links this call for political activism to that certain "quality" in nature he came to call "wildness": "Ability to see the cultural value of wilderness boils down, in the last analysis, to a question of intellectual humility. The shallow-minded modern who has lost his rootage in the land assumes that he has already discovered what is important; it is such who prate of empires, political or economic, that will last a thousand years. It is only the scholar who appreciates that all history consists of successive excursions from a single starting-point, to which man returns again and again to organize yet another search for a durable scale of values. It is only the scholar who understands why the raw wilderness gives definition and meaning to the human enterprise" (SCA 200–201).

Susan Flader has written that "[w]hile his reference to 'the scholar' may sound elitist, the context makes clear that by scholar Leopold means a person of intellectual humility — one who still asks questions and knows that the quest for understanding never ends" ("Let the Fire Devil" 93). Though Leopold certainly meant his scholar to be humble, the context also makes clear that he meant his scholar to be elitist — in the best sense of the word.

Leopold was likely influenced in his thinking about elitism by José Ortega y Gasset, the Spanish existentialist, whose *Revolt of the Masses* (1929) Leopold had read soon after its English translation became available in 1932. Leopold referred to the book in "The Conservation Ethic" (1933), portions of which eventually became part of "The Land Ethic": "The ultimate issue, in conservation as in other social problems, is whether the mass-mind *wants to* extend its powers of comprehending the world in which it lives, or, granted the desire, *has the capacity to do so*. Ortega, in his *Revolt of the Masses*, has pointed the first question with devastating lucidity. The geneticists are gradually, with trepidations, coming to grips with the second. I do not know the answer to either" (RMG 192).

Ortega had warned against the "tyranny of the majority" in *The Revolt of the Masses*, arguing that modern society is composed of masses of individuals content to live a common life, as opposed to a select minority who challenge themselves intellectually. Leopold hardly accepted this conclusion uncritically — he hardly accepted any conclusion uncritically — as his claim not to know the answer to Ortega's question makes clear. But he did believe there was a difference between the "shallow-minded modern" and the "scholar," and that difference was the scholar's appreciation of wildness — the "single starting-point" of evolutionary history. It is this that underlies all human efforts at establishing "a durable scale of values" and which — in its purest form, in the wilderness — "gives definition and meaning to the human enterprise."

The second way in which we might have interpreted Leopold differently had *A Sand County Almanac* ended with "Wilderness," therefore, is that more readers might have been inclined to agree with Max Oelschlaeger, who observed that "[b]y the time *Sand County Almanac* was published Leopold viewed wilderness as a necessity for the human animal: as an ontic foundation underlying culture and a backdrop essential to any measure of the human estate that sought to escape the merely transitory and contingent categories of culture" (*Idea* 220–21).

Leopold's focus on the scholar rather than the scientist reflects the fact that *A Sand County Almanac* is as much a work of environmental history as it is a work of environmental ethics, although it has primarily been seen as the latter.[98] In fact, one could say, following Oelschlaeger, that the land ethic emerges from, and is thus dependent on, a deep sense of one's own environmental history — exactly the kind of knowledge Leopold had attempted to model in parts 1 and 2. Without a historical understanding of one's self and one's culture, Leopold seemed to be saying, no land ethic of any kind is possible. Seen from this perspective, Leopold's writing and advocacy on behalf of wilderness were not "milestones along his route to a land ethic," as Susan Flader and other scholars have suggested, but the very foundation of the land ethic itself ("Aldo Leopold" 4). The land ethic, it could be said, was built on Leopold's understanding of wilderness, both theoretically and biographically.[99]

Today, Leopold's legacy rests mainly on A *Sand County Almanac*, a fact that is due in part to the efforts of the Wilderness Society. Only a year after its publication Benton MacKaye wrote to Howard Zahniser to say that the Wilderness Society "should push Aldo's book to the limit" (Fox, *John Muir* 271). Since then, the book has taken on near-legendary status. Writing in the pages of *Wilderness* in 1985, on the occasion of the fiftieth anniversary of the Wilderness Society, Wallace Stegner praised the book about as highly as anyone could. "When this forming civilization assembles its Bible," he said, "its record of the physical and spiritual pilgrimage of the American people, the account of its stewardship in the Land of Canaan, Aldo Leopold's A *Sand County Almanac* will belong in it, one of the prophetic books, the utterance of an American Isaiah" (Stegner, "Living" 15). Two years later *Wilderness* editor T. H. Watkins called A *Sand County Almanac* "one of the central documents — some would say, *the* central document — of the modern conservation movement" (Editor's Note 57).

What to do with Leopold's insights into wilderness and the wild remains an open question more than fifty years after the publication of A *Sand County Almanac*. Leopold himself had held out hope — like Roosevelt, Wright, and Muir before him — that education and legislation would eventually turn the tide of "progress" in favor of conservation. "[I]f education really educates," he wrote in "Wilderness," "there will, in time, be more and more citizens who understand that relics of the old West add meaning and value to the new" (SCA 199). After thirty years more of "progress," however, Bob Marshall's memorable invitation to Leopold and others to join the Wilderness Society — "We want no straddlers" — became a motto of far more utopian ambitions in the hands of Earth First! — "No Compromise in Defense of Mother Earth," and Leopold's questions about the desires and capacities of the mass-mind were put to a more challenging test.

CHAPTER FIVE

Toward Ecotopia

Edward Abbey
and Earth First!

Don't talk to me about other worlds, separate realities,
lost continents, or invisible realms — I know where I belong.
Heaven is home. Utopia is here. Nirvana is now.

EDWARD ABBEY, "Science with a Human Face"

S PRING EQUINOX, 21 March 1981. Under a cloudless, bright blue sky, a crowd gathers at the visitor's center parking lot near Glen Canyon Dam in southeastern Utah. About seventy-five protesters — members of a radical new environmental group named Earth First!—chant slogans and hold placards reading "Free the Colorado!" and "Let It Flow." As the dam's security force becomes occupied with the demonstration, four men and one woman quickly scale the fence surrounding the dam and move toward the center of the structure carrying a one-hundred-pound roll of black plastic sheeting.[1] To the delight of the crowd, the protestors secure the top of the plastic roll to a series of grilles on the dam and drop the rest of the roll over the edge, unfurling what soon becomes a three-hundred-foot wedge, which tapers from twelve to two feet in width and resembles nothing less than a long, narrow "crack" in the dam's face (Foreman, *Confessions* 21–22; Lee, *Earth First!* 45–46; McBride 34–36; McLeod).

As the "monkeywrenchers" complete their task and escape, Edward Abbey rises to speak to the crowd from the back of a pickup truck. Dressed in a blue parka, red bandana, and white cowboy hat, the author and environmentalist informs the onlookers that

the industrialization, urbanization, and militarization of the American West continues. More dams are proposed, more coal-burning and nuclear-power plants projected, an MX system that would desolate much of Nevada and western Utah, more river-diversion projects, more strip mining of our mountains, more clearcutting of our forests, the misuse of water, the abuse of the land. All for the sake of short-term profit, all to keep the industrial-military empire going and growing until it finally reaches the point where it must self-destruct and destroy itself.

What is the sake of building a great city if you haven't got a tolerable planet to put it on? Earth First!

How can we create a civilization fit for the dignity of free men and women if the globe itself is ravaged and polluted and defiled and insulted? The domination of nature leads to the domination of human beings.

Meanwhile, what to do? Here I can offer nothing but more of the same. Oppose. Oppose the destruction of our homeland by these alien forces from Houston, Tokyo, Manhattan, Washington, D.C., and the Pentagon. And if opposition is not enough, we must resist. And if resistance is not enough, then subvert.

After ten years of modest environmental progress, the powers of industrialism and militarism have become alarmed; the empire is striking back. Well, we must continue to strike back at the empire by whatever means available to us. Win or lose, it's a matter of honor. Oppose, resist, subvert, delay, until the empire itself begins to fall apart.

And until that happens, enjoy. Enjoy the great American West — what's left of it. Climb those mountains, run those rivers, hike those canyons, explore those forests, and share in the beauty of wilderness, friendship, love, and the common effort to save what we love. Do this, and we'll be strong and bold and happy. We will outlive our enemies, and as my good old grandmother used to say, we'll live to piss on their graves. (McLeod)

The first public action of Earth First! — which came nearly eleven years after the first Earth Day was held on 22 April 1970 — the "Cracking of Glen Canyon Dam" is now recognized as a critical moment in the history of American environmentalism. It must also be seen as a critical moment in the life and career of Edward Abbey. In Abbey's speech that morning can be seen all the threads that tie his vision as an environmentalist to his work as a novelist and essayist. Abbey follows Dwight Eisenhower in warning of the threat of the "military-industrial complex" to the future of the American Dream; he connects these forces to the urbanization of the West and the destruction of western environments; and he attributes this growth to greed and forecasts the eventual collapse of industrial civilization.[2] Abbey summarizes his arguments in accessible slogans; he uses well-known analogies to make his points (George Lucas's film *The Empire Strikes Back* was released in 1980); and he suggests that environmental protest should be the concern of all patriotic Americans.[3] In his comments, Abbey also reminds the crowd that he has been sounding these themes for more than a quarter century, having written of individual resistance to oppressive authority in his early fiction, having envisioned the demolition of Glen Canyon Dam in *Desert Solitaire* (1968), his best-known work, and having advocated the practice of "monkeywrenching" in his popular novel *The Monkey Wrench Gang* (1975).[4] Finally, Abbey invokes a coming golden age of freedom and wilderness, which his listeners can at least enact on a temporary basis by climbing mountains, running rivers, and engaging in collective action. In closing, Abbey invokes his well-known frontier humor, encapsulating the rebelliousness of the dam-cracking itself, which one observer described as "a wisecrack, a daring bit of humor in an environmental movement that had become glum and solemn" (Scarce 57).

This chapter explores the rich relationship between Abbey's novels, nature writings, and essays and the actions and philosophies of Earth First! which Mark Dowie calls "a bastard child of the Wilderness Society" (209). In particular, I argue that Abbey's dual interests in anarchism and desert environments helped to foster the development of a utopian narrative that directly affected the goals and methods of Earth First![5] Furthermore, I claim that by linking environmental activism with the philosophy of biocentrism, Abbey encouraged the use of illegal tactics to protest practices many environmentalists considered illegitimate. In light of the recent rise in incidents of domestic and international terrorism — such as the Oklahoma City bombing, the serial killings of the Unabomber, and the attacks on the World Trade Center and the Pentagon — I question the firm line Abbey draws between "ecosabotage" and "ecoterrorism," suggesting that the usefulness of monkeywrenching must be judged not only on what it harms but also on what it helps. Finally, although Abbey disliked being labeled a "nature writer," I argue that his adoption of a deliberately provocative persona and his conflation of fictional and nonfictional characters and events in support of environmental protection place him squarely in the ranks of those modern nature writers — such as Annie Dillard, Barry Lopez, and Terry Tempest Williams — working at the boundaries of the genre.

This last point deserves further scrutiny because no nature writer has more vigorously resisted the "nature writer" label than Abbey, who began protesting this designation soon after the publication of *Desert Solitaire*. In the introduction to *The Journey Home*, the essay collection that followed *Desert Solitaire*, Abbey claimed, "I am not a naturalist. I never was and never will be a naturalist. I'm not even sure what a naturalist is except that I'm not one. I'm not even an amateur naturalist. . . . I never studied botany or zoology or ecology or any other branch of natural science" (xi). "Much as I admire the work of Thoreau, Muir, Leopold, Beston, Krutch, Eiseley and others," Abbey continued, "I have not tried to write in their tradition. I don't know how" (xii). In an interview conducted a few months prior to the release of *The Journey Home*, Abbey voiced a similar complaint. "I never wanted to be an environmental crusader, an environmental journalist. I wanted to be a fiction writer, a novelist. Then I dashed off that *Desert Solitaire* thing because it was easy to do. All I did was copy out of some journals that I'd kept. It was the first book that I published that had any popularity at all, and at once I was put into the 'Western Environmentalist Writer' bag, category, pigeonhole" (Hepworth, "Poetry" 56). For the rest of his life, Abbey would express similar sentiments, resisting any kind of label — naturalist, nature writer, environmental writer — that he perceived as either inaccurate or restrictive.[6]

Wendell Berry — whose career as a multigenre writer and whose reputation as a "crank" closely parallels Abbey's — vigorously defends Abbey's claims in "A Few Words in Favor of Edward Abbey," an essay first published in 1985.[7] "Mr. Abbey is not an environmentalist," writes Berry. "He is, certainly, a defender of some things that environmentalists defend, but he does not write merely in defense of what we call 'the environment'" (3). Berry then asks: "If Mr. Abbey is not an environmentalist, what is he? He is, I think, at least in the essays, an autobiographer. He may be writing on one or another of what are now called environmental issues, but he remains Edward Abbey, speaking as and for himself, fighting, literally, for dear life. This is important, for if he is writing as an autobiographer, he cannot be writing as an environmentalist — or as a special ist [sic] of any other kind. As an autobiographer his work is self-defense. As a conservationist, he is working to conserve himself as a human being. But this is self-defense and self-conservation of the largest and noblest kind, for Mr. Abbey understands that to defend and conserve oneself in the fullest, truest sense, one must defend and conserve many others and much else" (5).[8] James Bishop Jr. agrees with Berry's reading, noting that Abbey was "a singular member of a vanishing breed, the independent social critic, his primary subject being himself — and human nature — against the backdrop of deserts, rivers, and canyons. Read in that context, the essence of much of his work is that he was writing in defense of himself as part of nature. This is what separates him from such nature writers as John Muir and Henry Thoreau" (31).

The problem with these arguments is not their misreading of Abbey's work as something more than "nature writing," but their misreading of "nature writing" as a category not capacious enough to contain the breadth of Abbey's writing. Abbey may have disliked being labeled a "nature writer," but his provocative persona and blending of fictional and nonfictional techniques in fact mark him as a premier example of the contemporary nature writer at work. In his eulogy for Abbey in *Sierra*, for example, Peter Wild observed that contemporary literary historians will think of Abbey "as combining the rapier of Thoreau with the large-souled righteousness of John Muir. Either way, he was smack in the middle of traditional American nature writing, carrying forward its heat and light, and the smoke of its magical trickery, into our own decades" ("Into the Heart's Wild Places" 100). Though their claims are not without merit, Abbey and Berry and Bishop all underestimate the expansiveness of the genre of nature writing to "contain multitudes," as Walt Whitman put it. In fact, the hallmark of contemporary nature writing may be the very substance of Abbey's protest: the ability to recognize that environmental issues are tied to a wide range of related concerns, both personal and political.

Westward I Go Free

Abbey's introduction to the American West resembled that of Theodore Roosevelt's, another easterner who fell in love with the freedom he found in the openness of the western landscape and who then proceeded to write about that landscape and argue for its preservation. To suggest that Abbey and Roosevelt shared more than a common pattern of experience, narration, and argument would be a grave mistake, however, because the origins of these two men could not be more distinct. Whereas Roosevelt's roots were in the urban, upper-class world of power and privilege, Abbey's were in the rural, working-class world of suffering and struggle; and whereas Roosevelt began his career writing works of nonfiction, Abbey first turned to fiction to represent the southwestern landscape that had captured his heart.

Early Life and Works

The oldest of five children, Abbey was born in the Allegheny mountain town of Indiana, Pennsylvania, on 29 January 1927.[9] His most important influence was his father, Paul Revere Abbey, a woodsman, farmer, salesman, and school bus driver. Paul Abbey was a socialist and agnostic, a "fierce and self-centered idealist" who could quote Walt Whitman at length (Bishop 55–56). "Dad was anti-capitalist, anti-religion, anti–prevailing opinion, anti-booze, anti-war, and anti–anyone who didn't agree with him," recalls Abbey's younger brother Howard (Bishop 56). Among Paul Abbey's favorite topics of conversation were Soviet Communism, the Socialist leaders Eugene Debs and Norman Thomas, and the time he shook the hand of William Dudley ("Big Bill") Haywood, an early leader of the International Workers of the World, or Wobblies (Bishop 61).[10] "Our family stuck out like a sore thumb because we were so politically radical," claims Abbey's sister Nancy (Bishop 62).

Like his father, who hitchhiked west at eighteen and worked for a time as a cowhand in Montana, Abbey traveled across the country at seventeen, in the summer of 1944, the year before his graduation from high school. As he recounted in "Hallelujah on the Bum," a 1970 essay later reprinted in *The Journey Home* (1977), Abbey hitched from Pennsylvania to Seattle and then on to San Francisco, returning home "via boxcar, thumb, and bus" by way of Arizona and New Mexico.

"I started out with twenty dollars in my pocket," he wrote, "and a piece of advice, cryptic I'd say, from my old man: 'Don't let anybody take you for a punk'" (*Journey* 1). By the time he reached California, Abbey recognized that for the first time he was "getting close to the West of my deepest imaginings — the place where the tangible and the mythical become the same" (*Journey* 5). When he finally saw the Southwest, "it was love at first sight," Abbey claimed, although he later admitted that he was in love with the region long before he saw it. "I guess I had too much Zane Grey, John Wayne and Hopalong Cassidy," Abbey told Grace Lichtenstein in 1976 ("Edward Abbey" 24). Still, as he rode along the great plateau of northern Arizona and New Mexico in a boxcar, he was transfixed by the passing landscape: "Telegraph poles flashed by close to the tracks, the shining wires dipped and rose, dipped and rose; but beyond the line and the road and the nearby ridges, the queer foreign shapes of mesa and butte seemed barely to move at all; they revolved slowly at an immense distance, strange right-angled promontories of rose-colored rock that remained in view, from my slow altering perspective, for an hour, for two hours at a time. And all of it there, simply there, neither hostile or friendly, but full of a powerful, mysterious promise" (*Journey* 10–11). For two years after this trip, Abbey recalled, "I kept bright in my remembrance, as the very picture of things that are free, decent, sane, clean, and true, what I had seen and felt — yes, even smelled — on that one blazing afternoon on a freight train rolling across the Southwest" (*Beyond* 53).

Abbey's first experience with the southwestern landscape offers an important early indication of the utopian meanings the desert would eventually come to hold for him. But even before he left for the West, Abbey's utopian leanings had been slowly developing. In December 1941, for instance, his freshman year of high school, Abbey wrote an anti-Hitler editorial entitled "America and the Future," which appeared in his school newspaper, the *Marion Center Independent*. The article concludes: "Men like Hitler cannot stem the upsurge of the human race! They may try, and partly succeed, but they will always fail. . . . A new world of peace, security, liberty and happiness is about to unfold! The old forces of feudalism and ignorance and slavery are making their last stand. But they will be conquered" (Cahalan, "Edward Abbey" 235). With its arid climate, unfamiliar land forms, and great expanses of uninterrupted space, the Southwest seemed to augment Abbey's forward-looking disposition, both in terms of the "powerful, mysterious promise" it augured for him personally, and also for the manner in which it represented all that was "free, decent, sane, clean, and true."

After serving with the U.S. Army in Alabama and Italy from 1945 to 1946, Abbey attended the University of New Mexico on the G.I. bill from 1948 to 1951, where he studied English and philosophy and edited the student literary magazine. He returned again to the University of New Mexico to study philosophy beginning in

1954, after attending the University of Edinburgh on a Fulbright fellowship from 1951 to 1952.[11] Abbey's years as a student in New Mexico further developed his knowledge of the desert landscape. During a long weekend during college, Abbey and a friend traveled around the Four Corners area of New Mexico, Utah, Arizona, and Colorado, finally ending up atop Comb Ridge, south of Bluff, Utah, looking out over Monument Valley—a landscape, Abbey later recounted

> that I had not only not seen before but that did not *resemble* anything I had seen before. I hesitate, even now, to call that scene beautiful. To most Americans, to most Europeans, natural beauty means the sylvan — pastoral and green, something productive and pleasant and fruitful — pastures with tame cows, a flowing stream with trout, a cottage or cabin, a field of corn, a bit of forest, in the background a nice snow-capped mountain range. At a comfortable distance. But from Comb Ridge you didn't see anything like that. What you see from Comb Ridge is mostly red rock, warped and folded and corroded and eroded in various ways, all eccentric, with a number of maroon buttes, purple mesas, blue plateaus and gray dome-shaped mountains in the far-off west. Except for the thin track of the road, switchbacking down into the wash a thousand feet below our lookout point, and from there climbing up the other side and disappearing over a huge red blister on the earth's surface, we could see no sign of human life. Nor any sign of any kind of life, except a few acid-green cottonwoods in the canyon below. In the silence and the heat and the glare we gazed upon a seared wasteland, a sinister and savage desolation. And found it infinitely fascinating. (*Beyond* 54–55)

In addition to exploring the southwest terrain, Abbey was further developing his political radicalism during his years as a student in New Mexico. In 1947, just before moving to the West, Abbey had attracted the interest of the FBI after he posted a notice on a bulletin board at the nearby Indiana State Teachers College (now Indiana University of Pennsylvania) asking students and faculty members either to mail their draft credentials to President Truman or to burn them. "This sounds like a foolish, crackpot scheme, but it is not," read the notice. "It is much more than that. It is much worse than that—it is a form of civil disobedience" (Bishop 75; Loeffler, *Adventures* 30). As editor of the *Thunderbird*, the University of New Mexico student literary magazine, he helped produce the March 1951 issue, in which he included his own story, "Some Implications of Anarchy." On the cover, he also placed a defiant quotation from Diderot—"Man will never be free until the last king is strangled with the entrails of the last priest"—which he sardonically attributed to Louisa May Alcott. As a result, most of the copies of this issue were seized, the staff of the magazine reprimanded, and Abbey fired as editor (Bishop 16; Cahalan, *Edward Abbey* 45; Loeffler, *Adventures* 36–37; McCann 6–7).

By the time he returned to New Mexico for postgraduate study, Abbey's interest in anarchism had grown significantly, and he chose to write his master's thesis on anarchism and the morality of violence. Abbey's thesis posed two questions: "To what extent is the traditional association of anarchism and violence warranted?" and "In so far as the association is a valid one, what arguments have the anarchists presented, explicitly or implicitly, to justify the use of violence?" ("Anarchism" 3). The bulk of the thesis consists of a survey of the views of two groups of anarchists: European theorists, such as William Godwin, Pierre-Joseph Proudhon, Michael Bakunin, Peter Kropotkin, and Georges Sorel, and active revolutionaries and sympathizers, such as the Haymarket anarchists, Emma Goldman, and Albert Camus.[12] In his conclusion, Abbey argued that "violence and rebellion, when exercised in the name of a cause which we hold to be morally just, and after peaceful means have been attempted and failed, can be justified as being — under the pressure of extreme circumstances — both a true and necessary expression of the human aspiration toward the good" (73–74). Violence, in other words, is justified when a "critical situation" arises "in which all moral alternatives have been eliminated . . . but two: passive submission to unquestioned wrong, or the exercise of violence" (74). Abbey remained troubled, however, by the absence of "a precise and convincing description of what constitutes such a 'critical situation'" (74). Insofar as the anarchist revolutionaries failed to justify the presence of this "critical situation," Abbey concluded, "they also failed to justify violence" (75). In some sense, Abbey's entire body of work can be seen as an attempt to provide such a "precise and convincing description" of this "critical situation."[13]

At the same time he was writing his thesis, Abbey was also beginning to dramatize his ideas in fiction. His first novel, *Jonathan Troy* (1954), concerns a self-involved young man who yearns to escape the confines of his Pennsylvania home for the wide open spaces of the West. Semiautobiographical, it chronicles the development of Jonathan Troy's anarchistic tendencies, which appear partly in response to the failures of his father, who, like Abbey's own father, was also a Wobbly. Although the book was largely ignored by the critics (the *New York Times* termed it "a symphony of disgust") and Abbey himself later called it "a very bad novel," *Jonathan Troy* does reflect Abbey's interest in the West as an ideal environment and also anticipates the conflict between wilderness and civilization that appears in his subsequent works (P. Carlson 63; Ronald, *New West* 5; West 25).

Abbey's second novel, *The Brave Cowboy* (1956), enjoyed greater success and also became the basis for the film *Lonely Are the Brave* (1962), starring Kirk Douglas and Walter Matthau. Subtitled "An Old Tale in a New Time," the novel features Jack Burns, a nineteenth-century-style cowboy whose rugged individualism has become anachronistic in modern New Mexico. When his friend Paul Bondi is jailed for refusing the draft, Burns attempts to free him, only to learn that Bondi has no desire to be part of an outdated, romantic rescue. Forced by this situation to break jail himself, Burns manages to elude both the law and the military after an elaborate chase — only to be killed by a truck carrying bathroom fixtures while trying to cross a highway on horseback, a symbol of the individual's resistance to bureaucracy and the unintended consequences of technological "progress."[14]

Fire on the Mountain (1962), the final novel of Abbey's early career, follows the struggles of John Vogelin as he unsuccessfully attempts to prevent the White Sands Missile Range from encroaching on his southern New Mexico ranchland. Based on the true story of John Prather, who fought the U.S. government over the same issue in 1955 and won, *Fire on the Mountain* continues Abbey's preoccupation with quixotic individualists engaged in battle with the military-industrial state. *Fire on the Mountain* differs from *The Brave Cowboy*, though, in its form of narration, with Vogelin's twelve-year-old grandson, Billy Vogelin Starr, explaining the events as he observes them, thereby allowing the novel to function in part as a bildungsroman. An important landmark in Abbey's evolving sense of place, *Fire on the Mountain* also has young Billy identify the southwestern landscape as a present and a future utopia: "These mountains — they seemed at once both close and impossibly remote, an easy walk away and yet beyond the limits of the imagination. Between us lay the clear and empty wilderness of scattered mesquite trees and creosote shrubs and streambeds where water ran as seldom as the rain came down. Each summer for three years I had come to New Mexico; each time I gazed upon that moon-dead landscape and asked myself: what is out there? And each time I concluded: *something* is out there — maybe everything. To me the desert looked like a form of Paradise. And it always will" (4). *Fire on the Mountain*, as Ann Ronald has pointed out, was "the final preparation for Abbey's mature writing" (*New West* 44).

Defining Utopia

Abbey's early fiction combines his developing anarchism with his love for the southwestern deserts, but unlike *Desert Solitaire* and *The Monkey Wrench Gang*, these first three novels are not themselves utopian, even though they do introduce aspects of Abbey's utopian imagination. In considering the ways in which Abbey's nature writing provides a more thorough utopian vision, we first should examine the identity and character of utopias generally.

Like most questions of definition, the identification of a literary utopia depends on where one wishes to place the boundaries of utopian writing. One of the more restrictive definitions appears in Glenn Negley and J. Max Patrick's anthology *The Quest for Utopia* (1952), in which the editors distinguish the utopia from other forms of literature or speculation on the basis of three characteristics: (1) it is fictional; (2) it describes a particular state or community; and (3) its theme is the political structure of that fictional state or community (2–3). Given Abbey's conflation of fictional and nonfictional techniques in *Desert Solitaire*, and given an especially broad interpretation of "political structure," such a definition could be made to fit both *Desert Solitaire* and *The Monkey Wrench Gang*, but doing so would certainly stretch the intended meaning of Negley and Patrick's definition to the breaking point. A more liberal definition of utopia, as offered by most recent interpreters of utopian writing, is better suited to categorizing these works.

Choosing to avoid the difficult, if not impossible, task of delineating the formal characteristics of literary utopias, contemporary critics have instead attempted to develop a functional definition of utopian discourse. For instance, Frank E. Manuel, the foremost modern historian of utopian thought and writing, claims that the boundaries of utopian writing "need not be demarcated with nice precision." According to Manuel, it is not "the literary form that establishes the universe of discourse . . . but the intent to evoke a vision of the life of man in an earthly paradise that would be radically different from the existing order and would presume to render its inhabitants happier in some significant sense of that ambiguous yet unavoidable word" ("Toward" 70). Ruth Levitas, in her excellent survey of utopian scholarship, finds a similarly inclusive definition to be the most useful. "Utopia is the expression of the desire for a better way of being," she writes. "This includes both the objective, institutional approach to utopia, and the subjective, experiential concern of disalienation. It allows for this desire to be realistic or unrealistic. It allows for the form, function and content to change over time" (8). Paul Sears likewise argues that to consider utopian thought "restricted to literary forms that bear its label is to underestimate its wide prevalence at many levels and in all cultures. However expressed, it is essentially a critique of the defects and limitations of society and an expression of hope for something better" (137).[15]

The idea of utopia, of course, comes from Thomas More's *Utopia* (1516), the title of which alludes to two Greek words: *eutopia*, "the good place," and *outopia*, "no place." More's usage also points to the dual function of utopian writing: it both describes an ideally perfect place and offers a generally impractical, visionary scheme for reform.[16]

Throughout the sixteenth century, utopian authors posited the New World, and particularly North America, as this "ideally perfect place." According to historian Jack P. Greene, "it is significant for both emerging expectations about America and the subsequent development of the utopian tradition that More located Utopia in the Atlantic and used as his central literary device the experienced traveler just returned from a voyage with Vespucci from the 'unknown peoples and lands' of the New World" (26). After More, and continuing through Jonathan Swift and beyond, "utopian writers continued to identify the dream of a perfect society with America and to locate their fairylands, their New Atlantis, their City of the Sun in some place distant from Europe and in the vicinity of America" (Greene

28). In the seventeenth century, however, as knowledge about the American land-scape grew more detailed, increasing numbers of Europeans "thought in terms not of finding an existing utopia but of founding one in the relatively 'empty' and inviting spaces of North America," according to Greene (51). The North American continent, he writes, "seemed to offer the unlimited and, even more important, the as yet unoccupied and unorganized space in which a new society, free from the imperfections and restraints of the old, might be created" (51–52).

The European conception of North America as both an existing and potential utopia is significant to an understanding of Abbey's work in that the discoverers and colonizers of the New World were influenced by the Judeo-Christian identification of the wilderness with the arid lands of the ancient Near East. As Roderick Nash points out, "[t]he Old Testament reveals that the ancient Hebrews regarded the wilderness as a cursed land and that they associated its forbidding character with a lack of water" (*Wilderness* 14). Thus paradise for the Hebrews was not a desert "wilderness" but rather a well-watered "Garden of Eden." Indeed, says Nash, "the story of the Garden and its loss embedded into Western thought the idea that wilderness and paradise were both physical and spiritual opposites" (15). After forty years of wandering in the wilderness, the Israelites had developed several specific meanings for this landscape, all of which were associated with aridity. "It was understood, in the first place, as a sanctuary from a sinful and persecuting society. Secondly, wild country came to signify the environment in which to find and draw close to God. It also acquired meaning as a testing ground where a chosen people were purged, humbled, and made ready for the land of promise" (16).[17]

In suggesting that the desert wilderness of the American Southwest is in fact a paradise, Abbey was offering a strikingly new vision of both the desert and paradise. (In fact, *Desert Solitaire* was originally titled *A Season in Paradise: Pages from a Desert Journal.*[18]) In Abbey's eyes, the desert was no mere "wasteland," but rather a richly diverse landscape of "rock and tree and cloud," beautiful in its own right.[19] Paradise, he likewise suggested, need not resemble the Fertile Crescent. Abbey was not, however, the first writer to look to the southwestern landscape for utopian purposes. In a study of four mid-twentieth-century utopian novels — Edward M. House's *Philip Dru: Administrator* (1920), Aldous Huxley's *Ape and Essence* (1948) and *Brave New World* (1946), and Ellery Queen's *And on the Eighth Day* (1964) — Fred Erisman concluded that all four books "share a belief that the Southwest is the site of ultimate reality. It has, they suggest, all that other regions have, the imperfection and instability as well as the beauty and goodness, but it lacks the damning artificiality of the other locales. It does not disguise itself. Its strengths and weaknesses are open, for all to see — a quality that makes the Southwest an obvious setting for utopia. Here man and life can meet on equal terms" ("Where" 142).[20]

If the desert for Abbey resembles Thomas More's *eutopia*, or "good place,"

Abbey's anarchism could likewise be seen as the "impractical, visionary scheme for reform" that defines More's *outopia,* or "no place." His best friend, Jack Loef-fler, has argued that Abbey's "greatest single contribution to Western culture has been to meld environmentalism and anarchism" ("Edward Abbey" 39), a melding Loeffler sees as "a single, complex fundament" of Abbey's being ("Edward Abbey" 38). The best mature summary of Abbey's own views on anarchism can be found in his essay "Theory of Anarchy," which — significantly — first appeared in the *Earth First! Journal* in 1986.[21] Anarchism, writes Abbey, "means maximum democracy: the maximum possible dispersal of political power, economic power, and force — military power. An anarchist society consists of a voluntary association of self-reliant, self-supporting, autonomous communities. The anarchist community would consist (as it did in preagricultural and preindustrial times) of a voluntary association of free and independent families, self-reliant and self-supporting but bound by kinship ties and a tradition of mutual aid" (*One Life* 25–26).[22]

Although Abbey calls such a plan "[d]ifficult but not utopian" (*One Life* 27), his rejection of the utopian label here is clearly a calculated attempt to prevent his reader's dismissal of what he himself admits will not be an easy societal change to bring about; "anarchy means and requires self-rule, self-discipline, probity, [and] character," Abbey concedes (*One Life* 27). Despite his rejection of the utopian la-bel, Abbey closes the essay with a prediction that is nothing if not utopian: "Even without the accident of a nuclear war, I predict that the military-industrial state will disappear from the surface of the earth within a century. That belief is the ba-sis of my inherent optimism, the source of my hope for the coming restoration of a higher civilization: scattered human populations modest in number that live by fishing, hunting, food gathering, small-scale farming and ranching, that gather once a year in the ruins of abandoned cities for great festivals of moral, spiritual, artistic, and intellectual renewal, a people for whom the wilderness is not a play-ground but their natural native home" (*One Life* 28).

Many anarchists share Abbey's reluctance to adopt the utopian label, but as An-drew Hacker points out, "[a]narchism must be understood as a variety of utopi-anism — although differing from other utopian thought in that it considers not only ends but also means to the achievement of those ends. Like all utopianism, it is at least partly an attitude of mind rather than a rigorous theory" (284). Indeed, the idea of a fully articulated anarchistic utopia would be a contradiction in terms, as several critics have noted. "There is no significant utopian novel or full-bodied description of a future utopian society whose author would identify himself as an anarchist," claim Frank E. and Fritzie P. Manuel in their survey *Utopian Thought in the Western World* (1979). "A utopian blueprint of anarchy would be self-contradictory, internally inconsistent, and anathema to anarchists" (737). One could also object that Abbey's anarchistic vision is more "primitivist" than utopian, especially considering Abbey's well-known desire to "keep it like it was" (*Monkey* 77; *Journey* 145).[23] But the Manuels also disagree with this claim, arguing that "[a]ny strict compartmentalization of future utopia and nostalgia for an idealized bygone human condition is invalidated by their constant interplay in Western thought" (5). Not only is Abbey's description of the desert as a paradise properly utopian, therefore, but his interweaving of this paradisaical realm with his vision of a future free from environmental threats is in fact characteristic of utopian writing as a whole.

Abbey's vision of the future may best be summarized by turning to Lewis Mumford, whom Abbey said "fully deserves the Nobel Prize for literature" for offering "the best critique yet of our modern military-industrial culture" ("Abbey on Books" 156). In addition to writing *The Myth of the Machine* (1967–70), which Abbey singled out for special praise (Vaz 57), Mumford was also the author of *The Story of Utopias* (1922), in which he outlined the shape he expected Thomas More's eutopias, or "good places," would take. "The inhabitants of our eutopias," wrote Mumford, "will have a familiarity with their local environment and its resources, and a sense of historic continuity, which those who dwell within the paper world of Megalopolis and who touch their environment mainly through the newspaper and the printed book, have completely lost" (305). "The aim of the real eutopian," according to Mumford, "is the culture of his environment, most distinctly not the culture, and above all not the exploitation, of some other person's environment" (307). Even more striking than these sentiments is a statement Mumford made in a 1966 essay, "Utopia, the City, and the Machine." Summarizing the contents of utopian writing, Mumford wrote that "[c]ompared with even the simplest manifestations of spontaneous life within the teeming environment of nature, every utopia is, almost by definition, a sterile desert, unfit for human occupation" (10). In taking the *actual* desert as his utopia, then, Abbey simultaneously was able to participate in the long tradition of utopian writing and completely reverse its definition, according to Mumford — a paradox with which the rebellious Edward Abbey would no doubt be greatly pleased.[24]

A Rebel for the Future

It is fair to say that when *Fire on the Mountain* was published in 1962, it did not have quite the same impact on readers as did another book released that same year, *Silent Spring*, by Rachel Carson. Widely recognized as the book that launched the modern environmental movement,[25] *Silent Spring* also employed the conventions of the dystopia or antiutopia, which in modern times has sought to alert its readers to the horrors of industrial and scientific "progress."[26] Carson opened her book with "A Fable for Tomorrow," a portrait of "a town in the heart of America where all life seemed to live in harmony with its surroundings"—at least until "a strange blight crept over the area and everything began to change" (13). After that, it seemed as if "[s]ome evil spell had settled on the community. . . . Everywhere was a shadow of death" (13–14). The spell, of course, was a pesticide, "a white granular powder . . . [that] had fallen like snow upon the roofs and the lawns, the fields and the streams" some weeks before (14).

If environmental reform succeeds to the degree its advocates express themselves in the vocabulary of their times, both Rachel Carson and Edward Abbey showed themselves to be masters of the metaphor of "utopia," perhaps the single most important concept in 1960s America. Just as Carson drew the attention of middle America to the perils of pesticide use through her use of antiutopian rhetoric — "Elixirs of Death," "Needless Havoc," and "And No Birds Sing" are some of her chapter titles—Edward Abbey galvanized the more rebellious members of the fledgling "environmental movement" by giving voice to their own vision of an ecological utopia, or "ecotopia."

Like many nature writers, Abbey is often read ahistorically, as if his representation of the natural world was unaffected by developments in the human world surrounding him.[27] Abbey himself helped to cultivate such a reading by providing only glancing references to current events in his books. Abbey's journals, however, suggest that this ahistorical stance is as much a fiction as anything else in Abbey's writing. His journal entries from the late 1950s, for instance, show that Abbey considered himself very much a part of the Beat Generation, the literary movement of alienated bohemians that served as a precursor to the extended cultural rebellion of the 1960s. Following a party he attended in Berkeley in October 1957, Abbey noted in his journal: "*I* say, hurrah for Ginsberg, hurrah for Rexroth, hurrah for Kerouac, hurrah for Miller and Jeffers and Mailer and Abbey and Williams and Dean Moriarty!" (*Confessions* 141). He called Ginsberg's *Howl* "the best poem written in America by an American since — well, since Pearl Harbor. . . . a beautifully shaggy little book" (*Confessions* 146). And in 1959 he wrote from the southwestern desert: "*San Francisco!* Miller, Jeffers, Ferlinghetti, Rexroth [. . . .] Damnit, maybe that's where we should be! I'm homesick for the sea, and the fog, and the sweet city in the hills! Sometimes I think . . . ah, but no, I am a desert rat! A desert rat!" (*Confessions* 156).

It is wise, therefore, to remember that when Abbey published *Desert Solitaire* in 1968, American society was in a state of upheaval. Students filled the streets protesting the war in Vietnam; violence broke out at the political conventions in Miami and Chicago; and assassins took the lives of Martin Luther King Jr. and Robert F. Kennedy. The upheaval of the entire decade was vividly reflected in many of the other titles published in 1968, such as Allen Ginsberg's *Airplane Dreams*, Norman Mailer's *Armies of the Night*, and Tom Wolfe's *Electric Kool-Aid*

Acid Test. Even Abbey himself could not ignore the political realities unfolding around him — though, of course, he had his own distinctive reactions. "Seventeen Vietcong commandos seize the U.S. Embassy in Saigon and hold it for *seven hours!*" he wrote in his journal on 31 January 1968. "Never before in human history have men armed with little more than courage, boldness and conviction fought so splendidly against such terrible, incredible odds. Men against machines, just as in Budapest, Santo Domingo, etc. Fantastic!" (*Confessions* 214). Ever the rebel against a future that contained unrestrained industrial and governmental forces, Abbey can also be seen as a rebel *for* a different kind of utopia, a distinctively sixties future of peace, love, and "absolute presence." As Peter Wild has written, Abbey was "[a] natural-born rebel . . . [who] caught the spirit of the youth culture of the 1960s and applied it to nature writing" ("Sentimentalism" 140). The only difference was, Abbey's ecotopia was a desert.

Desert Solitaire

Desert Solitaire, the book that established Abbey's career, grew out of the two seasons Abbey spent as a ranger at Arches National Monument (now a national park) near Moab, Utah.[28] Although *The Monkey Wrench Gang* is usually cited as Abbey's principal contribution to the radical environmental movement, most of the themes and philosophical underpinnings of that work first took shape in *Desert Solitaire*.[29] Moreover, *Desert Solitaire* itself had a direct impact on the development of environmentalism throughout the 1970s. Douglas Peacock, one of Abbey's closest friends and the inspiration for the character of Hayduke in *The Monkey Wrench Gang*, says that "*Desert Solitaire* was something larger than just a book about the desert. It was about the power of the land, the human connectedness to the Earth, an idea of freedom — it was a call to arms" (57). "This book," claims Peacock, "changed lives" (56).[30] Equally important, *Desert Solitaire* also changed national park policy, with portions of Abbey's policy agenda becoming the basis for the Conservation Foundation's recommendations in its 1972 report, *National Parks for the Future* (Little 56). The book's influence continues today, with eighteen printings having appeared in mass-market paperback by 1989 (Hoagland 44).[31]

In the most influential review of *Desert Solitaire*, which was published in the *New York Times Book Review*, Edwin Way Teale described the book as "a voice crying in the wilderness, *for* the wilderness" (7), a statement that helped establish Abbey's reputation as a doomsayer. According to Ann Ronald, however, Abbey "communicates to his readers not only a prophecy of the wilderness's doom but a happier perception of possibilities for its salvation" (*Fifty* 11). In *The New West of Edward Abbey* (1982), the only book-length study of Abbey's writing, Ronald uses the terminology of Renaissance scholarship to distinguish between an imagined, idyllic green world and a real and often unpleasant red one, both of which she thinks form the backdrop to Abbey's writing. In *Desert Solitaire*, she suggests, Abbey attempts "to construct a third alternative to the red and green that will successfully subsume the best parts of the other two. Without fully articulating its characteristics, since to do so would be to employ a substantiality alien to dreams, Abbey leaves the reader free to imaginatively design a vision that draws from the best of both green and red, or, more specifically, to predicate an alternative world from the factors of his experiences" (*New West* 83). Abbey himself repeatedly affirmed this forward-looking aspect of his writing. In a letter sent in response to a reviewer who called him a "smirking pessimist," Abbey wrote, "I resent . . . being called a pessimist, smirking or not, because it is false. I am not a pessimist" (Hepworth, "*Canis*" 135). Similarly, in an interview with the *Bloomsbury Review* he claimed, "I'm an idealist. I still think it's possible to find some better way to live, both as an individual and as a society" (Solheim and Levin 155).

Seen in the context of such statements, the structure of *Desert Solitaire* can usefully be compared to that of a utopian travelogue.[32] According to Tom Moylan, "The traditional way in which the author of a utopia conveys the alternative world to the reader is by the perambulations and confused, cynical, or excited questionings of the main protagonist of this genre, the visitor to utopia. More of an investigator or explorer than a hero who conquers villains and reaps rewards, the visitor serves to represent in the text the compelling advantages which the alternative society has over the visitor's own, usually coterminous with the one in which author and contemporary readers live" (37). Bertrand de Jouvenel provides another slightly more detailed version of the same structure: "An explorer who ventures into an unknown land firstly encounters one person or a small group; he is struck by their appearance and manners; they take him to their own dwellings, he notes the setting of their daily lives and conceives some notion of their occupations and entertainments. It is only later that he is brought to a center, and the journey thither allows him to observe the landscape before he discovers the main monuments. Thus he gains many visual impressions of these strange people before engaging upon conversations which shall explain to him the institutions of this society. That such lecturing should occur only after the traveler has seen for himself, this is essential to any well composed utopian tract" (220). The central difference, of course, between *Desert Solitaire* and the typical utopian narrative is also the central achievement of the book: its nonanthropocentrism. Whereas most utopian narratives are focused on the human inhabitants of the utopian landscape, *Desert Solitaire* concerns itself principally with the landscape itself and with the nonhuman inhabitants of that landscape.

Like a novelist — and also like Thoreau in *Walden* — Abbey selects and frames his material carefully to give *Desert Solitaire* the structural unity a utopian narrative requires. He compresses the two years of his stay at Arches into the single "season in the wilderness" (April to September) of his subtitle; he maintains a consistent point of view (which is violated only once, in "Rocks"); he employs recurring images (such as the lone juniper, the red bandana, the trailer, the natural stone terrace, and the fire); and he both arrives and departs in darkness, wind, and snow (winter is the one season not covered in the book).[33] More to the point, Abbey fulfills the true meaning of his job as a park *ranger*, disdaining the authority such a position usually conveys and instead ranging widely in and around Arches, as if he were a visitor entranced by some foreign land. Slowly becoming familiar with the strange desert landscapes that surround him, Abbey introduces the reader to those landscapes in the first four chapters, describing the desert's distinctive land forms (the arches), plants (cliffrose, prickly pear, yucca, juniper), animals (the "serpents of paradise" and the "wicked rabbit"), and even two of its human inhabitants, the superintendent, Merle McRae, and the chief ranger, Floyd Bence. Like the utopist who waits until his fictional traveler has "seen for himself" before lecturing his readers, Abbey waits until the fifth chapter before delivering his scathing polemic about "industrial tourism and the national parks."[34]

This distinction between the utopist and the traveler could fruitfully be compared to the distinction Ann Ronald suggests readers must make between Edward Abbey the author and the character she calls "Ed" who appears in *Desert Solitaire*. "Ed is an original creation, like Billy Vogelin Starr, manipulated by Abbey in similar ways and for similar purposes" (*New West* 67).[35] We know little about Ed, who appears to have no responsibilities to any wife or family and seems to maintain no substantive relationships with others — a stance, Ronald notes, that allows him to "behave like an apprentice to the Monkey Wrench Gang, leveling a billboard with a bucksaw borrowed from his employer, or pulling up survey stakes and cutting bright little ribbons that mark what will be a new road into his Arches domain. The anarchic gesture, unbecoming for a solid citizen with a wife and sons, or ironically inconsequential for a Paul Bondi, has more impact when performed by the unfettered Ed" (*New West* 68).[36] Clearly, this is a peculiar kind of utopia, and a unique brand of utopian traveler. Yet without the presence of the utopian element in *Desert Solitaire*, the monkeywrenching activities of Ed would have little purpose. Instead, by positing the desert as utopia and his fictionalized narrator/traveler as an ironic anarchist, Abbey is able to offer the ultimate justification for acts of eco-sabotage: the preservation of paradise.

Abbey spells out the character of this paradise in a key passage from the "Down the River" chapter of *Desert Solitaire*, which requires quotation at length — in part because Abbey originally titled the chapter "A Last Look at Paradise."[37] The love of wilderness, Abbey writes,

> is more than a hunger for what is always beyond reach; it is also an expression of loyalty to the earth, the earth which bore us and sustains us, the only home we shall ever know, the only paradise we ever need — if only we had the eyes to see. Original sin, the true original sin, is the blind destruction for the sake of greed of this natural paradise which lies all around us — if only we were worthy of it.
>
> Now when I write of paradise I mean *Paradise*, not the banal Heaven of the saints. When I write "paradise" I mean not only apple trees and golden women but also scorpions and tarantulas and flies, rattlesnakes and Gila monsters, sandstorms, volcanos and earthquakes, bacteria and bear, cactus, yucca, bladderweed, ocotillo and mesquite, flash floods and quicksand, and yes — disease and death and rotting of the flesh.
>
> Paradise is not a garden of bliss and changeless perfection where the lions lie down like lambs (what would they eat?) and the angels and cherubim and seraphim rotate in endless idiotic circles, like clockwork, about an equally inane and ludicrous — however roseate — Unmoved Mover. . . . That particular painted fantasy of a realm beyond time and space which Aristotle and the Church Fathers tried to palm off on us has met, in modern times, only neglect and indifference, passing on into the oblivion it so richly deserved, while the Paradise of which I write and wish to praise is with us yet, the here and now, the actual, tangible, dogmatically real earth on which we stand. (167)

Abbey's paradise resembles that presented in the gnostic Gospel of Thomas, in which Jesus proclaims that "the Kingdom of the Father is spread out upon the earth, and men do not see it" (M. Meyer 130). Indeed, Abbey couches his definition in explicitly religious language, heretical though his perspective may be, arguing that the earthly paradise is all that matters, because the paradise of the afterlife — if it exists — is beyond the reach of the living. As a result, original sin for Abbey is a very specific kind of greed: the greed that results in natural destruction, not just the greed represented by the eating of the fruit of the tree of good and evil. He extends this argument by claiming that paradise is "not only apple trees and golden women," but in fact all the natural world, both that which humans consider "good" and that which they consider "evil." Abbey's humorous question about what the lions would eat if they were to lie down with the lambs masks his serious desire to celebrate the immediate landscape, "the here and now, the actual, tangible, dogmatically real earth on which we stand."[38]

Such a belief in the presentness of utopia shares many of the characteristics of the "continuous present" narration by which Ed conveys his experiences to the reader. "I became aware for the first time today of an immense silence in which I was lost," Ed tells the reader in "Solitaire," the second chapter of the book. "Not a silence so much as a great stillness — for there are a few sounds: the creak of some

bird in a juniper tree, an eddy of wind which passes and fades like a sigh, the tick-
ing of the watch on my wrist — slight noises which break the sensation of absolute
silence but at the same time exaggerate my sense of the surrounding, overwhelming peace. A suspension of time, a continuous present" (11). Several critics have
pointed out this aspect of Abbey's narration in *Desert Solitaire,* including Ann
Ronald, who has also noted the importance of this passage and compared the
"timeless, eternal mood" of *Desert Solitaire* to that of Dickens's *Bleak House* and
Gertrude Stein's *Three Lives* (*New West* 67). Garth McCann has similarly observed that "there seems to be little growth or expansion of the narrator's consciousness. The real experiences of the author may well have had upon him the
effect of growth and development, but those of the narrator do not. Although complex and contradictory and fascinating, the 'I' remains essentially unchanged
throughout the book" (24).[39] One of Abbey's journal entries (22 November 1967)
from his time at Arches reveals the fullness of his understanding of the continuous
present: "Past, present, future: mystery. To live fully in the present — yes — but
could the present have any meaning, any value for us if we did not also believe in
the ineluctable reality of the past? And therefore, also, inevitably, of the future"
(*Confessions* 213).

Paul Bryant has argued that "this sense of the presence of the past, and the germ
of the future, in present time, has become a hallmark of our most sophisticated nature writers" ("Time" 319). In Abbey's case, the use of the continuous present also
has a utopian dimension similar to that described by the German sociologist Karl
Mannheim in *Ideology and Utopia.*[40] According to Mannheim, anarchism is the
most recent manifestation of a form of utopianism called "chiliasm," the essential
features of which he describes as follows: "The Chiliast expects a union with the
immediate present. Hence he is not preoccupied in his daily life with optimistic
hopes for the future or romantic reminiscences. His attitude is characterized by a
tense expectation. He is always on his toes awaiting the propitious moment and
thus there is no inner articulation of time for him. He is not actually concerned
with the millennium that is to come; what is important for him is that it happened
here and now, and that it arose from mundane existence, as a sudden swing over
into another kind of existence. The promise of the future which is to come is not
for him a reason for postponement, but merely a point of orientation, something
external to the ordinary course of events from where he is on the lookout ready to
take the leap" (195). Mannheim called this sense of time "absolute presentness"
(215), and he saw it as a function of both traditional millenarian movements and
modern-day anarchism (211–19, 248–49). In Richard David Sonn's words, it is a
kind of "revolutionary ecstasy . . . a quasireligious belief that the millennium is at
hand, that the world is liable to change totally at any moment, that the new
Jerusalem is here and now" (155).

Abbey finds in the desert the same "tense expectation" Mannheim finds at the core of chiliasm. "The desert says nothing," Abbey writes in the chapter "Episodes and Visions": "Completely passive, acted upon but never acting, the desert lies there like the bare skeleton of Being, spare, sparse, austere, utterly worthless, inviting not love but contemplation. In its simplicity and order it suggests the classical, except that the desert is a realm beyond the human and in the classicist view only the human is regarded as significant or even recognized as real. Despite its clarity and simplicity, however, the desert wears at the same time, paradoxically, a veil of mystery. Motionless and silent it evokes in us an elusive hint of something unknown, unknowable, about to be revealed" (240–41). Exactly what is about to be revealed remains a mystery in Abbey's desert, yet it is precisely this resistance to human understanding that allows Abbey to extract the moral lessons he does from the desert and then to translate those moral lessons into practical actions aimed at preserving his utopian landscape. To suggest, therefore, as Tom Pilkington does, that "[t]he surface account, . . . the desert travelog — and even the writer's professed reason for writing the book, his affirmation of the necessity for wilderness and freedom — are only incidental to the real purpose of *Desert Solitaire*" and that "their function is to serve as vehicles for conveying the mind of the author, that mind being the actual landscape that the book explores" is to miss the point of *Desert Solitaire* (22). Pilkington is correct, of course, in noting that Abbey is very much concerned with "the gap (and the possibility of bridging that gap) between reality and an individual's perception of reality" (22), but he is mistaken in maintaining that "the desert — the world of sun and rock — is important (to the reader) because it is important to Abbey's thought" (23). Abbey's purpose in *Desert Solitaire* is precisely the opposite: to introduce the reader to the desert *as desert*, not as linguistic description.

Time and again Abbey makes the claim that "the desert is a realm beyond the human." In "Cliffrose and Bayonets," for example, the narrator explains that "[a] weird, lovely, fantastic object out of nature like Delicate Arch has the curious ability to remind us — like rock and sunlight and wind and wilderness — that out there is a different world, older and greater and deeper by far than ours, a world which surrounds and sustains the little world of men as sea and sky surround and sustain a ship. The shock of the real" (37). Near the end of the book, as Ed prepares to leave Arches, he likewise observes that "[t]he finest quality of this stone, these plants and animals, this desert landscape is the indifference manifest to our presence, our absence, our coming, our staying or our going" (267). And a few pages earlier, Ed says he discovered, in conversation with a visitor, "that I was not opposed to mankind but only to man-centeredness, anthropocentricity, the opinion that the world exists solely for the sake of man" (244). It is this thought — that all creation is not for man — that "injects a truly radical perspective into Abbey's nature writings — a perspective implicit in Thoreau, in John Muir, in Aldo Leopold," according to Bill McKibben ("Desert Anarchist" 42).

Abbey did not fully explore the implications of this perspective until the appearance of *The Monkey Wrench Gang*, but the seeds of that novel were clearly planted in *Desert Solitaire*. As Ann Ronald notes, the narrator's lack of responsibilities allows him to pull up survey stakes and cut down billboards with impunity, but it bears repeating that the purpose of his doing so is fundamentally utopian. As Abbey later wrote in *The Journey Home*, "the war against the encroaching industrial state . . . may seem utopian, impossibly idealistic. No matter. There comes a point at every crisis in human affairs when the ideal must become real — or nothing" (235–36). In *Desert Solitaire* that utopian vision takes the form of Abbey's wish that "some unknown hero with a rucksack full of dynamite strapped to his back will descend into the bowels of the [Glen Canyon] dam; there he will hide his high explosives where they'll do the most good, attach blasting caps to the official dam wiring system in such a way that when the time comes for the grand opening ceremony, when the President and the Secretary of the Interior and the governors of the Four-Corner states are in full regalia assembled, the button which the president pushes will ignite the loveliest explosion ever seen by man, reducing the great dam to a heap of rubble in the path of the river" (165).[41] In *The Monkey Wrench Gang*, this ideal comes one step closer to becoming a reality.

The Monkey Wrench Gang

"No movement is complete without its utopian text," writes British environmental historian Anna Bramwell, and environmentalism can lay claim to several such texts, all of which contain a strong component of anarchism. As Bramwell points out, however, *The Monkey Wrench Gang* is a tough and rambunctious book, "the individualist side of the utopian coin," while other books offer a more traditional, socialist approach (*Fading* 73). The earliest of these other books is *News from Nowhere* (1890), William Morris's socialist fantasy of the transformation of London and the surrounding countryside into a pastoral paradise in which men and women engage in communal craftwork and agriculture, free from the oppressive aspects of large-scale technology. Aldous Huxley's *Island* (1962), Ursula LeGuin's *Dispossessed* (1974), and Ernest Callenbach's *Ecotopia* (1975) all update Morris's socialist utopia for the modern world, offering portraits of decentralized communities living in harmony with the earth. *Ecotopia* in particular, which first offered a name for this kind of "ecological utopia," has been a favorite text of social ecologists living in the Pacific Northwest, the setting for Callenbach's fiction.

Yet none of these novels quite had the effect of *The Monkey Wrench Gang*, published along with *Ecotopia* in 1975. A fast-paced adventure story of four "ecoteurs"

who roam throughout southeast Utah and northern Arizona committing industrial sabotage in the name of environmental protection, *The Monkey Wrench
Gang* crystallized the latent desire of many young activists for a new kind of
resistance to environmentally destructive activities. Only four months after the
book's publication in September 1975, Abbey had become "an underground cult
hero throughout the West among students, environmentalists, and would-be 'eco-
raiders,'" according to the *New York Times* (Lichtenstein, "Edward Abbey" 24). Although publicly Abbey said "it would be a fate worse than death to become a cult
figure, especially among undergraduates" (Lichtenstein, "Edward Abbey" 24), in
private he told Edward Hoagland that the word-of-mouth success of the paperback
edition pleased him more than anything (44). By 1989 the book had sold half a million copies and inspired thousands of environmentalists to take matters into their
own monkeywrenching hands (Hoagland 44). *The Monkey Wrench Gang*, says
Earth First! cofounder Dave Foreman, was "exactly what the staid environmental
movement needed. . . , [something that] would kick us in our plump, comfortable
butts" (Vaz 57).

Foreman's statement suggests one way in which Abbey's novel was able to have
such an effect: in it, Abbey gave free reign to his own provocative persona. As
Abbey told writer and photographer Stephen Trimble, "I write in a deliberately
outrageous or provocative manner because I like to startle people. I hope to wake
up people. I have no desire to simply soothe or please. I would rather risk making
people angry than putting them to sleep. And I try to write in a style that's enter-
taining as well as provocative. It's hard for me to stay serious for more than half
a page at a time" (27). As Abbey discovered, provocation and entertainment working in tandem are more effective than provocation working alone. "When I started
writing *The Monkey Wrench Gang*," Abbey told Trimble, "my original motive was,
I guess, anger. Trying to get some sort of revenge for the destruction I had witnessed in the American Southwest. But I soon discovered that the anger in itself
would lead to a sort of dead end, get me nowhere as an artist, as a writer. I found
that I could communicate my contempt and my disgust much better by trying to
make people laugh" (28).

Responding to Abbey's sense of playfulness in *The Monkey Wrench Gang*, Scott
Slovic argues that the novel, "far from being ideological, calls into question the
very notion of allowing a static ideology, whether pro-environment or pro-
development, to govern our behavior in the wilderness" (*Seeking* 101). The aesthetic element in Abbey's writing, Slovic claims, "is there not only to be enter-
taining, not only to make serious material more palatable, but chiefly to *conflict*
with the moral strata of the texts" (103). According to Slovic, "instead of merely
presenting an environmental ideology or even a group of fictional role models for
would-be activists, Abbey is trying to prompt a more basic kind of consciousness

among his readers, to provoke not a single-minded political movement but rather an awareness on the individual level of the need to question moral and aesthetic assumptions. *The Monkey Wrench Gang* is less a clear-cut call to action than a call to feeling" (103–4).

Slovic is certainly correct in identifying the importance of aesthetics in Abbey's writing, but his suggestion that Abbey's provocation and wordplay are not in the service of any ideology are worth revisiting. Far from being ideologically uncommitted, Abbey's aesthetics are quite clearly meant to serve the anarchistic environmentalism that Earth First! eventually came to espouse. Moreover, the often jarring linguistic playfulness of the text complements the very oppositions that are at the heart of utopian discourse. As Peter Ruppert explains, "Utopias set out to challenge existing social values, to undermine existing norms, to transform existing social beliefs. They engage us in a dialogue between social fact and utopian dream. What initiates this dialogue is the recognition of contradictions and disparities: the noncoincidence between social reality and utopian possibility, the incongruity between 'what is' and 'what might be' or 'what ought to be,' the discrepancy between history and utopia. The effectivity of literary utopias, the central experience and most important effect of these texts on readers, is a sharpening of our perception of these contradictions and disparities — confrontations of opposites that seek to ignite a fertile clash in the reader's mind and to arouse his own utopian desires" (5). Ann Ronald gets closer to the spirit of this text when she observes that *The Monkey Wrench Gang* "proposes a new doctrine of frontier behavior" and "projects a fictive version of Edward Abbey's wildest nonfiction dreams" (*New West* 182, 184). The novel, she writes, is "an old-fashioned Western designed to eradicate a new-fangled foe. . . . Whereas the traditional Western looks to the past, Abbey looks to the future" (*New West* 191).

Three passages in particular help to announce the utopian vision of this novel in its earliest pages. The first is Abbey's Mark Twain–like disclaimer that appears on the copyright page of the book: "This book[,] though fictional in form, is based strictly on historical fact. Everything in it is real and actually happened. And it all began just one year from today" (vi).[42] Even without the striking coincidence of events that followed the publication of the novel, this statement quite obviously sets the reader's sights on the future transformations the book intends to make manifest.

The second passage occurs near the end of Abbey's "Prologue: The Aftermath," after a newly constructed bridge across the Glen Canyon is demolished during its ribbon-cutting ceremonies, much in the fashion of Abbey's hope for the destruction of the dam itself in *Desert Solitaire*. Following a lengthy description of these events from the human point of view, the narrator changes perspective and takes the reader skyward, to where a "lone vulture spirals in lazy circles higher and higher, contemplating the peaceful scene below." From here, the full significance of the scene can be assessed: "Like a solitary smoke signal, like the silent symbol of calamity, like one huge inaudible and astonishing exclamation point signifying *surprise!* the dust plume hangs above the fruitless plain, pointing to heaven and downward to the scene of the primal split, the loss of connections, the place where not only space but time itself has come unglued. Has lapsed. Elapsed. Relapsed. And then collapsed" (7). This is Mannheim's moment of "tense expectation," in which "there is no inner articulation of time" and in which the millennium "happened here and now." Moreover, both the "Prologue: The Aftermath" and the "Epilogue: The New Beginning" are written in the present tense — Abbey's "continuous present" — suggesting that the new Jerusalem is quite clearly on its way.

The third and final suggestion of the novel's utopian aims appears in the second chapter, in which Hayduke, the novel's principal monkeywrencher, is introduced. The chapter begins: "George Washington Hayduke, Vietnam, Special Forces, had a grudge. After two years in the jungle delivering Montagnard babies and dodging helicopters . . . and another year as a prisoner of the Vietcong, he returned to the American Southwest he had been remembering only to find it no longer what he remembered, no longer the clear and classical desert, the pellucid sky he roamed in dreams. Someone or something was changing things" (15). This is the same desert — both "classical" and "clear," as Abbey wrote in *Desert Solitaire* — that "evokes in us an elusive hint of something unknown, unknowable, about to be revealed." Hayduke, of course, attempts to change things back to what they were, to reclaim paradise, an idea Abbey plays with later in the book by linking Hayduke's utopian vision of the desert to his sexual quest for fellow monkeywrencher Bonnie Abbzug. Following a highly charged exchange in which Bonnie tells Hayduke she is a "full-grown woman" who can take care of herself, Abbey writes: "Hayduke, by the window, gazed out at the scenery, that routine canyon country landscape — grandiose, desolate, shamelessly spectacular. Among those faraway buttes and pinnacles, rosy red against the sky, lay the promise of something intimate — the intimate in the remote. A secret and a revelation. Later, he thought, we'll get into all that" (110).

A few of the many elements that frame *The Monkey Wrench Gang* as a utopian quest, these three passages set the stage for the novel's more serious attempt at illustrating the value of anarchistic environmentalism. Most prominent is its vivid illustration of the need for such renegade action, a good example of which is the visit of Bonnie and Hayduke to the Kaibab National Forest, southwest of Glen Canyon: "He stopped the jeep. In silence they looked around at a scene of devastation. Within an area of half a square mile the forest had been stripped of every tree, big or small, healthy or diseased, seedling or ancient snag. Everything gone but the stumps. Where the trees had been were now huge heaps of slash waiting to be burned when the winter snows arrived. A network of truck, skidder and bulldozer tracks wound among the total amputees. 'Explain this,' she demanded. 'What happened here?'" (209). Hayduke then attempts to explain the clear-cutting of the natural forest ("what the industrial forester calls weed trees") and the planting of a tree farm in its place ("all one species of tree in neat straight functional rows like corn, sorghum, sugar beets or any other practical farm crop"). He also explains that the national forest does not really belong to the people, that the Forest Service builds the logging roads for the timber companies, and that alternative means of shelter could reduce Americans' reliance on the forest for building materials. "Let them build houses that will last a while, say for a hundred years, like my great-granpappy's cabin back in Pennsylvania," says Hayduke, echoing the outlines of Abbey's own upbringing. "Then we won't have to strip the forests" (210). To which Bonnie replies, "All you're asking for is a counter-industrial revolution." "Right," says Hayduke. "That's all" (211).

Like anarchists whose fully articulated utopia would be a contradiction in terms, Abbey's "band of four idealists" (75) do not lose sleep over their lack of a detailed mission statement.

> "Do we know what we're doing and why?
> "No."
> "Do we care?"
> "We'll work it out as we go along. Let our practice form our doctrine, thus assuring precise theoretical coherence." (65)

Hayduke, the closest thing to the gang's spokesman, has a vision of the future but is unable to articulate it. "When the cities are gone, he thought, and all the ruckus has died away, when sunflowers push up through the concrete and asphalt of the forgotten interstate freeways, when the Kremlin and the Pentagon are turned into nursing homes for generals, presidents, and other such shitheads, when the glass-aluminum skyscraper tombs of Phoenix Arizona barely show above the sand dunes, why then, why then, why then by God maybe free men and wild women on horses, free women and wild men, can roam the sagebrush canyonlands in freedom — goddammit! — herding the feral cattle into box canyons, and gorge on bloody meat and bleeding fucking internal organs, and dance all night to the music of fiddles! banjos! steel guitars! by the light of a reborn moon! — by God, yes! Until, he reflected soberly, and bitterly, and sadly, until the next age of ice and iron comes down, and the engineers and the farmers and the general motherfuckers come back again" (101). "Thus George Hayduke's fantasy," writes Abbey. "Did he believe in the cyclical theory of history? Or the linear theory? You'd find it hard to pin him down in these matters" (101). Whether his utopian fantasy would become a permanent condition was not Hayduke's immediate concern, of course. Instead, he was focused on Mannheim's here-and-now, the matter at hand. When Bonnie asks Hayduke how he proposes to bring about his counter-industrial revolution, Hayduke replies, "My job is to save the fucking wilderness. I don't know anything else worth saving. That's simple, right?" (211).[43]

The progress of Hayduke's response to the ecological destruction he witnesses can be seen as representative of similar transformations occurring around him — both inside and outside the gang, and also outside the novel itself. Inside the gang, Doc Sarvis, a billboard-leveling surgeon from Albuquerque, gradually grows more comfortable with the anarchist's use of violence. At first, his fear of dynamite appears quite serious: "it suggested anarchy, and anarchy is not the answer" (70). Later, after Doc calls the use of explosives "[b]ad public relations" and repeats that "[a]narchy is not the answer" (156), he not only participates in the use of dynamite but embraces a theory of anarchism: "I don't believe in majority rule. . . . I don't believe in minority rule either. I am against all forms of government, including good government. I hold with the consensus of the community here. Whatever it may be. Wherever it may lead. So long as we follow our cardinal rule: no violence to human beings" (158). The next time he repeats the phrase, he does so largely in jest, telling an inquisitive park ranger (tellingly named "Edwin P. Abbott, Jr."), "I've said it before and I'll say it again. . . . Anarchy is not the answer" (191).

The novel also alludes to the presence of other monkeywrenchers operating within its fictional sphere and according to its anarchistic methods. At one point Hayduke tells Bonnie,

> "I'll bet right this very minute there's guys out in the dark doing the same kind of work we're doing. All over the country, little bunches of guys in twos and threes, fighting back."
>
> "You're talking about a well-organized national movement."
>
> "No I'm not. No organization at all. None of us knowing anything about any other little bunch. That's why they can't stop us." (169)

Hayduke's intuition is confirmed by a comment made by a Lone Ranger–like masked man — an unidentified Jack Burns — who confronts Hayduke as he is disabling a bulldozer: "I can see you do a good job. Thorough. . . . Not like some of them half-assed dudes I seen up on the Powder River. Or them kids down around Tucson. Or them nuts that derailed — " (220).

The most remarkable aspect of the novel, though, must be its extraordinary ability to chronicle as well as foretell the nonfictional development of the radical environmental movement. Just as Abbey used fictional techniques in writing *Desert Solitaire* (not to mention taking liberties with some of the facts and perhaps even inventing a few scenes out of whole cloth),[44] so too did he base much of *The Monkey Wrench Gang* on real-life people and incidents. The earliest reference to

Abbey's own monkeywrenching appears in a 1976 interview with Grace Lichten-stein, in which Abbey admits cryptically that he and his friends "used to go out every Friday night in 1947 while I was at the University of New Mexico" and that he was once arrested while monkeywrenching in San Mateo, California ("Edward Abbey" 24). The first mention of *The Monkey Wrench Gang* in Abbey's journals appears on 12 February 1952, in which he writes: "*Journey to the Moon:* Ten miles of flaming billboards lighting up the night; bandits in a jeep" (*Confessions* 25). Jack Loeffler also says Abbey "led nightly attacks on the billboards that desecrated the land along Route 66" during his years at the University of New Mexico (*Adventures* 38), and Abbey himself claims to have "cut down one gigantic Cadillac billboard on steel posts outside Albuquerque" when he was an undergraduate (Niklaus E1).

Abbey's friend John DePuy, the painter, says the roots of the novel were set in the late 1950s, when Abbey was editor of a Taos newspaper: "Some fool in Las Vegas, New Mexico, the Melody Sign Company, put up about 12 immense 40 foot signs, so everybody on the paper went out in the middle of the night and sawed them down. And the next week, the owner of the company came to put an ad in the paper for the apprehension of these criminals, and Ed being the editor took the ad and burst out laughing, so Mr. Melody asked him what was so funny. He said 'Nothing, I'm thinking of something else'" (Temple). DePuy expands on this comment in Jack Loeffler's *Adventures with Ed*: "Then we decided to take out some of the heavy equipment that the developers were using. We'd pour sand into the crankcase. We didn't really know how to stop them in those days. But we became very interested in this new occupation. One day, . . . [we] were sitting around and Ed said, 'We really ought to throw a monkey wrench in it.' That was the first time I ever heard him use that term. We talked about the *sabot*, the root of the word sabotage. The Luddites" (72).[45]

Abbey's "night work" continued long after this period, as other sources indicate. The novelist William Eastlake admits to having accompanied Abbey on an expedition outside Flagstaff, while Abbey was working at Sunset Crater in the summer of 1963. "[W]e carved down a huge Las Vegas girlie sign that was hiding the West," he writes. "I can't say this is true, because that is illegal, but someone did it while we were in that area. Some bad people carved down all the expensive signs between Albuquerque and Santa Fe" (15). In the mid-1970s Abbey also fought against the Peabody Coal Company's efforts to build a series of power plants on the Colorado Plateau. According to Jack Loeffler, "he schemed on every conceivable means of liberating the land from the avarice of man," but "[o]nly on occasion would he inflict damage on an earthmoving machine" (*Adventures* 105).[46] Compared to his dreams of demolishing Glen Canyon Dam, most of Abbey's monkey-wrenching was relatively minor. Loeffler notes that Abbey "salted roadways with nails and other sharp objects to slow down the endless trucks. He pulled up surveyor's stakes . . . [and] experimented with the effect on motors of Karo syrup, sand graphite, and various other substances" (*Adventures* 106). Some of Abbey's actions, though, were more substantial. John DePuy recalls one foray in which he and Abbey "went in a rented 4-wheel drive, courtesy of *National Geographic*. It had a winch. We had to take direct action. We stayed out there for a week and pulled up miles of sensors. Luckily, we had some industrial garnet and we did in a couple of drills. Then we camped somewhere else. We went back a week later and discovered that they had replaced the sensors. So we pulled them all out again and threw them over the side of the plateau. Apparently, their insurance rates went up so high that it helped cripple the company" (Loeffler, *Adventures* 126). As these examples show, what in *Desert Solitaire* Abbey called "the nights of desperate laughter with brave young comrades, burning billboards, and defacing public institutions" (42) were far from the "romantic dreams" he claimed they were.

In fact, in several interviews Abbey admitted that he had done quite a bit of what he called "field research" for *The Monkey Wrench Gang*. In some cases he was coy, replying, "Let's just say that I've knocked over some billboards in my time" (John F. Baker 7). In others he attempted to distance himself from any illegal activity: "Yeah, I did some . . . night work. Yes. I'll admit that I did it 10, 15 years ago" (Temple). At other times he was more forthright, telling *People* magazine, "I did quite a bit of field research for that book. . . . I spent whole nights on construction sites in Utah, putting sand in transmissions, shooting holes in truck tires and radiators. I was full of rage and it made me feel good temporarily" (P. Carlson 63).[47]

Despite his hesitance about revealing the details of his personal involvement in monkeywrenching, Abbey consistently maintained that the characters in *The Monkey Wrench Gang* were only "inspired by people I know. They're not portraits of anybody I know" (Hepworth, "Poetry" 54; Hafen and McCowan 22). "[A]s I began writing the story," Abbey explained, "they became more and more fictional, more and more imaginary" (Temple). As Abbey and others have pointed out, the character of George Hayduke was roughly based on the ex–Green Beret Doug Peacock; Seldom Seen Smith was based on Utah river guide Ken Sleight; Doc Sarvis was a composite of Abbey's friends Al Sarvis, Brendan Phibbs, Jack Loeffler, and John DePuy; and Bonnie Abzugg most closely resembles Ingrid Eisenstadter and other women Abbey had known.[48] John DePuy claims that "[i]t was pretty informal. It wasn't as cohesive as the book, and most of the characters came later. In the early days it was a different group. But then Peacock came in and Ken, and Ed said he changed the names to protect the guilty!" (Temple). "He didn't totally make it up," notes Doug Peacock (Temple).[49]

According to Peacock, he and Abbey "started doing casual monkeywrenching in the early '70s. It was more talk than anything else. It was more recreational than methodical. We knocked down some billboards, etc., etc." (Laughlin 32). But he didn't know anything about *The Monkey Wrench Gang* until he and Abbey took a trip to the Cabeza Prieta National Wildlife Refuge around 1973–74: "Ed was quizzing me. I had been cross-trained in demolitions when I was a Green Beret medic in Vietnam and knew a little of this and that. He was asking me all these technical questions about ecotage. Actually, I had a bunch of old special warfare books that were classified at the time I stole them. They certainly aren't anymore. Finally over the campfire, the day after New Years, he said that he had been working on this book. And I had no idea what the hell it was about. He said the hero of the book was going to be a guy named Hayduke. That was the first I had heard of Hayduke. It came out about a year later" (Laughlin 32).

Abbey was also influenced by several other individuals and groups who shared his antitechnological bias. The earliest were the Luddites, bands of English craftsmen in the early nineteenth century who destroyed the textile machinery that was rendering their skills increasingly unnecessary. Generally masked and operating at night, the Luddites claimed to be led by Ned Ludd, an apparently mythical figure, to whom Abbey dedicated *The Monkey Wrench Gang*. (Earth First! would later adopt "Ned Ludd Lives!" as one of its slogans; cofounder Dave Foreman would publish its books under the "Ned Ludd Books" imprint; and letters on monkeywrenching sent to the *Earth First! Journal* would be published in a column entitled "Dear Ned Ludd.") Like the Monkey Wrench Gang, the Luddites also discouraged violence against people (Sale, *Rebels*). Another kindred spirit was Henry David Thoreau, who in *A Week on the Concord and Merrimack Rivers* (1849) mourned the inability of the shad to bypass the Billerica Dam in the Concord River. "I for one am with thee," Thoreau wrote of the fish, "and who knows what may avail a crow-bar against that Billerica Dam?" (37).

Additional inspiration came from a handful of ecosaboteurs operating throughout the United States in the early 1970s. One was middle-school science teacher James F. Phillips, who called himself "the Fox" after the Fox River in Illinois, and who plugged drainage pipes, capped factory smokestacks, and famously dumped industrial waste from a U.S. Steel plant into the office of the company's chief executive (D. Martin F6). Such tactics, he said, were no more illegal "than if I stopped a man from beating a dog or strangling a woman" (Manes, *Green Rage* 185). Another were the "Billboard Bandits," Michigan environmentalists who took to roadside signs with chainsaws (Scarce 55). A third were the "Eco-Commandoes," who used yellow dye and a flotilla of messages-in-bottles to trace the destination of sewage pollution in Dade County, Florida (Love and Obst 13). Perhaps most influential, though, were the "Eco-Raiders," a group of college-age boys intent on slowing suburban growth in and around Tucson, Arizona, Abbey's adopted hometown. Like the Monkey Wrench Gang, they burned billboards, disabled bulldozers, and vandalized development projects, causing more than half a million dollars of damage and becoming local folk heroes in the process (Lee, *Earth First!* 26–27; Zakin, *Coyotes* 59–60). In *The Monkey Wrench Gang,* Abbey refers to the gang in press reports as the "eco-raiders" (43).

If *The Monkey Wrench Gang* was strongly influenced by these bands of renegade environmentalists, the completed novel seems to have had a similar impact upon other would-be saboteurs, even before Earth First! appeared on the scene in 1980. In one sense, the novel can be said to have functioned as an instruction manual for ecosabotage, a prelude to Dave Foreman's 1985 book, *Ecodefense: A Field Guide to Monkeywrenching,* which was itself modeled on William Powell's 1971 *Anarchist Cookbook* (Manes, *Green Rage* 82).[50] Although the large number of scenes of sabotage in the novel may seem to be a weakness from a literary perspective, from a technical perspective they are clearly a strength, allowing Abbey to detail several different techniques for "decommissioning" bulldozers, blowing up bridges, and disabling power lines. And readers seem to have been paying attention, because in 1979 the residents of Moab, Utah, noticed some uncanny resemblances between art and life. Sam Taylor, publisher of the weekly *Moab Times-Independent,* recounted the incidents: a $250,000 drilling rig was driven over a cliff, bulldozers were started up and left to run dead, and construction signs were stolen. "The method of operation was right out of 'The Monkey Wrench Gang,'" Taylor told the *Washington Post.* "That book has been responsible for a million dollars worth of industrial sabotage" (Hornblower A3). Similar instances of ecological resistance were reported across the country after the book's publication. In 1978 and 1979 a group of Minnesota farmers called the "Bolt Weevils" successfully disabled fourteen electrical towers that were part of a high-voltage power line being built across the prairie (Zakin, *Coyotes* 284–85).[51] At about the same time, Oregon residents who were opposed to the spraying of herbicide, despite several temporary injunctions against the spraying, responded by slashing the tires of spray vehicles, occasionally firing at helicopters, and finally burning a helicopter (Kane 102). And in 1979 Mark Dubois, a founder of Friends of the River, chained himself to a cliff along California's Stanislaus River to stop construction of the New Melones Dam, in the process becoming a symbol to other environmentalists, including Earth First! cofounder Mike Roselle (Zakin, *Coyotes* 247–49).[52] Not all these acts of civil disobedience can be linked to *The Monkey Wrench Gang,* of course, and some may have been more directly inspired by the actions of Greenpeace (founded in 1969). As M. Jimmie Killingsworth has pointed out, "[t]he interrelation of fictional and historical actions surrounding the practice of monkeywrenching is indeed complex, with influences doubling back upon influences, and with 'life' and 'art' ever exchanging places" (193). Nevertheless, the role of utopian fiction in the environmental community cannot be underestimated. As essayist Jack Turner has written, "One *Monkey Wrench Gang* . . . is worth a thousand monkey wrenchings. We can all drive a spike into a tree, but few can produce visionary fiction . . . that transform[s] our beliefs and extend[s] the possibilities of what we might come to love" (95).

Earth First!

By the time *Hayduke Lives!*—the sequel to *The Monkey Wrench Gang*—appeared in 1990, Earth First! had splintered into several rival factions, its cofounder Dave Foreman had been arrested by the FBI and charged with conspiracy, and its chief inspiration, Ed Abbey, had died of esophageal varices and was buried, according to his wishes, at an illegal site in the Cabeza Prieta wilderness of Arizona.[53] Reviewing *Hayduke Lives!* in the *Washington Post*, Grace Lichtenstein, former Rocky Mountain bureau chief of the *New York Times*, wrote that "somehow the entire theme of ecotage comes off shopworn. In 1975, action-oriented environmentalism was still new, even radical. Now, it's so mainstream (except in the state of Utah) even some Republicans embrace it" (5).[54] That monkeywrenching could go from radical to shopworn in the short space of a few years can be seen as a measure of the success of Abbey and the Earth First! movement at publicizing both the practice of monkeywrenching and the causes for which it was carried out. In the final section of this chapter I examine Abbey's influence on and involvement in the specific activities of Earth First!—particularly monkeywrenching. Although Abbey's last years were filled with controversy regarding his views on immigration, feminism, and the livestock industry, ultimately he will be remembered most for his identification and popularization of ecosabotage, a legacy that took concrete form with the appearance of Earth First! in 1980.[55]

Out of the Desert

As Mark Dowie has pointed out, Earth First! could be called "a bastard child of the Wilderness Society" (209) because several of its founders began their careers with that organization. Of equal importance, though, is the fact that several of the original leaders of Earth First! had significant ties to the Southwest and that the idea for the group itself was born in the Pinacate Desert of Mexico, a place Abbey once called "the final test of desert rathood" (Lee, *Earth First!* 31, 162 n. 33; Abbey, *Beyond* 151). Of the group's founders, Dave Foreman, who was born in Albuquerque, New Mexico, had been the Wilderness Society's chief lobbyist in Washington, D.C.; Bart Koehler had worked for the Wilderness Society in Wyoming;

Howie Wolke, the Wyoming representative for Friends of the Earth, had inventoried roadless areas for Koehler; Mike Roselle, a Texan and veteran of the Vietnam War counterculture, had helped Wolke organize support for wilderness issues; and Ron Kezar, the conservation chair of the Sierra Club in El Paso, Texas, had been a longtime hiker of the southwestern mountains (Manes, *Green Rage* 66–68; Scarce 59–61; Zakin, *Coyotes* 101–14).

Earth First! was born out of the frustration these and other wilderness advocates felt in 1979 following the conclusion of the U.S. Forest Service's second Roadless Area Review and Evaluation (RARE II), which recommended that less than one-fourth of the roadless areas in the United States be protected with wilderness status (15 million acres). The rest were to be either immediately opened for development (36 million acres) or considered for future planning (11 million acres). Foreman and others saw this defeat as symptomatic of the accommodation, moderation, and compromise brought about by the professionalization of mainstream environmentalism. Discouraged and disillusioned with this state of affairs, Foreman left his job as chief lobbyist for the Wilderness Society in January 1979 and resumed his old position in New Mexico as the society's southwest regional representative.[56] He soon discovered, though, that the frustrations of environmental politics were not limited to inside the beltway. Back in New Mexico, Foreman received death threats from local ranchers and witnessed the birth of the Sagebrush Rebellion, which he described as "a move by chambers of commerce, ranchers, and right-wing fanatics in the West to claim federal public land for the states and eventual transfer to private hands" (Foreman, *Confessions* 16).

By April 1980 Foreman had had enough; he was ready to leave the Wilderness Society for good. That month he invited Koehler, Wolke, Roselle, and Kezar to accompany him on a weeklong camping trip to the Pinacate Desert of Mexico, in part because of Abbey's vivid description of the place in *Cactus Country* (Cahalan, *Edward Abbey* 191; Manes, *Green Rage* 68). The Pinacate, Abbey had written, "is the bleakest, flattest, hottest, grittiest, grimmest, dreariest, ugliest, most useless, most senseless desert of them all. It is the villain among badlands, most wasted of wastelands, most foreboding of forbidden realms" (*Beyond* 151). There the five men drank beer, ate shrimp, told stories, and mourned the fate of the environmental movement (Manes, *Green Rage* 69). Although the precise origins of Earth First! have become shrouded in folklore and mythology, the most reliable account seems to be that given by Rik Scarce, who says the group was founded in Foreman's Volkswagen minibus, while Foreman, Wolke, and Roselle were returning to Albuquerque after the Pinacate trip. As talk turned to the creation of a series of bioregionally based ecological land preserves, Foreman suddenly called out "Earth First!" and Roselle drew what became the group's clenched-fist logo (61).[57]

Earth First! and *The Monkey Wrench Gang*

According to Foreman *The Monkey Wrench Gang* was "indirectly inspirational" to the formation of Earth First! "We talked about encouraging that idea as a mythos, as a style as much as anybody actually doing it. But I think as the wilderness crisis became much more severe, as the forest service began to destroy more areas, roads penetrated deeper into the wilderness, more clear cuts sprang up, a lot of folks realized that it was time to really implement *The Monkey Wrench Gang*" (Temple).[58] Abbey himself argued that Earth First! would have been created even without *The Monkey Wrench Gang*, but at the very least both he and his novel played important roles in establishing the climate of opinion that fostered the growth of the radical environmental movement.[59] According to Rik Scarce, although other nature writers have influenced radical environmentalism, none of them has been "as consistently explicit as Abbey" in the advocacy of the destruction of anthropocentric ideas, institutions, and technologies. "Rather, they are political in the sense of offering alternatives," says Scarce. "The impact of their writings is measured on individuals and in a personal way, not on Earth First! or any other aspect of the movement as a whole in the same way that Abbey's writings give voice to some of the core values commonly held by eco-warriors" (242). In fact, writes Scarce, Abbey's influence among radical environmentalists was so widespread that many people "give *The Monkey Wrench Gang* a disproportionate amount of credit for inspiring the foundation of Earth First! Its primary importance was probably in forming the ideas and values that Earth First! espouses" (241). Mike Roselle, for instance, says he rarely came upon a copy of the book in the late 1970s "that was not dog-eared from being passed from person to person and being read countless times" (Scarce 241). According to Roselle, "You could discuss things with your friends after reading this book that for some reason you may not have discussed with them before. . . . I noticed that when I was living in Wyoming, amongst our circle of friends when we found somebody who hadn't read the book, we'd say, 'Here! You gotta read this book!' They'd read it, and when we asked, 'What did you think,' they'd say, 'Aw, it was great! Let's go cut down a billboard.' It had that kind of effect" (Scarce 241). Darryl Cherney, another Earth First! activist, was similarly struck by Abbey's foresight in *The Monkey Wrench Gang*. "Our principles have changed very little since Edward Abbey wrote *The Monkey Wrench Gang*," said Cherney after rereading the book. "I was astounded at how many casual remarks Abbey might make that have become an integral part of Earth First! philosophy" (Scarce 241). Bill McKibben agrees, noting that "[p]erhaps Earth First! . . . would have sprung up without Abbey's book. But it would have been a different movement, for it found in *The Monkey Wrench Gang* a rude good cheer, a fondness for beer, and a ready-made mythology" ("Gleam" 36).

The Monkey Wrench Gang appealed to the founders of Earth First! for three reasons: (1) the gang was a utopian group, composed of individuals unwilling to compromise in pursuit of their ideals; (2) it was a grassroots group, committed to local issues and local knowledge; and (3) it was a direct action group, more interested in monkeywrenching than bargaining with the enemy.

The utopian character of Earth First! can be seen most clearly in its motto — "No Compromise in Defense of Mother Earth" — a powerful indictment of the willingness of mainstream environmentalism to make concessions with advocates of "growth" and "development." Michael McCloskey, chairman of the Sierra Club in 1986, criticized Earth First! for its unwillingness to compromise, arguing that its members were "just utopians." The Sierra Club, McCloskey countered, "may be 'reformist' and all, but we know how to work within the context of the basic institutions of the society — and they're just blowing smoke" (Sale, "Forest" 32–33). Howie Wolke, however, disagrees, claiming that "Earth First! proposals and tactics make sense. . . . Who gives a damn if a bureaucrat thinks we're unrealistic?" (Manes, *Green Rage* 70).[60]

Earth First! proposals and tactics "made sense" to Wolke because they were not prepared in response to the desires of business and industry, as were those of reform environmentalism, but were rooted in "deep ecology," a philosophical movement that gained ground at about the same time *The Monkey Wrench Gang* appeared. In an important early description of deep ecology published in 1973, the Norwegian philosopher Arne Naess distinguished between "shallow ecology" — anthropocentric environmentalism concerned mostly with issues of pollution and resource depletion — and "deep ecology" — biocentric environmentalism that accords all species *"the equal right to live and blossom"* (96; emphasis in original). Naess termed this way of thinking "ecological egalitarianism" (96), in contrast to the utilitarian environmentalism that preserved the natural world for "the health and affluence of people in the developed countries" (95). A central component of the deep ecological outlook, Naess later wrote, is the idea of "self-realization," in which the "self" is understood to include not just an individual's consciousness but all human and nonhuman nature (what Emerson called the "not me").[61] Deep ecology, in other words, can be seen as a contemporary restatement of the ecocentrism earlier articulated in the writings of John Muir and Aldo Leopold. As Earth First! cofounder Mike Roselle put it, "Muir and Leopold are the old-time religion for us" (Manes, *Green Rage* 72).[62] The utopian outlook of deep ecology can perhaps best be seen in *Deep Ecology* (1985), the landmark book by Bill Devall and George Sessions, which includes chapters on both "ecotopia" and "ecological resisting."[63]

Just as Earth First! shares the utopian vision of the Monkey Wrench Gang and deep ecologists, so too does it share their emphasis on grassroots activism and the avoidance of "professionalism." Like Abbey, the founders of Earth First! considered the American political structure to be corrupt and instead favored a "tribal" organization similar to the "voluntary association of self-reliant, self-supporting, autonomous communities" Abbey outlined in his "Theory of Anarchy" (*One Life* 26). "[W]hen you take on the structure of the corporate state," Dave Foreman claimed in an interview, "you develop the ideology and the bottom line of the corporate state. So what is the one kind of human organization that's really worked? The hunter/gatherer tribe, so we tried to model ourselves structurally after that" (Lee, *Earth First!* 35). As Rik Scarce put it, Earth First! wanted to have "no bureaucracy, no lobbyists, no organizational spokespeople, just a force of devoted, unpaid, grassroots activists occupying a niche they had created in the environmental movement — in short, an anarchy" (62). As a result, Earth First! considered itself a "movement" and not an "organization" and its supporters claimed to be "Earth First!ers" and not "members."[64] Nevertheless, in their study of Earth First! sociologists Kimberley D. Elsbach and Robert I. Sutton found the movement "to be an organization and Earth First!ers to be its members because it has many trappings of an organization. Its fund-raising, media, and direct action committees indicate that a differentiated social structure is used to achieve collective goals. Mailing lists of people affiliated with Earth First! are maintained, and most people on such lists describe themselves as Earth First!ers. And local chapters operate under the Earth First! banner" (702).

If the organizational structure of Earth First! did not fully reflect Abbey's vision of anarchy, its members nevertheless shared the anarchist's fear of a fully articulated utopia. Echoing Abbey's Hayduke, Dave Foreman has often stated, "Let our actions set the finer points of our philosophy" (Manes, *Green Rage* 21), an assertion he expanded upon in a letter to the editor of *Environmental Ethics.* "Too often," wrote Foreman, "philosophers are rendered impotent by their [in]ability to act without analyzing everything to an absurd detail. To act, trust your instincts[;] . . . to go with the flow of natural forces . . . *is* an underlying philosophy. Talk is cheap. Action is dear" ("More" 95).

Abbey himself voiced a version of this claim in several articles he published in the *Earth First! Journal.* In the 1982 essay "Abbey on Books — and Gurus" Abbey told Earth First!ers that "writing, reading, thinking are of value only when combined with effective action. Those I most admire in the conservation movement are those who act: such men as David Brower, Paul Watson, and the legendary Bulgarian brigand Georges Heiduk.[65] Sentiment without action is the ruin of the soul. One brave deed is worth a hundred books, a thousand theories, a million words. Now as always we need heroes. And heroines! . . . As my Aunt Minnie used to say, back in Stump Crick West Virginny, 'Too much readin' rots the mind" (156–57).[66] Similarly, in a 1983 letter to Earth First! activists, Abbey offered one of his most stirring calls to arms: "It is not enough to write letters to Congressmen, deliver sermons, make speeches, or write books. The West we love is under violent attack; the Earth that sustains us is being destroyed. Words alone will not save our country or ourselves. We need more heroes and more heroines — about a million of them. One brave deed, performed in an honorable manner and for a life-defending cause, is worth a thousand books.[67] At some point we must draw a line across the ground of our home and our being, drive a spear into the land, and say to the bulldozers, earth-movers, government and corporations, *thus far and no far-ther*. If we do not we shall later feel, instead of pride, the regret of Thoreau, that good but overly-bookish man, who wrote, near the end of his life, 'If I repent of anything it is likely to be my good behavior. What demon possessed me that I be-haved so well?'" ("Ed Abbey to Earth First!" 248; emphasis in original).

Abbey's own support of Earth First! merged impassioned writing with direct ac-tion on behalf of the natural world. A frequent contributor to the *Earth First! Jour-nal*, Abbey published original articles, book reviews, and letters to the editor in the journal, and he also allowed it to reprint several of his essays. He offered his sup-port for the movement in several mainstream publications, such as his statement in *Mother Jones* that Earth First! is "precisely the sort of spontaneous, anarchic, ex-temporaneous uprising I most admire" (Petersen, "Earth's" 8). He wrote the "For-ward!" [sic] to Dave Foreman's *Ecodefense* and claimed in *Sierra* that the book was "an essential handbook for those who wish to take part in the ongoing, last-ditch defense of the little that remains of the great American wilderness, basis of our primary American freedoms. This book, like the flag, the Bible, and the demo-cratic rifle, should be among the few, fundamental possessions of all who call themselves patriots" (Vaz 57). He donated the royalties from all his books sold through the journal to Earth First! (Abbey, Letter 3). And in the 1 May 1984 issue of the *Earth First! Journal*, Abbey even lent his name to a 6 million acre wilder-ness proposal for the national forests of Arizona, a gesture both utopian in content and humorous in delivery. Compared to both the 750,000 acres proposed by Ari-zona congressman Morris Udall and the 1.8 million acres requested by a coalition of mainstream Arizona conservation organizations (including the Sierra Club, the Audubon Society, and the Wilderness Society), Abbey's proposal would have brought the total amount of protected wilderness in Arizona to 30 million acres, or about 40 percent of the state's land surface. Although this amount was still 10 percent short of the ideal fifty-fifty balance he desired between industrial growth and wilderness preservation, Abbey declared his proposal to be a tongue-in-cheek "gesture of goodwill," noting that "we in Earth First! are willing to lean over back-ward in the effort to be fair and reasonable, trusting that other interested parties will follow our example" (Abbey and Desierto 8).[68]

Abbey also supported Earth First! through his participation in its protests, rallies, and meetings. His activism began with his appearance at the cracking of Glen Canyon Dam, for which he donated two hundred dollars to aid in the purchase of the black plastic "crack" (Manes, *Green Rage* 6). His speech at the dam also became a critical part of early recruiting for Earth First! thanks to *The Cracking of Glen Canyon Damn* [*sic*], a film made about the protest by Toby McLeod and Randy Hayes, which was shown by Dave Foreman and Bart Koehler as part of the "Road Show" they took to forty cities in the fall of 1981 (R. Arnold 231). Abbey was also a regular participant in Earth First!'s annual meeting, held on or near Independence Day and called the "Round River Rendezvous" in honor of Aldo Leopold's essay, "The Round River — A Parable."[69] During the third Round River Rendezvous in 1982, Abbey helped to "desurvey" a five-mile-long road into the drainage area of Little Granite Creek in the Gros Ventre Wilderness of Wyoming, where Getty Oil was planning to drill an exploratory well (McBride 71). At one point during the rendezvous, Mike Roselle recalls seeing Abbey "walking down the trail with a survey stake sticking out of his belt and doing an interview with the local paper. It was open warfare on the road at that point" (Scarce 65). Most notable was Abbey's participation in the eighth Round River Rendezvous, held 6–10 July 1987 on the North Rim of the Grand Canyon. There Abbey gave a stirring speech in which he "warned of the coming government repression and urged folks to 'monkeywrench with parental permission only.' He also warned of the severe financial and spiritual tools which will be exacted from those caught in our corrupt legal system. 'Avoid arrest. Avoid jail. Avoid doing anything to further enrich the legal profession'" (Don Morris, "Earth First!" 19).[70] Abbey also spoke at several Earth First! rallies, including one in Jackson Hole, Wyoming, in the summer of 1983, and one in Tucson in February 1986 (Petersen, "Plowboy" 18; Untitled caption). Abbey's last public appearance was at an Earth First! rally in Tucson on 4 March 1989, where — ironically — he was introduced by a woman who would later be revealed to be an FBI informant (see page 256; Davis, "View"; Lee, *Earth First!* 126).

That the FBI would develop an interest in Earth First! should come as no surprise, given the group's rapid growth and its stated desire to undermine industrial civilization. In its first year the membership of Earth First! — measured by subscriptions to its newsletter — exceeded fifteen hundred; by 1989, membership had reached about ten thousand (Manes, *Green Rage* 67). Monkeywrenching, meanwhile, was estimated to be costing business and industry from $20 to $25 million a year in 1990 (Manes, *Green Rage* 9).[71] The term "monkeywrenching," of course, could be understood to cover a broad spectrum of behaviors, and thus it is important to distinguish between *monkeywrenching* proper, which involves sabotage, and *civil disobedience*, which usually does not.[72] As Martha Lee points out, "Monkeywrenching was never condoned or actively undertaken by all Earth First!ers;

Edward Abbey at a Tucson, Arizona, Earth First! rally on 4 March 1989, at which
he spoke in opposition to the development of an astronomical observatory on
Mount Graham. This is the last known photograph of Abbey, taken at his final
public appearance, ten days before his death. (Courtesy Charles Hedgcock,
© 1989 Charles Hedgcock)

indeed, its moral justification and relative efficacy were debated throughout the
movement's history. Nevertheless, monkeywrenching's occasional spectacular
consequences and its controversial nature insured that it would be this aspect of
Earth First! that would attract the most media coverage and draw public attention"
(Lee, *Earth First!* 54).[73] For these same reasons, it deserves our attention here.

Monkeywrenching: Ecosabotage or Ecoterrorism?

Although Abbey had explored the morality of violence in his master's thesis, the
growing interest in monkeywrenching challenged him to articulate his beliefs
about environmental sabotage in a more public fashion. In an interview given to
promote the release of *The Monkey Wrench Gang* in 1975, Abbey said that in general he preferred using traditional legal and political means to stop environmental destruction, "but when all else fails . . . perhaps you should try illegality. The

Boston Tea Party was a highly illegal act, after all" (John F. Baker 7). In another interview published the following year, Abbey repeated his advocacy of monkeywrenching "as a last resort if other means of resistance failed," but he emphasized
that no sabotage should endanger human life (Lichtenstein, "Edward Abbey" 24).
Abbey expanded on these statements in response to a 1982 editorial in the journal
Environmental Ethics, in which Eugene Hargrove said that monkeywrenching
seemed "closer to terrorism than civil disobedience" (292). "Let's have some precision in language here," Abbey implored. "[T]errorism means deadly violence —
for a political and/or economic purpose — carried out against people and other living things. . . . Sabotage, on the other hand, means the application of force against
inanimate property, such as machinery. . . . [S]abotage — for whatever purpose —
has never meant and has never implied the use of violence against living creatures" ("Earth First!" 94).[74] The characters in *The Monkey Wrench Gang,* Abbey
added, engage in industrial sabotage "only when it appears that in certain cases
and places all other means of defense of land and life have failed and that force —
the final resort — becomes . . . a moral obligation, as in the defense of one's own
life, one's own family, one's own home, one's own *nature,* against a violent assault"
("Earth First!" 94–95).

In these public statements Abbey makes a number of important points that
deserve further discussion. First, he argues that monkeywrenching should be attempted only as a last resort, after all other means of resistance have failed. Second, he claims that in such circumstances, breaking the law is not only morally
justified but also patriotic, citing the Boston Tea Party as an example. Embedded
in both of these points is an argument Abbey developed further in his "Forward!"
to *Ecodefense,* in which he claimed that representative government in the United
States "represents money, not people, and therefore has forfeited our allegiance
and moral support" (*One Life* 30). Undemocratic actions, in other words, can be
morally justified if committed in response to a fundamentally undemocratic system. Third, Abbey makes a distinction between living things and property, a distinction that — when its full implications are examined — reveals Abbey's belief in
the value of biodiversity over the value of private property. Fourth, Abbey defines
sabotage (which he supports) as an assault on inanimate objects, reserving the
term *terrorism* (which he deplores) to define an assault on living things. The di-
vergence of these definitions can be explained by the central defense of monkeywrenching Abbey offers.

Of all the charges leveled against the practice of monkeywrenching, the charge
of "ecoterrorism" has attracted the most attention and been leveled by the most
opponents of the practice, including everyone from Ron Arnold, father of the
Wise Use movement, to Jay Hair, president of the National Wildlife Federation.[75]
In Abbey's view, however, monkeywrenching is *not* terrorism because it is funda-

mentally *self-defense* — an argument that draws on the ecocentric insight of deep ecology that the "self" is in fact connected to all of nature. All of nature is one's home, Abbey claims in his "Forward!" to *Ecodefense*:

> If a stranger batters your door down with an axe, threatens your family and yourself with deadly weapons, and proceeds to loot your home of whatever he wants, he is committing what is universally recognized — by common law and in common morality — as a crime. In such a situation the householder has both the right and the obligation to defend himself, his family, and his property by whatever means are necessary. This right and this obligation is universally recognized, justified, and praised by all civilized human communities. Self-defense against attack is one of the basic laws not only of human society but of life itself, not only of human life but of all life.
>
> The American wilderness, what little remains, is now undergoing exactly such an assault. . . .
>
> For many of us, perhaps for most of us, the wilderness is more our home than the little stucco boxes, wallboard apartments, plywood trailerhouses, and cinderblock condominiums in which the majority are now confined by the poverty of an overcrowded industrial culture.
>
> And if the wilderness is our true home, and if it is threatened with invasion, pillage, and destruction — as it certainly is — then we have the right to defend that home, as we would our private quarters, by whatever means are necessary. (*One Life* 29–31)

By conflating "one's own life, one's own family, one's own home, one's own *nature*" into a single object worthy of defense, Abbey turns the tables on those who would label monkeywrenchers "terrorists" and throws their accusation back at them. "A bulldozer ripping up a hillside to strip-mine for coal is committing terrorism," Abbey wrote in *Environmental Ethics;* "the damnation [*sic*] of a flowing river followed by the drowning of Cherokee graves, of forest and farmland, is an act of terrorism" ("Earth First!" 94). David Brower, archdruid of the environmental movement, said as much of Earth First!ers. "They're not terrorists," Brower claimed. "The real terrorists are the polluters, the despoilers" (Kane 102).[76]

The fifth and final aspect of Abbey's defense of monkeywrenching that deserves scrutiny is his belief that monkeywrenching should not endanger human life, a point called into question by his inclusion of a murder at the end of *Hayduke Lives!* Paul Bryant has noted that although "[o]ne might argue that the tone of protest against exploitation of the West becomes more strident in the later fiction, culminating in an actual killing in *Hayduke Lives!* . . . , the basic vision is clearly expressed in *Desert Solitaire*" ("Structure" 18). In particular, Abbey famously claimed in *Desert Solitaire* that he was "a humanist; I'd rather kill a *man* than a snake" (17). Abbey alludes to this passage in the murder scene of *Hayduke Lives!* when Seldom Seen Smith tells Jasper Bundy, "You wouldn't have the nerve to shoot a snake," and Bundy replies, "I'd rather shoot you, mister, than any snake I ever seen" (288). In the end, Jack Burns kills Bundy by accident, in a failed attempt to knock Bundy's shotgun out of his hand, "like the Lone Ranger hisself always done in the funny papers" (290).

Abbey, says Jack Loeffler, "did everything he could think of to thwart the juggernaut of so-called human progress *save one thing* — he never, ever caused harm to another human being" ("Edward Abbey" 38–39). What, then, is the reader to make of Jasper Bundy's death? For one thing, it is important to note Abbey's irony in his statement in *Desert Solitaire*, which both alludes to a line from Robinson Jeffers's "Hurt Hawks" — "I'd rather, except the penalties, kill a man than a hawk" (*Cawdor* 154) — and transforms Jeffers's philosophy of "inhumanism" into "humanism."[77] Although Abbey was a great lover of Jeffers's poetry, his reference to "humanism" reveals Abbey's willingness to poke fun at even the most serious of topics and suggests that he may, in fact, have harbored an appreciation for *all* life, human as well as herpetological. It is also important to consider that Abbey composed the final portion of *Hayduke Lives!* on his deathbed, in a race against time, as his journal entry from 2 February 1989 makes abundantly clear: "On page 423 of HL! today. I've failed the contract deadline of February first. No matter. Two more weeks will finish the job. I may skip the courtroom trial [scene], however, just in case my guts don't hold out much longer. Let Doc, Bonnie and Seldom escape free and clear from the hijacking of the GEM, get off undetected, unidentified, and therefore never arrested or indicted. That way, we'd still have a complete novel, satisfy the contract, and I can croak, if necessary, in peace" (*Confessions* 352).[78] Thus, in having Jasper Bundy restate Abbey's own words from *Desert Solitaire*, only to be shot himself, Abbey may have been commenting on both the ultimate surrender all humans must make to death and also their foolishness in engaging in such swagger and bravado. That Jack Burns would kill Bundy by accident in an attempt to replicate art could perhaps also be seen as a final warning by Abbey about the dangers of taking *The Monkey Wrench Gang*, or any fiction, too seriously. It need not, in other words, repudiate rule number one of the "Code of the Eco-Warrior" — "Nobody gets hurt. Nobody. Not even yourself" (*Hayduke* 110) — nor Abbey's lifelong condemnation of violence against human beings.[79]

Since Abbey's death in 1989, the attention paid to violent forms of political protest has increased dramatically, especially following the events of September 11.[80] How are we to assess Abbey's legacy in this new context? It seems wise to ask three questions: (1) Is Abbey's distinction between *ecosabotage* and *ecoterrorism* valid? (2) Is monkeywrenching morally justified? (3) Is monkeywrenching an effective form of political protest? The complexity of addressing these questions in this new context is perhaps best illustrated by the fate of Neil Godfrey, a twenty-two-year-old Philadelphia resident, who was prevented from boarding a United

Airlines flight to Phoenix on 10 October 2001 because he was carrying a copy of *Hayduke Lives!*—the cover of which features an illustration of a man's hand holding several sticks of dynamite. After passing through security at Philadelphia International Airport, Godfrey was approached by a National Guardsman who told him to step aside, took his copy of the book, and asked him why he was reading it. Within minutes, according to the *Philadelphia City Paper*, "Philadelphia Police officers, Pennsylvania State Troopers and airport security officials joined the National Guardsman. About 10 to 12 people examined the novel for 45 minutes, scratching out notes the entire time." Eventually, the officials let Godfrey go, but a United Airlines employee nevertheless prevented him from boarding his plane, because, she said, he was "reading a book with an illustration of a bomb on the cover" (G. Shaffer). At a time of heightened awareness about so many things that previously seemed innocuous, it is that much more important that we think carefully about monkeywrenching and Abbey's position regarding it.

As Abbey recognized, the legitimacy of an activity lies in its definition, and defining *ecoterrorism* is no easy task.[81] Bron Taylor argues that we would be wise to "eschew broad definitions of the term terrorism" when considering radical environmental action ("Religion" 24). According to Taylor, "placing non-violent blockades, loud, 'scary' and obnoxious protests, and injury-risking sabotage all under the 'terrorism' label . . . misleads the public about the social movements engaged in them. . . . Moreover, such oversimplifications reduce the possibility that society will recognize and respond to the legitimate grievances such movements may express" ("Religion" 25). Taylor claims not only that "there is little evidence of violence being deployed [by radical environmentalists] to cause injuries or death," but also that "the martial symbolism and apocalyptic worldviews found within radical environmental subcultures has not and probably will not yield widespread or proliferating terrorist violence" ("Religion" 3, 5). The philosopher Robert Young develops Taylor's point, claiming not only that monkeywrenching is more accurately described as sabotage than as terrorism but also that it is actually a form of civil disobedience, despite its use of violence. According to Young, "it is a mistake to think that civil disobedience is essentially a non-violent form of protest. Sometimes the use of violence serves to highlight an injustice in a way that no other form of protest can match. Sometimes the violence may be an inescapable means to the resistance of an injustice or a rights violation (especially where tyranny reigns). And sometimes, as has been pointed out by protestors who have resorted to violence, including some radical environmentalists, it is not until there is violent protest that any meaningful response to wrongs is likely to be made in many a society" (206).[82] Just as Abbey seeks to legitimize monkeywrenching by describing it as sabotage rather than as terrorism, Young seeks to legitimize sabotage by describing it as civil disobedience.[83]

Unfortunately, the "precision in language" Abbey so fervently desired is not to be found — at least not yet. Like it or not, human interests are intimately tied to property, and thus doing harm to inanimate objects can and often does do harm to humans and other living creatures — usually indirectly, but sometimes quite violently. Ecosabotage is in fact built on this assumed relationship, since little would be gained by harming inanimate objects that had no meaning or value to human beings. The same could be said, however, about nonviolent forms of civil disobedience, which would be equally pointless if they did not somehow harm other humans, whether politically, economically, or socially. It may thus be best to recognize that forms of political protest exist on a spectrum of harms, whose increments are far from clear. As Bruce Barcott observed in his profile of the Earth Liberation Front (ELF) — a group even more radical than Earth First! — "Much of America's political conversation since Sept. 11 has focused on the definition of borders, of lines crossed. . . . When does legal political protest become terrorism?" The answer, unfortunately, is far from clear.

The better question might seem to be not "does monkeywrenching harm people?" but "is monkeywrenching morally justified?" and "is it an effective form of political protest?" Linguistic imprecision, however, remains a problem here, since different kinds of monkeywrenching inflict different kinds of harms, and determining which harms, if any, are either morally justified or politically effective is extremely complex. Pulling up survey stakes, disabling bulldozers, cutting down billboards, spiking trees, and blowing up dams are all very different kinds of activities, with equally different moral implications and political valences. Although this is not the place for a detailed analysis of each of these activities, some general observations about their commonalities are certainly warranted.

In perhaps the most thoughtful review of *The Monkey Wrench Gang* to appear at the time of the book's publication, Sam Love, a former coordinator of Environmental Action and coeditor of *Ecotage*, attempted to address some of these issues, and a portion of his review deserves quotation at length:

> For sheer adventure and superb writing, Abbey is great reading. But whether he is a sound theorist is an entirely different question. I understand the impulse for sabotage; we certainly need to do something to temper our pell-mell rush to self-destruction. But the use of sabotage raises some important social questions:
>
> *Is the anger misfocused?* Bulldozers are merely the cutting edge of a vast social complex that is running amok. Perhaps the proper targets are the institutions and cultural values that direct the use of bulldozers.
>
> *Does sabotage help articulate alternatives which people can embrace?* Our society is so obsessed with property that sabotage is perceived as destructive and gets confused with violence. Constructive visions are lost.

Isn't the power to rebuild greater than the power to destroy? An explosion here and there may be personally gratifying and produce the feeling that the monster is being stopped. But when the smoke and debris settle, the maintenance and construction crews start putting Humpty Dumpty back together again.

Abbey doesn't really deal with these questions. And that is *The Monkey Wrench Gang's* major weakness. All he offers for a vision is some form of naturalistic retribalization of the plains. ("Maverick Raiders" 43–44)

After September 11 these questions seem all the more prescient, and all the more pointed, but Love's diagnosis of *The Monkey Wrench Gang's* "major weakness" nevertheless lacks context. Abbey's utopian vision is considerably more detailed than Love describes, though he is correct that it is not fully articulated in *The Monkey Wrench Gang*. Still, his point is well taken, since anarchists are often said to know better what they are fighting against than what they are fighting for; they have utopian impulses but no clear vision of utopia.[84] Indeed, the same has been said about environmentalists generally.

Abbey recognized the significance of constructive visions in his master's thesis, in which he argued that "violence and rebellion, when exercised in the name of a cause which we hold to be morally just, and after peaceful means have been attempted and failed, can be justified as being — under the pressure of extreme circumstances — both a true and necessary expression of the human aspiration toward the good" (73–74). The morality of violence, in other words, depends not only on the existence of a "critical situation" but also on a vision of the good life that is threatened by such a crisis.

Abbey's vision of the good life is built primarily on the notion of freedom, and the crisis that threatens this freedom is the destruction of the wilderness — especially the desert wilderness, which Abbey identifies as freedom's ultimate home. Tom Lynch takes Abbey to task on this account, arguing that "Abbey's wilderness ideology is firmly rooted in the mythology of the frontier," which "leads him to decry the destruction of his wilderness and the freedom it represents even as he unwittingly abets that destruction by espousing an anarchic individualism that makes him deaf to the stories and songs embedded in the landscape and to the ecologically responsible communalism such stories celebrate" (100, 103). Lynch's criticism is directed most at Abbey's exclusion of American Indians from *Desert Solitaire*, but his larger point is clear. In his focus on the freedom of the individual, Abbey failed to emphasize fully its correlate: the responsibility of the individual to the community, especially the human community. This is, of course, the basic criticism of the wilderness idea: celebrating "wilderness" as distinct from "civilization" furthers a false dualism between "nature" and "culture" and helps to maintain the historic exclusivity of landscapes in terms of race, class, and gender.[85]

Yet despite these conceptual problems with the wilderness idea, there are several good reasons to preserve wilderness landscapes: they have value for humans — recreational, aesthetic, scientific, and cultural, to name just a few human values — as well as value for nonhumans — such as their abilities to maintain a rich diversity of species and function as the preferred habitat for many rare and endangered species, especially charismatic megafauna. Abbey's vision of the wilderness as a utopian space, although not as fully developed as Leopold's, is not that far afield. Nevertheless, one major criticism of the moral justification of monkeywrenching remains the incompleteness of the utopian vision on which it rests: by excluding much of civilization as we know it from their vision of the good life, monkeywrenchers may — in some cases — be unjustly discounting the validity of certain human interests to trump other interests, whether human or nonhuman.

Assuming *some* aspects of Abbey's vision of the good life have value, however, the question remains whether a critical situation exists that so threatens these values as to justify the use of violence to protect them. In his excellent study of the late twentieth-century debate about the future of the Pacific Northwest forest, William Dietrich quotes Earth First! member George Draffan, who defends the tactics of Earth First!: "It depends whether you believe there's a crisis or not. . . . If you believe there is a crisis, then you need to use crisis tactics to wake people up" (156). Yet the comments of Mitch Friedman, another Earth First! activist, make clear that the moral justification of monkeywrenching cannot easily be separated from its political effectiveness. Recalling the 1980s, Friedman observed: "At that time I thought this was one of those crisis points, I thought this is going to help. Now it's hard to tell. This is a complex world, and media perceptions are everything. Earth First! was never portrayed as Robin Hood, it was portrayed as terrorist. Society doesn't want a crisis dealt with through crisis tactics" (156).

Will the rest of society eventually come to value the nonhuman world in the way these activists do, and will it therefore come to see this moment in history as worthy of crisis tactics? Geographer Martin W. Lewis certainly doesn't think so. As he put it in *Green Delusions*, his critique of radical environmentalism, "the anarchic utopianism that marks the dominant strains of radical environmentalism stands little chance of gaining public acceptance, much less of creating a feasible alternative economy" (18). The "greatest strength" of the radical environmental movement, he says, is its "consistently utopian vision": "Imagining a world in which human beings live in harmony with each other and with nature is a rewarding and comforting exercise, and the utopian imagination deserves credit for enriching global culture," says Lewis. "But for all its attractions, utopia remains, and will always remain, 'no place.' Although the vision is easy to conjure, the reality is elusive" (249). Yet Lewis, I would argue, is too quick to dismiss the utopian imagination, whose function is not simply prediction but also implementation. As Edward Rothstein has observed, "The significance of utopias is not that they imagine versions of perfection, but that they imagine cures for imperfection. A utopia is not, like Peter Pan's Neverland, an impossible place; that would turn utopianism into mere fantasy. The promise of utopia is that while seeming to be Neverland and Noplace, it has a chance of becoming This Land and This Place. That is why something seemingly imaginary becomes compellingly urgent. Utopianism defines a political program; utopianism inspires progress" ("Paradise Lost" B7).[86]

The Function of Utopia

"In a large, quasi-metaphorical sense," says David Lodge, "all significant American literature is utopian in spirit, and saturated in the myths of paradise lost or regained, either celebrating the potentialities of the American Adam, or brooding over where he went wrong" (74). Likewise, all environmentalism could be said to be fundamentally utopian, engaged in a visionary struggle to preserve, sustain, and restore natural landscapes in the name of ecological health. In the novels, nature writings, and essays of Edward Abbey, and in the actions and philosophies of Earth First! these two utopian impulses came together more clearly than perhaps anywhere else.

According to Martha Lee, "Earth First! began as a small, tightly knit group of individuals who were convinced that they were living at the most important moment in human history but also that they had a crucial role to play in that history. In a world reborn, their community and its relationship with all other species would stand as the model and foundation for a new human civilization" (*Earth First!* 111–12). Over time, however, "the movement split into two factions, one that emphasized biocentrism, and one that emphasized the interrelated nature of biodiversity and social justice" (x).[87] Abbey's death, says Lee, was one of the events that "initiated the final stage of its [Earth First!'s] fragmentation" (125).

Abbey's impact on Earth First! was so profound primarily because he was able to offer a utopian narrative of environmental resistance upon which would-be monkeywrenchers could model themselves and their actions, particularly during the 1980s, when Ronald Reagan and James Watt became lightning rods for environmentalist scorn. M. Jimmie Killingsworth and Jacqueline S. Palmer say as much in their discussion of the potential role of utopias in American environmental politics. "Under the right conditions. . . ," they claim, "such radical visions may well model real revolutionary actions by expressing in language — our chief tool for mediating thought and action — what would otherwise be the stuff of insubstantial fancy. . . . The utopian impulse embodied in poetic performance may be a necessary first step in developing the kind of character needed for direct action, or it may provide a language experiment for testing the extremes of potential action" (235).

The impact of visionary nature writing is by no means limited to Abbey; it occurs throughout the last century of American environmental organizing. In his fine eulogy of Abbey in the *New York Times Book Review*, for instance, Edward Hoagland suggests that Earth First! was "perhaps no more radical than John Muir's Sierra Club appeared to be when that organization was formed in 1892" (44).[88] Among contemporary nature writers, though, Abbey manifested a singular ability to marshal both art and politics in service to the wild. "What sets Abbey apart—" wrote Doug Peacock, alias Hayduke, "even from writers of distinction like John McPhee and Barry Lopez—was that he saw the absolute danger of our times, the global crisis, the planet burning from a way of living encouraged and praised by governments and corporations. The world is on fire and Edward Abbey was here—is still here in his books—to get angry and make us mad too" (57).

The Island as Metaphor

Most of us are still related to our native fields as the
navigator to undiscovered islands in the sea.

HENRY DAVID THOREAU, *Wild Fruits*

U TOPIA, it must be remembered, was an island. It was so for Thomas
More — whose *Utopia* was modeled on a New World island — and it
was so even for writers working before More, whenever the image
of paradise was figured as an enclosed space, distinct from the rest of the fallen
world — the Garden of Eden, to give the most prominent example (see page
267). "The island seems to have a tenacious hold on the human imagination,"
Yi-Fu Tuan observes in *Topophilia*. "Above all, it symbolizes a state of prelapsarian innocence and bliss, quarantined by the sea from the ills of the continent"
(118).[1]

Although utopia may still be figured as an island, the island itself, sad to say, can
no longer be figured as a utopia. Island biogeography, the scientific study of population dynamics in island ecosystems, has changed our view of islands entirely.
Now, as the nature writer David Quammen explains, islands are no longer where
paradise may be found; instead, they are "where species go to die" (*Song* 258).

In *The Song of the Dodo* (1996), Quammen details the rise of this new science,
which began in 1967 with the publication of *The Theory of Island Biogeography* by
Robert H. MacArthur and Edward O. Wilson. One of the most frequently cited
books in ecology and population biology, *The Theory of Island Biogeography* articulates the importance of two major variables for determining the distribution of
species on an island: the size of the island and the distance of the island from the
mainland or other islands. The smaller the island, argue MacArthur and Wilson,
the fewer the number of species it will contain; the closer the island to the mainland or other islands, the greater the number of species it will contain. Small, isolated islands, in other words, support far fewer species than do large islands located
close to other land masses.

Although this conclusion may seem obvious, *The Theory of Island Biogeography* has had a profound effect on the scientific community because its implications are so disturbing. "There's been an explosion of island studies, island talk, is-

The island of Utopia seen from above, as envisioned by the illustrator of
the first edition of Thomas More's *Utopia* (1516). (Courtesy New York
Public Library, Henry W. and Albert A. Berg Collection of English and
American Literature)

land-framed theoretical thinking, in the years since the publication of MacArthur and Wilson's little book," writes Quammen (*Song* 87). The reason for this is that island biogeography is not just about actual islands. It is also about *metaphorical* islands: areas of the environment that have become isolated from their surroundings, either through natural means, cultural means, or some combination of the two. What holds for an island in the Galapagos, in other words, also holds for a distant mountaintop, a prairie pothole, or a square mile of old-growth timber left standing in the middle of a clear-cut. As Quammen describes it, "ecological isolation — either by seawater or by other sorts of delimitation — correlates strongly with risk of extinction" (*Song* 381). MacArthur and Wilson say as much in a comment in their first chapter: "The same principles apply, and will apply to an accelerating extent in the future, to formerly continuous natural habitats now being broken up by the encroachment of civilization" (4).[2]

Throughout this book, I have been arguing for the importance of metaphor in understanding how nature writing has influenced the formation and development of environmental organizations, and I have suggested that the metaphoric frames within which these writers and groups were operating were significant because they enabled narratives that in turn conveyed values about the human relationship to nature. Working from within these metaphoric frames, these writers were able not only to persuade those who shared their values to join them in solidarity but also to convince those who did not share their values to see the world from another perspective. At the same time, I have also tried to be careful about claiming too much for metaphor, suggesting that its function must be understood as part of a larger ecology of influence that is always historically, culturally, and geographically specific.

Two questions remain to be answered. First, how do we choose from among these metaphors and the narratives they enable? Is the metaphor of nature as island any better than the other geographic metaphors we have examined? How do we know? Second, what does the future hold for nature writers and environmental organizations? Does the "explosion of island studies, island talk, island-framed theoretical thinking" suggest a new direction for the environmental movement? Has *island* become the new conserving word?

Choosing from Among Metaphors

The question of how we are to choose from among competing metaphors is complex, since it raises the issue of relativism. If metaphors are not literal descriptions of the world but imaginative constructions, are they all equally valid? Does it matter whether we see nature as a frontier, garden, park, wilderness, utopia, or island? Sallie McFague recognizes the importance of this question in *Metaphorical The-*

ology: "It should be evident that no one model . . . is able to interpret adequately the networks of relationships that constitute the world, whether these be the structures intrinsic to physical phenomena or to human existence. The complexity of the subject matter makes such pretension impossible: metaphorical thinking is an acknowledgment of multiple interpretations and relativism in dealing with our world at this level. Therefore, the criteria for our choice of models, for adequate and inadequate models, for dominant models, for the criticism of models, for the introduction of new models, are the critical issue" (137).[3]

One set of criteria we might select for choosing from among metaphors are the narratives those metaphors enable. We might say, for instance, that certain metaphors are better or worse to the degree that they enable better or worse stories about how human beings should interact with the natural world. Metaphors that figure nature as enemy or machine, for instance, enable very different stories about the human place in the world than do metaphors that figure nature as friend or organism. Indeed, environmentalism could be said to arise as much out of opposition to the stories enabled by certain metaphors as it does out of adherence to the stories enabled by others. But this still begs the question: why are certain stories better or worse? Roger J. H. King asks this question in terms of the various "voices" first-person environmental narratives express: "whose voice should we be listening to: the resort developer's, the agribusiness entrepreneur's, the hunter's, the tourist's, the weekend athlete's? These voices are not all compatible with one another, nor are they all interested in the well-being of the natural world" ("Caring" 84).

My goal is not to provide a detailed exploration of the criteria for making value judgments, so I want to address this question by briefly expanding on what I called, in the introduction, the "constructive" and "productive" functions of metaphor. While it is not possible to prove that any particular metaphor of "nature" is false, we can nevertheless make judgments about the way particular metaphors both construct our ideas of nature and produce certain outcomes that affect nature's materiality. If metaphors help construct our understanding of a concept, concealing as well as revealing different aspects of it, we can ask which aspects of "nature" are hidden by certain metaphors and which aspects are disclosed. And if metaphors produce certain outcomes, encouraging some actions while discouraging others, we can ask which actions have resulted from metaphors of "nature" and which have failed to materialize.

These criteria are similar to those offered by other critics of metaphor and narrative, such as Sallie McFague and Walter Fisher. In *Metaphorical Theology* McFague argues that our criteria must be both systematic and empirical, addressing not only a metaphor's internal consistency and comprehensiveness but also its external "fit" with human experience (137–44). And in *Human Communication as Narration* Fisher claims that an audience judges a narrative not only by the narrative's "probability" (or internal coherence) but also by its "fidelity" (or whether it offers "good reasons" for belief or action).[4] Asking which aspects of "nature" a metaphor hides and reveals is a component of its coherence and comprehensiveness, and asking which outcomes it produces is a component of its empirical and pragmatic fidelity. Among the other questions we might ask about the fidelity of a metaphor are, does the narrative it enables make sense?[5] does it correspond to what we know about the world through personal experience and scientific investigation? does it work well in practice? does it promote environmental health and environmental justice? does it cultivate relationships of care? does it allow for individual freedom? does it foster an attitude of respect?[6]

If these are some of the criteria we might use to choose from among metaphors and the narratives they enable, we might then ask, based on these criteria, whether the metaphor of nature as island is preferable to other such metaphors. As for its coherence and comprehensiveness, the idea of nature as island might at first appear to neglect the idea of connectedness that most clearly defines the modern science of ecology. But this is not actually the case, particularly for island biogeography. Rather, islands provide a means to discuss webs and networks and systems of influence while still preserving a sense that actual *things* are being connected. They model a way for us to perceive these systems of interconnected things as existing in time and space, and in so doing they help emphasize the significance of *place* as a geographical signifier. The metaphor of the island, in other words, may help us to see that frontiers, gardens, parks, wilderness areas, and utopias are all versions of islands — distinct places, certainly, but places connected to other places.[7]

In fact, connecting these islands is precisely the purpose of the Wildlands Project, which Dave Foreman helped to organize after leaving Earth First! in 1989. Central to the group's mission is the establishment of migration corridors between large areas of wild habitat so that top predators, such as grizzly bears and gray wolves, can move unimpeded throughout their pre-Columbian range. According to the group's mission statement, existing parks, wilderness areas, and wildlife refuges "are too small, too isolated, and represent too few types of ecosystems to perpetuate the continent's biological wealth" ("Wildlands Project" 11). As a result, the project seeks "to heal nature's wounds by designing and creating wildlands networks and by creating and restoring critical species and ecological processes to the land" ("Wildlands Project" 13).

In terms of practical consequences, envisioning nature as an island makes any number of competing narratives possible, but two in particular — exploitation and protection — deserve our attention here. "What happens . . . when you are shipwrecked on an entirely strange island?" asks the philosopher Mary Midgeley. "As the history of colonization shows, there is a tendency for people so placed to drop any reverence and become exploitative. But it is not irresistible. Raiders who settle down can quite soon begin to feel at home, as the Vikings did in East Anglia, and can, after a while, become as possessive, proud and protective towards their new land as the old inhabitants" ("Duties" 179). These two narratives of exploitation and protection have dominated the literature and history of islands, as Diana Loxley and Richard Grove have shown, but they have also dominated the literature and history of nature — precisely because islands have functioned as microcosms of the whole.[8] Since the Apollo 8 astronauts captured the "Earth Rise" image in 1968, however, the planet itself has increasingly come to be seen as an island floating in space, occasioning equal amounts of despair and hope.[9] On the one hand, environmental scientists compare the ecological collapse of Easter Island in the seventeenth and eighteenth centuries to the potential future of Earth Island, while on the other hand, environmental activists use the metaphor of the island to organize a variety of island-themed groups, such as the Earth Island Institute, founded in 1982 by David Brower.[10] As the environmental historian J. Donald Hughes has written, "with the worldwide expansion of industrial technology and the market economy, the Earth has become an island, and a pattern like the trajectories of population growth, resource exploitation, depletion of biota and intergroup conflict observed on islands is now occurring on a global scale. The question is just which island history the global trajectory will turn out to resemble most" (124).

Although the metaphor of nature as island is no more true or accurate than any other metaphor, it may well turn out to be more useful, particularly because it reminds us that islands have limits; they cannot be endlessly exploited. In addition, it calls our attention to the question of *scale*, which will likely become the defining issue for conservation in the twenty-first century. Just as the notions of nature as external and universal can be seen as compatible rather than contradictory, so can the ideas of local and global islands be seen as complementary rather than competitive. As J. Baird Callicott, Larry B. Crowder, and Karen Mumford have pointed out, the protection of biodiversity reserves (or local islands of external nature, from which humans are separate) and the management of inhabited, human-altered landscapes (or the global island of universal nature, of which humans are a part) reflect two different schools of conservation philosophy that need not be mutually exclusive. "The preservation of islands of biological diversity and integrity and ecological restoration necessarily occurs at present in a humanly inhabited and economically exploited matrix," they observe. "Hence the success of nature preservation and restoration necessarily depends on ecologically rehabilitating and maintaining the health of these matrices. And that, circling back, will require the preservation of biological diversity-and-integrity reserves, if Leopold is right, as databases of normal ecosystem function. Such reserves are also important to the health of surrounding matrices as a source of recruitment" (32). In other words, as I have been suggesting, preserving the pieces will be an essential part of protecting the planet, and vice versa.

What Does the Future Hold?

In her 1997 presidential address to the American Society for Environmental History, environmental historian Susan Flader observed that whether contemporary environmentalists are members of grassroots groups, mainstream groups, or reformist groups such as Earth First! they all share two common beliefs: "a commitment to the tradition of citizen action in the shaping of environmental policy at various governmental levels" and "an appreciation of the importance of place, or at least a love of their particular place" ("Citizenry" 18). In the remainder of this conclusion, I want to explore briefly (and speculatively) the relationship between these two beliefs and the two major variables of island biogeography — the size of the island and the distance of the island from other land masses — with the goal of considering how the metaphor of nature as island might prove useful for both the environmental movement and the nature writers who will shape it in the twenty-first century.

The Size of the Island

"In 1493 the New World dawned on the European imagination as small delectable island-gardens," writes Yi-Fu Tuan. "By the seventeenth century the New World had stretched to an interminable continent, and the original vision of isles of innocence and sunshine turned to incredulity as colonists stood before the immeasurable and the horrifying" (119). As Tuan's comment suggests, islands always seem either too small or too big. To the earliest European explorers of North America, the islands they encountered were too small, with the prospect of Asia's riches still looming large over the horizon. To seventeenth-century settlers the continent had become frightening in its extensiveness, with the Western Ocean still thought to lie just beyond the sunset, but with frequent reports suggesting that the sun set much farther away than they had first anticipated.

The experiences of the early explorers and settlers of the New World vividly illustrate the way in which the question of scale has dominated thinking about the North American continent from the very beginning. For modern nature writers and environmental activists, the question of scale has assumed a new significance, with the nature writer Wendell Berry proclaiming "the futility of global thinking" in favor of local issues and concerns, while former Sierra Club director David Brower takes issue with Berry's claim, considering the international repercussions of global climate change.[11]

When Alexis de Tocqueville praised the democratic individualism of free associations in *Democracy in America* (1835–40), he was speaking only of small, community-based organizations, unable from his mid-nineteenth-century perspective to foresee the growth of the state or the corporation, much less the threat of greenhouse gases. In the twentieth century, however, and especially in the last quarter century since *Silent Spring*, the United States has witnessed the rapid growth of environmental organizations from regional clubs to national and international organizations, an expansion driven in part by the threats to environmental health and safety posed by those very same forces Tocqueville could not foresee: the state, the corporation, and global ecosystem change. Just as island biogeography suggests that species diversity is dependent in part on having an island composed of an optimal amount of land, so too might we see the effectiveness of environmental organizations as being dependent in part on having the organization match the size of the problem at hand.

In *The Good Society* Robert Bellah and his colleagues argue that the idea of subsidiarity is a vital component to a "good society." Subsidiarity, in their definition, "implies that high-level associations such as the state should never replace what lower-level associations can do effectively, but it also implies their obligation to help when lower-level associations lack resources to do the job alone" (262). Subsidiarity suggests not only that environmental organizations play a vital role in democratic societies but also that social change occurs on a variety of levels, including changes in individual behavior, group beliefs, and governmental policy. Subsidiarity, in short, reminds us that global sustainability is meaningless without local efforts, and vice versa. We all have various loyalties — to ourselves, our families, our communities, our bioregions, our nations, and our world — and ideally we need not disregard any of these. Likewise, ecological justice must involve participation on all levels of society, from government and industry to advocacy groups and individual citizens, each participating in the ways to which they are best suited.[12]

Describing subsidiarity specifically in terms of environmental groups, Michael E. Kraft and Diana Wuertz argue that although environmental discourse in the early twenty-first century will continue to depend on the mainstream national and international organizations, it will also necessarily involve local and regional groups. Grassroots groups, they note, "have limited capabilities for analysis and action on state, national, and international issues such as population growth, climate change, and loss of biological diversity," and sometimes "are not even well equipped to deal with technical issues at the local level . . . without considerable assistance." Moreover, grassroots groups "tend to emphasize a negative agenda" and "have difficulty building broad coalitions and fashioning acceptable public policies." Nevertheless, Kraft and Wuertz stress that "some local and regional environmental groups have been at the forefront of successful efforts to promote the goal of sustainable communities. They have encouraged a broad vision of environmental sustainability and have contributed in important ways to the search for new approaches to environmental protection, such as incentive-based initiatives, public education, and public-private partnerships" (118).

The Distance of the Island from Other Land Masses

One of the virtues of the principle of subsidiarity is its downward emphasis: social change should occur on the lowest level possible. Such a principle not only makes for good politics but also makes for good environmentalism, which shares the downward emphasis of subsidiarity in its interest in historically, geographically, and culturally particular places. Global ecosystem health, in other words, matters in part because local landscapes depend upon it. In fact, one of the difficulties of "saving the planet" may derive from the inability of humans to appreciate global problems with anything approaching the intimate understanding they have of their local landscapes. As David Abram has written, "it is only at the scale of our direct, sensory interactions with the land around us that we can appropriately notice and respond to the immediate needs of the living world" (*Spell* 268).

Similarly, we cannot understand writers apart from the landscapes they inhabit, because their own personal identities are intimately bound up with the identities of these places. To know who Theodore Roosevelt, Mabel Osgood Wright, John Muir, Aldo Leopold, and Edward Abbey are, we must also know something about the Dakota Badlands, the fields and forests of Connecticut, the Sierra Nevada, the sand counties of Wisconsin, and the southwestern deserts. Furthermore, to understand the origins of the Boone and Crockett Club, the National Audubon Society, the Sierra Club, the Wilderness Society, and Earth First! we must also know something about the places in which the ideas for these groups were conceived. Peter Steinhart has crystallized this idea in his discussion of John Muir, when he notes that in "describing a place," Muir "prescribed a conduct" ("Place" 49).

The love all these writers have for their particular places, not to mention their appreciation of the importance of place generally, takes on a heightened significance in light of the conclusion of island biogeographers that the fragmentation of habitat leads to species loss or what these scientists call "ecosystem decay." Whether it is Roosevelt's Yellowstone, Wright's Birdcraft, Muir's Yosemite, Leopold's wilderness areas, or Abbey's Arches, the landscapes these writers celebrate — and upon which the success of their organizations partly depends — can all be seen as islands in an encroaching sea of urbanization and industrialization. "But it isn't just Yellowstone," writes Quammen. "All over the world, the exigent needs and demands of people have left natural landscapes reduced and fragmented. Nature itself, in the form of richly diverse ecological communities, has been separated from humanity and compartmentalized, the compartments being these smallish reserves, refuges and national parks that we feel we can conveniently afford to set aside" ("National Parks" 13).[13]

As the tide of humanity gradually turns more and more natural spaces into islands of diminished ecological diversity, the borders between these islands also become increasingly meaningful. In a largely unrelated development, in the past few years the idea of the "border" has captured the imagination of many writers, such as Gloria Anzaldua, who have begun to explore the borderlands that exist not only between nations but also between racial and ethnic groups, economic classes, sexualities and genders, and even families, neighborhoods, and linguistic communities. Nature writers are especially well suited to appreciate the value of borders, not only because borders play such an important role in the natural world but also because nature writing itself is a border genre. John Elder, for instance, begins the introduction to *American Nature Writers* by noting that "[e]cologists speak of the 'edge-effect' created where two ecosystems meet. The joining of marine and terrestrial environments along a rocky shoreline and the brushy margin between a meadow and a forest are examples of such edges or 'ecotones.' These mixed, dynamic habitats are particularly rich in a couple of ways. They contain more species than are found in either constituent ecosystem, and they have a greater density of organisms within a given species. The special interest and importance of nature writing come from the ways in which it too represents a vivid edge — between literature and science, between the imagination and the physical processes of observation, and between humanity and the many other forms of life with which we share this earth" (xiii).[14]

Scientifically speaking, an ecotone is "a transitional zone between two communities containing the characteristic species of each," and the word derives from the Greek *oikos,* meaning house, and *tonos,* meaning a stretching, tension, or intensity (*American Heritage Dictionary of the English Language,* 3d ed.). For nature writers, then, the "ecotone" could be said to stretch or intensify the idea of the island to encompass both human and nonhuman "nature" on a variety of different scales, from the single cell awash in the body to the island we call home, Earth.

Many nature writers have already begun to employ the island metaphor in their work, especially since Apollo 8. Josephine Johnson's *Inland Island* (1969), Gary Snyder's *Turtle Island* (1974), Richard Nelson's *Island Within* (1989), and Gretel Ehrlich's *Islands, the Universe, Home* (1991) all meditate upon the connections between the human and the nonhuman, the self and nature, taking as their subject what Phillip Lopate calls "the contractions and expansions of the self" that are characteristic of the personal essayist in general (xxvii). Richard Nelson, for instance, writes of the island on which he lives in the Pacific Northwest in *The Is-*

land Within: "Living from wild nature joins me with the island as no disconnected love ever could. The earth and sea flow in my blood; the free wind breathes through me; the clear sky gazes out from within my eyes. These eyes that see the island are also made from it; these hands that write of the island are also made from it; and the heart that loves the island has something of the island's heart inside. When I touch myself, I touch a part of the island. It lives within me as it also gives me life" (250).

Notably, this identification has caused Nelson to become active in organizing—on both the national and local levels—to protect the Tongass National Forest that borders his island in Sitka Sound. "Although I work as a nature writer," Nelson explains, "I devote as much time these days to conservation activism. I belong to national environmental organizations that bring tremendous power and influence to bear on a wide range of issues that concern me; but here on the home grounds, where my body and soul are anchored, I need more direct, hands-on involvement. So I volunteer for the Sitka Conservation Society—a vigorously engaged, tightly organized, and highly effective local group that has worked for three decades to protect Tongass rainforests" ("Forest Home" 60). Whether *The Island Within*—which, like Quammen's *Song of the Dodo,* won the John Burroughs Medal for outstanding natural history writing—has helped to influence the debate on old-growth logging in the Tongass, or even membership in the environmental organizations Nelson supports, is an open question. But clearly Nelson believes in the power of collective action to effect social change, which he says "saves me from the despair of watching helplessly as the places, the trees, and the creatures I love are threatened" and "strengthens my grasp on the hope I find whenever I hike or hunt or fish on the home terrain" ("Forest Home" 63). And he also believes in the power of the written word to help bring such change about, as his books and essays so eloquently demonstrate.

Other contemporary nature writers who share Nelson's concerns have also been active in defending particular places through their affiliation with environmental organizations. In 1995 Stephen Trimble and Terry Tempest Williams coedited *Testimony,* a chapbook of twenty-one essays in support of Utah wilderness, which they presented to the U.S. Congress with the help of the Southern Utah Wilderness Alliance. The essays, published for the mass market by Milkweed Editions, helped convince President Bill Clinton to protect 2 million acres of Utah wildlands as the Grand Staircase–Escalante National Monument in 1996. That same year, thirty-one writers contributed to *Heart of the Land,* a collection of essays edited by Joseph Barbato and Lisa Weinerman in support of the Nature Conservancy's "Last Great Places" conservation program.

The success of both these volumes spawned several subsequent collections. *Voices from a Sacred Place,* edited by Verne Huser, was published through funding from Sacred Sites International and Friends of the Albuquerque Petroglyphs. *Off the Beaten Path*, edited by Joseph Barbato and Lisa Weinerman Horak, collected short stories inspired by visits to places protected by the Nature Conservancy, while *Uncommon Wealth*, edited by Robert M. Riordan, was a local version of *Heart of the Land* published by the Nature Conservancy's Virginia chapter. Carolyn Servid — who, notably, is director of the Island Institute in Sitka, Alaska — coedited two essay collections published by Milkweed, both about Alaskan landscapes: *The Book of the Tongass*, coedited with Donald Snow, about the temperate rain forest of southeastern Alaska, and *Arctic Refuge*, coedited with Hank Lentfer in response to proposals to drill for oil in the Arctic National Wildlife Refuge. And Rick Bass — a board member of several environmental organizations — edited *The Roadless Yaak*, a collection of essays about the Yaak Valley of northwestern Montana (Sumner 147–59).

Perhaps the most heartening development of all, though, is the increased recognition — by all the parties involved in the ecology of influence I have been tracing — that nature and culture are ultimately not dissociable, that the islands of "nature" these writers seek to protect cannot be separated, either intellectually or physically, from the islands of "civilization" whose borders they share. By using the metaphor of the "island" to represent the Pacific Northwest landscape in which he lives, Richard Nelson — like Theodore Roosevelt, Mabel Osgood Wright, John Muir, Aldo Leopold, and Edward Abbey before him — is helping to lead the conversation about "nature" into new rhetorical terrain. Although his use of the island metaphor reflects the discourse of his time and place ("local residents," he notes, "tend to think of the Tongass not as one expansive entity but as a myriad of special places, each endowed with unique qualities of beauty, richness, and history" ["Forest Home" 62]), Nelson also extends the idea of the island to embrace the entirety of the world around him — the earth and sea, the wind and sky — with which he claims communion. "I am the island and the island is me," as he says in the title chapter of *The Island Within* (250). In collapsing the distinction between the human and the nonhuman, Nelson also articulates what may be the most important contribution of American nature writers who have sought to represent "nature" in both language and politics: the realization that representing "nature" is, at the deepest level, self-representation, and that by speaking for "nature" one is, in fact, speaking for oneself.

Abbreviations

ALP Aldo Leopold Papers, Univ. of Wisconsin–Madison Archives
AMNH American Museum of Natural History
BMS Birdcraft Museum and Sanctuary
BPL Bridgeport Public Library
CAS Connecticut Audubon Society
EAP Edward Abbey Papers, Univ. of Arizona Library, Special Collections
FHS Fairfield Historical Society
FPL Fairfield Public Library
GP   George Bird Grinnell Papers, Sterling Memorial Library, Yale Univ.
MOW Mabel Osgood Wright
NYPL New York Public Library
SCB *Sierra Club Bulletin*
TRP Theodore Roosevelt Papers, Manuscript Div., Library of Congress
WSP Wilderness Society Papers, Denver Public Library

Notes

Introduction. The Ecology of Influence

1. See also Payne's "Talking Freely around the Campfire"; and Will Nixon's "Natural Causes."

2. Other nature writers have been involved in environmental organizations, but these five provide sufficient illustration of my argument. Sigurd Olsen, for instance, was active in the Wilderness Society; Rachel Carson served as honorary chairman of the Maine chapter of the Nature Conservancy; and Lois Gibbs founded the Citizens Clearinghouse for Hazardous Waste (now the Center for Health, Environment, and Justice), which she later wrote about in *Love Canal: My Story* (1982).

3. My subtitle alludes to Brooks's: *How Literary Naturalists from Henry Thoreau to Rachel Carson Have Shaped America.*

4. I use the term "ecosystem" metaphorically, as an example of a complex system, and refer to "ecology" in the broadest sense, as the science of the relationships between organisms and their environments. Like many scientific concepts, the term "ecosystem" is highly contested. For more on the history of ecosystem ecology, see Golley; and Hagen. I prefer the term "influence" to "power," not only because of the historical relationship between the idea of influence and the rhetorical concept of persuasion but also because of the rather sinister implications "power" has come to have in contemporary criticism. I also want to ecologize Harold Bloom's influential *Anxiety of Influence*. I recognize, of course, the influence of Michel Foucault on discussions about how power circulates through discourse. See, for instance, his *Archaeology of Knowledge*. For a collection of essays on Foucault and the environment, see *Discourses of the Environment*, ed. Éric Darier. For an ecosystemic theory of communication, see Niklas Luhmann, *Ecological Communication*. For a discussion of social movements as interpretive systems, see chapter 2 of Stewart, Smith, and Denton. For an "ecological model of writing, whose fundamental tenet is that writing is an activity through which a person is continually engaged with a variety of socially constituted systems" (367), see Marilyn M. Cooper, "The Ecology of Writing." For a related network theory of intellectual change, see Randall Collins, *The Sociology of Philosophies*.

5. Brulle also uses an ecological model to describe the changes in these discursive frames in "Environmental Discourse" (79).

6. Another relevant contribution to frame analysis is that of sociologist David A. Snow and his colleagues in "Frame Alignment" (464).

7. A number of other typologies of environmental discourses exist. See, for instance, Doremus; Dryzek; and Killingsworth and Palmer.

8. "All history," writes Donald Worster, "has become a record of disturbance and that disturbance comes from both cultural *and* natural agents" (*Nature's Economy* 424).

9. The notion that ethics is fundamentally narrative is a rich one for exploration. See, for instance, Booth, *The Company We Keep*; Coles, *The Call of Stories*; Newton, *Narrative Ethics*; and Nussbaum, *Love's Knowledge*. Walter Fisher argues that all forms of human communication can be understood as stories that enact a set of values in *Human Communication as Narration*. Among the most influential works on narrative and ethics are: David Carr, *Time, Narrative, and History*; Alasdair MacIntyre, *After Virtue*; Paul Ricoeur, *Time and Narrative*; and Charles Taylor, *Sources of the Self*. For a discussion of narrative and environmental history, see Cronon, "A Place for Stories." On the significance of narrative to environmental ethics, beyond those I cite below, see K. Warren, *Ecofeminist Philosophy*; A. Peterson, *Being Human*; Gare; and the responses to Gare by Cafaro and by Philip Ryan. Donald A. Schön's "Generative Metaphor" links metaphor, frames, and narrative with regard to social policy.

10. See, for instance, Burke's *Language as Symbolic Action*, *A Grammar of Motives*, and the essay "Dramatism." Burke's contributions to environmental rhetoric are examined in Roorda, "KB in Green"; and Coupe, "Kenneth Burke." See also Benford and Hunt.

11. For more on injustice frames, see William A. Gamson, Bruce Fireman, and Steven Rytina's *Encounters with Unjust Authority*.

12. Compare Burke's well-known statement about the "unending conversation" of our lives in *The Philosophy of Literary Form* (110–11). Compare also Alasdair MacIntyre's observation that "[w]e enter upon a stage which we did not design and find ourselves part of an action that was not of our making" (201).

13. See, for example, Whit Gibbons, *Keeping All the Pieces*; and Rocky Barker, *Saving All the Parts*.

14. See, for instance, Vogel. As Richard White has put it, "Without nature, there is no environmental history" ("Nationalization" 978 n. 7).

15. For a review of this early scholarship, see Mazel, *A Century of Early Ecocriticism*. It is an interesting and by no means minor point that nature writing scholarship has evolved roughly in tandem with the environmental movement. At the same time conservation developed into environmentalism in the late 1960s, nature writing scholarship began to change from more traditional literary scholarship into what has come to be known as "ecocriticism." For a thorough review of nature writing scholarship, see the "Bibliographical Essay" in Scheese, *Nature Writing*. For two recent meditations on the genre of nature writing, see Elder's introduction to his *American Nature Writers*, as well as Michael P. Cohen's essay "Literary Theory and Nature Writing" in the same publication.

16. Lyon is careful to admit this ("Nature writing is not in truth a neat and orderly field" [*This Incomperable Lande* 3]), but he still attempts to generalize. See Fritzell, *Nature Writing and America*; Scheese, *Nature Writing*; and Murphy, *Farther Afield*. For a full discussion of genre maps, see Fowler 239–50. For a textual, rather than graphic, genre map, see the appendix ("Nature's Genres: Environmental Nonfiction at the Time of Thoreau's Emergence") of Buell (397–423).

17. While some would identify nature writing as a "subgenre" of the essay "genre"—itself a subcategory of the "mode" of prose writing—my argument extends in the opposite direction. I follow the more common, less precise usage of "genre" to describe the kind of "super-genre" I am calling nature writing.

18. Compare Frank Stewart's passing description of the genre as "this literary conversation called nature writing" (xxi).

19. Compare John Elder's discussion of these two terms in the introduction to his *American Nature Writing*. For more on going "beyond nature writing," see also *The Greening of Literary Scholarship*, ed. Steven Rosendale.

20. Further discussion of this rhetorical understanding of genre can be found in the two volumes edited by Freedman and Medway.

21. For more on the relationship of fiction and nonfiction, see C. L. Rawlins, "Dillard's Cat"; and Sarah Heekin Redfield, "Surveying the Boundaries."

22. For a review of this history, see Coates, *Nature*.

23. In *An Ethics of Place* Mick Smith emphasizes the need to acknowledge "the difference between constructivism as an epistemological thesis, of whether our knowledge of nature is socially constructed, and constructivism as an ontological thesis, of whether nature is nothing more than a social construct" (118).

24. Richard White and David Mazel also quote portions of this passage. See White, "'Are You an Environmentalist?'" 182–83; and Mazel, *American Literary Environmentalism* 29–34.

25. For more on paradox, see Proctor, "Geography, Paradox, and Environmental Ethics," in which Proctor observes: "Nature and culture are not one, nor are they quite two" (242).

26. Humans are not different in *kind* from other creatures, but we are different in *degree*, and language is one of our distinguishing traits. Although chimpanzees are capable of limited forms of symbolic communication, only humans are fully capable of language—a consequence of evolution, not "design." The human brain is also larger and more complex than the brain of chimpanzees; humans are uniquely self-conscious (as far as we know); and humans have many ways to transmit information between generations, allowing for cultural evolution in addition to biological evolution. For a summary, see Barbour, *Religion and Science* 254–55. For more on language as a trait of human evolution, see chapter 7 of Paul Ehrlich's *Human Natures*.

27. I quote from the original version of Manes's essay, which first appeared in the journal *Environmental Ethics*. The essay has since been reprinted in both Oelschlaeger, *Postmodern Environmental Ethics* (43–56), and Glotfelty and Fromm, *The Ecocriticism Reader* (15–29), a measure of its significance to the ecocritical community.

28. Others have attributed this shift to different factors, such as Christianity, agriculture, and technology. For a related critique of alphabetic literacy, see Shlain. For a discussion of Abram in the context of literacy studies, see Roorda, "Great Divides."

29. For a related diagnosis of the abstraction of "nature" in human discourse, see Jack Turner, *The Abstract Wild*. For a discussion of the ways in which nature writers have attempted to avoid this natural abstraction, see chapter 6 ("Nature's Personhood") of Buell. For a rhetorical perspective that shares Abram's interest in phenomenology, see Maxcy. A wide range of titles reflect the prominence of the oral dimension in environmental rhetoric; see,

for instance, J. J. Clarke, *Voices of the Earth*; A. Gilliam, *Voices for the Earth*; Roszak, *The Voice of the Earth*; Payne, *Voices in the Wilderness*; and Schwartz, *Voices for the Wilderness*.

30. Peter Fritzell makes a similar point in *Nature Writing and America* (290).

31. See also Oelschlaeger, "Wilderness, Civilization, and Language."

32. These include Anna L. Peterson (religion), Kate Soper (philosophy), James D. Proctor (geography), N. Katherine Hayles (literature), William Cronon (history), and Anne Whiston Spirn (landscape architecture), just to name a few.

33. Our biology also shapes our perception in nonlinguistic ways. Nature writing and natural history writing, observes Gary Snyder, are both "'naively realistic' in that they unquestioningly accept the front-mounted bifocal human eye, the poor human sense of smell, and other characteristics of our species, plus the assumption that the mind can, without much self-examination, directly and objectively 'know' whatever it looks at" (*Place in Space* 164). Christopher J. Preston develops this insight in "Conversing with Nature" (238–39).

34. That certain forms of social constructionism can teach humility is often overlooked. William Cronon, however, emphasizes this in "The Uses of Environmental History" (15). An earlier, underappreciated recognition that nature teaches both relativism and humility can be found in George Santayana's 1911 address, "The Genteel Tradition in American Philosophy" (*Genteel Tradition* 62–64).

35. Others have made similar points. See Raymond Williams's "Ideas of Nature" and "Nature" (184); and Hay 336.

36. Furthermore, ideas do not simply influence behaviors, as Anna L. Peterson observes: "Mental attitudes . . . are connected to behavioral changes, but the relationship between them is complex, variable, and mutually reinforcing, rather than univocal and unidirectional" (208).

37. Many writers have explored the role of metaphor in environmental discourse. A good survey is Meisner. Noteworthy books include Botkin; Dryzek; Eisenberg; Harré, Brockmeier, and Mühlhäusler; and Kolodny.

38. In *Why We Garden* Jim Nollman notes that even the idea of the garden has metaphorical varieties (14).

39. For two good surveys of the definitions, critical views, history, and contemporary theories of metaphor, see the entries on "metaphor" by Wallace Martin in *The New Princeton Encyclopedia of Poetry and Poetics* and Richard Coe in *The Encyclopedia of Rhetoric and Composition*. Lakoff and Johnson develop their views in *Philosophy in the Flesh*. See also M. Johnson's *Moral Imagination*.

40. For a clever discussion of this and other figures of speech, see Quinn.

41. See, for instance, Borg, *The God We Never Knew*; and McFague, *The Body of God*.

42. M. Johnson develops this point in *The Body in the Mind* (132).

43. They generally avoid metaphors that express other kinds of instrumental values, such as technological or economic values. Three important works that attempt to catalog the varieties of environmental values are Kellert, *The Value of Life*; Kempton, Boster, and Hartley, *Environmental Values in American Culture*; and Rolston, *Environmental Ethics*.

44. Keep in mind the contested nature of the terms "species" and "ecosystem."

45. See also C. Preston's *Grounding Knowledge*.

46. This focus on place should not imply either a condemnation of rootlessness or a denial of difference within a place, both of which Sanders addresses in *Staying Put*. Scott Slovic has commented on the issue of rootlessness in "Literature" (261–62), and Daniel Berthold-Bon has observed that "any philosophy of place must place itself within an ethics which enables us to take seriously the (often conflicting) interests (and/or rights, depending on the ethics) of all who dwell in that place" (19). I address this point in the conclusion.

47. By saying that ethics is "rooted" in this way, I do not mean to imply that it has a geographical *foundation* but rather that it *emerges* as a property of a complex system. It is neither predictable from nor reducible to the lower-level properties and relations out of which it arises, that is, self and place, mind and body, reason and emotion, fact, and value. Jim Cheney makes a similar claim in "Postmodern Environmental Ethics," although not in the context of systems theory (132). See, however, Mick Smith's response in "Cheney and the Myth of Postmodernism" (7). My meaning is closest to that Karen Warren first articulated in "The Power and Promise of Ecological Feminism": "Narrative provides a way of conceiving of ethics and ethical meaning as *emerging out of* particular situations moral agents find themselves in, rather than as being *imposed* on those situations as a derivation of some predetermined, abstract rule or principle" (*Ecofeminist Philosophy* 103). For more on emergence, see Steven Johnson's *Emergence*.

48. Roger J. H. King makes a similar point in "How to Construe Nature" (106).

49. Lakoff and Johnson say as much in *Metaphors We Live By* (145).

50. Slovic's identification of the rhetorical modes of nature writing parallels the observations of Thomas Lyon in "Nature Writing" (8) and Peter Fritzell in *Nature Writing and America* (6).

51. An exception is Thoreau's notation in his journal in 1859 that "[e]ach town should have a park, or rather a primitive forest, of five hundred or a thousand acres, where a stick should never be cut for fuel, a common possession forever, for instruction and recreation" (12:387). He argued further in January 1861 that "natural objects of rare beauty" should be held in public ownership (14:305). As Robert Kuhn McGregor points out, Thoreau's incorporation of this sentiment into "The Allegash and East Branch"—which, along with his other Maine woods travel essays, was published posthumously in 1864 as *The Maine Woods*—"represented one of the first published calls for legislated wilderness protection" (184).

52. See, for instance, Chase; Fiedler; Lawrence; and R. Lewis.

53. For other statements about the tendency of nature writers working in the Thoreauvian tradition to underrepresent community, see Buell 128; Elder and Wong 3; and Fritzell, *Nature Writing and America* 155.

54. For a brief survey of this response, see the section "The Politics of Natural History" in the introduction to Don Scheese, *Nature Writing*.

55. For an overview, see my entry "Environment and Environmentalism" in the *Encyclopedia of American Studies*. For a brief analysis of terminology, see Dunlap, "Conservationists and Environmentalists." On the relationship of conservation and preservation, see James Turner, "Charting American Environmentalism's Early (Intellectual) Geography." Histories of the transition from conservation to environmentalism in America include Fox, *John Muir;*

Gottlieb; Hays; Nash, *Wilderness*; Rubin; Sale, *Green Revolution*; and Shabecoff. Discussions of the development of environmental groups in general include Ingram and Mann; R. Mitchell; Mitchell, Mertig, and Dunlap; and Petulla.

56. For a list of these groups, see Allin, *Politics* 29.

57. According to Theodore Cart, "[a]lthough game protective efforts go back to colonial times, the earliest 'modern' sportsman's group is thought to be the New York Association for the Protection of Game organized in 1844" (10). Cart also notes that "[f]rom 1874, sportsmen's clubs repeatedly tried to coordinate and enforce State statutes through the agency of regional and national confederations" (79). For a list of these groups, see Cart 78 n. 2.

58. Although the chronological organization of these chapters may suggest a linear, progressivist notion of history — in which these writers, metaphors, and organizations get closer to the "truth" over time — this is not my intent. Nature writing does not "improve" over time any more than metaphoric usage becomes more sophisticated or newer environmental organizations overtake older ones. Rather, particular metaphors are used at particular times and places by particular people with particular effects. For a general introduction to theories of social change, see Boudon; for a discussion of theories of social change from a postmodern perspective, see Featherstone.

1. *The Closing of the Frontier*

1. Letter dated 13 Nov. 1888. Winner of the Pulitzer Prize for biography in 1980, Edmund Morris's *Rise of Theodore Roosevelt* is the best biography for the period covered by this chapter, Roosevelt's life before becoming president. McCullough is also a good reference for this period, as is Putnam. The best one-volume biography is Dalton.

2. I cite from the National edition of the *Works*. For a comparison of the National and Memorial editions, see Hart and Perleger x–xi.

3. The precise date of the dinner is unknown. M. Collins (98) incorrectly gives the date as 8 December, a misreading of E. Morris, *Rise* 383.

4. "My Life as a Naturalist" first appeared in the *American Museum Journal* in May 1918.

5. Both Cutright's *Theodore Roosevelt: The Making of a Conservationist* (1985) and his earlier *Theodore Roosevelt: The Naturalist* (1956) are invaluable examinations of Roosevelt's interest in nature. Although some overlap occurs between these volumes, I generally quote from the more recent volume, which examines Roosevelt's youth in greater detail.

6. Osborn (254–55) says the museum was on the porch. For more on natural history museums, see Asthma.

7. See, for instance, Robert Barnwell Roosevelt, *Superior Fishing* 184–85; and Reiger, *American Sportsmen* 55–56.

8. In his third year, for instance, he received a 92 in Natural History 1 and a 97 in Natural History 3 (Cutright, *Making* 122).

9. For more on "Sou'-Sou'-Southerly," see my introduction to the *North Dakota Quarterly* reprint.

10. In addition to those publications cited parenthetically, the reader interested in Roosevelt's Dakota years should consult Broach; A. Carlson; Mathes; and Mattison.

11. For one prominent criticism of Erikson's stage theory of human development, see C. Gilligan.

12. Within the first year of publication, there were three American editions and one British (E. Morris, *Rise* 792 n. 8). Reviews of the book, all enthusiastic, appeared in the *New York Times* (13 July 1885), the *New York Tribune* (6 Oct. 1886), the *Spectator* (16 Jan. 1886), and the *Saturday Review* (29 August 1885). The Modern Library recently reissued *Hunting Trips* and *The Wilderness Hunter* in a new edition, with an introduction by Stephen A. Ambrose.

13. Roosevelt often refers to the differences between eastern sportsmen and western ranchmen in *Hunting Trips*. See, for instance, *Works* 1:67–68, 171–72, 179, 191–92.

14. For more on this episode, see Cutright, *Theodore Roosevelt: Making* 150–51; Hagedorn 95–96; Lang 156–58; and Putnam 454.

15. This is not to deny the humor with which Roosevelt and his readers viewed the result. See Hagedorn 173, 235–36; Morison 77; and E. Morris, *Rise* 281.

16. TRP, ser. 1, microfilm reel 75. No letterbook volume or pages given.

17. TRP, ser. 2, vol. 74, p. 45.

18. Although I restrict my discussion of the "frontier" to its role in Roosevelt's nature writing and advocacy, the term has generated a substantial scholarly literature. An excellent introductory synthesis is Nobles, *American Frontiers*.

19. Roosevelt frequently emphasizes the importance of bringing books on his hunting trips. See *Works* 1:150, 219.

20. Elsewhere Roosevelt notes how the badlands can deceive the hunter about the extent of his shooting skill (*Works* 1:32); how quicksands and mud holes engulf the unperceptive horseback rider into dangerous situations (*Works* 1:155); how one of his cowboys mistook some dark-colored ponies for bears (*Works* 1:170–71); and how he himself had mistaken charred logs for bears (*Works* 1:235). He explains the need for accurate observation at length in *Works* 1:153. In *The Young John Muir*, Holmes shows that John Muir shared Roosevelt's interest in the deceptiveness of perceptions (178, 194).

21. In its review of *Hunting Trips*, the *Saturday Review* called Roosevelt "thoroughly trustworthy" and said that the reader "may receive all his sporting experiences for gospel" (290–91). Another reviewer noted that many parts of the book "present the appearance of having been taken straight from notes day by day," which suggests Roosevelt may occasionally have recorded his impressions of the landscape on the spot for later reference (G. Johnson 8). Roosevelt's memory was legendary, however, and he would have had no trouble calling up detailed images of the Dakotas from just a few words jotted in his diary. See E. Morris *Rise* 26, 796 n. 25.

22. This essay originally appeared in 1893 as "Realism in Literature and Art." I quote from a reprint of the essay in Darrow's *Persian Pearl* (1899).

23. Compare Stewart Edward White on Roosevelt: "He was always somewhat impatient with the sentimentalist on the subject of killing. The killing of an animal is no more — and no less — important than the killing of a tree, or a flower, or a vegetable. All are manifestations in form of one thing — the essence of life" (*Works* 2:xviii).

24. The *Spectator* classified *Hunting Trips* alongside Izaak Walton's *Compleat Angler* as a book "in which the animal-killing is only a peg or skeleton for the lover of Nature, the bota-

nist, geologist, humourist, to hang his sketches or finished pictures on" (rev. of *Hunting Trips* 82). Paul Brooks, however, argues that "[w]hile it is demonstrably true, as Roosevelt asserted, that the finest sportsmen are also nature lovers, one cannot help feeling that on occasion he pushed that paradox to the limit" (110).

25. For more on market hunters, see Kimball and Kimball.

26. The only year Roosevelt missed his annual hunting trip was 1895, when he was serving as New York police commissioner.

27. In his introduction to *Hunting Trips* in the National Edition of the *Works*, Grinnell minimizes this aspect of his initial review (*Works* 1:xiv–xv).

28. Collins mistakenly places the meeting of Roosevelt and George Bird Grinnell in 1887, when Grinnell himself states plainly that the meeting occurred "[n]ot long after" his review appeared in the 2 July 1885 issue of *Forest and Stream* (M. Collins 97; Roosevelt, *Works* 1:xv).

29. The arrival of high-speed printing, low-cost paper, advertising revenue, and nationwide mail delivery facilitated the growth of these periodicals, some of the more prominent of which were *Fur, Fin, and Feather* (1868–91), *American Sportsman* (1871–77), *Field and Stream* (now *American Field* [1874–]), *Field and River* (1877–82), *Game Fancier's Journal* (1879–1910), *Forest, Forge, and Farm* (1880–86), *American Angler* (1881–1900), and *Outing* (1882–1923) (Dunlap, *Saving* 10). According to Tober, "[a]n 1889 survey of American sporting periodical literature [by *Recreation* magazine] included fifty-six journals covering a wide variety of sports" (62 n. 19). Schneirov examines the treatment of nature and the outdoors in the popular, general-interest magazines of the Progressive era (139–45). For more on sporting journalism, see Betts; and Estes. For more on *Forest and Stream* in particular, see Neuzil and Kovarik.

30. The magazine's full title suggests the scope of its interests: *Forest and Stream, a Weekly Journal Devoted to Field and Aquatic Sports, Practical and Natural History, Fish Culture, the Protection of Game, Preservation of Forests, and the Inculcation in Men and Women of a Healthy Interest in Outdoor Recreation and Study* (Tober 62 n. 19). In 1874, the year after the magazine's founding, G. W. Martin, the president of the Kennebec Association for the Protection of Game, attributed American interest in sporting to *Field and Stream*, Frank Forester, and the Smithsonian Institution (Tober 46).

31. Peter Steinhart has similarly noted that "[c]onservation made its way in America through the pages of magazines, rather than through those of newspapers" ("Longer View" 10). Thomas Dunlap also suggests that sporting journals organized hunters for political action (*Saving* 11).

32. In the winter of 1874–75 "nearly 100 sportsman's organizations were organized all over the country, ten or twelve state associations and one national association" (Burnham 13). The Schuylkill Fishing Company, perhaps the first such group, was founded in 1732 (Reiger, *American Sportsmen* 265 n. 46).

33. In New York, the Audubon Society was predated by the New York Association for the Protection of Game, established in 1844 as the New York Sporting Club (Trefethen, *Crusade* 17).

34. Roosevelt's greatest contribution to the Boone and Crockett Club, writes Paul Russell Cutright, "was his success in persuading men of prominence to join the club" (*Theodore Roosevelt: Making* 183)

35. The first formal meeting of the club, held on 29 February 1888 in New York City included seventeen members: the attendees at the December dinner meeting (with the exception of E. P. Rogers) and seven new members, Albert Bierstadt, Heber R. Bishop, William B. Bristow, Arnold Hague, William H. Merrill Jr., William Austin Wadsworth, and John E. Roosevelt, another cousin of Theodore.

36. The constitution and bylaws (to 21 January 1959) of the club are reprinted in Trefethen, *Crusade* 356–61.

37. Dunlap agrees that "hunters were the first organized group to press for wildlife preservation," despite his belief that "[i]t is too much to claim . . . that hunting was the cradle of the conservation movement" (*Saving* 9). For discussion of Reiger's thesis, see (in chronological order): Runte's review of the first edition of *American Sportsmen* in the *Journal of Forest History*, as well as the followup letters by Reiger, Runte, and Albright; Altherr, "American Hunter-Naturalist"; Dunlap, "Sport Hunting"; Reiger, "Commentary"; Reiger, "Wildlife"; and Altherr and Reiger, "Academic Historians."

38. For other examples, see Reiger, *American Sportsmen* 180–81, 185–86.

39. In a markedly unenthusiastic letter, Grinnell wrote to Madison Grant on 1 June 1904 saying, "[t]he club gets together once or twice a year and eats a dinner and talks about what ought to be done; a few of its members talk from time to time with influential people, trying to push or prevent this or that measure, and that is really all that we do" (Fox, *John Muir* 108).

40. "An Exclusive Club," undated, unidentified newspaper clipping, published ca. 1899–1901, GP, Box 31, Folder 152.

41. For a list of organizations of which Roosevelt was a member, see E. Morris, "Theodore Roosevelt" 26–27. The irony that a man who celebrated the individualism of the frontier joined so many groups is matched only by the irony that preserving natural spaces required strengthening the power of the state to restrain the individualism valued by the frontiersman (Ward 367).

42. Though they had yet to meet, Grinnell praised Roosevelt's support for the Adirondack legislation in the pages of *Forest and Stream* 22 (13 March 1884): 121–22.

43. The meeting was held on 14 January 1891 at the Metropolitan Club in Washington, D.C. Also present were Secretary of War Redfield Procter and Speaker of the House Thomas B. "Czar" Reed of Maine. Procter was present because the park had been under the control of the army since the summer of 1886.

44. According to James B. Trefethen, "[t]he same situation prevailed in nearly all other states, although Michigan and Wisconsin already had taken the lead in outlawing some of these abuses. As early as 1876 Wisconsin had outlawed the dogging of deer, and in 1881 Michigan had prohibited the shooting of deer in deep water and the taking of deer in traps and snares" (*Crusade* 76).

45. As governor of New York (1899–1900), Roosevelt appointed Major W. Austin Wadsworth, then president of the Boone and Crockett Club, to the presidency of the commission, which accomplished much under his leadership, including "the enactment of laws to protect the forests from fire, to outlaw spring waterfowl shooting, and to protect female deer as a method of increasing the state's depleted deer herds" (Trefethen, *American* 158).

46. GP, Box 30, Folder 142.

47. The sixty-four illustrations used in the magazine article were increased to eighty-two for the book (A. Norton 94).

48. The *Book Buyer* also noted that Roosevelt "adds a thorough familiarity with his subject, happily combining accuracy with entertainment" (484). Other reviews of the book appeared in *Overland Monthly* 28 (Nov. 1896): 604; the *New York Times* (30 Nov. 1888): 3; and the *Dial* 15 (16 Sept. 1893): 149.

49. Roosevelt's biographer Edmund Morris calls *The Wilderness Hunter* "arguably his finest book" and describes it as "richly-detailed" and "sweet-natured" (*Rise* 471, 818 n. 51). Other reviews of the book include the *New York Times* (6 Aug 1893): 19; the *Spectator* 73 (1894): 468–69; the *Nation* 57 (1893): 200; and the *Dial* 15 (1893): 149.

50. One essay *not* included in *American Big-Game Hunting* was an account by Albert Bierstadt that described the facts surrounding his supposed killing of a record-setting moose. See Eric W. Nye and Sheri I. Hoem, "Big Game on the Editor's Desk." Reviews of *American Big-Game Hunting* include: the *Nation* 57 (1893): 399–400; and the *Spectator* 73 (1894): 468–69. The book, released on 5 October 1893, was an immediate success and went into a second printing; profits from its sale were used to finance the publication of *Hunting in Many Lands* (Trefethen, *Crusade* 24–25).

51. Reviews of *Hunting in Many Lands* include: the *Spectator* 76 (1896): 744; and, by C. Hart Merriam, *Science* n.s.3 (1896): 246.

52. Reviews of *Trail and Camp-Fire* include: the *Nation* 66 (1898): 273–74; and, by C. Hart Merriam, *Science* n.s. 7 (1898): 320–21. The New York state librarian ranked *Trail and Camp-Fire* as one of the best fifty books published during 1897–98 (Reiger, *American Sportsmen* 181).

53. GP, Box 4, Folder 8.

54. TRP, ser. 2, vol. 1, p. 250.

55. GP, Box 4, Folder 9. For an examination of humor in American nature writing, see Peiffer.

56. TRP, ser 2, 2, vol. 2, p. 326.

57. TRP, ser. 2, vol. 2, p. 339.

58. TRP, ser. 2, vol. 2, p. 349. Robert Wilson Shufeldt (1850–1934) was the author of *The Mythology of the Raven* (New York: Macmillan, 1890).

59. A version of the romanticism-realism tension would surface again during Roosevelt's presidency in the form of the "nature fakers" controversy, which Ralph Lutts has chronicled in detail in *The Nature Fakers*. Gail Bederman briefly discusses the nature fakers in *Manliness and Civilization* 208. See also Lutts's *Wild Animal Story*; and Mighetto.

60. Wrote Grinnell, "Roosevelt's services to science and to conservation were many, but perhaps no single thing he did for conservation has had so far-reaching an effect as the establishment of the Boone and Crockett Club" (Roosevelt, *Works* 1:xviii).

2. The Garden, You, and I

1. See K. Jackson, *Crabgrass Frontier*.

2. For more on Osgood and his achievements, and a more detailed set of notes generally, see my edition of Wright's *Friendship of Nature*.

3. Osgood had two other daughters, Agnes Haswell and Bertha Stevens.

4. Mabel married James Osborne Wright (1852–1920), a British bibliographer and rare book dealer who appears as "Evan" in some of Mabel's novels, on 25 September 1884.

5. See Whetten for an examination of three Connecticut suburbs neighboring Farifield: Windsor, Norwich, and Wilton.

6. For more on domesticity, see P. Baker, "Domestication"; Cott; Kelley; Kerber; and Sklar.

7. The original essay appeared in *Horticulturist* 3 (1849): 449–55. For more on Downing, see Fishman 123–24; Major; Schuyler, *Apostle*; Sweeting; and Tatum and MacDougall. For more on domestic architecture generally, see the volumes by Clark; and Handlin. Citing the explosion of gardening books for American women following the English publication of Jane Loudon's *Gardening for Ladies*, Norwood argues that mid-nineteenth-century women of the middle and upper classes "really never quit their flower beds except, perhaps, in the imaginations of the intellectual elite" (101). She also notes that "[i]n preparing Loudon's book for the American audience, Downing deleted her chapters on kitchen gardens, thus reinforcing the image of the leisured American woman in an ornamental floral landscape" (299 n. 3).

8. For the history of gardens in general, see Adams; Berrall; Anthony Huxley; Hyams; and Thacker. For the history of American gardens in particular, see Hedrick; Punch; and the three volumes by Leighton. For recent garden theory, see Ross; and especially John Dixon Hunt's thought-provoking *Greater Perfections*.

9. For a detailed examination of the etymology of *garden*, see Erp-Houtepen.

10. "Women's garden literature (both in America and Great Britain) is heavily class-coded to this day," Norwood notes (101). Class is notoriously difficult to define, however, especially "middle class." See Blumin.

11. Robert Fishman says the same thing about the suburbs: "Suburbia kept alive the ideal of a balance between man and nature in a society that seemed dedicated to destroying it" (207).

12. During her European travels, Wright published a series of letters from abroad in the *Bridgeport Standard* that — apart from some poetry published in the *New York Evening Post* (with the aid of William Cullen Bryant) — constitute her first published work (Marble). In *The Garden of a Commuter's Wife*, Wright offered a fictionalized version of her European journey (17).

13. In a 17 October 1893 letter, Stedman was more cautious than Wright suggests. After reading the entire book in manuscript, Stedman grew more enthusiastic in a 16 April 1894 letter. See also his 15 May 1894 letter (MOW Autograph Album, FPL).

14. Brett moved to Darien, Connecticut, in 1891, and to Greenfield Hill in Fairfield in 1903. James Wright submitted the book to Brett on 3 February 1894, without mentioning that his wife was the author. On 21 February, Brett replied to James Wright, requesting a meeting with the author. Two days later, Brett spoke to Mabel and suggested that the book be revised and resubmitted. On 2 April, Brett conveyed the substance of a reader's report, which recommended changing some words, standardizing the botanical names, omitting some poems and an entire chapter ("By the River"), and asking Wright to double-check some factual information. Apparently Wright made the requested changes (Macmillan Company Records, Brett Letterbooks, NYPL).

15. Wright's memory fails her slightly. *The Friendship of Nature* was first published on 15 May 1894. It was reprinted in June and July 1894; in May, August, and October 1895; in July 1898; and in a new edition in September 1906. The book originally appeared in two editions, in a smaller duodecimo size and a larger "large paper" edition limited to 250 copies. An unbound preview copy of the book is located at the CAS Burr Street Office.

16. Holmes's letter appears in MOW's Autograph Album (FPL).

17. The letters appear in MOW's Autograph Album (FPL).

18. Writers who express the "complex pastoral," according to Marx, "invoke the image of a green landscape — a terrain either wild or, if cultivated, rural — as a symbolic repository of meaning and value. But at the same time they acknowledge the power of a counterforce, a machine or some other symbol of the forces which have stripped the ideal of most, if not all, of its meaning. Complex pastoralism, to put it another way, acknowledges the reality of history" (362–63).

19. Wright expressed similar sentiments in an article she wrote for the *Fairfield News* (MOW, "Conn. Audubon" 5).

20. John Burroughs to MOW, 8 July 1895 (MOW Autograph Album, FPL). See also Henry Van Dyke's letters of praise in the Autograph Album.

21. The only serious criticism of the book was leveled against its illustrations. For more information, see my edition of *The Friendship of Nature*.

22. For a brief biographical profile of Nice, see Bonta 222–31.

23. MOW to J. A. Allen, 11 May 1894, 18 Oct. 1894, 11 March 1895 (Ornithology Dept., AMNH).

24. For more on Bailey, see my profile of him in the *Encyclopedia of Gardens*.

25. Wright detailed her teaching method in "Bird Class" 100–101.

26. Although Wright was christened Mabel, her name at home was "Tommy" for many years, according to one source. Similarly, Wright used her middle name ("Gray") in the title of her 1907 book, *Gray Lady and the Birds* ("Passing of Mabel Osgood Wright").

27. Chapman also read and made corrections to *Tommy-Anne* in draft (MOW to Chapman, 17 June 1896 [Ornithology Dept., AMNH]). In his history of birdwatching, *A World of Watchers*, Joseph Kastner claims that Wright "owed a good deal to her collaborators" (166) on *Citizen Bird*, but many of the 250 letters Wright and Coues exchanged during and after their collaboration reveal Wright's contribution to be the larger, a fact Coues wished to hide. For more information, see my edition of *The Friendship of Nature*.

28. See Chapman, *Autobiography of a Bird-Lover* 183; and MOW, "Nature as a Field for Fiction."

29. For correspondence about fact and fiction in Wright's children's books, see the letters from MOW to George Brett, 16 May 1899, and Henry Van Dyke to MOW, 21 October 1899, (MOW Autograph Album, FPL).

30. See also *The Solitary Summer*, a sequel; *The Enchanted April*, recently adapted for the screen; and Usborne's biography of Russell.

31. Wright refers to *Elizabeth and Her German Garden* in *The Garden of a Commuter's Wife* 87–88.

32. Beverly Seaton discusses *The Garden of a Commuter's Wife* (1901) and *The Garden, You, and I* (1906) in the context of what she calls "garden autobiographies."

33. See also "The Lounger."

34. Especially interesting are *The Woman Errant* (1904) and *Eudora's Men* (1931).

35. For a discussion of Wright's garden books within the context of early-twentieth-century gardening, see Begg.

36. For more on early suburbs, see Archer.

37. Wright was a skilled amateur photographer whose photographs appeared in the works of Abbott, Child, Earl, and McCauley. Sometimes she would mount her landscapes on heavy boards and provide them with such pastoral titles as "Sheepfold" and "Evening Shadows" (Moeller 126). She would also re-create scenes from Fairfield's past, using costumed models posed in and around colonial buildings. For additional context on domestic photography, see Johnston; and the colonial revival writings of Nutting, such as *Connecticut Beautiful*. For background on Nutting's work, see Stilgoe, "Popular Photography." For more on the colonial revival in Connecticut, see Butler.

38. See MOW, *The People of the Whirlpool*; and Gissing, *The Whirlpool* (1897).

39. As Paul Brooks notes, Wright was "an early exponent of the doctrine that all living creatures, not just human beings, had their natural rights" (168).

40. For an important early exception, see Merchant.

41. For the *Science* supplement, see the AOU, "Supplement." Wright was named an associate member of the AOU in 1895 and a member in 1901 (the category of "member" resides between that of "associate member" and "fellow"). In response to her election to membership in 1901, in which she was joined by Florence Merriam Bailey and Olive Thorne Miller, Wright wrote to William Dutcher on 23 Nov., "Of course this does not make me rank with Mr. Chapman & others for to this I have no claim, for, in a scientific . . . sense[,] I have discovered nothing" (NAS Records, Box A-9, NYPL). For more on the AOU, see Barrow; Batchelder; Cart; Gibbons and Strom; Orr; D. Preston; and Welker.

42. Shooting clubs had used the "Audubon" name much earlier. James W. Cochrane, a friend of Audubon's widow, started the Audubon Club of Chicago in 1852. Other Audubon Clubs were organized in Rochester, New York, and Franklin County, Iowa, for field and trap shooting; occasionally, they organized support for improved game laws (Cart 12 n. 24, 68 n. 51).

43. In an 11 March 1895 letter to J. A. Allen, Wright recounted her first meeting with Miller: "I met Mrs Miller last week; her 'Talk about Birds,' was interesting, even if very primitive [*sic*]; but when *I* tried to talk to *her*!!! — She has all the irresponsive firmness of a setting hen" (Ornithology Dept., AMNH). Though they shared common goals, these writers obviously did not always share close friendships!

44. Wright was also instrumental in the founding of the Fairfield Garden Club in 1915 and an informal reading club in the 1920s (Leach and Field). For more on the changing domestic ideal in the Progressive era and after, see Hayden; and Schneider and Schneider. For more on women's clubs, see Scott.

45. For more on the founding of the Massachusetts Audubon Society, see Leahy, Mitchell, and Conuel.

46. An active member of the DAR, Wright first read her poem, "A Hymn to Our Flag," at a regional meeting of the group in 1898. On 4 July 1916 the "Connecticut Hymn of the Flag" was sung for the first time to Wright's own music, and in Feb. 1917, the Connecticut legislature reviewed a bill designating it the state anthem (DAR, Eunice Dennie Burr Chapter Records, FHS; "Outstanding").

47. The society's official name at this time was "Audubon Society, State of Connecticut." Due to an oversight, the society was not formally incorporated until 13 June 1914.

48. The first Bird Day was held in the Oil City, Pennsylvania, public school system in 1894 at the suggestion of superintendent Charles A. Babcock; Connecticut created Bird Day in 1899. Bird Day was modeled after Arbor Day, begun in 1872 by Julius Sterling Morton. See Babcock, "Bird Day"; and Palmer, *Bird Day*. See also the *Auk* 11 (1894): 342; the *Auk* 13 (1896): 349; and *Forest and Stream* 47 (18 July 1896): 41.

49. Information on the membership and activities of the society can be found in the occasional reports published in the Audubon department of *Bird-Lore* during the magazine's early years.

50. MOW to Frank Chapman, 11 July 1905 (Ornithology Dept., AMNH).

51. MOW to T. Gilbert Pearson, 5 Sept. 1913 (NAS Records, Box A-64, NYPL).

52. After Dutcher was elected president of the new group, he moved its office from his home to a room on Broadway; T. Gilbert Pearson was elected secretary. The relationship between the state societies and the national association has been a source of tension since the formation of the national committee in 1901. The national association has gradually grown in power, financial strength, and membership since 1901, and today only eleven state Audubon societies exist independently from the National Audubon Society. Interestingly, as early as 1903 Wright recognized that the future of bird protection would require more than just *national* associations. "Not only national but international cooperation is the only cement that will hold together the stones of individual effort that are to build the protective wall against which the shot of plume- and pot-hunter is to rattle in vain," she wrote in "The Spread of Bird Protection" (37). For more information, see my edition of *The Friendship of Nature*.

53. Not until 1940 did the association change its name to the National Audubon Society.

54. T. Gilbert Pearson to MOW, 2 Nov. 1928 (NAS Records, Box A-136, NYPL). For more on the history of the Audubon movement, see Graham; Line; and Orr. Other useful sources include J. H. Baker; Barrow; Buchheister and Graham; Chapman's "Relation"; Doughty; Dutcher's "History" and "National Association"; Gibbons and Strom; Pearson's *Adventures* and "Audubon Association"; Welker; and early issues of *Auk* and *Bird-Lore*. The Audubon movement also receives mention in Mighetto; Tober; and Trefethen, *American* and *Crusade*. Chapter 2 of Price offers an intriguing cultural studies approach.

55. Wright's correspondence with Chapman reveals the central role she played as an administrator in the first years of the Audubon movement (Ornithology Dept., AMNH).

56. Contributors to *Bird-Lore* during the journal's early years included John Burroughs, Henry Van Dyke, Bradford Torrey, Ernest Thompson Seton, Olive Thorne Miller, Florence Merriam Bailey, and William Brewster. In 1935 *Bird-Lore* was bought by the National Association of Audubon Societies; in 1941 its name was changed to *Audubon Magazine*; and in 1961 its name was shortened simply to *Audubon*. For more on *Bird-Lore*, see Chapman's

Autobiography; Peterson's "Evolution"; and the histories of the early Audubon Society cited above (n. 54).

57. NAS Records, Box A-31, NYPL.

58. MOW to William Dutcher, 28 Dec. 1900 (NAS Records, Box A-6, NYPL).

59. Willard G. VanName to MOW, 13 Jan. 1908 (CAS Records, BMS).

60. MOW to T. Gilbert Pearson, 8 May 1912 and 8 Oct. 1912 (NAS Records, Box A-50, NYPL).

61. MOW, draft letter regarding preservation of the Bald Eagle, n.d. (CAS Records, BMS). MOW to T. Gilbert Pearson, 30 May 1919 (NAS Records, Box A-87, NYPL).

62. In all of these initiatives, Wright was following in a long tradition of concern for game laws in Connecticut, which passed the first game law in America in 1677 (Palmer, *Chronology* 13).

63. MOW to William Dutcher, 28 September 1908 (NAS Records, Box A-31, NYPL). In a later letter to T. Gilbert Pearson (5 Dec. 1924) regarding her resignation as CAS president, MOW revealed more about her attitude toward hunting: "I've always preached moderation and fair hunting. . . . Old as I am, I love the sight of the dogs skirting the brush lots of a grey day in autumn & the tired & muddy booted men that follow them home at evening" (NAS Records, Box A-117, NYPL).

64. See also Bowdish.

65. See MOW to T. Gilbert Pearson, 1 Jan. 1916 (NAS Records, Box A-78, NYPL).

66. For more on the scenic cemetery movement, see Bender; French; Harris 200–8; Huth, *Nature* 66–70; and Schuyler, "Evolution," which is included in the special issue of the *Journal of Garden History* 4.3 (July–Sept. 1984) on cemetery and garden.

67. The performance at the Astor Place Theater drew an audience of two thousand, a capacity crowd. See also R. Allen, "Wild-Life," in which MOW says that she heard her father describe Mosswood as "the Sanctuary of the Birds" as early as 1862 (83). Allen incorrectly gives the date of the Meriden sanctuary's founding as 1911.

68. CAS, *Minutes*, 10 July 1914 (CAS Records, BPL).

69. Wright's legacy in this area can be seen in part by such books as Kress, *Audubon Society Guide to Attracting Birds*.

70. In his article "Collections of Birds in the United States and Canada" in the fiftieth-anniversary volume of the AOU, Chapman said the Birdcraft Museum and Sanctuary "should be seen by every one contemplating the development of similar projects" (148).

71. See also MOW to Helen Glover, 16 Sept. 1923 (CAS Records, BPL). The Roosevelt Sanctuary, located adjacent to the president's grave, was established on land donated to the National Audubon Society by the Roosevelt family after Roosevelt's death in 1919. Wright, whom T. Gilbert Pearson asked to serve on the committee to select a fountain design for the sanctuary, thought the fountain "should represent the rigorous modern Rooseveltian side of conservation, not the sentimental & idealistic side." The sentimental sculpture of a lightly clothed nymphet and prepubescent boy that was selected, Wright protested, was "totally unfit for its purpose of being a Roosevelt memorial." See the exchange of letters between MOW and T. Gilbert Pearson (NAS Records, Boxes A-112 and A-113, NYPL).

72. Compare John Burroughs's 1885 essay, "Bird Enemies."

73. Frederick C. Walcott to MOW, 11 May 1922 (CAS Records, BMS).

74. Modern ecologists call this the "Mother Goose syndrome," in which animals are designated as "good" or "bad" depending on their perceived effects.

75. See also MOW, "Encouraging Signs" 146.

76. Compare Andrew Jackson Downing: "As a people descended from English stock, we inherit much ardent love of rural life and its pursuits which belongs to that nation" (qtd. in Harris 23). For primary sources on nativism and conservation, see Grant; and Osborn. For secondary sources see Bramwell, *Ecology*; Cart 38–42; Fox, *John Muir*; Gottlieb; Schrepfer; and Tober 52–53. Pollan questions the philosophy behind the modern native-plant garden in "Against Nativism." See also the southern agrarian tract, *I'll Take My Stand*, by "Twelve Southerners," for an influential merger of regionalism and racism.

77. Visits numbered sixty-two hundred in its third year of operation.

78. CAS, *Minutes*, 27 June 1957 (CAS Records, BPL).

79. CAS, *Minutes*, 24 July 1958 (CAS Records, BPL). In 1958 a much smaller parcel of land was condemned by the Town of Fairfield for the Roger Ludlow High School (now Tomlinson Middle School), for which the society received $7,900 (CAS, *Minutes*, 15 Dec. 1958 [CAS Records, BPL]).

80. The thruway greatly affected the number of migrating birds counted at the sanctuary, according to Birdcraft's warden, Frank Novak, speaking in 1970 (F. Novak).

81. After being used as a schoolhouse and then falling into disrepair, Mosswood was eventually destroyed and replaced with 136 luxury apartments known as Mosswood Condominiums.

82. MOW to Helen Glover, 1 July 1922 (CAS Records, BPL). For additional reactions to her husband's death, see MOW to T. Gilbert Pearson, 1 Oct. 1920 (NAS Records, Box A-97, NYPL); MOW to Helen Glover, 19 Aug. 1924 (CAS Records, BPL); MOW to Frank Chapman, 3 Dec. 1932 (Ornithology Dept., AMNH).

83. For a discussion of the bungalow negotiations, see MOW to Frank Chapman, 7 March and 14 April 1933 (Ornithology Dept., AMNH), and the 3 April and 17 April 1933 entries of the CAS, *Minutes of the Meetings of the Board of Governors of . . . Birdcraft Sanctuary* (BMS).

84. See also MOW to Frank Chapman, 31 October 1922 (Ornithology Dept., AMNH).

85. MOW to Frank Chapman, 21 Dec. 1917 (Ornithology Dept., AMNH).

86. MOW to Frank Chapman, 31 Oct. 1922 (Ornithology Dept., AMNH). Wright was even more critical of the women of the new generation in a 9 Oct. 1925 letter to T. Gilbert Pearson (NAS Records, Box A-117, NYPL).

87. MOW to Frank Chapman, 7 March 1933 (Ornithology Dept., AMNH).

88. See also MOW to Frank Chapman, 23 Sept. 1923: "T.R.'s father and mine were friends in the old days of New York, before 1900, all our frirnds [sic] were mutual and our paths ran parallel" (Ornithology Dept., AMNH).

3. *Our National Parks*

1. Although more has been written about the entire career of Theodore Roosevelt, the work of no conservationist has received as much attention as that of John Muir. More than sixty editions of books by or about Muir are in print (Parshall 58). For biographies of Muir, see, in ad-

dition to Badè: James Clarke; M. Cohen, *Pathless*; G. Ehrlich, *John Muir*; Fox, *John Muir*; Holmes; Melham and Grehann; Stanley; F. Turner, *Rediscovering*; Watkins and Jones; Wilkins; and L. Wolfe, *Son*. I have relied on Turner as my principal biographical source, with reference to others as needed; Turner discusses the strengths and weaknesses of previous biographies in *Rediscovering America* (354–57).

2. See, for example, Clements; Fox, *John Muir*; L. Greene; Ise; Jones, *John Muir*; Nash, *Wilderness*; Richardson, *Politics* and "Struggle for the Valley."

3. In making the decision to limit my focus to the pre–Hetch Hetchy years, I follow Michael L. Smith, who argues in *Pacific Visions* that "[t]he political and educational activities of the Sierra Club in its first decade, before Hetch Hetchy became a major campaign, offer a clearer picture of the issues behind the club's emerging political identity" (144).

4. For a complete account of the Muir-Emerson meeting, see Branch, "Angel."

5. Roosevelt originally made this claim in "John Muir: An Appreciation," *Outlook* 109 (6 Jan. 1915): 27–28.

6. Roosevelt developed this statement in the pages of the *Outlook* (*Works* 11:289).

7. Leslie Paul Thiele makes a similar claim in *Environmentalism for a New Millennium* (186).

8. As this summary suggests, although my emphasis on the domestic in Muir's writing agrees with Steven J. Holmes's focus on these elements in his revisionist biography, my outline of Muir's life follows more traditional accounts. Readers interested in a more detailed discussion of Muir's first three decades, particularly from a psychoanalytic perspective, should consult Holmes.

9. John Muir, *The Story of My Boyhood and Youth*, in *Nature Writings*, ed. William Cronon (New York: Library of America, 1997), 25. Subsequent references to this volume, which also contains *My First Summer in the Sierra*, *The Mountains of California*, *Stickeen*, and selected essays, are made parenthetically in the text as NW. *The Story of My Boyhood and Youth* was originally dictated to Edward H. Harriman's personal secretary in 1908 before being revised and published in 1913 when Muir was seventy-five years old. On the trustworthiness of this text, see M. Cohen, *Pathless* 342–46; and F. Turner, *Rediscovering* 358n.

10. In *The Story of My Boyhood and Youth*, Muir says he attended the university for four years (NW 136).

11. For more on romanticism and transcendentalism, see Fleck.

12. L. Wolfe suggests that Muir did not run from the draft (*Son* 88–89), but Fox (*John Muir* 42–43) and F. Turner (*Rediscovering* 109–11) think otherwise.

13. Holmes cautions that because this description "was not written until a few years after the experience itself" and "uses language that he [Muir] had probably learned in the interim" (121), it may tell us more about Muir's thoughts at the time of composition than during the experience itself (139–40).

14. For the convenience of readers, I refer both to *Letters to a Friend* and to Bonnie Gisel's *Kindred and Related Spirits* when citing Muir's letters to Carr.

15. As Lyon and other critics have observed, "[t]he intensity of the experience, which parallels the sickness and conversion episodes in the lives of such religious figures as John Woolman and Jonathan Edwards, is reflected by the immense importance Muir gives to Light

again and again in his subsequent writings" (*John Muir* 28). Compare Holmes 143, 177–78; and Ewart 52.

16. In this and subsequent quotations from *A Thousand-Mile Walk to the Gulf*, I do not distinguish between the original journal of the walk (1867–68) and the book published posthumously (1916), as edited by William Frederic Badè. For a discussion of the differences and their relative importance, see M. Cohen, *Pathless* 1–27; F. Turner, *Rediscovering* 373–75n; and appendix B of Holmes 261–63. For my purposes here, the differences are not significant.

17. As Frederick Turner has observed, the word "escape" occurs with telling frequency in Muir's journal entries (*Rediscovering* 133).

18. For approaches that better contextualize Muir within the Christian tradition, see Austin; Limbaugh, "The Nature of John Muir's Religion"; and Stoll. See also D. Williams's *God's Wilds*, "John Muir, Christian Mysticism, and the Spiritual Value of Nature," and "John Muir and an Evangelical Vision for Western Natural Resources Management." M. Cohen reconsiders *The Pathless Way* in "A Brittle Thesis." David Robertson (38) and Don Scheese (*Nature Writing* 64) describe Muir as a panentheist. Most recently, Sandra Sizer Frankiel has claimed that Muir "did not give up traditional beliefs, only narrow interpretations of them" (122–23).

19. Compare Emerson in "The American Scholar": "When he can read God directly, the hour is too precious to be wasted in other men's transcripts of their readings" (89).

20. His other items of baggage included his plant press, a few toilet articles, a change of underwear, *Paradise Lost*, and the poems of Robert Burns (F. Turner, *Rediscovering* 133). At the time Muir was unfamiliar with William Bartram's *Travels* (1791), which he would not read until 1897 (F. Turner, *Rediscovering* 141n).

21. I agree with Holmes, who argues that "it is most correct to say that Muir was neither ecocentric nor anthropocentric but *religiocentric*, placing the divine — whether found in a deity or in the natural world — at the center of value and power" (183).

22. Compare the comments of Harlean James, executive secretary of the National Conference on State Parks and of the American Civic Association, who in 1926 declared that "[t]he term park has come to be a generic designation which includes a number of highly differentiated species" (196). See also A. Matthews.

23. Catlin's sentiments were not published until 1841, nine years later.

24. For a detailed history of the idea of the "park," see part 1 of Doell and Fitzgerald. For a more recent discussion of the role of the national park in the social construction of "nature," see chapter 9 of Benton and Short.

25. In his article "The Treasures of the Yosemite," Muir first suggested that the Sierra should instead be called the Range of Light (483).

26. In 1833 Joseph R. Walker had led a group of mountain men across the Sierra and looked down into the valley from somewhere along the north rim; because of the rugged terrain, however, the men were unable to descend into the valley and explore it, as the Mariposa Battalion subsequently did (Runte, *Yosemite* 10). The Sierra redwoods were discovered in 1852. For detailed histories of the Yosemite, see Farquhar; L. Greene; Runte, *Yosemite*; C. Russell; and Sanborn.

27. For more on the visual representations of Yosemite, see Ogden; Robertson; and chapter 6 of J. Sears, *Sacred Places*.

28. United States, *Statutes at Large* 13 (1864): 325. The measure was officially accepted by the state two years later.

29. See chapter 3, "Worthless Lands," of Runte, *National Parks*.

30. Olmsted read his report before a meeting of the commission in August 1865, but apparently Josiah Dwight Whitney, the director of the California Geological Survey, and William Ashburner, another geologist with the survey, prevented Olmsted's report from reaching the California legislature. According to Olmsted biographer Laura Wood Roper, who recovered the report and published it for the first time in 1952, Whitney and Ashburner may have feared competition with Olmsted's thirty-seven-thousand-dollar request for funding (287).

31. Between 1855 and 1863, only 653 people came to Yosemite; between 1864 and 1870, that number increased to 4,936 people (Runte, *Yosemite* 38). The trend would continue, with nearly 20,000 people visiting the valley in the 1870s, a fourfold increase (Runte, *Yosemite* 40). For more on early tourism in Yosemite, see Blodgett; and Hyde, "From Stagecoach to Packard."

32. Kevin DeLuca and Anne Demo make a similar point in "Imagining Nature and Erasing Class and Race" 554. Nevertheless, Thomas Vale argues compellingly that "the Yosemite landscape at the time of European contact could have been mostly pristine" (232). See Vale's "Myth of the Humanized Landscape."

33. For an earlier (1895) reference to this account, see Muir, "National Parks" 281. Badè gives the date of Muir's arrival as 27 March (1:177); L. Wolfe, *Son*, gives it as 28 March (116). Frederick Turner suggests that the arrival account Muir gave to Melville Anderson is more plausible: that Muir simply asked the man the nearest way out of the city and was directed to the Oakland Ferry. See F. Turner, *Rediscovering* 163; and Anderson.

34. Notably, Muir dedicated the book "to the Sierra Club of California, Faithful Defender of the People's Playgrounds" (NW 148).

35. According to Earl Pomeroy, "cold statistics show . . . that Easterners and foreigners far outnumbered Californians in the Yosemite Valley in the early years. Those who had fought the elements across the continent for a home were relatively less interested in climbing mountains for amusement" (88).

36. In a related observation, Robert Underwood Johnson writes of Muir's "mock contempt for man" and observes that "he was deeply interested in human nature" (*Remembered* 282).

37. William Cronon also links this transformation to tourism in "The Trouble with Wilderness" (75).

38. Muir first read Thoreau during his time in Yosemite, apparently at the urging of Jeanne Carr (*Letters* 84; Gisel 111). His first reading of *Walden* apparently came when Abba G. Woolson sent Muir her copy of the book in March 1872 (Fox, *John Muir* 395n). For more on Thoreau and Muir, see Allin, *Politics* 44; Fox, *John Muir* 83; Millard 596; and Nash, *Wilderness* 160.

39. See also Lyon, *John Muir* 43; and Michael Smith, *Pacific Visions* 97.

40. In *Dramas of Solitude* Randall Roorda discusses this passage as a paradigm of the retreat (21–26).

41. See also, for example, Muir's letters of 26 July 1868 and 24 February 1869 to Jeanne Carr, and his letter of 15 August 1868 to his sister Annie (reprinted in part in F. Turner, *Rediscovering* 166). Holmes also notes Muir's loneliness during the Yosemite years (208, 241). Of course, Muir was not always desirous of human contact, as his 8 September 1871 letter to Carr makes clear (*Letters* 105; Gisel 147).

42. For more on the Martinez years, see P. J. Ryan.

43. See also Millard 599.

44. See also Clarken 126; Strother, "John Muir" 8804; and F. Turner, *Rediscovering* 276n.

45. Earlier versions of Robert Johnson's portrait of Muir in *Remembered Yesterdays* appeared as "Personal Impressions of John Muir," *Outlook* 80 (1905): 303–6, and "John Muir as I Knew Him," *SCB* 10 (1916): 9–15. The latter essay also appeared as "John Muir" in the *Proceedings of the American Academy of Arts and Letters* 9 (1916): 63–70, and was reprinted in the Academy's *Commemorative Tributes, 1905–41* (New York: Spiral, 1942).

46. Compare Muir's brief account of this trip in "National Parks" 275.

47. Not until 1951 did the club bylaws change from "[t]o explore, enjoy and *render accessible* the mountain regions of the Pacific Coast" to "to explore, enjoy and *preserve* the Sierra Nevada and other scenic resources of the United States" (Jones, "John Muir" 78; emphasis added). For histories of the club, see: M. Cohen, *History*; Hyde, "Temples and Playgrounds"; Jones, *John Muir*; the two articles by Strong; and T. Turner, *Sierra*. See also Proffitt, which is part of a special issue of *California History* (71.2, summer 1992) devoted to the centennial of the Sierra Club.

48. Graber also cites these passages in J. Jackson.

49. Compare Muir, "National Parks" 272–73; and R. Johnson, *Remembered* 289.

50. Other reviews include an evaluation in the *Athenaeum* 105 (1895): 77–78; and brief notices in the *Annals of the American Academy of Political and Social Science* 5 (1894): 783, and *Academy* 47 (1895): 503.

51. Compare Emerson's famous passage in *Nature* (1836): "I become a transparent eyeball; I am nothing; I see all; the currents of the Universal Being circulate through me; I am part or parcel of God" (39).

52. See also Wyatt 45.

53. I disagree, therefore, with Oravec's belief that "Muir suggested that his armchair readers abandon an image of themselves as sightseers, scenic appreciators, tourists, to a life of strenuousness and commitment" (253). Muir certainly would have preferred that his readers embrace "a life of strenuousness and commitment," but he did not — indeed, could not — actually suggest this, lest he risk alienating his largely eastern audience. For an example of Muir's talkativeness, see F. Turner, *Rediscovering* 294.

54. Colby remained as leader of the outings until 1930.

55. By the time of the appearance of *Our National Parks* a decade later, Presidents Harrison, Cleveland, and McKinley had set aside approximately 46 million acres of public land as forest reserves.

56. For an earlier (1895–98) selection of Muir's "Thoughts Upon National Parks," see L. Wolfe, *John* 350–54.

57. For another review of the book, see the *Annals of the American Academy of Political and Social Science* 20 (1902): 419. An enlarged edition of the book was also reviewed in the *Dial* 47 (1909): 460–61.

58. Environmental philosopher Mark Sagoff offers an alternative to this utilitarian view of spirituality, arguing that aesthetic and spiritual ideals "have to do not with the utility but with the meaning of things, not with what things are used for but what they express" (63).

59. Dennis Williams speculates that "perhaps there was something deeper in the preservation issue than money that led Muir and Harriman to respect one another" (*God's Wilds* 186).

60. Colby, Richard G. Lillard writes, "was for letting cars drive along the rim to Glacier Point and for improving the road from Inspiration Point down. He saw no harm in mixing cars and horses. The mountain roads were no different from Market Street. There were drunken drivers and accidents in both places" (31). Automobiles had been allowed in Yosemite for a brief period, from 1900 to 1907, before the acting superintendent banned them, claiming they were "constantly a source of annoyance and friction" and "constantly endangering the lives of tourists in the Valley" (Lillard 68).

4. The Call of the Wild

1. Of the other essays in *A Sand County Almanac*, only "Thinking Like a Mountain" may rival "The Land Ethic" as Leopold's best-known piece of writing, in part because it documents an evolution in Leopold's attitude toward deer, wolves, and forests, as Susan Flader has so well described *(Thinking)*. But Leopold's essay "Wilderness" also documents an evolution in his thought, though the evolution is less obvious, because the essay presents his ideas about wilderness as overlapping instead of displacing one another, as in "Thinking Like a Mountain."

2. Others have made similar statements, including Oelschlaeger, "Taking" 336; and M. Nelson, "Amalgamation" 169.

3. Aldo Leopold, *The River of the Mother of God and Other Essays*, ed. Susan L. Flader and J. Baird Callicott (Madison: U of Wisconsin P, 1991) ix. Subsequent references to this volume are made parenthetically in the text as *RMG*.

4. Leopold's life paralleled Roosevelt's in other ways, including their boyhood interest in natural history and their lifelong love of hunting, but the literary parallel has not received much attention. An exception is Meine, "Utility" 138.

5. In his biography of Turner, Allan Bogue indicates that while Turner crossed paths with both Leopold and the ecologist Henry C. Cowles, "there is no suggestion that he sensed the stature they would eventually be accorded in the realms of ecology and environmentalism" (414).

6. For biographical information on Leopold, I rely primarily on Curt Meine's magisterial *Aldo Leopold: His Life and Work*. Marybeth Lorbiecki's popular, illustrated biography, *Aldo Leopold: A Fierce Green Fire*, also proved helpful, as did the first chapter of Susan Flader's *Thinking Like a Mountain*.

7. Aldo Leopold was made an associate member of the Boone and Crockett Club in 1923 (Trefethen, *Crusade* 248).

8. See my "'Such Pictures and Poems, Inimitable.'"

9. He also read Darwin's *Vegetable Mould and Earthworms* with "much interest and surprise" (Meine, *Aldo Leopold* 55).

10. Leopold replaced this original, autobiographical foreword with a more philosophical one in 1948.

11. As Flader notes, "the congressional mandate for preservation of timber and watershed values dates from the Sundry Civil Appropriations Act of June 4, 1897" (*Thinking* 11). For a detailed discussion of Leopold's role in turning the local commons of New Mexico into national hunting grounds, particularly through tourism, see chapters 3 and 4 of L. Warren, *Hunter's Game.*

12. For a thorough discussion of the sources and effects of increased visitor demand for recreation in the national forests, particularly as a foundation for Leopold's early wilderness thought, see Sutter, *Driven Wild* 56–67.

13. Frederick Law Olmsted Jr. authored the statement of purpose (Runte, *National Parks* 103–4; Sellars 38).

14. The Grand Canyon was made a national park on 26 February 1919, a recognition, in part, that the National Park Service was better equipped than the Forest Service to manage tourism on a large scale. Theodore Roosevelt had died nearly two months earlier, on 6 January 1919.

15. Timothy W. Luke harshly criticizes the Wilderness Society along these lines in "The Wilderness Society." I share the concern of John M. Meyer that Luke's work, while "penetrating in many respects," has a "single-minded focus on critique" (159 n. 31).

16. Carhart was employed by district 2; Trappers Lake is in the White River National Forest. On the basis of Carhart's work, historian Donald N. Baldwin believes Carhart deserves to be recognized as originating the wilderness concept in the national forests. See Baldwin, "Wilderness: Concept and Challenge," and *The Quiet Revolution.* Carhart, however, never used the word "wilderness" in the proposals Baldwin cites as evidence for his claim, and Carhart's and Leopold's ideas differed significantly in both size and scope.

17. The article originally appeared in the *Journal of Forestry* 19.7 (Nov. 1921): 718–21. I quote from its reprint in *RMG.*

18. This increase in user demand came in response to legislative initiatives and promotional campaigns, including the Term Permit Act of 1915; the Federal Aid Highway Acts of 1916, 1919, and 1921; the "See American First" campaigns; and the Good Roads movement. See Sutter 60–67; and M. Shaffer.

19. Grazing was also a means to reduce the fire hazard of grass (Flader, "Let the Fire Devil" 89). In a later report, Leopold also proposed that existing trails, phone lines, and stations for fire protection be retained in the wilderness area (Meine, *Aldo Leopold* 201; Lorbiecki 91). L. Warren comments on this in *Hunter's Game* 116.

20. For more on El Río Madre de Dios, see Flader, "The River of the Mother of God: Introduction."

21. That Leopold saw "adventure" as a version of "curiosity" can be seen from his comments to a group of students at the University of New Mexico in 1920 in an address entitled "A Man's

Leisure Time" (Meine, *Aldo Leopold* 182–83). A much-revised version of this address appears in *Round River* 3–8.

22. Leopold borrowed this image from John Burroughs, as he indicates in his 1923 manuscript, "Some Fundamentals of Conservation in the Southwest" (*RMG* 97). Leopold liked the image so much he used it again in "Wilderness as a Form of Land Use" (*RMG* 137).

23. Only three of these articles appear in *RMG* because Susan Flader thought all five were "too similar to one another, albeit rhetorically varied, to include more than a few," notes J. Baird Callicott ("Wilderness Idea" 337).

24. The article originally appeared in *Sunset* 54.3 (March 1925): 21, 56. I quote from its reprint in *RMG*.

25. "Gopher Prairie" is an allusion to Sinclair Lewis's *Main Street* (1920), a thinly disguised, savagely satirical portrait of Sauk Center, Minnesota, Lewis's hometown. Leopold's essays are littered with references to the works of Lewis, particularly *Babbitt* (1922), whose protagonist, George F. Babbitt, defined "Babbittian" narrow-mindedness for Leopold.

26. The magazine was named after its New Orleans–to–Los Angeles Sunset Limited train.

27. "The Pig in the Parlor" originally appeared in *USFS Service Bulletin* 9.23 (8 June 1925): 1–2. I quote from its reprint in *RMG*.

28. "The Last Stand of American Wilderness" originally appeared in *American Forests and Forest Life* 31.382 (Oct. 1925): 599–604. It was subtitled "A Plea for Preserving a Few Primitive Forests, Untouched by Motor Cars and Tourist Camps, Where Those Who Enjoy Canoe or Pack Trips in Wild Country May Fulfill Their Dreams."

29. "The Vanishing Wilderness," *Literary Digest* 90.6 (7 Aug. 1926): 54, 56–57.

30. According to the committee, Leopold's article "presents with remarkable clearness and force the wilderness motive and objectives" (Joint Committee 86).

31. "Wilderness as a Form of Land Use" originally appeared in *Journal of Land and Public Utility Economics* 1.4 (Oct. 1925): 398–404. I quote from its reprint in *RMG*.

32. "A Plea for Wilderness Hunting Grounds" originally appeared in *Outdoor Life* 56.5 (Nov. 1925): 348–50. I quote from its reprint in Brown and Carmony.

33. Former USFS chief Richard E. McArdle disagrees with this argument. See his "Wilderness Politics."

34. Robert Sterling Yard to AL, 30 April 1940 (ALP, record group 9/25, series 10, subseries 2, box 9). Subsequent references to materials from this source will be made by series-subseries and box (e.g., 10-2, 9).

35. AL to Robert Sterling Yard, 8 May 1940 (ALP 10-2, 9).

36. "The Conservation Ethic" originally appeared in the *Journal of Forestry* 31.6 (Oct. 1933): 634–43. The address was the fourth annual John Wesley Powell Lecture. I quote from its reprint in *RMG*.

37. For more on this well-known episode, see chapter 3, "The Gila Experience," in Flader, *Thinking*.

38. Flader calls this a "puzzling reference" ("Let the Fire Devil" 92) and "an intriguing lapse of memory" (*Thinking* 102 n. 29).

39. Like Theodore Roosevelt, Leopold was involved in many organizations, both professional associations and advocacy groups.

40. Similarly, Craig W. Allin argues that "Leopold's greatest contributions to wilderness preservation predate his ecological views" ("Leopold Legacy" 34).

41. Notably, Marshall quoted from Leopold's defense of wilderness on cultural grounds. In recognition of its significance, the *Sierra Club Bulletin* reprinted "The Problem of the Wilderness" in May 1947. As Michael P. Cohen has observed, however, in titling the essay, the *Bulletin* "pluralized Marshall's *Problem* into 'The *Problems* of the Wilderness'" (M. Cohen, "ProblemS" 72). See Robert Marshall, "The Problems of the Wilderness," *Sierra Club Bulletin* 32.5 (May 1947): 43–52. See also George Marshall, "On Bob Marshall's Landmark Article," *Living Wilderness* 40.135 (Oct.–Dec. 1976): 28–30; which is followed by another reprinting of the article on 31–35.

42. Robert Marshall to AL, 21 Feb. 1930 (ALP 10-3, 4).

43. In 1928 MacKaye had commented positively on Leopold's "Wilderness as a Form of Land Use" in *The New Exploration* (202–4).

44. Robert Marshall to AL, 25 Oct. 1934 (ALP 10-2, 9).

45. AL to Robert Marshall, 29 Oct. 1934 (ALP 10-2, 9).

46. AL to Robert Marshall, 3 Dec. 1934, (ALP 10-2, 9).

47. AL to Robert Marshall, 1 Feb. 1935 (ALP 10-2, 9).

48. Robert Marshall to AL, 14 March 1935 (ALP 10-2, 9).

49. AL to Robert Marshall, 3 April 1935 (ALP 10-2, 9).

50. Robert Marshall to Benton MacKaye, 9 April 1935 (WSP 2:100–200).

51. The society was incorporated on 29 April 1937. Five new individuals — L. A. Barrett, Irving M. Clark, Dorothy Sachs Jackson, George Marshall, and Olaus Murie — joined the eight original organizers to become a thirteen-member governing council. The society also began charging dues of one dollar, to augment the $2,000 to $3,700 Bob Marshall annually gave to the society, which remained its main source of income (J. Glover 208–9). For more on the society's council, see G. Marshall, "The Wilderness Society's Council."

52. Robert Sterling Yard to AL, 23 June 1935 (ALP 10-2, 9).

53. The others were "Origin and Ideals of Wilderness Areas" (July 1940), "Wilderness as a Land Laboratory" (July 1941), "Wilderness Values" (March 1942), and "The Last Stand" (Dec. 1942). "Wilderness as a Land Laboratory" was reprinted in *Outdoor America* 7.2 (Dec. 1941): 7; and was condensed in *Forest and Bird* (New Zealand) 65 (Aug. 1942): 2. "Wilderness Values" was reprinted from the 1941 *Yearbook, Park and Recreation Progress*, published by the National Park Service. "The Last Stand" was reprinted from *Outdoor America* 7.7 (May–June 1942): 8–9; and also appeared in the *Wisconsin Conservation Bulletin* 9.2 (Feb. 1944): 3–5 (Meine, *Aldo Leopold* 616).

54. On the significance of Leopold's choice of the prairie biome as an example, see Meine, "Reimagining" 154.

55. The two articles are "*Naturschutz* in Germany," *Bird-Lore* 38.2 (March–April 1936): 102–11; and "Deer and *Dauerwald* in Germany: I. History; II. Ecology and Policy," *Journal of Forestry* 34:4 and 34:5 (April and May 1936): 366–75, 460–66.

56. Note that Leopold defines "wilderness areas" broadly here; he does not distinguish between the domains of the different agencies.

57. For an investigation of how the term "biodiversity" has been socially constructed, see

Takacs, who argues that Leopold is a twentieth-century forerunner of contemporary conservation biologists and that "wilderness" is another name for "biodiversity" (11–21).

58. AL to Herbert A. Smith, 20 Dec. 1935 (ALP 10-2, 9).

59. AL to Robert Sterling Yard, 6 Jan. 1936 (ALP 10-2, 9). Leopold made a similar comment in a 28 May 1940 letter to Morris L. Cooke, noting, "The members will want to educate everybody else, but many will be unwilling to study themselves" (Fox, *John Muir* 334). Other printed replies to Smith's editorial came from Bob Marshall, Lincoln Ellison, and Adolph Murie.

60. "News and Comment Number 1" (ALP 10-2, 9).

61. "News and Comment Number 2" (ALP 10-2, 9).

62. AL to Gaston Burridge, 20 Jan. 1936 (ALP 10-2, 9).

63. "Wilderness News No. 3" (ALP 10-2, 9).

64. "Marshland Elegy" originally appeared in *American Forests* 43.10 (Oct. 1937): 472–74. I quote from the version published in *A Sand County Almanac*, subsequent references to which will be made parenthetically in the text as *SCA*.

65. Leopold made several such statements throughout *A Sand County Almanac*. See *SCA* 172 and 150.

66. Gary Nabhan revisits Leopold's encounters with the Sierra Madre in "Sierra Madre Upshot."

67. "Conservation Esthetic" originally appeared in *Bird-Lore* 40.2 (March–April 1938): 101–9. I quote from the *SCA* version.

68. Leopold made a similar point equating hunting to perception in "The Deer Swath" (*Round River* 128).

69. In early 1940 Leopold also began work on a manuscript entitled "Biotic Land-Use." See Leopold, *For the Health of the Land* 198–207.

70. Regulation U-1 governed "wilderness areas," and Regulation U-2 governed "wild areas." Only the secretary of agriculture could establish, modify, or eliminate a "wilderness" area, but the chief of the Forest Service could do so for a "wild" area. An additional regulation, U-3(a), governed "roadless areas."

71. AL to Robert Sterling Yard, 18 Nov. 1939 (ALP 10-2, 9).

72. AL to Robert Sterling Yard, 4 June 1940 (ALP 10-2, 9).

73. AL to Robert Cushman Murphy, 8 June 1940 (ALP 10-2, 9).

74. "Resolution" (ALP 10-2, 9).

75. Robert Sterling Yard to AL, 18 June 1940 (ALP 10-2, 9).

76. Minutes of the Meeting of the Wilderness Society Executive Committee, 19 March 1941 (WSP 1:100).

77. Robert Griggs to the Executive Committee of the Wilderness Society, 21 Sept. 1944 (WSP 1:100).

78. For more on these tensions within the ESA, see Tjossem.

79. After receiving the manuscript, Bob Yard asked Leopold whether he could revise the article to say that Leopold was the first to start the idea and title of the wilderness area. In a revealing reply, Leopold claimed that he couldn't in good conscience revise his paper, as he saw "too much of this staking claims to glory; if it is to be done it will have to be done by somebody else" (AL to Robert Sterling Yard, 8 May 1940; ALP 10-2, 9).

80. AL to Robert Sterling Yard, 26 Jan. 1942 (ALP 10-2, 9).

81. AL to Robert Sterling Yard, 13 Feb. 1942 (WSP 4:410).

82. "Wilderness Values" originally appeared in *1941 Yearbook, Park and Recreation Progress* (National Park Service, 1941) 27–29. It was reprinted in *Living Wilderness* 7.7 (March 1942): 24–25.

83. "The Last Stand" originally appeared in *Outdoor America* 7.7 (May–June 1942): 8–9. It was reprinted in *Living Wilderness* 7.8 (Dec. 1942): 25–26. I quote from the *Living Wilderness* version, which varies slightly from the *Outdoor America* version reprinted in *The River of the Mother of God*.

84. "Council Meeting of the Wilderness Society," 14 July 1945 (ALP 10-2, 9).

85. AL to Robert Sterling Yard, 21 Nov. 1938 (WSP 3:106).

86. AL to Benton MacKaye, 1 May 1946 (ALP 10-2, 9).

87. AL to Howard Zahniser, 6 Nov. 1946 (WSP 1:100).

88. "Continental Wilderness System Advocated," July 1947 (WSP 14:100).

89. Benton MacKaye, memo to Wilderness Society members, 9 Nov. 1947 (WSP 14:100).

90. That the campaign was effective is clear from a four-page selection of member correspondence printed in the winter 1948–49 issue of *Living Wilderness* under the headline "On Preserving Our 'Wildland Patches.'" Three years after the campaign was announced, the Wilderness Society devoted the entire winter 1950–51 issue of *Living Wilderness* to "a project in cooperation" with the ESA: a preliminary inventory of nature sanctuaries in the United States and Canada (inside front cover).

91. AL to Howard Zahniser, 25 August 1947 (ALP 10-2, 9). Murie responded on 17 September 1947 with a few suggestions but mostly praise. "I am a very poor one to read anything of yours with a view to offering criticism. I am so carried away by what you write, and your manner of presenting it, that I can only feel 'yes, yes' all along the line, and feel an elation and a desire to show it to everyone. I say this very sincerely" (ALP 10-6, 5). I could not locate a response from Zahniser in the portion of the Leopold papers I examined.

92. Killingsworth and Palmer's analysis of this essay neglects the history of its composition and publication, a crucial component of its importance (57–64). For more on the composition of *A Sand County Almanac*, see Meine, "Moving Mountains."

93. Alfred G. Etter, "Criticism of *Great Possessions*," 10 June 1948 (ALP 10-6, 5).

94. Leopold, "Notes for a Paper on Writing" (ALP 10-6, 16).

95. Olaus Murie commented on this passage in his 17 September 1947 letter to Leopold: "I wonder if we should use the term 'museum piece.' I have used it also, but I now wonder if it does not denote in the minds of many readers too small an area, and thus militate against our efforts to maintain wilderness on an adequate scale. Also, I feel that adequate wilderness preservation may *continue* to influence culture. Can both ideas be included, past and continuing?" (ALP 10-6, 5).

96. "Threatened Species" originally appeared in *American Forests* 42.3 (March 1936): 116–19. It is reprinted in *RMG* 230–34.

97. It is difficult not to think of the proponents of Earth First! here. Indeed, Dave Foreman has said that *A Sand County Almanac* "is not only the most important conservation book ever

written, it is the most important book ever written, and the clearest way home, except for a visit to the wilderness itself" (Vaz 56).

98. Stephen Fox is one of the few who have noted this in print. Although "large claims" have been made for the book's ethical conclusions, Fox observes, "*Sand County* ultimately seems grounded in history, not philosophy. The book is studded with some two dozen references to history or historians" (*John Muir* 248).

99. Similarly, although Alfred Etter claimed that the 1948 foreword of *A Sand County Almanac* "refers seemingly almost specifically to the concepts" contained in "The Land Ethic," in fact it depends almost wholly on Leopold's essay "Wilderness." In the 1948 foreword Leopold claims that progress is at odds with wildness and suggests "reappraising things unnatural, tame, and confined in terms of things natural, wild, and free" (ix). Only within the context of "Wilderness" could such a statement possibly make sense. For a further refinement and development of this concept, see Gary Snyder's "Etiquette of Freedom" in *The Practice of the Wild*.

5. *Toward Ecotopia*

1. The men and woman were Dave Foreman, Howie Wolke, Tony Moore, Bart Koehler, and Louisa Willcox (Zakin, *Coyotes* 149).

2. Eisenhower warned of the influence of the military-industrial complex in his farewell address, 17 Jan. 1961.

3. The most philosophical of the *Star Wars* films, *The Empire Strikes Back* offered an especially effective analogy for students of ecological thought.

4. Abbey later described the "cracking" of the dam as merely "symbolic," adding that he did not want Earth First! to take *The Monkey Wrench Gang* literally (Kaufmann 119). Elsewhere, Abbey suggests otherwise.

5. John W. Delicath claims that radical environmental discourse is "fundamentally anti-utopian," an argument with which I disagree. I also take issue with Susan M. Lucas, who argues that Abbey resembles Thoreau in the sense that Abbey's "opposition emerges from the pen rather than through collective protests, petitions, laws, or acts of sabotage" (266).

6. Interestingly, though, Abbey was disappointed not to have been included in a special issue of *Antaeus* devoted to nature writing (Loeffler, *Adventures* 256). Other nature writers, such as John McPhee, Robert Finch, and John Hay, also deny the "naturalist" label (Trimble 3–5).

7. I quote from the revised version published in Hepworth and McNamee. Berry himself acknowledges his reputation as a "crank" in *Another Turn of the Crank* (1995). For an interesting dialogue between Berry and Abbey over the issue of "wilderness," see Abbey's "Stewardship" and Berry's "My Answer."

8. See also "Abbey the Artist," Berry's letter to the editor of *Orion*.

9. Despite this fact, Abbey repeatedly claimed he was born in the nearby town of Home. For a full discussion of Abbey's use of place-names, see James M. Cahalan's *Edward Abbey: A Life*, the definitive biography.

10. Paul Abbey was himself a member of the IWW and remained so until his death (Zakin, *Coyotes* 363n). As Zakin points out, Earth First! adopted the Wobblies use of "silent agitators," such as bumper stickers and T-shirts, to convey their message (*Coyotes* 361). In addition, a "Bill Haywood" is listed as the coeditor with Dave Foreman of *Ecodefense*, for which Abbey wrote the "Forward!" [*sic*]. Although the identity of this author has never been revealed, it may have been Mike Roselle, or Foreman may have written the book alone.

11. As James Cahalan points out, "Abbey thought he was escaping from the overrun East to a more pristine Southwest; instead, he relocated to what would become major sites of over-development" (*Edward Abbey* 38).

12. Abbey's thesis suggests that Dave Foreman was not entirely correct when he said, in an article marking Abbey's death, that Abbey's ideas "were *American* ideas, not stale leftovers from the intellectual dustbins of Europe" (Foreman, "Edward Abbey" 36–37).

13. See Alderman for a detailed examination of Abbey's anarchism.

14. After a reader pointed out to Abbey in 1975 that Burns seemed to have been reincarnated as the one-eyed stranger in *The Monkey Wrench Gang*, Abbey deleted the final paragraph from *The Brave Cowboy* in the 1977 paperback edition, thus leaving Burns's fate ambiguous and allowing him to resurface again as the shadowy, anarchistic Lone Ranger in *Good News* (1980) and *Hayduke Lives!* (*Confessions* 244; Ronald, *New West* 28).

15. For an early overview of the problem of defining utopian literature, see Sargent. For a comprehensive discussion of the major studies of utopian thought, see Levitas.

16. W. H. Auden makes an important distinction between past and future visions of para-dise in "Dingley Dell and the Fleet" (409–10). On the one hand is the lost paradise: Eden in the Christian version and Arcadia in the secular. On the other hand is the future paradise: the New Jerusalem in the Christian version and Utopia in the secular. While Abbey's vision of paradise did contain some elements of the pastoral Arcadia, I argue that it was primarily Utopian. Rebecca Solnit comments on Auden's Arcadia and Utopia in *Savage Dreams* 112–17.

17. For the English colonists in New England, the vacancy of the wilderness became more important than its aridity, given the well-watered landscape they encountered. Eleazar Whee-lock, for instance, chose for the college seal of Dartmouth College the phrase Vox Claman-tis in Deserto (a Voice Crying in the Wilderness), a phrase Abbey himself used as the title of his collection of aphorisms (G. Williams, *Wilderness* 108, 123–24). New England, of course, was no more "vacant" than it was arid. See also Heimert.

18. EAP, Box 11, Folder 5.

19. See Abbey's title for the tenth (unnumbered) chapter in *Desert Solitaire:* "The Heat of Noon: Rock and Tree and Cloud."

20. For other perspectives on the desert, see Peter Wild's *Desert Reader* and Scott Slovic's *Getting Over the Color Green.*

21. Originally published as "A Response to Schmookler on Anarchy," it was reprinted in *One Life at a Time, Please,* from which I quote. The *Earth First! Journal* has seen several name changes as it evolved from a newsletter to its current tabloid format; for simplicity's sake, I refer to all incarnations of the publication as the *Earth First! Journal.*

22. For a fine overview of anarchist thought, plus a comprehensive bibliography of primary and secondary sources on anarchism, see Sonn.

23. Note, however, that Abbey balances primitivist arguments in *The Monkey Wrench Gang* against arguments for civilization (332), just as he argues in *Desert Solitaire* that "wilderness complements and completes civilization" (129).

24. For another vision embracing the desert, the idea of America, and utopia, see Baudrillard.

25. See, for instance, Sale, *Green* 3–6.

26. Buell discusses *Silent Spring* as an example of environmental apocalypticism in *The Environmental Imagination* (290–96).

27. Consider, for instance, SueEllen Campbell's observation that *Desert Solitaire* "says nothing about the civil rights movement; close to nothing about the war in Vietnam; almost nothing about the Cold War" (43).

28. Until 1979 Abbey continued to work as a seasonal National Park Service ranger and U.S. Forest Service fire lookout in various western locations (Petersen, "Plowboy" 17).

29. Abbey's four other nonfiction books — *The Journey Home* (1977), *Abbey's Road* (1979), *Down the River* (1982), and *One Life at a Time, Please* (1988) — mix essays on travel, politics, and personal history. Because I agree with Don Scheese that Abbey's philosophy "is not so much refined as merely repeated in subsequent works," I have chosen to limit my discussion of Abbey's nonfiction to *Desert Solitaire* (*"Desert Solitaire"* 224). Nevertheless, Abbey's other essay collections also manifest his utopian vision. See Ronald, *New West* 112.

30. Compare David Quammen: "A man wrote a book, and lives were changed. That doesn't happen often" ("Bagpipes" 25).

31. According to Earth First! cofounder Dave Foreman, "I can encounter people that I don't know when I give speeches and if they love the book *Desert Solitaire* like I do we're instantly friends and have an instant bond. There is a family of us out there, there is a clan of us out there. And I think the writings of Ed Abbey are the common denominator. They define a group of people in the west and we know we belong together. And that may have been Ed's real genius" (Temple). Foreman also remarked that *Desert Solitaire* was "the first book I'd ever read that I totally agreed with" (Zakin, *Coyotes* 26).

32. Abbey's claim that *Desert Solitaire* is "not a travel guide but an elegy" suggests more about the effect Abbey wished the book to have than about the character of its contents. He describes the book as a "memorial . . . a tombstone . . . [a] bloody rock" and asks the reader to "throw it at something big and glassy" (xiv). Here and elsewhere I quote from the original 1968 edition and not the 1988 revised edition.

33. See Bryant, "Structure and Unity," for a full discussion of these techniques.

34. Recognizing the change of tone this chapter enacts, Abbey says — with characteristic frankness — that it "protrudes, like an enflamed member, in the midst of an otherwise simple pastorale" in his 1988 preface to the book (*Desert Solitaire* 12). Abbey shares the younger Muir's distaste for tourism, but he must live with the consequences of the elder Muir's reconciliation with it.

35. For similar comments, see Hepworth, "Poetry" 60; Abbey, *Abbey's Road* xv, *Confessions* 246–47. David Copland Morris takes Ronald's argument a step further, claiming that Abbey displays not one voice, but several in *Desert Solitaire*.

36. In fact, at the time of his first season at Arches, Abbey was married to his second wife,

Rita Deanin, and had just become a father; Joshua Abbey was born on 12 April 1956. In a sense, Arches also functions as *personal* utopia for Abbey, as a refuge from domestic responsibilities. In the first draft of the foreword to *Desert Solitaire*, Abbey offers a chronology of his time in Arches, specifically noting the presence of his wife and son (EAP, Box 11, Folder 5). This chronology does not appear in the revised, published version of the book, a change similar to the revised foreword to Leopold's *Sand County Almanac*. In the preface to the 1988 edition of *Desert Solitaire*, Abbey continued to cultivate his solitary persona, claiming that during his first season at Arches, he "worked and lived alone" (9).

37. EAP, Box 11, Folder 5.

38. The book of Isaiah answers Abbey's question, although the answer would hardly satisfy him: "the lion shall eat straw like the ox" (Isaiah 11:7).

39. John Tallmadge (*Meeting* 102) and John R. Knott (339) make similar observations.

40. Mannheim calls "ideological" those mental constructs that "serve the purpose of glossing over or stabilizing the existing social reality"; "utopian" mental constructs, on the other hand, "inspire collective activity which aims to change such reality to conform with their goals, which transcend reality" ("Utopia" 201).

41. According to Scott K. Miller, Abbey was "the first on record to entertain the idea of removing Glen Canyon Dam" (150 n. 206). For an extensive history of subsequent responses to the dam, see Miller's "Undamming Glen Canyon."

42. I quote from the Avon paperback edition of the book, which contains a chapter — chapter 24, "Seldom Seen at Home" — not present in the original hardcover publication. See Erisman, "Variant."

43. Patricia Greiner argues that the activism of the Monkey Wrench Gang "is ultimately a dead end because it is not part of a thoroughly considered plan incorporating constructive as well as destructive acts" (11), but Abbey himself disagreed with this notion in *Desert Solitaire*, when he quoted Bakunin: "There are times when creation can be achieved only through destruction. The urge to destroy is then a creative urge" (162). Robert Ostman expressed his sympathy with Abbey on this point, noting that "'The Monkey Wrench Gang' . . . should not be regarded as a complete manifesto for a new theory of ecological politics or a flawless treatise on the solutions to America's problems. That is not Abbey's intent. . . . The book is the story of people who feel and respond, in their own faulting and inconsistent ways, to the personal traumas and inadequacies of modern life and the institutional rape of nature in America which, because of its magnitude, defies human response and tends to render impotent any response that is made" (n.p.).

44. In "Rocks" Abbey invented the story of the boy who dies; in "The Moon-Eyed Horse" he took liberties and may have invented the tale out of whole cloth; in "Dead Man at Grandview Point" he took great liberties (some rangers say he was not even present during the search); and in "Tukuhnikivats" he probably exaggerated or improvised the snow-sliding incident. See Petersen, "Cactus." Abbey's fictionalizing technique thus involved both false absences (omitting the presence of his wife and son) and false presences.

45. *Sabot*, French for "wooden shoe." On 19 January 1963, Abbey noted in his journal that his projected books included: "*The Wooden Shoe Gang* (or) *The Monkey Wrench Mob* (a

novel about the 'Wilderness Avenger' and his desperate band; sabotage and laughter and wild wild fun)" (*Confessions* 185).

46. It is unclear to what degree Abbey was related to the "Arizona Phantom," a supporter of the Black Mesa Defense Fund, who tore up the tracks of the Black Mesa railroad and disabled the coal company's construction equipment (Zakin, *Coyotes* 25, 56–57). Although the Black Mesa railroad is one of the targets in *The Monkey Wrench Gang*, the issues surrounding the railroad's presence are not explored in detail, a fact that disappointed Jack Loeffler, who initiated the Black Mesa Defense Fund (Zakin, *Coyotes* 179). Loeffler addresses these issues in chapter 5 of *Adventures with Ed.* See also Cahalan, *Edward Abbey* 138.

47. Cahalan details Abbey's participation in damaging a fleet of bulldozers being used to pave state route 95 west of Blanding, Utah. According to Cahalan, Abbey did more than twenty thousand dollars' worth of damage to the bulldozers. See *Edward Abbey* 160–61.

48. In *Down the River* Abbey refers to Doug Peacock as "a Green Beret named Douglas Heiduk" (226). In his journal entry for 6 November 1975, Abbey also noted: "Hayduke, of course, is *hajduk, heiduk*: a Magyar, Serbian, Turkish word meaning 'brigand' or 'robber' or Balkan bandit-resister (Oxford English Dictionary); or . . . , in Hungarian, 'foot soldier'" (*Confessions* 244). For more on the sources for these characters, see Cahalan, *Edward Abbey* 157–59.

49. Calvin Black, the model for Bishop Love in the novel, claimed that Abbey and his friends "would sit and watch the construction crews and then go in and sabotage equipment. . . . They'd put sand in gear boxes. Cut down highway signs. Over $200,000 damage was done to one construction company. Abbey had a lawyer look at that book so it could not be used as evidence." To which Abbey responded, "How flattering. I admit I'd be delighted if somebody blew up the Glen Canyon Dam. I'd do it myself if I had the materials." As to Black's specific accusations, "I did a little field research," he confessed (Hornblower A3).

50. Abbey himself had "pored over" *The Anarchist Cookbook*, according to Jack Loeffler (*Adventures* 105). Another possible source for *Ecodefense* was Sam Love and David Obst's 1972 *Ecotage*.

51. The Fox, the Eco-Raiders, and the Bolt Weevils were among the several monkey-wrenching groups to which Dave Foreman's *Ecodefense* was dedicated.

52. Abbey commented on Dubois in *Down the River* (234).

53. In 1986 Abbey predicted the coming campaign of repression against Earth First!, telling Susan Zakin it was likely that the group's leaders "will be in some sort of serious trouble sooner or later" (*Coyotes* 303). According to Charles Bowden, shortly before Abbey died, Abbey told Dave Foreman "that he could feel a bust was coming, that the government would come down, and come down hard" (49).

54. Lichtenstein was no doubt unaware that Dave Foreman was a registered Republican.

55. Lest anyone doubt how closely Abbey's legacy is tied to ecosabotage, in March 1990 three conservative legal groups — the Wilderness Impact Research Foundation, the Mountain States Legal Foundation, and the Pacific States Legal Foundation — held a conference in Salt Lake City, "Sabotage-Ecotage: The Legacy of Edward Abbey and His Monkeywrench Gang." The gathering was intended to help ranchers, loggers, and farmers combat "the sabotage of our resources in the name of preservation" (Short 181).

56. In April, Wolke had quit the society altogether. He did so on his birthday, 21 April, which also happened to be the date of John Muir's birth and Aldo Leopold's death. In fact, Wolke was born the same day Leopold died, 21 April 1948 (Scarce 60).

57. The logo, according to Roselle, was meant to represent "the Earth, the cycle of life, and the coffee stain on an environmental impact statement" (Manes, *Green Rage* 70).

58. Looking back on the ten-year anniversary of the publication of *The Monkey Wrench Gang*, Foreman asked, "Was it only ten years ago that *The Monkey Wrench Gang* by Edward Abbey radicalized so many of us?" ("Around" 2). He has also stated that "the way I defined Earth First! in the beginning stages was that Earth First! was made up of Ed Abbey style of conservationists" (Temple). Two weeks before Earth First! was founded, "'The Monkey Wrench Gang,' a group of 'concerned citizens,' . . . admitted the weekend theft of light bulbs from the star on Flagstaff Mountain" in Boulder, Colorado (Cahalan, *Edward Abbey* 192).

59. Abbey described *The Monkey Wrench Gang* as "a useful, convenient device, a symbol" for the founders of Earth First! (Bishop 15). Kezar voiced similar sentiments about Earth First! itself, saying that "If Earth First! hadn't come along, somebody else would have come along with something like it. . . . It was an idea whose time had come" (Scarce 59). As Bron Taylor points out, exactly what constitutes "radical environmentalism" is far from clear ("Religion" 33–34 n. 48). Steven C. Steel explores the role of Earth First! literature in "iterating and reiterating the movement's frame" (448).

60. Dave Foreman agreed with the characterization of Earth First! as utopian in Zakin, "Goodbye" 88. See also Loeffler, *Headed Upstream* 155. Another "bureaucrat" who thought Earth First! was unrealistic was Wilderness Society executive director Bill Turnage (Kaufmann 118).

61. See, for instance, the several essays by Naess in Sessions's *Deep Ecology for the Twenty-first Century*.

62. Dave Foreman speaks at length about the role of deep ecology in Earth First! in "The Plowboy Interview." As George Sessions points out, however, comments made by some Earth First! activists have been antithetical to deep ecological philosophy (xiii). For a detailed examination of the role of deep ecology in environmental politics, see Cramer.

63. Both Devall and Sessions were regular contributors to the *Earth First! Journal* during the 1980s.

64. In a 1989 interview, Dave Foreman said, "I consider myself a tribalist, not an anarchist" (Scarce 38). Here Foreman seems to have been defining "anarchy" as a chaotic lack of order, not the tribal organization Abbey envisioned it as.

65. Paul Watson, the controversial leader of the Sea Shepherd Conservation Society, declared himself an Earth First!er after Abbey gave him a subscription to the *Earth First! Journal* (Watson 1). The society also named one of its "marine ecological patrol vessels" the *Edward Abbey* (Sea Shepherd 70).

66. Compare "propaganda by deed," the anarchist slogan coined by Enrico Malatesta of Italy.

67. Jack Turner may have been playing on this line when he wrote, "One *Monkey Wrench Gang* . . . is worth a thousand monkey wrenchings" (95).

68. The proposal also appeared under Abbey's name alone as a column in the *Tucson Citizen*.

69. See Leopold, "Round River." Bart Koehler chose the Leopold reference; Foreman chose the term "Rendezvous" to recall "the get-togethers that the Indians and the mountain men of the Old West used to have" (Scarce 62). The first Round River Rendezvous was held in Dubois, Wyoming, in 1980. The second Rendezvous, held at Arches National Park in 1981, included a speech by Ken Sleight, the model for Seldom Seen Smith in *The Monkey Wrench Gang* (Lee, *Earth First!* 52).

70. Abbey later fictionalized this event in *Hayduke Lives!*

71. According to Lee, timber industry spokespersons, if pressed, admit that the property damage from monkeywrenching goes far beyond published estimates. On the other hand, many Earth First!ers admit that the negative publicity brought by some forms of monkey-wrenching, especially tree-spiking, render them less effective (*Earth First!* 167 n. 67).

72. Abbey himself made such a distinction, writing in the preface to Howie Wolke's *Wilderness on the Rocks*, "Monkey wrenching is not like civil disobedience. Monkey wrenching is an illegal act, carried out by person or persons unknown, with the intention of getting away with it, for the purpose of making the greenheaded goons of Big Industry and Big Government pay the whole cost of your trouble and time" ("George Hayduke's Code" xiv).

73. As Dave Foreman noted, "While Earth First! doesn't officially engage in monkey-wrenching, or even officially advocate it, we also don't *not* advocate it. It's an individual decision" ("Plowboy Interview" 21).

74. Abbey made this distinction on several occasions. See, for instance, R. Arnold 29 n. 28; Loeffler, *Headed Upstream* 8–9; Petersen, "Plowboy" 18; and Temple. In his 1985 "Plowboy Interview," Dave Foreman described monkeywrenching as "nonviolent," although his point was similar to Abbey's (21). Foreman maintains the "nonviolent" description in his *Confessions*.

75. See R. Arnold's *Ecoterror*. Jay Hair once described Earth First! advocates as "terrorists" who "have no right being considered environmentalists" (Malanowski 569; Setterberg 71).

76. See also Foreman's comments in D. Russell, "The Monkeywrenchers"; and Foreman, *Confessions* 117–47.

77. In the preface to *The Double Axe and Other Poems* (1948), Jeffers defines inhumanism as "a shifting of emphasis and significance from man to not-man; the rejection of human solipsism and rejection of the transhuman magnificence" (vii). In a detailed survey of poetic allusions in *Desert Solitaire*, David J. Rothman agrees with this reading (66).

78. The courtroom scene was to involve the "necessity defense," which argues that under certain circumstances a criminal act may be a proper act. Abbey had been in contact with an attorney, who had sent Abbey several law review articles about the defense. See EAP, Box 29, Folder 3.

79. Bill McKibben agrees, but sees a darker significance in *Hayduke Lives!* than I do ("Gleam" 36).

80. See also Milbourn.

81. Defining *terrorism* is no easier. See deFiebre.

82. Michael Martin, in contrast, observes that ecosabotage "is clearly not an act of civil disobedience" according to typical definitions, all of which specify that the act be publicly performed, which most acts of ecosabotage are not (296). Notably, Martin does not believe

nonviolence is essential to the meaning of civil disobedience (296 n. 18). For a development of Martin's argument, see Thomas Young's "The Morality of Ecosabotage" and Jennifer Welchman's "Is Ecosabotage Civil Disobedience?" For other perspectives on ecoterrorism, see Eagan, "From Spikes to Bombs"; Hettinger, "Environmental Disobedience"; and Lee, "Violence and the Environment."

83. It is important to note that both Taylor and Young were writing before September 11.

84. See also Patricia Greiner's comment above (n. 43).

85. Joni Adamson makes a similar point. See especially her second chapter, "Abbey's Country."

86. See also Rothstein, "Utopia and Its Discontents."

87. Lee frames this split in terms of millenarianism and apocalypticism; the biocentrists, she says, became more apocalyptic and the social justice faction became more millenarian (*Earth First!*). See also her articles "Environmental Apocalypse" and "Violence and the Environment."

88. Kaufmann quotes a letter to Earth First! from an old-timer who heard John Muir speak about the Hetch Hetchy Dam in 1912: "My decades-long membership in the Sierra Club is drawing to a close as I see the tendency to stick closely to the middle of the road on so many issues. In other words, I've belatedly realized that, yes, we must begin tearing down some of the dams already built! I've become very much disillusioned by the steady 'backing up.' John Muir must be spinning in his grave" (116). Not everyone agrees with this assessment. Abbey's view, claims Peter Wild, "would have appalled gentle John Muir, who, in a different time, had faith in rational solutions" (*Pioneer Conservationists* 186–87). Interestingly, Abbey had been an active member of the Sierra Club, but in 1975, the year *The Monkey Wrench Gang* was published, he told John F. Baker he felt that his activist approach would do the organization — and others like it — more harm than good. "I think they're better off without people like me," he said (Baker 7). In 1984, however, Abbey addressed a Sierra Club fund-raiser in San Diego (P. Carlson 59).

Conclusion. The Island as Metaphor

1. Many others have said the same. Compare, for example, Carson, *Sea around Us* 83; Gillis 56; Holm 330; Worster, *Nature's Economy* 115; and L. Young 2.

2. Another reason for the increased prevalence of the island metaphor in environmental discourse is the appearance of the term "biodiversity" in 1986; see Takacs. In addition to Quammen, an accessible introduction to conservation biology, the science of biodiversity and species extinction, is Grumbine, *Ghost Bears*. A good practical guide is Noss and Cooperrider. A popular textbook is Meffe, Carroll, and contributors. See also Quammen's "Islands of Memory."

3. Wes Jackson makes the same point in "Natural Systems Agriculture" 193.

4. J. Baird Callicott offers another version of these criteria in *Beyond the Land Ethic* 311.

5. David Abram makes a similar point in *Spell of the Sensuous* 265.

6. How we answer these questions will depend, as I suggest in the introduction, on our own situatedness and embodiment. This does not mean, however, that all values are what philoso-

phers call "surds," or concepts not capable of being influenced by rational persuasion. For more on this, see Hay 2–3; and Livingston 117. Were all values surds, we would never be able to persuade one another of anything by means of reason. Because our values develop in the context of place and in the practice of history, they are influenced not only by our emotional impulses but also by the force of reason.

7. For an example of how this might work in practice, see Branch and Philippon, "Virginia's Blue Ridge Mountains."

8. Islands have been prominent subjects for John Donne ("No Man Is an Island," 1624), Daniel Defoe (*Robinson Crusoe*, 1719), Jonathan Swift (*Gulliver's Travels*, 1726), Robert Louis Stevenson (*Treasure Island*, 1882), H. G. Wells (*The Island of Dr. Moreau*, 1896), William Golding (*Lord of the Flies*, 1954), and many other writers, while the advent of film and television has brought us *Gilligan's Island*, *Fantasy Island*, the first season of *Survivor*, and *Cast Away*. For more on islands in literature and history, see Grove; Hannabuss; and Loxley. For another ecocritical approach to islands, see J. Arnold.

9. The "Earth Rise" image may be the new myth of our time, according to Joseph Campbell (32). See also Kennedy's "Earthrise," an interview with Campbell; and D. Oates's *Earth Rising*.

10. Almost every major environmental science textbook uses the story of Easter Island when discussing the carrying capacity of the earth. For a book-length treatment, see Bahn and Flenley, *Easter Island, Earth Island*. For a criticism of the comparison, see Lomborg, *Skeptical Environmentalist* 29. As Jean Arnold points out, however, "the island equally arouses impulses toward empire as we speak about global computer networks and use satellites for communication" (33).

11. See David Brower's foreword, and Wendell Berry's "Futility of Global Thinking." For an organizational perspective on the need for a global thinking, see Frank Biermann, "The Case for a World Environment Organization."

12. This comment reflects a larger trend in environmental ethics toward ethical contextualism. See, for instance, Gare; Midgeley, *Animals*; B. Norton; and Callicott, *In Defense*.

13. Roderick Nash has called for a reversal of this state of affairs, arguing in *Wild Earth* for "island civilization." A version of his argument is reprinted as part of the epilogue to the fourth edition of *Wilderness and the American Mind*. It also appears in T. Butler, *Wild Earth*, 131–38.

14. For more on the significance of edges and boundaries, see Thomashow, *Bringing the Biosphere Home* 98–102.

Works Cited

Untitled book reviews by unnamed reviewers are alphabetized under the title of the book being reviewed.

Abbey, Edward. "Abbey on Books — and Gurus." Davis, *Earth First! Reader* 156–57.

———. *Abbey's Road*. New York: E. P. Dutton, 1979.

———. "Anarchism and the Morality of Violence." Master's thesis. U of New Mexico, 1959.

———. *Beyond the Wall: Essays from the Outside*. New York: Holt, Rinehart, and Winston, 1984.

———. *The Brave Cowboy: An Old Tale in a New Time*. Afterword by Neal E. Lambert. 1956. Albuquerque: U of New Mexico P, 1977.

———. *Cactus Country*. New York: Time-Life Books, 1973.

———. *Confessions of a Barbarian: Selections from the Journals of Edward Abbey, 1951–1989*. Ed. David Petersen. Illus. Edward Abbey. Boston: Little, Brown, 1994.

———. *Desert Solitaire: A Season in the Wilderness*. 1968. Rev. ed. Tucson: U of Arizona P, 1988.

———. *Desert Solitaire: A Season in the Wilderness*. Illus. Peter Parnall. 1968. New York: Simon and Schuster, 1990.

———. *Down the River*. New York: E. P. Dutton, 1982.

———. "Earth First! and *The Monkey Wrench Gang*." *Environmental Ethics* 5 (1983): 94–95.

———. "Ed Abbey to Earth First!" Davis, *Earth First! Reader* 247–49.

———. *Fire on the Mountain*. Afterword by Gerald Haslam. 1962. Albuquerque: U of New Mexico P, 1978.

———. "George Hayduke's Code of the Eco-Warrior: A Preface to Howie Wolke's Book." [By George Hayduke as told to Edward Abbey.] *Wilderness on the Rocks*. By Howie Wolke. Foreword by Edward Abbey. Tucson, Ariz.: Ned Ludd Books, 1991. xiii–xvi.

———. *Good News*. New York: E. P. Dutton, 1980.

———. *Hayduke Lives!* Boston: Little, Brown, 1990.

———. *Jonathan Troy*. New York: Dodd, Mead, 1954.

———. *The Journey Home: Some Words in Defense of the American West*. Illus. Jim Stiles. New York: E. P. Dutton, 1977.

———. Letter to the Editor. *Earth First! Journal* 5.5 (1 May 1985): 3.

———. *The Monkey Wrench Gang*. 1975. New York: Avon, 1976.

———. *One Life at a Time, Please*. New York: Henry Holt, 1988.

———. "A Response to Schmookler on Anarchy." *Earth First! Journal* 6.7 (1 Aug. 1987): 22.

——. "Stewardship versus Wilderness." Rev. of *Home Economics*, by Wendell Berry. *Earth First! Journal* 8.3 (2 Feb. 1988): 32.

——. *A Voice Crying in the Wilderness: Notes from a Secret Journal*. New York: St. Martin's, 1989.

Abbey, Edward, and Pablo Desierto. "Earth First! Proposes 6 Million Acres National Forest Wilderness in Arizona." *Earth First! Journal* 4.5 (1 May 1984): 8.

Abbott, Katherine M. *Trolley Trips: The Historic New England Coast*. Lowell, Mass.: K. M. Abbott, 1899.

Abram, David. "The Mechanical and the Organic: On the Impact of Metaphor in Science." *Scientists on Gaia*. Ed. Stephen Schneider and Penelope Boston. Cambridge, Mass.: MIT Press, 1991.

——. *The Spell of the Sensuous: Perception and Language in a More-than-Human World*. New York: Pantheon, 1996.

Adams, William Howard. *Nature Perfected: Gardens through History*. New York: Abbeville, 1991.

Adamson, Joni. *American Indian Literature, Environmental Justice, and Ecocriticism: The Middle Place*. Tucson: U of Arizona P, 2001.

Albanese, Catherine L. *Nature Religion in America: From the Algonkian Indians to the New Age*. Chicago: U of Chicago P, 1990.

Albright, Horace M. Letter to the Editor. *Journal of Forest History* (Oct. 1976): 222–23.

Alderman, Harold. "Abbey as Anarchist." Quigley 137–49.

Allen, J. A. Rev. of *The Friendship of Nature*, by Mabel Osgood Wright. *Auk* 11 (1894): 314.

Allen, Robert P. "The Wild-Life Sanctuary Movement in the United States." *Bird-Lore* 36 (1934): 80–84.

Allin, Craig W. "The Leopold Legacy and the American Wilderness." *Aldo Leopold: The Man and His Legacy*. Ed. Thomas Tanner. Ankeny, Iowa.: Soil Conservation Society of America, 1987. 25–38.

——. *The Politics of Wilderness Preservation*. Westport, Conn.: Greenwood Press, 1982.

Altherr, Thomas L. "The American Hunter-Naturalist and the Development of the Code of Sportsmanship." *Journal of Sport History* 5.1 (spring 1978): 7–22.

Altherr, Thomas L., and John F. Reiger. "Academic Historians and Hunting: A Call for More and Better Scholarship." *Environmental History Review* (fall 1995): 39–56.

American Ornithologists' Union. Committee on Bird Protection. Bulletin No. 1, "Supplement." *Science* 7 (1886): 191–205.

Anderson, Melville B. "The Conversation of John Muir." *American Museum Journal* 15 (Mar. 1915): 116–21.

Anzaldua, Gloria. *Borderlands = "la frontera": The New Mestiza*. San Francisco: Spinsters/ Aunt Lute, 1987.

Archer, John. "Country and City in the American Romantic Suburb." *Journal of the Society for Architectural Historians* 42 (1983): 139–56.

Armbruster, Karla, and Kathleen R. Wallace, eds. *Beyond Nature Writing: Expanding the Boundaries of Ecocriticism*. Charlottesville: UP of Virginia, 2001.

Arnold, Jean. "Mapping Island Mindscapes: The Literary and Cultural Uses of a Geographical Formation." *Reading under the Sign of Nature: New Essays in Ecocriticism.* Ed. John Tallmadge and Henry Harrington. Salt Lake City: U of Utah P, 2000. 24–35.

Arnold, Ron. *Ecoterror: The Violent Agenda to Save Nature: The World of the Unabomber.* Bellevue, Wash.: Free Enterprise Press, 1997.

Asthma, Stephen T. *Stuffed Animals and Pickled Heads: The Culture and Evolution of Natural History Museums.* New York: Oxford UP, 2001.

Athearn, Robert G. *The Mythic West in Twentieth-Century America.* Foreword by Elliott West. Lawrence: UP of Kansas, 1986.

Auden, W. H. "Dingley Dell and the Fleet." *The Dyer's Hand and Other Essays.* New York: Random House, 1962. 407–28.

Austin, Richard Cartwright. *Baptized into Wilderness: A Christian Perspective on John Muir.* Atlanta: John Knox, 1987.

Babcock, Charles A. *Bird Day: How to Prepare for It.* New York: Silver, Burdett, 1901.

Badè, William Frederick. *The Life and Letters of John Muir.* 2 vols. Boston: Houghton Mifflin, 1924.

Bahn, Paul G., and John Flenley. *Easter Island, Earth Island.* New York: Thames and Hudson, 1992.

Bailey, Florence Merriam. *A-Birding on a Bronco.* New York: Houghton, Mifflin, 1896.

——. *Birds of Village and Field: A Bird Book for Beginners.* New York: Houghton, Mifflin, 1898.

——. *Birds through an Opera Glass.* New York: Houghton, Mifflin, 1889.

Bailey, Liberty Hyde. *The Nature-Study Idea: Being an Interpretation of the New School-Movement to Put the Child in Sympathy with Nature.* New York: Doubleday, 1903.

Baker, John F. "Edward Abbey." *Publishers Weekly* 208 (8 Sept. 1975): 6–7.

Baker, John H. "Fifty Years of Progress in Furtherance of Audubon Objectives." *Audubon* 57 (1955): 8–9.

Baker, Paula. "The Domestication of Politics: Women and American Political Society, 1780–1920." *American Historical Review* 89 (1984): 620–47.

Baker, Ray Stannard. "John Muir." *Outlook* 74 (1906): 365–77.

Baldwin, Donald N. *The Quiet Revolution: Grass Roots of Today's Wilderness Preservation Movement.* Boulder, Colo.: Pruett Pub., 1972.

——. "Wilderness: Concept and Challenge." *Colorado Magazine* 44.3 (summer 1967): 224–40.

Barbato, Joseph, and Lisa Weinerman Horak, eds. *Off the Beaten Path: Stories of Place.* Intro. Barbara Kingsolver. New York: North Point, 1998.

Barbato, Joseph, and Lisa Weinerman, eds. *Heart of the Land: Essays on Last Great Places.* Foreword by Barry Lopez. New York: Vintage, 1996.

Barbour, Ian G. *Religion and Science: Historical and Contemporary Issues.* New York: HarperCollins, 1997.

Barcott, Bruce. "From Tree-Hugger to Terrorist." *New York Times Magazine* 7 Apr. 2002. <http://www.nytimes.com/>. Accessed 7 Apr. 2002.

Barker, Rocky. *Saving All the Parts: Reconciling Economics and the Endangered Species Act.* Washington, D.C.: Island Press, 1993.

Barrow, Mark V., Jr. *A Passion for Birds: American Ornithology after Audubon*. Princeton, N.J.: Princeton UP, 1998.

Bass, Rick, ed. *The Roadless Yaak: Reflections and Observations about One of Our Last Great Wilderness Areas*. Intro. Mike Dombeck. Guilford, Conn.: Lyons Press, 2002.

Batchelder, Charles Foster. *Memoirs of the Nuttall Ornithological Club, No. VII: An Account of the Nuttall Ornithological Club, 1873–1919*. Cambridge, Mass.: The Club, 1937.

Baudrillard, Jean. *America*. Trans. Chris Turner. New York: Verso, 1988.

Bederman, Gail. *Manliness and Civilization: A Cultural History of Gender and Race in the United States, 1880–1917*. Chicago: U of Chicago P, 1995.

Begg, Virginia Lopez. "Mabel Osgood Wright: The Friendship of Nature and the Commuter's Wife." *Journal of the New England Garden History Society* 5 (fall 1997): 35–41.

Bellah, Robert N., et al. *The Good Society*. New York: Knopf, 1991.

——. *Habits of the Heart: Individualism and Commitment in American Life*. 1986. Rev. ed. Berkeley: U of California P, 1996.

Bender, Thomas. "The 'Rural' Cemetery Movement: Urban Travail and the Appeal of Nature." *New England Quarterly* 47 (1974): 196–211.

Benford, Robert D., and Scott A. Hunt. "Dramaturgy and Social Movements: The Social Construction and Communication of Power." *Sociological Inquiry* 62 (1992): 36–55.

Bennett, Jennifer. *Lilies of the Hearth: The Historical Relationship between Women and Plants*. Ontario: Camden House, 1991.

Benton, Lisa M., and John Rennie Short. *Environmental Discourse and Practice*. Malden, Mass.: Blackwell, 1999.

Berrall, Julia S. *The Garden: An Illustrated History*. New York: Viking, 1966.

Berry, Wendell. "Abbey the Artist." Letter to the Editor. *Orion* 15.4 (autumn 1996): 2–3.

——. "A Few Words in Favor of Edward Abbey." Hepworth and McNamee 1–14.

——. "The Futility of Global Thinking." Willers 150–56.

——. "My Answer to Edward Abbey." *Earth First! Journal* 8.3 (2 Feb. 1988): 33.

——. "Preserving Wildness." *Home Economics: Fourteen Essays*. San Francisco: North Point Press, 1987. 137–51.

Berthold-Bond, Daniel. "The Ethics of 'Place': Reflections on Bioregionalism." *Environmental Ethics* 22 (2000): 5–24.

Betts, J. R. "Sporting Journalism in Nineteenth-Century America." *American Quarterly* 5 (1953): 39–56.

Biermann, Frank, "The Case for a World Environment Organization." *Environment* 42.9 (1 Nov. 2000): 22–31.

Binford, Henry C. *The First Suburbs: Residential Communities on the Boston Periphery, 1815–1860*. Chicago: U of Chicago P, 1985.

Bishop, James, Jr. *Epitaph for a Desert Anarchist: The Life and Legacy of Edward Abbey*. New York: Athenaeum, 1994.

Blair, Karen J. *The Clubwoman as Feminist: True Womanhood Redefined, 1868–1914*. New York: Holmes and Meier, 1980.

Blodgett, Peter J. "Visiting 'The Realm of Wonder': Yosemite and the Business of Tourism, 1855–1916." *California History* 69.2 (summer 1990): 118–33.

Bloom, Harold. *The Anxiety of Influence: A Theory of Poetry.* 2d ed. New York: Oxford UP, 1997.

Blumin, Stuart M. *The Emergence of the Middle Class: Social Experience in the American City, 1760–1900.* New York: Cambridge UP, 1989.

Bogue, Allan G. *Frederick Jackson Turner: Strange Roads Going Down.* Norman: U of Oklahoma P, 1998.

Bonta, Marcia. *Women in the Field: America's Pioneering Women Naturalists.* College Station: Texas A&M UP, 1991.

"The Book of Nature." Rev. of *The Mountains of California,* by John Muir. *Critic* 26, n.s. 23 (1895): 4.

Booth, Wayne C. *The Company We Keep: An Ethics of Fiction.* Berkeley: U of California P, 1988.

Borg, Marcus J. *The God We Never Knew: Beyond Dogmatic Religion to a More Authentic Contemporary Faith.* New York: HarperCollins, 1997.

Borus, Daniel H. *Writing Realism: Howells, James, and Norris in the Mass Market.* Chapel Hill: U of North Carolina P, 1989.

Botkin, Daniel. *Discordant Harmonies: A New Ecology for the Twenty-first Century.* New York: Oxford UP, 1990.

Boudon, Raymond. *Theories of Social Change: A Critical Appraisal.* Trans. J. C. Whitehouse. Cambridge, Eng.: Polity Press, 1986.

Bové, Paul A. "Discourse." *Critical Terms for Literary Study.* Ed. Frank Lentricchia and Thomas McLaughlin. Chicago: U of Chicago P, 1990. 50–65.

Bowden, Charles. "Dave Foreman! In the Face of Reality." *Buzzworm* 2.2 (Mar.–Apr. 1990): 46–51.

Bowdish, B. S. "The Relation of the Audubon Movement to the Sportsman." *Scientific American* 98.9 (29 Feb. 1908): 139.

Bradbury, Malcolm. "'Years of the Modern': The Rise of Realism and Naturalism." *American Literature to 1900.* Ed. Marcus Cunliffe. Vol. 8 of the *Penguin History of Literature.* New York: Penguin, 1993.

Bradley, Nina Leopold. "Good for the Soil, Good for the Soul." Part of "The Legacy Lives On: The Wilderness Society Salutes Aldo Leopold," a 16-page supplement to *Wilderness* 1998. 4–7.

Bramwell, Anna. *Ecology in the Twentieth Century: A History.* New Haven: Yale UP, 1989.

——. *The Fading of the Greens: The Decline of Environmental Politics in the West.* New Haven: Yale UP, 1994.

Branch, Michael P. "'Angel guiding gently': The Yosemite Meeting of Ralph Waldo Emerson and John Muir, 1871." *Western American Literature* 32 (1997): 126–49.

——. "Saving All the Pieces: The Place of Textual Editing in Ecocriticism." *Interdisciplinary Literary Studies* 3.1 (fall 2001): 4–23.

Branch, Michael P., and Daniel J. Philippon. "Virginia's Blue Ridge Mountains and Shenandoah Valley: A Place in the South." *Appalachian Heritage* 26.1 (winter 1998): 18–25.

——, eds. *The Height of Our Mountains: Nature Writing from Virginia's Blue Ridge Mountains and Shenandoah Valley.* Baltimore: Johns Hopkins UP, 1998.

Broach, Elise L. "Angels, Architecture, and Erosion: The Dakota Badlands as a Cultural Symbol." *North Dakota History* 59.1 (winter 1992): 2–15.

Brooks, Paul. *Speaking for Nature: How Literary Naturalists from Henry Thoreau to Rachel Carson Have Shaped America*. Boston: Houghton Mifflin, 1980.

Broome, Harvey."The Last Decade, 1935–1945." *Living Wilderness* 10.14–15 (Dec. 1945): 13–17.

———. "Origins of the Wilderness Society." *Living Wilderness* 5 (July 1940): 13.

———. "Thirty Years." *Living Wilderness* 29.91 (winter 1965–1966): 15–26.

Brower, David. Foreword. Willers xiii–xv.

Brown, David E., and Neil B. Carmony. *Aldo Leopold's Wilderness: Selected Early Writings by the Author of "A Sand County Almanac."* Harrisburg, Pa.: Stackpole Books, 1990.

Browning, Peter, ed. *John Muir in His Own Words: A Book of Quotations*. Lafayette, Calif.: Great West Books, 1988.

Brulle, Robert J. *Agency, Democracy, and Nature: The U.S. Environmental Movement from a Critical Theory Perspective*. Cambridge, Mass.: MIT Press, 2000.

———. "Environmental Discourse and Environmental Movement Organizations: A Historical and Rhetorical Perspective on the Development of U.S. Environmental Organizations." *Sociological Inquiry* 66 (1996): 58–83.

Bruner, Michael, and Max Oelschlaeger. "Rhetoric, Environmentalism, and Environmental Ethics." *Environmental Ethics* 16 (1994): 377–96.

Bryant, Paul T. "The Structure and Unity of *Desert Solitaire*." *Western American Literature* 28 (1993): 3–19.

———. "Time in Nature Writing." *North Dakota Quarterly* 59.2 (spring 1991): 319–30.

Buchheister, Carl W., and Frank Graham Jr. "From the Swamps and Back: A Concise and Candid History of the Audubon Movement." *Audubon* 75 (1973): 4–45.

Buell, Lawrence. *The Environmental Imagination: Thoreau, Nature Writing, and the Formation of American Culture*. Cambridge, Mass.: Harvard UP, 1995.

Bunnell, Lafayette Houghton. *Discovery of the Yosemite, and the Indian War of 1851, Which Led to that Event*. 1880. Freeport, N.Y.: Books for Libraries, 1971.

Burke, Kenneth. "Dramatism." *International Encyclopedia of the Social Sciences*. Ed. David L. Sills. New York: Macmillan, 1968. 7:445–52.

———. *A Grammar of Motives*. 1945. Berkeley: U of California P, 1969.

———. *Language as Symbolic Action: Essays on Life, Literature, and Method*. Berkeley: U of California P, 1966.

———. *The Philosophy of Literary Form: Studies in Symbolic Action*. 3d ed. 1941. Berkeley: U of California P, 1973.

Burnham, John. "The Old Era—and the New." *Bulletin of the American Game Protective [and Propagation] Association* 14 (Jan. 1925): 13.

Burroughs, John. "Bird Enemies." *Century* 31 (1885): 270–74.

———. "John Muir's 'Yosemite.'" *Literary Digest* 44 (1912): 1165–68.

Butler, Tom, ed. *Wild Earth: Wild Ideas for a World out of Balance*. Minneapolis: Milkweed Editions, 2002.

Butler, William. "Another City upon a Hill: Litchfield, Connecticut, and the Colonial Revival." *The Colonial Revival in America*. Ed. Alan Axelrod. New York: Norton, 1985. 15–51.

Cafaro, Philip. "Comment: Personal Narratives and Environmental Ethics." *Environmental Ethics* 21 (1999): 109–10.

Cahalan, James M. *Edward Abbey: A Life*. Tucson: U of Arizona P, 2001.

——. "Edward Abbey, Appalachian Easterner." *Western American Literature* 31 (1996): 233–53.

Callenbach, Ernest. *Ecotopia: The Notebooks and Reports of William Weston*. Berkeley, Calif.: Banyan Tree Books, 1975.

Callicott, J. Baird. *Beyond the Land Ethic: More Essays in Environmental Philosophy*. Albany: SUNY P, 1999.

——. *In Defense of the Land Ethic: Essays in Environmental Philosophy*. Albany: SUNY P, 1989.

——. "The Wilderness Idea Revisited: The Sustainable Development Alternative." Callicott and Nelson 337–66.

——, ed. *Companion to "A Sand County Almanac": Interpretive and Critical Essays*. Madison: U of Wisconsin P, 1987.

Callicott, J. Baird, Larry B. Crowder, and Karen Mumford. "Current Normative Concepts in Conservation." *Conservation Biology* 13 (1999): 22–35.

Callicott, J. Baird, and Michael P. Nelson. *The Great New Wilderness Debate*. Athens: U of Georgia P, 1998.

Campbell, Joseph. With Bill Moyers. *The Power of Myth*. Ed. Betty Sue Flowers. New York: Doubleday, 1988.

Campbell, SueEllen. "Foreword II: Magpie." Quigley 33–46.

Canby, Henry Seidel. "Back to Nature." *Yale Review* 6 (1917): 755–67.

Carlson, Alvar W. "Roosevelt and the Badlands: The Persistence of Error in Geographical Location." *Journal of the West* 9 (1970): 469–86.

Carlson, Peter. "Edward Abbey." *People Weekly* 21 (25 June 1984): 58–60+.

Carr, David. *Time, Narrative, and History*. Bloomington: Indiana UP, 1986.

Carson, Rachel. *The Sea around Us*. New York: Oxford UP, 1951.

——. *Silent Spring*. Boston: Houghton Mifflin, 1962.

Cart, Theodore Whaley. "The Struggle for Wildlife Protection in the United States, 1870–1900: Attitudes and Events Leading to the Lacey Act." Diss. U of North Carolina at Chapel Hill, 1971.

Cartmill, Matt. *A View to a Death in the Morning: Hunting and Nature through History*. Cambridge, Mass.: Harvard UP, 1993.

Catlin, George. *Letters and Notes on the Manners, Customs, and Conditions of the North American Indians*. 2 vols. New York: Wiley and Putnam, 1841.

Caton, John Dean. *The Antelope and Deer of America*. New York: Hurd and Houghton, 1877.

Chapman, Frank M. *Autobiography of a Bird-Lover*. New York: D. Appleton-Century, 1933.

——. "Collections of Birds in the United States and Canada." *Fifty Years' Progress of American Ornithology, 1883–1933*. Lancaster, Pa.: American Ornithologists' Union, 1933. 143–57.

——. Editorial. *Bird-Lore* 1 (1899): 28.

——. Editorial. *Bird-Lore* 17 (1915): 297.

——. "The Relation of *Bird-Lore* to the National Association of Audubon Societies." *Bird-Lore* 34 (1932): 284–328.

Chase, Richard. *The American Novel and Its Tradition*. Garden City, N.Y.: Doubleday, 1957.

Cheney, Jim. "Postmodern Environmental Ethics: Ethics as Bioregional Narrative." *Environmental Ethics* 11 (1989): 117–34.

Child, Frank Samuel. *An Old New England Town*. New York: Scribner's, 1895.

Clark, Clifford E., Jr. *The American Family Home, 1800–1960*. Chapel Hill: U of North Carolina P, 1986.

Clarke, James Mitchell. *The Life and Adventures of John Muir*. 1978. San Francisco: Sierra Club Books, 1980.

Clarke, J. J. *Voices of the Earth: An Anthology of Ideas and Arguments*. New York: George Braziller, 1994.

Clarken, George Gerard. "At Home with John Muir." *Overland Monthly* 52 (1908): 125–28.

Clements, Kendrick A. "Politics and the Park: San Francisco's Fight for Hetch Hetchy, 1908–1913." *Pacific Historical Review* 48 (1979): 185–215.

Coates, Peter. *Nature: Western Attitudes since Ancient Times*. Berkeley: U of California P, 1998.

Coe, Richard M. "Metaphor." *The Encyclopedia of Rhetoric and Composition*. Ed. Theresa Enos. New York: Garland, 1996. 438–44.

Cohen, Michael P. "A Brittle Thesis: A Ghost Dance: A Flower Opening." *The Wilderness Condition: Essays on Environment and Civilization*. Ed. Max Oelschlaeger. Washington, D.C.: Island Press, 1992. 188–204.

——. *The History of the Sierra Club, 1892–1970*. San Francisco: Sierra Club Books, 1988.

——. "Literary Theory and Nature Writing." Elder, *American Nature Writers* 2:1099–113.

——. *The Pathless Way: John Muir and American Wilderness*. Madison: U of Wisconsin P, 1984.

——. "The ProblemS of Post Modern Wilderness." *Wild Earth* (fall 1991): 72–73.

Cohen, Ralph. "Genre Theory, Literary History, and Historical Change." *Theoretical Issues in Literary History*. Ed. David Perkins. Cambridge, Mass.: Harvard UP, 1991. 85–113.

Cokinos, Christopher. *Hope Is the Thing with Feathers: A Personal Chronicle of Vanished Birds*. New York: J. P. Tarcher/Putnam, 2000.

Colby, William E. "Proposed Summer Outing of the Sierra Club — Report of the Committee." *SCB* 3.3 (Feb. 1901): 250–53.

——. "Twenty-Nine Years with the Sierra Club." *SCB* 16.1 (Feb. 1931): 1–15.

——. "Yosemite and the Sierra Club." *SCB* 23.2 (Apr. 1938): 11–19.

Coles, Robert. *The Call of Stories: Teaching and the Moral Imagination*. Boston: Houghton Mifflin, 1989.

Collins, Michael L. *That Damned Cowboy: Theodore Roosevelt and the American West, 1883–1898*. New York: Peter Lang, 1989.

Collins, Randall. *The Sociology of Philosophies: A Global Theory of Intellectual Change*. Cambridge, Mass.: Harvard UP, 1998.

"Concerning Anonymities." *Bookman* 23 (Mar. 1906): 7.

Connecticut Audubon Society [Audubon Society of Connecticut]. *Annual Report*. June 1898. CAS Records, BMS.

——. *Minutes.* CAS Records, BPL.

——. *Minutes of the Meetings of the Board of Governors of . . . Birdcraft Sanctuary.* CAS Records, BMS.

Cooper, Marilyn M. "The Ecology of Writing." *College English* 48.4 (Apr. 1986): 364–75.

Cooper, Susan Fenimore. *Rural Hours.* Ed. Rochelle Johnson and Daniel Patterson. 1850. Athens: U of Georgia P, 1998.

Cott, Nancy F. *The Bonds of Womanhood: "Woman's Sphere" in New England, 1780–1835.* New Haven: Yale UP, 1977.

Coues, Elliott. *Birds of the Northwest.* Washington, D.C.: GPO, 1874.

Coupe, Laurence. "Kenneth Burke: Pioneer of Ecocriticism." *Journal of American Studies* 35 (2001): 413–31.

Cox, Thomas R. "From Hot Springs to Gateway: The Evolving Concept of Public Parks, 1832–1976." *Environmental Review* 5.1 (1980): 14–26.

The Cracking of Glen Canyon Damn [sic]: With Edward Abbey and Earth First! Dir. Christopher McLeod. Earth Image Films, 1982.

Cramer, Phillip F. *Deep Environmental Politics: The Role of Radical Environmentalism in Crafting American Environmental Policy.* Westport, Conn.: Praeger, 1998.

"The Creation of Yosemite National Park: Letters of John Muir to Robert Underwood Johnson." *SCB* 29.5 (Oct. 1944): 49–60.

Croker, Robert A. *Pioneer Ecologist: The Life and Work of Victor Ernest Shelford, 1877–1968.* Washington, D.C.: Smithsonian Institution Press, 1991.

Cronon, William. "Landscape and Home: Environmental Traditions in Wisconsin." *Wisconsin Magazine of History* 74.2 (winter 1990–1991): 83–105.

——. "A Place for Stories: Nature, History, and Narrative." *Journal of American History* 78 (1992): 1347–76.

——. "The Trouble with Wilderness; or, Getting Back to the Wrong Nature." Cronon, *Uncommon Ground* 69–90.

——. "The Uses of Environmental History." *Environmental History Review* 17.3 (fall 1993): 1–22.

——. "A Voice in the Wilderness." Part of "The Legacy Lives On: The Wilderness Society Salutes Aldo Leopold," a 16-page supplement to *Wilderness* 1998. 8–13.

——, ed. *Uncommon Ground: Rethinking the Human Place in Nature.* New York: Norton, 1996.

Cutright, Paul Russell. *Theodore Roosevelt: The Making of a Conservationist.* Urbana: U of Illinois P, 1985.

——. *Theodore Roosevelt: The Naturalist.* New York: Harper and Brothers, 1956.

Dalton, Kathleen. *Theodore Roosevelt: A Strenuous Life.* New York: Knopf, 2002.

Dana, Samuel Trask, and Sally K. Fairfax. *Forest and Range Policy: Its Development in the United States.* 2d ed. New York: McGraw-Hill, 1980.

Darier, Éric, ed. *Discourses of the Environment.* Malden, Pa.: Blackwell, 1999.

Darrow, Clarence S. *A Persian Pearl and Other Essays.* 1899. Chicago: C. L. Ricketts, 1902.

——. "Realism in Literature and Art." *Arena* 9 (Dec. 1893): 98–113.

Davis, John. "A View of the Vortex." *Earth First! Journal* 9.4 (21 Mar. 1989): 2.

——, ed. *The Earth First! Reader: Ten Years of Radical Environmentalism*. Foreword by Dave Foreman. Salt Lake City: Gibbs Smith, 1991.

deFiebre, Conrad. "Government Units Strain to Define What Terrorism Is." *Star Tribune* (Minneapolis) 14 Feb. 2002, 4B.

Delicath, John W. "In Search of Ecotopia: 'Radical Environmentalism' and the Possibilities of Utopian Rhetorics." *Earthtalk: Communication Empowerment for Environmental Action*. Ed. Star A. Muir and Thomas Veenendall. Westport, Conn.: Praeger, 1996.

DeLuca, Kevin, and Anne Demo. "Imagining Nature and Erasing Class and Race: Carleton Watkins, John Muir, and the Construction of Wilderness." *Environmental History* 6.4 (Oct. 2001): 541–60.

Demars, Stanford E. *The Tourist in Yosemite, 1855–1985*. Salt Lake City: U of Utah P, 1991.

Devall, Bill. "John Muir as Deep Ecologist." *Environmental Review* 6.1 (spring 1982): 63–86.

Devall, Bill, and George Sessions. *Deep Ecology: Living as If Nature Mattered*. Salt Lake City: Gibbs Smith, 1985.

Dietrich, William. *The Final Forest: The Battle for the Last Great Trees of the Pacific Northwest*. New York: Penguin, 1993.

Dodge, Richard Irving. *The Plains of the Great West and Their Inhabitants*. New York: G. P. Putnam's Sons, 1877.

Doell, Charles E., and Gerald B. Fitzgerald. *A Brief History of Parks and Recreation in the United States*. Chicago: Athletic Institute, 1954.

Doremus, Holly. "The Rhetoric and Reality of Nature Protection: Toward a New Discourse." *Washington and Lee Law Review* 11 (2000): 11–73.

Dorman, Robert L. *A Word for Nature: Four Pioneering Environmental Advocates, 1845–1913*. Chapel Hill: U of North Carolina P, 1998.

Doughty, Robin W. *Feather Fashions and Bird Preservation: A Study in Nature Protection*. Berkeley: U of California P, 1975.

Dowie, Mark. *Losing Ground: American Environmentalism at the Close of the Twentieth Century*. Cambridge, Mass.: MIT Press, 1995.

Downing, Andrew Jackson. *The Architecture of Country Houses*. New York: Appleton, 1850.

——. *Rural Essays*. Ed. George William Curtis. 1853. New York: DaCapo, 1974.

——. *Treatise on the Theory and Practice of Landscape Gardening*. New York: Wiley and Putnam, 1841.

Dryzek, John S. *The Politics of the Earth: Environmental Discourses*. New York: Oxford UP, 1997.

Duncan, David James. "Nonfiction = Fiction." *Orion* (summer 1996): 55–57.

Dunlap, Thomas R. "Conservationists and Environmentalists: An Attempt at Definition." *Environmental Review* 4.1 (1980): 29–31.

——. *Saving America's Wildlife*. Princeton, N.J.: Princeton UP, 1988.

——. "Sport Hunting and Conservation, 1880–1920." *Environmental Review* 12.1 (spring 1988): 51–60.

Dutcher, William. "History of the Audubon Movement." *Bird-Lore* 7 (1905): 45–57.

——. "The National Association — Its Needs and Aims." *Bird-Lore* 7 (1905): 39–40.

Eagan, Sean P. "From Spikes to Bombs: The Rise of Eco-Terrorism." *Studies in Conflict and Terrorism* 19 (1996): 1–18.

Earle, Alice Morse. Rev. of *The Mountains of California*, by John Muir. *Dial* 18 (1895): 75–77.

——. *Old Time Gardens Newly Set Forth.* New York: Macmillan, 1901.

Eastlake, William. "A Note on Ed Abbey." Hepworth and McNamee 15–17.

Ebenreck, Sara. "Opening Pandora's Box: Imagination's Role in Environmental Ethics." *Environmental Ethics* 18 (1996): 3–18.

Ecological Society of America. Committee on the Preservation of Natural Conditions. *Preservation of Natural Conditions.* Springfield, Ill.: Ecological Society of America, 1922.

Ehrenfeld, David. *The Arrogance of Humanism.* New York: Oxford UP, 1978.

Ehrlich, Gretel. *Islands, the Universe, Home.* New York: Viking Penguin, 1991.

——. *John Muir: Nature's Visionary.* Washington, D.C.: National Geographic Society, 2000.

Ehrlich, Paul. *Human Natures: Genes, Cultures, and the Human Prospect.* Washington, D.C.: Island Press, 2000.

Eisenberg, Evan. *The Ecology of Eden.* New York: Knopf, 1998.

Elder, John. Introduction. Elder, *American Nature Writers* 1:xiii–xix.

——, ed. *American Nature Writers.* 2 vols. New York: Scribner's, 1996.

Elder, John, and Hertha D. Wong. "Introduction: A Trail of Stories." *Family of Earth and Sky: Indigenous Tales of Nature from Around the World.* Ed. John Elder and Hertha D. Wong. Boston: Beacon Press, 1994. 1–10.

Ellison, Lincoln. Letter to the Editor. *Journal of Forestry* 34 (1936): 448–50.

Elsbach, Kimberley D., and Robert I. Sutton. "Acquiring Organizational Legitimacy through Illegitimate Actions: A Marriage of Institutional and Impression Management Theories." *Academy of Management Journal* 35 (Oct. 1992): 699–738.

Emerson, Ralph Waldo. "The American Scholar." *Selected Essays.* Ed. Larzer Ziff. New York: Penguin, 1987. 83–105.

——. *Journals and Miscellaneous Notebooks.* Vol. 9 (1843–1847). Ed. Ralph H. Orth and Alfred R. Ferguson. Cambridge, Mass.: Harvard UP, 1971.

——. *Nature. Selected Essays.* Ed. Larzer Ziff. New York: Penguin, 1987. 35–82.

The Empire Strikes Back. Dir. Irvin Kershner. 20th Century Fox/Lucasfilm, 1980.

Engberg, Robert, ed. *John Muir Summering in the Sierra.* Madison: U of Wisconsin P, 1984.

Engberg, Robert, and Donald Wesling, eds. *John Muir to Yosemite and Beyond: Writings from the Years 1863 to 1875.* Madison: U of Wisconsin P, 1980.

Entrikin, J. Nicholas. *The Betweenness of Place: Towards a Geography of Modernity.* Baltimore: Johns Hopkins UP, 1991.

Erisman, Fred. "A Variant Text of *The Monkey Wrench Gang.*" *Western American Literature* 14 (fall 1979): 227–28.

——. "'Where We Plan to Go': The Southwest in Utopian Fiction." *Southwestern American Literature* 1 (Sept. 1971): 137–43.

Erp-Houtepen, Anne van. "The Etymological Origins of the Garden." *Journal of Garden History* 6 (1996): 227–31.

Estes, D. C. "The Rival Sporting Weeklies of William T. Porter and Thomas Bangs Thorpe." *American Journalism* 2 (1985): 135–43.

Ewart, Arthur W. "John Muir and Vertical Sauntering." Sally Miller, *John Muir* 42–62.

"Fairfield Country Day School, in Beautiful Historic Setting, Shuns 'Theories', Stresses Time-Tested Fundamentals in Teaching." *Bridgeport Sunday Post* 6 Apr. 1941, n.p. MOW Clippings File, BPL.

"Fairfield Estate with Big History Soon to be Sold." *New York Times* 13 Oct. 1913, n.p. MOW Clippings File, FHS.

Farnham, Thomas J. *The Oak Lawn Cemetery.* Fairfield, Conn.: Oak Lawn Cemetery Assoc., 1993.

Farquhar, Francis P. *History of the Sierra Nevada.* Berkeley: U of California P, 1965.

Featherstone, Mike, ed. *Cultural Theory and Cultural Change.* Newbury Park, Calif.: Sage, 1992.

Fiedler, Leslie A. *Love and Death in the American Novel.* 3d ed. New York: Stein and Day, 1982.

Fill, Alwin, and Peter Mühlhäusler, eds. *The Ecolinguistics Reader: Language, Ecology, and Environment.* New York: Continuum, 2001.

Fisher, Walter R. *Human Communication as Narration: Toward a Philosophy of Reason, Value, and Action.* Columbia: U of South Carolina P, 1987.

Fishman, Robert. *Bourgeois Utopias: The Rise and Fall of Suburbia.* New York: Basic, 1987.

Flader, Susan L. "Aldo Leopold and the Wilderness Idea." *Living Wilderness* 43.147 (Dec. 1979): 4–8.

——— . "Citizenry and the State in the Shaping of Environmental Policy." *Environmental History* 3 (1998): 8–24.

——— . "'Let the Fire Devil Have His Due': Aldo Leopold and the Conundrum of Wilderness Management." *Managing America's Enduring Wilderness Resource: Proceedings of the Conference, Minneapolis, Minnesota, September 11–17, 1989.* Ed. David W. Lime. St. Paul: Tourism Center, Minnesota Extension Service and Minnesota Agricultural Experiment Station, U of Minnesota, 1990. 88–95.

——— . "The River of the Mother of God: Introduction." *Wilderness* 54.192 (spring 1991): 18–22.

——— . *Thinking Like a Mountain: Aldo Leopold and the Evolution of an Ecological Attitude toward Deer, Wolves, and Forests.* 1974. Madison: U of Wisconsin P, 1994.

Fleck, Richard F. "John Muir's Transcendental Imagery." Sally Miller, *John Muir* 136–51.

Flint, Howard R. "Wasted Wilderness." *American Forests and Forest Life* 32.391 (July 1926): 407–10.

Foreman, Dave. "Around the Campfire." *Earth First! Journal* 5.4 (20 Mar. 1985): 2.

——— . *Confessions of an Eco-Warrior.* New York: Harmony Books, 1991.

——— . "Edward Abbey, 1927–1989." *Utne Reader* (July–Aug. 1989): 36–37.

——— . "More on Earth First! and *The Monkey Wrench Gang.*" *Environmental Ethics* 5 (1983): 95–96.

——— . "The Plowboy Interview: Dave Foreman: No Compromise in Defense of Mother Earth." *Mother Earth News* (Jan.–Feb. 1985): 17–22.

———. "Wilderness Areas for Real." Callicott and Nelson 395–407.

Foreman, Dave, and Bill Haywood [pseud.], eds. *Ecodefense: A Field Guide to Monkeywrenching.* 2d ed. Tucson: Ned Ludd Books, 1987.

Foucault, Michel. *The Archaeology of Knowledge.* Trans A. M. Sheridan Smith. New York: Pantheon, 1972.

Fowler, Alastair. *Kinds of Literature: An Introduction to the Theory of Genres and Modes.* Cambridge, Mass.: Harvard UP, 1982.

Fox, Stephen. *John Muir and His Legacy: The American Conservation Movement.* Boston: Little, Brown, 1981.

———. "'We Want No Straddlers.'" *Wilderness* 48.167 (winter 1984): 4–19.

Frankiel, Sandra Sizer. *California's Spiritual Frontiers: Religious Alternatives to Anglo-Protestantism, 1850–1910.* Berkeley: U of California P, 1988.

Freedman, Aviva, and Peter Medway, eds. *Genre and the New Rhetoric.* London: Taylor and Francis, 1994.

———. *Learning and Teaching Genre.* Portsmouth, N.H.: Boynton/Cook, 1994.

French, Stanley. "The Cemetery as Cultural Institution: The Establishment of Mount Auburn and the 'Rural Cemetery' Movement." *American Quarterly* 26 (1974): 37–59.

Rev. of *The Friendship of Nature,* by Mabel Osgood Wright. *Dial* 17 (16 Sept. 1894): 159.

Fritzell, Peter A. "Aldo Leopold." Elder, *American Nature Writers* 1:525–47.

———. *Nature Writing and America: Essays upon a Cultural Type.* Ames: Iowa State UP, 1990.

Gamson, William A., Bruce Fireman, and Steven Rytina. *Encounters with Unjust Authority.* Homewood, Ill.: Dorsey Press, 1982.

Gare, Arran. "MacIntyre, Narratives, and Environmental Ethics." *Environmental Ethics* 20 (1998): 3–21.

Gibbons, Felton, and Deborah Strom. *Neighbors to the Birds: A History of Birdwatching in America.* New York: Norton, 1988.

Gibbons, Whit. *Keeping All the Pieces: Perspectives on Natural History and the Environment.* Washington: Smithsonian Institution P, 1993.

Gibbs, Lois Marie. *Love Canal: My Story.* Albany: SUNY P, 1982.

Gilliam, Ann, ed. *Voices for the Earth: A Treasury of the Sierra Club Bulletin.* Intro. Hal Gilliam. San Francisco: Sierra Club Books, 1979.

Gilliam, Harold. Introduction. A. Gilliam xvii–xxi.

Gilligan, Carol. *In a Different Voice: Psychological Theory and Women's Development.* Cambridge, Mass.: Harvard UP, 1982.

Gilligan, James P. "The Development of Policy and Administration of Forest Service Primitive and Wilderness Areas in the Western United States." Diss. U of Michigan, 1954. 2 vols.

Gillis, John R. "Places Remote and Islanded." *Michigan Quarterly Review* 40.1 (winter 2001): 39–58.

Ginsberg, Allen. *Airplane Dreams: Compositions from Journals.* Toronto: Anansi, 1968.

Gisel, Bonnie Johanna, ed. *Kindred and Related Spirits: The Letters of John Muir and Jeanne C. Carr.* Foreword by Ronald Limbaugh. Salt Lake City: U of Utah P, 2001.

Gissing, George. *The Whirlpool.* Ed. William Greenslade. 1897. Boston: Tuttle Publishing, 1997.

Glotfelty, Cheryl, and Harold Fromm, eds. *The Ecocriticism Reader: Landmarks in Literary Ecology.* Athens: U of Georgia P, 1996.

Glover, Deborah N. "Some of My Memories about the Audubon Society, State of Connecticut." Typescript. July 1972. CAS Records, BMS.

Glover, H[elen]. W. *Report of the Secretary of the Audubon Soc. State of Connecticut.* Typescript. 1917–18. CAS Records, BMS.

Glover, James M. *A Wilderness Original: The Life of Bob Marshall.* Seattle: The Mountaineers, 1986.

"God's Ten Acres for the Feathered Friends of Men in Fairfield Bird Sanctuary." *Bridgeport Telegram* [?] n.d., n.p. CAS Records, BPL.

Goffman, Erving. *Frame Analysis: An Essay on the Organization of Experience.* Cambridge, Mass.: Harvard UP, 1974.

Golley, Frank B. *A History of the Ecosystem Concept in Ecology: More than the Sum of Its Parts.* New Haven: Yale UP, 1993.

Gottlieb, Robert. *Forcing the Spring: The Transformation of the American Environmental Movement.* Washington, D.C.: Island Press, 1993.

Gotliffe, Harvey. "Sunset Magazine." *Regional Interest Magazines of the United States.* Ed. Sam G. Riley and Gary W. Selnow. New York: Greenwood Press, 1991. 305–10.

Graber, Linda H. *Wilderness as Sacred Space.* Washington, D.C.: Association of American Geographers, 1976.

Graham, Frank, Jr. *The Audubon Ark: A History of the National Audubon Society.* New York: Knopf, 1990.

Grant, Madison. *The Passing of the Great Race.* New York: Scribner's, 1916.

Greeley, Horace. *An Overland Journey from New York to San Francisco in the Summer of 1859.* New York: C. M. Saxton, Barker, 1860.

Greene, Jack P. *The Intellectual Construction of America: Exceptionalism and Identity from 1492 to 1800.* Chapel Hill: U of North Carolina P, 1993.

Greene, Linda Wedel. *Historic Resource Study: Yosemite: The Park and Its Resources: A History of the Discovery, Management, and Physical Development of Yosemite National Park, California.* 3 vols. Washington, D.C.: U.S. Department of the Interior, National Park Service, 1987.

Greiner, Patricia. "Radical Environmentalism in Recent Literature Concerning the American West." *Rendezvous* 19.1 (fall 1983): 8–15.

Grinnell, George Bird. "The Audubon Society." *Forest and Stream* 26 (1886): 41.

[———.] "The Boone and Crockett Club." *Forest and Stream* 31 (1889): 513.

[———.] "Boone and Crockett Club Meeting." *Forest and Stream* 36 (1891): 3.

———. "Brief History of the Boone and Crockett Club." *Hunting at High Altitudes.* Ed. George Bird Grinnell. New York: Harper and Brothers, 1913. 435–91.

[———.] "Game Protection Fund." *Forest and Stream* 20 (1884): 301.

[———.] "Hunting Trips of a Ranchman." Rev. of *Hunting Trips of a Ranchman,* by Theodore Roosevelt. *Forest and Stream* 24 (1885): 451.

———. "The Last of the Buffalo." *Scribner's Magazine* 12 (1892): 267–86.

[———.] "The Park Bill Hearing." *Forest and Stream* 34 (1890): 207.

[——.] "President Roosevelt as a Sportsman." *Forest and Stream* 61 (1903): 437.

[——.] "Snap Shots." *Forest and Stream* 30 (1888): 61.

[——.] "Snap Shots." *Forest and Stream* 38 (1892): 245.

Grinnell, George Bird, and Theodore Roosevelt, eds. *American Big-Game Hunting: The Book of the Boone and Crockett Club.* New York: Forest and Stream Publishing, 1893.

——. *Hunting in Many Lands: The Book of the Boone and Crockett Club.* New York: Forest and Stream Publishing, 1895.

——. *Trail and Camp-Fire: The Book of the Boone and Crockett Club.* New York: Forest and Stream Publishing, 1897.

Grove, Richard H. *Green Imperialism: Colonial Expansion, Tropical Island Edens, and the Origins of Environmentalism, 1600–1860.* New York: Cambridge UP, 1995.

Grumbine, R. Edward. *Ghost Bears: Exploring the Biodiversity Crisis.* Foreword by Michael E. Soulé. Washington, D.C.: Island Press, 1992.

——. "Using Biodiversity as a Justification for Nature Protection in the U.S." *Wild Earth* 6.4 (winter 1996–97): 71–80.

——. "Wild and Sustainable Uses: Revisioning Wilderness." *Wild Ideas.* Ed. David Rothenberg. Minneapolis: U of Minnesota P, 1995. 3–25.

Hacker, Andrew. "Anarchism." *International Encyclopedia of the Social Sciences.* Ed. David Sills. 16 vols. New York: Macmillan and the Free Press, 1968. 1:283–85.

Hafen, Lyman, and Milo McCowan. *Edward Abbey: An Interview at Pack Creek Ranch.* Santa Fe, N.Mex.: Vinegar Tom Press, 1991.

Hagedorn, Hermann. *Roosevelt in the Bad Lands.* New York: Houghton Mifflin, 1921.

Hagen, Joel B. *An Entangled Bank: The Origins of Ecosystem Ecology.* New Brunswick, N.J.: Rutgers UP, 1992.

Hallock, Charles. "Announcement." *Forest and Stream* 1 (1873): 8.

Halpern, Daniel, ed. *On Nature: Nature, Landscape, and Natural History.* San Francisco: North Point, 1987.

Handlin, David P. *The American Home: Architecture and Society, 1815–1915.* Boston: Little, Brown, 1979.

Hannabuss, Stuart. "Islands as Metaphors." *Universities Quarterly* 38.1 (winter 1983–84): 70–82.

[Hargrove, Eugene.] "Ecological Sabotage: Pranks or Terrorism?" *Environmental Ethics* 4 (1982): 291–92.

Harré, Rom, Jens Brockmeier, and Peter Mühlhäusler. *Greenspeak: A Study of Environmental Discourse.* Thousand Oaks, Calif.: Sage, 1999.

Harris, Neil. *The Artist in American Society: The Formative Years, 1790–1860.* 1966. Chicago: U of Chicago P, 1982.

Hart, Albert Bushnell, and Herbert Ronald Perleger, eds. *Theodore Roosevelt Encyclopedia.* New York: Theodore Roosevelt Association, 1941.

Hawkes, Terence. *Metaphor.* London: Methuen, 1972.

Hay, Peter. *Main Currents in Western Environmental Thought.* Bloomington: Indiana UP, 2002.

Hayden, Dolores. *The Grand Domestic Revolution: A History of Feminist Designs for American Homes, Neighborhoods, and Cities.* Cambridge, Mass.: MIT Press, 1981.

Hays, Samuel P. "From Conservation to Environment." *Beauty, Health, and Permanence: Environmental Politics in the United States, 1955–1985.* New York: Cambridge UP, 1987. 13–39.

Hedrick, U. P. *A History of Horticulture in America to 1860.* New York: Oxford UP, 1950.

Heimert, Alan. "Puritanism, the Wilderness, and the Frontier." *New England Quarterly* 26 (1953): 361–82.

Hepworth, James R. *"Canis Lupus Amorus Lunaticum."* Hepworth and McNamee 113–37.

———. "The Poetry Center Interview." Hepworth and McNamee 48–60.

Hepworth, James R., and Gregory McNamee. *Resist Much, Obey Little: Remembering Ed Abbey.* San Francisco: Sierra Club Books, 1996.

Herndl, Carl G., and Stuart C. Brown, eds. *Green Culture: Environmental Rhetoric in Contemporary America.* Madison: U of Wisconsin P, 1996.

Hettinger, Ned. "Environmental Disobedience." Jamieson 498–509.

Hoagland, Edward. "Edward Abbey: Standing Tough in the Desert." *New York Times Book Review* 7 May 1989, 44–45.

Holm, Bill. *Eccentric Islands: Travels Real and Imaginary.* Minneapolis: Milkweed Editions, 2000.

Holmes, Steven J. *The Young John Muir: An Environmental Biography.* Madison: U of Wisconsin P, 1999.

Hornblower, Margo. "A Clash of Values: Old and New at War amid Burnt Cliffs." *Washington Post* 31 Dec. 1979, A3.

House, Edward M. *Philip Dru: Administrator.* 1920. Upper Saddle River, N.J.: Gregg Press, 1969.

Howells, William Dean. "Criticism and Fiction." *American Thought and Writing: The 1890s.* Ed. Donald Pizer. New York: Houghton Mifflin, 1972. 69–77.

Huggard, Christopher J. "America's First Wilderness Area: Aldo Leopold, the Forest Service, and the Gila of New Mexico, 1924–1980." *Forests under Fire: A Century of Ecosystem Mismanagement in the Southwest.* Ed. Christopher J. Huggard and Arthur R. Gómez. Tucson: U of Arizona P, 2001. 133–79.

Hughes, Arthur H., and Morse S. Allen. *Connecticut Place Names.* Hartford: Connecticut Historical Society, 1976.

Hughes, J. Donald. "Ripples in Clio's Pond." *Capitalism Nature Socialism* 12 (2001): 119–24.

Hunt, John Dixon. *Greater Perfections: The Practice of Garden Theory.* Philadelphia: U of Pennsylvania P, 2000.

Rev. of *Hunting in Many Lands,* ed. George Bird Grinnell and Theodore Roosevelt. *Nation* 62 (1896): 314.

Rev. of *Hunting Trips of a Ranchman,* by Theodore Roosevelt. *Spectator* (16 Jan. 1886): 82–84.

Hurd, D. Hamilton, ed. *History of Fairfield County, Connecticut.* Philadelphia: J. W. Lewis, 1881.

Huser, Verne. *Voices from a Sacred Place: In Defense of Petroglyph National Monument.* N.p: Artcraft Printing, 1998.

Hutchings, James Mason. *Scenes of Wonder and Curiosity in California.* San Francisco: Hutchings and Rosenfield, 1860.

Huth, Hans. *Nature and the American: Three Centuries of Changing Attitudes.* 1957. Lincoln: U of Nebraska P, 1990.

———. "Yosemite: The Story of an Idea." *SCB* 33.3 (Mar. 1948): 47–78.

Huxley, Aldous. *Ape and Essence.* New York: Harper and Brothers, 1948.

———. *Brave New World.* New York: Modern Library, 1946.

———. *Island: A Novel.* New York: Harper and Row, 1962.

Huxley, Anthony Julian. *An Illustrated History of Gardening.* New York: Paddington, 1978.

Hyams, Edward. *A History of Gardens and Gardening.* New York: Praeger, 1971.

Hyde, Anne F. "From Stagecoach to Packard Twin Six: Yosemite and the Changing Face of Tourism, 1880–1930." *California History* 69.2 (summer 1990): 154–69.

———. "Temples and Playgrounds: The Sierra Club in the Wilderness, 1901–1922." *California History* 66 (1987): 208–36.

Ingram, Helen M., and Dean E. Mann. "Interest Groups and Environmental Policy." *Environmental Politics and Policy: Theories and Evidence.* Ed. James P. Lester. Durham, N.C.: Duke UP, 1989. 135–57.

Ise, John. *Our National Park Policy: A Critical History.* Baltimore: Johns Hopkins UP, 1961.

Jackson, Helen Hunt. *A Century of Dishonor: A Sketch of the United States Government's Dealings with Some of the Indian Tribes.* New York: Harper and Brothers, 1881.

Jackson, John Brinckerhoff. *American Space: The Centennial Years, 1865–1876.* New York: Norton, 1972.

Jackson, Kenneth T. *Crabgrass Frontier: The Suburbanization of the United States.* New York: Oxford UP, 1985.

Jackson, Wes. "Natural Systems Agriculture: The Truly Radical Alternative." *Recovering the Prairie.* Ed. Robert F. Sayre. Madison: U of Wisconsin P, 1999. 191–99.

Jakle, John A. *The Tourist: Travel in Twentieth-Century North America.* Lincoln: U of Nebraska P, 1985.

James, Harlean. *Land Planning in the United States for the City, State, and Nation.* New York: Macmillan, 1926.

James, William. *The Varieties of Religious Experience: A Study in Human Nature.* Intro. Reinhold Niebuhr. New York: Macmillan, 1961.

Jamieson, Dale, ed. *A Companion to Environmental Philosophy.* Malden, Mass.: Blackwell, 2001.

Jeffers, Robinson. *Cawdor and Other Poems.* New York: Horace Liveright, 1928.

———. *The Double Axe and Other Poems.* New York: Random House, 1948.

[Johnson, G. R.] "The Writings of Theodore Roosevelt." *Book Buyer* 18.1 (1899): 5–9.

Johnson, Josephine W. *The Inland Island.* New York: Simon and Schuster, 1969.

Johnson, Mark. *The Body in the Mind: The Bodily Basis of Meaning, Imagination, and Reason.* Chicago: U of Chicago P, 1987.

———. *Moral Imagination: Implications of Cognitive Science for Ethics.* Chicago: U of Chicago P, 1993.

Johnson, Robert Underwood. "John Muir as I Knew Him," *SCB* 10 (1916): 9–15.

———. "Personal Impressions of John Muir." *Outlook* 80 (1905): 303–6.

———. *Remembered Yesterdays.* Boston: Little, Brown, 1923.

Johnson, Steven. *Emergence: The Connected Lives of Ants, Cities, Brains, and Software.* New York: Scribner, 2001.

Johnston, Frances Benjamin. "What a Woman Can Do with a Camera." *Ladies Home Journal* (Sept. 1887): 6–7.

Joint Committee on Recreational Survey of Federal Lands. *Recreation Resources of Federal Lands.* Washington, D.C.: National Conference on Outdoor Recreation, 1928.

Jones, Holway R. *John Muir and the Sierra Club: The Battle for Yosemite.* San Francisco: Sierra Club, 1965.

———. "John Muir, the Sierra Club, and the Formulation of the Wilderness Concept." *Pacific Historian* 25.2 (summer 1981): 64–78.

Jouvenel, Bertrand de. "Utopia for Practical Purposes." Manuel, *Utopias and Utopian Thought* 219–35.

Kane, Joe. "Mother Nature's Army: Guerrilla Warfare Comes to the American Forest." *Esquire* Feb. 1987, 98+.

Karr, Alphonse. *A Tour Round My Garden.* Ed. J. G. Wood. New York: Routledge, 1855.

Kastner, Joseph. *A World of Watchers.* New York: Knopf, 1986.

Kaufmann, Elizabeth. "Earth-Saving: Here Is a Gang of Real Environmental Extremists." *Audubon* (July 1982): 116–20.

Keller, Evelyn Fox. *Refiguring Life: Metaphors of Twentieth-Century Biology.* New York: Columbia UP, 1995.

Kellert, Stephen R. *The Value of Life: Biological Diversity and Human Society.* Washington, D.C.: Island Press, 1996.

Kelley, Mary. *Private Woman, Public Stage: Literary Domesticity in Nineteenth-Century America.* New York: Oxford, 1984.

Kempton, Willett, James S. Boster, and Jennifer A. Hartley. *Environmental Values in American Culture.* Cambridge, Mass.: MIT Press, 1995.

Kennedy, Eugene. "Earthrise: The Dawning of a New Spiritual Awareness." *New York Times Magazine* 15 Apr. 1979, 14+.

Kerber, Linda K. "Separate Spheres, Female Worlds, Women's Place: The Rhetoric of Women's History." *Journal of American History* 75 (1988): 9–39.

Killingsworth, M. Jimmie. "Realism, Human Action, and Instrumental Discourse." *Journal of Advanced Composition* 12 (1992): 171–200.

Killingsworth, M. Jimmie, and Jacqueline S. Palmer. *Ecospeak: Rhetoric and Environmental Politics in America.* Carbondale: Southern Illinois UP, 1992.

Kimball, David, and Jim Kimball. *The Market Hunter.* Minneapolis: Dillon Press, 1969.

Kimes, William F., and Maymie B. Kimes. *John Muir: A Reading Bibliography.* Foreword by Lawrence Clark Powell. Palo Alto, Calif.: W. P. Wreden, 1977.

King, Roger J. H. "Caring about Nature: Feminist Ethics and the Environment." *Hypatia* 6.1 (spring 1991): 75–89.

———. "How to Construe Nature: Environmental Ethics and the Interpretation of Nature." *Between the Species* 6 (1990): 101–8.

———. "Narrative, Imagination, and the Search for Intelligibility in Environmental Ethics." *Ethics and the Environment* 4.1 (1999): 23–38.

Klein, Marcus. *Easterns, Westerns, and Private Eyes: American Matters, 1870–1900.* Madison: U of Wisconsin P, 1994.

Kniepp, Leon F. "What Shall We Call Protected Recreation Areas in the National Forests?" *American Planning and Civic Annual* 1 (1929): 34–36.

Knight, C. P. "About Road Hogs and Gentlemen: Experiences of a Motorist with Human Nature on Desert Trails." *Sunset* 54.3 (Mar. 1925): 49+.

Knott, John R. "Edward Abbey and the Romance of Wilderness." *Western American Literature* 30 (1996): 331–51.

Kolb, Harold H., Jr., *The Illusion of Life: American Realism as a Literary Form.* Charlottesville: UP of Virginia, 1969.

Kolodny, Annette. *The Lay of the Land: Metaphor as Experience and History in American Life and Letters.* Chapel Hill: U of North Carolina P, 1975.

Kraft, Michael E., and Diana Wuertz. "Environmental Advocacy in the Corridors of Government." *The Symbolic Earth: Discourse and the Creation of Our Environment.* Ed. James G. Cantrill and Christine L. Oravec. Lexington: UP of Kentucky, 1996. 95–122.

Kress, Stephen W. *The Audubon Society Guide to Attracting Birds.* New York: Scribner's, 1985.

Krutch, Joseph Wood. Prologue. *Great American Nature Writing.* New York: William Sloane Associates, 1950. 1–70.

Lakoff, George, and Mark Johnson. *Metaphors We Live By.* Chicago: U of Chicago P, 1980.

——. *Philosophy in the Flesh: The Embodied Mind and Its Challenge to Western Thought.* New York: Basic Books, 1999.

Lang, Lincoln A. *Ranching with Roosevelt.* Philadelphia: Lippincott, 1926.

Laughlin, Josh. "Livin' Like a Griz: An Interview with Doug Peacock." *Earth First! Journal* 21.1 (1 Nov. 2000): 32–33, 100–101.

Lawrence, D. H. *Studies in Classic American Literature.* 1923. New York: Penguin, 1977.

Leach, Mrs. Robert, and Mrs. John Field. *History of the Fairfield Garden Club, 1915–1948.* Fairfield, Conn.: Fairfield Garden Club, 1948.

Leahy, Christopher W., John Hanson Mitchell, and Thomas Conuel. *The Nature of Massachusetts.* Reading, Mass.: Addison-Wesley, 1996.

Lears, T. J. Jackson. "From Salvation to Self-Realization: Advertising and the Therapeutic Roots of the Consumer Culture, 1880–1930." *The Culture of Consumption: Critical Essays in American History, 1880–1980.* Ed. Richard Wightman Fox and T. J. Jackson Lears. New York: Pantheon, 1983. 1–38.

LeConte, Joseph. *A Journal of Ramblings through the High Sierra of California by the University Excursion Party.* 1875. San Francisco: Sierra Club, 1960.

Lee, Martha F. *Earth First! Environmental Apocalypse.* New York: Syracuse UP, 1995.

——. "Environmental Apocalypse: The Millennial Ideology of 'Earth First!'" *Millennium, Messiahs, and Mayhem: Contemporary Apocalyptic Movements.* Ed. Thomas Robbins and Susan J. Palmer. New York: Routledge, 1997. 119–37.

——. "Violence and the Environment: The Case of Earth First!" *Terrorism and Political Violence* 7.3 (1995): 107–27.

LeGuin, Ursula K. *The Dispossessed: An Ambiguous Utopia.* New York: Harper and Row, 1974.

Leighton, Ann. *American Gardens in the Eighteenth Century: "For Use or for Delight."* Boston: Houghton Mifflin, 1976.

———. *American Gardens of the Nineteenth Century: "For Comfort and Affluence."* Amherst: U of Massachusetts P, 1987.

———. *Early American Gardens: "For Meate or Medicine."* Amherst: U of Massachusetts P, 1970.

Lentfer, Hank, and Carolyn Servid, eds. *Arctic Refuge: A Circle of Testimony.* Minneapolis: Milkweed Editions, 2001.

Leopold, Aldo. "Comment." *American Forests and Forest Life* 32.391 (July 1926): 410–11.

———. "Deer and *Dauerwald* in Germany: I. History; II. Ecology and Policy." *Journal of Forestry* 34.4 and 34.5 (Apr. and May 1936): 366–75, 460–66.

———. Foreword (1947). Callicott, *Companion* 281–88.

———. *For the Health of the Land: Previously Unpublished Essays and Other Writings.* Ed. J. Baird Callicott and Eric T. Freyfogle. Washington, D.C.: Island Press, 1999.

———. "Game Conservation: A Warning, also an Opportunity," *Arizona* 7.12 (Dec. 1916): 6.

———. *Game Management.* Drawings by Allan Brooks. New York: Charles Scribner's Sons, 1933.

———. "The Last Stand." *Living Wilderness* 7.8 (Dec. 1942): 25–26.

———. "The Last Stand of American Wilderness." *American Forests and Forest Life* 31.382 (Oct. 1925): 599–604.

———. Letter to the Editor. *Journal of Forestry* 34 (1936): 446.

———. "*Naturschutz* in Germany." *Bird-Lore* 38.2 (Mar.–Apr. 1936): 102–11.

———. "Origin and Ideals of Wilderness Areas." *Living Wilderness* 5 (July 1940): 7.

———. *The River of the Mother of God and Other Essays.* Ed. Susan L. Flader and J. Baird Callicott. Madison: U of Wisconsin P, 1991.

———. *Round River: From the Journals of Aldo Leopold.* Ed. Luna B. Leopold. Illus. Charles W. Schwartz. New York: Oxford UP, 1953.

———. *A Sand County Almanac, and Sketches Here and There.* Illus. Charles W. Schwartz. New York: Oxford UP, 1949.

———. "Why the Wilderness Society?" *Living Wilderness* 1 (Sept. 1935): 6.

———. "Wilderness Values." *Living Wilderness* 7.7 (Mar. 1942): 24–25.

Levitas, Ruth. *The Concept of Utopia.* New York: Philip Allan, 1990.

Lewis, Martin W. *Green Delusions: An Environmentalist Critique of Radical Environmentalism.* Durham, N.C.: Duke UP, 1992.

Lewis, R. W. B. *The American Adam: Innocence, Tragedy, and Tradition in the Nineteenth Century.* Chicago: U of Chicago P, 1955.

Lichtenstein, Grace. "The Desert Fox." Rev. of *Hayduke Lives!* by Edward Abbey. *Washington Post Book World* 28 Jan. 1990, 5.

———. "Edward Abbey, Voice of Southwest Wilds." *New York Times* 20 Jan. 1976, 24.

"The Life Out of Doors." Rev. of *The Friendship of Nature*, by Mabel Osgood Wright. *New York Times* 28 May 1894, 3.

Lillard, Richard G. "The Siege and Conquest of a National Park." *American West* 5.1 (Jan. 1968): 28–32, 67–72.

Limbaugh, Ronald H. "The Nature of John Muir's Religion." *Pacific Historian* 29.2–3 (summer–fall 1985): 16–29.

——. "Stickeen and the Moral Education of John Muir." *Environmental History Review* 15.1 (spring 1991): 25–45.

Limerick, Patricia Nelson. *The Legacy of Conquest: The Unbroken Past of the American West.* New York: Norton, 1987.

Line, Les, ed. *The National Audubon Society: Speaking for Nature: A Century of Conservation.* Southport, Conn.: Hugh Lauter Levin Associates, 1999.

Little, Charles E. "Books for the Wilderness." *Wilderness* (summer 1988): 56–61.

Livingston, John A. *The Fallacy of Wildlife Conservation.* Toronto: McClelland and Stewart, 1981.

Lodge, David. "Utopia and Criticism: The Radical Longing for Paradise." *Encounter* 32 (Apr. 1969): 65–75.

Loeffler, Jack. *Adventures with Ed: A Portrait of Abbey.* Albuquerque: U of New Mexico P, 2002.

——. "Edward Abbey, Anarchism, and the Environment." Hepworth and McNamee 31–39.

——. *Headed Upstream: Interviews with Iconoclasts.* Tucson: Harbinger House, 1989.

Lomborg, Bjørn. *The Skeptical Environmentalist: Measuring the Real State of the World.* New York: Cambridge UP, 2001.

Lonely Are the Brave. Dir. David Miller. Universal Pictures, 1962.

Lopate, Phillip. Introduction. *The Art of the Personal Essay: An Anthology from the Classical Era to the Present.* New York: Anchor, 1994.

Lopez, Barry. "Searching for Ancestors." *Crossing Open Ground.* New York: Scribner, 1988. 165–80.

Lopez, Barry, et al. "Natural History: An Annotated Booklist." Halpern 283–97.

Lorbiecki, Marybeth. *Aldo Leopold: A Fierce Green Fire.* New York: Oxford UP, 1996.

Loudon, Jane Webb. *Gardening for Ladies.* Ed. A. J. Downing. New York: Wiley and Putnam, 1843.

Loudon, John Claudius. *Encyclopaedia of Cottage, Farm, and Villa Architecture and Furniture.* London: Longman, 1833.

"The Lounger." *Critic* 48 (1906): 291–308.

Louter, David. "Glaciers and Gasoline: The Making of a Windshield Wilderness, 1900–1915." *Seeing and Being Seen: Tourism in the American West.* Ed. David M. Wrobel and Patrick T. Long. Foreword by Earl Pomeroy. Lawrence: UP of Kansas, 2001. 248–70.

Love, Sam. "Maverick Raiders." *Progressive* 40.7 (July 1976): 43–44.

Love, Sam, and David Obst, eds. *Ecotage.* Foreword by Robert Townsend. New York: Pocket Books, 1972.

Loxley, Diana. *Problematic Shores: The Literature of Islands.* New York: St. Martin's, 1990.

Lucas, Susan M. "Counter Frictions: Writing and Activism in the Work of Abbey and Thoreau." *Thoreau's Sense of Place: Essays in American Environmental Writing.* Ed. Richard J. Schneider. Foreword by Lawrence Buell. Iowa City: U of Iowa P, 2000. 266–79.

Luhmann, Niklas. *Ecological Communication.* Trans. John Bednarz Jr. Chicago: U of Chicago P, 1989.

Luke, Timothy W. "The Wilderness Society: Environmentalism as Environationalism." *Capitalism, Nature, Socialism* 10.3 (Dec. 1999): 1–35.

Lutts, Ralph H. *The Nature Fakers: Wildlife, Science, and Sentiment.* Golden, Colo.: Fulcrum, 1990.

——, ed. *The Wild Animal Story.* Philadelphia: Temple UP, 1998.

Lynch, Tom. "Nativity, Domesticity, and Exile in Edward Abbey's 'One True Home.'" Quigley 88–105.

Lyon, Thomas J. *John Muir.* Boise, Idaho.: Boise State College, 1972.

——. "John Muir's Enlightenment." *Pacific Historian* 25.2 (summer 1981): 50–57.

——. "Nature Writing as a Subversive Activity." *North Dakota Quarterly* 59.2 (spring 1991): 6–16.

——, ed. *This Incomperable Lande: A Book of American Nature Writing.* Boston: Houghton Mifflin, 1989.

"Mabel Osgood Wright Recalls Pleasures of a Busy Literary Life." *Bridgeport Sunday Post* 8 Mar. 1925, n.p. MOW Clippings File, FHS.

MacArthur, Robert H., and Edward O. Wilson. *The Theory of Island Biogeography.* Princeton, N.J.: Princeton UP, 1967.

MacIntyre, Alasdair C. *After Virtue: A Study in Moral Theory.* 2d ed. Notre Dame, Ind.: U of Notre Dame P, 1984.

MacKaye, Benton. "Flankline vs. Skyline." *Appalachia* 20 (1934–35): 104–9.

——. *The New Exploration: A Philosophy of Regional Planning.* Intro. Lewis Mumford. Urbana: U of Illinois P, 1962.

MacKaye, Percy. *Sanctuary: A Bird Masque.* New York: Frederick A. Stokes, 1914.

Mailer, Norman. *The Armies of the Night: History as a Novel, the Novel as History.* New York: New American Library, 1968.

Major, Judith K. *To Live in the New World: A. J. Downing and American Landscape Gardening.* Cambridge, Mass.: MIT Press, 1997.

Malanowski, Jamie. "Monkey-Wrenching Around." *Nation* (2 May 1987): 568–70.

Manes, Christopher. *Green Rage: Radical Environmentalism and the Unmaking of Civilization.* Boston: Little, Brown, 1990.

——. "Nature and Silence." *Environmental Ethics* 14 (1992): 339–50.

Mannheim, Karl. *Ideology and Utopia: An Introduction to the Sociology of Knowledge.* 1929. New York: Harcourt, Brace, and World, 1968.

——. "Utopia." *Encyclopaedia of the Social Sciences.* Ed. Edwin R. A. Seligman; associate ed. Alvin Johnson. 15 vols. New York: Macmillan, 1930–35. 15:200–203.

Manuel, Frank E. "Toward a Psychological History of Utopias." Manuel, *Utopias and Utopian Thought* 69–98.

——, ed. *Utopias and Utopian Thought.* Boston: Houghton Mifflin, 1966.

Manuel, Frank E., and Fritzie P. Manuel. *Utopian Thought in the Western World.* Cambridge, Mass.: Harvard UP, 1979.

Marble, Annie Russell. "Mabel Osgood Wright—A Lover of Birds." *Boston Evening Transcript* 11 Dec. 1926, n.p. MOW Vertical File, FHS.

Marsh, George Perkins. *Man and Nature*. Ed. David Lowenthal. Cambridge, Mass.: Harvard UP, 1965.

Marsh, Margaret. *Suburban Lives*. New Brunswick, N.J.: Rutgers UP, 1990.

Marshall, George. "On Bob Marshall's Landmark Article." *Living Wilderness* 40.135 (Oct.–Dec. 1976): 28–30.

———. "The Wilderness Society's Council, 1935–1965." *Living Wilderness* (winter 1965–66): 25–26.

Marshall, Robert. Letter to the Editor. *Journal of Forestry* 34 (1936): 446–48.

———. "The Problem of the Wilderness." *Scientific Monthly* 30 (1930): 141–48.

Martin, Douglas. "James Phillips, 70, Environmentalist Who Was Called the Fox." *New York Times* 22 Oct. 2001, F6.

Martin, Michael. "Ecosabotage and Civil Disobedience." *Environmental Ethics* 12 (1990): 291–310.

Martin, Wallace. "Metaphor." *The New Princeton Encyclopedia of Poetry and Poetics*. Ed. Alex Preminger and T. V. F. Brogan. Princeton, N.J.: Princeton UP, 1993. 760–66.

Marx, Leo. *The Machine in the Garden: Technology and the Pastoral Ideal in America*. New York: Oxford UP, 1964.

Mathes, Valerie Sherer. "Theodore Roosevelt as a Naturalist and Bad Lands Rancher." *North Dakota History* 53.3 (summer 1986): 2–13.

Matthews, Albert. "The Word *Park* in the United States." *Publications of the Colonial Society of Massachusetts* 8 (1906): 373–99.

Matthews, Brander. *The Tocsin of Revolt and Other Essays*. New York: Scribner's, 1922.

Mattison, Ray H. "Roosevelt and the Stockman's Association." *North Dakota History* 17 (1950): 72–95, 177–209.

Maxcy, David J. "Meaning in Nature: Rhetoric, Phenomenology, and the Question of Environmental Value." *Philosophy and Rhetoric* 27.4 (1994): 330–46.

Mazel, David. *American Literary Environmentalism*. Athens: U of Georgia P, 2000.

———, ed. *A Century of Early Ecocriticism*. Athens: U of Georgia P, 2001.

McArdle, Richard E. "Wilderness Politics: Legislation and Forest Service Policy." *Journal of Forest History* 19 (Oct. 1975): 166–79.

McBride, Stewart. "The Real Monkey Wrench Gang: A Little Field Work with the Eco-Pranksters of Earth First!" *Outside* (Dec.–Jan. 1983): 34–38, 69–73.

McCann, Garth. *Edward Abbey*. Boise, Idaho: Boise State U, 1979.

McCauley, Lena May. *The Joy of Gardens*. Chicago: Rand McNally, 1911.

McCormick, Richard L. "Public Life in Industrial America, 1877–1917." *The New American History*. Ed. Eric Foner. Philadelphia: Temple UP, 1990.

McCullough, David. *Mornings on Horseback*. New York: Simon and Schuster, 1981.

McDowell, Michael J. "The Bakhtinian Road to Ecological Insight." Glotfelty and Fromm 371–91.

McFague, Sallie. *The Body of God: An Ecological Theology*. Minneapolis: Fortress, 1993.

———. *Metaphorical Theology: Models of God in Religious Language*. Philadelphia: Fortress, 1982.

McGregor, Robert Kuhn. *A Wider View of the Universe: Henry Thoreau's Study of Nature.* Urbana: U of Illinois P, 1997.

McKibben, Bill. "The Desert Anarchist." *New York Review of Books* 35 (18 Aug. 1988): 42–44.

———. *The End of Nature.* New York: Anchor Books, 1990.

———. "The Gleam of Open Sky." Rev. of *Hayduke Lives!* by Edward Abbey. *Hungry Mind Review* 14 (May–June 1990): 36.

McLeod, Christopher. *The Cracking of the Glen Canyon Damn [sic]: With Edward Abbey and Earth First!* La Honda, Calif.: Earth Image Films, [1981].

McNeill, John R. *Something New under the Sun: An Environmental History of the Twentieth-Century World.* New York: Norton, 2000.

Meffe, Gary K., C. Ronald Carroll, and Contributors. *Principles of Conservation Biology.* Sunderland, Mass.: Sinauer, 1997.

Meine, Curt. *Aldo Leopold: His Life and Work.* Madison: U of Wisconsin P, 1988.

———. "Moving Mountains: Aldo Leopold and *A Sand County Almanac.*" *Aldo Leopold and the Ecological Conscience.* Ed. Richard L. Knight and Suzanne Riedel. New York: Oxford UP, 2002. 14–31.

———. "Reimagining the Prairie: Aldo Leopold and the Origins of Prairie Restoration." *Recovering the Prairie.* Ed. Robert F. Sayre. Madison: U of Wisconsin P, 1999. 144–60.

———. "The Utility of Preservation and the Preservation of Utility: Leopold's Fine Line." *The Wilderness Condition: Essays on Environment and Civilization.* Ed. Max Oelschlaeger. Washington, D.C.: Island Press, 1992. 131–72.

Meine, Curt, and Richard L. Knight. Introduction. *The Essential Aldo Leopold: Quotations and Commentaries.* Ed. Curt Meine and Richard L. Knight. Madison: U of Wisconsin P, 1999. xiv–xix.

Meisner, Mark. "Metaphors of Nature: Old Vinegar in New Bottles?" *Trumpeter* 12.1 (1995): 11–18.

Melham, Tom, and Farrell Grehann. *John Muir's Wild America.* Washington, D.C.: National Geographic, 1976.

Merchant, Carolyn. "The Women of the Progressive Conservation Crusade: 1900–1915." *Environmental History: Critical Issues in Comparative Perspective.* Ed. Kendall E. Bailes. Lanham, Md.: UP of America, 1985. 153–75.

Merriam, C. Hart. Rev. of *Hunting in Many Lands,* ed. George Bird Grinnell and Theodore Roosevelt. *Science* n.s. 3 (1896): 246.

———. "Roosevelt, The Naturalist." *Science* 75 (12 Feb. 1932): 181–83.

Merrill, Samuel. "Personal Recollections of John Muir." *SCB* 13.1 (Feb. 1928): 24–30.

Meyer, John M. *Political Nature: Environmentalism and the Interpretation of Western Thought.* Cambridge, Mass.: MIT Press, 2001.

Meyer, Marvin W., ed. *The Nag Hammadi Library in English.* New York: Harper and Row, 1977.

Midgeley, Mary. *Animals and Why They Matter.* Athens: U of Georgia P, 1983.

———. "Duties Concerning Islands." *Environmental Philosophy: A Collection of Readings.* Ed. Robert Elliot and Arran Gare. New York: U of Queensland P, 1983. 166–81.

Mighetto, Lisa. *Wild Animals and American Environmental Ethics*. Tucson: U of Arizona P, 1991.

Milbourn, Todd. "In Wartime Climate, Legislators, FBI Target 'Eco-terrorism.'" *Star Tribune* (Minneapolis) 7 Apr. 2002, A10.

Mill, John Stuart. "Nature." *Essays on Ethics, Religion, and Society*. Ed. J. M. Robson. Intro. F. E. L. Priestley. Toronto: U of Toronto P, 1969.

Millard, Bailey. "A Skyland Philosopher." *Bookman* 26 (1908): 593–99.

Miller, Carolyn. "Genre as Social Action." *Quarterly Journal of Speech* 70 (1984): 151–67.

Miller, Olive Thorne [Harriet Mann]. *A Bird-Lover in the West*. New York: Houghton, Mifflin, 1894.

———. *Little Brothers of the Air*. New York: Houghton, Mifflin, 1892.

———. *The Woman's Club: A Practical Guide and Hand-book*. New York: United States Book Co., 1891.

Miller, Sally M., ed. *John Muir: Life and Work*. Albuquerque: U of New Mexico P, 1993.

Miller, Scott K. "Undamming Glen Canyon: Lunacy, Rationality, or Prophecy?" *Stanford Environmental Law Journal* 19.1 (Jan. 2000): 120–207.

Mitchell, John G. "A Man Called Bird." *Audubon* (Mar. 1987): 81–104.

Mitchell, Robert C. "From Conservation to Environmental Movement: The Development of the Modern Environmental Lobbies." *Government and Environmental Politics: Essays in Historical Developments since World War Two*. Ed. Michael J. Lacey. Washington, D.C.: Wilson Center Press, 1989. 81–113.

Mitchell, Robert C., Angela G. Mertig, and Riley E. Dunlap. "Twenty Years of Environmental Mobilization: Trends among National Environmental Organizations." *The U.S. Environmental Movement, 1970–1990*. Washington, D.C.: Taylor and Francis, 1992. 11–26.

Moeller, Madelyn Kay. "Ladies of Leisure: Domestic Photography in the Nineteenth Century." Master's thesis. U of Delaware, May 1989.

More, Thomas. *Utopia*. 1516. New Haven: Yale UP, 1966. Vol. 4 of *The Complete Works of St. Thomas More*. 21 vols. 1963–97.

Morison, Elting E., ed. *The Letters of Theodore Roosevelt*. Vol. 1. Cambridge, Mass.: Harvard UP, 1951. 8 vols.

Morris, David Copland. "Celebration and Irony: The Polyphonic Voice of Edward Abbey's *Desert Solitaire*." *Western American Literature* 28 (1993): 21–32.

Morris, Don. "Earth First! No Wimps." *Earth First! Journal* 7.7 (1 Aug. 1987): 19.

Morris, Edmund. *The Rise of Theodore Roosevelt*. New York: Ballantine Books, 1979.

———. *Theodore Rex*. New York: Random House, 2001.

———. "Theodore Roosevelt, the Polygon." *Theodore Roosevelt: Many-Sided American*. Ed. Natalie A. Naylor, Douglas Brinkley, and John Allen Gable. Interlaken, N.Y.: Heart of the Lakes Publishing, 1992. 25–32.

Morris, William. *News from Nowhere; or, An Epoch of Rest: Being Some Chapters from a Utopian Romance*. Ed. Krishan Kumar. New York: Cambridge UP, 1995.

Mott, Frank Luther. *A History of American Magazines*. 5 vols. Cambridge, Mass.: Harvard UP, 1938–68.

"A Mountain Enthusiast." Rev. of *The Mountains of California*, by John Muir. *Nation* 59 (1894): 366–67.

Rev. of *The Mountains of California*, by John Muir. *Athenaeum* 105 (1895): 77–78.

Moylan, Tom. *Demand the Impossible: Science Fiction and the Utopian Imagination.* New York: Methuen, 1986.

Muir, John. "Features of the Proposed Yosemite National Park." *Outlook* 40 (1890): 656–67.

——. *Letters to a Friend: Written to Mrs. Ezra S. Carr, 1866–1879.* 1915. Dunwoody, Ga.: Norman S. Berg, 1973.

——. Letter to the Editor. *Century* 49 (1895): 630–31.

——. "The National Parks and Forest Reservations." *SCB* 1.7 (Jan. 1896): 271–84.

——. *Nature Writings.* Ed. William Cronon. New York: Library of America, 1997.

——. *Our National Parks.* Foreword by Alfred Runte. 1901. San Francisco: Sierra Club Books, 1991.

——. *A Thousand-Mile Walk to the Gulf.* Foreword by Colin Fletcher. Intro. William Frederic Badè. 1916. San Francisco: Sierra Club Books, 1992.

——. "The Treasures of the Yosemite." *Century* 40 (1890): 483–500.

——. *The Yosemite.* Intro. Frederic R. Gunsky. 1912. New York: Doubleday, 1962.

——, ed. *Picturesque California.* New York: J. Dewing, 1888.

Muir, John, et al. "Statement Concerning the Proposed Recession of Yosemite Valley and Mariposa Big Tree Grove by the State of California to the United States." *SCB* 5.3 (Jan. 1905): 242–50.

Mumford, Lewis. *The Myth of the Machine.* 2 vols. New York: Harcourt, Brace, 1967–70.

——. *The Story of Utopias.* Intro. Hendrik Willem Van Loon. New York: Boni and Liveright, 1922.

——. "Utopia, the City, and the Machine." Manuel, *Utopias and Utopian Thought* 3–24.

Murie, Adolph. Letter to the Editor. *Journal of Forestry* 34 (1936): 641–43.

Murphy, Patrick D. *Farther Afield in the Study of Nature-Oriented Literature.* Charlottesville: UP of Virginia, 2000.

Murray, John A., et al. "The Rise of Nature Writing: America's Next Great Genre?" *Manoa* 4.2 (fall 1992): 73–96.

Nabhan, Gary. "Sierra Madre Upshot: Ecological and Agricultural Health." *Cultures of Habitat: On Nature, Culture, and Story.* Washington, D.C.: Counterpoint, 1997. 43–56.

Naess, Arne. "The Shallow and the Deep, Long-Range Ecology Movement: A Summary." *Inquiry* 16 (spring 1973): 95–100.

Nash, Roderick. "The American Invention of National Parks." *American Quarterly* 22 (1970): 726–35.

——. "Island Civilization: A Vision for Planet Earth in the Year 2992." *Wild Earth* 1.4 (winter 1991–92): 2–4.

——. *The Rights of Nature: A History of Environmental Ethics.* Madison: U of Wisconsin P, 1989.

——. *Wilderness and the American Mind.* 3d ed. New Haven: Yale UP, 1982.

National Conference on Outdoor Recreation. *Proceedings of the National Conference on Outdoor Recreation.* Washington, D.C.: GPO, 1926.

Negley, Glenn, and J. Max Patrick. *The Quest for Utopia: An Anthology of Imaginary Societies*. 1952. Garden City, N.Y.: Anchor Books, 1962.

Nelson, Michael P. "An Amalgamation of Wilderness Preservation Arguments." *The Great New Wilderness Debate*. Ed. J. Baird Callicott and Michael P. Nelson. Athens: U of Georgia P, 1998. 154–98.

Nelson, Richard. "Forest Home: Taking a Stand for Conservation and Community." *Orion* 16.3 (summer 1997): 58–63.

———. *The Island Within*. San Francisco: North Point Press, 1989.

Neuzil, Mark, and William Kovarik. "Specialized Media: *Forest and Stream* Magazine and the Redefinition of Hunting." *Mass Media and Environmental Conflict: America's Green Crusades*. By Mark Neuzil and William Kovarik. Thousand Oaks, Calif.: Sage, 1996. 1–32.

Newton, Adam Zachary. *Narrative Ethics*. Cambridge, Mass.: Harvard UP, 1995.

Nice, Margaret Morse. *Research Is a Passion with Me*. Toronto: Consolidated Amethyst Publications, 1979.

Niklaus, Phil. "Novelist Tore Down Billboards in Protest." *Albuquerque Journal* 18 Jan. 1976, E1.

Nixon, Will. "Natural Causes: Nature Writers' Pens Become Their Swords." *Taxi* 5.1 (Dec. 1989–Jan. 1990): 110–13.

Nobles, Gregory H. *American Frontiers: Cultural Encounters and Continental Conquest*. New York: Hill and Wang, 1997.

Nodier, Charles. *The Bibliomaniac*. Trans. Mabel Osgood Wright. New York: J. O. Wright, 1894.

Nollman, Jim. *Why We Garden: Cultivating a Sense of Place*. New York: Holt, 1994.

Norton, Aloysius A. *Theodore Roosevelt*. Boston: Twayne, 1980.

Norton, Bryan G. *Toward Unity among Environmentalists*. New York: Oxford UP, 1994.

Norwood, Vera. *Made from This Earth: American Women and Nature*. Chapel Hill: U of North Carolina P, 1993.

Noss, Reed F., and Allen Y. Cooperrider. *Saving Nature's Legacy: Protecting and Restoring Biodiversity*. Foreword by Rodger Schlickeisen. Washington, D.C.: Island Press, 1994.

Novak, Barbara. *Nature and Culture: American Landscape and Painting, 1825–1875*. Rev. ed. New York: Oxford, 1995.

Novak, Frank. Interview. Audiocassette. Oct. 1970. CAS Records, BPL.

Nussbaum, Martha C. *Love's Knowledge: Essays on Philosophy and Literature*. New York: Oxford UP, 1990.

Nutting, Wallace. *Connecticut Beautiful*. Framingham, Mass.: Old America, 1923.

Nye, Eric W., and Sheri I. Hoem, eds. "Big Game on the Editor's Desk: Roosevelt and Bierstadt's Tale of the Hunt." *William and Mary Quarterly* 60 (1987): 454–65.

Oakeshott, Michael. "The Voice of Poetry in the Conversation of Mankind." 1959. *Rationalism in Politics and Other Essays*. New ed. Foreword by Timothy Fuller. Indianapolis: Liberty Press, 1991.

Oates, David. *Earth Rising: Ecological Belief in an Age of Science*. Corvallis: Oregon State UP, 1989.

Oates, Joyce Carol. "Against Nature." Halpern 236–43.

Obituary of James O. Wright. *New York Times* 28 May 1920, 13.

Oelschlaeger, Max. *Caring for Creation: An Ecumenical Approach to the Environmental Crisis.* New Haven: Yale UP, 1994.

——. *The Idea of Wilderness: From Prehistory to the Age of Ecology.* New Haven: Yale UP, 1991.

——. "Taking the Land Ethic Outdoors: Its Implications for Recreation." *Wildlife and Recreationists: Coexistence through Management and Research.* Ed. Richard L. Knight and Kevin J. Gutzwiller. Washington, D.C.: Island Press, 1994. 335–50.

——. "Wilderness, Civilization, and Language." *The Wilderness Condition: Essays on Environment and Civilization.* Ed. Max Oelschlaeger. Washington, D.C.: Island Press, 1992. 271–308.

——, ed. *Postmodern Environmental Ethics.* Albany: SUNY P, 1995.

Ogden, Kate Nearpass. "Sublime Vistas and Scenic Backdrops: Nineteenth-Century Painters and Photographers at Yosemite." *California History* 69.2 (summer 1990): 134–53.

O'Grady, John P. *Pilgrims to the Wild: Everett Ruess, Henry David Thoreau, John Muir, Clarence King, Mary Austin.* Salt Lake City: U of Utah P, 1993.

Olmsted, Frederick Law. "The Yosemite Valley and the Mariposa Big Trees: A Preliminary Report." Introductory note by Laura Wood Roper. *Landscape Architecture* 43 (1952–53): 12–25.

Olwig, Kenneth R. "Reinventing Common Nature: Yosemite and Mount Rushmore — A Meandering Tale of a Double Nature." Cronon, *Uncommon Ground* 379–408.

"On Preserving Our 'Wildland Patches.'" *Living Wilderness* 13.27 (winter 1948–49): 11–14.

Oravec, Christine. "John Muir, Yosemite, and the Sublime Response: A Study in the Rhetoric of Preservationism." *Quarterly Journal of Speech* 67 (1981): 245–58.

Orr, Oliver H., Jr. *Saving American Birds: T. Gilbert Pearson and the Founding of the Audubon Movement.* Gainesville: UP of Florida, 1992.

Orsi, Richard J. "'Wilderness Saint' and 'Robber Baron': The Anomalous Partnership of John Muir and the Southern Pacific Company for Preservation of Yosemite National Park." *Pacific Historian* 25.2 (summer 1981): 136–56.

Ortega y Gasset, José. *The Revolt of the Masses.* London: Allen and Unwin, 1932.

Osborn, Henry Fairfield. *Impressions of Great Naturalists: Darwin, Wallace, Huxley, Leidy, Cope, Balfour, Roosevelt, and Others.* 2d ed. New York: Scribner's, 1928.

Osgood, Samuel. *Mile Stones in Our Life-Journey.* 1855. 3d ed. New York: Dutton, 1877.

Ostmann, Robert, Jr., "Guerrillas under Nature's Banner." Rev. of *The Monkey Wrench Gang,* by Edward Abbey. *Detroit Free Press* 21 Sept. 1975, n.p.

Rev. of *Our National Parks,* by John Muir. *Annals of the American Academy of Political and Social Science* 20 (1902): 419.

Rev. of *Our National Parks,* by John Muir. *Dial* 32 (1902): 163.

Rev. of *Our National Parks* (1909 ed.), by John Muir. *Dial* 47 (1909): 460–61.

Rev. of *Our National Parks,* by John Muir. *Nation* 74 (1902): 294–95.

"Outstanding Figures among Women of State in Last Half Century Named." *Bridgeport Post* 4 July 1926, n.p. MOW Vertical File, FHS.

Palmer, Theodore Sherman. *Bird Day in Schools.* U.S. Dept. of Agriculture, Div. of Biological Survey, Circular 17. Washington, D.C.: GPO, 1896.

———. *Chronology and Index of the More Important Events in American Game Protection, 1776–1911.* U.S. Dept. of Agriculture, Bureau of Biological Survey, Bulletin 41. Washington, D.C.: GPO, 1912.

Parshall, Gerald. "A Knight in the Wilderness: Sierra Club Founder John Muir Launched a Movement a Century Ago." *U.S. News and World Report* 20 July 1992, 57–58.

Parsons, Frances Theodora [Mrs. William Starr Dana]. *How to Know the Wild Flowers: A Guide to the Names, Haunts, and Habits of Our Common Wild Flowers.* Illus. Marion Satterlee. New York: Scribner's, 1893.

"Passing of Mabel Osgood Wright, Noted Novelist and Naturalist, Recalls Highlights of Her Splendid Life." *Bridgeport Sunday Post* 22 July 1934, n.p. CAS Records, BMS.

Paul, Sherman. *For Love of the World: Essays on Nature Writers.* Iowa City: U of Iowa P, 1992.

Payne, Daniel G. "Talking Freely around the Campfire: The Influence of American Nature Writing on American Environmental Policy." *Society and Natural Resources* 11 (1999): 39–48.

———. *Voices in the Wilderness: American Nature Writing and Environmental Politics.* Hanover, N.H.: UP of New England, 1996.

Peacock, Doug. "Edward Abbey." *In Praise of Nature.* Ed. Stephanie Mills. Washington, D.C.: Island Press, 1990. 55–57.

Pearson, T. Gilbert. *Adventures in Bird Protection: An Autobiography.* Intro. Frank M. Chapman. New York: D. Appleton-Century, 1937.

———. "The Audubon Association and the Spirit of Cooperation." *Bird-Lore* 31 (1929): 225–32.

———. "Fifty Years of Bird Protection in the United States." *Fifty Years' Progress of American Ornithology, 1883–1933.* Lancaster, Pa.: American Ornithologists' Union, 1933. 199–213.

Peiffer, Katrina Schimmoeller. *Coyote at Large: Humor in American Nature Writing.* Salt Lake City: U of Utah P, 2000.

Perényi, Eleanor Spencer Stone. *Green Thoughts: A Writer in the Garden.* New York: Random House, 1981.

Petersen, David. "Cactus Ed's Moveable Feast: A Preview of *Confessions of a Barbarian: Pages from the Journals of Edward Abbey.*" *Western American Literature* 28 (spring 1993): 33–41.

———. "The Earth's Guerrilla Army." *Mother Jones* (Feb.–Mar. 1986): 8.

———. "The Plowboy Interview: Edward Abbey: Slowing the Industrialization of Planet Earth." *Mother Earth News* (May–June 1984): 17–20+.

Peterson, Anna. L. *Being Human: Ethics, Environment, and Our Place in the World.* Berkeley: U of California P, 2001.

Peterson, Roger Tory. "The Evolution of a Magazine." *Audubon* 75 (1973): 46–51.

———. *Field Guide to the Birds.* New York: Houghton Mifflin, 1934.

Petulla, Joseph M. *Environmental Protection in the United States: Industry, Agencies, Environmentalists.* San Francisco: San Francisco Study Center, 1987.

Philippon, Daniel J. "Environment and Environmentalism: An Overview." *Encyclopedia of American Studies.* Bethel, Conn.: Grolier, 2001. 84–89.

———. "Liberty Hyde Bailey." *Encyclopedia of Gardens: History and Design.* London: Fitzroy Dearborn, 2001. 103–5.

——. "'Such Pictures and Poems, Inimitable': Nature and Language in Walt Whitman's *Specimen Days.*" *Reading the Earth: New Directions in Literature and Environment.* Ed. Michael P. Branch, Rochelle Johnson, Daniel Patterson, and Scott Slovic. Boise: U of Idaho P, 1998. 179–93.

Pilkington, Tom. "Edward Abbey: Western Philosopher, or How to Be a 'Happy Hopi Hippie.'" *Western American Literature* 9 (1994): 17–31.

Polanyi, Michael. *Personal Knowledge: Towards a Post-critical Philosophy.* 1962. Corrected ed. Chicago: U of Chicago P, 1974.

Pollan, Michael. "Against Nativism." *New York Times Magazine* 15 May 1994, 52–55.

——. *A Place of My Own: The Education of an Amateur Builder.* New York: Random House, 1997.

Pomeroy, Earl. *In Search of the Golden West: The Tourist in Western America.* 1957. Lincoln: U of Nebraska P, 1990.

Rev. of *Poppea of the Post Office*, by MOW. *New York Times Book Review* 7 Aug. 1909, 477.

Powell, William. *The Anarchist Cookbook.* Secaucus, N.J.: L. Stuart, 1971.

Preston, Christopher J. "Conversing with Nature in a Postmodern Epistemological Framework." *Environmental Ethics* 22 (2000): 227–40.

——. *Grounding Knowledge: Environmental Philosophy, Epistemology, and Place.* Athens: U of Georgia P, 2003.

——. "Intrinsic Value and Care: Making Connections through Ecological Narratives." *Environmental Values* 10 (2001): 243–64.

Preston, Daniel J. "The AOU's Fledgling Years." *Natural History* 92 (Sept. 1983): 10–12.

Price, Jennifer. *Flight Maps: Adventures with Nature in Modern America.* New York: Basic Books, 1999.

Proctor, James D. "Geography, Paradox, and Environmental Ethics." *Progress in Human Geography* 22.2 (1998): 234–55.

Proffitt, Merrilee. "The Sierra Club and Environmental History: A Selected Bibliography." *California History* 71 (1992): 271–75.

Punch, Walter T., gen. ed. *Keeping Eden: A History of Gardening in America.* Boston: Bulfinch, 1992.

Putnam, Carleton. *Theodore Roosevelt: The Formative Years, 1858–1886.* New York: Scribner's, 1958.

Quammen, David. "Bagpipes for Ed." *Outside* (June 1989): 25–29.

——. "Islands of Memory." *Audubon* 99.4 (July–Aug. 1997): 64–67.

——. "National Parks: Nature's Dead End." *New York Times* 28 July 1996, sec. 4, p. 13.

——. *The Song of the Dodo: Island Biogeography in an Age of Extinctions.* 1996. New York: Touchstone, 1997.

Queen, Ellery. *And on the Eighth Day.* New York: Random House, 1964.

Quigley, Peter, ed. *Coyote in the Maze: Tracking Edward Abbey in a World of Words.* Salt Lake City: U of Utah P, 1998.

Quinn, Arthur. *Figures of Speech: Sixty Ways to Turn a Phrase.* Salt Lake City: Peregrine Smith, 1982.

Rev. of *Ranch Life and the Hunting Trail,* by Theodore Roosevelt. *Book Buyer* 5.11 (Dec. 1888): 484.

Rev. of *Ranch Life and the Hunting Trail,* by Theodore Roosevelt. *Nation* 64 (1897): 92.

Rawlins, C. L. "Dillard's Cat." *Northern Lights* 13.3 (summer 1998): 16–18.

Redfield, Sarah Heekin. "Surveying the Boundaries: An Inquiry into Creative Nonfiction." *Poets and Writers* 27.5 (Sept.–Oct. 1999): 36–41.

Reiger, John F. *American Sportsmen and the Origins of Conservation.* 1975. 3d ed. Corvallis: Oregon State UP, 2001.

——. "Commentary on Thomas R. Dunlap's Article." *Environmental Review* (fall 1988): 94–96.

——. Letter to the Editor. *Journal of Forest History* (Oct. 1976): 221.

——. *The Passing of the Great West: Selected Papers of George Bird Grinnell.* New York: Winchester Press, 1972.

——. "Wildlife, Conservation, and the First Forest Reserve." *Origins of the National Forests: A Centennial Symposium.* Ed. Harold K. Steen. Durham, N.C.: Forest History Society, 1992. 106–21.

Ribbens, Dennis. "The Making of *A Sand County Almanac.*" Callicott, *Companion* 91–109.

Richardson, Elmo R. *The Politics of Conservation: Crusades and Controversies, 1897–1913.* Berkeley: U of California P, 1962.

——. "The Struggle for the Valley: California's Hetch Hetchy Controversy, 1905–1913." *California Historical Society Quarterly* 38 (1959): 249–58.

Ricoeur, Paul. *Time and Narrative.* Trans. Kathleen McLaughlin and David Pellauer. 3 vols. Chicago: U of Chicago P, 1984–88.

Riordan, Robert M., ed. *Uncommon Wealth: Essays on Virginia's Wild Places.* Intro. Jennifer Ackerman. Helena, Mont.: Nature Conservancy, 1999.

Robertson, David. *West of Eden: A History of the Art and Literature of Yosemite.* [Yosemite Natl. Park, Calif., and Berkeley]: Yosemite Natural History Association and Wilderness Press, 1984.

Robinson, Corinne Roosevelt. *My Brother, Theodore Roosevelt.* New York: Scribner's, 1921.

Rolston, Holmes, III. *Environmental Ethics: Duties to and Values in the Natural World.* Philadelphia: Temple UP, 1988.

——. "Nature for Real: Is Nature a Social Construct?" *The Philosophy of the Environment.* Ed. T. D. J. Chappell. Edinburgh: Edinburgh UP, 1997. 38–64.

Ronald, Ann. "Edward Abbey." *Fifty Western Writers: A Bio-Bibliographical Sourcebook.* Ed. Fred Erisman and Richard W. Etulain. Westport, Conn.: Greenwood, 1982. 3–12.

——. *The New West of Edward Abbey.* 2d ed. Afterword by Scott Slovic. Reno: U of Nevada P, 2000.

Roorda, Randall. *Dramas of Solitude: Narratives of Retreat in American Nature Writing.* Albany: SUNY P, 1998.

——. "Great Divides: Rhetorics of Literacy and Orality." *Ecocomposition: Theoretical and Pedagogical Approaches.* Ed. Christian R. Weisser and Sidney I. Dobrin. Albany: SUNY P, 2001. 97–116.

———. "KB in Green: Ecology, Critical Theory, and Kenneth Burke." *ISLE: Interdisciplinary Studies in Literature and Environment* 4.2 (fall 1997): 39–52.

Roosevelt, Robert Barnwell. *Game Birds of the Coasts and Lakes of the Northern States of America.* New York: Carleton, 1866.

———. *Game Fish of the Northern States of America and British Provinces.* New York: Carleton, 1865.

———. *Superior Fishing; or, the Striped Bass, Trout, and Black Bass of the Northern States.* New York: Carleton, 1865.

Roosevelt, Theodore. "The Boone and Crockett Club." *Harper's Weekly* 37 (1893): 267.

———. *Hunting Trips of a Ranchman: Sketches of Sport on the Northern Cattle Plains and the Wilderness Hunter: An Account of the Big Game of the United States and Its Chase with Horse, Hound, and Rifle.* Intro. Stephen A. Ambrose. New York: Modern Library, 1996.

———. Letter to the Editor. *Forest and Stream* 39 (1892): 514.

———. "'Sou'-Sou'-Southerly': An Unappreciated Nature Essay." Ed. Daniel J. Philippon. *North Dakota Quarterly* 64.1 (winter 1997): 83–92.

———. *The Works of Theodore Roosevelt.* National edition. Ed. Hermann Hagedorn. 20 vols. New York: Scribner's, 1926.

Roper, Laura Wood. *FLO: A Biography of Frederick Law Olmsted.* Baltimore: Johns Hopkins UP, 1973.

Rorty, Richard. *Philosophy and the Mirror of Nature.* Princeton, N.J.: Princeton UP, 1979.

Rosendale, Steven, ed. *The Greening of Literary Scholarship: Literature, Theory, and the Environment.* Iowa City: U of Iowa P, 2002.

Ross, Stephanie. *What Gardens Mean.* Chicago: U of Chicago P, 1998.

Roszak, Theodore. *The Voice of the Earth.* New York: Simon and Schuster, 1992.

Roth, Dennis. "The National Forests and the Campaign for Wilderness Legislation." *Journal of Forest History* 28.3 (July 1984): 112–25.

Rothman, David J. "'I'm a Humanist': The Poetic Past in *Desert Solitaire.*" Quigley 47–73.

Rothman, Hal K. "'A Regular Ding-Dong Fight': Agency Culture and Evolution in the NPS-USFS Dispute, 1916–1937." *Western Historical Quarterly* 20.2 (May 1989): 141–61.

Rothstein, Edward. "Paradise Lost: Can Mankind Live without Its Utopias?" *New York Times* 5 Feb. 2000, B7.

———. "Utopia and Its Discontents." *Visions of Utopia.* By Edward Rothstein, Herbert Muschamp, and Martin E. Marty. New York: Oxford UP, 2003. 1–28.

Rubin, Charles T. *The Green Crusade: Rethinking the Roots of Environmentalism.* 1994. New York: Rowman and Littlefield, 1998.

Runte, Alfred. Rev. of *American Sportsmen and the Origins of Conservation,* by John Reiger. *Journal of Forest History* (Apr. 1976): 100–101.

———. Letter to the Editor. *Journal of Forest History* (Oct. 1976): 221–22.

———. *National Parks: The American Experience.* 2d ed. Lincoln: U of Nebraska P, 1987.

———. *Yosemite: The Embattled Wilderness.* Lincoln: U of Nebraska P, 1990.

Ruppert, Peter. *Reader in a Strange Land: The Activity of Reading Literary Utopias.* Athens: U of Georgia P, 1986.

Russell, Carl P. *One Hundred Years in Yosemite: The Story of a Great Park and Its Friends.* Yosemite, Calif.: Yosemite Natural History Association, 1957.

Russell, Dick. "The Monkeywrenchers." *Amicus Journal* 9.4 (fall 1987): 28–42.

Russell, Mary Annette Beauchamp [Elizabeth von Arnim, pseud.]. *Elizabeth and Her German Garden.* Intro. Elizabeth Jane Howard. 1898. London: Virago, 1985.

———. *The Enchanted April.* Intro. Terence de Vere White. 1922. London: Virago, 1986.

———. *The Solitary Summer.* 1899. London: Virago, 1993.

Ryan, Philip. "Comment: Gare, MacIntyre, and Tradition." *Environmental Ethics* 22 (2000): 223–24.

Ryan, P. J. "The Martinez Years: The Family Life and Letters of John Muir." *Pacific Historian* 25 (summer 1981): 79–85.

Sagoff, Mark. *The Economy of the Earth: Philosophy, Law, and the Environment.* New York: Cambridge UP, 1988.

Sale, Kirkpatrick. "The Forest for the Trees: Can Today's Environmentalists Tell the Difference?" *Mother Jones* (Nov. 1986): 24+.

———. *The Green Revolution: The American Environmental Movement, 1962–1992.* New York: Hill and Wang, 1993.

———. *Rebels against the Future: The Luddites and Their War on the Industrial Revolution: Lessons for the Computer Age.* New York: Addison-Wesley, 1995.

Salisbury, Robert H. "Interest Groups." *Nongovernmental Politics.* Vol. 4 of *Handbook of Political Science.* Ed. Fred I. Greenstein and Nelson W. Polsby. 9 vols. Reading, Mass.: Addison-Wesley, 1975. 171–228.

Samuels, Edward A. *Among the Birds: A Series of Sketches for Young Folks, Illustrating the Domestic Life of Our Feathered Friends.* Boston: Nichols and Noyes, 1868.

Sanborn, Margaret. *Yosemite: Its Discovery, Its Wonders, and Its People.* New York: Random House, 1981.

Sanders, Scott Russell. "Speaking a Word for Nature." *Secrets of the Universe: Scenes from the Journey Home.* Boston: Beacon, 1991. 205–27.

———. *Staying Put: Making a Home in a Restless World.* Boston: Beacon, 1994.

Sanger, William Cary. "The Adirondack Deer Law." *Trail and Camp-Fire.* Ed. George Bird Grinnell and Theodore Roosevelt. New York: Forest and Stream Publishing, 1897. 264–78.

Santayana, George. *The Genteel Tradition: Nine Essays.* Ed. Douglas L. Wilson. Cambridge, Mass.: Harvard UP, 1967.

Sargent, Lyman Tower. "Utopia—The Problem of Definition." *Extrapolation* 16.2 (May 1975): 137–48.

Scarce, Rik. *Eco-Warriors: Understanding the Radical Environmental Movement.* Foreword by David Brower. Chicago: Noble Press, 1990.

Scheese, Don. "*Desert Solitaire*: Counter-Friction to the Machine in the Garden." *North Dakota Quarterly* 59.2 (spring 1991): 211–27.

———. *Nature Writing: The Pastoral Impulse in America.* New York: Twayne, 1996.

Schneider, Dorothy, and Carl J. Schneider, eds. *American Women in the Progressive Era, 1900–1920.* New York: Facts on File, 1993.

Schneirov, Matthew. *The Dream of a New Social Order: Popular Magazines in America, 1893–1914*. New York: Columbia UP, 1994.

Schön, Donald A. "Generative Metaphor: A Perspective on Problem-Setting in Social Policy." *Metaphor and Thought*. Ed. Andrew Ortony. 2d ed. New York: Cambridge UP, 1993. 137–63.

Schrepfer, Susan R. *The Fight to Save the Redwoods: A History of Environmental Reform, 1917–1978*. Madison: U of Wisconsin P, 1983.

Schullery, Paul. "Hope for the Hook and Bullet Press." *New York Times Book Review* 22 Sept. 1985, 1+.

———. Introduction. *Wilderness Writings*. By Theodore Roosevelt. Ed. Paul Schullery. Salt Lake City: Peregrine Smith, 1986. 11–29.

Schuyler, David. *Apostle of Taste: Andrew Jackson Downing, 1815–1852*. Baltimore: Johns Hopkins UP, 1996.

———. "The Evolution of the Anglo-American Rural Cemetery." *Journal of Garden History* 4.3 (July–Sept. 1984): 291–304.

Schwartz, William, ed. *Voices for the Wilderness*. New York: Ballantine Books, 1969.

Scott, Anne Firor. *Natural Allies: Women's Associations in American History*. Urbana: U of Illinois P, 1991.

Sears, John F. *Sacred Places: American Tourist Attractions in the Nineteenth Century*. New York: Oxford UP, 1989.

Sears, Paul B. "Utopia and the Living Landscape." Manuel, *Utopias and Utopian Thought* 137–49.

Sea Shepherd Conservation Society. "The Spirit of Edward Abbey Lives On: Enlist in the Sea Shepherd Navy." Advertisement. *Wild Earth* 1.1 (spring 1991): 70.

Seaton, Beverly. "The Garden Autobiography." *Garden History* 7.1 (spring 1979): 101–20.

Sellars, Richard West. *Preserving Nature in the National Parks: A History*. New Haven: Yale UP, 1997.

Servid, Carolyn, and Donald Snow, eds. *The Book of the Tongass*. Minneapolis: Milkweed Editions, 1999.

Sessions, George, ed. *Deep Ecology for the Twenty-First Century*. Boston: Shambhala, 1995.

Setterberg, Fred. "The Wild Bunch: Earth First! Shakes Up the Environmental Movement." *Utne Reader* (May–June 1987): 68–76.

Shabecoff, Philip. *A Fierce Green Fire: The American Environmental Movement*. New York: Hill and Wang, 1993.

Shaffer, Gwen. "Novel Security Measures." *Philadelphia City Paper* 18–25 Oct. 2001. <http://www.citypaper.net/articles/101801/news.godfrey.shtml>. Accessed 31 Oct. 2001.

Shaffer, Marguerite S. *See America First: Tourism and National Identity, 1880–1940*. Washington, D.C.: Smithsonian Institution Press, 2001.

Shelford, Victor E. "The Organization of the Ecological Society of America, 1914–19." *Ecology* 19.1 (Jan. 1938): 164–66.

Shepard, Paul. *Man in the Landscape: A Historic View of the Esthetics of Nature*. 2d ed. College Station: Texas A&M UP, 1991.

Shi, David E. *Facing Facts: Realism in American Thought and Culture, 1850–1920*. New York: Oxford UP, 1995.

Shlain, Leonard. *The Alphabet versus the Goddess: The Conflict between Word and Image.* New York: Viking, 1998.

Short, Brant. "Earth First! and the Rhetoric of Moral Confrontation." *Communication Studies* 42.2 (summer 1991): 172–88.

Sies, Mary Corbin. "North American Suburbs, 1880–1950: Cultural and Social Reconsiderations." *Journal of Urban History* 27.3 (Mar. 2001): 313–46.

Simonson, Harold P. "The Tempered Romanticism of John Muir." *Western American Literature* 13 (1978): 227–41.

Sipchen, Bob. "The Muir Mystique." *Los Angeles Times* 20 Apr. 1988, 1, 4.

"Sixtieth Anniversary of the Founding of the Audubon Society, State of Connecticut." Typescript. CAS Records, BPL.

Sklar, Kathryn Kish. *Catharine Beecher: A Study in American Domesticity.* New Haven: Yale UP, 1973.

Slotkin, Richard. *Gunfighter Nation: The Myth of the Frontier in Twentieth-Century America.* New York: Atheneum, 1992.

Slovic, Scott. "Epistemology and Politics in American Nature Writing: Embedded Rhetoric and Discrete Rhetoric." Herndl and Brown 82–110.

——. "Literature." Jamieson 251–63.

——. *Seeking Awareness in American Nature Writing: Henry Thoreau, Annie Dillard, Edward Abbey, Wendell Berry, Barry Lopez.* Salt Lake City: U of Utah P, 1992.

——, ed. *Getting Over the Color Green: Contemporary Environmental Literature of the Southwest.* Tucson: U of Arizona P, 2001.

Smith, Henry Nash. *Virgin Land: The American West as Symbol and Myth.* 1950. New York: Vintage, 1970.

Smith, Herbert A. "The Cult of the Wilderness." *Journal of Forestry* 33 (1935): 955–57.

Smith, Herbert F. *John Muir.* New York: Twayne, 1965.

Smith, Michael L. *Pacific Visions: California Scientists and the Environment, 1850–1915.* New Haven: Yale UP, 1985.

Smith, Mick. "Cheney and the Myth of Postmodernism." *Environmental Ethics* 15 (1993): 3–17.

——. *An Ethics of Place: Radical Ecology, Postmodernity, and Social Theory.* Albany: SUNY P, 2001.

Smith, Neil. *Uneven Development: Nature, Capital, and the Production of Space.* Oxford, Eng.: Basil Blackwell, 1984.

Snow, David A., E. Burke Rochford Jr., Steven K. Worden, and Robert D. Benford. "Frame Alignment Processes, Micromobilization, and Movement Participation." *American Sociological Review* 51 (1986): 464–81.

Snyder, Gary. *No Nature: New and Selected Poems.* New York: Pantheon, 1992.

——. *A Place in Space: Ethics, Aesthetics, and Watersheds.* Washington, D.C.: Counterpoint, 1995.

——. *The Practice of the Wild: Essays.* San Francisco: North Point Press, 1990.

——. *Turtle Island.* New York: New Directions, 1974.

Solheim, Dave, and Rob Levin. "The *Bloomsbury Review* Interview." Hepworth and McNamee 138–55.

Solnit, Rebecca. *Savage Dreams: A Journey into the Landscape Wars of the American West.* 1994. Berkeley: U of California P, 1999.

Sonn, Richard David. *Anarchism.* New York: Twayne, 1992.

Stanley, Millie. *The Heart of John Muir's World: Wisconsin, Family, and Wilderness Discovery.* Madison, Wis.: Prairie Oaks Press, 1995.

Steel, Steven C. "Literature as Community: The Essential Utility of the Literature of Earth First!" *Literature of Nature: An International Sourcebook.* Ed. Patrick D. Murphy. Chicago: Fitzroy Dearborn, 1998. 447–53.

Stegner, Wallace. "It All Began with Conservation." *Smithsonian* 21.1 (Apr. 1990): 34–43.

———. "Living on Our Principal." *Wilderness* 48.168 (spring 1985): 15–21.

———. "A Short History of Conservation." *Where the Bluebird Sings to the Lemonade Springs: Living and Writing in the West.* New York: Random House, 1992. 117–32.

Steinhart, Peter. "The Longer View: Conservation Has Made Its Way in America through the Pages of Magazines, Not Newspapers." *Audubon* (Mar. 1987): 10+.

———. "Place as Purpose: Muir's Sierra." *Orion Nature Quarterly* 7.4 (autumn 1988): 42–49.

Stewart, Charles J., Craig Allen Smith, and Robert E. Denton Jr. *Persuasion and Social Movements.* 4th ed. Prospect Heights, Ill.: Waveland, 2001.

Stewart, Frank. *A Natural History of Nature Writing.* Washington, D.C.: Island Press, 1995.

Stilgoe, John R. *Borderland: Origins of the American Suburb, 1820–1939.* New Haven: Yale UP, 1988.

———. "Popular Photography, Scenery Values, and Visual Assessment." *Landscape Journal* 3 (1984): 111–22.

Stoll, Mark. "God and John Muir: A Psychological Interpretation of John Muir's Journey from the Campbellites to the 'Range of Light.'" Sally Miller, *John Muir* 64–81.

Strong, Douglas H. "John Muir: Naturalist, Geologist, Interpreter of Nature." *World's Work* 13 (1907): 8804–8.

———. "The Sierra Club — A History; Part 1: Origins and Outings." *Sierra* (Oct. 1977): 10–14.

———. "The Sierra Club — A History; Part 2: Conservation." *Sierra* (Nov.–Dec. 1977): 16–20.

[Strother, French.] "A Conversation with John Muir." *World's Work* 13 (1906): 8249–50.

Sumner, David Thomas. "'Speaking a Word for Nature': The Ethical Rhetoric of American Nature Writing." Diss. U of Oregon, 2000.

Sutter, Paul. *Driven Wild: How the Fight against Automobiles Launched the Modern Wilderness Movement.* Seattle: U of Washington P, 2002.

Sweeting, Adam. *Reading Houses and Building Books: Andrew Jackson Downing and the Architecture of Popular Antebellum Literature, 1835–1855.* Hanover, N.H.: UP of New England, 1996.

Takacs, David. *The Idea of Biodiversity: Philosophies of Paradise.* Baltimore: Johns Hopkins UP, 1996.

Tallmadge, John. "John Muir and the Poetics of Natural Conversion." *North Dakota Quarterly* 59.2 (spring 1991): 62–79.

———. *Meeting the Tree of Life: A Teacher's Path.* Salt Lake City: U of Utah P, 1997.

Tatum, George B., and Elisabeth Blair MacDougall, eds. *Prophet with Honor: The Career of Andrew Jackson Downing, 1815–1852.* Washington, D.C.: Dumbarton Oaks, 1989.

Taylor, Bron. "Religion, Violence, and Radical Environmentalism: From Earth First! to the Unabomber to the Earth Liberation Front." *Terrorism and Political Violence* 10.4 (winter 1998): 1–42.

———. "Resacralizing Earth: Pagan Environmentalism and the Restoration of Turtle Island." *American Sacred Space*. Ed. David Chidester and Edward T. Linenthal. Bloomington: Indiana UP, 1995. 97–151.

Taylor, Charles. *Sources of the Self: The Making of the Modern Identity*. Cambridge, Mass.: Harvard UP, 1989.

Teale, Edwin Way. "Making the Wild Scene." *New York Times Book Review* 28 Jan. 1968, 7.

Temple, Eric. Draft Transcript for *Edward Abbey: A Voice in the Wilderness*. South Burlington, Vt.: Canyon Productions, 1993.

Tesh, Sylvia Noble. *Uncertain Hazards: Environmental Activists and Scientific Proof*. Ithaca, N.Y.: Cornell UP, 2000.

Thacker, Christopher. *The History of Gardens*. London: Croom Helm, 1979.

Thiele, Leslie Paul. *Environmentalism for a New Millennium: The Challenge of Coevolution*. New York: Oxford UP, 1999.

Thomas, Keith. *Man and the Natural World: A History of the Modern Sensibility*. New York: Pantheon, 1983.

Thomashow, Mitchell. *Bringing the Biosphere Home: Learning to Perceive Global Environmental Change*. Cambridge, Mass.: MIT Press, 2002.

———. *Ecological Identity: Becoming a Reflective Environmentalist*. Cambridge, Mass.: MIT Press, 1995.

Thoreau, Henry David. *The Journal of Henry D. Thoreau*. Ed. Bradford Torrey and Francis H. Allen. Boston: Houghton Mifflin, 1906. 14 vols.

———. *The Maine Woods*. 1864. Ed. Joseph J. Moldenhauer. Princeton, N.J.: Princeton UP, 1972.

———. *Walden*. 1854. Ed. J. Lyndon Shanley. Princeton, N.J.: Princeton UP, 1971.

———. "Walking." *The Natural History Essays*. Intro. Robert Sattlemeyer. 1862. Salt Lake City: Gibbs M. Smith, 1980. 93–136.

———. *A Week on the Concord and Merrimack Rivers*. Ed. Carl Hovde et al. Intro. Linck C. Johnson. Princeton, N.J.: Princeton UP, 1980.

———. *Wild Fruits: Thoreau's Rediscovered Last Manuscript*. Ed. Bradley P. Dean. New York: Norton, 2000.

Tichi, Cecelia. *New World, New Earth: Environmental Reform in American Literature from the Puritans through Whitman*. New Haven: Yale UP, 1979.

Tjossem, Sara Fairbank. "Preservation of Nature and Academic Respectability: Tensions in the Ecological Society of America, 1915–1979." Diss. Cornell U, 1994.

Tober, James A. *Who Owns the Wildlife? The Political Economy of Conservation in Nineteenth-Century America*. Westport, Conn.: Greenwood, 1981.

Tocqueville, Alexis de. *Democracy in America*. Ed. Richard D. Heffner. 1835–40. New York: Mentor, 1956.

Trefethen, James B. *An American Crusade for Wildlife*. New York: Winchester Press, 1975.

———. *Crusade for Wildlife: Highlights in Conservation Progress*. Harrisburg, Pa.: Stackpole, 1961.

"Tribute to Mabel Osgood Wright Is Read at Memorial Services." N.p.: n.p., n.d. CAS Records, BPL.

Trimble, Stephen. "Introduction: The Naturalist's Trance." *Words from the Land: Encounters with Natural History Writing.* Ed. Stephen Trimble. Salt Lake City: Gibbs Smith, 1989. 2–29.

Trimble, Stephen, and Terry Tempest Williams, eds. *Testimony: Writers of the West Speak on Behalf of Utah Wilderness.* Minneapolis: Milkweed Editions, 1996.

Tuan, Yi-Fu. *Topophilia: A Study of Environmental Perception, Attitudes, and Values.* Englewood Cliffs, N.J.: Prentice Hall, 1974.

Turner, Frederick. *Rediscovering America: John Muir in His Time and Ours.* New York: Viking, 1985.

Turner, Frederick Jackson. *The Significance of the Frontier in American History.* Madison: State Historical Society of Wisconsin, 1894.

Turner, Jack. *The Abstract Wild.* Tucson: U of Arizona P, 1996.

Turner, James Morton. "Charting American Environmentalism's Early (Intellectual) Geography, 1890–1920." *Wild Earth* 10.2 (summer 2000): 18–25.

Turner, Tom. *Sierra Club: 100 Years of Protecting Nature.* New York: Harry N. Abrams, 1991.

Twelve Southerners. *I'll Take My Stand: The South and the Agrarian Tradition.* Intro. Louis D. Rubin Jr. 1930. Baton Rouge: Louisiana State UP, 1977.

Ulman, H. Lewis. "'Thinking Like a Mountain': Persona, Ethos, and Judgment in American Nature Writing." Herndl and Brown 46–81.

Untitled caption to picture. *Earth First! Journal* 6.4 (20 Mar. 1986): 13.

Usborne, Karen. *"Elizabeth": The Author of "Elizabeth and Her German Garden."* London: Bodley Head, 1986.

Vale, Thomas. "The Myth of the Humanized Landscape: An Example from Yosemite National Park." *Natural Areas Journal* 18 (1998): 231–36.

VanDyke, Theodore S. *The Still-Hunter.* New York: Fords, Howard and Hulbert, 1883.

Vaz, Mark. "Leaves of Green." *Sierra* (May–June 1986): 56–61.

"Visit to Famous Garden of Past Discloses Shrine Dedicated to Many Poets." N.p.: n.p., n.d. MOW Clippings File, FHS.

Vogel, Steven. "Environmental Philosophy after the End of Nature." *Environmental Ethics* 24 (2002): 23–39.

Waage, Frederick O. "American Literary Environmentalism, 1864–1920." *Teaching Environmental Literature: Materials, Methods, Resources.* Ed. Frederick O. Waage. New York: MLA, 1985. 19–34.

Ward, George Baxter, III. "Bloodbrothers in the Wilderness: The Sport Hunter and the Buckskin Hunter in the Preservation of the American Wilderness Experience." Diss. U of Texas at Austin, 1980.

Warren, Karen J. *Ecofeminist Philosophy: A Western Perspective on What It Is and Why It Matters.* New York: Rowman and Littlefield, 2000.

———. "The Power and Promise of Ecological Feminism." *Environmental Ethics* 12 (1990): 125–46.

Warren, Louis S. *The Hunter's Game: Poachers and Conservationists in Twentieth-Century America.* New Haven: Yale UP, 1997.

Watkins, T. H. Editor's Note. *Wilderness* 51.179 (winter 1987): 57.

———. "The Shadow of a Man." *Wilderness* 48.168 (spring 1985): 3.

———. "A Signature on the Land." *American Heritage* 45.5 (Sept. 1994): 52–63.

Watkins, T. H., and Dewitt Jones. *John Muir's America*. New York: Crown, 1976.

Watson, Paul. "Occurrence in the Ferocious Isles: Sea Shepherd Takes on Whale Butchers." *Earth First! Journal* 6.8 (23 Sept. 1986): 1+.

Welchman, Jennifer. "Is Ecosabotage Civil Disobedience?" *Philosophy and Geography* 4.1 (2001): 97–107.

Welker, Robert Henry. *Birds and Men: American Birds in Science, Art, Literature, and Conservation, 1800–1900*. Cambridge, Mass.: Harvard UP, 1955.

Wesling, Donald. "The Poetics of Description: John Muir and Ruskinian Descriptive Prose." *Prose Studies, 1800–1900* 1.1 (fall 1977): 37–44.

West, Herbert F. "A Bitter Young Man." Rev. of *Jonathan Troy*, by Edward Abbey. *New York Times Book Review* 11 Apr. 1954, 25.

Whetten, Nathan Laselle. *Studies of Suburbanization in Connecticut*. 1936–39. New York: Arno, 1974.

White, G. Edward. *The Eastern Establishment and the Western Experience: The West of Frederic Remington, Theodore Roosevelt, and Owen Wister*. New Haven: Yale UP, 1968.

White, Gilbert. *The Natural History of Selborne*. Ed. Richard Mabey. 1789. New York: Penguin, 1977.

White, Richard. "'Are You an Environmentalist or Do You Work for a Living?'" Cronon, *Uncommon Ground* 171–85.

———. "Discovering Nature in North America." *Journal of American History* 79 (1992): 874–91.

———. "The Nationalization of Nature." *Journal of American History* 86.3 (Dec. 1999): 976–86.

Wild, Peter. "Into the Heart's Wild Places: Edward Abbey (1927–1989)." *Sierra* 74 (May–June 1989): 100–101.

———. *Pioneer Conservationists of Western America*. Intro. Edward Abbey. Missoula, Mont.: Mountain Press, 1979.

———. "Sentimentalism in the American Southwest: John C. Van Dyke, Mary Austin, and Edward Abbey." *Reading the West: New Essays on the Literature of the American West*. Ed. Michael Kowalewski. Cambridge, Eng.: Cambridge UP, 1996. 127–43.

———, ed. *The Desert Reader*. Salt Lake City: U of Utah P, 1991.

Rev. of *The Wilderness Hunter*, by Theodore Roosevelt. *Atlantic Monthly* 75 (1895): 826–30.

"The Wildlands Project: Mission, Vision, and Purpose (1992; revised 2000)." *Wild Earth: Wild Ideas for a World Out of Balance*. Ed. Tom Butler. Minneapolis: Milkweed Editions, 2002. 10–14.

Wilkins, Thurman. *John Muir: Apostle of Nature*. Norman: U of Oklahoma P, 1995.

Willers, Bill, ed. *Learning to Listen to the Land*. Washington, D.C.: Island Press, 1991.

Williams, Dennis C. *God's Wilds: John Muir's Vision of Nature*. College Station: Texas A&M UP, 2002.

———. "John Muir and an Evangelical Vision for Western Natural Resources Management." *Journal of the West* 35.3 (July 1996): 53–60.

——. "John Muir, Christian Mysticism, and the Spiritual Value of Nature." Sally Miller, *John Muir* 82–99.

Williams, George H. *Wilderness and Paradise in Christian Thought: The Biblical Experience of the Desert in the History of Christianity and the Paradise Theme in the Theological Idea of the University.* New York: Harper and Brothers, 1962.

Williams, Raymond. "Ideas of Nature." *Problems in Materialism and Culture: Selected Essays.* London: NLB, 1980. 67–85.

——. "Nature." *Keywords: A Vocabulary of Culture and Society.* New York: Oxford UP, 1976.

Woehlke, Walter V. "Transcontinental Motor Trails of the Far West — I. Southwestern Highways: The Open Road Is Calling." *Sunset* 54.3 (Mar. 1925): 24+.

Wolfe, Linnie Marsh. *Son of the Wilderness: The Life of John Muir.* 1945. Madison: U of Wisconsin P, 1979.

——, ed. *John of the Mountains: The Unpublished Journals of John Muir.* 1938. Madison: U of Wisconsin P, 1979.

Wolfe, Tom. *The Electric Kool-Aid Acid Test.* New York: Farrar, Straus and Giroux, 1968.

Wood, John George. *Homes without Hands: Being a Description of the Habitations of Animals, Classed According to Their Principle of Construction.* London: Longmans, Green, 1865.

Worster, Donald. *Nature's Economy: A History of Ecological Ideas.* 2d ed. New York: Cambridge UP, 1994.

——. *The Wealth of Nature: Environmental History and the Ecological Imagination.* New York: Oxford UP, 1993.

Wright, Mabel Osgood. "Annual Report to the National Association of Audubon Societies." Draft. [1911.] NAS Records, Box A-43, NYPL.

——. "Bird-Cities-of-Refuge." *Bird-Lore* 12 (1910): 159–60.

——. "A Bird Class for Children." *Bird-Lore* 1 (1899): 100–101.

——. *Birdcraft: A Field Book of Two Hundred Song, Game, and Water Birds.* New York: Macmillan, 1895.

——. "Birdcraft Sanctuary: After Sixteen Years — Facts and Phantasy." *Bird-Lore* 32 (1930): 401–3.

——. *Captains of the Watch of Life and Death.* New York: Macmillan, 1927.

——. *Citizen Bird: Scenes from Bird-life in Plain English for Beginners.* With Elliott Coues. New York: Macmillan, 1897.

——. "The Conducting of Audubon Societies." *Bird-Lore* 1 (1899): 64–65.

——. "Conn. Audubon Society Holds Annual Meet." *Fairfield News* 9 June 1923, 5.

——. "Encouraging Signs." *Bird-Lore* 3 (1901): 146–47.

——. "The End of the Beginning — Wild Flowers and Hawks." *Bird-Lore* 26 (1924): 104–7.

——. *Eudora's Men.* New York: Macmillan, 1931.

——. "Fees and Pledges." *Bird-Lore* 2 (1900): 63–65.

——. *Flowers and Ferns in Their Haunts.* New York: Macmillan, 1901.

——. *Four-Footed Americans and Their Kin.* Ed. Frank Chapman. New York: Macmillan, 1898.

——. *The Friendship of Nature: A New England Chronicle of Birds and Flowers.* Ed. Daniel J. Philippon. 1894. Baltimore: Johns Hopkins UP, 1999.

——. *The Garden of a Commuter's Wife*. New York: Macmillan, 1901.

——. *The Garden, You, and I*. New York: Macmillan, 1906.

——. *Gray Lady and the Birds: Stories of the Bird Year for Home and School*. New York: Macmillan, 1907.

——. "Inviting the Birds and Wild Flowers." *Garden Magazine and Home Builder* 40 (1924): 107–10.

——. "The Law and the Bird." *Bird-Lore* 1 (1899): 203–4.

——. "Life Outdoors and Its Effect upon Literature." *Critic* 42 (1903): 308–11.

——. "The Literature of Bird Protection." *Bird-Lore* 5 (1903): 137–38.

——. "Little Stories from Birdcraft Sanctuary: I. A Hummingbird Waif." *Bird-Lore* 24 (1922): 193–95.

——. "The Making of Birdcraft Sanctuary." *Bird-Lore* 17 (1915): 263–73.

——. "Meditations on the Posting of Bird Laws." *Bird-Lore* 5 (1903): 205–6.

——. *My New York*. Illus. Ivin Sickels II. New York: Macmillan, 1926.

——. "Nature as a Field for Fiction." *New York Times Book Review* 9 Dec. 1905, 872.

——. *People of the Whirlpool: From the Experience Book of a Commuter's Wife*. New York: Macmillan, 1903.

——. *Poppea of the Post Office*. New York: Macmillan, 1909.

——. "The Responsibility of the Audubon Society." *Bird-Lore* 1 (1899): 136–37.

——. "Song Bird Reservations." *Bird-Lore* 3 (1901): 114–15.

——. "The Spread of Bird Protection." *Bird-Lore* 5 (1903): 36–37.

——. "Three Years After: Some Notes on Birdcraft Sanctuary, Fairfield, Conn." *Bird-Lore* 20 (1918): 201–10.

——. *Tommy-Anne and the Three Hearts*. New York: Macmillan, 1896.

——. *Wabeno, the Magician: The Sequel to "Tommy-Anne and the Three Hearts."* New York: Macmillan, 1899.

——. "Wanted — The Truth." *Bird-Lore* 2 (1900): 32–33.

——. *The Woman Errant: Being Some Chapters from the Wonder Book of Barbara, the Commuter's Wife*. New York: Macmillan, 1904.

——. "Work! And after That More Work." *Bird-Lore* 4 (1902): 103–4.

Wyatt, David. *The Fall into Eden: Landscape and Imagination in California*. New York: Cambridge UP, 1986.

Young, Louise B. *Islands: Portraits of Miniature Worlds*. New York: W. H. Freeman, 1999.

Young, Robert. "'Monkeywrenching' and the Processes of Democracy." *Ecology and Democracy*. Ed. Freya Mathews. Portland, Oreg.: Frank Cass, 1996.

Young, Thomas. "The Morality of Ecosabotage." *Environmental Values* 10 (2001): 385–93.

Zakin, Susan. *Coyotes and Town Dogs: Earth First! and the Environmental Movement*. New York: Viking, 1993.

——. "Goodbye to All That. Again." *Orion* (winter 1999): 88.

Index

References to the major treatment of a subject are given in boldface. References to illustrations are given in italics.